ALSO BY THOMAS A. SCHWARTZ

The Strained Alliance: U.S.-European Relations from Nixon to Carter (editor, with Matthias Schulz)

Lyndon Johnson and Europe: In the Shadow of Vietnam

America's Germany: John J. McCloy and the Federal Republic of Germany

HENRY KISSINGER
AND AMERICAN POWER

HENRY
KISSINGER
AND
AMERICAN
POWER

A POLITICAL BIOGRAPHY

THOMAS A. SCHWARTZ

HILL AND WANG

A division of Farrar, Straus and Giroux | New York

Hill and Wang
A division of Farrar, Straus and Giroux
120 Broadway, New York 10271

Portions of this book have appeared, in different form, in the *Journal of Transatlantic Studies* (17, no. 1, 2019) and *US Presidential Elections and Foreign Policy* (University Press of Kentucky, 2017).

Library of Congress Cataloging-in-Publication Data
Names: Schwartz, Thomas Alan, 1954– author.
Title: Henry Kissinger and American power : a political biography / Thomas A. Schwartz.
Description: First edition. | New York : Hill and Wang, a division of Farrar, Straus and Giroux, 2020. | Includes bibliographical references and index. | Summary: "A biography of American secretary of state Henry Kissinger." —Provided by publisher.
Identifiers: LCCN 2020012452 | ISBN 9780809095377 (hardcover)
Subjects: LCSH: Kissinger, Henry, 1923– | Statesmen—United States—Biography. | Cabinet officers—United States—Biography. | United States—Foreign relations—1969–1974. | United States—Foreign relations—1974–1977.
Classification: LCC E840.8.K58 S39 2020 | DDC 327.730092 [B]—dc23
LC record available at https://lccn.loc.gov/2020012452

Designed by Richard Oriolo

Our books may be purchased in bulk for promotional, educational, or business use. Please contact your local bookseller or the Macmillan Corporate and Premium Sales Department at 1-800-221-7945, extension 5442, or by e-mail at MacmillanSpecialMarkets@macmillan.com.

www.fsgbooks.com
www.twitter.com/fsgbooks • www.facebook.com/fsgbooks

1   2   3   4   5   6   7   8   9   10

To my daughters, Helene, Evie, and Marigny.
They are the treasures of my life.

CONTENTS

HENRY KISSINGER
AND AMERICAN POWER

INTRODUCTION:
HENRY KISSINGER AND
AMERICAN POWER

W HEN I FINALLY GOT THE OPPORTUNITY to interview Henry Kissinger, and made my way through security into his Park Avenue office, the former secretary of state asked me what type of book I had planned. I told him I hoped to write a "short and concise" biography, using his career as a prism through which to explore the modern history of American diplomacy. Looking somewhat puzzled, he replied, in his inimitable German accent, "But you will leave things out."

Henry Kissinger is the most famous American diplomat of the twentieth century. He may well be one of the most heavily documented public figures in American history. He wrote not only three volumes totaling four thousand pages of memoirs, but also other books, articles, speeches, and op-eds that would fill several library shelves. When I began my research, the late Harry

Howe Ransom, a Vanderbilt University colleague who had worked with Kissinger in the 1950s, joked that "Henry never had an unpublished thought." As Kissinger continues his commentary on American foreign policy well into a seventh decade, Ransom may well be right. As national security adviser and secretary of state, Kissinger left an unprecedented paper trail of memoranda of conversations, policy papers, and telephone conversations that record almost every day of his eight years in office. His presence is also significant in the 3,700 hours of the Nixon tapes. Indeed, it was a formidable challenge to write anything "short and concise" about Henry Kissinger.

For these reasons it may be best to start out with explaining what this book isn't. This book is not a full biography of Kissinger the man, and it is not an attempt to make conclusions about his family life and personal relationships. The historian Niall Ferguson has undertaken that project, with the cooperation of Kissinger, and Ferguson has access to Kissinger's personal papers.[1] I have used Ferguson's first volume for my opening chapter, supplemented with materials I have discovered in my own research. Ferguson treats many of the personal matters of Kissinger's life before 1969 with great delicacy.[2] Still, his work is extremely important for the light it sheds on such topics as Kissinger's first years in the United States, his service during and after World War II, and his role in Vietnam negotiations before becoming national security adviser.

My book is also not an attempt to review every claim, accusation, and historical argument that has been made about Henry Kissinger. Covering the wide array of secondary literature about Kissinger would take a small army of historians. Although I make a number of judgments about Kissinger's diplomacy and political behavior, I shy away from the thundering moral pronouncements of condemnation that are commonplace among academics and political activists. Writing dispassionately about a man whom some call a war criminal and lump together with figures like Slobodan Milošević or Pol Pot is not easy. Greg Grandin's *Kissinger's Shadow* indicts Kissinger for not only the actions he took while in power but also the "endless wars" that have characterized American foreign policy ever since.[3] This strikes me as excessive— Kissinger has enough to answer for during the time he actually held governing responsibility. His advocacy of policies as a private citizen is worth studying, but making him responsible for every military action the United States has taken since 1977 is playing into Kissinger's own sense of self-importance. Neither do I find myself as taken with the claims of many of Kissinger's admirers, from his contemporary portrayal as "Super K" to the narratives of some establishment politicians and pundits who argue that Kissinger was the "20th century's greatest 19th-century statesman."[4] The extreme praise and vilification Kissinger receives does little to provide any real understanding of the historical role he has played, or the consequences and legacy of his public life and career. In studying Kissinger, I have attempted to gain an insight into a personality in power, a brilliant man who thought seriously and with great insight about the foreign policy issues of the time, but who was prone to deception and intrigue, highly skilled at bureaucratic infighting, and given to the ingratiating and fawning praise of the president as the source of his power. Kissinger was also a genius at self-promotion, becoming a celebrity diplomat, a man whose activities were chronicled in the entertainment and society pages as well as in the news sections. He was indeed larger than life, negatively as well as positively.

This book aims to reintroduce Henry Kissinger to the American people and to an international audience. It is not quite the "short and concise" book I had hoped it would be. It is much shorter than it would have been had I delved into every aspect of Kissinger's role in foreign policy. There are still many Americans, mostly now sixty and over, who well remember Kissinger. In the mid-1970s he ranked as the most admired American, enjoying close to universal acclaim. In the dawning age of globalization, he was internationally famous, one of the most recognizable figures on the planet. For a younger generation of Americans, the students I teach, Henry Kissinger is not very well known or understood. This book is written for them, as an attempt to explain who Henry Kissinger was, what he thought, what he did, and why it matters. Kissinger was an immensely powerful and important figure during a critical period in recent American history, and his career reflects on many of the enduring and important questions connected to U.S. foreign policy.

Each chapter of the book begins with a television news vignette, explaining in part how viewers saw the career of Henry Kissinger unfold in their living rooms. The first describes the course of Kissinger's life from refugee to presidential adviser, a life and career shaped by the extraordinary changes in America's world position as well as by the actions and sheer good fortune of the brilliant and ambitious Kissinger. His ascent owed much to his personal qualities, but it also provides an insight into America during the Cold War era, when universities like Harvard and politicians like Nelson Rockefeller needed the expertise and talents of men like him. The next three chapters cover Kissinger's role as national security adviser, a position that answers to a constituency of one, the president of the United States. Chapter 2 tells the relatively unhappy story of the first two years of the Richard Nixon administration, as its attempt to start fresh with American foreign policy largely failed because it could not end the Vietnam War. This failure did not detract from the rise of Henry Kissinger to a position as the president's principal adviser on foreign affairs, supplanting the secretary of state and controlling foreign policy from the White House. Chapter 3 takes the story through 1971, which began with the disastrous invasion of Laos but which saw Nixon and Kissinger surprise the world with the announcement of a trip to China. Kissinger's role in Nixon's foreign policy helped the president within the domestic political arena and also enhanced Kissinger's personal fame, despite a stumble in South Asia, as he became known as Nixon's "secret agent." Chapter 4 records what Kissinger called the "trifecta" of 1972—the trip to China, the Moscow summit, and the Paris Peace Accords with North Vietnam—that helped propel Nixon to a landslide electoral victory and Kissinger to international stardom. This marriage between geopolitical realism and American domestic politics, engineered by Nixon and Kissinger, was always a tenuous one, but it served the electoral purposes of Nixon and even won Kissinger a Nobel Peace Prize.

The second half of the book examines Kissinger at the height of his fame. Chapter 5 records Kissinger's appointment as secretary of state, an appointment Nixon was forced to make because of Watergate. Nixon's standing plummeted with the scandal, and Kissinger assumed the preeminent role within the administration. He achieved extraordinary success in launching the Middle East peace process, pushing the Soviet Union out of that region and putting the United States at the center of its diplomacy. His understanding and manipulation of the media, both print and electronic, enhanced the authority and power he exercised. By the time Nixon resigned, Kissinger had become the most powerful figure in Washington.

Chapter 6 examines Kissinger's role in the short-lived Gerald Ford administration. Ford deferred to Kissinger on foreign policy, making the decision to retain him one of the first he announced. Kissinger boasted to Soviet leaders in October 1974 that he had full negotiating authority because he enjoyed the approval of 85 percent of all Americans. Unfortunately, this would be an expression of pride before the fall. After the "Watergate elections" of November 1974, Kissinger faced a different political reality. During his last two years in office, he struggled with a hostile Democratic Congress and a changing national and international political environment. Kissinger himself became a political issue in the 1976 campaign, attacked from both the left and the right for his foreign policy realism and "Lone Ranger" style. When he left office at age fifty-three, after Ford's defeat, however, few would have thought Kissinger would not be back in an official role sometime in the future.

In chapter 7 I look at Kissinger's role in American foreign policy in the forty years since he left office and his effort to wield influence and to shape how Americans approach foreign affairs. During the Carter administration, Kissinger played the role of a shadow secretary of state, enjoying great influence, because the perception was that he would likely be back in power soon. After the Republican victory in 1980, however, Kissinger remained outside the White House. He constructed a role for himself as an influential commentator on foreign policy throughout the Reagan and Bush presidencies, writing newspaper opinion pieces and appearing frequently on network news shows. He also created an international business-consulting group, Kissinger Associates, Inc., and earned millions advising governments and large corporations about international events and trends. His public profile remained so prominent, and his actions as a policymaker so controversial, that he was one of the few American leaders whose mere presence at an event could provoke a hostile demonstration. Presidents Bill Clinton and George W. Bush, men young

enough to be his sons, called him in for advice and counsel. For potential candidates for president, a meeting with Henry Kissinger became seen as a sign of
seriousness, so much so that foreign policy novices like Sarah Palin and Her-
man Cain made the pilgrimage to his Park Avenue office. His brand of foreign
policy realism, reduced emphasis on human rights, and recognition of the limits of American power even enjoyed something of a comeback under Barack
Obama, with administration officials justifying their response to the Syrian
civil war and Iranian nuclear program in these terms.[5] When Kissinger was
photographed meeting with Donald Trump the day after the president fired
the FBI director, James Comey, to head off the investigation into Russian
meddling in the 2016 election, with echoes of Watergate resounding, it was
only another one of the many ironies of Kissinger's continuing presence in
Washington.

This book is based on extensive research in both published and unpublished sources, as well as interviews with a number of Kissinger's colleagues,
including Brent Scowcroft, Helmut Sonnenfeldt, and Winston Lord. Given
the sheer quantity of Kissinger materials available, I cannot, in good conscience, call my research "exhaustive" or "definitive." I have read thousands of
pages of Kissinger documents, listened to hundreds of hours of tapes, and
read numerous secondary accounts. One unique source, new to the study of
Henry Kissinger, is the holdings of the Vanderbilt Television News Archive,
which began recording the evening news on August 5, 1968. The media environment of the era when Henry Kissinger shot to fame was very different
from that of today. By the early 1960s, television news had surpassed newspapers as the principal source of information for most Americans. The half-
hour news broadcasts of the three networks originated in New York and
sought to present the news "objectively" to the American people.[6] For a variety of reasons, historians have largely neglected the study of television's impact on American thinking about most major public policy questions, even
while acknowledging its importance. As the Rutgers professor David Greenberg commented, "Television has clearly remained integral to the process by
which Americans learn about and interpret public events. It stands to reason

that historians, who strive to understand how people experienced their own worlds, should explore how TV portrayed the developments they are writing about."[7]

No political leader had a stronger sense of the importance of television than Richard Nixon. He believed television cost him the 1960 election. In 1968 he obsessively managed the coverage of his campaign.[8] While his administration will forever be remembered for Vice President Spiro Agnew's blistering attacks on the establishment media, both press and television, Nixon was particularly aware of how the television news presented his policies and wanted to manipulate it in his favor. Kissinger eventually became a key to this manipulation. The evening news documents Kissinger's ascendancy, from his relatively few and short appearances in 1969 and 1970 to a growing fascination with his role in the Nixon White House over the next two years, captured in his "peace is at hand" press conference on the eve of the 1972 election. During the following four years, as he became secretary of state during Watergate and engaged in his "shuttle diplomacy" in the Middle East, Kissinger made hundreds of appearances in American living rooms, serving as, in effect, the "president for foreign policy." Kissinger remained a dominant television personality after he left office, making exclusive deals with the major networks and becoming a leading commentator on American foreign policy.

His television role in promoting the Nixon and Ford administrations' foreign policy contributes to what is the central argument of this book. Most treatments of Henry Kissinger have highlighted his role as a foreign policy intellectual who advocated a policy of *realpolitik* for the United States, a foreign policy that eschewed moral considerations or democratic ideology and was geared to a "cold-blooded" promotion and protection of America's security and interests. This is not incorrect, but it is incomplete. To fully understand Henry Kissinger, it is important to see him as a political actor, a politician, and a man who understood that American foreign policy is fundamentally shaped and determined by the struggles and battles of American domestic politics. Kissinger frequently liked to portray himself as a foreign policy expert "above" politics, independent and nonpartisan in his political leanings, offering his wisdom and advice to leaders without concern for the political advantage or disadvantage it might bring. "The President never talks to me about domestic politics," Kissinger remarked, sitting at the Republican presidential convention in 1972 and answering a question about whether a peace settlement in Vietnam might help Nixon's reelection chances.[9] This was nonsense. Kissinger spoke with Nixon often about the domestic political impact of foreign policy. He well understood the importance of domestic politics in shaping foreign policy when he worked for Nelson Rockefeller, and his sensitivity to those issues grew—first as Richard Nixon's personal agent for foreign policy, scoring successes that brought Nixon's reelection; then, as Nixon declined during Watergate, as the president for foreign policy, acting unilaterally in the Middle East and elsewhere; and finally as secretary of state and effectively Gerald Ford's director of foreign policy. While not a traditional politician—Kissinger's foreign birth precluded him from running for president, and he did not hold rallies, kiss babies, or give formal campaign speeches—he recognized the centrality of politics to foreign policy and knew how deeply intertwined within the American system foreign policy and domestic politics were. He adjusted his perspective and recommendations accordingly. The French foreign minister Michel Jobert, who clashed with Kissinger during the 1973 Middle East crisis, remarked, "[Kissinger] was said to have a taste for stardom, that he was a foreign policy *prima donna*, but I believe [his taste] was for politics. He is a politician, above all else . . . He calculates like a politician."[10] Henry Kissinger sought political power for reasons of personal ambition, to enact his preferred policies, and to defend his perception of America's national interest.

In approaching Kissinger from this perspective, the issue of the role of partisan domestic politics in shaping foreign policy emerges, and remains a hotly contested issue.[11] Many Americans deeply believe that the United States should adhere to the famous words of Senator Arthur Vandenberg of Michigan that "politics stops at the water's edge." Vandenberg made this statement as the Soviet Union was emerging as the new threat to the United States and as President Harry Truman was rallying Americans behind such programs as the Marshall Plan and the NATO alliance. The bipartisan support for the containment policy in Europe was, however, more the exception than the rule in U.S. history. Hedrick Smith, the chief diplomatic correspondent of *The New York Times*, wrote, "By the unwritten rules of the power game, it is practically immoral for presidents to admit that domestic politics play a role in foreign policy decisions. But everyone knows they do, and presidents listen to those who heed the political winds."[12] The best way to approach the study of this question is to recognize that the influence of domestic politics should be considered along a spectrum, from being quite fundamental to some decisions and more peripheral to others. As unpleasant as it is to think that decisions about war and peace might be influenced by electoral considerations, it is better to recognize and accept it as the reality of our flawed but still democratic and pluralist republic. From a president's point of view, the best foreign policy for the country is useless if he is not elected or reelected to implement it. Even the great realist George Kennan, the father of the containment policy, acknowledged this. Kennan often despaired over the influence of American domestic politics and believed it would be best if there could be found "men independent of government and reluctant to participate" who could be drafted to serve as an enlightened elite to conduct the affairs of state. But he was grounded enough to realize this was an impossibility, and that the national interest was subject to interpretation and its promotion could never be totally disinterested or objective. Kennan knew that the direction of American foreign policy was shaped, at least in part, by "internal power struggles" and that while Americans might reach a bipartisan consensus on some issues, most of their history reflected bitter divisions and partisan arguments over how best to defend and promote the national interest.[13]

Kissinger, in his understanding of the politics of American foreign policy, and in the manner in which he came to personalize and project that foreign policy while he served in office, experienced considerable success and some tragic failures. But he did give American foreign policy a coherence and strategic purpose it has often lacked in the years since Kissinger was in office. At times he reflected an admirable sense of the proper limits of American power and sought to keep the United States from misguided commitments and unnecessary foreign adventures. Yet he also embodied a contradiction, as his preaching of limits was in tension with his own energetic search for new opportunities to assert American power. Hans Morgenthau, the legendary German analyst of international relations who preached realism in foreign policy, once characterized Kissinger as the Greek word *polytropos*, or "many-sided" or "of many appearances." Morgenthau was seeking to explain his former student's extraordinary skill as a negotiator and mediator, a "miracle worker" in the Middle East "who satisfies the interests of all within limits tolerable for all concerned, and thereby, holds out at least the promise of an end to strife."[14] This book recognizes the *polytropos* in Henry Kissinger and seeks to shed some light on the many sides of this complicated historical figure.

1.

THE MAKING OF
HENRY KISSINGER,
1923–1968

O N DECEMBER 2, 1968, Americans watching the evening news saw a relatively short, stout, curly-haired figure with horn-rimmed glasses standing next to their president-elect. Professor Henry A. Kissinger was Richard
Nixon's "first major foreign policy appointment," as Frank Reynolds of ABC
put it. Kissinger would be "the new assistant to the president for national security affairs, the job currently occupied by Walt Rostow." Commentators on
all three networks wondered whether it was significant that Nixon announced
Kissinger's appointment before he had selected a secretary of state. A nervous-
looking Kissinger stared at Nixon as the president praised him: "Dr. Kissinger
is a man who is known to all people who are interested in foreign policy as
perhaps one of the major scholars in America and the world in this area."
Nixon went on to note that Kissinger had never held a "full-time government

assignment" and that he was encouraging the Harvard professor to "bring in new men to develop new ideas and policies." All three networks reported Kissinger's unwillingness to label himself when asked whether he was a "hard- or soft-liner" on the Vietnam War. Kissinger stressed that Nixon wanted advisers "even if they didn't agree with the administration." Nixon answered a question about whether he wanted to be "his own secretary of state" by insisting that he had instructed Kissinger not to set himself up as a "wall" between the president and secretary of state, adding, "I intend to appoint a strong secretary of state."[1]

Kissinger's appointment was greeted with acclaim across the political spectrum.[2] William Buckley, the conservative editor of the National Review, wrote to him, "Not since Florence Nightingale has any public figure received such universal acclamation,"[3] while the liberal historian Arthur Schlesinger, Jr., simply referred to it as the "best appointment so far."[4] The New York Times columnist Tom Wicker noted "the collective sigh of relief that went up from the liberal Eastern Establishment, and the Ivy League."[5] Fearing Nixon's Cold Warrior image, most shared in the sentiment of Kissinger's Harvard colleague Adam Yarmolinsky: "We'll all sleep a little better each night knowing Henry is down there."[6]

How had this refugee scholar, who had arrived in the United States as a teenager three decades earlier and still spoke with a distinctive German accent, ended up on a stage with the American president? Henry Kissinger's life is interwoven with the global developments of the twentieth century: the rise of Nazism, World War II and the Holocaust, and the Cold War. America's rise to a new position as a superpower transformed its institutions and society, and shaped the lives of all Americans. This history, coupled with the extraordinary personal ambition and intelligence of Kissinger, is the necessary backdrop for understanding the meteoric ascent of the Jewish boy from a small city in Germany.

FÜRTH ON BOTH SIDES OF THE ATLANTIC

Henry Kissinger was born in the city of Fürth in the province of Bavaria on May 27, 1923. Heinz Alfred was the first child of Louis Kissinger, a schoolteacher, and Paula Stern, the daughter of Falk Stern, a prosperous cattle dealer whose wealth would help the Kissingers purchase their first home. The Kissingers were observant Orthodox Jews, conservative in their politics, and thoroughly middle-class German patriots. Kissinger grew up with his younger brother, Walter, in what seemed like a safe and secure community, developing a lifelong passion for soccer, reading voraciously, and enduring the other learning rituals of German *Bildung*, or "inward cultivation," including the piano lessons that the young Heinz disdained.[7] His parents enjoyed the close fellowship of friends largely but not exclusively from Fürth's small Jewish community, which could trace its origins to the fifteenth century and whose emancipation and active participation in the life of the town dated back more than seventy-five years.[8]

As secure as this world might have seemed, it was about to come apart at the seams. The first warning signs coincided with the year of Kissinger's birth. Germans used wheelbarrows full of banknotes to pay for a loaf of bread as their currency collapsed under the weight of reparations for World War I and the French occupation of the Ruhr. The city of Munich, only a little over a hundred miles from Fürth, saw Adolf Hitler attempt his "Beer Hall Putsch" in November, failing to overthrow the Weimar Republic but demonstrating the depth of nationalist opposition and the potential for anti-Semitic violence. Heinz Kissinger remembered little of the traumas of Weimar democracy. His family's position was not seriously affected by the inflation or the beginning of the Great Depression in 1929. The coming of the Nazis to power in January 1933, however, left its mark. His father lost his teaching job and fell into a state of immobility and psychological depression. "Permanently retired," Louis Kissinger "withdrew into his study," his son Walter later recalled.[9] As a young teenager, Kissinger and his brother saw the progressive segregation, isolation, and humiliation the Jews of Fürth experienced; even their attempt to watch soccer games came with the risk of their being beaten by young Nazi thugs. The world of Heinz's childhood rapidly collapsed, and his parents and the older generation of Fürth's Jews could not protect their young from the hatred around them. After the passage of the Nuremberg Laws of 1935, Kissinger's mother began to look for a way to leave Germany. A cousin in the

United States was willing to provide the financial support that would allow the Kissingers to emigrate. In August 1938, after a last visit with Paula's elderly parents in Leutershausen, where Heinz saw his father cry for the first time, the family headed to New York. Only three months later, during Kristallnacht, the synagogue in Fürth, like hundreds of others throughout Germany, burned to the ground in a night of orchestrated violence. Of the almost two thousand Jews in Fürth in 1933, fewer than forty were left by 1945. At least thirteen, if not more, members of Kissinger's family would perish in the Holocaust.

Kissinger recalled that "the deepest impact" of his early life in Germany and his immigration to the United States in 1938 was that "all the things that had seemed secure and stable collapsed and many of the people that one had considered the steady examples suddenly were thrown into enormous turmoil themselves and into fantastic insecurities. So in this case it was a rather unsettling experience."[10] "Rather unsettling" is a colossal understatement, but Kissinger regularly disdained any psychohistory, insisting, "That part of my childhood is not a key to anything."[11] Yet the family's forced exile from Germany and their difficult early years as immigrants in the United States were traumatic for Heinz, now Henry. It does not take Sigmund Freud to recognize that these experiences may have shaped or accentuated certain characteristics, such as Kissinger's legendary insecurity, paranoia, and extreme sensitivity to criticism. His intellectual emphasis on stability and equilibrium in international relations, and his fears about revolution and disorder, were natural outgrowths of a youth violently interrupted. The collapse of his gentle father in the face of Nazi persecution contributed to Kissinger's own sense that not only do the meek not inherit the earth, but that power is the ultimate arbiter in both life and international relations. Stanley Hoffmann, Kissinger's colleague from Harvard and a fellow victim of Nazi persecution, remarked that Kissinger's philosophy of life was that "good will won't help you defend yourself on the docks of Marseilles."[12]

After he achieved fame, Kissinger often romanticized his first experiences of America. He regularly told the story of walking down the street, seeing a group of boys, and then crossing the street to avoid the expected violence, only to remember that he was in America. As attractive a story as this is, the reality of New York in the late 1930s was not that of tolerance and tranquility. Ethnic violence was hardly uncommon. America in the late 1930s was more an indifferent and sometimes hostile environment, consumed with its own suffering and hoping to isolate itself from the world. Although Franklin Roosevelt's New Deal was entering its sixth year, unemployment still hovered near 20 percent, and immigrants were neither numerous nor wanted by most Americans. The Kissingers were fortunate to have family in New York, but their living conditions were difficult. They spent the first two years in a small two-bedroom apartment in the Bronx. In 1940, they moved to a larger apartment at 615 Fort Washington Avenue in Washington Heights, an area of Manhattan that received so many Germans it was nicknamed the "Fourth Reich." Louis Kissinger began to suffer from a gallbladder ailment and slipped deeper into depression, telling his wife he was the "loneliest person in this big city."[13] Although he eventually found work as a bookkeeper, it was Paula who took charge. Helped by the Council of Jewish Women, Paula became a caterer and quickly built a small business that helped keep the family afloat financially.[14]

Washington Heights was "a relatively homogeneous neighborhood consisting mainly of Jews from southern Germany rather than Berlin and the north," with "an emphasis on orthodoxy, not as practiced in Eastern Europe, but still quite pronounced."[15] In effect, the Kissingers moved to a Fürth on the other side of the Atlantic, and although Henry prided himself on learning how to take the subway to Yankee Stadium and understanding baseball, his life still revolved around the traditional Orthodox community and synagogue. He remained a shy and socially inept young immigrant teenager, an observant Orthodox Jew who played soccer for the neighborhood club but flunked his driving test. While he admired "American technology, the American tempo of work, American freedom," he shared a common European feeling about the superficiality of Americans. They took a "casual approach to life," Kissinger wrote, and "no youth of my age has any kind of spiritual problem that he seriously concerns himself with."[16] Kissinger found it difficult to make American friends. He started seeing Anneliese Fleischer, a fellow refugee from Nuremberg, although their relationship unfolded slowly and fitfully.[17] Kissinger graduated from George Washington High School and then attended the City College of New York at night. He worked during the day in a brush-cleaning factory owned by cousins of his mother and seemed destined for a career as an accountant, "a nice job," he later recalled.[18] As one biographer put it, "Nothing that happened to Kissinger during those years encouraged him to read more widely; his historical interests were as underdeveloped when he was twenty as when he arrived in New York as a boy of fifteen."[19]

THE UNITED STATES ARMY AND MR. HENRY

Henry Kissinger received his draft notice in January 1943 and became part of an extraordinary moment in American history—the mobilization of some 16 million Americans, more than 10 percent of the population, for the first truly global conflict. This mobilization caused untold suffering and led to almost 400,000 American deaths and thousands more wounded, both physically and psychologically. Nevertheless, it would also be an enormously liberating experience for millions of Americans, like both of the Kissinger brothers, who, although they had traveled far, had never been outside their insular community. The geographical and social mobility unleashed by World War II, furthered by the financial and educational benefits of the GI Bill, fundamentally altered the United States, not only making it the first superpower but also opening up unprecedented opportunities for millions of its citizens.[20]

Kissinger's career is impossible to imagine without World War II. After his induction, Kissinger went to the Infantry Replacement Training Center in Spartanburg, South Carolina. As one writer put it, "The army experience, which for so many Americans meant death or a hiatus in their prospective careers, meant a new life for Henry Kissinger."[21] He was both fascinated and appalled by this strange new world, sharing with his brother the resentments of an unhappy draftee, who had been "pushed around and inoculated, counted, and stood at attention." Although he would later say how much he liked "the middle Americans" from "Wisconsin and Illinois and Indiana" with whom he trained, he wrote to Walter, "Don't become too friendly with the scum you invariably meet there." Continuing his admonitions, he warned his younger brother against gambling and patronizing prostitutes, especially the "filthy, syphilis-infected camp followers." He also urged Walter, "Repress your natural tendencies and don't push to the forefront."[22] Kissinger himself ended up standing out in a different way. In a series of tests given by the Army at Clemson University, Kissinger scored high enough to be assigned to the Army Specialized Training Program (ASTP), which sent talented soldiers to colleges.[23] Along with this official recognition of his intellect, on June 19, 1943, Henry Kissinger became an American citizen.[24]

The ASTP program sent Kissinger to study engineering at Lafayette College in Easton, Pennsylvania, only about eighty miles west from his Washington Heights home. The ASTP students were expected to finish their degrees quickly, and in a little over six months, Kissinger completed twelve engineering courses. Despite the intense workload, he occasionally hitchhiked home, saw his girlfriend, and dutifully attended synagogue with his father. His roommates at Lafayette recalled him as the "brainiest of a very intelligent class." Charles Coyle remembered of Kissinger, "He didn't read books. He ate them, with his eyes, his fingers, with his squirming in the chair or bed, and with his mumbling criticism." Kissinger's intellectual intensity matched with his "unmilitary" appearance, as he was easily the sloppiest dresser of his cohort.[25]

Kissinger's ASTP experience confirmed his growing sense of his own intellectual abilities, but it may also have been the beginning of his doubts about his religion.[26] By "eating ham for Uncle Sam," Kissinger rebelled against an identity determined by his Orthodox community and completed his "Americanization," shedding his religion but keeping his German accent, with his keen intelligence distinguishing him within the melting pot.[27] As a clearly gifted student whom the professors depended on to explain complicated materials to the other soldiers, Kissinger achieved an academic status that he had not had before. When the manpower needs of D-Day in Europe led the Army to cancel the ASTP program and return the trainees to their lowly status as privates, Kissinger was among the twenty-five men selected to be tested for admission to medical school. He was not one of the final five chosen, losing out in a quota system that allowed only one Jewish student with the two Protestants and two Catholics. Along with 2,800 ASTP trainees, Kissinger was shipped to Camp Claiborne, Louisiana, and the Eighty-Fourth Infantry Division, arriving there on April 1, 1944. The April Fools' date contributed to the ASTP soldiers' sense of victimhood, as the drill sergeants treated the "college kids" unmercifully. In the midst of grueling training sessions in the Louisiana heat, Kissinger grew homesick, calling collect to say, "Mother, I want to walk out on my hands and crawl home."[28]

Even in the misery of Camp Claiborne, however, Kissinger stood out, selected by his commanders to provide soldiers with a weekly briefing on war news. Although he did the job well, Kissinger was more impressed with another older German refugee in an American uniform, Fritz Kraemer, who came to Camp Claiborne in May 1944 to speak about the meaning of the war. After Kraemer's impassioned talk, Kissinger wrote him a note: "Dear Private Kraemer: I heard you speak yesterday. This is how it should be done. Can I help you somehow?" Kraemer responded almost immediately to the simple "fan letter," returning a few days later to seek out Kissinger for conversation and dinner, insisting they speak in German, not English. The Lutheran Kraemer later said that he was taken with "this little Jewish refugee" he had met who, he believed, "as yet knows nothing, but already he understands everything." Kraemer became the first of Kissinger's significant mentors and patrons, helping him to achieve distinction within the Army and obtain positions and opportunities that might have been difficult to acquire on his own.

Fritz Kraemer was himself a caricature of a nineteenth-century Prussian conservative, wearing a monocle and riding boots, carrying a riding crop, and speaking in long harangues about the values of Western civilization. Ironically, both of Kraemer's divorced parents were Jews who had converted, and his father, about whom Kraemer never spoke, died in a concentration camp.[29] An informant described Kraemer in his FBI file as "probably 100 percent pro-German but also definitely anti-Hitler," and his political views mixed a respect for international law with a profound anti-materialism and emphasis on the moral basis of civilization.[30] Kraemer introduced Kissinger to the study of history, reinforcing Kissinger's conservatism and disdain for the radicalism of the Nazis and Communists. Kissinger later eulogized Kraemer as "the greatest single influence on my formative years," praising him for dedicating "his life to fighting against the expedient over the principled."[31] Kraemer was the proud teacher and Kissinger the devoted student, absorbing the historical lessons and reading the philosophers Kraemer told him to read. Fifteen years older than Kissinger, Kraemer had a forceful and dynamic character, eccentric as it was, that appealed to Kissinger and made of him a new father figure, a powerful man who had fought back against the Nazis.

With rumors of Germany's imminent collapse and the possibility that their only function might be serving as military government, Kissinger's regiment of the Eighty-Fourth Division arrived in Europe on November 2, 1944, the day Franklin Roosevelt was elected to a fourth term as president. Germany was not finished fighting, however, and the soldiers of the Eighty-Fourth faced combat. Kissinger was not among them, having been reassigned to the "G-2 section of divisional headquarters," interviewing German civilians and combing through captured German mail and documents for intelligence. His formal title was "Special Agent in charge of the reg[imental] CIC [Counter-Intelligence Corps] team."[32] This marked the beginning of Kissinger's twelve-year association with Army Intelligence, and the friendships and contacts he made there would play a role in his career. This assignment meant that Kissinger "was never called upon to fire his rifle in combat," but he still faced danger when he stayed behind in the Belgian town of Marche-en-Famenne during the German offensive in the Battle of the Bulge.[33] As Kraemer later praised him, Kissinger "did this with full knowledge that he would never get out if the Germans took the town."[34]

After the failure of the German offensive, Kissinger's division entered Germany in March 1945 and occupied the industrial city of Krefeld. Kissinger's chief role was in the Allied policy of "denazification," to both ferret out active Nazis and trap possible "Werewolves," the name given by Nazi propaganda to guerrilla resistance to the Allied occupation.[35] Kissinger was soon promoted to sergeant and officially assigned to the Eighty-Fourth Counter-Intelligence Corps. After the Eighty-Fourth moved into Hannover in April 1945, Kissinger was particularly effective at capturing Nazi and Gestapo members. He later joked about his method, noting that he simply "put up a poster that all those interested in police work should come to us," and that a former Gestapo officer promptly came in for a job. Kissinger continued, "I just gave him a driver and a police escort" and "he went out and rounded up 45 of his Gestapo colleagues!" The joking aside, Kissinger was good at this police work, "involving a mixture of detection, interrogation, and detention," and it helped him earn the Bronze Star.[36]

Kissinger never joked about April 10, 1945, when the Eighty-Fourth Division came upon the concentration camp at Ahlem. In fact, Kissinger did not speak of this event until much later, calling it "one of the most horrifying experiences of my life."[37] He described the "barely recognizable human" state of the prisoners and his "immediate instinct" to want to feed the starving men, only to discover that solid food killed some, as they were unable to digest it. One surviving prisoner later remembered Kissinger as the American GI who told him, "You are free." Shortly after the experience, Kissinger wrote an essay titled "The Eternal Jew," which was an ironic reference to Nazi propaganda. He recounted the painful question he asked himself at the liberation of the camp: "Who was lucky, the man who draws circles in the sand and mumbles, 'I am free,' or the bones that are interred in the hillside?" Kissinger also expressed a raw sentiment that many came to share when confronted by the camps: "This is humanity in the 20th century."[38]

On May 8, 1945, the war in Europe ended, and the Eighty-Fourth Division pulled back to the Heidelberg area in the American zone. Sergeant Henry Kissinger became the "absolute ruler of Bensheim," a small papermaking town about thirty miles south of Frankfurt. The twenty-two-year-old had the "absolute authority to arrest people," and Kissinger certainly enjoyed the perks of his position of power, appropriating a villa, commandeering a luxury car for his travels, and telling his parents, "We also took over the butler so that now we get our shoes shined . . . clothes pressed, baths drawn, & whatever else a butler does."[39] Kissinger acted like other Americans in military government, but he displayed no outward signs of vengeance against the Germans. When his father urged him to be "tough on the Germans," Kissinger responded that he was tough but that "somewhere this negativism must end, somewhere we must produce something positive or we'll have to remain here, as guardians over chaos, forever." Kissinger used an expression that he hoped might characterize the occupation: "Prove to them that you are here in Germany because you are better, not that you are better because you are here."[40] He referred to himself as "Mr. Henry" to the Germans, "because," he said, "I didn't want the Germans to think the Jews were coming back to take revenge."[41] Kissinger's "objectivity," as Fritz Kraemer called it, was atypical among Jewish veterans, most of whom, according to one recent history, "shunned and despised Germans," swearing "never to visit Germany as tourists, viewing it . . . as a cursed land."[42] Kissinger's approach to the Germans was generous and forward-looking, and his "feeling for his homeland would always resemble that of a political exile . . . [who] would despise the insurgent regime which had branded him a public enemy . . . [but] feel an overpowering affinity for the greater historical and cultural tradition into which he had been born."[43]

Because Germany later emerged as a peaceful democratic state, the American military government of Germany looks much better in historical perspective than it did to contemporary observers.[44] At the time, critics from the left complained about a lenient denazification that allowed too many former Nazis to remain in positions of power, while critics from the right derided the New Dealers who wanted to reform Germany but were unable to restore the economy. To many ordinary Germans the immediate postwar years were simply an era of hunger and deprivation, in which cigarettes became a common currency and the black market the difference between life and death. In this chaotic environment, Kissinger proved effective as the commandant in Bensheim, although he relied on some Germans of dubious character, including a police chief who was later convicted of taking bribes.[45] Kissinger remained in Bensheim only until April 1946, when an opportunity to teach at the European Command Intelligence School opened up. The job paid well and allowed the "unmilitary" Kissinger to stay in Germany as a civilian. The job also reunited him with Fritz Kraemer, who was responsible for organizing the curriculum. The school, designed for officers serving in military government, afforded Kissinger, still only a high school graduate with some college courses in accounting and engineering, the opportunity to lecture his former superiors on such topics as the structure of the Nazi state and German paramilitary organizations. As the political climate in Germany began to change in late 1946, and the Cold War loomed, Kissinger displayed his own anti-communist sentiments, advocating strict surveillance of German personnel and a ban on the employment of Communists at the school.[46] The academic milieu of the school also appealed to Kissinger, and among his talented colleagues would be his future assistant Helmut "Hal" Sonnenfeldt and, later, his Harvard colleague Henry Rosovsky. Kissinger showed his rebellious side as well, refusing to submit a lesson plan for approval and violating regulations by keeping his dog in the barracks. "He was a problem person," the director of education later recalled, a description of Kissinger articulated often over the course of his career.[47]

Kissinger was not in a hurry to return to the United States and stayed at Oberammergau for a year. He now had a girlfriend, Leonie Harbert, a fellow instructor and a German gentile. This caused tension with his parents, who feared he might marry her. He assured them that he was not in a "marrying or engaging mood," but his evident loss of his Orthodox Jewish faith contributed even further to their unhappiness. In several blunt and even hostile letters, Kissinger defended himself and criticized their traditional beliefs: "To me there is not only right or wrong but many shades in between. The real tragedies in life are not choices between right and wrong . . . Real difficulties bare difficulties of the soul, provoking agonies, which you in your world of black and white can't begin to comprehend." Kissinger's wartime experiences shattered many of the certainties that had guided his own life, and he lashed out at his parents when they repeated them. His defiance shocked them, but he assured his parents that he would readjust. "After all, not everybody came out of this war a psycho-neurotic."[48]

When Kissinger finally decided he should return to the United States and finish college, Fritz Kraemer told him, "A gentleman does not go to the College of the City of New York," and encouraged him to get away from "the city where your parents happen to be."[49] Kissinger applied late, but Harvard accepted him, giving him a year's academic credit for his City College experience and awarding him one of the two Harvard National Scholarships given to New Yorkers that year.[50] Kissinger arrived back in the United States, preceded by his dog, Smokey, dutifully shipped by Harbert. In one of his continuing small rebellions, Kissinger brought the dog to Cambridge, violating Harvard rules but providing him "with a wonderful link between a life that was & one that will be."[51]

The Henry Kissinger who returned to Washington Heights in July 1947 was a very different man from the one who had left four years earlier. The Orthodox Jew from Fürth no longer practiced his Judaism, the refugee had exercised power and authority over the people who expelled him, and the future accountant now planned to enter America's greatest university. There were other changes as well—changes in how Kissinger saw the world and what he believed about human nature and human beings. The Army experience deepened and matured Kissinger, opening new worlds, changing his expectations for his life, and fueling his indomitable ambition. It also forced him to confront the bitter reality of what happened to those of his family who had not left Germany.[52] Kissinger's harsh assessment of human nature was conveyed in a letter he wrote to the relatives of Helmut Reissner, a boyhood classmate of Kissinger's in Fürth who had survived the concentration camps and was now coming to the United States. Reissner's family, one of the wealthier Jewish families in Fürth, had been shipped to a concentration camp in Latvia, but Reissner had managed to survive and make his way back to Fürth, where Kissinger found him and helped him recover. Kissinger told Reissner's family not "to expect a broken boy. Helmut is a man. He has seen more than most people in a lifetime." Kissinger went on to explain that the camps were "testing grounds," where men "fought for survival" under the worst possible circumstances. "The intellectuals, the idealists, the men of high morals had no chance." Survival required "a singleness of purpose inconceivable to you sheltered people in the States. Such singleness of purpose broached no stopping in front of accepted sets of values, it had to disregard ordinary standards of morality. One could only survive through lies, tricks and somehow acquiring enough food to fill one's belly." Kissinger closed the letter with a telling statement: "They have seen man from the most evil side, who can blame them for being suspicious?"[53]

Although Kissinger resisted the idea of presenting himself as "some traumatized victim," there is no question that these experiences would inform his approach to politics and international relations. It is not difficult to detect in these letters aspects of Kissinger's later approach to international affairs, particularly his belief that the statesman could not be held to "ordinary standards of morality" in the struggle between nations. His dismissal of the "intellectuals, the idealists, the men of high morals" would also be a refrain throughout his career, especially in his critique of the policies of American leaders like Woodrow Wilson and their League of Nations. Yet Kissinger could also be flexible in the way he invoked the lessons of the Holocaust, and it is best to avoid too many facile connections between Kissinger's experiences in Nazi Germany and his policies and personality.[54] The Nazi experience contributed to Kissinger's strong sense of the tragedy in human life and his profoundly pessimistic view of human nature and society. However, the war years also opened up the world to him, contributing to his self-confidence; pride in his accomplishments as a soldier, occupier, administrator, and teacher; and strong faith, even arrogance, about his intellectual abilities and future promise.

HARVARD UNIVERSITY AND "WILD BILL" ELLIOTT

The two million veterans who streamed into America's colleges after World War II were a serious and mature lot, hardened by wartime experiences and filled with idealism, the hope of creating a better world, and the personal desire to get ahead in American society. None was more ambitious and serious than Henry Kissinger. Rooming with his illegal dog, Smokey, and two other Jewish veterans in Claverly Hall, Harvard's most dilapidated dormitory, Kissinger largely kept to himself. He recalled later, "I was completely unsure of myself. I had gotten out of the Army and felt like an immigrant again."[55] Roommates remembered Kissinger sitting in an overstuffed chair, reading at all hours of the day and night, biting his nails bloody. One recalled that Henry "worked harder, studied more . . . read till 1 or 2 a.m., had tremendous drive and discipline . . . he was absorbing everything."[56] Kissinger made "no lasting friendships with other students; he seemed scarcely aware of the extraordinary range of people gathered in Cambridge."[57] Kissinger's close friends were other veterans, and he remained a reserve Counter-Intelligence Corps officer, staying in close contact with Kraemer, who was now working in Washington, and spending his vacation time working in the CIC. After his second year at Harvard, he dutifully married Ann Fleischer, his longtime girlfriend, who had shortened her first name, and moved off campus.[58]

In his first semester, Kissinger took Development of Constitutional Government, taught by one of the legends in Harvard's Government Department, William Yandell Elliott, who would become the second great mentor in Kissinger's life. "Wild Bill" Elliott was anything but the typical Harvard professor of the 1950s. Athlete, poet, and scholar, he was a man of enormous energy and dynamism, possessing what Kissinger called the style of "grand seigneur." Other colleagues were less impressed. Stanley Hoffmann thought Elliott "slightly mad," and Daniel Ellsberg called him "a terrible fake with a Southern accent."[59] A Tennessee native proud of his roots, Elliott was an artillery commander in World War I and an all-American football player for Vanderbilt University, and even had a brief association with the Fugitives, the renowned band of poets and literary scholars who came together at Vanderbilt in the early 1920s to defend their conception of the South and its agrarian way of life. Elliott won a life-changing Rhodes Scholarship and attended Balliol College at Oxford, where he came to admire the individual tutorials of Oxford and eventually used them with his Harvard students. In the 1930s, he was an active campaigner against the Neutrality Acts and for intervention in Europe, a stance that was not popular on the Harvard campus.[60] During World War II he had served as vice president of the War Production Board. After 1945, he often spent two to three days a week consulting in Washington with the House Foreign Affairs Committee.

Elliott was a keen judge of student talent, and among his tutees were future leaders like John Kennedy, Dean Rusk, and McGeorge Bundy.[61] Kissinger enjoyed telling the story of nervously entering Elliott's office, where the busy professor kept him waiting before looking up and exclaiming, "Oh God, another tutee." Elliott assigned Kissinger a paper on the philosopher Immanuel Kant, whom Elliott also admired greatly, and rattled off a long list of books for him to read. Kissinger went directly to the library, got the books, read them, and wrote the paper. Elliott, as another student remembered, was "impressed to the gills." It marked the beginning of an important relationship in Kissinger's career. Elliott became a near tireless promoter of Henry Kissinger, describing him as "more like a mature colleague than a student" and "a combination of Kant and Spinoza." Elliott's high praise for Kissinger's "depth and philosophical insight" was sometimes mixed with disparaging references to his mind's "lack of grace" and "Teutonic" thoroughness, but Elliott recognized Kissinger's potential and was remarkably unselfish in opening up numerous opportunities for his prized student.[62]

Kissinger confirmed Elliott's faith in his intellectual talent and depth with his massive 388-page senior honors thesis, immodestly titled "The Meaning of History: Reflections on Spengler, Toynbee and Kant." Kissinger compared Immanuel Kant's moral philosophy with those of the lesser figures of Oswald Spengler and Arnold Toynbee. Kissinger's arguments were portentous and heavy: "Life is suffering, birth involves death. Transitoriness is the fate of existence. No civilization has yet been permanent, no longing completely fulfilled. This is necessity, the fatedness of history, the dilemma of mortality."[63] Kissinger chose to structure his work in a Hegelian dialectical form of thesis, antithesis, and synthesis: Spengler's philosophical pessimism about the inevitable decline of the West provided the thesis; Toynbee's more hopeful interpretation of history's meaning and purpose, the antithesis; and finally, Kant's emphasis on man's freedom and the spiritual meaning of history, the possible new synthesis.[64] Kissinger was not always careful to delineate his own views from his restatement of Spengler's and Toynbee's philosophies, with the result that some have seen Kissinger's pessimistic musings about America in the 1970s as a reflection of his attraction to Spenglerian historical pessimism.[65] In fact, Kissinger rejected what he perceived as Spengler's and Toynbee's historical determinism, along with their belief that history operated with "laws" similar to the natural world, which could be ascertained through empirical research. Kissinger was far more attracted to Kant's moral philosophy and its famous "categorical imperative . . . the general formulation of which enjoins men to act according to those maxims which can at the same time be made into a universal law."[66] Kissinger agreed with Kant that man had the freedom to shape his own history. But he did not draw Kant's optimistic conclusions from this assumption. In an idiosyncratic reading of Kant, he argued that the German philosopher's work *Perpetual Peace*, which maintained that "mankind was progressing slowly but surely in the right direction" toward universal peace with a league of free republics, undermined Kant's own argument against determinism. Kissinger saw a contradiction "between Kant's moral philosophy and his philosophy of history."[67] Reflecting on his own loss of religious faith, Kissinger rejected the notion of a transcendental meaning or purpose in history and criticized Kant's optimism about humanity's progress. Kissinger regarded much of history as the story of tragedy, something that Americans, in their optimistic national creed, had difficulty understanding and accepting. In the end, according to the historian Peter Dickson, Kissinger's own personal "philosophy of history" was "a curious amalgamation of ethical relativism and antimaterialism," in which "man must create his own meaning, his own values, and his own reality." Dickson characterizes this as "Kissinger's existentialist philosophy of history."[68]

Kissinger never published his thesis, a rather uncharacteristic action on his part. Though sympathetic to Kissinger, and using the thesis to develop his theme of Kissinger as an "idealist," his biographer Niall Ferguson has called the work "an exercise in academic exhibitionism," an undergraduate's showing off all that he has learned rather than a sustained original academic work.[69] Ferguson is right. The thesis, while containing many interesting historical formulations and impressive in its scale and sheer hubris, is designed to impress a favored mentor, not to offer a profound insight into the author's soul or his future. It accomplished its most important purpose though. Kissinger earned a summa cum laude degree and admission into the graduate program. (It also led the Government Department to enact the "Kissinger Rule" restricting future undergraduate theses to less than half the length of the Kissinger opus.)

Only a few weeks after Kissinger's undergraduate graduation, the Korean War began. Just as World War II had transformed his life and career goals, this new war in Asia opened up new opportunities. North Korea's attack on the South in June 1950 was the Pearl Harbor moment of the Cold War, convincing American leaders that the Soviet Union sought global domination and setting off a mobilization of the American state and its resources. America now was at war with international communism. After China's intervention in November 1950, President Truman issued a declaration of a national emergency, and fears grew over a possible atomic war. Senator Joseph McCarthy's hunt for domestic communists only intensified anxieties that America faced both a foreign and a domestic enemy. The Cold War was now a hot war, and it would shape Henry Kissinger's life for the next four decades.

Harvard University became a "Cold War university," reflecting both the strength of the Cold War consensus within American society as well as the university's dependence on financial support from the government, foundations, and corporations.[70] Elliott was poised to take advantage of this change.[71] He believed that the attack in Korea was a "testing of the civilization of the West . . . clearly and brutally" thrust upon the United States and its allies.[72] Kissinger shared his mentor's viewpoint, arguing in even stronger terms, "The stark fact of the situation is, however, that Soviet expansionism is directed *against our existence, not our policies.*"[73] Kissinger believed that containment had failed and that war with the Soviet Union was "inevitable, not because of the United States policies but because of the existence of the United States as a symbol of capitalist democracy."[74] Kissinger's viewpoint is striking although not unusual. The famous National Security Council Report 68 argued that the Cold War was a "total war," a life-and-death struggle, and that it required the total commitment of all parts of American society to wage it successfully.[75]

With the American government deeply concerned about the ideological struggle, and with Harvard eager to cooperate, Elliott made the case for two projects that Kissinger ended up directing.[76] Kissinger took charge of the International Seminar program, designed to bring young leaders from Europe to Harvard for a six-week course during the summer. Kissinger described the program as a way to create a "spiritual link" between future elites in Europe and the United States. In Kissinger's view, it was "primarily in the spiritual field that American stock is lowest in overseas countries due to a combination of Nazi and Communist propaganda which pictures the U.S. as bloated, materialistic, and culturally barbarian."[77] He hoped that by giving to "active, intelligent Europeans the opportunity to observe the deeper meaning of United States democracy," the program would strengthen the bonds of the Western unity. The program began with twenty European participants in the summer of 1951 and would continue for the next eighteen years, expanding to include students from Africa, Asia, and Latin America. Among the more than six hundred elite participants would be some who in the future became presidents and prime ministers of France, Japan, Belgium, Malaysia, and Turkey, as well as influential academics, artists, journalists, publishers, and corporate officials. The seminar quickly became Kissinger's show, as he organized both the academic and social programs. Kissinger recruited speakers for the seminar, engaging luminaries like Eleanor Roosevelt, Arthur Schlesinger, Jr., and other prominent Harvard and Washington figures.[78] Kissinger also hosted the group at his home, even giving his amused students a lecture in the rules of the American cocktail party. The seminar was an activity Kissinger attended to enthusiastically, showing his own embrace of the psychological tactic, later called "soft power," to help the United States in its Cold War struggle.

After the first seminar in 1951, Elliott and Kissinger conceived the idea of publishing a journal to embody many of the ideas and discussions from the seminar. *Confluence* was an effort "to reach wider audiences and in the form of something approaching an international forum."[79] Kissinger did not express his own views in the journal, arguing, "In a world increasingly threatened by a pervasive orthodoxy, there must be room for free inquiry, for discussion without polemic, and for a debate which assumes the good faith of all participants."[80] Kissinger emphasized, using the editorial "we," that "we are not neutralists," and that he would differ with many of the contributors. Critics later argued that *Confluence* was "a fake . . . primarily an enterprise designed to make Henry known to great people around the world."[81] That was certainly one result of the journal—it led to the first mention ever of Kissinger's name in the pages of *The New York Times*.[82] However, it also confused one result with the more admirable goals of the project. *Confluence* opened its pages to an impressive spectrum of European opinion, especially German, and was widely distributed in the new Federal Republic.[83] It achieved significant no-toriety for an academic journal, and it attracted prestigious authors and com-mentators in both the political and cultural realms, recruiting articles from figures like McGeorge Bundy, Reinhold Niebuhr, Hannah Arendt, Raymond Aron, André Malraux, Alberto Moravia, Enoch Powell, and Denis Healey.[84]

Confluence did not avoid controversy, as when Kissinger published an ar-ticle by Ernst von Salomon, a right-wing German writer who had been con-victed for his role in the assassination of Walther Rathenau, the German foreign minister in the Weimar Republic. This article provoked an angry let-ter from Shepard Stone of the Ford Foundation, who had provided money for both the International Seminar and the journal. Stone was appalled that Kissinger would publish an article by a criminal and Nazi-sympathizer like Salomon. Kissinger told Stone he disliked Salomon and opposed what he stood for, considering him "a damned soul driven by the furies." Demonstrat-ing a remarkable self-confidence for a graduate student, Kissinger defended himself for publishing the article: "I may err occasionally on the side of too great tolerance, partly because I believe our readers sufficiently mature to make their own judgments." Kissinger argued that what Salomon represented was "a symptom of certain tendencies of our age," but that by appearing in a liberal journal like *Confluence*, Salomon was the one who was "compro-mised."[85] Kissinger was not simply defending free speech. He had solicited the article from Salomon, telling the German about "having long admired your writings even if I could not share your point of view."[86] Kissinger com-plained in a letter to Kraemer, "I have now joined you as a cardinal villain in liberal demonology," mentioning his anger that his publishing of right-wing Germans was seen "as a symptom of my totalitarian and even Nazi sympa-thies."[87] Kissinger carried himself as a professional colleague of the aca-demics with whom he dealt, but he was acutely sensitive to criticism and sought constantly to please both ends of the political spectrum. He worked hard at appearing to sympathize with people of very different political sensi-bilities, a trait he would develop and perfect when he finally reached Washington.

Both the International Seminar and *Confluence* ran on tight budgets, and

Kissinger spent a considerable amount of time trying to raise money.[88] When Shepard Stone refused additional funds for *Confluence* in May 1954, Kissinger told him that it was "a bitter pill to swallow" and that Stone's reasoning for denying him funding was the equivalent "of committing suicide because of the fear of death."[89] *Confluence* lasted until 1958, when Kissinger decided to focus on the International Seminar. The CIA provided some money for both ventures, eventually using various front organizations—including the Farfield Foundation and a group called the Friends of the Middle East—to make its contributions. When this was revealed in 1967, along with the agency's funding of *Encounter* and other leading periodicals of the time, Kissinger denied knowing the true source of the money.[90] While his denial is hard to credit, it is also the case that the CIA's funding was extremely limited. As Ferguson rightly notes, "Kissinger's activities at Harvard were among the most staid operations of the cultural Cold War. In modern terminology, it was soft power at its softest."[91]

Along with the seminar and journal, Elliott helped Kissinger with his Washington contacts, including the State Department's policy planning staff. Kissinger undertook consulting jobs with the Operations Research Office, which sent him to Korea in 1951.[92] Kissinger also became a consultant to the Psychological Strategy Board (PSB), which sponsored his first return trip to Germany in May 1952. The PSB itself was "a natural outgrowth and supplement to the operations of the CIA," part of the "ideological struggle for the hearts, minds, and souls of people around the world."[93] Kissinger was also traveling in his role as director of the International Seminar, meeting with prominent German officials and soliciting opinions on U.S. policies. The former refugee now found himself the guest of a group of rich industrialists, some of whom had served the Nazi state, sitting in the dining room of the Krupp munitions plant. "Who would have thought," Kissinger told his parents, that they would hold a dinner in honor of Henry Kissinger.[94] Along with recruiting future students for the Seminar, Kissinger contributed a report on conditions within Germany to PSB. He had arrived shortly after the United States signed the contractual agreements. Designed as a substitute for a peace treaty, the agreements were meant to put an end to the occupation regime and speed the transformation of Germany into an ally of the West. These were coupled with the signing of the treaty for the creation of the European Defense Community, the European military force within which Germany would make a contribution. Secretary of State Dean Acheson attended the signing of the treaties, and the event was trumpeted as a success for America's European policy.[95]

Kissinger would have none of it. He summed up the German reaction to the "Peace Treaty," especially the idea of Germans enlisting into a new "European Army," as "hysterical," and leading to "an outburst of anti-American feeling totally out of proportion to the specific criticism advanced." The "present psychological climate" would render any German military contribution of "doubtful usefulness." The threat he perceived in Germany was not a Communist takeover but "a nationalist reaction fed on dogmatic anti-Americanism," which would bring to power "a government which will lean on the USSR to achieve independence from the West whatever its ideological differences." To combat this, Kissinger advocated that the United States pursue a program that "emphasizes the psychological component of its political strategy," including such measures as exchange programs that might send "a few, highly selected individuals to Germany, to give them a 'cover' which will permit them to travel widely and establish contacts." Using the language of an intelligence officer, Kissinger argued for "study groups, cultural congresses, exchange professorships, and intern programs, whenever possible under nongovernmental auspices." Kissinger even advocated infiltrating and influencing German military veterans' groups, "because their power is constantly growing." He recognized that some might find these groups "unpalatable," but the Cold War did not give Americans a choice.[96]

Within the overall Cold War consensus, Kissinger, the young graduate student, had penned a critique that was both incisive and self-serving. It would mark the beginning of a distinct pattern in Kissinger's critiques and writing before he actually achieved power. The criticism would be pessimistic, direct, and cogently expressed, but rarely linked to any person or specific leader and often phrased in a way that indicated his understanding and sympathy for the policymaker's dilemma. It would question tactics but never the basic assumptions undergirding the Cold War policy of containment. And in its self-serving element would either emphasize a project Kissinger was developing, support a political candidate Kissinger favored, or confirm the wisdom of views he had already published. As interesting and insightful as Kissinger's published writings often are, they should be approached as primarily instrumental, designed less for intellectual consistency than for political utility.

Along with editing *Confluence*, running the International Seminar, and doing consulting work for the government, Kissinger worked on his doctoral dissertation, finishing it in June 1954. Titled "Peace, Legitimacy, and the Equilibrium (A Study of the Statesmanship of Castlereagh and Metternich)," the dissertation was eventually published "almost unaltered" with a new title, *A World Restored: Metternich, Castlereagh and the Problems of Peace 1812–1822*. The book is an examination of the process of peacemaking undertaken by European diplomats after the Napoleonic Wars—an unusual choice of topic.[97] One of Kissinger's graduate student classmates, John Stoessinger, remarked that most of his cohorts looked on the study of history with skepticism and suspicion, believing that "the past could not help us much to unlock the secrets of the future."[98] Other graduate students sarcastically asked Kissinger if he had heard of the atomic bomb.[99] Kissinger responded that nuclear weapons did not make history irrelevant and that it made sense to study a successful example of peacemaking like the Congress of Vienna. In the preface, he wrote, "I have chosen for my topic the period between 1812 and 1822, partly, I am frank to say, because its problems seem analogous to those of our day. But I do not insist on this analogy. Even if it is denied, the significance of this period remains in the fact that it was faced with the construction of a new international order and therefore with all the dilemmas of foreign policy in their most immediate form: the relationship between domestic and international legitimacy, the role of the balance of power, the limits of statesmanship."[100]

Kissinger dedicated his work to Elliott, to whom he owed, he said, "more, both intellectually and humanly, than I can ever repay." The book is "a mixture of history, theoretical analysis of international relations, and personal reflections on the nature of leadership."[101] Kissinger's sympathies are with the conservative statesmen who sought to preserve the stability of the international order against the revolutionary forces unleashed by France. He argues strongly that diplomacy cannot be divorced from the use of military force, and that the search for peace cannot be the primary objective of the major powers, since it would place the international system "at the mercy of the most ruthless member of the international community." Rather, true peace comes only out of a balance of power, an international equilibrium created as nations pursued their national interests within a generally accepted, "legitimate" international order. The focus of his narrative is on the "two great men," Lord Castlereagh of Britain, "who negotiated the international settlement," and Klemens von Metternich of Austria, "who legitimized it."[102] Kissinger is particularly interested in the two statesmen's struggle to reconcile the political demands of their own domestic situations with the necessity for international leadership and cooperation. Kissinger admires Metternich for his skill at negotiation and ability to manage, and manipulate, other powers in Austria's interest. But he also criticizes the Austrian's "smug self-satisfaction" in not recognizing that Austria's domestic structures required reform and adaptation. On the other hand, Kissinger praises Castlereagh for leading a reluctant Britain into a role in Europe's concert of powers, but regrets his failure to make that achievement more lasting. In an often-quoted conclusion, Kissinger says, "The two statesmen of repose were therefore both defeated in the end by their domestic structure: Castlereagh by ignoring it, Metternich by being too conscious of its vulnerability."[103]

A World Restored is often read as an "overture" to Kissinger's career, and Kissinger would spend considerable time dismissing the idea that he was another Metternich, a crafty and secretive leader determined to manipulate the balance of power.[104] Kissinger's attempt to derive historical lessons from this analogy between the post-Napoleonic era and the Cold War, with the revolutionary Soviet Union taking the role of Napoleonic France, and the United States in the position of both Castlereagh's Britain and Metternich's Austria, is occasionally heavy-handed and simplistic. Kissinger's insights into the intimate relationship between foreign policy and domestic politics provide the most revealing insights into his later career, although less as a detailed plan and more in the spirit in which he behaved. Kissinger's focus on the importance of history—he wrote that "history is the memory of states" and always described himself as a historian—belies the fact that his book is not really history in the professional sense, a close examination based on original sources of the diplomacy of the early nineteenth century. Kissinger did not undertake any archival research to complete his dissertation. He constructed an ideal Metternich—a leader who advanced the "long range principles and plans of a constructive European statesman"—rather than the Metternich revealed in the primary sources of the time, a man "of short-range maneuvers and the expedients of a repressive Austrian diplomat."[105] Although *A World Restored* possesses many profound insights into the nature of statesmanship, Kissinger romanticized the leadership of nineteenth-century diplomats and molded history into a pattern more relevant to his own philosophical and contemporary concerns than to the actual record of the past. The leaders of his work were great individuals who acted to change history, statesmen who understood the limits of political action but had exercised their creativity and insight to provide a "structure of peace" in their time. Kissinger portrayed a heroic and even idealistic model of statesmanship, a great distance from the complicated and messy choices of the flawed but very human figures of Metternich and Castlereagh.

Having finished his dissertation, Kissinger needed a job. Elliott's influence in the Government Department could not overcome some of the jealousy and resentment toward Kissinger and his mentor, and the department did not immediately promote him to assistant professor. Kissinger taught as an instructor, continuing his work on the International Seminar and *Confluence*.[106] Nevertheless, Kissinger was a man in a hurry, impatient with the strictures of academia, and profoundly ambitious.[107] He approached and received offers of assistant professorships from both the Universities of Chicago and Pennsylvania. Neither of these moved Harvard to counter their offers, but Kissinger was reluctant to move away from Cambridge. He wrote a long letter of complaint to McGeorge Bundy, the Harvard dean, lamenting the lack of "joy" in academic life, bitterly criticizing the dependency on senior professors and the resulting "conformity" and "mediocrity," and even saying he was considering going to law school.[108]

THE COUNCIL ON FOREIGN RELATIONS AND
NELSON ROCKEFELLER

In his dissertation Kissinger wrote, "Luck, in politics as in other activities, is but the residue of design."[109] At this low point in his life, Kissinger got lucky. In September 1954, as Harvard's academic year was beginning, Kissinger ran into his friend, the Pulitzer Prize–winning historian and tenured professor Arthur Schlesinger, Jr., walking across Harvard Yard. Theirs was an unusual friendship. Although Schlesinger was only six years older than Kissinger, he took a paternal interest in the refugee scholar, and Kissinger admired and flattered the accomplished historian. They also shared a bond in their desire to make history as well as write about it.[110] Schlesinger had with him a letter from the former secretary of the Air Force Thomas Finletter, which defended the Eisenhower administration's policy of threatening "massive retaliation" as a way to deter Soviet expansionism. Schlesinger suggested that Kissinger write a response. Kissinger did, criticizing the administration's "New Look" defense policy. This was an argument very congenial to a Democrat like Schlesinger, who called it "the most interesting and useful discussion of the current foreign policy impasse I have read anywhere." Schlesinger circulated it among his powerful friends, and the result was its publication in the preeminent journal *Foreign Affairs* as "Military Policy and the Defense of 'Grey Areas.'"[111] McGeorge Bundy liked the article and recommended Kissinger to Hamilton Fish Armstrong, the editor of *Foreign Affairs*, who offered Kissinger a position as the head of a study group at the Council on Foreign Relations in New York working on the issue of nuclear weapons and American foreign policy.

For Kissinger, this was a decision not without risk but with extraordinary potential rewards. The Council constituted the unofficial State Department and was a vital part of the "Eastern Establishment" that dominated American foreign policy. Nuclear weapons were the critical issue of the time, and the Council wanted to make its statement about their role in diplomacy. Its study group, consisting of many of the most distinguished experts on the issue— among them, Gordon Dean, the former head of the Atomic Energy Commission; Paul Nitze, the former director of policy planning at the State

Department; Frank Pace, the former secretary of the Army; and General James Gavin—had already been meeting for a number of months before Kissinger was hired. Kissinger was rarely humble about his abilities, but even he admitted to J. Robert Oppenheimer, the "father of the atomic bomb," that "I find myself somewhat overawed by the enormity of the subject."[112] Kissinger would now be dealing directly with many of the key leaders he aspired to impress and influence.

Shortly after Kissinger settled into his new position at the Council, he received an invitation from Nelson Rockefeller, special assistant for foreign affairs to President Eisenhower, to participate "in a group study and review of the psychological aspects of future U.S. strategy," a meeting that would take place in August 1955 at the Quantico Marine Base, near Washington.[113] Rockefeller's first Quantico meeting had helped produce the "Open Skies" proposal at the Geneva Conference of July 1955, a proposal to allow the United States and the Soviet Union to operate reconnaissance flights over each country's territory. It proved a psychologically effective proposal, putting the Russians on the defensive over their extreme secrecy. Rockefeller was eager to repeat his success and strengthen his own position within the Eisenhower administration.

Nelson Aldrich Rockefeller was one of the most significant political leaders of mid-twentieth-century America, a man many assumed would become president. Heir to wealth and privilege, Rockefeller had already played an active role in U.S.–Latin American relations under Franklin Roosevelt. Ebullient, outgoing, and gregarious, Rockefeller was a natural politician, always working the room, backslapping and putting people at ease. He was a patrician who felt he had a social obligation to serve, and he truly believed in "the brotherhood of man and the fatherhood of God."[114] Kissinger remembered their first meeting at Quantico, as all the experts, himself included, were "intoxicated by the proximity to power." They offered Rockefeller tactical advice on certain political goals: "After we were finished, the smile left his face and his eyes assumed the hooded look which showed that we were now turning to things that mattered. 'What I want you to tell me,' he said, 'is not how to maneuver. I want you to tell me what is right.'"[115]

This August meeting marked the beginning of the "lasting odd-couple relationship between Kissinger and Rockefeller."[116] Rockefeller was the wealthy American aristocrat, an eternal optimist with an outgoing, warm personality, while Kissinger was the brooding intellectual, cold in his personal relationships and personally insecure to the point of paranoia. Kissinger worked hard at the courtship, seeing the Rockefeller family as the nearest equivalent to "the function of a good aristocracy."[117] Rockefeller came to see in Kissinger "the combination of brilliance and egotism" he found so appealing.[118] Kissinger was also drawn to Rockefeller's idea that America faced a "moral" challenge in the Cold War, and he jumped at the opportunity to draft two of the papers in the long report from the Quantico meeting, *Psychological Aspects of U.S. Strategy*, that Rockefeller sent to Eisenhower. When he finished, Kissinger wrote to "Mr. Rockefeller" that it "was a special gratification to be permitted to serve with a group of such undoubted moral courage and surprising agreement about the nature of our difficulties." He also flattered Rockefeller, telling him, "Whatever success our effort may have will be due to a large extent to your interest and participation." Rockefeller appreciated Kissinger's work, praising his "capacity to mobilize all the facts and arguments and to give both sides."[119] However, influenced by Secretary of State John Foster Dulles, President Eisenhower rejected Rockefeller's Quantico II report, and Rockefeller decided to resign. The resignation was a bureaucratic victory for Dulles, who wanted to retain his own dominance over foreign policy and distrusted the politically ambitious Rockefeller. It was an early lesson for Kissinger in the bureaucratic battles that frequently shaped American foreign policy. Kissinger immediately wrote to "Nelson," saying, "It has been both a comfort and an inspiration to know of your presence in the Government, and of your willingness to stand up for what you thought important without considering what might be administratively easiest." Kissinger assured him, "Time will vindicate what you have stood for."[120] Rockefeller thanked him for his "generous comments" and suggested that they meet soon to "find ways and means to continue [their] efforts together."[121]

Rockefeller and Kissinger met several times over the first few months of 1956, and Rockefeller eventually persuaded Kissinger to direct his Special Studies Project of the Rockefeller Brothers Fund. He even got the University of Chicago, where Kissinger had accepted a position, to release him for a three-month period to work for Rockefeller before beginning to teach.[122] Rockefeller described the Special Studies Project as an attempt to "define the major problems and opportunities facing the United States and clarify national purposes and objectives, and to develop principles which could serve as the basis of future national policy." The project, despite its emphasis on nonpartisanship and its recruitment of both prominent Democrats and Republicans, was the equivalent of a modern-day political think tank. Kissinger explained the project as attempting to fill a gap "between governmental planning and much of the research on international affairs," a project that would provide long-term planning on public policies for the next decade and help determine priorities by taking an "overall point of view and following it up over a long period of time."[123] With access to Rockefeller's enormous resources and contacts, Kissinger could now ask some of the most prominent people in America to join one of the seven subpanels concerned with political, social, and economic issues—ranging from Kissinger's subpanel, International Security Objectives and Strategy, to one reflecting Rockefeller's specific concerns, the Moral Framework of National Purpose.

The Special Studies Project was an enormous undertaking for the young professor, still tasked with finishing the Council on Foreign Relations' book on nuclear weapons and getting his dissertation published. In running this project, which involved a multitude of contributors, endless meetings, and very complex politics, Kissinger reflected, "We really do lead a bureaucratized life in this country in which the internal workings of whatever machine we are caught up in [are] more complicated than the problems for which the machine was designed in the first place"—a comment he would later make about the foreign policy bureaucracy when he became national security adviser. He often referred to the Special Studies Project as the "circus" he was directing, apologizing to one visiting official he was unable to meet with, "The only way I can retain my sanity is to be unavailable on certain days."[124] At one point, when Rockefeller's secretary requested he draft another speech, Kissinger wrote a plaintive memo: "I love NAR—but no more writing for a few weeks—*please*."[125]

What Kissinger did accomplish over these eighteen months was remarkable. He provided the Council on Foreign Relations with a bestselling critique of the Eisenhower administration's nuclear policies, and Nelson Rockefeller with an alternative policy to the "weakness" and "sterility" of the Eisenhower administration's. Kissinger's book *Nuclear Weapons and Foreign Policy* criticized the doctrine of "massive retaliation," whereby the United States would threaten a full-scale nuclear attack in the event of a case of Soviet aggression. Whatever merits the doctrine had when Dulles announced it in 1954 had largely diminished, especially as the Soviets grew their nuclear arsenal and tested long-range missiles. Most American foreign policy experts no longer found the threat of all-out nuclear war credible. Eisenhower's determination to limit military spending had also greatly reduced America's conventional military, especially the Army, with the result that a nonnuclear defense of Western Europe seemed doomed to fail. With his skill for simplifying and expressing complex ideas, Kissinger put the issue starkly: "The dilemma of the nuclear period can, therefore, be defined as follows: the enormity of modern weapons makes the thought of war repugnant, but the refusal to run any risks would amount to giving Soviet rulers a blank check."[126] Kissinger's conclusions were not original. The study group at the Council was almost unanimous in its desire to find some alternative to Eisenhower's stated policy, and many defense intellectuals, most notably Bernard Brodie and Basil Liddell Hart, had also written on the subject of limited nuclear war. Kissinger's book demonstrated his talent as a "creative synthesizer" of their ideas, drawing out the implications of their work and arguing that for America's Cold War diplomacy to have any real substance, the United States had to accept the possibility of the limited use of nuclear weapons.[127] That Kissinger's own solution of limited nuclear war was also highly problematic was less important to many contemporary observers than that it broke free from the straitjacket of the Eisenhower administration's policy.[128]

Kissinger's timing proved exceptionally fortunate. The book was published in June 1957, a little over half a year after the United States had experienced two foreign policy crises that made its nuclear arsenal seem useless: the Hungarian crisis, in which the Soviet Union crushed an uprising against communist rule, and the Suez crisis, during which the Soviet leader Nikita Khrushchev threatened America's allies, Britain and France, with nuclear attack if they did not end their invasion of Egypt. The unexpected result was that Kissinger's book sold seventeen thousand copies in its first year and was on the bestseller list for fourteen weeks. A front-page story in *The New York Times* proclaimed, "For the first time since President Eisenhower took office, officials at the highest government levels are displaying interest in the theory of the 'little,' or 'limited,' war. The theory of massive retaliation is re-examined."[129] General Andrew Goodpaster, White House staff secretary, prepared a summary of the book for President Eisenhower, who then recommended the book to Secretary Dulles as "interesting and worth reading."[130] Vice President Richard Nixon was photographed carrying the book. The British Foreign Office even commissioned an extensive secret study of the book and its implications for American foreign policy.[131]

Even before *Nuclear Weapons and Foreign Policy* appeared in 1957, Kissinger had developed a sharp critique of Eisenhower's foreign policy. He was particularly outspoken with his friends from military intelligence, telling Colonel Bill Kintner that the "cravenness of our behavior from the Aswan Dam to the Suez Crisis, to the United Nations is beyond belief." Kissinger lamented how "a nation that had an absolute superiority ten years ago has maneuvered itself into a position where all the long term trends are running against it."[132] He placed much of the blame for America's failures on the personnel running foreign policy, particularly the lawyers and businessmen like Dulles and his chief of the policy planning staff, Robert Bowie.[133] Although he was careful in expressing his own views during the meetings of the Rockefeller panels, Kissinger often put strong sentiments in letters to participants. He told Adolf Berle, the former assistant secretary of state under Roosevelt, that the American response to the Hungarian uprising "seems to me to indicate a moral weakness rather than an analytical one on the part of the free world." America needed a strong sense of purpose to compete against the "Messianic movement" of Soviet communism. Kissinger feared that America was too bound by "bureaucratic rationality" and lacked a sense of mission, without which "it is impossible to achieve great things." He concluded with a comparison that might seem unusual for the former Orthodox Jew: "At the risk of being blasphemous, one might say that if Christ had been advised by a policy planning staff, he would never have mounted the Cross."[134]

Kissinger's critique of the Eisenhower administration's caution in foreign policy reflected a broad sentiment among American elites of the time, but these ideas had not captured public attention. Eisenhower's prestige and political popularity remained high, and the country was both at peace and prosperous. When the Soviet Union stunned the world by launching the first man-made satellite on October 4, 1957, however, the psychological impact on the United States was extraordinary. The sudden sense of vulnerability and fear made the country extremely receptive to new ideas about national security. In that frenzied atmosphere, Rockefeller rush-released the panel report *International Security: The Military Aspect*, written by Kissinger, with proposals for major increases in defense spending and weapons development. The report stated somberly, "The willingness to engage in nuclear war when necessary is part of the price of our freedom," and it explicitly called for accepting the idea of limited war and developing the "modern sea lift and an air lift capacity we do not now possess." The report also called for a massive effort at civil defense, including the building of fallout shelters in every house.[135] When Rockefeller appeared on the *Today* show to discuss the report, the host, Dave Garroway, told viewers that anyone interested in a copy could get one by writing to the show. No one expected that the next day there would be forty-five thousand requests; as Rockefeller's aide Nancy Hanks put it, the report went like "hot cakes." There were two hundred thousand more requests the day after that. The Rockefeller report became known as "the answer to Sputnik," and Henry Kissinger's words circulated throughout the nation.[136]

On July 14, 1958, Professor Henry Kissinger appeared in a nationally broadcast television interview with the prominent journalist Mike Wallace. Wallace prefaced his questions by saying, "In the field of foreign policy and military affairs, Dr. Kissinger, you're acknowledged to be one of the most penetrating minds in the country."[137] Kissinger's star had risen, and with that came an academic bidding war for his services. Harvard won out over Chicago, much to the distress of Charles Percy, the president of Chicago's Bell and Howell Company and, later, a senator from Illinois. Percy told Rockefeller that the Special Studies Project was "a remarkable experience for all of us working with Henry Kissinger," who was "the best listener I have ever known . . . with the patience of Job." Percy saw Kissinger as "a doer, an original thinker, as well as a conciliator." Whenever Percy got discouraged about the potential leadership in the country, he wrote in the conclusion of his letter to Rockefeller, "I think of Henry Kissinger and feel better."[138] Percy's extraordinary praise demonstrates how well Kissinger handled his Rockefeller assignment, cementing his position as Rockefeller's principal consultant for foreign affairs. Kissinger's deftness at handling the relationships, egos, and rivalries of the corporate, legal, and governmental officials he worked with at the Council on Foreign Relations and on the Special Studies Project contrasts sharply with the problems he had with academic colleagues, where his fierce ambition, abrasive personality, and conspicuous networking inspired intense animosity and lingering resentments.

Kissinger's return to Harvard reflected this. He wanted Harvard to recognize his new status. McGeorge Bundy had procured a major grant from the Ford Foundation to establish the Center for the Study of International Affairs. Bundy convinced Robert Bowie, now a professor at Harvard Law School, to be the center's first director. He then offered Kissinger the post of associate director, in effect asking him to work with one of the government officials he had sharply criticized. Bundy no doubt believed that with a high-level government official like Bowie and an academic star like Kissinger, the center would have little difficulty raising funds and making an immediate impact. Although the center did survive and prosper, the two men did not cooperate and grew to despise each other. Kissinger was leery from the beginning. He told one of his old military friends, "It was a painful decision, but after consulting with friends we both admire like Bill Elliott, [George] Abe Lincoln, and Bill Kintner, I decided this would be my way of going to the barricades." Kissinger hoped that "a center for the advanced training of civilians and government officials would help and also undertaking major research efforts could be a force in the country."[139] Bowie, a distinguished lawyer and government official who had played an important role in the occupation government of Germany, resented what he saw as Kissinger's continuing ties to the Rockefellers and unwillingness to be "his assistant director" or do more for the center's development. Kissinger was still convinced that he did not "owe anything in particular to academic life" and that "the disparity between [his] reputation outside academic life and inside academic life is so great as to be ludicrous."[140] Despite having neighboring offices, the two men would go long periods without speaking, and rumor had it that they would sometimes check with their secretaries before coming out to avoid running into each other.

Kissinger's return to Harvard meant that he was back at the university when Senator John F. Kennedy of Massachusetts planned his campaign for the White House. Although Kissinger was linked to Rockefeller, he made a strong point of insisting in public, as he did in his Mike Wallace interview, "that I'm here as a nonpartisan, that I'm an independent."[141] He continued to network out of Harvard, taking over the Defense Studies Program and inviting prominent Washington figures to Cambridge to be guest lecturers. In a demonstration of his own ideological flexibility and eagerness to keep a foot in both camps, he also worked with the Harvard-MIT Arms Control Group, whose work, Kissinger later argued, "created the basis for what became known as arms control thinking."[142] As the election year 1960 approached, he helped Rockefeller on his speeches but was deeply disappointed when the New York governor pulled back from challenging Nixon. Kissinger kept his options open. He turned down an offer from the former secretary of state Dean Acheson to join the Democrats' Advisory Committee on Foreign Policy but assured Acheson that he would give advice on a "personal basis."[143] He also signaled his interest to the Kennedy camp through Arthur Schlesinger. In August 1960, he told Schlesinger that he had gone to see "Nelson" at his summer place in Seal Harbor, Maine, to tell him that he, Kissinger, would do nothing to help Nixon in the campaign, adding that Rockefeller "loathes Nixon." Kissinger told Schlesinger he hoped that Kennedy could bring "a shift into a new atmosphere, a new world."[144]

In early January 1961, just before the Kennedy inauguration, Kissinger published his book *The Necessity for Choice*, which laid out a vision for foreign policy for the 1960s. Kissinger's pessimism is striking: "The United States cannot afford another decline like that which has characterized the past decade and a half. Fifteen years more of a deterioration of our position in the world such as we have experienced since World War II would find us reduced to Fortress America in a world in which we had become largely irrelevant." He warned, "Our margin of survival has narrowed dangerously," echoing themes that Kennedy's advisers had developed, including the famous—and fictional—missile gap between the United States and the Soviet Union. Kissinger continued his own support for alternatives to "massive retaliation," although he now backed away from his support for limited nuclear war.[145] Critics of his *Nuclear Weapons and Foreign Policy* accused Kissinger of delusion in thinking that the United States and the Soviet Union would ever be able to limit a nuclear exchange, and said that he was proposing ridiculous "Marquis of Queensbury rules in the midst of a nuclear war."[146] Kissinger now advocated a conventional arms buildup, since "the dividing line between conventional and nuclear weapons is more familiar and therefore easier to maintain." He continued to insist that the United States develop smaller nuclear weapons, but he moved his own position to where he thought Kennedy's was. In effect, *The Necessity for Choice* was something of a job application, and Kissinger hoped Kennedy would make an offer.[147]

KISSINGER AND THE KENNEDY
AND JOHNSON ADMINISTRATIONS

Between 1961 and 1968, Kissinger learned about how Washington operated and became increasingly involved in significant issues, especially those related to Germany and Vietnam. Although he experienced considerable frustration, Kissinger cultivated the right people and developed a reputation for competence and discretion that made him, by the end of 1968, the leading candidate for a major foreign policy position, no matter who won the White House.

Kissinger told Arthur Schlesinger, who soon became a special adviser to Kennedy, that the president's inaugural address, with its stirring call to "pay any price, bear any burden," was "excellent" and that he "might become a registered Democrat" if the rumors of Schlesinger going to Washington were true.[148] Kissinger met with President Kennedy in February, after which McGeorge Bundy, now the new national security adviser, offered Kissinger a part-time consulting position. He told Kissinger, "I think you are one of the few people whose advice will be really helpful on this relatively informal basis" and stressed that the two areas where Kissinger could contribute would be "weapons and policy" and "all aspects of the problem of Germany."[149] Bundy suspected correctly that Kissinger was still advising Rockefeller, who was likely to challenge Kennedy in 1964, and that Kissinger might not be fully loyal to the new administration.[150] Kissinger certainly wanted to be more intimately engaged with a whole range of issues and to spend the summer working directly on policy matters. However, Bundy wanted Kissinger to work only on the two issues he had initially suggested, especially the Germans. Bundy, a brilliant man of almost Puritan reserve, was put off by Kissinger's flattery and distrusted him. Kissinger suggested that Bundy disliked him, at least in part, because he was both foreign and Jewish, writing that Bundy "tended to treat [him] with the combination of politeness and subconscious condescension that upper-class Bostonians reserve for people of, by New England standards, exotic backgrounds and excessively intense personal style."[151] When Bundy restricted Kissinger's access to Kennedy, Kissinger sought to use Schlesinger to see the president personally. Bundy had Kennedy tell Schlesinger, "You know, I do find some of what Henry says to be interesting, but I have to insist that he report through Bundy, otherwise things will get out of hand."[152] Although he resented Bundy, Kissinger learned valuable lessons about how the national security adviser could control access to the president.

Kissinger's most direct role in the Kennedy administration came in dealing with the growing crisis over Berlin and the German question. Germany remained divided and the frontline of the Cold War in Europe. Encouraged by the West Germans and their leader, Konrad Adenauer, the Western powers refused to recognize East Germany as a legitimate state and insisted on free elections to reunify the country. For his part, the Soviet leader, Nikita

Khrushchev, sought to secure East Germany's status and demanded that either the Western powers settle the German issue within six months—in effect recognizing Germany's division—or Khrushchev would sign a separate peace treaty with East Germany and unilaterally change the status of the divided city. With Berlin located deep within the communist part of Germany, the West feared that if Khrushchev went ahead with his plan, Western access to part of Berlin would then be controlled by East German soldiers, threatening West Berlin's freedom. Kissinger prepared a long paper for Bundy, which Bundy passed along to Kennedy with the comment that "it was a powerful document setting one strong line on Germany." Kissinger also produced a psychological profile of the German chancellor, Konrad Adenauer, before Adenauer's first meeting with Kennedy. Some of what Kissinger said about Adenauer echoed aspects of Kissinger's own life. Noting that the chancellor had experienced the collapse of Imperial Germany, the overthrow of Weimar, and the "total disintegration of Germany," Kissinger wrote, "To an extent hard to understand for an American, he is conscious of, perhaps obsessed by, the possibility of tragedy." Kissinger observed, "The chief lesson he has drawn from that history is that moderation and a sense of proportion are not a forte of the Germans. I agree with him." This "distrust of his compatriots" helped explain Adenauer's "rigidity."[153] Kissinger also traveled to Germany in May, trying to reassure the chancellor that "Germany could no longer be considered a foreign country and that our future and Europe's were intimately linked. A defeat in Europe would be as bad as the destruction of Chicago."[154]

After Kennedy's failed summit with Khrushchev in June 1961 in Vienna, Kennedy feared the Soviet premier would act against Berlin. With refugees leaving East Berlin at an alarming rate, it was clear that the very existence of the East German state was in peril. Dean Acheson, brought into the government by Kennedy for advice, prepared a hawkish policy memo arguing that any challenge to Berlin was a critical test of Western will and urging a military response if the Soviets cut off Western access to Berlin. Schlesinger opposed Acheson's approach and wanted Kissinger to balance Acheson's views and give Kennedy some diplomatic alternatives.[155] Kissinger composed a memorandum criticizing Acheson's emphasis on a military option while making it clear that he was not "suggesting that diplomacy is an alternative to an improvement in our readiness. I think it is a necessary corollary to the build-up I favor."[156] He stressed, "We must not permit the Communists to monopolize the diplomatic forums." Bundy supported Kissinger's view, telling Kennedy, "The current strategic planning is dangerously rigid and, if continued without amendment, may leave you little choice as to how you face the moment of thermonuclear truth."[157]

The communist decision on August 13, 1961, to build a wall and stop the population exodus from East Berlin caught the United States by surprise but brought a temporary relief to the Kennedy administration. Kennedy had insisted only on maintaining the status of West Berlin and was reputed to have said, "A wall is a helluva lot better than a war." Underlining this attitude was a frustration with Adenauer and the West Germans. Kennedy and his key advisers wanted to break the German "veto" over American foreign policy and were willing to accept the division of Germany as a reality of postwar Europe. Although Kissinger had not advocated a military response to the Wall, he wanted a more forceful response, concerned as he was about the feeling of betrayal among the Germans.[158] Kissinger pushed for a "Kennedy Plan for Central Europe," a positive American proposal to counter Khrushchev's aggressive propaganda.[159] He feared that Kennedy was moving toward recognizing East Germany, listening to those who claimed that "realism should impel us to confirm what we are incapable of changing." Kissinger rejected such realism, arguing that it would undermine West Germany's "trust in the United States."[160] By this point, however, Kissinger found himself in Washington simply reading cables, writing memos, and getting no response from Bundy. He felt his "contribution to Berlin planning is that of a kibitzer shouting random comments from the side-lines." Kissinger cleaned out his desk and left Washington shortly afterward, writing a long letter to Schlesinger to explain "the frustration and despair" that led to his decision.[161] He also asked Schlesinger to assure President Kennedy of his "continued moral support."[162]

Kissinger initially avoided a public resignation and continued to help the administration on German issues.[163] However, when Kissinger took a trip to South Asia in early 1962 and commented that Pakistan "would never do anything so foolish" as join an alliance with China—which Pakistan eventually did—Bundy told reporters that Kissinger no longer worked for the American government.[164] By summer 1962, Kissinger began publishing critical articles about the administration's foreign policy, focusing on alliance issues and nuclear weapons. He continued giving advice and writing foreign policy speeches for Nelson Rockefeller, preparing him for a possible presidential campaign. Privately Kissinger now attacked the Kennedy administration with extraordinary "vehemence," arguing that it had "demoralized the bureaucracy and much of the military."[165] Kissinger was particularly critical of plans for a multilateral nuclear force (MLF), which was designed to replace the independent nuclear forces of Britain and France with an Allied nuclear force under NATO command. Kissinger defended President Charles de Gaulle of France and his insistence on greater independence for Europe from the United States. He criticized the Kennedy administration for such actions as its support for an "opening to the left" in Europe, an American willingness to tolerate Socialist parties in coalition governments like Italy's. Ironically enough, Kissinger also attacked the administration for its belief that the Sino-Soviet split provided opportunities for the United States to engage the Soviet Union. Kissinger told Rockefeller, "While the split [between the Soviet Union and China] seems real enough at the moment, we must be careful not to make agreements which would not otherwise be justified by our national interest, simply for the sake of emphasizing this split."[166]

Kissinger maintained a friendly correspondence with Schlesinger even when he was writing critically about the administration. He sent along a friendly assessment of Kennedy's triumphant "Ich bin ein Berliner" trip to Germany in June 1963 that he had received from a conservative German industrialist, Kurt Birrenbach. Birrenbach, Kissinger noted, had not previously been "a great admirer of the administration." Birrenbach wrote that the president's trip was an "extraordinary success" and that the reaction of Germans "was incomparably more enthusiastic than to that of the trip of General de Gaulle." Kennedy, the German went on to say, "moved the masses in a way which I have not seen in decades." Knowing that Schlesinger would not miss the comparison between Kennedy's speeches and a certain German leader's of the 1930s, Kissinger added a handwritten P.S.: "I am not so sure I like the 'decades' implication. But then we can't have everything."[167]

While Kennedy's assassination on November 22, 1963, was a profound psychological shock to the country and placed the martyred young president in the pantheon of American heroes, Kissinger did not share the assessment. He told colleagues that Kennedy had been "leading the country to disaster."[168] Kissinger's own personal life was a disaster at the time, as he divorced his wife, leaving her with two children under the age of five. Kissinger threw himself into the 1964 Rockefeller campaign, even attending the Republican National Convention in San Francisco. He tried to keep Rockefeller from moving too close to the foreign policy positions of Barry Goldwater, at one point urging him not to recommend establishing "a government in exile" for Cuba. Kissinger emphasized to Rockefeller, "You have often said that you wanted to say nothing as a candidate that you are not prepared to implement as President." Kissinger told Rockefeller that such an approach would have almost no Latin American support and would make it "even more difficult than it is now" to get rid of Castro.[169] Kissinger opposed the right wing's rollback fantasies and Goldwater's cavalier policy toward nuclear weapons. He was bitter about the harsh treatment of Rockefeller at the convention and quickly made it clear to Bundy and other Harvard associates that he planned to vote for Lyndon Johnson.[170]

Despite his suspicions about Kissinger, Bundy continued to use him, especially on issues involving Germany. In late November 1964, Bundy circulated an analysis by Kissinger that questioned the German interest in the multilateral nuclear force. Kissinger's paper stated boldly that it was "simply wrong to allege that the future orientation of the Federal Republic depends on pushing through the MLF."[171] Bundy used the Kissinger memo to help convince President Johnson to reduce the American pressure on Europeans to adopt the MLF.[172] As the Vietnam War began to preoccupy the White House in the spring of 1965, Kissinger made sure that Bundy knew of his support. Sending Bundy a note about German politics, Kissinger included as a P.S., "I think our present actions in Vietnam are essentially right," adding that the administration had his respect "for the courage with which [it] is acting."[173] "Essentially right" was a Kissinger phrase that allowed a great deal of room for criticism, but Bundy accepted Kissinger's words gratefully. He told Kissinger in April 1965, "You may be somewhat lonely among all our friends at Harvard," an acknowledgment that opposition to the war at Harvard was already widespread.[174] Later that month, Bundy wrote to Kissinger that he had been "using your name in vain with a few people who want to know whether any respectable professors are with us."[175] However, Bundy still kept Kissinger at arm's length. When Kissinger told him that he was preparing to "answer the outrageous attack on you by the 100 Phi Beta Kappa members," Bundy replied that the "Phi Beta Kappa business has passed by cheerfully," noting, "I wonder if the matter is not best left where it is."[176]

Kissinger's "first government assignment in three years" originated not with Bundy but with Ambassador Henry Cabot Lodge, who asked Kissinger to come as his consultant to Vietnam in October 1965. Kissinger jumped at the opportunity, requesting a year's sabbatical from Harvard.[177] His briefings in Washington before he left introduced Kissinger to the confusion and chaos in Vietnam policy, with official optimism mixed with unofficial cynicism about the war effort. One Pentagon official told him bluntly, "At some point on this road we will have to cut the balls off the people we are now supporting in Vietnam, and if you want to do a really constructive study you ought to address yourself to the question of how we can cut their balls off."[178] Kissinger wrote in his diary, "How does one convince a people that one is prepared to stay indefinitely 10,000 miles away against opponents who are fighting in their own country?"[179] Kissinger spent two weeks in the country, meeting Vietnamese officials, religious leaders, and students. He was disillusioned by the optimism he observed among U.S. military officials as well as the difficulties of the Saigon government. When a story appeared in the *Los Angeles Times* citing him as a source for negative comments about Saigon's leaders, the White House quickly disavowed Kissinger. On his telephone taping system, Johnson plaintively asked Secretary of Defense Robert McNamara, "Who sent Kissinger out there, Bob?" To which McNamara replied, "I don't know," but suggested that it was Lodge. McNamara then read to Johnson from the *Times* story that "there are authoritative reports that Kissinger will tell the White House that there is not yet a cohesive national government here, because nowhere among the national leaders is there a sense of dedication to the nation." LBJ responded, "Who in the hell lets these folks get in?"[180]

Kissinger reacted furiously to the newspaper story, writing a two-page handwritten letter to Bundy denying he had said what was reported. He insisted that he had been pursuing his work for Lodge "quietly and unobtrusively." Kissinger claimed that he spoke only "three sentences" during the meeting with the eight reporters, and that he "went out of [his] way to endorse Administration policy." Bundy acknowledged Kissinger's right to be annoyed with the original White House statement, since the White House had forgotten that Kissinger was a consultant to Lodge. However, Bundy also asked his brother William, then the assistant secretary of state for East Asian Affairs, to intercede with Kissinger and not press for a correction: "I don't blame him for feeling agitated, but I think he should know that everyone else is pretty relaxed about this right now."[181] Bundy did not add what he likely suspected: that the newspaper story was an accurate reflection of Kissinger's views.[182]

Kissinger calmed down, but not before writing a letter to Johnson's political adviser Clark Clifford, telling him, "I am depressed and shaken that my effort to be helpful to the Administration and to Ambassador Lodge has ended so ignominiously."[183] Although he was determined not to lose his connection to the Johnson White House as he had to Kennedy's, this did not keep him from expressing doubts about the direction of the war. He told Bundy, "The situation in Vietnam is less encouraging than I had believed before I left," although he insisted this was not because of the "weakness of the Saigon government," which was "as good as any conceivable alternative." Kissinger's real doubts went beyond the current Saigon government and centered on the nation of South Vietnam itself. Kissinger's first drafts of his report to Lodge were "too hard-hitting," and he ultimately sent the ambassador a heavily edited version. He dutifully wrote, "I am deeply persuaded that Vietnam is the hinge of our national effort where success and failure will determine our world role for decades to come."[184] He continued to argue that the administration's policy was "essentially correct" and even appeared on one of the first satellite debates to argue the case for the war against the British Labour Party firebrand Michael Foot.[185]

Nearing the end of his sabbatical, Kissinger returned to Vietnam in July 1966.[186] On this trip, Kissinger was working for the State Department's Planning Group, sent to discuss with Lodge "questions arising in connection with possible initiation of negotiations, including cease-fires and cessation of hostilities, standfasts, inspection by ICC [International Control Commission] or other body, etc." As Secretary of State Dean Rusk's cable to Lodge added, "Kissinger is thoroughly familiar with our thinking and [we] recommend you make full use [of] his presence for analysis [of] these subjects."[187] After the trip, Kissinger published an assessment of the war in the popular magazine *Look* in August 1966. Kissinger's tone remained supportive of Johnson's policy, arguing that an American withdrawal from Vietnam would embolden enemies, dishearten allies, and weaken America's credibility. He also added a wrinkle that reflected the administration's view of the by then undeniable Sino-Soviet split. Kissinger stressed that a North Vietnamese victory would "strengthen the most bellicose factions in the internecine Communist struggle around the world," meaning the Chinese under Mao.[188]

As supportive as he seemed, Kissinger was slowly staking out a position distinct from the administration's. In part this was his response to the increasingly prevalent view among Americans that the war was a stalemate and that, despite the high body counts of enemy soldiers, the United States was bogged down in a "quagmire." The Johnson administration's optimistic claims were contributing to the "credibility gap," the belief that the government was exaggerating and even lying about the progress it was making in Vietnam. Kissinger began his *Look* article by stating, "The war in Vietnam is dominated by two factors: withdrawal would be disastrous and negotiations are inevitable." In September 1966, Arthur Schlesinger cited Kissinger positively in a prominent *New York Times Magazine* article titled "A Middle Way Out of Vietnam." Schlesinger invoked Kissinger's advocacy of a form of counterinsurgency doctrine, namely a strategy advocating "the creation and stabilization of secure areas where the South Vietnamese might themselves undertake social and institutional development."[189] Kissinger was trying to keep a foot in both camps, bridging the gap between the opponents of the war and the Johnson administration. The following month Kissinger attended the Annual Conference on Strategic Studies in London and bragged to British diplomats that he was "one of a small group of not more than a dozen in the White House, State Department, and the Pentagon who saw all the papers related to possible negotiations." He also told the British that one possibility Washington was pondering was direct talks with the southern arm of the insurgency, the National Liberation Front. Kissinger even confessed his own pessimism to the British, telling them his own hope was for an internal negotiation in South Vietnam that "could be a better face-saving device to enable an eventual American withdrawal than any full Geneva-type conference."[190]

Kissinger's most dramatic involvement in the attempt to start negotiations with the North Vietnamese came in the middle of 1967, in the initiative code-named Pennsylvania.[191] At a Paris meeting in June 1967, Kissinger approached two French intellectuals, Raymond Aubrac and Herbert Marcovich, about conveying messages to Hanoi about a possible opening of negotiations. Over a two-month period in the summer and early fall of 1967, Kissinger conducted his first form of "shuttle diplomacy," traveling between Boston, Washington, and Paris, bringing messages from American government officials to the Frenchmen and hoping for a positive response from Hanoi.[192] He even met with Mai Van Bo, the North Vietnamese representative in Paris. The North Vietnamese ultimately refused to give the Frenchmen entry visas, putting an end to the channel. At one point in a White House meeting, Kissinger made a strong argument for avoiding the bombing of Hanoi while the situation was still in play. Johnson grudgingly agreed, but "glowered at him and said, 'OK, we will do it the professor's way. But if it doesn't work, I will personally cut your balls off.'"[193]

Kissinger survived Johnson's threat to his manhood and even tried to revive the Pennsylvania initiative when he was in Moscow in December 1967. Kissinger acknowledged that the level of distrust on both sides "was very deep," and then suggested that when "so much depended on nuances, an intermediary, such as the Soviet Union, would play a useful role." To Kissinger, the Soviets seemed to be interested in this possible role, though they warned him that their competitive relationship with China affected their willingness to become involved in Vietnam. They also warned Kissinger that the "Vietnamese were not easy to deal with." When Kissinger responded that the South Vietnamese government showed great skill in pursuing its interests and was anything "but an American tool," his Soviet counterpart replied, "And you have 500 hundred thousand troops in South Vietnam. You can imagine the limits of our influence in Hanoi."[194] Although the Soviet warning proved prophetic, Kissinger retained his belief that the path to peace in Vietnam could run through Moscow and that secret diplomacy might provide the key.[195]

In early 1968 Kissinger turned again to presidential politics, advising and writing speeches for Nelson Rockefeller.[196] In his advice to Rockefeller, Kissinger was still preaching an idea he pushed in his earliest work, that "we live in a revolutionary age," and that the challenge to America was whether in conducting a complex foreign policy "we can mobilize the moral aspirations of [our] people for the tasks ahead."[197] Kissinger helped draft a key speech Rockefeller gave on Vietnam in May 1968. In the speech, Rockefeller criticized present policy and the "Americanization" of the war. He argued in favor of a policy that would eventually resemble Nixon's "Vietnamization," turning control of the war back over to the South Vietnamese. The speech also pushed an opening to China, arguing that nothing was gained from "aiding or encouraging the self-isolation of so great a people," and even suggested that through a type of triangular diplomacy "with communist China and the Soviet Union, we can ultimately improve our relations with each—as we test the will for peace of both."[198]

The violence, assassinations, and student unrest of 1968 had a deep impact on Kissinger. Shortly after the killing of Robert Kennedy in June, Kissinger wrote a memorandum to Rockefeller, arguing, "Many people will gag at the choice of Nixon and Humphrey." He urged Rockefeller to "appeal to idealism and the desire for commitment," especially prevalent among young people. In a meeting with Rockefeller and John Gardner, then president of the Urban Coalition, Kissinger sounded themes that echoed from his honors thesis almost two decades earlier, as he asserted: "We were now paying the price for two centuries of debunking. It was great fun to show the weakness of every philosophy and institution as long as there was a great capital of belief to draw on. But now this capital has been exhausted." Kissinger went on to claim, "The task is to restore a moral dimension together with a sense of the complexity of events." Kissinger's concern about America's moral crisis even found expression when he reviewed a book on the Nuremberg Nazi Party rallies and concluded that they were a "warning of what may happen if society neglects the inner being or if man loses faith in his future."[199]

Kissinger was deeply disappointed when Rockefeller lost the Republican nomination again, telling an interviewer a day after Nixon's nomination that he had "grave doubts" about Nixon as president and that he considered him "unfit" to be president.[200] Yet Kissinger was aware of the stature he now enjoyed among insiders in Washington, as Johnson's people felt strongly that Kissinger had handled his Vietnam assignments with great discretion and professionalism. Still maintaining he was an "independent," Kissinger refused an offer to serve on Nixon's foreign advisory board, telling Nixon's advisers that he could be of more help "behind the scenes." At the same time, he kept up his contacts with his Democratic friends, including Averell Harriman, who was handling the Paris negotiations. Kissinger sought to position himself for a high foreign policy position no matter who won the election. As one of his more sympathetic friends later put it, "Whether they were conservatives or liberals, each one felt that Kissinger understood their point of view and may have been sympathetic with it. This was a tribute to Kissinger's brilliance as well as his deviousness."[201]

Kissinger's behavior was later highlighted in the documentary *The Trials of Henry Kissinger*. It argues that Kissinger, acting solely for reasons of personal ambition, used his privileged access to the Paris negotiations to inform the Nixon campaign of the impending bombing halt of North Vietnam and thereby helped Nixon and the South Vietnamese government sabotage the chance for peace in Vietnam, defeat Humphrey in the election, and prolong the war for another four bloody years.[202] This is the most extreme view of Kissinger's behavior, and it overstates Kissinger's responsibility. As self-serving and deplorable as Kissinger's behavior was, it is unlikely that an acceptable peace agreement could have been negotiated by the Johnson administration in a matter of weeks, something that the sheer difficulty of the subsequent negotiations with the North and South Vietnamese suggests as unlikely. Furthermore, the assumption that Hubert Humphrey would have won the election if the South Vietnamese government agreed to attend the talks in Paris, and that the only reason the South Vietnamese didn't was because of the information Kissinger provided, is also problematic, as Saigon was fully capable of making that judgment on its own. As one South Vietnamese official later told a Kissinger critic, "Kissinger was totally irrelevant to our [South Vietnamese] deliberations . . . We had been uneasy with the Johnson Administration's discussion of negotiations . . . and had long planned to back out of any talks that the White House was using to score political points during the 1968 presidential election."[203] Close elections are also decided by a multiplicity of factors. Nevertheless, Kissinger's behavior was self-serving and egregious, with even Nixon commenting later, "Henry's role may not have been too admirable, as he seems to have had a foot in both camps."[204]

What is indisputable is that Kissinger did try to keep the Nixon camp informed about the progress in the Vietnam negotiations, although, as Ferguson notes, "there was nothing very secret about what was happening in Paris."[205] During the fall, Kissinger spoke a number of times to Nixon campaign officials, always insisting that his role be kept secret. Nixon certainly appreciated the information, though he also suspected that Kissinger might be providing disinformation, even if unintentionally.[206] Nixon had other sources close to the negotiations, including a close friend of his aide Bryce Harlow, who was in the White House and passing along information, and he monitored the talks closely. Nixon suspected that the Johnson administration was using the possibility of the election of the hard-line Cold Warrior Nixon as a negotiating tool with Hanoi. Nixon did become very careful in his public statements on Vietnam, a caution encouraged by Kissinger, who told the campaign "something big was afoot." At the same time, Nixon was also using his contacts with the South Vietnamese ambassador Bui Diem and Anna Chennault, the widow of the famed World War II aviator Claire Chennault, to tell Saigon not to rush into any deal.[207] Nixon's dealings with Chennault infuriated the Johnson White House and convinced LBJ that Nixon's behavior bordered on the "treasonous."[208] However, Johnson's information on these contacts was gained through wiretaps and other surveillance that the president did not want to reveal publicly. When Johnson announced the bombing halt, and hopes for a quick peace spiked, it did help Humphrey briefly in the polls. The South Vietnamese refusal to attend the talks may have stopped Humphrey's momentum, but the 1968 election revolved around so many variables that to say definitively that the refusal cost Humphrey the election is impossible, although many Humphrey supporters believed it.[209]

Those who are convinced that Nixon stole the election tend to underestimate the North and South Vietnamese governments and their knowledge of the American electoral process.[210] Both governments fully understood how an "October surprise" might affect their interests, and both acted accordingly.[211] Kissinger has argued he was a political independent, keeping both sides informed of the negotiations and trying to prevent a bad deal in Paris.[212] That his behavior also advanced his career was a happy by-product, a reflection of the degree to which both American political parties shared a consensus view on foreign policy that enabled Kissinger to walk the line between them. Both Democrats and Republicans understood how the election could be affected by even the appearance of the prospect of peace. Kissinger's behavior during these months certainly proved self-aggrandizing and did increase his "credibility" with Nixon, who appreciated the secrecy with which Kissinger operated and valued Kissinger for the "finer points of duplicity." Yet ironically, Hubert Humphrey remained an admirer of Kissinger's as well, a testament to his ability to charm politicians of all types.[213] Humphrey later commented that he would have appointed Kissinger his national security adviser. This may have been an exaggeration, but he remained on friendly terms with Kissinger throughout the Nixon years.[214]

By November 1968, Henry Kissinger was among the most well-regarded experts on American foreign policy and national security. Even Seymour Hersh, who was one of the first to write about Kissinger's secret dealings during the campaign, acknowledged that Kissinger "enjoyed a considerable reputation as an expert on the war" and "earned the respect of the top echelon of the Johnson Administration, including the President and Secretary of

Defense Robert S. McNamara, by his discreet involvement" in the Pennsylvania initiative.[215] Kissinger expected a job in the new administration, although he could hardly have foreseen its exact dimensions, and the opportunity to exercise power it would afford him.

THE PRESIDENTIAL TRANSITION AND
THE CREATION OF THE NSC SYSTEM

When on November 25, 1968, Richard Nixon asked Henry Kissinger to come to the Hotel Pierre in New York, it was only the second time the two men had met personally. The first had been at a Christmas party in 1967 at the home of Clare Boothe Luce, where the two had a brief conversation. Now the two men had a long and rambling conversation about foreign policy, with Nixon expressing his distrust of the State Department and the CIA—Kissinger recorded on a yellow pad Nixon's blunt "Influence of the State Department establishment must be reduced."[216] For Nixon, stealing away Nelson Rockefeller's prized academic adviser was a coup itself, both for its outreach to the liberal wing of his party and as a way of besting Rockefeller, his frequent and bitter rival. Nixon, although he appreciated Kissinger's help on Vietnam during the campaign, wanted to be sure of Kissinger's acceptance. Although the two men shared a professional love for foreign policy, and had a sense of themselves as outsiders not fully accepted by the elites, they were also possessed of markedly different temperaments and backgrounds. Nixon was from a lower-middle-class, Californian, Quaker background, and resented the Eastern Establishment, liberal Jews, and Ivy League intellectuals. He was, despite being in the most public of professions, a loner who hated confrontation with others and brooded over real and imagined slights. Kissinger was more gregarious than Nixon, enjoyed dealing with the media and people of different views, and was confident of his own intellectual superiority. They soon became the odd couple of American politics, brought together by their own love of intrigue and power, and by what William Safire observed was Kissinger's "tuning fork relationship with the president on the matters that mattered to them most."[217] It was Kissinger who tuned into Nixon's frequency, becoming more like him in some ways, but able to understand, anticipate, and, most important, manipulate Nixon better than many who had known him for years.[218]

Two days later, on November 27, 1968, Kissinger was summoned back to New York to see Nixon's campaign manager, and later his attorney general, John Mitchell, who asked him, "What have you decided about the National Security job?" When Kissinger replied that he did not know it had been offered to him, Mitchell exclaimed, "Oh, Jesus Christ, he has screwed it up again."[219] Mitchell, who had known Nixon long enough to understand his indirect and nonconfrontational style, must have guessed that Nixon did not make the offer because he was afraid of Kissinger turning him down in person. Mitchell quickly left the room and told Kissinger that the president-elect wished to see him again. This time the offer was made, but Kissinger asked Nixon for a week to "consult" with "friends and associates." Whether Kissinger had any real doubts about accepting the position is hard to credit, even though Ferguson claims he did have continuing doubts about Nixon.[220] On November 29, he called Nixon's aide Dwight Chapin to accept the position.[221]

During 1968, Kissinger had been involved in a Harvard-based study whose goal was to recommend ways to foster a smooth presidential transition, and some of its ideas, especially about presidential control over foreign policy and revitalization of the National Security Council (NSC), came from this project.[222] Kissinger always insisted the system he devised, which made the NSC—and Kissinger himself—the main adviser responsible to the president on foreign affairs, was what Nixon wanted. The president believed that he needed a more centralized and secretive approach to foreign policy and that the way to accomplish this was to bring foreign policy making directly into the White House, something both Kennedy and Johnson had also sought to do. Kissinger emphasized that Nixon would hardly have allowed him, still suspect as a Harvard and Rockefeller man, to put into place anything that did not conform to Nixon's own preferences.[223] While this is true, it leaves out some important qualifiers, especially Kissinger's own special touch in the new organization and how it could serve his own position. When he went to meet with Walt Rostow, who held the equivalent position of assistant on national security affairs under President Johnson, Rostow advised Kissinger that "the only right way to organize is to serve the President's needs." Kissinger certainly followed this advice. His NSC system served the needs of Richard Nixon, with his odd reclusive personality, high intelligence, and propensity for duplicity.[224] Like his great rival John Kennedy and in sharp contrast to his predecessor, Lyndon Johnson, Nixon believed that a president should focus on foreign policy, once saying, "This country could run itself domestically without a President," and joking that domestic policy amounted to "building outhouses in Peoria."[225] He had traveled extensively as vice president and during his years out of office and was extremely knowledgeable about other countries and their leaders. He was also convinced of the importance of foreign policy for a president's domestic political position. His national security adviser, as the position would soon become known, was a presidential choice who did not have to be approved by, or testify before, a Democratic Party–controlled Congress. Kissinger's constituency was one man and one man alone.

Nixon was rarely interested in the details of implementing his decisions, and for this he relied on Kissinger. Kissinger, working with his Harvard colleague Morton Halperin, a specialist in bureaucratic structures, delivered a system that made the NSC "the principal forum for issues requiring presidential determination. The nature of the issues to be considered may range from current crises and operational problems to middle and long-range planning."[226] On the practical side, this involved an almost immediate tripling of the size of the NSC's staff and a dramatic increase in its budget, making it a mini State Department, the vehicle through which Kissinger sought to control and tame the bureaucracy. Many of those Kissinger brought into government were Democrats or independents, unsympathetic to Nixon but deeply enamored of Kissinger. To manage the flow of information to the president, Kissinger proposed and put into operation a system of interdepartmental committees, all chaired by himself and covering most foreign policy issues, covert actions, intelligence, and defense issues.[227]

Bringing foreign policy into the White House was Nixon's way to ensure that the State Department did not prevent the foreign policy innovation—and claim the political credit for that innovation—that he sought to achieve. Kissinger was the key to this. When Nixon appointed his old friend, and Eisenhower's attorney general, William P. Rogers as secretary of state, the press immediately speculated as to whether Rogers, who had little background in foreign policy, could compete with Kissinger for the president's ear.[228] The NSC staffer and later Kissinger critic Roger Morris concluded that Nixon and Kissinger had executed "a seizure of power unprecedented in modern American foreign policy," calling it "the *coup d'état* at the Hotel Pierre."[229] There were limits to this coup d'état, and it was not quite the successful seizure of power over all foreign policy that Morris asserted. Secretary of Defense Melvin Laird secured Nixon's agreement before his appointment, giving him autonomy in running his department.[230] Laird's bureaucratic mastery and extensive political contacts in Congress made him a considerable rival to Kissinger.[231] The Treasury Department also operated outside Kissinger's control, although the implications of this for foreign policy were not as immediately apparent. Even though Rogers was put at a disadvantage before the Nixon presidency began, his personal friendship with Nixon went back to the Eisenhower years, and he had considerable access to, and occasionally influence with, the president.[232] Nixon recognized Kissinger's insecurity, and he used Rogers to exploit that weakness in the national security adviser. As Kissinger later wrote, Nixon "did not really mind the tug-of-war that developed between Secretary of State Rogers and me," and was convinced "my special talents would flourish best under conditions of personal insecurity."[233] He joked that the great thing about his job as national security adviser was that "you can be paranoid and have real enemies."[234] In a more serious vein, he reflected in his memoirs: "No one could survive the White House without Presidential goodwill, and Nixon's favor depended on the readiness to fall in with the paranoid cult of the tough guy. The conspiracy of the press, the hostility of the Establishment, the flatulence of the Georgetown set, were permanent features of Nixon's conversation which one challenged only at the cost of exclusion from the inner circle."[235] From January 20, 1969, Kissinger wanted to be in the inner circle, and it would take his intellectual brilliance, skill as a courtier, and Machiavellian maneuvering within and against the bureaucracy to stay there.

2

"YOU CAN'T LOSE THEM ALL"

Kissinger as National Security Adviser, 1969–1970

AS THE SECOND ANNIVERSARY of the Nixon presidency approached, *CBS Evening News* had an exclusive: an interview with National Security Adviser Henry Kissinger. Although news anchors often mentioned Kissinger, his press briefings were on background and not broadcast. Kissinger announced that he would not return to Harvard University and would stay in his National Security Council job for the remainder of President Nixon's term of office.[1] Kissinger, drumming his fingers on his desk, haltingly told the CBS correspondent Robert Pierpoint that being national security adviser was "a very satisfying job." He added, "I know that the power I now have is bound to be fleeting, and whether it lasts a year more or less is not decisive. The only thing that will be remembered is what we accomplish, not the exercise of power while we did it."[2] Unbeknownst to Pierpoint or his viewers, Kissinger had just come from an angry meeting with Nixon's top presidential aides, H. R. Haldeman and John Ehrlichman, during which he had threatened again to resign over his problems in dealing with William P. Rogers and the State Department. Haldeman calmed him down and Kissinger decided to stay, even though Haldeman suspected that Kissinger never had any real intention of resigning.[3]

Pierpoint then asked Kissinger about the FBI's announcement detailing a plot to kidnap him. The story had broken a month earlier, with reports that the FBI was now guarding the national security adviser. The government indicted eight antiwar activists, including the famous priests Daniel and Philip Berrigan, claiming that they conspired to kidnap Kissinger and blow up the heating ducts under federal buildings. Kissinger told Pierpoint that he knew nothing more about the kidnap plot than had appeared in the papers, and that he was certain it was only the work of "a very tiny minority." Many already regarded the prosecution as "farcical," as Eric Sevareid of *CBS Evening News* put it. Sevareid went on to joke, "What would they do with Kissinger—argue with him and lose?"[4] A *New York Times* editorial also made fun of the allegation, imagining the "fanatically pacifist priests" debating with the "German-accented *realpolitik* professor" in the "catacomb-like depths of a Federal building . . . A citation from St. Francis of Assisi is countered by one from Bismarck, the moral claims of John XXIII set against the wisdom of Metternich."[5] Kissinger himself even joked that many members of his staff wanted the KIDNAP KISSINGER buttons that were now popular in the protest movement.

Pierpoint's interview bears witness to Kissinger's growing national prominence. Dan Rather, the CBS Washington correspondent, even referred to him as Nixon's "vest-pocket secretary of state."[6] These references to Kissinger's influence came despite the fact that Nixon's foreign policy seemed stalled, with no major achievements. Along with the continuing social turmoil at home and a troubled economy, many observers were predicting defeat for Nixon in November 1972. Nixon later wrote, "The problems we confronted were so overwhelming and so apparently impervious to anything we could do to change them that it seemed possible that I might not even be nominated for re-election in 1972."[7] While this was unlikely, it reflects Nixon's frustration at the mid-point of his first term. Even Kissinger, with his irreverent sense of humor, recognized that things had not gone their way. When a brief crisis erupted in Jordan in September 1970, and the United States successfully backed King Hussein's efforts to secure his regime, Kissinger joked to one reporter that the administration's new motto would be "You can't lose them all."[8] Kissinger's joke stood in sharp contrast with the energy and confidence that both men possessed when they began their work together in January 1969.

BE LIKE IKE: NIXON, THE FIRST HUNDRED DAYS, AND THE EISENHOWER ANALOGY

Richard Nixon's presidential inauguration was the first to be met by angry street protesters in Washington, who staged a "counter-inaugural" and showered the parade with beer cans, rocks, and bottles. The civil unrest over the Vietnam War defined America's political landscape. In a conciliatory speech, Nixon pleaded with Americans to "lower our voices" and announced, "After a period of confrontation, we are entering an era of negotiation." Nixon made a "sacred commitment" to the "cause of peace among nations" but cautioned that "peace does not come through wishing for it—that there is no substitute for days and even years of patient and prolonged diplomacy."[9] Unlike John F. Kennedy's call to "pay any price, bear any burden," the Nixon inaugural signaled the beginning of a policy of retrenchment, of limiting America's commitments and reducing its footprint abroad.

Nixon and Kissinger realized that America's position in the world had changed profoundly since the Kennedy years. Throughout the globe, the United States seemed like a captive Gulliver, embroiled in conflicts it could not win and unable to escape commitments it no longer wanted. Vietnam was the overwhelming priority, with more than half a million Americans fighting a vicious war that was claiming more than a thousand dead a month. At home, the urban rebellions of the 1960s convinced many Americans that the nation could no longer afford both its international commitments and the expensive weaponry they required. Student protests highlighted the polarization and deep divisions within American society as well as a loss of the heady self-confidence of the Kennedy years. Abroad, the Soviet Union now stood as equal in nuclear arms, with its recent invasion of Czechoslovakia and border conflicts with China showing that it remained a dangerous adversary. Western Europe was increasingly preoccupied with its own domestic problems and search for greater unity, while the Middle East was on the verge of renewed conflict. The challenges for the United States appeared overwhelming.

Kissinger attacked his new job with a sustained energy and enthusiasm, but also made sure to court the media. A cover story in *Time* magazine in early February 1969 described Kissinger "working six days a week from 7:30 a.m. to near midnight" and engaging the brutal pace of government, which led him half-jokingly to say he didn't want to confront any more new ideas because he was living off his "intellectual capital." The article strongly implied his indispensability to Nixon: "'There cannot be a crisis next week,' he jokes in a softly Germanic accent. 'My schedule is already full.'"[10] Kissinger's rapid emergence as a key adviser did not escape notice. The British embassy, with its sensitivity to changes in Washington, attributed it to Secretary of State Rogers's leisurely style. Rogers embodied "the amateur approach to his job. He dislikes working over-long hours and is reluctant . . . to deal with official business after dinner. At weekends he is far more likely to be found on the golf-course than in his office or on the platform."[11] Congressional Democrats also worried. Senator J. William Fulbright, the chair of the Senate Foreign Relations Committee, warned that the new NSC organization might "move in the direction of taking very important matters out of the hands of the traditional agencies, most of which felt a responsibility to Congress."[12] As early as January 29, 1969, only nine days after the inauguration, CBS News reported that Nixon went to the State Department to combat the rumors about Kissinger's influence and reassure the Foreign Service officers that he regarded Rogers and the State Department as his prime source for foreign policy advice.[13]

Despite Nixon's efforts to promote Rogers, the profile in *Time* sympathetically allowed Kissinger to convey his own hope to change American attitudes toward foreign affairs, emphasizing the need for the United States to "get some reputation for steadiness [in foreign policy]. We will not get steadiness unless we have a certain philosophy of what we are trying to do."[14] He was careful not to define this "philosophy," or use an exotic term like "realpolitik" to describe it. Rather, he tried to position the administration's approach between the extremes of "excessive idealism" and "excessive pragmatism" in foreign policy, an approach that was trademark Kissinger. Both he and Nixon quickly began using a different vocabulary to describe America's objectives. In just his second press conference, Nixon answered a question about possible withdrawals from Vietnam by saying, "I do not want an American boy to be in Vietnam one day longer than is necessary for our national interest."[15]

Although Nixon and Kissinger used the language of realism and put the Vietnam commitment in terms of the national interest, their understanding of the term included the notion of credibility, both international and domestic. To Kissinger, no American president could accept the demand of an immediate and unilateral withdrawal of American soldiers, something advocated by one of the leading realist thinkers, Hans Morgenthau. Kissinger sympathized in part with Morgenthau's position but thought such an approach was politically unacceptable: "By 1969 the over half-million American forces, the 70,000 allied forces, and the 31,000 who had died there had settled the issue of whether the outcome was important for us and those who depended on us."[16] For Kissinger, the credibility of the United States was on the line. "What is involved now is confidence in American promises. However fashionable it is to ridicule the terms 'credibility' or 'prestige,' they are not empty phrases; other nations can gear their actions to ours only if they can count on our steadiness."[17] Although Nixon also stressed that a rapid American withdrawal would have "disastrous" effects in Asia, the president tended to emphasize the domestic effects: "The most serious effect would be in the United States. When a great power fails, it deeply affects the will of the people. While the public would welcome peace initially, they would soon be asking why we pulled out and this would in turn lead to an attack on the leadership and establishment and the U.S. role in the war."[18] Nixon believed that a rapid withdrawal, with a likely collapse of Saigon and victory for the North Vietnamese, would cause an intense political crisis within the United States. Critics would rightly ask, What was the sacrifice in American blood and treasure for? Why did my father or son or brother have to die? Who was responsible for this failure? Nixon believed this would destroy his capacity to govern. He shared the sentiment that Kissinger's mentor, Fritz Kraemer, penned in a memo Kissinger forwarded to the president: "The 'people' are not very just, they forgive the victor, but always make scapegoats of their own leaders who are not victorious."[19]

Ending the Vietnam War was the first priority of Nixon and Kissinger. Nixon knew Americans elected him because they believed he would end the war in Vietnam, and he worked with a historical analogy. It was based on what he believed had happened when Dwight Eisenhower, Nixon's own political hero and the man he served as vice president, came into office.[20] Nixon believed that Eisenhower had implicitly threatened the Soviets that he would use all means to end the Korean War, including nuclear weapons. Like Eisenhower, Nixon hoped that a combination of secret diplomacy with the Russians and promises of an arms control deal and a settlement in the Middle East, coupled with threats of more forceful military action against North Vietnam, would yield an "honorable peace" that afforded South Vietnam a "reasonable" chance for survival. Nixon recognized that even though many Americans in 1953 had regarded the end to the Korean War as a "defeat," that the outcome had freed Eisenhower to devote his attention to more important issues, such as organizing NATO and quieting the McCarthy furor over domestic communism. Similarly, Nixon wanted to restore America's leadership over the European allies and quiet the antiwar protests at home. For Nixon, getting a Korean-like result in South Vietnam would be the best outcome the United States could achieve.[21]

Nixon's plan to imitate Eisenhower helped Kissinger establish his prominence among Nixon's advisers. Nixon wanted an early trip to Europe, telling congressional leaders that Americans had been looking "too much to collateral areas" of the world and not enough to what "some would still call the blue chip."[22] Europe was "blue chip" and Kissinger's specialty, and he accompanied Nixon throughout his trip, even when it created problems with diplomatic protocol.[23] Nixon met first with de Gaulle, whose alienation from the Johnson administration afforded Nixon the opportunity for a clear contrast. Along with secretly promising cooperation with the French nuclear program, Nixon flattered the French leader publicly, making it clear he valued France's role in the Western alliance.[24] He told the French leader that he wanted to pursue détente with the Soviet Union, but he also vowed to be "hard and pragmatic" in his dealings. De Gaulle downplayed his own outspoken opposition to the Vietnam War and encouraged Nixon's caution, telling him that he "should not rush to Moscow and lay out the red carpet before Brezhnev."[25] Nixon also visited with the British prime minister, Harold Wilson, in London and the German chancellor, Kurt Kiesinger, in Bonn. Nixon wanted to believe that his trip was a great success, and Kissinger told him it was: "I am convinced that your trip drove the key message home: we are sensitive to the critical problems; we respect and value the opinions of our Allies, we will approach talks with the Soviets with great prudence and only in full consultation with our friends; and we do not intend to try to dictate solutions to international problems anywhere at any time."[26]

Kissinger's praise echoed the type of critique he had often written about how American leaders dealt with Europe, but this advice would soon encounter the reality of a Europe turning inward and not receptive to a renewal of a 1950s Eisenhower-style American leadership.[27] All the European leaders Nixon met were gone within the next fifteen months, with the resignation of de Gaulle in April 1969 a harbinger of this change. As Nixon and Kissinger began their approach to the Soviet Union, the real limits Nixon placed on multilateral consultation became clear. Kissinger himself admitted in a phone call to Rogers that Nixon "is not so much for consultation in practice as in theory."[28] Nixon understood that his image as a leader of the alliance was important to the American public, but despite this early attention to Europe, he quickly began to focus solely on Vietnam and the Soviet Union. Nixon believed that a new strategic arms agreement might be enough of an incentive to encourage the Soviets to use their influence with Hanoi to end the war in Vietnam.

Despite his personal ties to Europe, Kissinger shared Nixon's view that ending the Vietnam War quickly should be the priority of American foreign policy.[29] To engage the Soviet Union, Nixon instructed Kissinger to become his confidential emissary in a series of "back channel" meetings with the Soviet ambassador Anatoly Dobrynin, meetings kept secret from the State Department. Within the first days of taking office, Kissinger conveyed Nixon's message to Soviet officials that the United States was "determined to end the war in Vietnam one way or another." Kissinger also conveyed his idea of linkage by telling Dobrynin that Soviet assistance in ending the war would yield progress on other issues like the strategic arms negotiations and the Middle East.[30] Kissinger emphasized to Dobrynin that the United States had "a good understanding of our overall approach and values the role of the Soviet Union in seeking a peace settlement." Kissinger went on to stress that the administration "for foreign and domestic policy reasons 'simply cannot' allow any lengthy procrastination in resolving the Vietnam question," and that if a settlement did not come "within some fairly limited time frame," "the question of using other means will inevitably arise," which Dobrynin told Moscow meant military means.[31]

In order to drive home to the Soviets and the North Vietnamese that he was serious, Nixon believed he needed a military option, especially after the North launched its post-Tet offensive in February 1969, ending a lull in the fighting and killing more than a thousand American soldiers in a short period. Kissinger shared his view, having argued much of his public life that "our insistence on divorcing force from diplomacy caused our power to lack purpose and our negotiations to lack force."[32] Kissinger pushed the military to suggest possibilities that "could convey to the North that there is a new firm hand at the helm."[33] Even though Nixon wanted to strike at the North, he quickly recognized, and was told by Rogers and Laird, that a renewal of the bombing of North Vietnam might reignite domestic protests and damage the president's early honeymoon with the American public. As an alternative, General Creighton Abrams proposed the possibility of B-52 raids on enemy sanctuaries and positions within Cambodia. The North Vietnamese occupied significant parts of eastern Cambodia, in violation of that country's neutrality, and although the United States had authorized covert operations against some of the sanctuaries, no large-scale operations had been undertaken. Kissinger argued that such a military action, bizarrely code-named Breakfast, if coupled with an offer of private talks with the North Vietnamese, "will serve as a signal to the Soviets of the Administration's determination to end the war." Kissinger added that it would also "be a signal that things may get out of hand," appealing to Nixon's oft-expressed "madman" strategy—the idea that his reputation for anti-communist fanaticism might serve to frighten both the Russians and the North Vietnamese into believing that he might escalate even further and thus into making concessions.[34] Nixon approved the bombing on March 16, and as Haldeman noted in his diary the next day: "Historic Day. K[issinger]'s Operation Breakfast finally came off at 2:00 pm our time. K[issinger] really excited, as was P[resident.]"[35] Prince Norodom Sihanouk, the Cambodian leader, did not protest the raids in a public statement, unable to stop either the Americans from bombing his country or the North Vietnamese from occupying it.

The bombing of Cambodia was undertaken in secret from the American people, primarily to prevent "domestic critics" from seizing on the issue to renew their attacks on the war and "pressure for a quick US withdrawal."[36] It was not a secret to the Cambodians or the North Vietnamese, and there were contingency plans to claim that it was a mistake if the North Vietnamese or Cambodians went public. (The secret did not last long in the United States. On May 9, 1969, William Beecher published a fairly complete account of the bombings in *The New York Times*.)[37] When there was no outcry from the North Vietnamese, Nixon and Kissinger took the next step of a direct approach to the Soviet Union, with an implicit threat of greater military action against North Vietnam. On April 14, 1969, in a setting that smacked of a Hollywood movie script, Kissinger invited Dobrynin to his home late in the evening, telling the ambassador that their meeting was so confidential "he gave the maid the evening off and set the tea table himself." He also told the Secret Service to check on whether any journalists were lurking outside or had followed Dobrynin to his house. Kissinger dramatically announced to the Soviet ambassador, "The President had therefore decided to make one more direct approach on the highest level before drawing the conclusion that the war could only be ended by unilateral means." In Dobrynin's account of the meeting, Kissinger also put forth a straightforward domestic political account for Nixon's motivation and thinking, noting that Nixon "is not seeking a military victory, but he cannot go down in American history as the first U.S. president to have lost a war in which the U.S. participated." Kissinger explained that Nixon believed Hanoi was counting on a collapse of American will in the wake of mounting protests. However, Kissinger told Dobrynin that Hanoi was wrong and that American public opinion, including those who voted for Nixon and "the more than 12 million who voted for Wallace," supported "ending the war as soon as possible by any means, if necessary by using even greater military force." Alternatively, "dragging out the war in its present form for three more years, until the next election, will inevitably lead to electoral defeat." Kissinger even showed Dobrynin the president's signed approval of his talking points for the discussion and stressed that relations with the Soviet Union were at a crucial turning point. A Vietnam settlement would allow them to move forward on a host of issues, including arms control and the Middle East. The talking points also suggested the possibility of sending a "high level representative" to Moscow to meet with a North Vietnamese representative to negotiate a settlement. (Kissinger wanted to send the former deputy secretary of defense Cyrus Vance.) Kissinger concluded that Nixon believed if he succeeded in improving relations with the Soviet Union, "he will be assured of winning the next election, since at least 80 percent of the electorate will then vote for him."[38]

Haldeman recorded in his diary that Kissinger was so "pleased with his plan" that he could not "resist telling someone outside his shop," so he stopped by Haldeman's office. But Kissinger's excitement about this plan did not last long. On April 15, 1969, the North Koreans shot down an EC-121 unarmed American reconnaissance plane. Even though both Nixon's and Kissinger's first reaction was to consider this a "test" from the Communist world that demanded a strong response, the crisis actually underlined how weakened America's military capacity had become. The military advised the president that it would take at least a week to plan a successful air strike.[39] The fears of setting off another war in Asia weighed heavily on Nixon, as did the advice he got from Rogers and Laird that military action would be too dangerous as well as likely to spark protests in the United States. Although Nixon decided against a military response, Kissinger's forceful advocacy of bombing won Nixon's sympathy and strengthened his personal standing in the White House.[40] Frustrated by his inaction in Korea, Nixon approved additional bombing missions over Cambodia, hoping to signal his resolve to the Soviets and North Vietnamese.[41]

Two weeks before the Korean incident, on March 28, 1969, Dwight Eisenhower died. Nixon, informed of the news, uncharacteristically broke down and wept openly in front of a group of his aides, including Kissinger, Haldeman, and Rogers. "He was such a strong man," Nixon said. Nixon hoped to begin his presidency following Eisenhower's example. The North Korean action made clear, however, that the world Nixon inherited was not that of the thirty-fourth president. The United States no longer enjoyed the overwhelming military and economic power it had when Eisenhower became president. The Communist world was not the unified monolith Eisenhower faced in the Korean War. In early March 1969, the Soviet Union and China engaged in their first serious military clash in the northeastern border region, a signal that the Sino-Soviet split now was dangerously violent. The world was different, American power had limits, and Nixon needed a new approach.

VIETNAMIZATION, "SALTED PEANUTS," AND THE MAKING OF A WASHINGTON CELEBRITY

Kissinger had hoped that his appeal to Ambassador Dobrynin to arrange secret talks would yield a breakthrough in the Vietnam stalemate, but the Soviet government never replied. Instead, on May 8, 1969, the Vietnamese Communists put forward a ten-point peace program, demanding unconditional American withdrawal and a new coalition government in Saigon. Nixon felt pressured to respond. Kissinger, who told Haldeman that Hanoi "may be folding," put together a fourteen-point plan that called for both sides to withdraw their forces within a year under international supervision. In a formula that echoed the original 1954 Geneva arrangements, the international supervisors would see to it that elections were held in South Vietnam. Nixon emphasized, in words that Kissinger hoped might help in possible peace talks, that although reports from Hanoi indicated it was counting on a "collapse of American will in the United States . . . there could be no greater error in judgment." But Nixon also acknowledged that he could not ask for "unlimited patience" from Americans "whose hopes for peace have too often been raised and cruelly dashed over the last four years."[42]

The problem with Nixon's message was that there were clear signs that the American people's patience was wearing thin and that they were anxious to see an end to American involvement. The spring of 1969 saw a renewal of antiwar protests in Washington as well as a surge in campus unrest, over both the war and racial issues. Fears of growing anarchy and violence were widespread. The picture of militant black students exiting a Cornell University building with rifles and shotguns "sent a shudder through this country," in the words of James "Scotty" Reston, a New York Times columnist.[43] Kissinger's own Harvard came under siege with a two-week strike by radical students. When antiwar students came to Washington, Kissinger met with a delegation led by Roger Black of the University of Chicago. Kissinger was quoted on CBS Evening News as asking the students to give the administration more time and to be patient, and saying, in words that would come back to haunt him, "If you come back in a year and things haven't changed, we won't have a morally defensible position."[44] While many Americans both feared and opposed the campus protests, the agitation kept the frustrating war in the news and encouraged the type of sentiment, captured in a CBS Evening News report, of a Harvard professor telling a group of prominent business executives: "How do you get out of Vietnam? In ships!"[45] There were also clear signs that the congressional moratorium on criticism was ending. After the May 1969 battle of Hamburger Hill in Vietnam, when American soldiers seized Hill 937 and then abandoned it, at a cost of 633 North Vietnamese and "fewer" than 100 Americans, Senator Edward Kennedy, the presumed favorite for the Democratic nomination in 1972, called the policy "senseless and irresponsible."[46]

Kennedy had already become a leader in trying to stop the administration's development of an antiballistic missile (ABM) system, an expensive weapons system designed to counter the Soviet Union's increasing number of intercontinental ballistic missiles (ICBMs). The fact that the Soviets were also developing ABMs made the prospect of a new arms race in defensive systems likely and invigorated Senate opponents. Nixon's staff saw the Kennedy-led fight as the "first battle of '72."[47] Nixon's policy of retrenchment was unfolding too slowly to appease the public mood, and the "Pentagon presented a large, conspicuous target for those in Congress worried about military domination of foreign policy, militarization of American society, and out-of-control defense spending."[48] Public and congressional sentiment was clearly shifting away from the automatic Cold War support for the Pentagon budget. The demand now was for spending at home, and President Eisenhower's famous farewell address, warning of a "military-industrial complex," received renewed attention and respect in the wake of his death. The New York Times reflected this sentiment, arguing that "excessive military spending has contributed to a misallocation of national resources [and] society has already suffered irreparable harm from the pressures and distortions thus created."[49]

Secretary of Defense Melvin Laird was acutely sensitive to this changing public mood. Laird quickly became the administration's most fervent proponent of disengagement from the war through Vietnamization, the program of training and equipping the South Vietnamese army to take over combat responsibilities from the United States. Laird's knowledge of Capitol Hill, shaped by sixteen years on committees dealing with appropriations, foreign policy, and intelligence, led him to recognize the danger posed by the burgeoning appeal of the antiwar, anti-defense-spending attitudes.[50] He wanted to preserve as far as possible the Defense Department's budget for the central tasks of containment, a nuclear balance with the Soviet Union, and the defense of Europe.[51] Laird's Vietnamization brought the troops home, bought time for the administration, and did not depend on getting Soviet and North Vietnamese agreement. Nixon recognized the political benefits of Vietnamization, announcing the first troop withdrawal of twenty-five thousand men during his meeting with President Nguyễn Văn Thiệu on Midway Island in June 1969. At a press conference only a few days later, Nixon reacted angrily to a question about former secretary of defense Clark Clifford's call for the withdrawal of all ground combat forces by the end of 1970. Pointing out how Clifford's own tenure as defense secretary had corresponded with high casualties and an increasing number of troops in Vietnam, Nixon said, "I would hope we could beat Mr. Clifford's timetable, just as I think we have done a little better than he did when he was in charge of our national defense."[52]

Nixon's statement "shook Kissinger pretty badly," Haldeman reported.[53] Kissinger regarded Nixon's impromptu bid to outdo Clifford's plan as damaging to any possibility of negotiations with Hanoi for mutual withdrawals.[54] He speculated to Haldeman that this could cause the collapse of the Saigon government and worried that this meant the president had lost confidence in him. Haldeman thought Kissinger was overreacting, but there was a larger context to Kissinger's uncertainty. It was no secret that many of the people Kissinger had brought to Washington were not Nixon supporters, and Nixon and his close advisers mistrusted them. Kissinger himself exploded in anger when the Beecher story about the Cambodian bombing appeared in the *Times*. In the atmosphere of suspicion within the White House, Kissinger himself and the men he brought with him were prime suspects for the news leaks Nixon most despised. As a result of the White House concern, and in order to preserve his own position, Kissinger "set out to prove to Nixon and his Prussian staffers that he was more fervent than anyone in enforcing the cult of secrecy."[55] Kissinger called FBI director J. Edgar Hoover and gave him a list of those staffers in his office with access to the information, telling Hoover that he would "destroy whoever did this if we can find him, no matter where he is."[56] Among the first to be wiretapped was Morton Halperin, who had helped devise the NSC system; Helmut Sonnenfeldt, Kissinger's fellow German Jewish refugee; and even Winston Lord, the man Kissinger later called his "conscience" on foreign policy issues.[57] In all there would be seventeen FBI wiretaps ordered by the White House, thirteen on government employees including Kissinger's staff and four on newsmen, among them Kissinger's British friend who was a reporter for London's *Times* Henry Brandon, the *New York Times* journalist Hedrick Smith, and the columnist Joseph

Kraft. The wiretapping underscores the insecurity and fragility of Kissinger's position within the Nixon White House as well as Kissinger's determination to fight by any means necessary to stay within the president's inner circle.[58]

Despite the public prominence of Vietnamization, Kissinger convinced Nixon to try his plan for ending the war through secret negotiations combined with a military ultimatum. As part of this plan, Kissinger conducted talks with the North Vietnamese in early August. At those talks, Kissinger assured Nixon, he "laid down the deadline on them very hard."[59] Kissinger was referring to Nixon's letter to Ho Chi Minh, sent through a French intermediary, Kissinger's friend Jean Sainteny.[60] The idea for the letter emerged after a key meeting on the presidential yacht, the *Sequoia*, on July 7, after which Nixon resolved, "I decided to 'go for broke' in the sense that I would attempt to end the war one way or the other—either by negotiated agreement or by an increased use of force."[61] Nixon's letter told Ho, "The time has come to move forward to the conference table toward an early resolution of this tragic war." Nixon emphasized that without a breakthrough in the talks, he would have to resort to "measures of greater consequence and force." Operation Duck Hook set a deadline of November 1, 1969, the one-year anniversary of President Johnson's bombing halt over North Vietnam.[62]

The NSC, under Kissinger's direction, was to come up with some type of "savage, punishing blow" to destroy much of the North in a short campaign. Although all sorts of military contingencies were considered for Duck Hook, including the destruction of the system of dikes that prevented the flooding of the Red River, the use of tactical nuclear weapons, and even a ground invasion of the North, the most likely scenario was an intense bombing campaign "attacking 29 significant targets in North Vietnam ... and aerial mining of the deep water ports."[63] Of Kissinger, Haldeman noted, "He wants to push for some escalation—enough to get us a reasonable bargain for a settlement within six months."[64] Over the summer of 1969, Kissinger tried to prepare Nixon for the escalation. He told Haldeman and Ehrlichman that Nixon needed to make a "total mental commitment and be prepared to take the heat" that would come with the proposed military action.[65]

These secret considerations about escalation went on during a period of time when the American public's mood, the world political situation, and even the administration's own policies pointed in a very different direction. During his world trip in July 1969, Nixon proclaimed his "Nixon Doctrine," a post–Vietnam War policy in which the United States announced that it would provide political and economic support to endangered allies in Asia but not provide American soldiers. These countries would need to supply their own men to fight insurgencies. Nixon emphasized, "We must avoid that kind of policy that will make countries in Asia so dependent upon us that we are dragged into conflicts such as the one we have in Vietnam." Although Nixon argued that his doctrine was an answer to those who wanted the United States to withdraw fully from Asia, the general understanding of the policy was that it reflected a retreat from an interventionist stance. Nixon's successful trip to Romania, where he was greeted with real public enthusiasm from the people of the maverick communist state, coupled with the renewed military clashes between the Soviet Union and China in early August, also created an image of a communist enemy in disarray, no longer the fearsome monolith of the early Cold War. Within the United States, the summer of the moon landing—and Woodstock—saw an intense Senate debate over whether to continue building an ABM system. This debate came to a head in early August and dominated the news. The Nixon administration barely won the Senate vote, needing Vice President Agnew's tie-breaking vote to win approval of the ABM. Television coverage of the vote was extensive, and also included sharply critical comments from the NBC anchor David Brinkley, who noted that days of "giving the military everything it wanted" were finally over.[66]

The most important indicator of the public mood came as the antiwar movement announced plans for a massive mobilization and demonstrations on Washington, to begin October 15 and continue every month until the war was ended. The "moratorium" movement would seek to bring protest into the mainstream of middle-class American life. Nixon announced another withdrawal of thirty-five thousand American troops from Vietnam on September 16, 1969, as well as plans for a fifty-thousand-man reduction in draft calls for the upcoming months. The steps were taken with the beginning of the fall's college semester in mind, recognizing the potential for trouble on campuses. Newspaper columnists speculated, "The President hopes that this combination of troop withdrawal and draft suspensions will give him a longer spell of freedom from domestic confrontation."[67] The New York Republican senator Charles Goodell proposed legislation to set a deadline for the withdrawal of U.S. troops from Vietnam by the end of 1970.[68]

It was in this atmosphere that Kissinger prepared a memorandum for Nixon that would later achieve notoriety as the "salted peanuts" memo.[69] The memo reflected Kissinger's foreign policy analysis combined with his recognition of how the domestic politics of the Vietnam question were playing out. Kissinger bluntly told the president that time "runs more quickly against our strategy than theirs" and that his "pessimistic view" was based on this perception. The pressure of public opinion in the United States to end the war would "increase greatly" in the coming months. Kissinger did not believe that Vietnamization would reduce that pressure and warned Nixon, "You will then be somewhat in the same position as was President Johnson, although the substance of your position will be different." In the most often repeated line of the memo, Kissinger told Nixon that the "withdrawal of U.S. troops will become like salted peanuts to the American public: The more U.S. troops come home, the more will be demanded. This could result, in effect, in demands for unilateral withdrawal—perhaps within a year." To Kissinger, Vietnamization, with its regular—and unreciprocated—troop withdrawals, undermined whatever slim hope there was of a diplomatic settlement. "It looks as though they are prepared to try to wait us out," Kissinger wrote, saying that approach "fits both with its doctrine of how to fight a revolutionary war and with its expectations about increasingly significant problems for the U.S." Nixon underlined this concluding sentence, well aware that Kissinger had put his finger on the central politically driven contradiction within his Vietnam policy.[70]

As the deadline neared for Operation Duck Hook, Nixon tried to keep his options open, one minute speaking of his hopes for a new era of peace and negotiations, and the next telling Republican senators that he was considering a plan to blockade Haiphong harbor and invade North Vietnam, promising them that he would not be "the first American president to lose a war" and that "by the 1970 elections, one way or another, it is going to be over with."[71] Sharing Kissinger's sense of the importance of force to effective diplomacy, Nixon was genuinely ambivalent, recognizing Hanoi's strategy for waiting him out but not wanting to inflame the domestic protest movement through a military escalation whose prospects were unpredictable. He looked for possible reasons to delay, at one time speculating with Kissinger that Ho Chi Minh's death in September might contribute to the North's intransigence.[72] Kissinger noticed the president's ambivalence and gave him more reasons to put off military action. After a press conference in which Nixon stated starkly that he would not be affected by the domestic protests scheduled in October, Nixon asked Kissinger whether he could make "the tough move" before October 15 so that it would not appear that he had been affected by "the rioting at home." Kissinger cautioned against the idea, saying that there was a "ten percent chance Hanoi might want to move" and that Hanoi should be given until November 1.[73]

As the date approached, Nixon confessed to Haldeman that he understood that support for the war was "more tenuous every day."[74] He resented both Laird and Rogers for strongly advising him that any military escalation would tear the country apart and cripple his presidency. Kissinger told the president that he thought there were only two alternatives, "to bug out or accelerate," and that he favored escalation. The main question, as Kissinger put it to Nixon, was whether he could hold the country together for the six months or so necessary for this strategy to work. Haldeman, who often sympathized with Kissinger on the issue, thought Kissinger underestimated the scale of domestic resistance toward any military escalation, even one that might bring the war to a successful conclusion. He thought Kissinger's "contingency plans" didn't "include the domestic factor."[75] What Kissinger's plan did do was cement in Nixon's mind that his national security adviser understood his instincts, even though in this case the president would choose differently. In early October, Nixon decided against any military strike on November 1.[76] It was a painful decision for Nixon, running against his own self-image as a leader unafraid to buck the public opinion polls. Kissinger also worried once again that it might mean that Nixon had lost faith in him, and might even be trying to ease him out.[77] Nixon wanted to try a bluff, however, wagering on his "madman" theory to see if he could get progress on a settlement. He plotted with Kissinger to telephone him while Kissinger was meeting with the Soviet ambassador, Dobrynin. During the call, Nixon emphasized that "Vietnam was the critical issue" and that the Soviet Union "should not expect any special treatment until Vietnam was solved." Nixon also had Kissinger tell Dobrynin that it was a "pity that all our efforts to negotiate had failed" and that "the train had just left the station and was now headed down the track." While these words were intended to convey an ominous sense of threat, Dobrynin seemed unmoved. He told Kissinger simply that he hoped "it was an airplane and not a train and could leave some maneuvering room."[78]

To strengthen his bluff, Nixon ordered the U.S. military to go on nuclear alert on October 13.[79] This alert, however, was nothing like the very public DEFCON 2 alert that President Kennedy initiated at the time of the Cuban Missile Crisis, with missiles and bombers placed on high alert. Rather, Nixon asked Laird to order U.S. military forces to take a series of measures designed to convey to the Soviets an increasing readiness by U.S. strategic forces. Nixon and Kissinger wanted the highest level of secrecy within the government and military, and wanted to avoid any measures that might lead to public disclosure. In effect, they wanted an alert loud enough for the Russians to hear but soft enough to avoid public notice. Unfortunately, the combination diminished whatever impact the alert had on the Soviet Union. After the alert began, Nixon called Kissinger to give him advice on his meeting with Dobrynin. Nixon told Kissinger to play the "good cop, bad cop" routine, and that when the subject of Vietnam was raised, "Shake [your] head and say 'I am sorry, Mr. Ambassador, but he is out of control. Mr. Ambassador, as you know, I am very close to the president, but you don't know this man—he's been through more than any of the rest of us put together. He's made up his mind and unless there's some movement,' just shake your head and walk out."[80] Nixon himself warned Dobrynin, "If the Soviet Union would not help us to get peace, the U.S. would have to pursue its own methods for bringing the war to an end. It could not allow a talk-fight strategy without taking action." He again promised Dobrynin that if the Soviet Union did something in Vietnam, "the U.S. might do something dramatic to improve Soviet-U.S. relations, indeed something more dramatic than they could now imagine." But Nixon insisted, "We would not hold still for being 'diddled' to death in Vietnam."[81] In his report of the conversation to his superiors, Dobrynin did not try to translate "diddled," but he noted that "events surrounding the Vietnam crisis now wholly preoccupy the U.S. President" and that Nixon worried that he will share the "fate of his predecessor Lyndon Johnson." This was taking on "such an emotional coloration," he said, that Nixon was "unable to control himself even in a conversation with a foreign ambassador."[82] The Russians were not moved to act, and Nixon's bluff came up empty.[83]

Nixon and Kissinger overestimated both Moscow's ability and its willingness to try to influence Hanoi. The Russians competed with the Chinese for influence with North Vietnam, and the North Vietnamese skillfully manipulated the two communist superpowers for their own interest. By 1969 the Soviet Union provided about a half-billion dollars in aid to Hanoi, but as the historian Ilya V. Gaiduk concluded, its assistance was "not converted into proportional political influence." Soviet leaders complained, but they were never willing to tie their aid to changes in North Vietnamese behavior. In addition, the Soviets hoped that North Vietnam would play an important role in their long-term plans for influence in Southeast Asia, and even though they grumbled about Vietnamese "intransigence," they remained supportive throughout the war. As Gaiduk characterized it, to the Kremlin, Vietnam was "not only an issue of ideology but also a question of geopolitics."[84]

The Soviets also may have viewed the enormous public demonstrations during the October moratorium and the shrinking levels of support for the war as an indication that America was indeed on its way out of Indochina, not about to escalate or even threaten military action. Television news coverage of the October moratorium demonstrations was overwhelmingly positive. NBC devoted more than half its broadcast to detailing events around the nation, acknowledging some counterdemonstrations but focusing on the peaceful and largely middle-class nature of the protests.[85] The demonstrations had an impact on Nixon and Kissinger, although each responded in characteristic fashion. Although he canceled Duck Hook primarily because of a fear of public protest, Nixon said he would not be affected, telling a Georgetown college student who wrote to him that "to allow government policy to be made in the streets would destroy the democratic process . . . It would invite anarchy." Nixon also recognized the need for a political counterattack and sent Vice President Agnew out to criticize the moratorium as a "reflection of the confusion that exists in America today." Agnew went on to blast many of those whom Kissinger might have considered colleagues: "A spirit of national masochism prevails, encouraged by an effete corps of impudent snobs who characterize themselves as intellectuals."[86] For his part, Kissinger, although he supported an escalation of the war, was unnerved by the demonstrations and kept talking with many of his friends and colleagues who strongly opposed the war. The newspaper columnists Frank Mankiewicz and Tom Braden asked him to appear at the Georgetown Day School as a speaker, teasing him that they had found the last "hawk" in America among the parents at the school. Kissinger joked, "It can't be me," noting that they must want him as speaker to show the students "a sample of human depravity."[87] In a long conversation with Robert Kennedy's former speechwriter Adam Walinsky, Kissinger pleaded for "a little compassion and understanding" for the fact that the administration wanted peace. But Walinsky stridently insisted that "your boss" Nixon was "finished," and "is not going to get reelected . . . [and is] worse than LBJ was two years into his term in 1966." Kissinger thanked Walinsky for his "friendship and confidence" and promised to tell Nixon of their conversation.[88] That same day Nixon asked Haldeman to try to keep Kissinger "on an even keel and stop his worrying."[89]

Nixon's own counterattack against the moratoriums and the peace movement came November 3 in his famous "Silent Majority" speech. Kissinger provided the core of the speech, though, as he later wrote, Nixon added "rhetorical flourishes throughout."[90] Nixon offered a defense for the war and made the case "that a nation cannot remain great if it betrays its allies and lets down its friends." In the most famous part of the speech, Nixon appealed to the "great silent majority of my fellow Americans" to support him in ending the war "in a way that could win the peace." Nixon coldly insisted, "North Vietnam cannot defeat or humiliate the United States; only Americans can do that."[91] Coupled with the speeches of Vice President Agnew attacking the media, the administration's offensive won immediate results in public opinion polls. Kissinger was a keen observer of this example of how foreign policy could be used for domestic political purposes, noting, "Nixon was elated. Professing indifference to public adulation, he nevertheless relished those few moments of acclaim that came his way."[92] The president's popularity soared into the high 60s and 70s, and public support coalesced around what Kissinger called the administration's "dual-track strategy of Vietnamization and negotiations."[93] Even though the Vietnam moratorium in mid-November brought new demonstrations to Washington, the fervor of antiwar protest began to decline. The television news coverage of the November moratorium was not as positive, with significant attention now focused on "silent majority" groups and counter-demonstrators.[94] There were no significant December demonstrations. The president had, as Haldeman put it, "pretty thoroughly gotten into the position of calming down the war opposition, killing the mobilizations, and assuring the people he's got a plan and that it's working."[95] Kissinger concluded that for "the first time since January the Administration had some maneuvering room."[96]

There was considerable irony in Henry Kissinger's stature as the first year of the Nixon administration drew to an end. Kissinger had advised the president to pursue linkage with the Soviet Union on arms control and set a deadline for military escalation against North Vietnam to end the Vietnam War. In the end, the United States resumed the Strategic Arms Limitation Talks (SALT) without linkage, and Nixon backed down from his threat against Hanoi. Despite the overall failure of his advice, Kissinger emerged as the most celebrated public figure in the Nixon administration within Washington, appearing in both news columns and the society pages.[97] Maxine Cheshire, the *Washington Post*'s society columnist, regularly wrote about Kissinger's comings and goings and provided one of the most famous stories about him. Kissinger arrived late to a party at the Washington socialite Barbara Howar's house, clutching a manila envelope with "The White House" stamped on it. Kissinger "never put the packet down all evening, not to eat or to drink or to talk," and when someone questioned him about it, he jokingly remarked, "It's my advance copy of Playboy." When Sally Quinn, another *Washington Post* reporter, remarked, "Oh so you're really a swinger underneath it all," Kissinger answered, "Well you couldn't call me a swinger because of my job. Why don't you just assume I'm a secret swinger?"[98] The "secret swinger" appellation took off. Kissinger enjoyed the publicity even when reporters teased him about his new title. The columnist Rowland Evans called and asked, "Are you the famous White House swinger?" Kissinger exclaimed, "Jesus Christ! I don't have to do anything more." Evans went on to tell him that he would never live down the title, to which Kissinger replied, "I just hope everyone will remember when I am teaching at Arizona State."[99]

Kissinger's joke about ending up forgotten in a university distant from the Ivy League captured the self-deprecating humor that won over critics. Kissinger understood that in Washington society "the appearance of power is therefore almost as important as the reality of it; in fact, the appearance is frequently its essential reality."[100] Although Kissinger still provided briefings to the media only on an anonymous "background" basis, reporters' knowledge of his close relationship to the president contributed to this "appearance of power." Kissinger consciously courted the publicity, spending hours on the phone with journalists not only explaining the administration's policy but also making it clear his important role in shaping it. One assistant estimated that Kissinger spent "at least 35 percent of his time and energy on press matters," while another put the figure at 50 percent.[101] Kissinger could be carefully ambiguous with reporters, cultivating an image as a restraining influence and even a "dove" within Nixon's inner circle.[102] Joseph Kraft, a liberal journalist who remained friendly with Kissinger despite having his phone tapped, later wrote, "Kissinger tries to come on as the secret good guy of the Nixon foreign policy Establishment. Actually . . . he works to reinforce and legitimize the President's hardline instincts on most major international business."[103] A few weeks after the "secret swinger" story, Cheshire phoned Kissinger to ask if he had the Apollo 12 astronauts bring one of his woman friend's earrings to the moon. Kissinger practically yelled in reply, "For God's sake no," but as the conversation continued, Cheshire told him that she got calls all the time with readers reporting Kissinger sightings, adding, "People are more interested in you than President Nixon."[104] A few months later, when Kissinger represented the administration at the hundredth birthday party for Lenin at the Soviet embassy, Kissinger was described as "the center of attention," surrounded by foreign diplomats and enjoying his reputation as a "ladies' man." "Two years ago, before I got this reputation as a swinger, I was much more resistible," he said. "Now it's great to be irresistible."[105]

Kissinger worried at times that his new image might hurt him in the White House, where some of Nixon's close advisers resented Kissinger's prominence and mocked his playboy image. He asked Nixon's speechwriter William Safire, "Do you suppose people will think the President's national security adviser is gaga?" (Safire thought it amusing that Kissinger used the word "gaga.") He did not yet appear on television, as the administration felt that his foreign accent would not "play in Peoria."[106] Nixon encouraged Kissinger to take the initiative with the Georgetown set, seeing it as an opportunity to defuse his critics and sell his policies.[107] Kissinger's swinger image may have, as Safire put it, reassured Americans that "their national security was in the hands of a red-blooded American boy," as well as helped Kissinger within the hypermasculine culture of the Nixon White House.[108] What is clear is that by the end of 1969, Kissinger enjoyed Nixon's confidence and had Nixon's ear, even if his advice was not always followed or successful. As Safire observed, "Henry was changing, gaining confidence, feeling his oats, expanding his authority, stepping on toes. Richard Nixon observed all this, shook his head admiringly, and said, 'Henry plays the game hard, all right.'"[109]

KISSINGER AND THE "NEW REALISM" OF AMERICAN FOREIGN POLICY

In early January 1970, Richard Nixon warned his staff that the year ahead might well be the "worst year" of his presidency, especially as America faced its first economic recession in almost nine years. They would have to "ride it through," expecting that things would improve in 1971 and 1972.[110] Nixon hoped his foreign policy would be one of the bright spots in the year ahead, with a possible summit with the Soviets and progress on ending the war in Vietnam. Kissinger would continue to provide the coordination and control Nixon wanted to exercise from the White House. Yet the overall retrenchment the administration signaled would have consequences.

This became particularly clear in Western Europe, where the United States had long exercised its "empire by invitation."[111] As a European specialist himself, Kissinger explained at a press briefing toward the end of 1969 that "for about 20 years after the end of the war, American foreign policy was conducted with the maxims and the inspiration of the Marshall Plan, that is, the notion of a predominant United States, as the only stable country, the richest country, the country without whose leadership and physical contribution nothing was possible, and which had to make all the difference for defense and progress everywhere in the world." Now, at the beginning of the 1970s, Kissinger explained, "We have run out of that particular vision." The recovery of Europe and Japan, the independence of formerly colonial nations, the fracturing of the communist monolith—all these now required that the United States seek to "build international relations on a basis which may be less unilaterally American." Kissinger told the reporters that "we have no permanent enemies, and that we will judge other countries . . . on the basis of their actions and not on the basis of their domestic ideology." This "new realism" was also the theme of Kissinger's *First Annual Report to the Congress on United States Foreign Policy,* issued in February 1970 and designed to convey a "new approach to foreign policy to match a new era in international relations."[112]

As innovative and politically astute as this new approach was, it wasn't always comfortable for Kissinger, especially as he confronted the new assertiveness of his former homeland. In October 1969, Willy Brandt, the famous and charismatic mayor of West Berlin, took office as chancellor with a determination to initiate his *Ostpolitik,* a new opening toward Eastern Europe and the Soviet Union. Brandt's key adviser, Egon Bahr, told Kissinger that the Germans would practice their own form of informing, rather than consulting with, the United States.[113] Kissinger replied that America wanted to "deal with Germany as partner, not a client," but these words belied the real concerns about Brandt taking the leadership of Europe and unleashing a "détente euphoria" at a time when the United States found its own movement toward better relations with the Russians bogged down. Kissinger knew of Nixon's deep distaste for Brandt, a figure who reminded him of the Kennedys, and Kissinger's own approach to Germany would find him trying to keep a foot in both camps, explaining his former countrymen's policies to his unsympathetic boss.

Over the next several months, despite private misgivings, frequent predictions of failure, and constant appeals from Germany's political opposition to intervene, the United States found itself essentially led by its ally. Brandt's determination to move in directions that earlier U.S. administrations had suggested—including the recognition of the Oder-Neisse border with Poland established after World War II, exchanges with East Germany, and talks with Moscow—accelerated the movement toward European détente far more quickly than Kissinger and Nixon wanted. The drive toward détente in Europe, a movement that the French president Charles de Gaulle had pushed earlier in the 1960s, had seemed to stall after the Soviet invasion of Czechoslovakia in August 1968. Brandt gave it new life, but Kissinger, given his personal—and conflicted—history with Germany, feared that Brandt's efforts might rekindle a "debate about Germany's basic position" within the West, "not only inflaming German domestic affairs but generating suspicions among Germany's western associates as to its reliability as a partner." As he concluded in one memo to Nixon, "[Brandt's] problem is to control a process which, if it results in failure could jeopardize their political lives and if it succeeds could create a momentum that may shake Germany's domestic stability and unhinge its international position."[114] Kissinger preferred the stability of a divided Europe to a renewed push for German reunification, especially if that might lead to weakening Germany's ties to the West. The United States, however, could do little to control Brandt, a reflection of the "new era in international relations" that Kissinger himself had proclaimed.

Nixon disliked "the assumption that is gaining disturbing currency abroad and in the United States—that this Administration is on an irreversible course of not only getting out of Vietnam but of reducing our commitments around the world." Kissinger, however, understood the reality of America's relative decline.[115] He believed that if the United States could negotiate an end to the Vietnam War, it could regain a more effective, if not dominant, role in international relations, and he wanted to play the central role in these negotiations. When North Vietnam agreed to another secret meeting in Paris in February 1970, this time sending Lê Đức Thọ, a key member of the politburo, Kissinger believed that the North was now ready to deal. Both Nixon and Kissinger loved the intrigue and secrecy involved in the meeting, though, as Haldeman sarcastically noted, "In typical K[issinger] fashion, with all the secrecy, he then leaves by chopper from the Ellipse."[116]

Over the next two months Kissinger engaged in three secret meetings with the North Vietnamese. He told Haldeman after the second meeting, "If we can hold here in the United States for two to four months . . . we'll have it."[117] Kissinger sought to convince the North Vietnamese that a negotiated agreement with the United States was in their interest.[118] Kissinger referred to himself as "a professor on leave" who heard that the North Vietnamese thought he was trying to trick them. "But we are not," Kissinger said, "trying to do so—not because we are particularly benevolent but because it would not be in our interest." Kissinger observed that after a settlement, Hanoi "would be closer to South Vietnam than we . . . [and that] we want a settlement which is in their interest," a geography lesson with a clear implication. Kissinger sought to dispel Hanoi's view of the peace movement's strength, claiming that President Nixon had strong support from Americans. He alluded to the Sino-Soviet conflict by saying, "The international situation has complications which may make Vietnam no longer the undivided concern of other countries and may mean that Vietnam will not enjoy the undivided support of countries which now support it." He concluded his remarks by joking that "Harvard professors always speak for 55 minutes." The transcript recorded "North Vietnamese smiles" as the reaction, but not the reason why.[119]

Kissinger used charm, self-deprecating humor, and even a reference to his growing celebrity status, hoping to establish a personal connection with the determined revolutionaries of the Vietnamese side. In trying to set a date for their next session, he told the North Vietnamese that he would prefer a

Sunday, joking, "If I leave on Sunday, everyone will think I have a girl."[120] Kissinger told Nixon after the first encounter that he thought the atmosphere of the meeting was "remarkably frank and free of trivia" and that "it was certainly the most important [meeting] since the beginning of your administration and even since the beginning of the talks in 1968."[121] However, the Communist insistence that the United States act to replace the "military agents, people like Thiệu, Ky, Khiem," before an agreement could be reached presented the most difficult problem for Kissinger. The North Vietnamese were interested in the outcome, not the process Kissinger suggested. As their negotiator Lê Đức Thọ put it, "Our proposals are realistic, they reflect reality, they conform to the aspirations of the South Vietnamese people. Only such methods will reflect correctly the political relationship in South Vietnam and register it in a political process."[122] The rigidity in the North Vietnamese position leads to the conclusion that Kissinger's optimism about a negotiated settlement came only because he was the one doing the negotiating.[123]

Kissinger's devotion to a negotiated settlement and his relationship with Nixon were tested when Nixon decided to send American forces into Cambodia in April 1970. During the previous month, General Lon Nol, the pro-American minister of defense, surprised the Nixon administration when he led a successful coup against Prince Norodom Sihanouk.[124] Relations between the United States and Cambodia improved despite the secret bombing. When full diplomatic relations were restored, Sihanouk even made what Kissinger called "an unabashed pitch for aid" and endorsed the Nixon Doctrine.[125] When news of the coup reached Washington, Nixon immediately told Kissinger to ask the CIA "to develop and implement a plan for maximum assistance to pro U.S. elements in Cambodia," and instructed him to handle this like "our air strikes"—namely in secret from the bureaucracy.[126] After objections from Rogers and Laird that such a quick decision to aid Lon Nol would confirm suspicions that the United States was behind the coup, Nixon decided to wait.[127] But covert assistance soon began, as it became clear that the new Cambodian government was taking a strong anti–North Vietnamese stance. Nixon was especially pleased when the new government cut off

Hanoi's access to the port of Sihanoukville, which was supplying its forces in the South.

North Vietnamese attacks in Cambodia soon increased, and there were serious doubts about whether the Lon Nol government would survive. Prince Sihanouk allied himself with the communist Khmer Rouge, and North Vietnam announced its support for his return to power. Nixon and Kissinger now considered an assault on North Vietnamese sanctuaries in Cambodia. As with Operation Duck Hook, however, both Laird and Rogers weighed in against the idea of sending any U.S. forces into Cambodia, concerned primarily with the political consequences at home. Laird argued that the South Vietnamese forces, the Army of the Republic of Vietnam (ARVN), could do the job alone and would stir up little of the domestic unrest that an American operation would. Kissinger remained skeptical of the ARVN's capacity to conduct such a large operation. He recognized that Nixon wanted to help Lon Nol, and in his capacity as the chair of the Washington Special Action Group (WSAG), he directed operations to funnel military assistance to the Cambodians.[128] (WSAG, the subcommittee of the National Security Council that handled crisis management, had been formed in the wake of the North Korean downing of the American intelligence plane in April 1969.)[129] He also hoped that a military operation that changed the facts on the ground might push Hanoi to negotiate seriously.[130]

Kissinger recognized that Nixon was leaning toward action. During a quick trip to the Pacific to greet the astronauts returning home from the near-disastrous Apollo 13 mission, Nixon was briefed by the Pacific commander, John McCain (the father of the future senator). McCain so impressed Nixon on the "need for speed in view of the precarious situation in Cambodia" that Nixon asked him to return to the United States and brief Kissinger. After this briefing, Nixon told Kissinger he had decided to order an incursion but was unsure about whether to use American troops. Still, he did not want South Vietnam "to get in there and then get the hell kicked out."[131] In his memoirs, Kissinger argued that Nixon might have chosen the more limited option of only South Vietnamese–led attacks if not for Vice President Agnew's outspoken complaint at the National Security Council meeting on April 22 that "either the sanctuaries were a danger or they were not," and that if they were, he favored an American role in the attack. Nixon hated "being shown up in a group as being less tough than his advisers," Kissinger wrote.[132] Kissinger's reference to Agnew was likely a way to lessen his own role in encouraging Nixon to act. He was pessimistic about Vietnam at this point, and he told his aide David Young that Vietnamization was "not working" and that the only thing keeping the North Vietnamese at bay was Nixon's unpredictability—the "madman" image.[133] Haldeman suspected that Kissinger wanted Nixon to act if only to assert Nixon's presidential authority against the naysayers and his rivals, Laird and Rogers, in the cabinet.[134] Kissinger agreed with Nixon when the president told Haldeman we "can get [Vietnam] wound up this year if we keep enough pressure on, and don't crumble at home."[135]

Even as these secret deliberations about Cambodia were going on, Nixon delivered a major TV address on April 20, 1970, announcing that he would withdraw 150,000 troops from Vietnam over the next year. This was the climax of a sharp internal debate about how to handle the announcement of troop withdrawals. Despite his misgivings about the policy, Kissinger actually preferred the larger number to more frequently announced smaller withdrawals. His reason was that it would allow the military the flexibility to keep more combat troops in Vietnam until near the end of the deadline and prevent the American negotiating position from deteriorating further. The problem was that the president's speech, with its dramatically higher number than expected, served to encourage the public to view the war as winding down. Nixon celebrated the withdrawal announcement as proof of the success of his Vietnamization program and praised Americans for their "steadiness and stamina," which would achieve the goal of a "just peace" in Vietnam. Even though the speech also contained warnings about communist advances in Laos and Cambodia, the major thrust of Nixon's message was that he was indeed ending the Vietnam War through troop withdrawals. Nixon's speech contributed to the psychological atmosphere within the country that intensified the surprise and outrage at the decision to go into Cambodia.[136]

Kissinger might have warned Nixon of the danger of this approach, but he was consumed with the bureaucratic conflict with Rogers and Laird, and with strengthening his own personal position with the president. He continued to argue with Rogers, challenging him with the question, "Do you think there is a prayer for Vietnamization if Cambodia is taken over?"[137] Kissinger helped Nixon exclude Laird and Rogers from some of the key deliberations and lined up military support for the action by going directly to the acting chairman of the Joint Chiefs of Staff, William Westmoreland. He explained that the president "can understand the political people thinking of reasons why we shouldn't, but the military usually stands with the Commander-in-Chief and he wants to do something." Kissinger welcomed Westmoreland's offer of support, but ended the conversation with a revealing joke: "I hope you need a political analyst in the army. I'll never be able to go back to Harvard." His humor may have been a nervous response as well to the dissent he faced from his own NSC staff. Roger Morris, Winston Lord, and Anthony Lake, three of his closest aides, warned their boss, among other things, "that U.S. troops in Cambodia would have a strong and damaging political effect in the U.S., which would both hurt the President's Vietnam policies and divide the country further."[138] (Morris, Lake, and William Watts, another NSC official, would all resign because of the Cambodia decision.)

On April 30, 1970, Nixon announced his decision to send American forces into Cambodia. Working with his most bellicose speechwriter, Pat Buchanan, Nixon sought to repeat the success of his November 3 "Silent Majority" speech, rallying his supporters "with the bark on—patriotic, angry, stick-with-me-or-else, alternately pious and strident."[139] When he read the speech to Haldeman and Kissinger, both applauded and thought, "It will work" and that it was a "very strong and excellent wrap-up."[140] Nixon started by dramatically announcing an increase in North Vietnam's "military aggression" in Cambodia that endangered "the lives of Americans that are in Vietnam now." He then lied—or as Kissinger euphemistically described it, included "a sentence that was as irrelevant to his central thesis as it was untrue"—saying that the United States had "scrupulously" respected the neutrality of the Cambodian people, ignoring both covert actions and the secret B-52 bombing. In describing the actions America would now take,

Nixon emphasized that the American attack was directed at the "head-quarters for the entire communist military operation in South Vietnam," known as COSVN, creating the image of American GIs storming a communist Pentagon.[141] Nixon did make a more reasonable case for how the Cambodian incursion could speed Vietnamization and end American involvement in the war. He reminded Americans: "We have stopped the bombing of North Vietnam. We have cut air operations by over 20 percent. We have announced withdrawal of over 250,000 of our men. We have offered to withdraw all of our men if they will withdraw theirs." Then the president decided to employ Churchillian rhetoric and declared, "If when the chips are down, the world's most powerful nation, the United States of America, acts like a pitiful, help-less giant, the forces of totalitarianism and anarchy will threaten free nations and institutions throughout the world." It was a startling contrast to his words of only ten days earlier, whipsawing the country's mood and challenging his opponents. As Safire sympathetically noted, "Nixon had done what only Nixon could do—made a courageous decision and wrapped it in a pious and divisive speech."[142]

Nixon's overheated rhetoric may have come from his frustration with not taking action over the EC-121 that was shot down and backing away from Operation Duck Hook. Encouraged by Kissinger, he believed that the Communists saw him as weak and indecisive and that he needed to change that perception.[143] The invasion was not the irrational action of an out-of-control president; it made sense as a limited military strike, defensive in orientation, and designed to protect American soldiers in South Vietnam as they withdrew. Nixon, however, decided to present it to the American people in apocalyptic terms, complete with exaggerations about its possible impact as well as outright deception of what had been American policy. This was hardly unprecedented—almost every American president during the Cold War had behaved in a similar way about some foreign policy issues, beginning with Truman's decision in 1947 to "scare the hell out of the American people" in selling the Truman Doctrine. This time, however, the mood of the country was very different.

Initial public response to the Cambodian invasion was supportive but not as overwhelming as after the November 3 speech. More significant was the outcry from Capitol Hill, other parts of the government, and the campuses, which immediately placed the administration on the defensive. Nixon agreed to meet with the Senate Foreign Relations Committee on his terms, which meant including the more supportive House members.[144] Nixon's offhand comment about "bums burning up the books and blowing up the campuses," meant as a reference to a Stanford incident when a researcher's work was completely destroyed, came to be seen as Nixon's characterization of all campus demonstrators. The killing of four students at Kent State University on May 4 brought what Kissinger called a "shock wave" to the nation, as thousands of campus strikes erupted at even conservative colleges and universities. Washington was besieged with thousands of demonstrators coming to protest the war and the action in Cambodia. The protests so affected Nixon that after an evening press conference on May 8, he wandered around the Lincoln Memorial in the early-morning hours trying to talk with students. (Egil Krogh, an aide to John Ehrlichman, thought Nixon was drunk and only vaguely aware of what he was doing.)[145] In New York, the student demonstrators in the financial district were set upon by construction workers, who beat the protesters with clubs. With the polarization and bitterness so intense, Kissinger met frequently with both faculty and student groups to explain the policy. ABC News reported on Kissinger's meeting with fifteen Stanford students who accused him of presenting the "illusion of dialogue."[146] He even had to move into the basement of the White House to get any sleep, as demonstrators ringed his apartment and loudly protested. The protests took a toll on him. Nixon himself later noted that Kissinger came to see him and, staring disconsolately out the window, said, "I still think you made the right decision as far as foreign policy considerations were involved. But in view of what has happened I fear I may have failed to advise you adequately of the domestic dangers."[147] Kissinger's anguish was so visible on his face and in his body language that Nixon regarded it as a sign of weakness, telling Kissinger, in an unusual biblical reference, to "remember Lot's wife, and never look back."[148]

Kissinger even faced off with old colleagues from Harvard, including many, like Richard Neustadt, Francis Bator, and Adam Yarmolinsky, who had served in government during the Kennedy-Johnson years. Kissinger was willing to go off-the-record to explain policy, but his "close colleagues and friends" would not accept the offer. They were determined to take a public stance against administration policy. The most telling and insightful comment came from the historian Ernest May, who told Kissinger, "You're tearing the country apart domestically," and that this "would have long-term consequences for foreign policy as tomorrow's foreign policy is based on today's domestic situation." The economist Thomas Schelling told Kissinger, "There are two possibilities: Either one, the president didn't understand when he went into Cambodia that he was invading another country; or two, he did understand. We just don't know which is scarier." Kissinger "sat in pained silence, and just listened," Schelling later remembered. Francis Bator, who had the NSC portfolio for Europe under President Johnson, remarked that Kissinger "behaved with great grace and dignity and courage under intense emotional pressure from his peer group."[149]

Kissinger, however, later denounced the "lack of compassion, the overweening righteousness," and the hyperbole that characterized many of the professors' comments. He was likely the source for those stories that appeared suggesting that the Harvard group threatened he would not be welcome to return after his government service. For his part, Kissinger remarked that the "meeting completed my transition from the academic world to the world of affairs."[150] It also strengthened his standing with Richard Nixon, who disliked his anguish but appreciated his loyalty. A few weeks after the Cambodian decision, on a short break in Key Biscayne, Florida, Nixon called Kissinger, Haldeman, and Ehrlichman to his cabin on Air Force One and told them that they deserved an award like the Purple Heart because they had taken the brunt of the criticism over the last few weeks. He then presented them with the "Blue Heart," a blue cloth heart made for those who were "true blue," hand-sewn by a girlfriend of Nixon's close friend Bebe Rebozo.[151] A month later, Kissinger's office was moved from the White House basement to far more spacious and luxurious quarters in the West Wing, just a few yards from the Oval Office. This led to a new nickname, with its allusion to a famous play: the "Playboy of the Western Wing."[152]

Nixon announced the departure of American troops from Cambodia on June 30, 1970, deliberately avoiding any mention of the communist military headquarters COSVN and emphasizing instead the enormous amounts of supplies seized, especially weapons and foodstuffs, and the disruption to enemy attempts to undermine Cambodia's government.[153] Getting out by June 30 itself had been, as Kissinger noted, a "panicky decision" and a "concrete result of public pressures."[154] In his speech, Nixon returned to the more optimistic portrayal of the military situation he had been giving before Cambodia and reaffirmed his intention to withdraw 150,000 American soldiers from Vietnam and not to send any more American forces into Cambodia. In part he was responding to the Senate, which had just passed the Cooper-Church Amendment restricting such American ground efforts in Cambodia.

As the uproar over Cambodia began to fade, the crisis in the Middle East intensified. Nixon and Kissinger had not given the Middle East much attention during 1969. Kissinger did compare the situation to the Balkans before 1914, a place where the great powers could be drawn into war by the actions of their small but militant allies.[155] Israel fit the bill, as it now possessed nuclear weapons. Kissinger warned Nixon, "The Israelis, who are one of the few peoples whose survival is genuinely threatened, are probably more likely than any other country to actually use their nuclear weapons."[156] In his first talks with the Israeli prime minister Golda Meir in September 1969, Nixon urged that the Israelis not introduce or test nuclear weapons in the region, maintaining a policy of "nuclear ambiguity."[157] Nixon gave official responsibility for the Middle East to Rogers, in part because he believed Kissinger's Jewish background made it impossible for him to be impartial about Israel. However, he also encouraged Kissinger to discuss Middle Eastern questions with the Soviet ambassador, Dobrynin. Kissinger also developed his own back-channel arrangement with the Israeli ambassador, Yitzhak Rabin, providing him with information outside State Department channels.[158] This guaranteed conflict. In December 1969, Rogers unveiled his initiative, the Rogers Plan, a comprehensive framework to bring peace to the region through an Israeli withdrawal from occupied territories in return for an end to hostilities and diplomatic recognition.[159] Nixon, who regarded himself as the president most independent of the "Jewish lobby," was determined to open up channels of communication to the Arab world to draw it away from the Soviet embrace. When American Jewish protesters roughed up the French president, Georges Pompidou, and his wife during a visit to Chicago in February 1970, Nixon was outraged and delayed the sales of advanced Phantom jets to the Jewish state. At the same time, Nixon had Kissinger warn the Soviets that their sending of "combat personnel in the Middle East" would be of the "gravest concern."[160] The warning came far too late. The Soviets had already decided to send thousands of their soldiers and pilots, along with surface-to-air missiles (SAMs), to help defend Egypt from deep-penetration air raids launched by Israel.[161] Dobrynin assured the Kremlin that Americans, worried about "a new Vietnam" in the Middle East, would be reluctant to act forcefully against such a Soviet move.[162]

During spring 1970, while America was consumed with the Cambodia debate, the military situation in the Middle East grew more threatening. Soviet fighters challenged the Israeli Air Force, and Soviet SAM sites became operational in defense of Egypt. In April, an Israeli Air Force jet mistakenly bombed an Egyptian schoolhouse, killing forty-seven children and producing an international outcry. At the end of June, Egyptian and Soviet fighters attacked Israeli rear areas in the Sinai Peninsula. The fear that these attacks could trigger a superpower confrontation led Secretary of State Rogers to intensify his efforts. He met privately with Dobrynin and received assurances that the Egyptians were prepared to make important concessions for a ceasefire, including ending their state of war with Israel and controlling the Palestinian fedayeen who were attacking from bases in Egypt. Nixon was supportive of the department's efforts, hoping that these might lead to a summit meeting in Moscow before the midterm elections. Nixon arranged his own private appointment with Dobrynin, bringing Kissinger along. Nixon explained to Dobrynin that he faced a domestic political problem: "I don't want to anger the Jews, who hold important positions in the press, radio, and television, from which they can exert a powerful influence on other groups of American voters." (What Kissinger must have thought of Nixon's statement is not in Dobrynin's record of the conversation.) Nixon, however, added that he did not want to be accused of "selling out" Israel. He concluded by telling Dobrynin that although it would be very difficult for the two countries, as well as for the Arabs and Israelis, he was prepared to seek a "compromise settlement."[163]

Nixon still wanted to control White House dealings with the Russians, and that meant Kissinger should take the lead. He told Dobrynin, "You should regard everything Kissinger says as coming personally from me," an endorsement that in Dobrynin's experience was unprecedented. Dobrynin recorded that Kissinger "positively glowed with pleasure and from the acknowledgment of his importance."[164] Kissinger, however, had long had serious reservations about the State Department's efforts in the Middle East, telling Haldeman in March, "I have not believed in what we are doing on the Middle East for ten months," and that it would "blow up."[165] Kissinger believed Rogers's efforts for a cease-fire gave the Soviets a "blank check" for their new military presence in Egypt, a presence that would "enhance [Soviet] geopolitical influence."[166] In a background briefing at the end of June, Kissinger told reporters that the United States was "trying to expel the Soviet military presence" from the Middle East, a formulation that provoked anger at the State Department.[167] When the *New York Times* columnist Max Frankel called to ask Kissinger if he had been "expelled" from the California White House, an exasperated Kissinger replied, "Sometimes I give up. What do you want us to say—we want a Soviet presence in the Middle East?"[168] Kissinger feared correctly that his own position with the president had slipped, and he angrily complained about Rogers: "The SOB is trying to prove that everything the White House has done since January 20, 1969, has been wrong and he is trying to save the country."[169] Kissinger's resentment of Rogers led him to identify with the Israelis even more. He told William Safire that his struggle with Rogers was "like the Arabs and the Israelis. I'll win all the battles, and he'll win the war. He only has to beat me once."[170]

Kissinger was correct to recognize that he was vulnerable on the Middle East. Nixon used a news conference to soften Kissinger's use of the word "expel" and explained his own preference for a "peaceful" Soviet withdrawal from the Middle East. He told Haldeman that Kissinger was "overly concerned about anything that affects Israel" and that Kissinger's battles with Rogers over the issue deeply disturbed him.[171] When Egypt accepted Rogers's terms of cease-fire on July 22, Kissinger had a hard time concealing his disappointment. With Israel's acceptance on August 7, 1970, came, in Kissinger's grudging words, the "first uncontroverted achievement of the Nixon Administration in foreign policy."[172] *The Washington Post* reported, "Secretary of State William Rogers is in an ebullient mood" over the success of his Middle Eastern initiative and might even renege on his earlier statement that he would serve only one term.[173] Kissinger was skeptical about the cease-fire, quickly sharing the Israeli belief that the Soviets and Egyptians were violating it. He leaked stories to his media friends, especially Joseph Alsop, depicting Rogers as naive in trusting the Russians to abide by the agreement.[174] Nixon suspected that Kissinger was simply "jealous" that he had not achieved this foreign policy success, and that he was even trying to make it fail. (He once told his speechwriter Safire that he regretted the struggle between Kissinger and Rogers: "Henry thinks Bill isn't very deep, and Bill thinks Henry is power crazy." When Safire added that each thought the other an egomaniac, Nixon concluded, "They're both right.")[175] Nixon worried that Kissinger had "reached the end of his usefulness." Haldeman disagreed, telling Nixon that Kissinger's behavior was "the price we pay for his enormous assets."[176] Even when the CIA confirmed Egyptian and Soviet violations of the cease-fire, Nixon still ordered Haldeman to "get K[issinger] off the Middle East."[177] In late summer 1970, Kissinger was in trouble with his boss, and Nixon was seriously considering cutting his losses with the Harvard professor.

KISSINGER'S AUTUMN OF CRISES: JORDAN, CUBA, AND CHILE

In his memoirs, Henry Kissinger wrote ominously about the three-week period in September 1970 when "three major crises descended upon the administration in corners of the world thousands of miles apart." He acknowledged that the "causes of these events were fundamentally different," but then he insisted, "They all represented—or seemed to us to represent—different facets of a global Communist challenge." The inclusion of the phrase "seemed to us" may well have been Kissinger's awareness that future writers might disaggregate the three crises and criticize the administration for thinking they were all related to the Soviet Union. Few contemporaries saw this short time period as a particularly frightening or crisis-filled one. Each crisis, however, reflected both Kissinger's strengths and weaknesses as a presidential adviser, illuminating his wisdom and his recklessness. More important, these crises changed the dynamic of his rivalry with Secretary of State Rogers, underlining Kissinger's importance to Nixon and establishing his position as the second most powerful man in the White House.

The most dramatic crisis came in the Middle East, where the radical Popular Front for the Liberation of Palestine (PFLP) hijacked three airliners to Jordan and held the passengers hostage in the desert, surrounded by television cameras and the international media. The hostages were eventually taken off the planes, which were then destroyed in spectacular explosions, a frightening visual symbol of the potential dangers of the Middle East.[178] These events were part of the larger struggle for power within Jordan, where the moderate King Hussein faced challenges from both the PFLP and the Palestine Liberation Organization (PLO) under Yasser Arafat. Nixon and Kissinger almost immediately saw the conflict as encouraged by a Soviet Union willing to help its radical allies get rid of the pro-Western Hussein. Kissinger told Nixon, "It looks like the Soviets are pushing the Syrians and the Syrians are pushing the Palestinians. The Palestinians don't need much pushing."[179]

Nixon and Kissinger recognized that the fall of Hussein itself would be a major blow to Western interests and could lead to another war between Israel and the Arab states. Kissinger took control of the WSAG to coordinate the crisis response.[180] Following the initial deliberations, Nixon, acting in accord with Kissinger's advice, ordered the Sixth Fleet to move to the eastern Mediterranean and placed various U.S. forces, including the Eighty-Second Airborne Division, on alert. He gave an "off-the-record" interview that threatened U.S. intervention if Syria or Iraq tried to depose Hussein.[181] When Hussein finally decided to act against the Palestinians, American concern focused on the possibility of either Syrian or Iraqi intervention against the king. If those two nations moved to intervene, Nixon told Kissinger, "We should use American air and knock the bejesus out of them."[182] Kissinger liked the opportunity to have Nixon's support for a forceful response, but he showed deliberation and caution in handling the crisis. In the midst of the confusing situation, with frequently contradictory intelligence reports flowing in to Washington, Kissinger kept the WSAG in session, deliberating about all the possible scenarios. He stayed in close touch with the Israelis, especially Ambassador Yitzhak Rabin, and steered American policymakers toward the position that Israeli intervention might ultimately be necessary to save Hussein, with American force acting as a deterrent to any Soviet intervention.[183]

Kissinger saw Israeli power in the region as a strategic asset in the Cold War. When Syrian tanks rumbled into Jordan, Kissinger favored a tough message to the Soviets, direct action by the Israelis, and a complete Syrian withdrawal, contrasting his view with that of Rogers, who favored a "slow and measured escalation" and was willing to wait to see whether the Syrians pushed farther than northern Jordan. Rogers was worried more about the Soviet response and the effect that any ground operations by the Israelis would have on the chances for peace. Rogers wanted to keep some separation between the United States and Israel, and believed that Kissinger was pushing the president toward a rash decision.[184] Kissinger convinced Nixon to support an Israeli strike but was relieved when the Soviets indicated they would act to restrain Syria.[185] During a twenty-four-hour period starting late on the evening of September 20, the WSAG met repeatedly, evaluating the reports of the Syrian invasion and Jordanian counterattack. They weighed King Hussein's request for air strikes against the Syrians, waiting to see how the situation developed.

In reality, the Syrian action was part of an internal power struggle within Damascus, and the Syrian air force leader, General Hafez al-Assad, refused to deploy air cover to defend the tank invasion of his rivals for power. Assad soon emerged triumphant in the struggle.[186] The Jordanian air force destroyed almost a hundred Syrian tanks, and the Syrians withdrew. King Hussein had triumphed, and the Palestinians were defeated—and the U.S. and Israeli threats may have helped. Nixon told Haldeman that the Israeli ambassador, Yitzhak Rabin, called him and told him that things worked out well for these reasons: "First, the tough U.S. position; second, the Israeli threat; third, Russian pressure on Syria and Iraq as a result of the U.S. position; fourth, superb fighting by Jordanian troops."[187] As Kissinger told Nixon later that day, "I think that we are over the hump of this one."[188]

While a tough-but-cautious U.S. position helped yield results in Jordan, Nixon still wanted to improve relations with the Soviets, and he told Kissinger, "We can't gloat." Nixon and Kissinger followed this approach concerning the possibility that the Soviets were building a submarine base in Cuba.[189] Unlike the famous Cuban Missile Crisis of October 1962, the "Cienfuegos crisis" is one of the least-known crises in recent history, with critics convinced it was a "false crisis" and "fantasy."[190] The story begins with Kissinger bursting into Haldeman's office, slamming down photographs on his desk, and telling Nixon's chief of staff, "It's a Cuban seaport, Haldeman, and these pictures show the Cubans are building soccer fields . . . These soccer fields could mean war, Bob." When Haldeman asked why, Kissinger replied, "Cubans play *baseball*. Russians play *soccer*."[191] Kissinger's dramatic moment might be excused, since it occurred in the midst of the Jordanian crisis. But Kissinger's way of illustrating his point also leaves him open to criticism and even ridicule, as Cubans played soccer as well as baseball.

Although Kissinger used the crisis in his struggle with Rogers, his personal motive does not exclude the existence of a genuine national security issue. The declassified diplomatic exchanges between Kissinger and the Soviet ambassador Dobrynin, especially the Russian documents themselves, lend weight to the American accusation. The "understanding" that resolved the Cuban Missile Crisis—the Soviets removed their missiles in return for a promise that the United States would not invade Cuba—remained vague, and the idea that the Soviets might test this understanding by basing submarines armed with nuclear weapons in Cuba was not implausible. Dobrynin was not shocked or outraged by Kissinger's claim that the Soviets were challenging the "understanding" that resolved the Cuban Missile Crisis.[192] American reconnaissance flights determined that the Soviets were building something on

Cienfuegos Bay, and this intelligence indicated SAM sites, communication towers, barracks, and other facilities that could be used to service submarines. In the midst of the Soviet challenge in the Middle East, Kissinger was hardly being irrational in wondering whether this constituted "a process of testing under way in different parts of the world."[193]

Nixon initially sided with Secretary of State Rogers, who proposed having a "quiet talk" with the Soviet foreign minister Andrei Gromyko when he was in New York in October for the annual meeting of the United Nations General Assembly. Kissinger went to Haldeman and told him the issue could not wait, that Rogers's "softness will mislead them—as [Secretary of State Dean] Rusk did in '62." Kissinger was convinced that the Soviets would achieve a "fait accompli" of a submarine base in Cuba and this would be a "real kick in teeth to RN." Knowing Cuba's political sensitivity, in both domestic politics and foreign policy, Kissinger crafted a message clearly designed to manipulate Nixon, and it worked. Nixon decided to have Kissinger handle the matter in his confidential channel with Dobrynin. Before Kissinger could meet with Dobrynin, however, the Defense Department inadvertently released details of the Soviet naval activity in Cuba, and Kissinger held a press backgrounder to both warn the Soviets and tamp down any sense of crisis. Kissinger used language that echoed Kennedy's warning in 1962 when he said, "The Soviet Union can be under no doubt that we would view the establishment of a strategic base in the Caribbean with the utmost seriousness." But Kissinger coupled the warning with an assurance to the press: "We are in excellent communication. Nothing very rapid or dramatic is likely to occur, and we are going to be in very close touch with the situation."[194]

When Kissinger did finally meet with Dobrynin, he described the ambassador's face as "ashen." Dobrynin may have believed that he was again being blindsided by his government's policies, as had happened in 1962 when Khrushchev had not informed him of the Soviet missiles. Kissinger outlined what he described as a Soviet campaign of misinformation about its recent activities in Cuba. He told the ambassador that the U.S. government knew there was a submarine base, but that its public announcement was designed to give the Soviets "an opportunity to withdraw without a public confrontation." As Kissinger told Dobrynin, "If the ships—especially the tender[195]—left Cienfuegos we would consider the whole matter a training exercise." Kissinger also made it clear that Nixon deliberately used the secret channel with Dobrynin as a way to avoid anything like the 1962 public confrontation. He insisted that the United States and the Soviets were at "a turning point in their relationship" and that it was up to the Soviets whether they "wanted to go the route of conciliation or the route of confrontation. The United States is prepared for either." When Dobrynin suggested that the United States was about to begin "a big press campaign on this Cuban business," Kissinger assured him that it would not, but that it was not going to allow the Soviets to have submarine-based missiles in Cuba.[196]

The Nixon administration remained low-key in its approach to the crisis. At their next meeting, the Soviet ambassador told Kissinger that the Soviet government reaffirmed the 1962 understanding but had some "clarifying questions" of what constituted a base. The Americans gave them a set of stipulations that defined a "base" in terms of support for ships "carrying offensive weapons; i.e., submarines or surface ships armed with nuclear capable, surface to surface missiles."[197] Although there were occasional protests, the Soviets held to their side of the agreement. Nixon and Kissinger were extremely pleased with their success, and Kissinger told Nixon that it might not hurt matters to "tell a few of those Senators who we gave a briefing the bare essence of the thing."[198] Kissinger told one reporter that "this was done with minimum humiliation for the Soviets." When the reporter challenged Kissinger that both the resolution of the Middle East crisis and the Cuba issue were based on understandings between Washington and Moscow, Kissinger responded sharply, "That's not true. I wish it were. There is nothing we would rather have than an understanding with the Russians. Anyone who's been through the last twenty-five years realizes there are no victories in confrontation."[199]

Kissinger believed that the outcome of his efforts on both the Middle East and Cuba had demonstrated his value to Nixon, as well as highlighted the importance of his secret channel to Dobrynin.[200] He was certain that the strength, caution, and moderation the administration demonstrated would set a pattern for relations with the Soviet leaders that facilitated the "understanding" Kissinger wanted. However, the third crisis that was part of Kissinger's autumn casts a different shadow over the wisdom of his diplomatic efforts. On September 4, 1970, Salvador Allende, a Marxist Socialist running in coalition with the Communist Party of Chile, came in first, winning 36.6 percent of the vote in the country's presidential race. Allende had close ties to Fidel Castro and the Soviet Union, and the Communist world celebrated his victory as a historic defeat for American imperialism.[201] The American ambassador in Chile, Edward Korry, wrote to Washington, "Chile voted calmly to have a Marxist-Leninist state, the first nation in the world to make this choice freely and knowingly."[202] That this defeat occurred in the area of the world so often considered the United States' "backyard" helped give rise to exaggerated fears in Washington.[203]

Allende's victory caught the Nixon administration by surprise. In the past, American covert efforts to influence Chilean elections had helped moderate Chilean figures like Eduardo Frei win their elections against leftist candidates. In the 1970 election, however, the U.S. effort had been negative and anti-Allende, and it had failed. Nixon was furious, equally mad about the prospect of another communist state in the western hemisphere and his bureaucracy's failure to stop it. He told Kissinger, "I want a personal note to State that I want to see all cables to Chile."[204] When Kissinger told him that the State Department preferred an approach that would allow Allende to come to power and see what could be done then in dealing with him, Nixon reacted strongly: "Like against Castro? Like in Czech.[oslovakia]? The same people said the same thing. Don't let them do that." On September 15, 1970, Nixon called in Kissinger; the attorney general, John Mitchell; and the CIA director, Richard Helms, and told the group that he wanted to "save Chile" from Allende even if there was only a one-in-ten chance of success. Nixon threw out the idea of spending some $10 million to support a military coup and talked of making the Chilean economy "scream." Kissinger claimed that he recognized some of the "Nixonian posturing" at the heart of this outburst, and consequently did not set aside the $10 million.[205] He did recognize how important "doing something" on Chile was to Nixon, and he did not want to disappoint him. The CIA's Helms, on the other hand, tried to dissuade Nixon, arguing that Allende would most probably be confirmed by the Chilean Congress and that there was only a slim possibility of a coup. But Helms recounted Nixon's determination, remarking, "Standing mid-track and shouting at an oncoming locomotive might have been more effective."[206]

Kissinger's role in Chile remains one of the most controversial questions surrounding his career.[207] Before becoming national security adviser, Kissinger had never shown much interest in Latin America. At a meeting with the Chilean foreign minister in 1969, Kissinger was quoted as saying, "Nothing important can come from the South," as well as "What happens in the South has no importance." When the minister responded that Kissinger knew nothing of Latin America, Kissinger replied, "You're right. And I don't care."[208] Before September 1970, Kissinger ignored Chile and denigrated its significance. He joked, "Chile was a dagger aimed at the heart of Antarctica." He also told his colleagues, with a mix of arrogance, dark humor, and cynicism, "I don't see why we have to let a country go Marxist just because its people are irresponsible."[209]

Yet Kissinger also understood Nixon's passions, and he played to them. With recent history in his thinking, Nixon did not want "a Cuba in his administration."[210] Kissinger quickly recognized that Chile afforded him another opportunity to show Nixon how important Kissinger's control over foreign policy was to Nixon. Ambassador Korry, reflecting the State Department consensus, complained about the "grievous defeat" suffered by the United States, but he believed that an American effort to promote a coup was "to court a failure as massive and damaging to American interests as the Bay of Pigs."[211] With the State Department reluctant to intervene, and the president still insistent, Kissinger stepped into the role with determination, as much to promote his relationship with Nixon as out of any deep-seated concern with the dangers posed by Chile. When Secretary of State Rogers warned him of undertaking anything in Chile that might "backfire" on the United States, Kissinger told him, "The President's view is to do the maximum possible to prevent an Allende takeover, but through Chilean sources and with a low posture."[212]

Kissinger's staff also warned him of the dangers of an American attempt to block Allende. Viron Vaky, a deputy to Kissinger in the National Security

Council, echoed Korry's argument about a "Bay of Pigs," adding, "What we propose is patently a violation of our own principles and policy tenets." He went on to say, "If these principles have any meaning, we normally depart from them only to meet the gravest threat to us, e.g., our survival. Is Allende a mortal threat to the U.S.? It is hard to argue this."[213] Kissinger rejected his argument. As the deliberations on Chile proceeded, Kissinger was preternaturally inclined to see the Soviet challenge in Chile as connected to the other crises in the Middle East and Cuba. This link was not just his imagination. The KGB spent considerably to help Allende in the election, and they remained active in the country after the election.[214] The Soviets were opportunists, and along with Cuba's extensive involvement, this set off alarms for Kissinger.[215] In Kissinger's mind, to wait until American "survival" was at stake before acting was ultimately too rigid and simplistic a position for the complex clash between the superpowers and their proxies during the Cold War. When Kissinger wrote, "The reaction [to Chile] must be seen in that context," it was his way of explaining—and rationalizing—the flaws in judgment and excess of zeal toward the "dagger aimed at Antarctica."[216] His approach to Chile also almost perfectly complemented his personal and bureaucratic interests within the Nixon administration.

As the chair of the "40 Committee," the group that oversaw U.S. covert operations, Kissinger engineered approval of Track I, a measure designed to find ways to convince the Chilean Congress to avoid selecting Allende.[217] When this approach failed, Kissinger helped launch Track II, which involved finding Chilean generals who would undertake a coup to prevent Allende's selection by the Congress. With American intelligence agents spreading money around and eager for quick results, the possibility for tragedy was rife. As one critic later noted, "It assumed too much reliability from people over whom we had no control."[218] The search for willing generals led the CIA into contact with Roberto Viaux, an extreme, right-wing retired general who lacked allies within the Chilean military. The CIA operatives in Santiago were also in contact with other anti-Allende forces, some of which were plotting to kidnap General René Schneider, the chief of Chile's armed forces and an opponent of any interference in the political process. By mid-October, only a week before the Chilean Congress would meet, Kissinger called Nixon and told him that the Track II effort "looks hopeless," and that he "turned it off. Nothing would be worse than an abortive coup." Nixon's response was to affirm that policy toward Allende be "coolly detached" and to insist that the United States cut off any financial assistance to the Allende government. Nixon went on to say that this was the "worst diplomatic mess" that the United States had gotten into, and Kissinger quickly agreed.[219]

Even after Track II was turned off, Kissinger told the CIA that it should continue keeping the pressure on Allende, "until such time as new marching orders are given." Kissinger's attitude reflected what Nixon wanted, and undoubtedly encouraged Allende's opponents, who assumed that they would receive Washington's support no matter what they did.[220] These Chileans went ahead with their attempts to kidnap Schneider, and he was killed in a botched effort on the morning of October 22, 1970. The result was to only deepen the determination of the Chilean Congress to go forward with the democratic process and select Allende as president. The coup attempt had backfired miserably.

Shortly after Allende was inaugurated president, the National Security Council met to decide on future American policy toward Chile. Kissinger encouraged the president to study the issue carefully, using a warning that must have set off alarm bells in Nixon's brain: "Chile could end up being the worst failure in our administration—'our Cuba'—by 1972."[221] Kissinger's memo for the meeting was almost a textbook case of Cold War exaggerations covering up bureaucratic maneuvering. Chile "poses for us one of the most serious challenges ever faced in the hemisphere," it said, noting that Nixon's decision about what to do "may be the most historic and difficult foreign affairs decision you will have to make this year." Kissinger emphasized that the "example of a successful elected Marxist government in Chile" would lead to "similar phenomena elsewhere" and "significantly affect the world balance and our own position in it . . . If all concerned do not understand that you want Allende opposed as strongly as we can, the result will be steady drift toward modus vivendi approach." Kissinger recommended to Nixon, "You make a decision that we will oppose Allende as strongly as we can and do all we can to keep him from consolidating power, taking care to package those efforts in a style that gives us the appearance of reacting to his moves."[222] Kissinger knew that Nixon wanted a tough policy, and the wording of his memo reflected Nixon's desire to keep "maximum pressure on the Allende government to prevent its consolidation and limit its ability to implement policies contrary to U.S. and hemisphere interests." The "publicly cool and correct posture" would conceal the ongoing American effort to oppose and undermine the Allende government.[223]

Kissinger had done his president's bidding in getting a tough policy toward Chile imposed on a resistant American bureaucracy. The two men were particularly worried about the "contagion" of the Chilean example. As Nixon put it, "If [Allende] can prove he can set up a Marxist anti-American policy, others will do the same thing," to which Kissinger affirmed that it would have its effect in Europe as well as Latin America.[224] Kissinger did not maintain a close involvement with Chilean issues, but over the next three years the United States undertook a significant effort to undermine Allende. More than $3.5 million went to opposition political parties, along with some $2 million to newspapers and various media outlets, and $1.5 million to business, labor, and other organizations.[225] The United States also organized a "credit squeeze" that exacerbated the Allende government's economic problems. Even with all these measures, and recognizing that the American policy was an overreaction to the threat posed by Chile's socialist experiment, the idea that Kissinger was the author of Allende's demise gives him too much blame—or credit—for Chilean circumstances he did not control or dictate.[226]

VIETNAM, THE MIDTERM ELECTIONS, AND KISSINGER'S ASCENDANCY

In a formulation strikingly similar to Kissinger's, Nixon concluded his own assessment of the "autumn of crises" by remarking, "Communist leaders believe in Lenin's precept: Probe with bayonets. If you encounter mush, proceed; if you encounter steel, withdraw . . . While our effort to prevent Allende from coming to power failed, at least in 1970 in Jordan and in Cuba, their probing had encountered unmistakable steel."[227] As important as these shows of strength were to Nixon and Kissinger, both men recognized that the American people's basic foreign policy concern was still summarized in one word: Vietnam. With the midterm elections approaching, Nixon hoped to demonstrate progress on ending the war and becoming a "peacemaker."[228] After Cambodia, American casualties had decreased markedly, and the level of combat had sharply fallen off. Within the American government, proposals for a cease-fire acquired momentum. Kissinger sought to play a key role in these considerations, twice in September 1970 heading to Paris for secret talks with the North Vietnamese.[229] Kissinger put forward a twelve-month schedule for troop withdrawals but maintained that the United States would still not agree to the forcible overthrow of the South Vietnamese government. Kissinger tried to entice the North Vietnamese with the idea of a "political process that would offer opportunities for each side to achieve whatever popular support it could muster," but insisted, "We could not in advance guarantee to such or such party that it would win and we should both agree to respect the outcome."[230] Kissinger thought Hanoi wanted to "get rid of organized non-Communist opposition. Then they can form a coalition with the non-organized non-Communists who cannot possibly survive under those circumstances."[231] The North Vietnamese simply reiterated Hanoi's earlier positions, and their inflexibility led the North Vietnamese to note in their records that Kissinger "seemed to be sad, thinking that no result could be secured at this forum." Kissinger did say, however, that even if their political differences were large, on the military side of the question, the differences between the United States and North Vietnam "are small enough so that everything else can be settled."[232]

Nixon still wanted some type of dramatic gesture before the midterm elections, but Kissinger tried to keep the president's speech from being too "pacifist" in tone. He told Safire, "I am worried about the impact on the North Vietnamese. The North Vietnamese think we are down, we are finished. They have fought for 50 years and they don't think war is horrible."[233] Nixon heightened the drama of the speech by telling reporters a day before that it would be "the most comprehensive statement ever made on this subject since the beginning of a very difficult war."[234] On October 7, 1970, Nixon gave the speech in prime time, beginning, "Tonight I would like to talk to you about a major new initiative for peace."[235] Nixon's call for a cease-fire and an all-Indochina peace conference had obvious political motives, but it was still extremely well received by many Senate doves and other opinion makers, especially his call for a halt to American bombing throughout Indochina. All three network newscasts presented the speech in favorable terms, with many featuring calls for unity from prominent Democratic senators such as Mike Mansfield, Edmund Muskie, and George McGovern.[236] After the speech, Kissinger acknowledged that the idea of a "standstill cease-fire" was designed to indicate some flexibility on the idea that North Vietnam would have to withdraw its forces from the South, a major concession the United States confirmed a few months later. Nevertheless, Hanoi continued to reject Nixon's proposals.[237]

Although the war in Vietnam would prove less important in the midterm elections than the increase in unemployment and continuing inflation, Nixon tried to tie the disruptions of antiwar protesters to the more general fears of crime and disorder that were a part of the electorate's mood.[238] "Permissiveness is the key theme," Nixon told his advisers, and the Republican campaigns targeted the "social issue," seeking to connect Democrats with the perceived "anarchy" of the era.[239] For his part, Kissinger endeavored to stay away from the campaigning, but Nixon wanted to use him in the California Senate race, where the Republican senator George Murphy faced a tough challenge from John Tunney, the son of the famous boxer and a close friend of Ted Kennedy's. Kissinger resisted, telling Robert Finch, the campaign director, that he hated "to be used in the Jewish community." When Finch responded that it was a briefing for "friends of the president," Kissinger replied, "But they are all Jewish." Finch then promised to throw in a few gentiles, and Kissinger ended by saying, "If [Nixon] wants me to do it, I will."[240] Kissinger later boasted to a reporter that his event raised more money for the Murphy campaign in California than they had ever raised, but he still insisted, "The one group I hate to talk to is a Jewish group."[241]

On Election Day, November 3, 1970, when the journalist Marilyn Berger called Kissinger in the early evening, he started their conversation by saying, "What are you taking me away from, a Republican landslide?" When she asked if he was serious, he replied, "I can't see it."[242] The midterm elections were a disappointment to the Nixon White House, intensifying Nixon's fear that he would be a one-term president. Nixon could take some comfort in the defeat of a few of his adversaries in the Senate, such as Charles Goodell in New York, Joseph Tydings in Maryland, and Albert Gore, Sr., in Tennessee. However, most of the candidates the president campaigned for lost, including Murphy in California and George H. W. Bush in Texas. The Republican attempt to capitalize on a violent protest against Nixon in San Jose, California, had backfired. Republicans did gain two seats in the Senate but lost nine House seats and eleven governorships—the overall Democratic margin in House elections increased from 1.1 million votes in 1968 to 4.5 million in 1970.[243]

Nixon was shaken by the results. His own popularity was slipping below 50 percent, and he was angry when a Gallup poll showed that Americans thought the country's prestige abroad had fallen during his presidency. "We are not getting credit for foreign policy," he angrily told Haldeman.[244] In a long memorandum in early December, Nixon told Haldeman he wanted a meeting with special counsel Dick Moore, speechwriter Safire, and Kissinger. Nixon had "reluctantly concluded that our entire effort on the public relations front has been misdirected and ineffective." What was needed in Nixon's view was "to get across those fundamental decencies and virtues which the great majority of Americans like—hard work, warmth, kindness, consideration for others, willingness to take the heat and not to pass the buck and, above all, a man who always does what he thinks is right, regardless of the consequences." Nixon knew Haldeman might wonder about including Kissinger in this group, but Nixon was direct: "The reason is that he will love sitting in such a meeting. He will keep it absolutely confidential; he will not contribute anything on how to get the ideas across, but above everything else, he is our big gun in the area where we have had our greatest success, and while he does not know it, he is the one who has been measured the favorite."[245]

That Nixon thought Kissinger would keep such a meeting "absolutely confidential" is surprising, and reflective of how little he understood his assistant. But who "measured" Kissinger "the favorite"? In Nixon's view, the establishment media—the TV networks and the Eastern liberal newspapers—had anointed Kissinger, and for political reasons it was important for the administration to use that popularity. Although the administration had been cautious about having Kissinger on television, Nixon delighted in an October 1970 *60 Minutes* profile of his adviser and now encouraged Kissinger to do more TV appearances. Others in the administration's press office reacted with the same enthusiasm. Safire told Kissinger, "That was the most fantastic show I have ever seen; it not only reflected well on you, but also on the President and the Administration." The British TV personality David Frost now wanted Kissinger on his program, and Nixon himself arranged for the *Today* show's Barbara Walters to interview Kissinger.[246]

The connection between the domestic politics of foreign policy and Kissinger's ascendancy is also suggested by Haldeman's detailed record of the almost-daily Kissinger-Rogers struggle. Early in the fall, Nixon was still concerned about the ongoing rivalry between the two men, telling Haldeman that he would have to "get them both to quit acting like little children, trying to nail the other and prove him wrong." Nixon agreed with Haldeman that it might be good to suggest to Kissinger that he think of leaving, if only "to shake him a little." If one had to go, it would probably be Kissinger, and Nixon then said he would put Kissinger's deputy, Al Haig, into his position.[247] Only two months later the positions of Rogers and Kissinger were reversed. Haldeman complained to Nixon about Rogers's disloyalty to the administration, and Nixon asked him to put together a documented case against the secretary of state. Haldeman suspected Nixon wanted a case for the removal of Rogers, though he knew how difficult it would be for Nixon to fire his old friend.[248] Nixon recognized how important success in foreign policy, and getting the credit for that success, would be for his reelection. The best bet for those political benefits was Kissinger. He was now, as Haldeman told Kissinger, "indispensable to the President, and both he and the President know it, and he's got to stay here."[249]

By this point Kissinger had become the consummate courtier, recognizing Nixon's desperate need for praise, especially after his televised speeches and press conferences.[250] He could almost read Nixon's mind in talking about political figures, aware of the president's resentments and manipulating his grievances. After his October 1970 cease-fire speech, Kissinger called Nixon to tell him it went very well, and that Senator Charles Percy, a leading dove, called him to say that it was "a brilliant speech, one of his finest ever." Before conveying that sentiment, Kissinger, knowing Nixon's mixed feelings, remarked, "That son of a bitch Percy called," and when Nixon asked whether he should call him, Kissinger replied, "I hate to see an opportunist rewarded."[251] After a courteous conversation with his former staff member Anthony Lake, who had now joined up with Muskie's campaign, Kissinger called Nixon and told him of his conversation with that "snake Lake."[252] Nixon also loved the flattery Kissinger provided. When Kissinger called after a press conference in December, Nixon asked him to tell his daughter Tricia his reaction. "I thought your father was spectacular," Kissinger said. "This was by far the best press conference he has ever held." A skeptical Tricia asked him why it was "the best," and Kissinger explained that it was because her father was "conciliatory and tough." Even after Nixon got back on the phone, he continued to tell Tricia all of Kissinger's various compliments.[253] The next month, after another press conference, Kissinger told Nixon that the British journalist Henry Brandon had told him that Nixon was better at press conferences than Kennedy was, "more articulate and more disciplined." Nixon replied, "Really? That's like talking against Christ."[254]

As deferential as Kissinger could be to Nixon, he also continued to cultivate his own standing, both in his continuing media contacts—which Nixon alternately resented and encouraged—and his attempt to carry on a dialogue with opponents of the administration's Vietnam policy. During the Cambodian protests, Kissinger had met a pacifist student, Brian McDonnell, who was fasting to protest the American invasion. He admired McDonnell for the strength of his convictions and maintained a dialogue with him, meeting without publicity to debate him about the war. After the indictments against the Berrigan brothers for plotting to kidnap him were announced, Kissinger sought to downplay the issue, and even continued his own meetings with antiwar activists, including some of those indicted in the plot against him. When Lloyd Shearer, a *Parade* magazine celebrity journalist, and perhaps the only person ever to call Kissinger "Hank," asked him why he now had a body-guard, the normally loquacious Kissinger replied, "Because of threats." When Shearer joked that Kissinger was "being protected from hordes of girls," Kissinger replied stiffly, "That's not the reason."[255]

Kissinger's ascendancy owed much to his bureaucratic maneuvering, his skill with the media, and his relationship with Nixon. It also stemmed from his ability to discuss foreign policy in new ways, and his language of retrench-ment and realism was perfectly coordinated with the political mood of the nation. In year-end briefings for the press, Kissinger used the language of re-alism to discuss foreign policy. "It is really our interests that should get us in-volved, not our commitments." America needed a debate "on what and where are our interests, and only then should we look at our commitments." Kis-singer understood the real limits of American power. He told the journalists of his occasional frustration that "one of the great dangers with trying to deal with such a high number of issues and problems is that the urgent ones seem to displace the more important ones." Kissinger noted, "It is a constant fight to find time to address those questions which have long range implications."[256] As Nixon entered the second half of his first term, he and Kissinger attempted to deal with those long-range issues, hoping to complete a significant change in American foreign policy that would reverberate domestically and win the president reelection in 1972.

3

"NIXON'S SECRET AGENT"

Kissinger as the New Face of
American Foreign Policy, 1971

I N JANUARY 1972, Richard Nixon delivered a nationally televised speech on Vietnam, outlining a proposal for a cease-fire, American withdrawal, return of the POWs, and new elections. Nixon dramatically and surprisingly highlighted the role of "Dr. Kissinger" as "my personal representative," who had traveled secretly to Paris twelve times to negotiate with the North Vietnamese. The next day Kissinger's press briefing was the lead story on all three network newscasts. CBS's Dan Rather listed a series of titles for Kissinger: "Secretary of State without title, swinging bachelor ladies' man, masterful explainer, propaganda artist, skilled briefer"—and then noted the strange White House rule that still prevented news organizations from playing the audio of Kissinger's briefing.[1] On NBC, John Chancellor called the rule against broadcasting Kissinger's accented voice "inexplicable."[2] Kissinger was seen but not heard, explaining the secret negotiations he had conducted over a thirty-month period, making it clear how far the Nixon administration had gone in meeting Communist demands.

Both *Time* and *Newsweek* featured Kissinger on their covers with the title "Nixon's Secret Agent." On CBS, Eric Sevareid saw Kissinger's role in a raw political light; he was an emissary of the president who was not accountable to Congress and could be used as a way to defuse Vietnam as a political issue. ABC's Howard K. Smith praised Kissinger, saying that now the Democrats would find it "hard to make [Vietnam] a political issue."[3] The announcement of Kissinger's role capped off a year in which Kissinger had become the public face of American foreign policy. It was a year that had started with military defeat in the jungles of Laos and antiwar protests in Washington, then transitioned through a cloak-and-dagger trip to Beijing and a summit announcement with Moscow, and ended with the embarrassment of supporting an incompetent and genocidal ally fighting a losing war in Southwest Asia. Kissinger figured in all of it.

VIETNAM, LAOS, AND THE "DECENT INTERVAL"

The second half of the first Nixon presidential term did not begin well. The news from Vietnam, despite the decline in casualties and fighting, was frustrating and increasingly grim. A well-executed raid on a POW camp in North Vietnam came up empty, as the American prisoners had already been moved. With soldiers "fragging" their officers, high rates of heroin and marijuana use, and racial conflict within units, the U.S. Army seemed on the verge of collapse. In December 1970, Nixon told Kissinger that he wanted to go to Vietnam in April, tour the country, give speeches touting the achievements of Vietnamization, and then make "a basic end of the war announcement." Kissinger, sounding more political than his boss, told Nixon that if the United States pulled out all its forces in 1971, and South Vietnam came under attack in 1972 and collapsed, "We'll have to answer for [it] at the elections."[4] Kissinger's blunt argument swayed Nixon, although he asked Kissinger to draw up plans that might allow him some type of popular move later in 1971, such as announcing that no more draftees would be sent to Vietnam. Nixon knew and stated publicly that he expected "to be held accountable by the American people" if he failed to end American involvement in the war.[5]

Nixon remained drawn to more aggressive plans—military measures that might end the war sooner, get the POWs back, and even give Saigon more of a chance to survive long-term. Although conscious of a possible domestic backlash, Nixon approved a dry-season offensive against the primary supply route for the North Vietnamese and Viet Cong, the Ho Chi Minh Trail in Laos. Originating in Kissinger's NSC and coordinated with Saigon, "Lam Son 719," the Vietnamese name given to the Laotian invasion, was both a military and political undertaking. American military planners had long wanted to move against the Ho Chi Minh Trail, whose importance as a supply line to Communist forces had increased substantially after Cambodia's new rulers cut off the port of Sihanoukville. Despite the domestic turmoil it had unleashed, the Cambodian operation was a limited military success in disrupting the Communist war effort, and it encouraged the idea of going after North Vietnamese forces in Laos. Congressional restrictions prevented the United States from sending its ground troops into Laos, but ARVN forces could undertake the attack. President Thiệu, running for reelection later in the year, also saw the appeal of a military victory in enhancing his image. For Kissinger, given the plan for American troop withdrawals, Lam Son 719 was probably the last opportunity to mount any sort of military operation that might push Hanoi toward a negotiated settlement. If nothing else, a military success might set back any North Vietnamese military offensive for two years, a long enough time for the United States to finish its withdrawal from Vietnam and for the president to be safely reelected.

To avoid the cabinet dissension that had occurred over Cambodia, Nixon used a series of low-key meetings, orchestrated by Kissinger, to convince potential opponents of the action.[6] The most important potential critic was Secretary of Defense Melvin Laird. Initially Laird did not see the need for action in Laos and worried that a setback could damage Vietnamization. However, after a trip to Saigon and talks with General Abrams, Laird came to see the Laotian invasion as a way to both demonstrate the success of the

Vietnamization program *and* speed up the withdrawal of American forces. Now allied with Kissinger, he presented the advantages of the operation, arguing that it would attack the crucial supply hub of the North Vietnamese. Given the planned withdrawal of American units, this was now the time to act. Even if the North Vietnamese proved willing to stand and fight, American air power would decimate their forces. Nixon and Kissinger were pleased with Laird's presentation, and both remarked that the operation could prove "decisive in the overall conduct of the war."[7]

It was left to Secretary of State Rogers to raise objections to the plan, objections that Kissinger later admitted were "right on target." Rogers argued that the risks of the invasion were excessive, that the enemy knew the operation was coming, and that the ARVN, with only three divisions and about seventeen thousand men, was being asked "to conduct an operation that we refused to do in the past because we were not strong enough." If the South Vietnamese were set back in the operation, it would be a defeat for Vietnamization, Thiệu's future would be in doubt, and "we would be giving up everything we had achieved."[8] Rogers was prophetic, but he was in an increasingly weakened position within the administration. Just as the planning for the Laotian operation was being discussed, *The New York Times* ran two stories on consecutive days headlining the decline of the State Department and the key role played by Kissinger. Presenting Kissinger as at the "hub" of foreign policy, the *Times* wrote, "Hardly a proposal of consequence on foreign affairs reaches the President without Mr. Kissinger's covering memo giving his analysis of the problem, the proposals of other agencies, and his recommendations." The article concluded, "Nixon may hear all the options . . . but he seems to listen most of the time to one voice."[9] Rogers complained bitterly to Nixon, who wanted to put out a statement denouncing the article. Haldeman convinced him to wait, commenting that the article had enough basis in fact and accuracy that a statement would not be wise.[10]

As if to confirm the *Times* stories, Kissinger played the key role in carrying out the Laotian operation.[11] He coordinated support within the government, briefed sympathetic journalists, and kept Nixon apprised of the military situation and the political reaction within the United States. He was in frequent touch with the military, calling Admiral Thomas Moorer, chairman of the Joint Chiefs of Staff, to remind him that the president wanted him to know "how much we have riding on this one."[12] Kissinger encouraged a *Newsweek* story that put the odds for success in Laos "at 5 to 1" and that suggested the United States was on the verge of a major victory.[13] When the ARVN forces met only light resistance from the North Vietnamese during the first two weeks, Kissinger told Nixon, "Having made strides we ought to stay in there now through the rainy season . . . and just chew them up." To Nixon's question "The South Vietnamese are going to fight. They're going to stand and fight. Aren't they?," Kissinger reassured his boss: "Oh yeah. So far they have."[14] Kissinger bragged to Safire, "Laos would not have happened if I had not been here . . . because the two of us are here, the President and myself, we have a chance of *winning* this thing."[15]

Kissinger's optimism faded quickly as the operation unraveled. Only a little over two weeks after the invasion, South Vietnamese forces were bogged down and facing determined opposition from the North Vietnamese. Only American airpower was preventing retreat. In what was one of the biggest intelligence failures of the war, analysts had gravely overestimated the time it would take the North Vietnamese to reinforce their forces near the trail. The South Vietnamese had walked into a trap and soon found themselves surrounded by as many as five North Vietnamese divisions—more than forty thousand men with heavy artillery and antiaircraft guns. For the first time in the war, the North Vietnamese attacked with Soviet tanks. The South Vietnamese were badly outmanned and outgunned, and heavily dependent on American air support, which bad weather frequently prevented. To salvage a symbolic victory from the operation, President Thiệu ordered his commanders to conduct a rapid airborne assault on the original objective, the town of Tchepone. Once the already-deserted town was taken on March 6, Thiệu, concerned about the political effect of the growing number of casualties on his own reelection, ordered his forces to withdraw from Laos as quickly as possible. The ARVN units were not disciplined enough to conduct an orderly withdrawal, especially under heavy pressure from North Vietnamese attacks. Their retreat became a rout, with American television showing demoralized

South Vietnamese soldiers clinging to helicopter skids as they sought to escape.[16] By March 25, when the last ARVN soldier crossed back into Vietnam, the image of Lam Son 719 as a humiliating defeat was firmly established. Although the North Vietnamese losses were estimated at 20,000, largely from U.S. air strikes, over 7,000 ARVN soldiers were killed or wounded, with the United States, although not fighting on the ground, losing more than 700 helicopters and planes, with 257 men killed and more than 1,100 wounded.[17]

Despite the rules against having his voice heard, Kissinger took on a more prominent public role on Laos, appearing on CBS News to defend the administration's policy. Kissinger stressed that regardless of what happened in Laos, the administration would continue its troop withdrawals. He even managed a slight smile when Bernard Kalb asked him about the possibility that the South Vietnamese might invade North Vietnam. It was not the "dominant probability," Kissinger replied, adding that the United States would not assist any such military action.[18] Behind the scenes Kissinger engaged in a flurry of back-channel messages to the American embassy in Saigon. Kissinger told Ambassador Ellsworth Bunker, "You know what we are up against here . . . We will do our best to hold the fort. But we must know what we are up against. There is no chance to keep panic from setting in if we are constantly outstripped by events."[19] As the news from Laos grew worse, public opinion polls showed that by a margin of two to one, most Americans believed the Laotian incursion would lengthen rather than shorten the war.[20] When Kissinger heard of Thiệu's plan for a quick withdrawal after the South Vietnamese took Tchepone, he sent an angry message to Bunker, telling him to tell Thiệu that this was the "last chance" for the ARVN to have support for such an operation and that they should continue to disrupt the enemy's supply operation and stay in Laos at least until the end of April.[21] His effort was in vain, and when he found out a week later that the ARVN was leaving Laos at full speed, he angrily told his military briefer, "Those sons of bitches. It's their country and we can't save it for them if they don't want to. We would never have approved the plan if we thought they were only going to stay for a short time."[22] He wrote to Ambassador Bunker, warning, "I hope Thiệu understands that the President's confidence is an asset he should not lightly dissipate and that this may be his last crack at massive U.S. support."[23] Even more bluntly, he told Moorer that the South Vietnamese withdrawal would "kill us domestically."[24] When reports came that enemy soldiers had been drinking large quantities of rice wine to drive them to a suicidal frenzy, Kissinger, aware that ARVN also faced a drug problem, cynically remarked, "This ought to be a great battle, one army hopped up on drugs and the other . . . on booze."[25] To his assistant Haig, who had been a strong advocate of the operation, Kissinger raged, "Well Al, your military finally got what it wanted and they've fucked it up!"[26]

Nixon appreciated Kissinger's efforts to ride herd on the operation, and both men complained bitterly in their private conversations about the military's poor performance and the media's negative coverage. Laos increased Nixon's reliance on and trust in Kissinger. Kissinger had learned a lesson from his "agonizing" over Cambodia that had so irritated Nixon. Now he made it a point to tell the president, "If I had known before it started that it was going to come out exactly the way it did, I would still have gone ahead with it."[27] When Senator Stuart Symington created a public controversy in early March by saying that Kissinger was "Secretary of State in all but the title," Nixon told Haldeman that Kissinger was "irreplaceable" and far more valuable to him than Rogers, and if someone had to fall on their sword for the president, Kissinger would do it. Haldeman conceded the point, but added, "If Henry did do it, he would do it with loud kicking and screaming and make sure the blood spurted all over the place so he got full credit for it."[28]

Kissinger recognized how badly the Laos operation affected public support for the war. He told Nixon, "Laos has again brought the war to the front pages, in a way which shows that no early and easy end is in sight."[29] On a personal level, Kissinger continued to reach out to antiwar critics, even meeting such prominent figures as Senators Eugene McCarthy and George McGovern, as well as the economist John Kenneth Galbraith, his Harvard friend.[30] But he raised the hackles of the White House staff with a Saturday-morning session with three co-conspirators in the case of the alleged plot to kidnap him.[31] After the meeting, one of the activists remarked, "The scary part of it is that he really is a nice man . . . He sees himself as the conscience of the Administration."[32] Kissinger denied using that exact expression, telling

Dan Rather, "My megalomania takes extreme forms but not quite that."[33] Kissinger sought to cultivate an image of being more dovish than he really was, and he could never quite give up on his attempt to convince his critics.[34]

Nixon scrapped his original plan to use the success of Lam Son 719 to visit Vietnam and declare an end to the war. However, he still intended, with Kissinger's encouragement, to take a page from Senator George Aiken's famous suggestion to declare victory and bring the troops home. In this case, Nixon decided to give a nationally televised speech proclaiming that the Laotian operation proved that Vietnamization was working successfully and that therefore he could increase the rate of American troop withdrawals. Shortly before the speech, Kissinger alerted Ambassador Bunker that the administration recognized that this increase in the rate of withdrawal "will undoubtedly pose some difficult problems for President Thiệu. At the same time holding public opinion here after Lamson [sic] is an absolute imperative and is in the long run more useful to Thiệu than anything else we might do."[35] Two days before the speech, a group of Republican senators met privately with Defense Secretary Laird and told him bluntly that they would not be able to hold the party together if Nixon did not set a date for withdrawal.[36] Laird told Nixon, whose sense that his own party was deserting him intensified his resentment and anger.

Nixon's speech of April 7, 1971, tried to defend the Laotian invasion and his overall Vietnam policy, emphasizing with a simple chart the scale of troop withdrawals he had undertaken. Nixon still refused to set a final date for withdrawal, arguing that in setting such a date, "we would have thrown away our principal bargaining counter to win the release of American prisoners of war, we would remove the enemy's strongest incentive to end the war by negotiation, and we will have given enemy commanders the exact information they need to marshal their attacks against our remaining forces at their most vulnerable time." He also posed the question of America's responsibility to the South Vietnamese: "Shall we leave Vietnam in a way that—by our own actions—consciously turns the country over to the Communists? Or shall we leave in a way that gives the South Vietnamese a reasonable chance to survive as a free people?"[37] Nixon's "reasonable chance" was Kissinger's "decent interval," a recognition that the odds against the South Vietnamese state surviving were long, but that the key was not having the collapse seem the direct responsibility of the United States, or as critics would argue, the political responsibility of the Nixon administration.[38]

Kissinger called Nixon almost immediately after the speech to tell him, "It was by far the best delivery I've heard you give. It was dignified, strong. It was not ingratiating." Kissinger continued to pour on the compliments and called Nixon back some four times with the positive reaction of others to the speech. Nixon, however, was in a defiant mood, angry with his cabinet, particularly Laird and Rogers, but also at the Republican leadership, who were pressing him to set a definite deadline for withdrawal. "Those leaders were a miserable lot," he told Kissinger, particularly angry with Senator Hugh Scott, the Senate minority leader, and Robert Griffin, the Republican whip. Reassured by Kissinger that he was heroically "saving the country," Nixon defiantly added, "If Congress wants to take over, fine, but they have to take the responsibility if this goes down the drain, and that is clear, gentlemen."[39] He went on to tell Kissinger that if the United States couldn't make progress in negotiations with the help of the Soviets, he was prepared to turn right "so goddamn hard it will make your head spin," adding, "We'll bomb those bastards right off the earth." When pressed for his agreement, a hesitant Kissinger provided a more measured response: "We have to make fundamental decisions."[40] Faced with the continuing drain of Vietnam on his presidency and fearing its impact on his reelection prospects, feeling besieged and without supporters, Nixon freely vented his anger to Kissinger. The next day he told Kissinger and Haldeman that he would never forget their loyalty to him and that they had stood up when no one else, especially in his cabinet, had done so.[41]

The aftermath of Lam Son 719 was a low point for the Nixon presidency and reflected a pervasive disenchantment in the country as a whole. The British Foreign Office assessed the mood of the United States in early 1971 and titled its paper "No Longer God's Own Country."[42] Americans were angry and dissatisfied with almost all the leading institutions of their society. The Vietnam War remained central to that unhappiness. Antiwar demonstrators besieged Washington in April 1971, including a substantial number of Vietnam veterans, among them John Kerry, who tossed their medals back at the White House. Although their attempt to shut down Washington failed, it led to police confrontations, mass arrests, and scenes of Marines landing by helicopter on the National Mall. Polls showed almost 73 percent of Americans wanted the United States out by the end of 1971, 60 percent wanted withdrawal even if the South Vietnamese government collapsed, and 58 percent believed it morally wrong for the United States to fight in Vietnam.[43]

CHINA, SALT, AND THE PENTAGON PAPERS

Nixon and Kissinger frequently lapsed into talking about their various diplomatic moves as a "game," imagining international relations as something like the famous Parker Brothers board game Risk, in which players compete for world domination.[44] So there was a certain irony when the Chinese government decided to make its own move in the game of diplomacy by having its champion Ping-Pong team invite the American team to visit China. The invitation came on April 7, 1971, the same day as Nixon's Laos speech, as if the Chinese had timed their invitation as a response to Nixon's announcement that the United States was withdrawing even faster from Vietnam. Over the next ten days, "ping-pong diplomacy" dominated the media, with favorable images of China and positive assessments of the "thaw" in relations between the United States and China.[45] *Time* magazine titled its coverage "The Ping Heard Round the World," speculating, "China has finally decided to turn outward again."[46] Haldeman noted, "The big thing now is to make sure we get credit for all the shifts in China policy, rather than letting them go to the State Department."[47] Kissinger even told Nixon that the extensive media attention was a needed "diversion from Vietnam" and something necessary for "our game" with the Soviets.[48] Neither man seemed aware of how quickly and decisively that change was coming, even though they had been working toward it for over two years.

In an October 1967 *Foreign Affairs* article titled "Asia After Vietnam," the then candidate Richard Nixon had argued, "We simply cannot afford to leave China forever outside the family of nations, there to nurture its fantasies, cherish its hates, and threaten its neighbors."[49] Less than two weeks into his presidency, Nixon instructed Kissinger, "We should give every encouragement to the attitude that this Administration is 'exploring possibilities of raprochement [sic] with the Chinese.'"[50] Nixon insisted that this be handled quietly.[51] Kissinger was initially skeptical of an approach toward Beijing.[52] "Our Leader has taken leave of reality," Kissinger remarked to Haig, but he ordered an NSC study of relations with the Communist giant.[53] When Haldeman told Kissinger in July 1969—during a worldwide trip in which Nixon was asking the Pakistanis and Romanians to signal China of his interest—that Nixon "seriously intends to visit China before the end of the second term," Kissinger replied, "Fat chance."[54]

There was good reason for Kissinger's skepticism. China's revolutionary militancy and the fear it produced in Asia were among the key factors leading to U.S. intervention in Vietnam. China provided Hanoi with "the bulk of the small arms and ammunition used" by its forces during the early years of the war, and by 1967 some 170,000 Chinese military personnel were estimated to be stationed in North Vietnam.[55] The Cultural Revolution had convulsed China since 1966, isolating Beijing from the rest of the world but securing the unrivaled power of Mao Zedong. Mao's rivalry with the Soviet Union for leadership of the world's communist movement, dating back to his disputes with Nikita Khrushchev, finally led to armed clashes between their armies near the Ussuri River in March 1969. During one of their first back-channel meetings, Dobrynin gave Kissinger "a gory account of the atrocities committed by the Chinese." Kissinger told Nixon that he listened politely and said to Dobrynin that this was a problem for China and the Soviet Union and "we did not propose to get involved."[56]

Kissinger's neutrality did not last long. His personal conversion on the possibilities of a China opening was jump-started after the renewal of border clashes in August 1969, especially when Soviet diplomats began asking Americans what U.S. policy might be in the event of war between the two communist countries.[57] At an NSC meeting that same month, Nixon posed what he called "rhetorical questions" about the possibility of a Soviet attack on China, saying, "I am not sure if it is in our long term interest to let the

Soviets knock them off."[58] Nixon encouraged the resumption of the Warsaw talks between the two countries in February 1970. The Chinese actually proposed that "if the US wished to send a representative of ministerial rank or a special Presidential envoy to Peking," they would be prepared to receive him.[59] Although this seemed to indicate some progress, it almost immediately elicited sharp protests from the nationalist government in Taiwan, more delays in arranging another meeting, and then a suspension of the talks in the wake of the Cambodian invasion of May 1970.

The suspension of the talks underlines the often-overlooked fact that the opening to China was also contingent on the mercurial, impulsive, and aging Mao Zedong, whose foreign policy attitudes alternated between revolutionary fantasies and sophisticated realism. Some officials in Mao's government had come to recognize the danger in which China had been placed through its isolation, and Zhou Enlai had led a group that hoped to reopen China's ties with the world, including the United States. Mao's word remained decisive, and his influence could change the direction of policy. The Cambodian incursion, and the protests against it, led Mao to condemn Nixon's "Fascist aggression."[60] The Chinese leader argued that the "current international situation has developed to the high tide of world revolutionary movement of anti-U.S. imperialists and its running dogs. We must make use of it."[61] The succession struggle around the aged Chinese dictator also meant that policy could fluctuate. On July 10, 1970, Beijing released Bishop James Walsh, an American citizen who had been serving a twenty-year sentence for espionage. Yet only a few days earlier, Chinese aircraft, in a move reminiscent of the North Korean incident a year earlier, tried to intercept and shoot down an American aircraft gathering intelligence almost one hundred miles off the coast. Had they succeeded, as Kissinger told the president, "they would have finished off the slight movement toward a Sino-U.S. thaw." Kissinger further reasoned that the "most plausible hypothesis is that somebody in the power structure *did* want to wreck Sino-U.S. relations."[62]

Although the silence from China continued into the fall of 1970, Nixon remained hopeful.[63] He started to use the proper title, the "People's Republic of China," in public and gave an interview to *Time* magazine in which he said that he still hoped for rapprochement with China even if it took five or ten years, adding, "If there is anything I want to do before I die, it is to go to China."[64] On December 9, 1970, the Pakistani ambassador, Agha Hilaly, visited Kissinger, carrying with him a message from Prime Minister Zhou Enlai. In a formulation that was surprisingly simple and almost comic, Zhou noted, "We have had messages from the United States from different sources in the past but this is the first time that the proposal has come from a Head, through a Head, to a Head." Although confining the subject of negotiations to the evacuation "of Chinese territories called Taiwan," the Chinese said that a special envoy from the United States would "be most welcome in Peking." Kissinger asked Hilaly to take a message back to the Chinese, offering preliminary talks not limited to Taiwan and suggesting himself as the American emissary. Kissinger also dangled the carrot that "it would not be difficult to comply with the Chinese request for withdrawing American forces from Taiwan."[65]

When the Chinese delayed responding, Nixon worried, "We may appear too eager. Let's cool it."[66] In late January, the United States and South Vietnam launched Lam Son 719. It seemed the Laos operation, as with the Cambodia invasion a year earlier, might cause the Chinese to hesitate. In the United States, there was even speculation that China might intervene in Vietnam, and Bernard Kalb asked Kissinger during a CBS interview if the North Vietnamese were correct in "brandishing" the threat of Chinese intervention. Kissinger nervously stared straight ahead, beginning his answer with an oddly philosophical note: "In foreign policy the most intractable problems are those where both sides are right." He went on to note that the North Vietnamese were correct to say that China would intervene if the United States "threatened [North Vietnam's] national existence." But he emphasized, in his distinctively slow cadence, that this was not what the United States was doing. There was palpable relief in his voice when he finished the answer, as he undoubtedly hoped the Chinese got the message.[67]

They did. On April 27, 1971, Pakistan's Hilaly came with an urgent message from the Chinese government. The Nixon administration was stunned to learn that the Chinese were prepared "to receive publicly in Peking a special envoy of the president of the U.S. (for instance Mr. Kissinger) or the

U.S. Secretary of State or even the President of the U.S. himself for direct meeting and discussions."[68] Nixon and Kissinger knew the importance of the message they received—it "spoke for itself, . . . the most important message an American President had received since World War II."[69] Nixon called Kissinger to discuss possible envoys, including Kissinger's great patron, Nelson Rockefeller, as well as David Bruce, George Bush, and even the recently deceased Thomas Dewey. Kissinger said in his memoirs, "Originally there was no thought of sending me," but this claim is disingenuous since Kissinger had already suggested himself and the Chinese note listed him by name. Nixon may not have been deliberately torturing his national security adviser by talking about every other possibility, including poor Dewey, but the suspicion that he was playing with Kissinger is inescapable. The only one Kissinger warmed to was Rockefeller—because on foreign policy, Kissinger said, Rockefeller "would take my advice"—and he praised the idea as "original" and Rockefeller as a "tough" negotiator. Kissinger, however, quickly affirmed a Nixon comment that Rockefeller would have great "visibility" and that the Chinese would "jump" at the possibility, thereby feeding the suspicion in Nixon's mind that Rockefeller might overshadow the president. By the end of the conversation, Nixon was even asking Kissinger to figure out a way to tell the Chinese not to invite Senate majority leader Mike Mansfield before Nixon's own trip was confirmed.[70] Kissinger believed Nixon's "overriding" motive for selecting him was that Kissinger best understood the foreign policy of the administration and what Nixon sought to achieve. However, Kissinger also understood the domestic political motives Nixon had: "Of all the potential emissaries I was the most subject to his control . . . my success would be a Presidential success."[71] Nixon instinctively knew, as he told Kissinger, "we played a game and we got a little break," and this break could have a tremendous political impact.[72]

But only if the "game" were handled correctly. In the Nixon and Kissinger view, this meant cutting out the State Department bureaucracy and Secretary of State William P. Rogers.[73] Nixon also tried to dampen speculation about changes in China policy—as he put it, "What we have done has broken the ice; now we have to test the water to see how deep it is."[74] Nixon was determined to keep other American politicians, particularly Democrats like Mansfield and rivals like Edward Kennedy, from getting invitations to China before he went. Kissinger asked Hilaly to convey to the Chinese as his own idea that "President Nixon will find it more difficult to move quickly in the matter if American politicians come into it."[75] Nixon also wanted the arrangements kept secret, and Kissinger asked the Chinese to handle the preparations in a "preliminary *secret* meeting" between Kissinger and Zhou.[76] The original Chinese message indicated their preference for a public visit, and Kissinger said he later learned that the Chinese were suspicious about the American demand for secrecy, perhaps considering it as a way to allow the United States to change its mind abruptly. Kissinger argued that secrecy would protect the initiative against hostile forces within the bureaucracy or from other countries.[77] There were advantages to secret diplomacy, but the real danger in public knowledge would be diminishing the psychological and political impact of the announcement of the visit. Nixon hoped to catch his political opponents completely off guard and strengthen his claim to be the "peace" candidate in 1972.[78]

As Kissinger was still sorting out the details of his China trip, in May 1971 the White House was preparing to announce a "procedural breakthrough" in the Strategic Arms Limitation Talks, which had been underway since late 1969. Nixon had always regarded his management of U.S.-Soviet relations as central to the success of his presidency. In setting up Kissinger's back channel to Dobrynin, Nixon hoped for dramatic results. Nixon and Kissinger both understood that the massive Soviet nuclear arms buildup during the 1960s had changed the nature of the superpower relationship. Nixon recalled, "At the beginning of the administration I began to talk in terms of *sufficiency* rather than *superiority* to describe my goals for our nuclear arsenal."[79] The Soviet buildup increased Soviet confidence and the "aggressiveness of their foreign policy." To Nixon, whose understanding of nuclear issues was shaped in the Eisenhower era, extended deterrence, the nuclear umbrella the United States had once held over Europe, was now "a lot of crap," and a flexible response, its corollary, was "baloney." In Nixon's view, there now existed a genuine "balance of terror."[80] With the United States no longer possessing the overwhelming superiority in nuclear weapons it had in the 1950s, Nixon doubted whether America's commitment to Europe's defense was still believable, through either a nuclear response to a Soviet attack across the German frontier or the conventional armed resistance that flexible response once promised.

Nixon and Kissinger had fought hard and successfully in 1969 for the approval of the ABM missile system. Although he argued for the strategic necessity of the ABM, Nixon, the inveterate poker player, wanted to have some chips available for bargaining with the Soviet Union. Consequently, Nixon was very disappointed at the lack of Soviet interest in an early summit meeting in 1970 that Nixon hoped might boost Republican chances in the midterm election.[81] Although Nixon could be dismissive of arms control, disparaging it as reflecting the "pathetic idealism" of Americans, by 1971 he recognized that it was a political and economic imperative, especially because there was so little domestic support for increased defense spending.[82] By January 1971, when Nixon sent Kissinger to see Dobrynin to suggest the outline of a possible strategic arms agreement, he was prepared to bargain ABM away, provided the Soviets would link such an agreement to a "freeze" on offensive land-based weapons and start negotiations aimed at an agreement on such offensive weapons. Nixon, who had little interest in the technical details of arms control, nevertheless knew "the SALT thing would be enormously important" to his political prospects.[83]

In early 1971, the Soviets also believed that Nixon might be ready to deal, largely for domestic political reasons. When Senator Edmund Muskie, then the front-runner for the Democratic presidential nomination to oppose Nixon, planned a trip to Moscow in January 1971, Kissinger repeatedly told Dobrynin that President Nixon "hopes that Moscow will not do anything to make these trips a big issue in the purely internal contest within the U.S." Dobrynin suggested to his superiors, "It is important that the incumbent President constantly remain alert (but without excessively annoying him personally) to the fact that we can still play a role in the upcoming 1972 U.S. presidential election campaign, especially if he ignores our interests or directly opposes them."[84] Dobrynin told the politburo how Kissinger remarked at the end of their talks that Nixon "continues to attach a great deal of importance to his meeting with the Soviet leadership."[85]

By May 1971 the Nixon administration's foreign policy looked like it might be turning a corner, and at the center stood Henry Kissinger.[86] The secrecy with which Kissinger operated created a range of bureaucratic nightmares, from the Soviets putting forth conflicting proposals to the American arms control negotiators in Helsinki, to the problem of telling Secretary of State Rogers about the breakthrough on SALT crafted without his knowledge.[87] The key was the political impact of SALT, and the importance of the president receiving the political benefits from it. Gerard Smith, the chief State Department negotiator in Helsinki, believed that "Kissinger was more interested in the major political thrust that this accord would give the negotiation than in its specific provisions."[88] As the SALT announcement neared, Nixon, always reluctant to have personal confrontations, instructed Haldeman to break the news to Rogers. During a week in which the administration had also prevailed in a Senate vote against the Mansfield Amendment to cut U.S. forces in Europe, Nixon told Kissinger in a phone call that Rogers should be pleased to be part of the administration that is now "winning a few." Kissinger reinforced Nixon's feelings by adding that in the "history books," it would not really matter who did what to get the agreement and that the important thing was that the president got the "personal credit."[89]

The announcement of the breakthrough in the SALT talks, that the United States and the Soviets would now strive for an ABM agreement and at the same time begin consideration of limits on offensive weapons, was the featured news item on all three networks, with the CBS commentator Eric Sevareid noting directly how it would improve Nixon's chances for reelection.[90] Nixon called Kissinger the evening of the announcement and praised his negotiations with Dobrynin, telling him he "couldn't have handled it better." Nixon was pleased at the "hell of a television wallop" the announcement got.[91] The establishment newspapers, especially *The New York Times* and *The Washington Post*, could still stir Nixon's anger. He told Kissinger that the *Times* headline "U.S. and Soviet to Stress ABMs" was "a deliberate shaft." Kissinger reassured him that he would speak to the *Times* columnist Max Frankel about it, and then reinforced one of Nixon's deeper prejudices, telling him that although the TV coverage was very good, it was "certainly not as much as Kennedy would've done."[92] In the days after the SALT announcement, Kissinger repeatedly told Nixon that reporters, after his briefings, were now writing how he was "creating a whole new era of American foreign policy, one of the most significant in 20 years."[93] Kissinger added, "In terms of achievements—this sounds self-serving—but who has had a 3-year period like this? If you had said on January 20th that you would get 400,000 troops out of Vietnam in 2 years, open the way to a visit to Peking, a visit to Moscow, a SALT Agreement, you'd have all of that done at the end of your third year—" Nixon interrupted, "That'd be incredible, wouldn't it?" Kissinger added, "They would have said, That's insanity."[94]

Kissinger's position still rested on Nixon's trust in him, and that remained vulnerable. On June 13, 1971, *The New York Times* began printing excerpts from the secret study commissioned by Secretary of Defense Robert McNamara of American involvement in the Vietnam War—what would come to be known as the Pentagon Papers. The *Times* had received the papers from Daniel Ellsberg, a brilliant if erratic defense strategist who had known Kissinger for a number of years and actually worked as a consultant to the NSC for the Vietnam policy review in early 1969. Haldeman later claimed that Nixon's immediate reaction to the release of the papers was "muted," since they had nothing to do with his presidency and were focused on the actions of his predecessors. Haldeman reported Kissinger taunting Nixon, "It shows you're a weakling, Mr. President," and saying that it "could destroy our ability to conduct foreign policy." After Kissinger was done telling Nixon that Ellsberg had "weird sexual habits, used drugs, and enjoyed helicopter flights in which he would take potshots at the Vietnamese below," Nixon was "as angry as his foreign affairs chief."[95]

Haldeman clearly wanted to blame Kissinger for Nixon's reaction to the Pentagon Papers. Kissinger's role is more complicated than Haldeman describes but hardly flattering to Kissinger.[96] In their first discussion of the papers, on June 14, it is Nixon who tells Kissinger that what the *Times* did was "unconscionable," having already been given that interpretation by Al Haig, who told the president that it was a "devastating security breach."[97] Nixon made an analogy between the case and his career-defining role in the Alger Hiss prosecution. Kissinger, as was his tendency in their conversations, quickly agreed with Nixon but also agreed when the president commented that the Pentagon Papers centered on Kennedy and Johnson and showed "massive mismanagement of how we got there." Kissinger told Nixon that the release of the papers would hurt in negotiations with Hanoi because it showed a "further weakening of our resolve." When Nixon called the action "treasonable," Kissinger readily agreed and suggested that he talk to Attorney General Mitchell.[98] Kissinger told Mitchell that the leaks were "an attack on the whole integrity of government ... If whole file cabinets can be stolen and then made available to the press, you can't have orderly government anymore."[99] When Ellsberg's role became clear, Kissinger described Ellsberg as a "genius," the "brightest student" he'd ever had, and someone who was "so nuts that he'd drive around all over Vietnam with a carbine when it was guerrilla-infested ... and he'd shoot at peasants in the fields." Kissinger added that in "late '67, [Ellsberg] suddenly turned into a peacenik," though one moderate enough that "even as late as the transition period," Kissinger confessed, "I talked to him ... because he is so bright." But as Ellsberg adopted a more "intransigent, radical position," Kissinger claimed to have distanced himself from the man, saying that he had not seen him since earlier in the year at an MIT event where Ellsberg had heckled him as a "murderer."[100] Kissinger left out a meeting in 1970 when Ellsberg tried to get Kissinger to read the Pentagon Papers study.[101] In another conversation with Nixon, Kissinger referred to Ellsberg as "the most dangerous man in America today ... who must be stopped at all costs."[102]

Kissinger was selective in what he told Nixon about Ellsberg, and his emphasis on Ellsberg's allegedly unstable personality could only have encouraged the disastrous idea of discrediting Ellsberg through stealing his psychiatric records. As with the wiretaps of 1969, Kissinger's attack on Ellsberg may have served to preempt Nixon's suspicions about his own loyalty. From the beginning of the scandal, Nixon's suspicion focused on "Henry's shop" and his NSC staff.[103] Haldeman told Nixon that the FBI was investigating

Ellsberg. Nixon remarked, "I must say, Henry certainly knows all these people, doesn't he?" Haldeman went on to tell Nixon that there were stories that Kissinger was a frequent visitor to Ellsberg's apartment in Santa Monica. Nixon remarked, "Henry must be torn on the Jewish business. Every one of them is a Jew," although Haldeman quickly added, "Henry doesn't back off of this one at all . . . His argument is that we've got to fight."[104] Nixon's anti-Semitism came to full expression as he complained to Haldeman that "the government is full of Jews" and that "most Jews are disloyal." But Nixon excepted his national security adviser and foreign policy partner. "You have a [White House consultant Leonard] Garment and a Kissinger—and frankly a [speechwriter William] Safire, and by God, they're exceptions. But Bob, generally speaking, you can't trust the bastards. They turn on you."[105] Two days later Nixon remarked again that the fact that Ellsberg was Jewish must "tear a fellow like Henry to pieces," but he still concluded, "Jews are born spies."[106]

Nixon may have believed Kissinger was an exception to his Jewish-conspiracy-filled view of the world, but by this point he was also deeply dependent on him. Kissinger sensed his potential vulnerability to Nixon's prejudices and clearly sought to appease his boss.[107] In public, Kissinger used his sense of humor to deal with the Pentagon Papers. He told *The Washington Post* that to lessen the possibility of unauthorized leaks from the Nixon administration, "all secret documents are being written in German—without any verbs."[108] In the midst of the furor over the Pentagon Papers case, Kissinger threw his "first big Washington party," borrowing the home of the columnist Tom Braden and inviting many Democrats as well as Republicans in what he called the "ecumenical spirit of the Nixon Administration."[109] Kissinger was also soon preoccupied with other issues, flying to Paris to negotiate with Lê Đức Thọ, meeting with Dobrynin to discuss a possible Soviet summit, and preparing for his secret trip to China. When he met with Nixon on July 1 before leaving for Asia, the president pushed Kissinger to be tough with the Chinese, using what Kissinger called the "invariable hard-line rhetoric with which he sent me off on every mission."[110] Kissinger was to stoke Chinese fears about a resurgent Japan, the Soviet army divisions on its border, and the possibility that Nixon would take tougher action on Vietnam. But true to his domestic political concerns, Nixon also reminded Kissinger again to tell the Chinese that "we expected them to institute a severe limit on political visitors" prior to his own visit.[111] While Nixon told Kissinger "not to indicate a willingness to abandon much of our support for Taiwan until it was necessary to do so," he closed their meeting by mentioning again that the six thousand U.S. troops on Taiwan were connected to the war in Vietnam and that "as that issue was solved the requirement for these troops would disappear."[112]

Kissinger's stature in Washington was now prominent enough that the American news media covered his Asian trip, and the false report of his stomachache in Pakistan merited attention on *CBS Evening News*.[113] Pakistan's leader, Yahya Khan, enjoyed playing the role of intermediary between the United States and China, arranging the report of Kissinger's illness and then arranging for Kissinger to leave for his secret trip to Beijing from Islamabad. Kissinger's meeting with the Chinese began awkwardly, with Zhou offering cigarettes to the nonsmoking Americans, and Kissinger apologizing for reading a prepared statement. He again explained the reasons for secrecy, this time emphasizing that the president wanted it so they could "meet unencumbered by bureaucracy, free of the past, and with the greatest possible latitude."[114] By the end of the two-day visit, however, Kissinger described the talks in enthusiastic terms to Nixon as "the most searching, sweeping and significant discussions I have ever had in government." For a man who prided himself on being "cold-blooded" and realistic in his understanding of international politics and foreign personalities, Kissinger wrote of the visit as "a very moving experience," which left an "indelible impression on me and my colleagues." The discussions with Zhou "had all the flavor, texture, variety and delicacy of a Chinese banquet." He assured Nixon that he and Zhou "have laid the groundwork for you and Mao to turn a page in history," and that if the United States could handle its dealings with the Chinese with "reliability, precision, and finesse, . . . we will have made a revolution."[115]

Kissinger's reaction to his Chinese encounter was uncharacteristically enthusiastic and extravagant.[116] He believed that the opening to China would deeply engage Americans, showing that despite Vietnam and the decline in its relative power, the United States could still play a decisive and creative role in diplomacy. The sheer mystique of Chinese civilization, with its thousands of years of history and sense of cultural superiority, obviously affected Kissinger. Shortly after the trip became public knowledge, Arthur Schlesinger found Kissinger still "enchanted" with the Chinese, whom he found "less doctrinaire" and "more idealistic" than the Russians, and possessed of an "elegance of manners." Although he could never understand a young militant dedicating himself to the "dreary and sterile" Soviet Union, Kissinger told Schlesinger, "I could fully understand it if someone decided to dedicate himself to Communist China."[117] Kissinger was also taken with the elegant Zhou, whom he would later say was one of the most impressive public figures he had ever met.

The transcripts of the talks between Zhou and Kissinger do not fully capture Kissinger's enthusiasm. From the very beginning of their conversations, Kissinger sought to erase any stigma of John Foster Dulles's famous refusal to shake hands with Zhou at the Geneva Conference in 1954, stressing that the talks were taking place now in a complete "basis of equality and mutual respect." Kissinger went even further, explaining to the Chinese that Dulles "believed that it was America's mission to fight communism all around the world and for the U.S. to be the principal force to engage itself in every struggle at every point in the world at any point in time." Kissinger emphasized, "President Nixon operates on a different philosophy." In explaining the Nixon Doctrine, Kissinger put America's concessions dramatically before the Chinese. Acknowledging Zhou's point that had the Korean War not come along, Taiwan would probably have fallen under Beijing's control back in 1950, Kissinger said that the United States planned to reduce its commitment to Taiwan. "As a student of history," he expected a "political evolution" in the direction of reunification with China. On Vietnam, he emphasized, "We are realists" and "we know that after a peace is made we will be 10,000 miles away, and they will still be here." He told Zhou, "We want to base our foreign policy on the realities of the present and not on the dreams of the past."[118]

Along with his frankness about America's need to reduce its military commitments in Asia went Kissinger's attempt to convince the Chinese of the importance of a continuing American presence. He assured Zhou that the United States would not collude with any third power against China and made disparaging comments about the Soviet Union's style of negotiating, which elicited knowing grins from Zhou. America's role in policing Japan's power remained important, and Kissinger implied that without the United States, Japan might become threatening toward China. He donned the role of a professor to describe how the United States had found itself engaged all over the world in the aftermath of World War II, espousing both a military doctrine of containment and a social welfare doctrine of development. But he also made a starkly political argument that would later become a cliché of American politics: "President Nixon, precisely because his political support comes from the center and right of center, cannot be attacked from that direction, and won't be attacked by the left in a policy of moving toward friendship with the People's Republic of China." He then begged Zhou not to tell a visiting American reporter what he said; otherwise, Kissinger joked, "I will have to ask for a job as an adviser in your Ministry of Foreign Affairs," a comment that the transcript noted elicited "considerable laughter from the Chinese." The Chinese even agreed to a Thursday, July 15, simultaneous evening announcement to allow the Americans to get the most publicity from the weekly news magazines like *Time* and *Newsweek*. Kissinger reminded the Chinese of Nixon's request that they not invite other American politicians, and he taught the Chinese an American expression by asking them to prevent the issue from becoming a "political football."[119]

Kissinger returned to the United States on July 13, and he and Nixon went about the task of informing the rest of the government, including the secretary of state. The secret was so well handled that when Nixon asked for television time from the networks for the evening of July 15, the reporters speculated that his speech would have something to do with a breakthrough in the Vietnam peace talks.[120] Instead, Nixon announced that he would visit China to "seek a new relationship with the People's Republic of China," but "not at the expense of our old friends." In a line directed at the Soviet Union, he added, "[Our action] is not directed against any other nation." Nixon also came back to the central theme he wanted to reinforce on every occasion, his role as a peacemaker: "I will undertake what I deeply hope will become a journey for peace, peace not just for our generation but for future generations on this earth we share together."[121] Nixon's announcement received an overwhelmingly favorable reception from the media. Commentators fell over themselves seeking historical analogies, with Howard K. Smith of ABC calling it "the most dramatic development in international affairs since the Hitler-Stalin pact," and others calling it "stunning," "unbelievable," and "incredible." Nixon's own news summary reported, "There has not been a Presidential action which has brought such wide comment and speculation," most of which was favorable.[122] Senator Mansfield commented, "I am astounded, delighted, and happy," and even George McGovern said, "I applaud the president's imagination and judgment."[123] Negative comments came from conservatives like Barry Goldwater and William Buckley, but the overwhelming national and international approval heartened Nixon, and as Haldeman noted, the president asked him to conduct a poll.[124] One showed the public approved of his trip by a 68 to 19 percent margin.[125] Other polls had Nixon leaping ahead of Muskie for the first time in over a year, a clear indication that the good news in foreign policy was translating into political support.[126]

In the midst of celebration over the China trip, Kissinger's mentor, Fritz Kraemer, sent Kissinger a cautionary and gloomy memo, which Kissinger felt compelled to send along to Nixon. Kraemer warned that in the euphoria over the Americans' "playing with China," what was lost was the continuing advance of Soviet power and America's retreat. Running down a list beginning with "S. Vietnam and Thailand, as well as in Korea, the Ryukyus, and Japan" (the United States signed a treaty with Japan in June 1971 returning Okinawa to Japanese rule), Kraemer painted a picture of worldwide withdrawal and American weakness. Kraemer believed that Soviet leaders would see the American opening to China not as part of a game of triangular diplomacy but as a "symptom of our overwhelming desire to seek reconciliation and disengagement anyway and everywhere."[127] Nixon scrawled at the bottom of Kraemer's memo, "K—this memo brilliantly points up the dangers of our move—e.g. Mansfield et al. applaud it for the *wrong* reasons. Our task is to play a hard game with the Soviets and to see that wherever possible—including Non Communist Asia—our friends are reassured."[128] Nixon even called a sleepy Kissinger at midnight to discuss the memo, remarking that "he really paints a gloomy picture, doesn't he?" Kissinger acknowledged Kraemer's tendency "to go a little bit in the apocalyptic direction," but he told Nixon, "There's something in what he says if we don't play it carefully." Nixon defended the move toward China in electoral terms, explaining, "If we hadn't done something and we'd been tossed out, everything would have come apart at the seams, and all we're doing is to frankly buy some time and to turn around if we can still turn around." Nixon kept coming back to the powerful domestic political impact of the China opening: "The way this thing has shocked . . . particularly our usual critics . . . the left—the liberals, the peacenik types—they are just up a wall. They don't know what to do with this . . . The mood really in the country has significantly changed."[129]

When he spoke of the "mood" in the country, Nixon was referring to the political mood, but what had also changed dramatically was the standing of his national security adviser. Before the China trip, Kissinger had cultivated the Washington media successfully. Now his return from Beijing "catapulted" him to national fame and a role as America's celebrity diplomat.[130] In addition to appearing on both *Time*'s and *Newsweek*'s covers, major newspapers and magazines competed with one another to do profiles on the man. *The New York Times* headlined its profile "The Inscrutable Occidental," remarking that Kissinger "manages the development of Presidential diplomacy while creating the illusion that he is a full-time permanent floating cocktail party guest of honor. That takes dazzling intellect, fancy footwork, beguiling aplomb, and, it sometimes seems, mirrors."[131] The extravagant praise annoyed Nixon, but his response was characteristically schizophrenic: on the one hand he tried to stop Kissinger from talking to the press on backgrounders, while on the other he gave his adviser ideas on how to promote Nixon's own role, such as comparing Nixon's career and manner with Zhou Enlai's. Kissinger did so in an interview with the *Time* correspondent Hugh Sidey, but even as he praised Nixon, Kissinger's star ascended. *Time* reported, "At the height of a brilliant career, he enjoys a global spotlight and an influence that most professors only read about in libraries."[132]

But Kissinger's celebrity appeal now went well beyond the political world. The proximity of Nixon's "Western White House" at San Clemente to Hollywood meant that Kissinger also had the time to throw "himself into the Hollywood social scene with an enthusiasm he had previously shown only for backchannel negotiations."[133] Kissinger now appeared frequently with Hollywood celebrities and was a sought-after guest for film premieres and other events. He developed a range of fast friendships with the actors Kirk Douglas and Gregory Peck, the producer Robert Evans, and the former Kennedy friend and leader of the Rat Pack Frank Sinatra. Even Kissinger taking his children to meet teen heartthrob Bobby Sherman made it into the national press.[134] The media's fascination with Kissinger contributed further to his power and influence within the Nixon administration. Kissinger's relationship with the media, however, was a double-edged sword, and he soon discovered its dangers.

KISSINGER STUMBLES: THE INDIA-PAKISTAN WAR AND THE RADFORD AFFAIR

In the aftermath of the China opening, Nixon's foreign policy dominated the headlines. On August 15, 1971, Nixon stunned both the country and the world again by cutting the link between the dollar and the price of gold, imposing across-the-board tariffs on imports, and adopting domestic wage and price controls, a heresy for most Republicans. Kissinger had little direct involvement with these decisions, but on returning from a Paris negotiating session with the Vietnamese, he made sure to call Nixon to say, "Congratulations, you scored another coup."[135] By the end of the month, using his back channel with Dobrynin, Kissinger finished the Berlin Agreement, providing guaranteed Western access to the divided city. He also finalized the scheduling for a summit meeting with the Soviets, whose shock at the China trip led them to be more agreeable to American demands.[136] The administration did suffer a defeat in the United Nations at the end of that month, when its effort to appease Taiwan and its conservative American backers by promoting a two-China policy, seating both the People's Republic and Taiwan in the General Assembly, was rejected by that body. Taiwan was then expelled, a defeat that Nixon deeply resented and for which Kissinger was partially responsible. The American position was fatally weakened by the timing of Kissinger's second—this time public—visit to China, just before the UN vote. That trip, designed to make the arrangements for Nixon's journey, was covered extensively in the international and domestic media, with *NBC Nightly News* noting that Kissinger's arrival received a special announcement on Chinese radio.[137] Kissinger brushed off the criticism of his visit by some, including the U.S. ambassador to the United Nations, George H. W. Bush, who thought that this "two State Departments thing" was not a very effective way to run foreign policy.[138] (Bush would long remember Kissinger's role in this fiasco.) Kissinger was now playing an increasingly prominent public role in the administration's political battles. References to him on the evening news multiplied, and though he was rarely recorded speaking, he was now extensively cited, photographed, and filmed. Only three days after he returned from China, Kissinger received the credit for single-handedly lobbying enough senators to defeat the Cooper-Church Amendment, with its legislative deadline for troop withdrawals from Vietnam. Kissinger was "everywhere," NBC reported, and he turned a potential administration defeat into a victory.[139]

The avalanche of favorable publicity Kissinger received after his China trip and its importance to his position in the Nixon administration are essential background to Kissinger's behavior and reactions during the India-Pakistan War and its aftermath. In November 1971 *The New York Times Magazine* rolled out an eleven-page glossy profile of Kissinger titled "The Road to Peking, or How Does This Kissinger Do It?" Along with other accolades, including a description of Kissinger as the "second most powerful man in the world," the article quoted Dan Rather describing Kissinger as "the best briefer in Washington," adding that Kissinger "has the reputation that he never lies." Another reporter praised Kissinger as one of the few officials who "will always tell you if something is secret and that he can't talk about it. He'll never just out and out lie like other bureaucrats might." Kissinger was quoted telling the *Times* that he "was always available to talk to the press," and that he knew this was one of the reasons he had "been treated so well." He added, "I have no competitors for that job among my colleagues in this Administration."[140] This extraordinary praise, along with Kissinger's boasting of his status with the media, would seem ludicrous only a few weeks later as war in South Asia and a spying scandal damaged Kissinger's rapport with the media and relationship with Nixon so seriously that he considered resigning and Nixon considered firing him—after suggesting that Kissinger needed psychological help.[141]

The South Asia crisis developed over the course of 1971. It began with the attempt of the Pakistani government of Yahya Khan to put down a separatist rebellion led by Sheikh Mujibur (Mujib) Rahman, the leader of the Awami League, in the Bengali-dominated East Pakistan. Rather than allow autonomy, on March 25, 1971, Yahya ordered Mujib's arrest and the violent suppression of his movement. The Pakistani army swept into East Pakistan with tremendous brutality and violence, shooting, bombing, and burning thousands of people to death. The Pakistani army's terror precipitated a massive refugee movement into India's province of West Bengal, threatening its political stability and imposing huge costs. Archer Blood, the U.S. consul general in Dacca, reported these atrocities to Washington in horrific detail. Met with a Washington response that Blood described as a "deafening silence," he and his fellow diplomats vigorously protested what they perceived as a policy of "moral bankruptcy" in its failure to denounce the atrocities or intervene against "genocide."[142] The "Blood telegram" was widely circulated and increased demands for a stronger American policy against Pakistan.[143]

Nixon resisted this pressure, and Kissinger played the role of his dutiful deputy. Because of his sympathy for Pakistan's position as a U.S. ally, as well as its crucial role in the China initiative, Nixon opposed any American involvement, characteristically observing to Kissinger, "The people who bitch about Vietnam bitch about it because we intervened in what they say is a civil war . . . Now some of the same bastards . . . want us to intervene here—both civil wars."[144] Although Nixon approved a Kissinger policy paper that the

United States would "make a serious effort to help Yahya end the war and establish an arrangement that could be transitional to East Pakistani autonomy," his sympathy for Pakistan, as well as the timing of the China move, strongly influenced the American approach. Nixon added to the memo in his own handwriting, "Don't squeeze Yahya at this time."[145] In May 1971 India began massing troops along its border with East Pakistan, and Prime Minister Indira Gandhi was pushing her generals to take action. Kissinger told her that the Nixon administration was "strongly opposed to military action." Nixon told Kissinger that if India intervened, "by God we will cut off economic aid." Kissinger responded with a clear reference to the China opening "that it is the last thing we can afford now to have the Pakistani government overthrown, given the other things we are doing." Playing to Nixon's prejudices, Kissinger called the Indians "the most aggressive goddamn people around there," while Nixon callously added that what India deserved was a "mass famine." Both men agreed that India had no right to invade "no matter what Pakistan does in its territory," although Kissinger added inaccurately, and without a trace of irony, "Besides the killing has stopped."[146]

The Pakistani atrocities elicited outrage, and the plight of the Bengali refugees stirred up humanitarian concerns in the United States.[147] The former Beatle George Harrison put on the first huge rock star benefit, the Concert for Bangladesh, which Nixon lambasted to Kissinger as another "screwball cause" of soft-hearted Americans.[148] The involvement of his political rival Senator Edward Kennedy, who visited the refugee camps and criticized the administration's policy, only intensified Nixon's anger. Nixon conceded, as he told the NSC in July 1971, that "world opinion is on the side of the Indians," but he added that they were "a slippery, treacherous people."[149] Whatever doubts Kissinger might have personally held about American policy—and he recognized Yahya's limitations as a leader—he remained loyal to Nixon's preferences, telling the U.S. ambassador to India, Kenneth Keating, that Nixon wanted to give Yahya a few months to fix the situation, but that they understood that East Pakistan would eventually become independent. Kissinger added, "The President has a special feeling for President Yahya. One cannot make policy on that basis, but it is a fact of life."[150]

Kissinger tried to head off the outbreak of war and made that his recurring message to both the Indians and the Soviets. He feared that war "could blow up everything," by which he meant the American summits with China and Russia, and by implication the domestic and foreign policy benefits that would flow to Nixon.[151] After the Chinese leader Zhou Enlai spoke against the Indian and Soviet position on Bangladesh during his secret trip, Kissinger's worries about the impact of a war only increased.[152] In August 1971 India signed a "Friendship Treaty" with the Soviet Union, the effect of which, Kissinger wrote, was like "throwing a lighted match into a powder keg." It led Kissinger to redouble his own efforts to prevent a conflict; he told the Indian ambassador that a "war between India and Pakistan would set back Indian-American relations for half a decade."[153] Nixon and Kissinger hoped that with U.S.-Soviet relations improving and a summit in sight, the Soviets would have a "shared interest" with the United States in averting a war in South Asia. At the same time, they also suspected that the Soviets might be behaving with India the same way they were with North Vietnam, saying one thing but doing another. In early October, Kissinger told Dobrynin that the president "attached the most urgent importance to the prevention of an India-Pakistan war and was hoping that the Soviet Union would act in the same way." Dobrynin reassured him but counseled that the "Indians were getting extremely difficult."[154]

Nixon and Kissinger better understood Dobrynin's statement when Gandhi visited Washington in early November. Nixon warned the prime minister against any military action and stressed that "the American people would not understand if India were to initiate military action against Pakistan." Gandhi, who had already decided to act, told Nixon that it was no longer realistic to expect West and East Pakistan to remain together and emphasized the importance of Mujib's role as the "symbol of the imperative for autonomy." She refused to engage Nixon on the possibility of any withdrawal of Indian forces from the border. Nixon promised that the United States would continue to "assist with humanitarian relief efforts," but he stressed again toward the end of their conversation that "the initiation of hostilities by India would be almost impossible to understand."[155] The next day

Nixon and Kissinger engaged in sexist bravado, calling Gandhi a "bitch" and referring to the Indians as "bastards." The two men believed that they had successfully "slobbered over the old witch."[156] Kissinger assured the president that Gandhi would "not be able to go home and say that the United States didn't give her a warm reception and therefore, in despair, she's got to go to war." But they also recognized that Gandhi had refused to respond to the concessions they had offered on Yahya's behalf and that the likelihood of war remained.[157] They continued to hope the Soviet Union might play a key role in restraining India.[158]

South Asia was not a matter of great national concern for most Americans, and few believed that the United States had significant national interests in the region. Nevertheless, the crisis drew the attention of the American media, and a substantial pro-India sentiment existed among elites. In late November 1971, the outbreak of war threw the Nixon administration into crisis mode. Gandhi sent significant Indian military forces, along with the guerrilla force she had helped organize, the Mukti Bahini, into East Pakistan.[159] In response, Pakistan decided on an air attack on India on December 4, allowing India to portray the war as a response to Pakistani aggression. It was a lopsided contest from the beginning. The Pakistani government was, as one of their top diplomats put it, "totally unprepared for war," and the "whole situation had an air of unreality about it."[160] The Pakistani army in the East was quickly surrounded, and its defeat by India's regular army and the Mukti Bahini guerrillas was only a matter of time. Nixon conceded, "Looking at the balance there, the Indians are going to win." The president wanted to "tilt" policy toward Pakistan and in support of Yahya, but he emphasized, "I don't want to get caught in the business where we take the heat for a miserable war that we had nothing to do with."[161]

Kissinger again assumed leadership of the Washington Special Action Group, reprising the role he had played in the Jordanian crisis a year earlier. The bureaucracy was more sharply divided than ever, with both State Department and Defense Department representatives expressing caution and uncertainty about the American response. Kissinger, however, was determined to be the president's man in the deliberations. Although formally the

United States announced it was following a neutral policy toward the conflict, Kissinger told the WSAG early on that he was "catching unshirted hell every half-hour from the President who says we're not tough enough" and wanted a "tilt toward Pakistan."[162] Nixon wanted to examine every "possibility of how we can squeeze India."[163] Facing considerable resistance from the State Department, Kissinger still proved enthusiastic in searching for ways to please Nixon's strong anti-India sentiments. He was willing to operate at what some have called the "edge of legality" by encouraging countries like Iran and Jordan to send American military equipment and aid to Pakistan, and he pushed hard in the United Nations for resolutions demanding a ceasefire and the withdrawal of forces.[164]

Why was Kissinger so determined to do everything possible to help Pakistan? Underlying Kissinger's approach, along with demonstrating his loyalty to Nixon, was the overwhelming desire to reassure China. Kissinger put it in graphic language in a phone call to Treasury Secretary John Connally: "The thing that concerns the President and me is this: here we have Indian-Soviet collusion, raping a friend of ours. Secondly, we have a situation where one of the motives that the Chinese may have had in leaning towards us a little bit is the fear that something like this might happen to them."[165] Nixon and Kissinger believed that the crisis would be perceived by the Chinese as a test of whether the United States could offer effective support in the event of a Soviet threat to China. They convinced themselves that China would see any American weakness toward India, a Soviet ally, as a sign that stronger ties with the United States were worthless. This was not an irrational belief—China had long-standing ties to Pakistan and had expressed a very public anti-Indian and anti-Soviet stance. The political turmoil in China—Mao's designated heir, Lin Biao, had been killed in September attempting to escape after supposedly trying to overthrow the regime—also contributed to Nixon's and Kissinger's sense of the fragility of their new relationship with the Chinese. China had helped turn around Nixon's domestic political fortunes as well as contributed to the perception of Kissinger's foreign policy genius. Nevertheless, Nixon's and Kissinger's belief that supporting Pakistan was essential to China was only an assumption, resting on the hubris of the two men who thought they understood Chinese national interests better than the Chinese themselves.

Nixon and Kissinger attempted to convince the Soviet Union to restrain its ally India. In Dobrynin's absence, Kissinger called in the Soviet chargé d'affaires, Yuri Vorontsov, and told him that the president "did not understand how the Soviet Union could believe that it was possible to work on the broad amelioration of our relationships while at the same time encouraging the Indian military aggression against Pakistan." The president, Kissinger emphasized repeatedly, viewed the crisis in South Asia as a "watershed" in relations between the two superpowers.[166] The Soviets, however, coolly dismissed Nixon's concept of a "watershed" and appealed for a "business-like search for realistic solutions." Ironically, the Soviets then attacked Pakistan's repression and defended self-determination, in this case the idea of "a political settlement in East Pakistan on the basis of respect for the will of the population."[167] This ideological confusion—the Soviets supporting Indian democracy while the United States backed a Pakistani dictatorship—was not lost in the American media's portrayal of the war, rendering the position of Nixon and Kissinger even more tenuous. The cheering crowds of Bengalis greeting Indian soldiers on the American evening news made the Soviet argument all the more compelling.[168]

As the "best briefer in Washington," Kissinger sought to use his skill with the press to make the administration's case in a long backgrounder he held on December 7. Before he met the press, he had complained to Haldeman again about the State Department and Secretary Rogers's lack of support in the crisis, threatening again to resign. His threat lost some of its power when Kissinger added that he still wanted to go to China with the president. Haldeman told him that would not be possible, and that if he resigned, he would be out immediately.[169] Kissinger went ahead with his briefing and said that the claim that the administration was anti-India was "totally inaccurate." He argued that the administration had sought to encourage a peaceful settlement of the East Pakistan issue, describing American efforts to deal with the refugee issue. He concluded his prepared statement by maintaining that the administration was deeply disappointed when India resorted to an armed invasion to settle the issue. Kissinger's problems began when he started answering questions. He implied that relations with China were not a factor in the American position by arguing that the administration came to its position "independently" of the Chinese. He stated baldly that he was "not aware of the President's preference for Pakistan leaders over Indian leaders," dismissing the idea that "personal pique" had played any role in shaping policy.[170] Kissinger called Nixon after the briefing to tell him how effective he had been.[171] Kissinger added that he had canceled a "reconciliation" dinner in his honor at Harvard after an argument with John Kenneth Galbraith, who was a former ambassador to India and one of the organizers. "India-lovers are a breed apart," Nixon lamented, and Kissinger assured him, "No one likes the Indians." That evening the United Nations General Assembly had voted overwhelmingly in favor of a cease-fire and withdrawal-of-forces resolution. Nixon was very pleased, and he repeatedly emphasized to Kissinger the need to go on the attack against India.[172]

The next day the administration's perception of the dangers within the crisis intensified. Fueled by an unverified and raw intelligence report coming from a source inside Gandhi's cabinet, Kissinger told a WSAG meeting that India intended to occupy Azad Kashmir, a southern part of that disputed territory, and to smash Pakistan's air and tank forces.[173] Reminding them of Gandhi's comments during her meeting with the president a month earlier, Kissinger went on to assert that India planned to detach Baluchistan from West Pakistan and turn the country into a "vassal state." Later in the day Kissinger told Nixon that if India succeeded in its war goals, they "would have been achieved by Soviet support, Soviet arms, and Indian military force," and would have a serious effect on countries looking to the United States for support. In particular China might conclude that the United States was "just too weak" to have prevented this humiliation and would turn elsewhere for an ally.[174] Nixon decided to send an American carrier task force to the Bay of Bengal, under the cover of evacuating American citizens but designed to be a show of strength to the Indians. After the meeting ended, Nixon called Kissinger and told him, "Maybe we have to put it to the Russians and say that we feel under the circumstances we have to cancel the summit."[175]

At this point a decidedly surreal aspect entered the Nixon-Kissinger conversations. Both men wanted to come off as tough and masculine, and they exaggerated the stakes of their decisions wholly out of proportion to the actual situation developing on the ground in South Asia. On that battlefield, the war was coming to a speedy end, with Indian soldiers and their guerrilla allies making rapid progress. Nixon recognized this, at one point remarking to Kissinger, "You see those people welcoming the Indian troops when they come in . . . why . . . Henry, are we going through all this agony?"[176] Kissinger answered, "We're going through this agony to prevent the West Pakistan army from being destroyed. Secondly, to maintain our Chinese arm. Thirdly, to prevent a complete collapse of the world's psychological balance of power, which will be produced if a combination of the Soviet Union and the Soviet armed client state can tackle a not so insignificant country without anybody doing anything."[177] Whether Nixon needed Kissinger's reassurance that they were on the right path is not completely clear. Nixon probably recognized the political effect of the images coming out of East Pakistan with more clarity than his national security adviser, while Kissinger trusted the questionable intelligence that India wanted to destroy all of Pakistan. Nevertheless, Nixon still took a hard line later that day, telling a Soviet official, "If India moves forces against West Pakistan, the United States cannot stand by," and Brezhnev must "recognize the urgency of a cease-fire and political settlement of the crisis."[178]

The next day Kissinger traveled to New York to tell the new Chinese ambassador to the United Nations, Huang Hua, that the United States would support China if the country decided to move against India. Kissinger used the conversation to offer satellite intelligence on the disposition of Soviet forces and to argue, "Both of us must continue to bring pressure on India and the Soviet Union." Two days later, when the Chinese requested another meeting, Kissinger was certain they had decided to act. He told Nixon, "If the Soviets move against them and then we don't do anything, we'll be finished." Nixon responded, "So what do we do if the Soviets move against them? Start lobbing nuclear weapons in, is that what you mean?" The two men went back and forth with apocalyptic scenarios, until Kissinger concluded that a successful move by the Soviets against China "will be a change in the world balance of power of such magnitude . . . that the security of the United States for, maybe forever, certainly for decades—we will have a ghastly war in the Middle East." Not to be outdone, Nixon added, "Now we really get into the numbers game. You've got the Soviet Union with 800 million Chinese, 600 million Indians, the balance of Southeast Asia terrorized, the Japanese immobile, the Europeans, of course will suck after them, and the United States the only one, we have maybe parts of Latin America and who knows."[179]

This bizarre exchange has been called "one of the eeriest of the Nixon Presidency—and perhaps of the whole Cold War."[180] The two men eventually calmed down, recognizing, as Nixon concluded, that "Russia and China aren't going to go to war," with Kissinger adding, "We don't have to lob nuclear weapons." Less than an hour after discussing these Armageddon-like scenarios, Kissinger came back to the Oval Office to tell Nixon they had just received word from the Russians assuring them that India had no plans to attack West Pakistan.[181] Kissinger now told Nixon that he believed they had "broken the back of" the crisis and flattered Nixon that the president's strong measures had led the Soviets and Indians to back down.[182] The two went ahead with their plan to draft another message to Brezhnev urging an immediate cease-fire and send it via the Washington–Moscow hotline. Then they left for the Azores and a meeting with the French leader, Georges Pompidou, to discuss new international monetary arrangements. The Chinese request for a meeting had not been to signal any military action but only to tell the Americans they would now support the United Nations resolution for a standstill cease-fire. The crisis was almost over, and the surrender of Pakistani forces in East Pakistan was only a matter of days away, perhaps even hours.

Kissinger continued to try to manage the American response from the Azores, but his emotional behavior on the trip, especially his open resentment toward Rogers and shouting at Haig on the phone, got Nixon's attention. The president told Haldeman that he planned to talk with Kissinger because "he didn't want to have to keep putting up with that." Now that the actual danger was gone, and to curry favor with Nixon, Kissinger told reporters on the flight back from the Azores that if the Soviet Union did not restrain

India further, the president might cancel his summit meeting in Moscow. CBS News played up Kissinger's statement, with Marvin Kalb discussing it as an "extraordinary warning" that demonstrated that the mood in U.S.-Soviet relations was worsening.[183] Nixon, however, decided quickly to pull the rug out from under Kissinger and have his press secretary, Ron Ziegler, disavow the threat while at the same time *The Washington Post* named Kissinger as the source.[184] Partly to justify his action, Kissinger told Haldeman that since he fully expected the Russians to bring the Indians along, the president would "get the credit for it" since it would seem like it was in response to his threat.[185] Nixon did not seem to be all that unhappy with what Kissinger did, since the next day the Indians declared a cease-fire and hostilities ended.[186]

As the cease-fire news reached Washington, Kissinger called Nixon to assure him, "We have come out of this amazingly well and we scared the pants off the Russians." Nixon wanted Kissinger to do another press backgrounder and tell them, "If we hadn't used our influence as strongly as possible, it never would have come out the way it did."[187] Nixon and Kissinger wanted to make the claim that they "saved" West Pakistan from destruction, convincing the Soviets to restrain India at its moment of victory. This was, however, thin gruel for a foreign policy success. Whatever satisfaction the two men shared with this achievement was tempered by the newspaper and television coverage of the Pakistani surrender. The Nixon administration had backed the discredited loser in the conflict, and U.S. policy appeared not only ineffective but incompetent and, even worse, immoral. Television reporters showed cheering Bengalis treating Indian forces as liberators, and the CBS correspondent Bert Quint described Pakistani forces as an "occupying force" in East Pakistan that "never had a chance" to prevail.[188] In frustration and perhaps psychological denial, Kissinger complained bitterly to Haldeman that Rogers was behind the criticism that the State Department was leaking stories about White House "blundering" and seeking revenge against him for not following their pro-India sentiments.

In addition to the negative press the administration was receiving about its South Asia policy, Kissinger faced another problem. On December 14, the Washington newspaper columnist Jack Anderson headlined his "Washington

Merry-Go-Round" column "U.S., Soviet Vessels in Bay of Bengal," with direct excerpts from the WSAG meetings that Kissinger had chaired. Anderson's column revealed the infamous "tilt" toward Pakistan that Kissinger denied, undermining his credibility with the Washington press corps. When *ABC Evening News* reported Anderson's allegations, its correspondent, Tom Jarriel, remarked that there had been "hardly a more believable source" in the White House than Kissinger, but that the administration now seemed "more determined to find the source of the leak than to defend Kissinger's credibility."[189] The Nixon administration's "plumbers" quickly determined that the leak came from Kissinger's National Security Council. Charles Radford, the Navy stenographer assigned to the NSC, had been passing thousands of documents to his superiors, who were then giving them to Admiral Thomas Moorer, the chairman of the Joint Chiefs of Staff. Radford himself disliked the policy tilt toward Pakistan and sympathized with India's position in the conflict. Moorer and the Joint Chiefs of Staff were less concerned with the policy's direction and more with the process, especially the surprise they had already faced with China. The secrecy with which Nixon and Kissinger had formulated their foreign policy had come back to haunt them. The Pentagon was spying on the president and his national security adviser.[190]

Already feeling that he had been made the scapegoat for the failed policy with India, Kissinger saw the Radford affair as another example of a conspiracy against him. At first he refused to believe Ehrlichman and Haldeman when they told him. He did not accept this until he listened to the tape of Radford's superior officer, Admiral Robert Welander, discussing the spying. He reacted angrily when he learned that Nixon intended to cover up the whole affair and reappoint Moorer as Joint Chiefs of Staff chairman. To Kissinger, it was in line with Nixon's other actions, especially his tolerance of Rogers and the State Department defying his policy. Kissinger told Ehrlichman, "If he won't fire Rogers—impose some discipline in this Administration—there is no reason to believe he'll fire Moorer. I assure you all this tolerance will lead to very serious consequences for this Administration."[191] The next day, Christmas Eve, a despondent Kissinger stopped by the Oval Office to deliver the same message to Nixon, who was meeting with

Ehrlichman. Nixon explained to Kissinger that if he fired Moorer, "the shit's going to hit the fan." Rationalizing his decision to keep Moorer and defend the military, Nixon added, "You need to protect . . . the only hard line institution in the damn government." After Kissinger left the meeting, Nixon and Ehrlichman discussed Kissinger's reaction to the negative press coverage he received over the India-Pakistan War. Nixon suggested that Kissinger should ignore his press critics. He lamented, "Henry thinks the whole world thinks that he's failed, and that we've failed, and so forth. That's bullshit." More important, Nixon said, the American people just did not care about South Asia. Ehrlichman speculated that Kissinger was "interested in what Marquis Childs writes, and what Joe Kraft writes, and what [James] Reston thinks" because these reporters were "Henry's world. Those are the people because he has no family, no personal life, so that's his cosmos." And Ehrlichman suggested to Nixon they should "get him some psychotherapy."[192]

Kissinger later wrote that in the wake of the India-Pakistan War, "The policy became *my* policy. For several weeks Nixon was unavailable to me. Ziegler made no statement of support, nor did he deny that I was out of favor . . . I did not take kindly—or even maturely to my first experience of sustained public criticism and presidential pressures."[193] Kissinger exaggerated how long he was out of contact with Nixon. Their lack of phone contact during this period, the Christmas holidays, was less than a week. However, for the first time Kissinger was subject to harsh media criticism, with Bernard and Marvin Kalb writing that it was "a personal disaster. His image as candid articulator of U.S. policy was badly tarnished."[194] When Kissinger collaborated with the columnist Joseph Alsop for a defense of his role in the crisis, having Alsop refer to him as a "positive authority," Harry Reasoner, one of the anchors of *ABC Evening News*, sarcastically referred to the term as meaning "someone pretty damned important." Reasoner went on to deliver a blistering editorial accusing Kissinger of speaking in "the discredited argot of geopolitics" as well as sounding like Dr. Strangelove in his discussions of the crisis. Responding to Kissinger's defense that the Anderson stories had been taken out of context, Reasoner remarked that Kissinger's unaccountable and secretive position in the government meant that "his whole role is out of context."[195]

Such commentaries stung, and Kissinger continued to complain bitterly to Haldeman that the president had lost confidence in him and that perhaps he should resign. On January 10, hearing that Defense Secretary Laird, his rival, had convinced the president to announce a higher number for troop withdrawals from Vietnam, Kissinger bitterly commented to Haldeman, "As usual we're following our policy of rewarding traitors." Kissinger went on to tell the chief of staff, "The latest thing today, now, is that there are rumors all around that he [Kissinger] is resigning, and he said the real question that they ask is why is a Presidential assistant under attack with no word of support from his boss?"[196]

Kissinger's behavior continued to worry Nixon, and he and his aides pondered what to do about the "Henry problem." Nixon considered getting rid of his national security adviser, telling Haldeman, "We've got to bite the bullet now and get him out," since Kissinger would otherwise be in a strong position during the campaign, and "We've got to remember that he did leak things to us in '68 and we've got to assume he's capable of doing the same thing to our opponents in '72." Yet as remarkable as this statement is—that Nixon feared his closest adviser on foreign affairs would betray him—Nixon also recognized Kissinger's extraordinary value. He told Haldeman that Kissinger was indispensable to the success of his China trip and much more important to him on foreign policy than Secretary of State William P. Rogers.[197]

Ironically, it would actually be Jack Anderson's columns that contributed to Kissinger's quick rebound in public standing. With the presidential election now only ten months away, Nixon was concerned by polls that showed him tied or with only a narrow lead over his Democratic opponents. His diplomatic achievements had led *Time* to name him "Man of the Year" and pronounce his leadership "refreshingly flexible and disconcertingly unpredictable."[198] However, Vietnam still hung like an albatross on his political prospects, with some opponents, like Senator George McGovern, calling Nixon a liar for saying that he had offered an American withdrawal in return for the release of the prisoners.[199] President Thiệu's unopposed "reelection" in September was another embarrassment to the administration, and it drained away what little sympathy still existed for defending the South Vietnamese from the communists. Even Kissinger acknowledged to Nixon that "no one gives a damn" about Thiệu.[200] Nixon feared that the Anderson papers might contain hints of Kissinger's secret talks and the offers he had made to the North Vietnamese in Paris. To gain the domestic political impact he wanted, Nixon sought once again to surprise the nation, and he feared Anderson might beat him to the punch and reveal the secret talks. Nixon hoped that the revelation of the talks and his offer to withdraw all U.S. troops six months from the signing of an agreement and a cease-fire would buy him time with the American public.[201]

Nixon's January 1972 Vietnam speech reignited the media's fascination with Kissinger, and the national security adviser reveled in the attention, enjoying the opportunity of a quick rehabilitation of his standing. The night after the speech, Kissinger appeared before the Washington Press Club and poked fun at his reputation by making a joke about the feminist leader Gloria Steinem's recent statement that she had never been a girlfriend of his: "She did not say, if nominated, I will not run, or if elected, I will not serve." While Washington media figures appreciated his sense of humor, Kissinger may have sensed that his speech also called for a more serious reflection on the contemporary scene. He closed his talk with a somber and even gloomy assessment of this "most difficult" period in American history by arguing that Americans' belief in "Utopia" as "our logical destination" was no longer in evidence, and that "in traveling we will not find utopia but only ourselves. The realization of our essential loneliness accounts for so much of the frustration and the rage of our time."[202]

Kissinger's pessimism would come back to haunt him in a few years when the political climate changed. In the Washington of January 1972, however, his approach captured the national mood. Kissinger was now back in the media's favor, the most colorful and interesting figure in the otherwise bland Nixon administration. Russell Baker, a *New York Times* columnist, pronounced Kissinger as "Mister Professident," a figure who "transcended academia" and has "become something new in American life." Baker's humorous approach even embraced the Anderson revelations but used them to show Kissinger as he "pushes around lumpish bureaucrats, tells foot draggers to shape up, orders the Indian ambassador given the cool treatment." Compared to the dull life of President Nixon, who was "watching television with Bebe Rebozo," Kissinger "sneaks into Paris in dark glasses and false whiskers ready to play bloody chess with cunning men from Asia and, afterward, to dine well with a lovely woman." "Red-blooded American boys looking about for a hero must find his life irresistible," Baker concluded.[203] The irony was that although Nixon might have brooded about the invidious comparison Baker was making, the president's own political needs and decisions had helped catapult Kissinger back into the limelight.

"PEACE IS *REALLY* AT HAND"

Kissinger, the "Trifecta,"
and the 1972 Presidential Election

O N JANUARY 24, 1973, at 11:00 a.m. Eastern Standard Time, all three television networks interrupted their usual programming for a briefing by Henry Kissinger. ABC's Howard K. Smith referred to Kissinger's famous statement when he told his viewers, "Peace is *really* at hand now." Since Kissinger was typically late, Smith filled in the time by remarking that this announcement would be the "remarkable climax of a remarkable diplomatic year for Henry Kissinger," complete with the trip to China, the SALT agreement with the Soviet Union, and now the peace treaty ending the Vietnam War. These achievements were also those of President Nixon, but as venerable an establishment institution as *Time* magazine had chosen to make both Kissinger and Nixon its "Men of the Year."[1]

That same night all three networks led their evening broadcasts with the settlement and Kissinger, showing White House footage of him signing the agreements with the North Vietnamese in Paris, and then summarizing his long press conference. In particular, they stressed Kissinger's assurance that American prisoners would be released within two weeks of the formal signing of the agreement. On CBS, Marvin Kalb called Kissinger's briefing a "typical Kissinger seminar," meaning that it was "long, articulate, and occasionally vague."[2] With the signing of the Paris Peace Accords, Nixon and Kissinger had achieved their diplomatic "trifecta"—China, SALT, and now peace in Vietnam. Kissinger had become the face of a successful American foreign policy that had helped bring about Richard Nixon's landslide reelection victory. During this pivotal election year of 1972, Kissinger played a central role in the maneuvering and articulation of the "realist" revolution in American foreign policy that was designed for maximum domestic political effect. The "trifecta" was as much about the struggle for power at home as it was about Kissinger's new international "structure of peace."

CHINA, THE EASTER OFFENSIVE, AND THE MOSCOW SUMMIT

Nixon's Vietnam speech of January 25, 1972, in which he revealed Kissinger's secret talks with the North Vietnamese, gave him a brief boost in the polls. Despite the ongoing primary campaigns, Vietnam was not the major political issue, at least temporarily. Nixon and Kissinger worried about North Vietnam launching a military offensive that would damage the political impact of the upcoming China trip. Nixon authorized a series of bombing raids in early February to try to head off any attack, which he feared might be tied to the Vietnamese Lunar New Year and become another Tet Offensive. At the same time, Kissinger himself remained indirectly in the media eye on a Vietnam issue, as the "Harrisburg Seven" finally went on trial. The trial, which drew wide media coverage and lasted until April, ultimately embarrassed both the FBI and the Justice Department. The jury refused to believe an informer, and the case ended in a mistrial on the most serious charges, including the plot to kidnap Kissinger.[3]

As the departure for China approached, Kissinger received word that the North Vietnamese wanted to meet with him secretly in mid-March. The national security adviser was "ecstatic" and told Nixon he was certain this meant that there would be no major offensive and that perhaps there would be a "breakthrough" in the talks. A skeptical Nixon questioned him sharply on this, arguing that the negotiations could be another Vietnamese ploy.[4] Nixon even reflected that it was a "mistake" for the United States to have ever gotten involved in Vietnam, "because the way it's been conducted has cost us too much compared with what it would cost us to let it go." The two men agreed, however, that they could not have gotten out of Vietnam in 1969. Their firmness in Vietnam had been a "demonstration of strength," which, Kissinger argued, had actually led to the China trip. In defense of his negotiating efforts, Kissinger asserted, "We gained a helluva lot more from the secret meetings than they did." He still hoped for a breakthrough, even alluding to a decent interval: "If they are willing to maintain a non-Communist structure in the south for a while, I think we can find a solution."[5]

As they were concluding their conversation, Nixon, whose mental preparation for the trip was extraordinarily intense, told Kissinger, "I'm a little more Chinese than many Americans." Nixon was referring to growing up in California and having gone to school with Chinese children, but he also reassured Kissinger that the two of them, compared with "Connally or Agnew or Rogers," were the only ones who really understood the significance of the trip.[6] Indeed, the China trip proved to be a bonding experience for the two men. Although they could be intensely jealous and petty rivals, Nixon and Kissinger relished the secretive and conspiratorial way they pulled off this diplomatic coup, all to their mutual benefit. For Nixon, it was central to his reelection campaign, "Nixon's primary," the press corps joked. For Kissinger, it was a crucial step in his ascendancy over William P. Rogers and the State Department, making him the number two man in Washington.

Television coverage was central to the China trip, both in the symbolism of the reconciliation of former enemies and in the political point that it was Richard Nixon who was doing this. In his memoirs, Kissinger evinces a snobbish disdain for the "obsessive single-mindedness of the advance men" who accompanied him on his planning trips to China, comparing them to past "barbarians" with whom the Chinese had dealt.[7] He worried about their overwhelming presence and complained, "We don't want [the Chinese] thinking we're using the summit for political purposes."[8] For all of Kissinger's philosophical musings about China, Nixon cared most about its importance to the American electorate. This was to be a "journey for peace," and Nixon's team went all out to convey that message. China offered a particular bonus for American television coverage, as early-evening events could be transmitted live on American morning programs, while morning events could headline the evening news. Nixon's advance team, led by Dwight Chapin but under Haldeman's supervision, carefully choreographed events to ensure maximum coverage.[9] They made sure that both Nixon's arrival and departure occurred in prime viewing hours and that such events as the welcoming banquet, Nixon's trip to the Great Wall, and Mrs. Nixon's tours of schools and collective farms fit the timing of television news.[10] Critics observed, "Nixon was finally getting the kind of 'p.r.' he had sought for more than three years."[11] A Gallup poll registered an awareness of the China visit at 98 percent, a record at the time, and public approval of Nixon's trip was 84 percent.[12]

Kissinger was not the star of the television coverage in China. The cameras stayed focused on the president and Mrs. Nixon, with Zhou Enlai the principal Chinese celebrity. But Kissinger's position was enhanced even without the TV time. His participation in the first day's historic meeting with Mao, and the absence of Secretary Rogers, spoke volumes, or, as one State Department official crudely put it, was "a great big cow turd in Rogers' face."[13] Nixon's praise for Kissinger in front of Mao, referring to him as a "doctor of brains," and then teasing that "anyone who uses pretty girls as a cover must be the greatest diplomat of all time," confirmed his stature to the Chinese. The networks duly reported that in Nixon's subsequent negotiations with Zhou, he was accompanied by Kissinger, not Rogers.[14] Two days into his talks, Nixon told Zhou that he needed Kissinger because he could take "the long view" while he, Nixon, had a schedule so filled with practical matters that, he said, "I don't have as much time to take the long view as he does." He went on to assure Zhou that if he were reelected, he would keep Kissinger, adding, as he had told Haldeman a month earlier, that he could not afford to have him leave, since "the book he would write would tell too much."[15]

The reason Kissinger was rarely in front of TV cameras was that he was involved in long negotiating sessions with his Chinese counterpart, trying to secure a joint communiqué.[16] The underlying agreement about the Soviet threat, which had brought them together in the first place, laid the basis for compromise on more difficult issues. With the Chinese refusal to help on the Vietnam issue, the main subject of discussion was the status of Taiwan. Nixon told Zhou that this was a major political issue with conservatives in the Republican Party, and that the two countries needed "to find language which will meet your need yet does not stir up the animals so much that they gang up on Taiwan and thereby torpedo our initiative."[17] After long hours of negotiation, the final communiqué used an unusual formulation: It affirmed that the United States did not "challenge" the belief of all Chinese that there was but one China and that Taiwan was a part of China. It affirmed as well that a peaceful resolution of the Taiwan question would allow for an American withdrawal from the island.[18] Kissinger's efforts to produce a compromise faltered, however, when Secretary Rogers and Assistant Secretary Marshall Green noted the absence from the communiqué of any mention of America's defense treaty with Taiwan.[19] Nixon was angrier with Rogers for pointing out the omission than he was with Kissinger for failing to have the treaty mentioned, in part because he feared an attack by right-wing critics of a "sellout" of Taiwan. Unable to get the Chinese to alter the communiqué at the last minute, Kissinger simply reaffirmed the defense treaty during his news conference.[20] The tactic worked, and the television networks broadcast reports on the Shanghai Communiqué and Kissinger's briefing, as well as Nixon's toast, with his extravagant claim that "this was the week that changed the world."[21] Kissinger concluded the controversy about the communiqué was subsumed by the very television coverage he had once disdained. "Pictures overrode the printed word," he wrote. "The public simply was not interested in the complex analyses of the document after having watched the spectacle of an American president welcomed in the capital of an erstwhile enemy."[22]

Nixon was extremely happy with the results of the trip, relishing the public acclaim as well as the praise from establishment journalists like James Reston, whose *New York Times* column on the visit was titled "Mr. Nixon's Finest Hour." Nixon praised Kissinger's work during the trip, particularly the communiqué, and told Haldeman to call his friend Bebe Rebozo in Key Biscayne and "have him give Henry all of his phone numbers of girls that are not over thirty."[23] He was particularly pleased when Kissinger reported that his phone call to Ronald Reagan had elicited strong support. Reagan, unlike other conservatives such as the *National Review*'s William Buckley, recognized the politics behind Nixon's trip.[24] But Nixon also quickly began to fear that Kissinger was not doing enough for Nixon's image and needed to stress more how the president was "a big league operator" and that this was a "classic battle between a couple of heavyweights." He kept pushing Haldeman and Kissinger to come up with ways to highlight the achievements of the trip. But when Marvin Kalb offered a TV interview for Kissinger, Nixon rejected it. He told Haldeman, "We've got to be concerned about his proclivity to build himself as the power behind the throne. Maybe we just can't change him."[25]

(Kissinger's NSC staff was keenly aware of how the president approached his summit diplomacy. In a moment of brilliant satirical effort, they composed a briefing memorandum "authored" by Nixon's friend the Reverend Billy Graham, with advice on his forthcoming "Summit Meeting with God." Mimicking Kissinger's language, the memo advised the president that the meeting had come about because of a desire to reassure the Almighty that "your recent summit with Satan" was not an attempt "to exploit the Heaven-Hell split." Recognizing Nixon's preference for one-on-one meetings, "Graham" described how "you and the Almighty will be meeting alone for the first hour" but then joined by "Dr. Kissinger and St. Peter." The memo added, "We turned down His bureaucracy's request that we include his Son and a third figure, who remains obscure." In a knowing reference to the domestic politics of Nixon's summits, "Graham" advised, "Wide distribution of photos by [Nixon political aide Charles] Colson and the RNC [Republican National Committee] should ensure the success of the Southern strategy and help considerably in the Middle West. Distribution in New York City and Cambridge area is inadvisable." Kissinger probably enjoyed his staff's humor, although he sent the fake memo on to Haldeman with a covering note saying, "If my staff worked as hard on things that are important, we might have been out of Vietnam by now.")[26]

As he assumed responsibility for planning the president's trip to Moscow, Kissinger believed the United States had dodged a bullet. Even though the North Vietnamese canceled their March meeting with him, he still thought the chances of a major offensive had dropped. He argued that because of the "triangular diplomacy" with the Chinese and Russians, Hanoi was isolated and its leaders would try to settle the conflict sometime before the November election. He even advised Nixon against approving General Abrams's new requests for major air strikes into North Vietnam to blunt a possible offensive, fearful of provoking a political uproar at home and damaging the China relationship. Kissinger did worry that the communists might launch an offensive in October, right before the presidential election. But he assured Nixon, "It's a hell of a gamble for them to take, because if they don't tip you over in October, then they've had it."[27]

North Vietnam, however, decided to gamble well before October. Buoyed by the success of its forces in Laos, the Vietnamese politburo, led by Lê Duẩn and Lê Đức Thọ, believed that a complete military victory was within their grasp. Shortly before they began the offensive, Lê Duẩn, *primus inter pares* in the North Vietnamese politburo, accused Zhou Enlai of saving a "drowning" Nixon by allowing him a successful visit and warned the Chinese that Hanoi would not tolerate another "betrayal" as had occurred at the Geneva Conference in July 1954.[28] The North Vietnamese feared that their Chinese and Soviet allies would once again pressure them to accept the division of their country because they wanted to pursue good relations with the United States. Within the politburo, those who favored the offensive argued that Nixon's concern for his new relationships with China and the Soviet Union would restrain him from retaliating. They also believed that antiwar public opinion and the presidential election in the United States would prevent Nixon from escalating the war.[29] Some politburo members, however, urged caution, arguing, "Nixon is a very daring individual who might take that risk, no matter what the consequences. We should not underestimate him."[30]

On March 30, 1972, in the "Easter Offensive," thousands of North

Vietnamese soldiers attacked across the demilitarized zone, armed with Soviet and Chinese tanks and weaponry, with their objective the provincial capital of Quang Tri and the imperial capital of Hue. Military attacks also took place in two other regions of South Vietnam, one in the Central Highlands, threatening to divide the country and seize the city of Kontum, and the other in the Tay Ninh region near Saigon, where An Loc was threatened. Unlike the Tet Offensive of 1968, these attacks were launched by regular North Vietnamese units and were conventional military assaults. They achieved initial success in the DMZ, sweeping aside South Vietnamese defenders and surrounding Quang Tri. The offensive also played out on American television. Evening news reports showed ragged South Vietnamese soldiers and civilians fleeing the fighting. The CBS correspondent Bob Simon repeated the administration's argument that the offensive would be a test of Vietnamization, but added, "So far the results are not encouraging."[31] By the time Kissinger walked into Nixon's office on Monday morning, April 3, and remarked, "It is clear there's a massive attack," Nixon replied, "Well, we knew that yesterday."[32]

Throughout the first weeks of the offensive, Kissinger and Nixon reinforced each other's suspicions and concerns about the lassitude and weakness of the military services, the civilian leadership in the Defense Department, and the entire foreign policy bureaucracy in not recognizing the urgency of the situation and the need for drastic action. They echoed each other's historical analogies—the Battle of the Bulge proved that bad weather should not prevent the Air Force from flying sorties—and often repeated each other's words: both talked about bombing the "bejeezus" out of North Vietnam. Although the crisis initially found them thinking and acting in almost complete harmony, it also revealed a key difference. When Kissinger actually raised the prospect of military defeat, seeming resigned to it, Nixon reacted strongly: "If the ARVN collapses a lot of other things will collapse around here." He emphasized, "If they were going to collapse, they had to a year ago. We can't do it this year, Henry." Nixon made it clear to Kissinger that, in his view, "we're playing a much bigger game. We're playing a Russian game, a Chinese game, an election game."[33] Throughout the discussions, Nixon equated defeat

in Vietnam with his political defeat in the United States, and he was determined to use almost every element of his power to prevent this.[34]

Kissinger acted quickly to implement Nixon's policies in the immediate
days after the North Vietnamese attack. Kissinger's extraordinary energy and
stamina, along with his almost unlimited access to Nixon, placed him at the
center of both military and diplomatic decision-making. He immediately
began to pressure Admiral Moorer for a buildup of American power in the
region, and even arranged for General John Vogt to meet with Nixon and
then sent him out to Saigon to take over the air campaign. He also served as
Nixon's ally in dealing with Defense Secretary Laird and General Abrams in
Saigon, both of whom Nixon thought were not responding to the offensive with
enough imagination or aggressiveness. Although there would be considerable
friction with the military, Nixon and Kissinger's efforts brought "to bear firepower beyond anything" the North Vietnamese had anticipated: six aircraft
carriers, five cruisers, forty destroyers, and more than one thousand war-
planes, including over 150 B-52s.[35] On the diplomatic front, Kissinger told
Nixon that he would use his back channel to Ambassador Dobrynin to press
the Russians to intervene with Hanoi. With Nixon's eager approval, he suggested threatening to use American influence with the West Germans to prevent the approval of their treaties with the Soviet Union and even the survival
of Willy Brandt's government, with which the Soviets had forged important
links.[36] Kissinger also assured Nixon that Dobrynin was "slobbering" for him
to come to Moscow for a secret visit to plan the summit and that this more
than likely meant the Russians were preparing to "screw" their North Vietnamese ally.[37]

Nixon valued Kissinger's assistance, but he was more suspicious than
Kissinger of Russian policy. Nixon also suspected that Kissinger was interested in the personal glory and media attention connected to another secret
mission to Moscow. "Henry, with all of his many virtues, does seem too often
to be concerned about preparing the way for negotiations with the Soviets,"
Nixon wrote in his diary, noting that Kissinger seemed to believe that even
if the United States failed in Vietnam, "we can survive politically." Nixon,

however, "had no illusions whatever on that score." Not only would the United States not have "a credible foreign policy," but, Nixon recognized, defeat in Vietnam would also spell the end for his reelection efforts.[38] He told Kissinger that he was considering calling off the summit, ordering a blockade of North Vietnam, and looking "for a successor," since he would clearly be unable to stand for reelection. An emotional Kissinger rejected the idea, all the while suspecting that Nixon just needed reassurance that he was indispensable to the country. Nixon emphasized that if he allowed Kissinger to go to Moscow, Vietnam must be the priority of his trip.[39] Kissinger remembered Nixon's threats to cancel the summit during the Indo-Pakistani conflict and suspected Nixon might change his mind. Kissinger wanted desperately to go to Moscow.[40] Using politics to manipulate the president, he told Nixon that a liberal columnist like Joseph Kraft, who was "violently opposed to everything we're doing," had said that the United States should "knock off the summit," and this was clear evidence that "the Democrats" would like nothing better than to see the summit fall through. Nixon relented and decided to let Kissinger go to Moscow, but he insisted that he must stress Vietnam above all. In a melodramatic moment, he told Kissinger, "I'm willing to throw myself on the sword. We are not going to let this country be defeated by this little shit-ass country."[41]

Kissinger secretly left Washington in the early-morning hours of April 20, taking with him on Air Force One the Soviet ambassador Dobrynin. Even before the flight arrived in Moscow, Nixon had sent another long memorandum, critiquing Kissinger's briefing book and again stressing, "Your primary interest, in fact your indispensable interest, will be to get them to talk about Vietnam." His suspicions about Kissinger's motives and intentions had not disappeared, and he feared Kissinger would spend "hours and hours and hours on philosophical bullshit," with the result that the meeting would never get to Vietnam.[42] He was not far wrong. Disregarding Nixon's injunctions, and confident in his own style of negotiation, Kissinger began his talks with Soviet leaders in a cordial manner. He allowed the Soviet leader Leonid Brezhnev to dominate their first discussion with his appeals for superpower cooperation and hope that Nixon would adhere to the words of his inauguration and move from an "era of confrontation to an era of negotiation." When Kissinger was finally able to turn the discussion to Vietnam, he placed the Vietnamese behavior in a historical context, arguing that they were haunted by their experience of Geneva in 1954. He tried to appeal to the Kremlin's self-interest in not facilitating a North Vietnamese victory that "would deprive an American president of any authority to have the sort of discussions with the General Secretary that it has been the principal objective of his Administration to bring about." When Brezhnev criticized the bombing of North Vietnam, Kissinger commented, "In your own experience, when a leader has necessities and a country has necessities, he must take painful steps which he doesn't like to do." Brezhnev responded, "You were hinting at Czechoslovakia." Kissinger insisted that he meant the comment in a "spirit of understanding," but he was trying to turn the Brezhnev Doctrine against its author. Brezhnev was not about to concede. The general secretary went on to question whether the bombing would help Nixon win reelection, but then focused on the Chinese, who, he asserted, were behind the Vietnamese offensive, since "we have nothing to do with the planning of the war."[43]

Nixon was furious about Kissinger's report on the first negotiating session and wanted him to return home immediately. Kissinger later acknowledged that he had "stretched whatever authority [he] had to include other subjects to the limit."[44] Over the next few days, in cables that are remarkable for their indignation, bluntness, and defiance, Kissinger rejected the criticisms coming from Nixon through his deputy Alexander Haig and insisted that he had been "more brutal on Vietnam than in any talk with any leader of any country." Although he had convinced the Soviets to forward a peace proposal and arrange for talks with Hanoi in Paris on May 2, Kissinger defended the Russians and concluded, "I am not sure they are able to deliver on Vietnam." Kissinger's sharp and defensive reaction reflects how his own vision for American foreign policy was diverging from Nixon's. He believed strongly that negotiating with the Soviets, balancing them with the Chinese, and being at the center of this triangular diplomatic structure were far more important to the future of the United States than what happened in Vietnam. Kissinger believed the difficulties of Brezhnev's domestic position, commenting, "We may have an election in November; he acts as if he has one next week and every week thereafter." Kissinger recognized that Nixon would not be as sympathetic to Brezhnev, given his own problems, and turned his appeal quickly back to American domestic politics. Brezhnev wanted a "summit at almost any cost," and this fact could be helpful "to control the uproar in the U.S." that might greet further escalation in Vietnam. Nixon sarcastically referred to this argument as "typical Kissinger gobbledygook," and Haldeman reported he was "driven up the wall" by Kissinger's "unbelievable ego" and emphasis on the summit instead of Vietnam. However, despite his angry words, Nixon continued to see the advantages in Kissinger's diplomatic coups and the reverence with which the media treated them. He made a special point to ensure that the timing of the public announcement of Kissinger's Moscow trip would receive "solo ride on the Tuesday evening news cycle."[45]

Kissinger arrived at Camp David on the evening of April 24, the same day the news reported another "catastrophic" North Vietnamese attack in the Central Highlands.[46] Nixon "was all primed to really whack Henry," as Haldeman wrote, but, in characteristic Nixon fashion, backed off once Kissinger arrived. (It did not help Nixon's projection of presidential authority that his fly was unzipped throughout the meeting.)[47] The next morning Nixon jokingly asked where Kissinger was when he was trying to reach him, and Nixon's secretary Rose Mary Woods interjected, "Probably out with some babe." Kissinger laughed and said no, but "it wasn't through a lack of offers." He then regaled Nixon with an account of how the Soviets had offered him "a whole bunch of girls, all 25 years and younger," and that "the crudeness of these guys is not to be believed."[48] Nixon told Kissinger of having "mixed emotions" about Kissinger's emphasis on the summit in his talks with Brezhnev. Although "we're going to be sorely tempted to save the summit at almost any cost," Nixon said, he wanted to go further to risk it. Putting the question in domestic terms, Nixon stressed again his feeling that the United States could not lose in Vietnam, "that this is the great struggle between the left and the right, the great struggle between the peaceniks and the patriots." Kissinger disarmed Nixon by agreeing with him, but made the case that the Russians were now trying to be helpful by passing American peace proposals to Hanoi. He flattered Nixon, telling him a story from Dobrynin: He, Kissinger, had been very tough with Gromyko. Dobrynin then told his Central Committee colleagues, "If you think Kissinger is tough, wait till you meet the President." It was exactly the type of reputation Nixon wanted with the Russians.[49]

Nixon went ahead with having Kissinger conduct an on-the-record briefing about the trip, and then was delighted when it led all the TV news broadcasts. Nixon remarked that the press must be "out of their goddamn minds" at both Kissinger's trip and the fact that the summit was still on despite the bombing of North Vietnam.[50] Television reporters took Kissinger's remark that "Lê Đức Thọ does not travel lightly" as an indication that the secret talks in Paris would soon resume. John Chancellor remarked that since Kissinger's trip was secret, the fact that the White House announced it at all meant that it was a success.[51] Journalists poured on the praise for Kissinger. Reston wrote, "How [Kissinger] performs this delicate and dangerous role is a *miracle* which defies physical and intellectual endurance." Hugh Sidey, another journalist whom Nixon disdained, gushed, "You can't help but admire the man." Both accounts quoted Kissinger's humorous response as to why he went to Moscow: "I'd do anything for caviar."[52]

Nixon followed up the positive coverage of the Kissinger trip with another prime-time Vietnam speech.[53] Nixon announced that Vietnamization "has proved itself sufficiently" to allow a withdrawal of an additional twenty thousand American soldiers from Vietnam, for a total of a half-million men since he became president. Nixon quoted a report from General Abrams, stating, "The South Vietnamese are fighting courageously and well in their self-defense. They are inflicting very heavy casualties on the invading force, which has not gained the easy victory some predicted for it three weeks ago." Nixon announced that the United States would return to the public peace talks in Paris but that he would not suspend air attacks on North Vietnam. Reminding viewers of his "historic journey for peace" to China, he assured them that based on "Dr. Kissinger's report," he expected to make a similar journey to Moscow. However, he also warned that such a trip would not be possible for future presidents "if the United States betrays the millions of people who have relied on us in Vietnam."[54]

The television commentators were not kind to Nixon's speech. Eric Seva-reid, the CBS analyst, remarked that Nixon's speech was clearly intended for a domestic audience and reminded him of Shakespeare's "Prince Hal in modern dress" rallying the troops with optimistic talk about progress in Vietnam "that people have heard before." Dan Rather emphasized that even though Nixon stressed troop withdrawals in the speech, there had been a tremendous increase in American strength in Southeast Asia, particularly in air and naval forces. The relationship of Nixon's speech to Kissinger's trip led the reporters to a discussion of "how difficult it is to separate the two men" in analyzing a possible superpower deal on Vietnam.[55] Only four days after his speech, the news from Vietnam turned decidedly worse. North Vietnamese forces finally overran the provincial capital of Quang Tri and seemed well on their way to threatening Hue. *The New York Times* described panicking South Vietnamese soldiers "streaming south down Route 1 like a rabble out of control."[56] General Abrams now cabled Washington that Saigon's military leadership was "losing its will and cannot be depended on to take the measures necessary to stand and fight."[57]

The Abrams cable arrived Monday evening, May 1, as Nixon, who had just returned to Washington from a Texas fundraiser, was meeting in the White House with Kissinger and Haldeman.[58] On the flight from Texas to Washington, Nixon remarked to Haldeman that he suspected, because of Kissinger's commitment to the summit and to the possibility of a breakthrough in negotiations with the North Vietnamese, that "Kissinger was not playing it straight with him on Vietnam," and that his national security adviser was "wrong on public opinion."[59] Nixon brooded over the Abrams cable and finally concluded that if South Vietnam collapsed, the United States could impose a blockade and demand its prisoners back. Kissinger agreed that would be the only choice. Nixon added solemnly, "But then we're defeated." Kissinger tried to provide some reassurance, uttering the tired cliché "We'll have to tighten our belts." Nixon "sort of laughed" at the comment. The "sort of laugh" captured Nixon's sentiment, as he recognized that "we may have had it in Vietnam" and that this would spell the end of his political career.[60]

Kissinger left for Paris the next day, instructed by Nixon "not to give anything" and knowing that the president was willing to sacrifice the summit and order "hard strikes" unless the North Vietnamese showed some willingness to negotiate seriously.[61] "Settle or else" is how Nixon summarized his message to Hanoi. Given the events on the battlefield, however, the North Vietnamese felt no need to make concessions. Kissinger spent three hours with Lê Đức Thọ and Xuân Thủy, time that consisted of the simple restatement of past positions. Kissinger proposed a cease-fire and American withdrawal in four months in return for the POWs. The Vietnamese irritated Kissinger with continual references to American domestic politics, leading him to snap angrily, "Our domestic discussions are of no concern of yours." As they were leaving the session, Lê Đức Thọ pulled Kissinger aside to remark on how "good" the prospects for the North Vietnamese now looked.[62] "The man was as defiant as if he had won the war after all," Kissinger later told Dobrynin.[63]

Nixon was not surprised that Kissinger had no luck with the North Vietnamese, commenting in his diary that Kissinger's "weakness" was his obsession "with the idea that there *should* be a negotiated settlement." Nixon saw that "there really isn't enough in it for the enemy to negotiate at this time."[64] He believed now that he needed strong military action against the North and to take a step that even Lyndon Johnson had shied away from—mining the harbor at Haiphong. Because the North's conventional military offensive relied so heavily on a daily flow of imported fuel for its tanks and armored vehicles in the South, a disruption in the supply could have serious effects in a way that previous bombing campaigns had not. Mining Haiphong, however, meant the possibility of direct interference with Soviet shipping, and was, in Kissinger's words, "crossing the Rubicon." It put into jeopardy the Moscow summit and posed the question of whether the United States should cancel it before the Soviets did.[65] Nixon also made it clear that there was no way he could attend the summit, make agreements with the Soviets, trade toasts, and drink champagne while the North Vietnamese, armed with Soviet tanks and weaponry, marched into Hue or Kontum. Both Haldeman and John Connally made the case that the United States should not act first in canceling the summit and that it should take whatever military action it chose and leave it to the Russians to decide whether to cancel the summit. Nixon was persuaded by Connally's "animal-like decisiveness" in saying to him, "You can do without the summit, but you cannot live with a defeat in Vietnam."[66]

Kissinger made arguments for and against each policy option, but he remained "horrified" by the prospect of losing the Moscow summit.[67] His secret talks had made significant progress toward a SALT treaty, with the Russians showing their willingness to compromise on both the inclusion of submarine-launched ballistic missiles (SLBMs) in the treaty and on the ABM question.[68] Kissinger thought that the prospect of signing the first significant arms control agreement between the superpowers was far more meaningful than the fate of South Vietnam. He made it clear to sympathetic journalists that he was "uncomfortable" with the direction Nixon was heading and that Vietnam "still had the capacity to distort the nation's diplomatic priorities." He was also "agonizing about his image with the liberal community," hoping to avoid becoming what he often referred to as "the Walt Rostow of the Nixon Administration."[69] He feared that renewed bombing "would trigger every goddamn peace group in this country."[70]

Kissinger could see the direction that Nixon was moving and decided to reassure the president. He compared the situation to what they had faced in Laos, when critics thought the operation had doomed any opening to China and yet "three months later we were there." He wholeheartedly agreed as Nixon graphically spoke of how he wished they could "flush Vietnam down, flush it, and get out of it in any way possible and conduct a sensible foreign policy with the Russians and with the Chinese." Kissinger exclaimed, "Goddamnit, let's face it, if they had accepted our May 31st proposal last year, they would have taken over Vietnam within a year or two." Nixon replied, "See, if we can survive past the election, Henry, and then Vietnam goes down the tubes, it really doesn't make any difference." Nixon then came back to the point that had driven him since the beginning of the offensive: "We must not lose in Vietnam. It's as cold as that." Kissinger agreed, although when Nixon emphatically added, "We're going to bomb those bastards all over the place," Kissinger rejoined, "The only point I disagree is we can do all of this without killing too many civilians." To this Nixon readily agreed, though adding, "Don't be so careful that you don't knock out the oil for their tanks."[71]

Once Nixon made his decision, Kissinger adapted, although he remained convinced that the Russians would cancel the summit. He pushed for Nixon's speech to be "low key and calm," as well as "very conciliatory to the Russians," an implicit contrast with Nixon's over-the-top speech on Cambodia. Again, Nixon agreed, but told Kissinger, "The only place where you and I disagree, at the present time, is with regard to the bombing. You're so goddamned concerned about the civilians." Kissinger defended his concern by appealing to Nixon's self-interest, noting, "I'm concerned about the civilians because I don't want the world to be mobilized against you as a butcher." After Kissinger left the room, Nixon told Haldeman, "Henry's always saying he's going to get something out of the Russians," and he "really shouldn't be lunching with Dobrynin today."[72] But Nixon did not stop him, and Kissinger met his Russian counterpart, telling him that Nixon had made the decision to go to the summit but not warning him about the mining. The result was that Dobrynin advised his Kremlin superiors that until the summit, "the White House will try to refrain from making particularly major decisions on far reaching military measures" against North Vietnam.[73]

In a departure from usual form, Nixon did not have Kissinger provide a briefing for journalists before his dramatic May 8 speech to the nation. He began with an emphasis on the "peace efforts" he had undertaken in response to the North Vietnamese attack and then again revealed that "Dr. Kissinger" had conducted secret talks with the Vietnamese on May 2. The failure of these efforts led Nixon, more in sorrow than in anger, to announce that the United States needed to take action to keep "the weapons of war out of the hands of the international outlaws of North Vietnam." The mining of Haiphong was now necessary to protect the remaining American forces in Vietnam as well as prevent America's "humiliation." Nixon added that America's peace terms were straightforward and simple: an internationally supervised cease-fire, the return of American POWs, and then an American withdrawal within four months. Nixon closed the speech with a strong appeal to the Soviet Union not to see the mining as directed against them, but simply "as our right to defend our interests." Nixon urged that the United States and the Soviet Union "not slide back toward the dark shadows of a previous age" but continue to build "a new relationship that can serve the interests of our two countries." He also clearly placed the question of the summit in Soviet hands, saying that the United States was prepared to continue building a new relationship and "that the responsibility is yours if we fail to do so."[74]

Media commentary on the Nixon speech assumed the worst.[75] Dan Rather reminded viewers that there had been no advance briefing as he asked Eric Sevareid for his reaction. Sevareid appeared stunned and commented that this was "very solemn business," as well as a clear admission by Nixon that "Vietnamization had failed." Marvin Kalb remarked that the Nixon move was a "frontal challenge" to the Soviet Union and placed the summit "very, very much in jeopardy."[76] The other networks shared in this tone of deep pessimism, with ABC referring to Nixon's decision as "a slap in the face" to the Russians, and NBC saying that the "Soviets will have to react." The political reaction from the Democrats was equally passionate and pessimistic. McGovern called the move "reckless, unnecessary, and unworkable, a flirtation with World War III." Edward Kennedy said Nixon's action "demonstrates the desperation of the President's Indochina policy."[77] Small protests broke out throughout the country, although the campus unrest was nowhere near the scale it had been after Cambodia.[78]

To deflect and calm the opposition, Nixon encouraged Kissinger to brief reporters the next day. Although Marvin Kalb was convinced that "Henry didn't have his heart in it," other reporters described how Kissinger gave an "impassioned defense" of the president's action. In a voice "choked with emotion," Kissinger called the action a "very painful and difficult decision" made "only because it was believed that no honorable alternative" existed. Expressing hope that the Soviets would understand the American decision, Kissinger said that the summit meeting was still on, but he would not predict the Soviet reaction. Still not allowed to use the audio of Kissinger's briefing, CBS reported that his voice rose "in anger" as he accused North Vietnam of attempting to humiliate the United States.[79] Kissinger calmed down to spend much of the briefing reassuring the Soviets of the benefits of cooperation with the

United States and appealing to them to "work out some principles of international conduct" that would allow such troublesome peripheral conflicts like
Vietnam to be managed successfully.[80] Behind the scenes, Kissinger called
Dobrynin to tell him that he had called Egon Bahr, Willy Brandt's assistant,
and was reassured that the German treaties would be ratified. Kissinger
added, "I wanted you to know at least in areas outside Southeast Asia, we have
continued to do business as we promised."[81]

To a large extent, the American media and Nixon's political opponents
were overlooking the degree to which superpower relations had changed
since the Cuban Missile Crisis of 1962, or even since the Middle East crisis of
1970. Nixon and Kissinger's move to bring China into the dynamic with the
Soviets, as well as the moves to stabilize the European and German situations, had all created incentives to keep the Soviets from overreacting to
Nixon's Vietnam moves. Nevertheless, as Kissinger suspected, there was an
intense struggle within the Soviet politburo over whether to cancel the
summit. Having relied on Dobrynin's rosy assessment, the Soviet leaders
were caught off guard by Nixon's action. Brezhnev faced the objections of
strong rivals like Nikolai Podgorny, chairman of the Supreme Soviet, and his
ally Petro Shelest, the Ukrainian party leader, as well as the military leadership under Marshal Andrei Grechko. Mikhail Suslov, the party's ideological
voice, was also skeptical about moving ahead with the summit in light of the
American action. Brezhnev was "a walking bundle of nerves, popping in and
out of the room, smoking one cigarette after another." For Brezhnev, as for
Nixon in a different manner, foreign policy was ultimately about domestic
legitimacy, and promoting his image as a peacemaker was as essential to the
Soviet leader as it was to his American counterpart. Brezhnev's "personal
emotional investment" in the summit and the entire range of policies associated with détente—a slowing of the arms race, ratification of the German
treaties, obtaining Western capital for economic development—helped to
carry the day. Ironically enough, the winning argument within the politburo
debate "was that the North Vietnamese should not be allowed to exercise a
veto over Soviet relations with the United States."[82]

The suspense did not last long. On Thursday, May 11, when the Soviet foreign trade minister Nikolai Patolichev and Ambassador Dobrynin arrived at the White House for a meeting with President Nixon, Kissinger asked Dobrynin if he could arrange some publicity, and the Russian agreed. The result was a lead report on NBC's evening newscast, showing a convivial meeting between Nixon, Kissinger, and the two Russians, followed by a reporter's shouted question to Patolichev asking if the president's visit was still on, and Patolichev's response through his interpreter, "We never had any doubts about it."[83] Kissinger's estimate of the summit's probability shifted dramatically, and he now told Nixon of a number of signs that were pointing away from a cancellation. The next morning he called Nixon to say that it was "slightly better than 50–50" the Soviets would not cancel, adding that if they canceled now, it would take them eighteen months to get back to another summit. Nixon realized the political meaning, telling Kissinger, "If they cancel this they're gambling on somebody else winning the election."[84] By late afternoon the same day, Kissinger reported to Nixon that he'd met with Dobrynin, who was "busily working away at the summit," and they were discussing various gifts to give to each of the leaders. Kissinger now thought it "99 percent" likely that the summit would take place. And he added, "Hanoi must be beside itself."[85]

Both Nixon and Kissinger were aware that the media would compare their meetings in Moscow with the China trip, both in terms of the atmosphere and the substance. A key priority was to make sure that the wide-ranging set of agreements being signed in Moscow—arms control, trade, scientific cooperation, cultural exchange—were seen as presidential initiatives. Kissinger assured Nixon, "We can demonstrate that of these agreements not one could have been done without your personal channel to Brezhnev."[86] Nixon had Kissinger bring Dobrynin to Camp David a few days before the summit and told him that it was very important for the Russians not to reveal the Kissinger-Dobrynin back channel in their statements. Nixon expressed a preference for meetings with Brezhnev to be kept "to the smallest number possible," and bluntly told Dobrynin, "I do not rely on Rogers." Nixon hoped that the Soviet foreign minister Gromyko could be used to keep Secretary of State Rogers "busy" at the summit, so that Nixon and Kissinger could conduct the serious negotiations.[87] Away from Dobrynin, Nixon and Kissinger engaged in crude banter about Rogers and the State Department, convinced that they would "piss" on either SALT or the "principles agreement" as they had with the Shanghai Communiqué.[88] When Nixon heard that Rogers planned a press briefing to talk about the summit, Nixon exploded, telling Haldeman that he was going to do the briefing and that Rogers "doesn't know the first thing about what is going on."[89]

Along with the bureaucratic politics of the summit, Nixon worried about the domestic political reaction to any agreements he might bring home. He warned Kissinger that the real problem with a SALT agreement would come from the right, and it would be "terribly difficult" for them to accept that we "put our arms around our enemies."[90] It would be equally difficult for them to accept the numerical inferiority inherent in a SALT agreement, even if Kissinger could make the case for the overall strength of the American deterrent. The specific details of the numbers of missiles, the size of silos, and the location of radars never really concerned Nixon. When Kissinger called to mention a discussion with Dobrynin about the number of radars that could be allowed at an ABM site, Nixon remarked, "As you and I both know, it doesn't make a hell of a lot of difference. Just so we can defend it."[91] In the wake of his Vietnam decisions, which his conservative supporters had enthusiastically backed, Nixon became increasingly concerned with avoiding "a massive right wing revolt on the SALT agreement." The hawks in Congress would have to be consoled by the assurance that the president was committed to moving ahead on new weapons systems like the B-1 bomber or technical advances like the multiple independent reentry vehicle (MIRV) for warheads, which were not covered by the agreement.[92]

Much of the SALT agreement was arranged before the summit, but some technical issues—among them, the radars for the ABMs, the manner of counting submarines and SLBMs, and a way of regulating improvements in the size of ICBMs and their silos—still required last-minute bargaining.[93] Nixon's absolute determination to receive the political credit for SALT reinforced Kissinger's own determination to keep the threads of all these issues in his own hands. As a result, the American experts in the SALT talks who had been negotiating with the Russians in Helsinki were minimally consulted and not brought to Moscow until the last minute. Kissinger himself acknowledged that their exclusion contributed to some of the problems in the final agreements. Furthermore, outside of the ABM agreement, which actually limited both sides to two facilities and required Senate ratification, the five-year "freeze" on offensive weapons actually allowed both sides to continue to build up their arsenals, although the ceiling on submarines and SLBMs would keep the United States from falling further behind. Kissinger argued that America's technological superiority, particularly its absolute lead in the number of warheads and the MIRV system, offset the Soviet advantage. The central political problem for Nixon came in allowing the Soviets to have more ICBMs (1,618 to 1,054) and more SLBMs (740 to 656) and the way those "inequalities" might be exploited by opponents of the agreement.[94]

None of these details, however, was as important to Nixon as the sheer theater of the summit, which Nixon's advance men had once again carefully orchestrated. The Soviets told Nixon that because of Vietnam, there would be a more "subdued" public welcome, but reporters estimated that about one hundred thousand Muscovites came out to see Nixon's motorcade— compared with the empty streets of Beijing. The network anchors went out of their way to talk about how "remarkable" it was that the summit was occurring given what had happened in Vietnam.[95] The signing of the various agreements, timed for each nightly newscast, also highlighted the contrast with the China summit, stressing the "substance" of these meetings. The media duly noted the environmental and health agreements on the first night, and presented the agreement on cooperation in space as a true "twenty-first century" achievement of the summit.[96] They gave considerable broadcast time to ceremonial events, including Nixon placing a wreath at the Tomb of the Unknown Soldier, attending the Bolshoi Ballet, and speaking directly to Russians on Soviet TV. In the background of many of their stories was Kissinger, referred to by John Chancellor, NBC's anchor, as "the second most important American" at the summit. Kissinger used his briefings with journalists to encourage them to recognize the historic importance of the meetings, as the two superpowers were "learning to be equal partners in the preservation of peace."[97] He also portrayed the meetings as a true turning point in history, possibly "the end of the Cold War," and a "healthy and civilized" way for the two superpowers to deal with each other.[98]

Although Nixon's people choreographed much of the summit, there were moments of unexpected drama. On the third day, Brezhnev effectively "kidnapped" Nixon and Kissinger for a high-speed ride to his dacha outside Moscow. There the Kremlin triumvirate, Brezhnev, Alexei Kosygin, and Nikolai Podgorny, harangued the Americans for more than three hours about Vietnam. Nixon suffered through the verbal assault with great patience, occasionally interjecting a pointed question like, "Who elected the president of North Vietnam?" When he finally was allowed to speak longer, he offered a spirited defense of his actions, but closed his comments by remarking, "We will think matters over," and, "Perhaps Kissinger will use his brain to come up with a new proposal." This prompted Kosygin to declare, "He must certainly do that," and Brezhnev then drew the meeting to an end.[99] News of the meeting contributed to turning the media coverage more doubtful and pessimistic. Reporters began depicting Vietnam as "clouding the summit" and suggested that the arms control and trade talks were stalled because the "thorn of Vietnam remains" in the U.S.-Soviet relationship.[100]

In reality, Vietnam had not affected the SALT talks in any significant way. Nixon authorized Kissinger to accept the previously agreed numerical limits on missiles and to continue to push the Russians for concessions. Kissinger described Nixon giving him this authorization while lying naked on a massage table in his Kremlin suite, "a heroic position from a decidedly unheroic posture."[101] Although Kissinger contended that Brezhnev needed SALT even more than Nixon did, and Nixon insisted, "The hell with the political consequences," it is difficult to imagine that Nixon would have left Moscow without signing the first strategic arms agreement.[102] Kissinger and Gromyko conducted an agonizingly long negotiation late into the night, working against a Friday deadline. The result was a last-minute compromise on increasing the dimensions of silos and calculating the Soviet SLBMs, both of which proved confusing and favorable to the Soviets and would come back to haunt Kissinger when he began negotiating the SALT II agreement.[103]

However, the television networks hailed it as "the most important arms agreement ever," with Chancellor noting, "It was quite a day for Richard Nixon." Amid the extensive praise for the president's triumph, with its clear political overtones, it was also clear how important Kissinger was to this image of success. Kissinger played a decisive role in briefing reporters about the agreement. *The New Republic's* John Osborne described how Kissinger "labored with all the eloquence and brilliance at his command, along with a dash of sardonic humor, to minimize the vulnerabilities."[104] Kissinger's defense of the agreement, his description of SALT as in "the common interest of humanity," and claim that "both sides won" were picked up in the newscasts, along with his careful explanation of why the agreement was balanced despite the numerical advantage the Soviets had in ICBMs and SLBMs. He made clear to reporters that the freeze on ICBM production and ceiling on submarines would keep the United States from falling even further behind the Soviets in the arms race. He used his trademark humor as well. After answering a question by detailing the Soviet production of missiles, something never discussed publicly in the Kremlin, Kissinger deadpanned, "If I get arrested here for espionage, gentlemen, we will know who is to blame."[105]

The signing of the SALT agreement was followed by the final act of the summit, the "Basic Principles" agreement defining relations between the superpowers. The document proclaimed that the two countries "will proceed from the common determination that in the nuclear age there is no alternative to conducting their mutual relations on the basis of peaceful coexistence."[106] The CBS anchor Walter Cronkite now declared that Nixon's trip exceeded expectations, and that although there had been no final deal on trade or agreement on Vietnam, that "paled into insignificance" compared with SALT and the Basic Principles agreement. All this, Cronkite said, was "the personal accomplishment of President Nixon's diplomacy," and he had, along with Kissinger, created a basis of mutual respect and friendship with the Soviet leaders.[107] Nixon's dramatic return to the United States, an evening landing in a helicopter on the steps of the Capitol to report to Congress and a live national audience on his visit, added further to the pageantry of the summit and its treatment as "historic" by the commentators.[108] Nixon's rhetoric in the speech was not restrained, as he called for seizing this "unparalleled opportunity to build a new structure for peace" and for America "to lead the world up out of the lowlands of constant war, and onto the high plateau of lasting peace."[109] In the congressional gallery, sitting next to Mrs. Nixon, was the smiling and laughing Henry Kissinger. The newscasters joked about the morning's newspaper picture of Kissinger in a nightclub in Tehran, where the presidential party stopped briefly after Moscow.[110] The national security adviser was photographed with a belly dancer sitting in his lap, and when asked, Kissinger remarked that they had discussed "how you convert the SLBMs on a G-class submarine."[111]

Kissinger was now, as Peter Lisagor of the *Chicago Sun-Times* put it, "a legend," a diplomat who was "the compleat cosmopolitan, urbane without swagger, self-centered without smugness." He was now "a global superstar, the first and thus far only celebrity diplomat of the media age."[112] His masterful press briefings during the summit had journalists searching for more superlatives. Marvin Kalb described one late-night briefing in almost mythic terms: "All eyes were on the star, enveloped in a soft yellow spotlight, crooning his melody of détente through SALT, and cracking a couple of jokes, as if he were the lead in a Hasty Pudding production called *Everything You Ever Wanted to Know About Diplomacy, But Never Dared to Ask*."[113] When Kissinger spoke to congressional leaders on the SALT I agreement in mid-June, Dan Rather described it for CBS viewers as "a briefing that almost all who attended" regarded as "brilliant, fair, and persuasive."[114] After Kissinger returned from another trip to China to brief Zhou Enlai on the Moscow talks, the Nixon administration finally relented from its earlier media rules and allowed television crews to record Kissinger's voice as well as his image. Kissinger remarked to the reporters that there would be "simultaneous translation" of his comments, a self-deprecating joke that only further enhanced his image.[115]

During the summer of 1972, Kissinger became a regular fixture on the nightly news, with his world travels chronicled and his words parsed for any indication that progress was being made on the Vietnam peace talks. Now described as a "man with one of the world's toughest jobs," and the president's "number one envoy," Kissinger's secret trips had become a thing of the past, with reporters following him like the paparazzi of more recent times. After traveling to Paris in August for talks with the North Vietnamese, Kissinger went off to celebrate his parents' fiftieth wedding anniversary in Switzerland with his children and other relatives. CBS News was there, hoping to get some assessment of the peace talks.[116] Kissinger was a featured guest at the Republican National Convention, where Walter Cronkite announced that the floor reporter Dan Rather had gained an interview with a "celebrity," Henry Kissinger. During this interview, Kissinger stressed that the administration was making "a very serious effort" to negotiate an end to the war, and that "peace is much too important to be engaged in partisan politics." With a very straight face he also remarked that the president "never talks to me about domestic politics," a statement designed for the image Kissinger wished to project rather than its accuracy. He also appeared in the Republican campaign film about Nixon, which highlighted both the China trip and the Moscow summit. In his contribution, Kissinger at first confessed that, like "most of [his] colleagues," he had opposed Nixon, but that he had watched and observed him and now thought there was "a certain heroic quality about how he conducts his business," and that his impact on foreign policy would be "historic."[117]

VIETNAM: THE FINAL LEG OF THE TRIFECTA

When William Safire and Henry Kissinger strolled through downtown Warsaw, reflecting on the results of the Moscow summit, Safire remarked, "Been one hell of a week, Henry. What does the President do for an encore?" Kissinger did not hesitate: "Make peace in Vietnam."[118] In the months before he reached the tentative October agreement, Kissinger emphasized to Nixon that one of the president's great heroes, Charles de Gaulle, had achieved French withdrawal from Algeria as an act of national policy, that "he left under his own steam," even though this turned Algeria over to his enemies. Kissinger believed that Hanoi found itself isolated from the Soviet Union and China, with both pushing their communist ally to settle with Nixon. The North Vietnamese Easter offensive had failed, and hopes that George Mc-Govern would capture the presidency imploded at the end of July with the

Eagleton fiasco. (McGovern had hastily selected Senator Thomas Eagleton as his running mate, a man who had been treated for serious depression with electric shock therapy. After the embarrassing public controversy and indecision, McGovern replaced him with Kennedy brother-in-law Sargent Shriver, but the decline in the opinion polls was dramatic.)[119] Kissinger was certain that the North Vietnamese would want to settle with the United States before the election, fearful of what a reelected Nixon might do.

Both Nixon and Kissinger wanted to end the war, though they occasionally clashed over specific tactics and the timing of initiatives.[120] When they discussed Vietnam in early August, both expressed pessimism about South Vietnam's long-term viability, but Nixon's basic concern was that the Saigon regime had to remain intact until after the November election. With the domestic political implications foremost in his mind, Nixon emphasized, "We also have to realize, Henry, that winning an election is terribly important, it is terribly important this year." Kissinger agreed, and in response to Nixon's question of whether the United States could have a "viable foreign policy" if North Vietnam conquered South Vietnam in a year or two, Kissinger added that if they could get a proper settlement by October, "by January '74 no one will give a damn."[121] Kissinger was more optimistic about the negotiations than Nixon, while Nixon worried more about raising expectations among voters within the United States each time Kissinger met with the North Vietnamese in Paris, as disillusionment could be harmful politically—a lesson learned from the 1968 election.[122] Nixon, however, did not stop Kissinger, who continued his meetings in Paris.

Kissinger's reading of his adversaries proved correct. Hanoi's politburo changed its policy in the summer of 1972, most likely because of a combination of Soviet and Chinese pressures, the failure of its military offensive, and the general war weariness of its population.[123] North Vietnam finally accepted the proposals in Nixon's May 8 speech and the decoupling of the military and political aspects of the negotiations. Hanoi would agree now to a cease-fire in place—North Vietnamese troops would remain in the South—and the return of American prisoners in return for a complete American withdrawal from Vietnam. The Thiệu government could remain, and the issues between the Communists and Saigon could be settled "peacefully" in vaguely defined elections. Hanoi now insisted on a settlement before November 7, the date of the American presidential election.[124]

Saigon, however, did not want a settlement. The success of the ARVN forces in defeating the offensive led President Thiệu to believe the war was now being won. The South Vietnamese resisted the prospect of complete American withdrawal, especially with the North Vietnamese forces remaining in the South. In contrast to its continued presence in South Korea, the United States did not plan to leave behind any American military forces that might deter a North Vietnamese attack. (The North Vietnamese insisted upon complete withdrawal in return for the release of the American POWs.) The Vietnamese, although well equipped and financed, would be on their own militarily against their dedicated and determined Northern brothers. Reflecting the feelings of many of his compatriots, Thiệu was terrified by the prospect and determined to resist it, as he had in November 1968. As Kissinger admitted, "Thiệu's domestic imperatives imposed intransigence."[125]

After a meeting on September 15, Kissinger, sensing the change in Hanoi's attitude, reported to Nixon, "They repeatedly, and almost plaintively, asked how quickly we wished to settle and there was none of their usual bravado about how U.S. and world opinion was stacked against them." Kissinger flattered Nixon when he reported to him his warning to the North Vietnamese: "You and your friends have turned this election into a plebiscite on Vietnam. And after November, the President is going to have a majority for continuing the war."[126] Nixon was more ambivalent, warning Kissinger that his polls showed that Americans were opposed to forcing Saigon to accept a coalition government with the Communists, that they favored continued bombing, and that some even wanted "to see the United States prevail after all these years." Yet Nixon also realized the public mood was very "fragile" and likely to change, and that the new relationships with Russia and China could suffer from continuing the war.[127] Although he remained worried about a public confrontation with Thiệu, Nixon was tempted by the political advantages of a peace settlement before the election and having the POWs "home by Christmas."[128] This would require more pressure on Thiệu. At Kissinger's request, on October 6, 1972, Nixon sent a letter to Thiệu urging the Vietnamese leader to "take every measure to avoid the development of an atmosphere which could lead to events similar to those we abhorred in 1963 and which I personally opposed so vehemently in 1968."[129] Both references tapped into Thiệu's fears. In 1968, Thiệu feared that Johnson was plotting to overthrow him if he did not agree to go to Paris for the peace talks. Even worse was the reference to the Diem assassination of 1963, as ominous a threat as any American leader could have given. Paradoxically, Ambassador Bunker reported to Kissinger that the message "had a reassuring and steadying effect on Thiệu," although it is hard to see why.[130]

Two days later, Kissinger had a meeting with Lê Đức Thọ, which Kissinger would describe as "the moment that moved me most deeply" in his career in public service.[131] The Vietnamese diplomat announced that the U.S. proposed plan "represented an acceptance of our proposals," a separation of the military and political elements of the settlement, a cease-fire, and an American military withdrawal and the return of the prisoners of war. Hanoi also conceded that Thiệu's government could remain in power. Kissinger asked for a recess and then shook hands with his long-suffering aide Winston Lord and said, "We've done it."[132] Others in his staff, notably John Negroponte, were more restrained in their reaction, recognizing the great difficulty they would have in convincing President Thiệu to accept the continued North Vietnamese troop presence in the South. Kissinger remained in a triumphant mood and went off to take a walk in Paris, leaving Lord and Negroponte to work on Lê Đức Thọ's document. He sent an urgent telegram to Ambassador Bunker in Saigon telling President Thiệu to order his commanders to seize as much territory as possible since a cease-fire might be coming. He told Haldeman to tell the president that there had been some "definite progress" in the talks and that he "can harbor some confidence that the outcome will be positive."[133] For the next few days, Kissinger sent similarly vague but hopeful messages to Nixon, saving the unveiling of the agreement until he could personally deliver the message.

Back in the United States, Senator George McGovern delivered his own Vietnam plan on October 10 in a nationally televised paid political broadcast.

McGovern declared that on Inauguration Day he would halt the bombing of North Vietnam and halt all aid to South Vietnam. He would then withdraw American forces within ninety days, expecting that this would lead to the return of the POWs.[134] Although Defense Secretary Laird criticized it as "unconditional surrender," McGovern's speech made it clear that he still believed there was political gain in a strong antiwar stance and that the Nixon administration's commitment to the survival of the Thiệu regime was a domestic political vulnerability. With Nixon buoyed by a relatively strong economy, only the Watergate scandal—*The Washington Post* ran a front-page story on Republican espionage against Democratic candidates the same day as McGovern's speech—and Vietnam remained as issues working against Nixon's prospective landslide.

On October 12, 1972, Kissinger and Haig arrived at the White House for dinner, having just returned from Paris. Kissinger showed no signs of jet lag as he told Nixon, "Well, you got three out of three, Mr. President. It's well on the way." Nixon responded with a surprised, "You got an agreement? Are you kidding?"[135] Kissinger then proceeded to give him the details of the Vietnam cease-fire and peace agreement he had reached with the North Vietnamese. As Kissinger slowly made his presentation, emphasizing that "this was a much better deal by far than we had expected," Nixon grew increasingly excited—"cranked up," as Haldeman described him—interrupting Kissinger to emphasize all the problems and crises he had faced in getting to this point and thinking about the best ways to convince Thiệu to accept the treaty. Eventually Nixon decided to summon his valet, Manolo Sanchez, and ask him to get the good wine, his '57 Lafite Rothschild, to toast the achievement.[136] Nixon surely realized that McGovern's Vietnam plan was asking so much less from the North Vietnamese than they now indicated they were prepared to grant to Nixon, and that Kissinger's deal was not only another foreign policy success but also the final nail in the coffin of McGovern's candidacy.

Kissinger had negotiated a tight schedule with the North Vietnamese. The timetable called for him to go to Saigon to get Thiệu's approval, then to Hanoi for final talks, with Nixon's announcement of the agreement on October 26 and the signing in Paris on October 31, seven days before the election. If he could pull it off, it would be a spectacular media event, and Kissinger would be at the center of it. Indeed, some of his more skeptical aides suspected that he was so enthralled with the prospect "that the scenario was almost more important than the words," and that a sloppiness about the specific provisions would be caused by the rush to settle by Election Day.[137] Although there were numerous indications otherwise, Kissinger was certain Thiệu would accept the agreement, as he told Haldeman that it was "the best he's ever going to get and, unlike '68, when Thiệu screwed Johnson, he had Nixon as an alternative. Now he has McGovern as an alternative, which would be a disaster for him, even worse than the worst possible thing that Nixon could do to him."[138] Nixon assured Kissinger he would do whatever he could to convince Thiệu, although shortly before Kissinger left, Nixon again reminded him, "We cannot have a collapse in South Vietnam prior to the election." Kissinger assured Nixon that would not happen. Nixon ultimately told Kissinger, "If you can make the deal, do it now. If you can't, do the next best thing." Kissinger then asked, "Politically it'd be better for you to do the latter?" Nixon replied, "Henry, don't even think of the politics. Let me say: either has an advantage."[139]

Nixon was thinking of the politics involved, but believed that he was far enough ahead in the polls that he could spin either result in a way that favored his candidacy.[140] The president thought that the settlement Kissinger had negotiated was the best they could do, but if Thiệu refused to go along now, he was prepared to wait until after the election. Kissinger wanted the settlement before the election. He believed this favored the U.S. bargaining position, with Hanoi clearly wanting to settle rapidly and seemingly willing to make more concessions. Kissinger knew the personal glory and media applause he would receive if he succeeded with this personal trifecta of diplomatic achievements; it also would serve to make him indispensable in Nixon's second term. Kissinger was clearly growing more worried about his relationship with Nixon. He told one reporter who wanted to do a story on him "at home," "If I survive the next four weeks, you can do it," and he joked with his friend Max Frankel, who called for an appointment, "I am sometimes tempted to squeeze anybody in ahead of the President."[141] In a number of telephone conversations with sympathetic friends, he referred to "my Leader" in talking about Nixon, while Nixon occasionally teased Kissinger about going back to academic life, perhaps at Pomona in California, and then mentioned that "poor Rostow, poor fellow's got to be in Texas and he's a brilliant fellow. Henry we'll get you a good college out here."[142]

Kissinger's deputy, Al Haig, suspected this insecurity. A decorated Vietnam combat veteran, Haig had advanced in rank rapidly within the Nixon White House, and Nixon admired Haig's physical courage and liked his blunt manner and loyalty. Haig's organizational abilities and military efficiency contrasted with Kissinger's lack of attention to such matters and kept the National Security Council functioning smoothly. Some in the White House even considered Haig to be Kissinger's "alter ego," although this underestimated the rivalry between the two men for Nixon's attention.[143] Haig's own close relationship with Nixon, developed during Kissinger's frequent absences, contributed to Kissinger's uneasiness about where he stood with Nixon.

Haig told Haldeman that it was important to give Kissinger "total support" so that he would not feel he had to prove anything.[144] Given Haig's own doubts about the settlement, however, Haig was likely playing a double-sided game, as he also cautioned Nixon about Thiệu's reluctance to settle. For his part, Kissinger said later that the White House staff wanted to "cut [him] down to size," claiming, "Of all of Nixon's Assistants I was the least involved in the election campaign . . . On the principle that foreign policy was bipartisan, I had refused to attend any fund-raising functions."[145] This was not the real issue. The central problem was Kissinger's cavalier and dismissive assumptions about the South Vietnamese, for whom he had less respect than he did for their communist compatriots. Kissinger believed that Thiệu had no choice but to yield.[146] On the day of Kissinger's arrival in Saigon, one of the leading Vietnamese newspapers ran the *Harvard Lampoon*'s fake naked picture of the national security adviser—posed on a rug as the magazine *Playgirl* had posed the actor Burt Reynolds—with the caption "Kissinger has no more secrets."[147] This was a signal to Kissinger that his treatment in the Vietnamese city would not be as respectful or reverential as he had come to expect.

The atmosphere of the meeting, as his assistant John Negroponte recalled, was "very tense and very unpleasant."[148] Kissinger's confrontations with Thiệu's advisers, particularly his cousin and adopted nephew Hoang Duc Nha, were particularly intense, with Nha challenging Kissinger about the Vietnamese text of the agreement and particularly a reference to only "three" nations of Indochina, a reference in effect accepting the Communists' insistence on Vietnam as one country. Thiệu continually arrived late and canceled meetings, leading Kissinger to exclaim in frustration, "I am the Special Envoy of the President of the United States. You know I cannot be treated as an errand boy." Thiệu bluntly rejected Kissinger's agreement. Kissinger told Nixon that it was "hard to exaggerate the toughness of Thiệu's position. His demands verge on insanity." Kissinger still wanted to keep to the schedule he had given Lê Đức Thọ and go to Hanoi to try to get a final deal, but Nixon thought that would now look like "a complete surrender."[149] The president wanted him to continue to press Thiệu and wrote another letter warning Thiệu of the political dangers of a break with the United States. The United States had already initiated Operation Enhance Plus, a massive military aid program to Saigon that was designed to bolster the regime before a cease-fire, and Nixon thought this might give Kissinger some leverage with Thiệu. But Kissinger's last meeting went as badly as the first. Thiệu refused to accept the continued presence of a North Vietnamese army in the South, rejected the proposed National Council of Reconciliation, and accused the United States of wanting to abandon South Vietnam. Kissinger angrily responded, "We have fought for four years, have mortgaged our whole foreign policy to the defense of one country. What you have said is a very bitter thing to hear."[150]

After Kissinger's return to the United States, he feared that Hanoi would now go public with the agreement, demonstrating its willingness to settle and creating a political embarrassment for the administration. So Kissinger, determined to get the story out, lunched with the *New York Times* journalist Max Frankel and gave him the basic outlines of the agreement—and his own personal role in securing it. When Radio Hanoi did go public with its broadcast of the agreement on the morning of October 26, Kissinger was ready to spring into action. In a nationally televised press conference, he declared, "We believe that peace is at hand," and his bold words led the evening news.

Kissinger's words had an electric effect across the country, with commentators like Dan Rather remarking that they guaranteed Nixon's landslide, while others also remarked on Kissinger's centrality in negotiating an agreement.[151] After the press conference ended, Kissinger launched a full-scale media offensive, giving countless interviews and briefings and building up, in the words of the Kalb brothers, "an extraordinary journalistic momentum behind the idea of "peace is at hand."[152] Even Haldeman, who often worried about Kissinger upstaging Nixon, was pleased with Kissinger's press conference and called it "the best lucky break of the campaign" because it "takes the [Watergate] corruption stuff off the front pages, totally wipes out any other news."[153] Nixon called Kissinger later that evening and jokingly began by saying, "I understand that all the three network news shows were about Vietnam and I wonder why." Kissinger chuckled and responded by noting that he had talked to Colson, who believed that "we had wiped McGovern out now." Kissinger added that he thought the president was getting the credit without the agreement being finalized. Nixon was very pleased, telling Kissinger that he was glad Kissinger made the announcement, since if he himself had made it, people would think it was a political move.[154]

Kissinger closed his press conference with a comment that was little noted at the time but captured his own sentiments. After mentioning that the United States would not be "stampeded" into an agreement, which was a reference to North Vietnam, nor "deflected from an agreement when its provisions are right," a reference to South Vietnam, he closed by saying he hoped that "we can restore both peace and unity to America very soon."[155] Kissinger truly believed that a negotiated peace would help to heal the domestic divisions of the war. It was also his way of expressing a strong political message supporting Nixon while appearing as the nonpolitical expert. But his "peace is at hand" soon became a target for critics, who questioned why the agreement was still out of reach. Only a few days after Kissinger's press conference, Senator McGovern appeared on *Meet the Press* to argue that Kissinger's statement was all about electoral politics, and then at a November 5 campaign rally, he accused Kissinger of lying, saying, "Peace is not at hand; it is not even in sight."[156]

In the days leading up to the election, Kissinger was in a very confident mood, certain that the war would soon end and that his own vision of a nego-tiated settlement would be vindicated. It was in this mood that he had what he later called the "most disastrous conversation I ever had with any member of the press."[157] Two meetings with the Italian journalist Oriana Fallaci led Kissinger to a number of statements he would deeply regret, including his comment that the key to his "movie star status" arose "from the fact that I've always acted alone. Americans like that immensely. Americans like the cow-boy who leads the wagon train by riding ahead alone on his horse." The sheer absurdity of the imagery leads one to wonder whether he might have been flirting with the beautiful Italian, whose other questions—"If I put a pistol to your head and ask you to choose between having dinner with Thiệu and hav-ing dinner with Lê Đức Thọ, whom would you choose?"—were designed to provoke him. Kissinger's explanation of the cowboy—"this amazing, roman-tic character suits me precisely because to be alone has always been part of my style or, if you like, my technique"—leads to the conclusion that Kissinger believed in his own magic, as enraptured journalists discussed the Vietnam negotiations and paired these with China and the Soviet Union. Kissinger rejected Fallaci's suggestion that he was "Nixon's mental wet nurse," insisting that Nixon was "a very strong man" with a "consuming interest" in foreign policy and claiming, "What I've done has been possible because he made it possible for me."[158] However, such statements paled against Kissinger's claims to have acted alone, especially on China. Ironically, they also reflected an attitude that existed among some of Nixon's most extreme critics, especially on the right, whose exaggeration of Kissinger's role was thinly veiled anti-Semitism. Campaigning for president as the candidate of George Wallace's American Party, John Schmitz told voters that if the American people were "fooled by all this talk of peace" in Vietnam, "they deserved President Kissinger for four more years."[159]

When Nixon arrived back at the White House on election night, he found a handwritten note from Kissinger on the pillow of his bed. It saluted Nixon's "historic achievement—to take a divided nation, mired in war, losing its con-fidence, wracked by intellectuals without conviction, and give it a new purpose and overcome its hesitations," and thanked Nixon for his "unfailing human kindness and consideration," and for the "privilege of the last four years."[160] Nixon's overwhelming electoral victory—forty-nine states and 60.7 percent of the popular vote—was a remarkable personal achievement in which Kissinger had played a decisive role. Kissinger called Nixon late on election night to extend his "warmest congratulations," as Nixon harshly described McGovern as a "prick" for what he regarded as an ungracious concession speech. Kissinger agreed, calling the South Dakota senator "ungenerous, unworthy," and, playing to Nixon's prejudices, reminded him that the media and "all the intellectuals" were against him but he triumphed nevertheless.[161] Kissinger's expression of support, however, could not defuse Nixon's anger when the Fallaci interview became public a week and a half after the election. Nixon called Haldeman in astonishment, particularly at Kissinger's claim that the China initiative was an example of Kissinger's acting alone. Nixon even told Haldeman that he should tell Kissinger about the White House taping system as a way to remind him that there was a record of how decisions were made, and that, as Nixon put it, "[Henry] doesn't make the decisions, and when they are made, that he wavers the most."[162]

Kissinger spent the postelection period readying for his return to Paris while hoping that Haig would deal with Saigon and get concessions from President Thiệu. Haig's meetings with Thiệu proved more productive than Kissinger's, but the issue of North Vietnamese troops in South Vietnam remained. Haig was reluctant to press the issue to the point of an open break, commenting, "To have done so would have hardened his position and confronted him with a test of manhood in front of his advisers that he could not have gone back from."[163] Kissinger helped Nixon draft another strong letter to Thiệu, in which Nixon tried to sweeten his hard line with Thiệu by promising that in the event of a North Vietnamese violation, "It is my intention to take swift and severe retaliatory action."[164] Thiệu's continuing defiance led Kissinger to complain to Nixon, "That goddam Thiệu—he's going through his stalling act." Although he thought it a "terrible" alternative, Kissinger told Nixon that he could favor making a simple bilateral agreement with the North Vietnamese. Nixon worried that antiwar critics would then be able to say, "Hell you could have done that all along." Kissinger feared that the North Vietnamese would toughen their stance but told Nixon, "At this moment they are less of a problem than Thiệu."[165] Both men recognized that the newly elected Congress might vote to cut off assistance to Thiệu if he continued to resist the agreement.[166]

Kissinger's renewed Paris discussions began on November 20 and took place in a media circus, with hundreds of television reporters and journalists covering Kissinger's every move in Paris. At his arrival press conference, Kissinger made a point of stressing repeatedly that he was consulting closely with "our allied country, the Government of the Republic of Vietnam," a classic case of overcompensation. Kissinger added that if the North Vietnamese reflected the same constructive attitude they had in October, a "rapid" end to the war was possible.[167] Over the next weeks, the television coverage of the talks was consistently optimistic about the possibilities of a settlement, with Kissinger's smiling countenance and walks in the garden with Lê Đức Thọ seen as signs that an agreement was near. Behind the scenes, Kissinger made little headway with the North Vietnamese on the sixty-nine changes Thiệu asked for in the October agreement. He characterized Thiệu's changes as "so preposterous, they went so far beyond what we had indicated both publicly and privately, that it must have strengthened Hanoi's already strong temptation to dig in its heels and push us against our Congressional deadlines."[168] The North Vietnamese responded by withdrawing some of their earlier concessions, most notably now insisting that Thiệu release some thirty thousand political prisoners at the same time they released American POWs. When Kissinger reported this to the president, Nixon responded by dispatching a "tough-sounding instruction" to Kissinger for use with the North Vietnamese, reminding them that he could take "strong action," as he had done before the Moscow summit. In his memoirs, Kissinger describes Nixon as "ensconced at Camp David, surrounded only by his public relations experts, . . . deep in the bog of resentments that had produced the darkest and perhaps most malevolent frame of mind of his presidency."[169] Kissinger portrays an isolated Nixon as much more eager to use military force than Kissinger thought wise. In reality, Nixon was genuinely undecided, and the next day he changed course and told Kissinger to keep talking with the North Vietnamese.

After a brief adjournment in the talks, during which Kissinger returned to Washington to join Nixon in pressuring the South Vietnamese to accept the agreement, and Nixon promised Thiệu he would react "with full force" in the event of violations, Kissinger returned to Paris.[170] His return on December 4 was greeted with a renewed wave of media optimism about the imminence of a Vietnam cease-fire and settlement. All three networks led their nightly news broadcasts with images of a smiling Kissinger and Lê Đức Thọ exchanging handshakes, and speculated about the possibility of some American POWs being home by Christmas.[171] The contrast between the positive coverage and the reality of the talks was striking. That evening Kissinger's report to Nixon began with the ominous words, "We are at a point where a break-off in the talks looks almost certain." Kissinger's attempt to get some concessions that could appease Saigon was met with a North Vietnamese withdrawal of more of their past concessions, including a demand for the withdrawal of American civilian advisers, something that would have rendered American military assistance ineffectual. Kissinger now believed that the North Vietnamese were playing for time, seduced by the "attractive vision they see of our having to choose between a complete split with Saigon or an unmanageable domestic situation." His own sense was that the United States now had only two choices: sign the original October agreement, with its implications for the Thiệu regime, or risk breaking off the talks, which might mean renewed military action against North Vietnam and the political consequences that would bring. Kissinger acknowledged that if the talks collapsed, "I will talk to you upon my return about my own responsibility and role." Along with these hints of his resignation, Kissinger also put forward what would prove unpalatable advice to Nixon. Kissinger advised the president to go on national television and make another "stirring and convincing case" to the people "to proceed with your principled course until there was a sound and just peace, and you would underline this stance by combining firm military actions and a reasonable negotiating position."[172]

Over the next two weeks Kissinger and Nixon exchanged countless messages, with Kissinger expressing optimism after one negotiating session and pessimism after the next, and Nixon counseling patience and negotiations in one cable and firmness and threats in the next. The television coverage expressed optimism and the expectation of an imminent settlement. Kissinger later portrayed his complex interaction with Nixon as rooted in his strained relationship with the president at the time, aggravated by Kissinger's sense of Nixon's isolated situation. Nixon, Kissinger said, was "cut off from the most knowledgeable senior advisers, all of whom (including Haig) were with me. He would ruminate, writing out the issues on his yellow pad, all the while showered with the advice of his public relations geniuses."[173] Nixon, for his part, thought Kissinger was still emotionally "up and down," weakened in his negotiations by the perception that the North Vietnamese now had "that he has either to get a deal or lose face." Nixon rejected out of hand Kissinger's proposal that he rally the nation to support a renewed bombing campaign, telling Ehrlichman, "Henry doesn't seem to understand that. Or does he? Maybe he just wants people to associate me with failure."[174] This personal strain and rivalry between the two men, aggravated by the Fallaci interview and the efforts of both to blame the other, misses the degree to which they ultimately reached the same conclusion: Hanoi was delaying a final settlement, playing for time until the split with Thiệu became insurmountable and Congress cut off funding. Kissinger told Nixon, "Hanoi may well have concluded that we have been outmaneuvered and dare not continue the war because of domestic and international expectations."[175] At the same time that Kissinger reached this conclusion about Hanoi's position, President Thiệu delivered another defiant speech to his National Assembly, demanding the complete withdrawal of all North Vietnamese troops and calling the National Council of Reconciliation a "disguised coalition government."[176] Nixon now recognized that he faced a difficult choice with both Vietnams: he was convinced that Hanoi was stalling because it was "aware of our difficulties with Thiệu and the threats we have made."[177] When Kissinger left the Paris talks on December 13 to return to Washington, reporters still focused on Thiệu's resistance, and Kissinger leaked a story to Reston in *The New York Times* that proclaimed "Thiệu's Sovereignty Bid at Issue" and identified the South Vietnamese leader as the primary obstacle to peace.[178]

On the morning of December 14, 1972, Nixon, Haig, and Kissinger met to discuss their choices. Kissinger later recalled that all those at the meeting "agreed that *some* military response was necessary," but that they were not in accord about what kind.[179] Nixon actually began with a long monologue, telling Kissinger not to be discouraged and to remember all that they had been through during the last four years—"November 3, Cambodia, May 8th"—and not to second-guess his recent actions, including the "peace is at hand" statement before the elections. Kissinger apologized for his "up and down reports," saying that "they had us on a roller coaster." He then gave a version of the Paris talks in a way that implied that there had been a sudden change in the attitude of the North Vietnamese at the end of the third day of talks, which he had not reported earlier, and that after that point, they had started dragging things out. He implied that the North Vietnamese had intelligence from within the Saigon government that provided them with the content of Washington's messages to Thiệu. Nixon already suspected this—in part because the United States itself was listening in on Thiệu's internal conversations as well—and Kissinger argued that Hanoi recognized that the greater the tension between the United States and Saigon, "the greater the possibility we would flush Thiệu down the drain." Kissinger explained that he had continued to negotiate seriously until the very end, emphasizing that on the last day he was there, "We had it down to two issues on the text, and one issue of substance." But in the end, Kissinger became convinced that "they're always going to keep it just out of reach." Without a deadline like Election Day, the North Vietnamese reverted to their "normal negotiating habit" of delay after delay. "They're shits," Kissinger exclaimed, "tawdry, miserable, filthy people. They make the Russians look good."[180]

Kissinger did not reserve his scatological venom for only the North Vietnamese. From his point of view, his "gamble" to get a settlement before the election was lost "80 percent because of Thiệu." The United States was "caught between Hanoi and Saigon, both of them facing us down in a position of total impotence, in which Hanoi is just stringing us along, and Saigon is just ignoring us." This was, in one of Kissinger's favorite expressions, his "cold-blooded analysis," and he could see nothing changing. Kissinger now volunteered to give a "low-key briefing" to the press to describe the deadlock in the talks. He acknowledged that they would attack him because he "was the guy who said, 'Peace is at hand.'" This act of self-sacrifice—done with a fair amount of self-pity—led Nixon to offer Kissinger reassurance and tactical guidance as to how to deal with the press. Nixon even coined the statement that Hanoi wanted a treaty that provided "peace in North Vietnam and perpetual warfare in South Vietnam." Using one of Nixon's own idioms, Kissinger then suggested, "We start bombing the bejeezus out of them within 48 hours of having put the negotiating record out." After two weeks of bombing, Kissinger thought the United States should offer a separate deal to Hanoi, excluding Thiệu's government, that would trade the withdrawal of U.S. forces in return for the POWs and would be timed just as Congress came back into session. He added, "If you are willing to go six months, they're going to crack." Nixon responded that six months was not "in the cards" given congressional attitudes, but they could bomb through Christmas and before Congress came back into session. When Haig added that the weather in North Vietnam "right now is absolutely bad," Nixon asked about using B-52s. Kissinger's guess was "that if you go bold," the chances were "75–25, because these guys are on their last legs." As the meeting drew to a close, Nixon worked himself up to the conviction that he had to order the bombing, that "we've got to play the big bullet." This time, however, he would not go on television "and make one of these asshole Vietnam speeches. This is not the time." Kissinger rapidly chimed in to reassure Nixon that he was right about this and that Kissinger had been wrong to suggest it. He even added, "It's painful for me . . . but if you don't do this, it will be like the EC-121," referring to the lack of retaliation after North Korea shot down the U.S. reconnaissance flight in April 1969. After Nixon reminded him again that "the press is the enemy" and the "professors are the enemy," Kissinger used an expression sure to get Nixon's attention. "Mr. President," he intoned, "if you don't do this, then you'll really be impotent."[181]

On Saturday, December 16, Kissinger went in front of the White House press corps to brief them on the stalemated negotiations. The day before, Nixon had spent considerable time coaching Kissinger, encouraging him to "make the President the tough guy all the way through" and telling Haldeman after Kissinger left that he "must try to be effective rather than brilliant."[182]

With Nixon's directions in hand, Kissinger sought to place the blame on Hanoi for the stalemate, while at the same time making it clear to Saigon that a settlement was near. Kissinger referred repeatedly in the briefing to the president—fourteen times compared with three times in the October press conference. One of his most quoted lines was, "The President decided we could not engage in a charade with the American people." Kissinger again emphasized that the United States would not be "stampeded into an agreement," adding that it would not be "charmed into an agreement until its conditions are right." He did include a conciliatory tone toward the end of the briefing, telling Hanoi, "We are prepared to continue in the spirit of the negotiations that were started in October."[183] The irony was that Nixon's insistence on making himself "the tough guy all the way through" would ultimately facilitate the stories that Kissinger favored diplomacy while Nixon wanted to bomb, stories that would lead to a Nobel Peace Prize for Kissinger and ignominy for Nixon.[184] At the time, Kissinger lamented that the story coming out of his briefing was the contrast between his report of a breakdown in the talks and his earlier "peace is at hand" statement. Even before the bombing resumed, *NBC Nightly News* on December 17 stressed this contradiction, prominently reporting George McGovern's claim that the administration deliberately misled the American people before the election. It also did a long feature on the death in Vietnam of Air Force Colonel Louis Taylor from Johnson City, Tennessee, and interviewed his wife, who had voted for Nixon but was now bitter that peace had been promised but not delivered and that her husband was dead as a result. Garrick Utley introduced the story by talking about the many—mostly Vietnamese but also Americans—who had died since Kissinger had announced that "peace is at hand."[185]

On December 18, Operation Linebacker II began, a twelve-day campaign—with a one-day pause for Christmas—involving some 739 B-52 sorties dropping 15,237 tons of bombs on the Hanoi and Haiphong areas. Air Force and Navy fighter-bombers dropped an additional 5,000 tons. The American bombing sought to convince the North Vietnamese to stop their delaying tactics and to reassure the South Vietnamese that the United States was not abandoning them, like a cowboy shooting his way out as he exited the saloon—not a comparison Kissinger would now have made. The North Vietnamese, using virtu-ally every SAM missile they possessed, shot down fifteen B-52s, nine fighters, a reconnaissance plane, and a rescue helicopter. North Vietnam announced casualties of 1,312 in Hanoi and some 300 in the Haiphong area. American losses amounted to some 31 crewmen captured and 93 lost in the operation.[186] The "Christmas bombing" unleashed a wave of angry criticism of American policy, both from domestic critics and internationally. The Swedish prime minister, Olof Palme, compared it with Nazi atrocities, Pope Paul VI called it "the object of daily grief," and press criticism throughout Europe was partic-ularly extreme. At home Nixon's critics vehemently denounced the bombing, with Senator William Saxbe from Ohio speculating that the president "ap-pears to have lost his senses" and the Senate Democratic leader Mike Mans-field calling it a "stone-age tactic." Press and television coverage was also intensely critical of the operation. "Terror Bombing in the Name of Peace" headlined *The Washington Post.* The *New York Times* columnist James Reston called it "war by tantrum." His colleague Tom Wicker said it amounted to "shame on earth" at the Christmas season, and Anthony Lewis referred to it as a "crime against humanity."[187] Some focused on Kissinger directly. Senator Stuart Symington said the White House had deceived the American people when Kissinger, the "number one representative of the administration in for-eign policy," said peace was at hand. He claimed to have been told by others in the Nixon administration that the administration was not as close to peace as Kissinger claimed.[188] The columnist Joseph Kraft accused Kissinger of be-ing "a good German" who provided respectability to "whatever monstrous policy" Nixon decided upon.

The intensity of the criticism had its impact on both men. Colson recalled that Nixon "got less and less sleep as he took the full weight of the criticism. I saw him aging before my eyes."[189] Nixon's popularity fell by 11 points, and ru-mors abounded of a rift between Nixon and Kissinger, which was reported on the evening news.[190] These rumors emerged just as both men were honored together as *Time*'s "Men of the Year." The magazine described them as an "odd couple, an improbable partnership," but as having created a "unique symbiosis—Nixon supplying power and will, Kissinger an intellectual framework and negotiating skills." Together they combined to change "the shape of the world, accomplishing the most profound rearrangement of the earth's political powers since the beginning of the cold war."[191] The article described Kissinger as "Nixon's creation, using the power base of the presidency to roam the world and speak for Nixon, to set the stage for summits, negotiate war and peace," and referred to his "servant's heart" for Nixon. The joint award infuriated Nixon, who told Haldeman that Kissinger should not see *Time*'s editors or talk to them at all, even insisting that the White House prevent Kissinger from calling or receiving calls, something Haldeman confessed in his diary he could not do.[192]

Kissinger had tried to head off the *Time* award, even appealing directly to the editors.[193] Now in his direct dealings with Nixon during the Christmas bombing, he tried something akin to damage control and sought to reassure Nixon that his bombing decision was the right one. He told Nixon that he had explained to the State Department's William Sullivan, who was with him at the Paris talks, that "the President is caught between the two Vietnamese parties," and it was their mistake to try to trap him. Flattering Nixon—but also making his own point about the difficulty of both Vietnams, especially Thiệu—Kissinger added, "I have no idea what [the president's] going to do, but my guess is he'll turn on both of them." Kissinger repeatedly blasted Thiệu in language much harsher than what he used for the North Vietnamese, referring to him as an "unmitigated selfish, psychopathic, son-of-a-bitch," and continually lamenting that he had prevented the October agreement. Kissinger also reassured Nixon that the public supported him, saying, "I must have 200 letters by now, or telegrams, all saying 'We are proud of what you're doing. Don't let the Communists push you around.'" He also told Nixon that by bombing, "if we now get the agreement it makes it enforceable."[194] Nixon quickly agreed, and sent Haig to see Thiệu as the bombing commenced to convey the message that the United States was preparing to settle, and to provide Thiệu the reassurance—testified to by the B-52 bombing—that the United States would act to prevent any flagrant North Vietnamese violation of the agreement.[195]

Kissinger was, however, stung by the harsh criticism he received from journalist friends and associates for the bombing, and clearly made some efforts to distance himself from the decision. In his memoirs, he notes that the White House staff tried to blame him for the collapse of the negotiations and accused him of overstepping his negotiating authority in the first place. However, Kissinger also admits, "Some of the journalists may have mistaken my genuine depression about the seeming collapse of the peace efforts for a moral disagreement."[196] Most notably, a Reston article depicted Kissinger as "undoubtedly" opposed to the bombing strategy and suggested that Kissinger might resign and "write the whole story of the Paris talks and why they broke down, and this would probably be highly embarrassing to Mr. Nixon."[197] Such articles infuriated Nixon, who ordered his aide Charles Colson to call Kissinger and tell him not to speak to anyone. "I will not tolerate insubordination," Nixon told Colson, and asked him to have the Secret Service keep a record of Kissinger's phone conversations.[198] Kissinger later admitted, with the same words he used in regretting the wiretaps on friendly journalists and his staff, that his effort to distance himself from Nixon on this issue "is one of the episodes in my public life in which I take no great pride."[199]

For all the animosity between the two men it created, Operation Linebacker II "worked."[200] While not justifying the level of force, Vietnamese civilian casualties, or the loss of B-52s and American lives, the bombing did convince the North Vietnamese leadership to return to Paris and helped give Nixon an argument he could use with President Thiệu.[201] Vietnamese sources indicate that the bombing did "inflict severe physical and psychological damage on North Vietnam." What helped drive Hanoi back to the talks was the sense of isolation it experienced from its Communist allies, despite the worldwide antagonism toward the American action. On December 26, the North Vietnamese leaders sent word that they were ready to resume negotiations with the United States on January 4. Washington ended the bombing on December 29.[202]

As word came to the Americans that Hanoi wanted to talk, Kissinger took the opportunity to rebuild his relationship with Nixon, calling him from a friend's home in California and reassuring him that despite all the criticism, "we've faced down the people again, and you have shown that you are not to be trifled with." Nixon was showing the strain he was under from both the American losses in the bombings and the relentless political attacks on the policy. When Kissinger started to assure him, "I am certain you will go down in history as having—" Nixon interrupted him and said, "Well forget history . . . you haven't run into a hell of a lot of flak out there, have you?" Kissinger sheepishly remarked that he was not running into anybody, since his friend's house was quite isolated and he was determined "to stay out of the social columns on this trip."[203] The next day, when Hanoi's decision was confirmed, Kissinger again called Nixon to say, "This has been another spectacular for you, Mr. President." Nixon softly replied, "Yeah. Well, hell, we don't know whether it's that . . . at least it pricked a boil, didn't it?" Kissinger poured it on, telling Nixon of a tense conversation he'd had with McGeorge Bundy, who called him to say he was writing a public letter protesting Nixon's policies. When Kissinger asked why, Bundy said, "Because what am I going to tell my son?" Kissinger told Nixon he replied, "Tell him: 'I got us into this war and now I'm preventing us from getting out,'" and then he hung up on him. Playing to Nixon's feelings against Harvard and the "New York establishment," as Kissinger referred to them, was always a bonding moment for the two men, but Nixon quickly brought the conversation back to the problems they still faced, particularly with Thiệu, saying, "We have to pull this off, and it's going to be tough titty."[204]

As Kissinger prepared to return to Paris in early January, he knew that most congressional Democrats were determined to cut off funding for the war. The Democrats enjoyed a healthy 56–42 advantage in the Senate and a 242–192 majority in the House, although there remained some conservative Democrats who would vote with the administration and some liberal Republicans who would oppose its policy on Vietnam. On January 2, the House Democrats voted overwhelmingly to cut off all funds as soon as arrangements could be made for the troops to be withdrawn and the POWs returned. The Senate Democrats passed a similar resolution. Nixon angrily told Kissinger to warn Mike Mansfield that his efforts to cut off funding would imperil his negotiations and threaten that the president would go to the American people with that message.[205] The congressional pressure angered Nixon and

Kissinger, but they also used it to apply even more pressure on the South Vietnamese to settle or face a cutoff in funding and support.[206]

Kissinger's mood switched quickly from tragedy to triumph as he began negotiating with the North Vietnamese again in Paris. On January 9, Nixon's sixtieth birthday, Kissinger called to tell him that there had been a "major breakthrough" in the talks and that "we settled all the outstanding questions in the text of the agreement." Nixon responded by saying that it was the "best birthday present [he'd] had in sixty years," but they agreed to maintain secrecy on the news. Unlike the talks in November and December, there was a real effort to downplay any progress and to put out the message that the talks might last for a long time.[207] Kissinger and Lê Đức Thọ basically returned to the October agreement with some minor differences.[208] Hanoi now accepted Kissinger's formulations on the demilitarized zone, with the irony being these would matter little, as North Vietnamese forces controlled the territory on both sides of the zone. The National Council of Reconciliation was described now in both the American and Vietnamese versions in ways that made it clear it was not a coalition government, a cosmetic change that helped Thiệu politically at home. Nixon and Kissinger had always been clear that they did not want to force Thiệu into a government with the Communists. Rather, they were simply allowing Thiệu to stay in power and continue the war. This is clear from the fact that there was no attempt to secure a withdrawal of North Vietnamese forces from South Vietnam, although there were formal—and completely unenforceable—restrictions against their resupply and reinforcement.

Kissinger and Nixon were pleased with the agreement, and determined to get Thiệu to accept it. Haig was sent again to Saigon, armed with letters from Nixon telling Thiệu that he "irrevocably decided" to sign the agreements on January 27, and that if Thiệu did not sign as well, the result would be "an inevitable and immediate termination of U.S. economic and military assistance." With Operation Linebacker II to demonstrate his credibility, Nixon assured Thiệu that the United States would "react strongly" in the event the agreement was violated.[209] Thiệu continued to resist, but Nixon asked Kissinger to get two key Senate conservatives, Mississippi's John Stennis and the former Republican presidential candidate Barry Goldwater, to tell Thiệu that he needed to accept the agreement or face a cutoff of American aid. Both Nixon and Kissinger believed that Thiệu knew that rejecting the agreement could lead to his own overthrow by political opponents. Without the backing of the United States, as Nixon put it, "They're down the tube." Nixon still worried that Thiệu might reject the agreement, ruining the mood of his second inauguration. He asked Kissinger if "we have a plan . . . to cut our losses but God damned fast?" Kissinger replied, in words that captured his own fatalism about Vietnam, "Mr. President, the fact is that now we are doomed to settle."[210]

Kissinger was right. President Thiệu hesitated up until the last moment, but he finally gave his consent. Kissinger ended up having to push Nixon to include more reassurances to the South Vietnamese in his speech announcing the agreement. He told Haig to reinforce his message to Nixon that "this thing is precarious" and that "Thiệu might just collapse" if he did not keep these assurances in the speech.[211] In his speech, Nixon did affirm American support for the Thiệu regime as the "sole legitimate government of South Vietnam," and he insisted, "Terms of the agreement must be scrupulously adhered to."[212] However, neither he nor Kissinger wanted to be more specific about what the United States would do if North Vietnam violated the accord. In Kissinger's nationally televised news conference outlining the agreement, when asked if the United States might again send troops to Vietnam, he replied that he did not want to speculate about a hypothetical situation that "we didn't expect to happen." Well aware of Nixon's many letters to Thiệu, he nevertheless denied there were any secret understandings, even though he also stressed that the United States would remain vigilant and would not withdraw its military from countries surrounding Vietnam.[213]

Kissinger gave an extended answer to a question about the almost 150,000 North Vietnamese troops remaining in South Vietnam. On the *NBC Nightly News* coverage of his briefing, Kissinger tried to make the agreement sound like something it was not by repeatedly using the words "flat prohibition" as though they carried extraordinary weight. First, he claimed there was a "flat prohibition" against any new forces being introduced to South Vietnam. He was suggesting that somehow natural attrition would reduce the number of North Vietnamese soldiers. Then he stated that there was a "flat prohibition" against any foreign forces in Laos and Cambodia, suggesting that since these were the routes of the Ho Chi Minh Trail, no new North Vietnamese soldiers would be able to take that route into the South. How Laos and Cambodia, both weak and war-torn, would enforce the prohibition was left unanswered. Third, he suggested there was a "flat prohibition" against any movement of forces across the demilitarized zone. Along with the provisions for the reduction and demobilization of forces, Kissinger concluded that there was no way North Vietnam could live up to this agreement and still threaten the South with its forces. He was quick to add, "It is not inconceivable that the agreement won't be adhered to," but he hoped that with the possible incentive of reconstruction aid and help from the Soviet Union and China, it would be adhered to. The next report on NBC after Kissinger featured Lê Đức Thọ proclaiming victory and denying that there were any North Vietnamese forces in the South. There was only one Vietnam, Lê Đức Thọ emphasized, and the report indicated that he believed he had won this point in the treaty.[214]

Kissinger and Nixon also stressed the importance of economic aid to both North and South Vietnam, and they thought this might provide some leverage over North Vietnamese behavior.[215] The North Vietnamese attempt to get "ironclad assurances" of this economic aid at the January 23 meeting in which the agreement was initialed undoubtedly reinforced Kissinger's sense that this might be an effective way to enforce the treaty.[216] But Kissinger's pessimism also surfaced. When John Ehrlichman asked him after the news conference how long he thought the South Vietnamese could survive under the agreement, Kissinger replied, "I think that if they're lucky they can hold out for a year and a half."[217]

Kissinger had pulled off his trifecta, and he had received a huge amount of credit and admiration from Americans. At the end of 1972, the Gallup Poll found him to be the fourth most admired American, behind Nixon, Billy Graham, and the late Harry Truman. Although angered and annoyed by Kissinger's behavior during the last stages of the Vietnam War, Nixon still understood the enormous value Kissinger brought to his presidency. As he told Haldeman after the Vietnam agreement became clear, Kissinger was "now the hottest property in the world."[218] Nixon was so aware of this that he could even tease Kissinger about it. As they were finishing the Vietnam negotiations, Nixon remarked to Kissinger, "Well I hope your morale is all right." When Kissinger started to respond, Nixon added, "You've been through a lot, haven't you?" Kissinger replied, "Well we've all been through a lot, but I think—" Nixon cut him off and said, "Well, that's my job. I mean, you're just a paid hand, you know." Kissinger started to protest, "Now, Mr. President," but Nixon cut him off again and said, "I'm the guy that gets all the glory." Kissinger did not want to acknowledge the subtle irony in Nixon's statement, and simply said, "No President has taken such a beating, on the contrary, whenever you do something great, the press is looking for some way to take away the glory from you," and Nixon readily agreed.

There remained an underlying competition as well as cooperation between the two men. Nixon occasionally mused about firing Kissinger, especially after stories like Reston's about the Christmas bombing. He was annoyed that Kissinger did not say more about his "courage" and other qualities in his January 24 press conference, complaining to Haldeman that, as Haldeman put it, "Henry should realize the way to show he and the P[resident] don't differ is for him to sell what the P[resident] did in his appearances, especially sell the hell out of the bombing."[219] Henry was "the big gun," and Nixon wanted him to praise the president more. When Harry Reasoner, who only a year earlier talked about how dangerous a figure Kissinger was, now nominated him for the Nobel Peace Prize, Nixon told Haldeman that Kissinger needed to answer Reasoner and affirm the president's role.[220] But Nixon himself contributed to Kissinger's lionization. In his first news conference after the Paris Peace Accords were signed, Nixon spoke of how Kissinger had "so brilliantly briefed the members of the press," and he speculated to Haldeman that part of Kissinger's problem was that "he's made all the big plays now and he's trying to look for ways to maintain the momentum, which is essentially impossible." As *Time* magazine had noted, Kissinger was Nixon's creation, and an extension of his authority and political power as president.

5

"HENRY KISSINGER DID IT"

Kissinger as President for Foreign Policy, 1973

"HENRY KISSINGER DID IT," exclaimed John Chancellor of *NBC Nightly News* on May 29, 1974. Secretary of State Henry Kissinger had successfully concluded a disengagement agreement between the Israelis and the Syrians along the border of the Golan Heights. This agreement, following up on one between Egypt and Israel in January, was a remarkable testimonial to Kissinger's monthlong "shuttle diplomacy," a term coined to describe his continuous travels between Damascus and Tel Aviv, as well as other Arab capitals, in search of a peace agreement. Commentators extolled Kissinger's achievement in glowing terms. It not only was a significant step toward an eventual Middle East peace and an end to future oil embargoes, but also, as NBC's David Burrington reported from the Golan Heights, stopped Israel from executing a military "blitz attack" against Syria planned in the days before the agreement was made. Now because of Kissinger's efforts, Burrington said, "hundreds of soldiers are alive today on both sides of the border." Chancellor closed out the broadcast by pronouncing that this was "one of the most remarkable diplomatic efforts ever made" and then showing the Israeli leader Golda Meir telling Kissinger that this was his day and his personal achievement. Kissinger was clearly, as all the networks designated him, "the man of the hour."[1]

Although Kissinger had enjoyed the "trifecta" success of the first Nixon term, the heights of celebrity and fame he now enjoyed were unprecedented. Congressman Jonathan Bingham even proposed a constitutional amendment to allow the foreign-born Kissinger to run for president. How had this happened? How had Kissinger become, in effect, the "president for foreign policy"? The simplest explanation was the devastating impact of the Watergate scandal on Nixon's authority and the president's increasing preoccupation with defending himself from impeachment. There was more to this story than Watergate, however, and to the changes in American foreign policy that Kissinger's ascendancy brought with it.

BEFORE WATERGATE ERUPTED:
ASIA, THE MIDDLE EAST, AND EUROPE

In his memoirs, Kissinger wrote of early 1973 that "rarely had a Presidential term started with such bright foreign policy prospects," and that "the United States had before it a rare opportunity for creativity in its foreign policy."[2] He added, however, that his own role in this would be limited, since he planned to resign by the end of the year.[3] Despite the tensions between the two men during the last months of 1972, Nixon and Kissinger simply continued to do business in the same way they had throughout the first four years. Nixon thought in terms of popular new initiatives in which he could use Kissinger. Among these would be the "Year of Europe," with a presidential trip and the signing of a new Atlantic Charter, revitalizing America's relationship with her oldest allies. Nixon also wanted to make a serious effort to forge a Middle East peace settlement. Successes in foreign policy would continue to strengthen Nixon politically at home. Although Nixon's hope to reorganize the executive branch, create a "New Majority" with the Republican Party, and realign American politics was not solely dependent on such foreign policy successes, he wanted to harness the acclaim and political support that success would bring, and Kissinger was still his weapon of choice.

Kissinger wanted to continue his role as the "second most powerful man in the world," but he was still concerned about the intense criticism he had received from many of his friends, especially in the media, about Operation Linebacker II, the Christmas bombing. Nixon remained angry and defiant over media coverage of the Vietnam settlement, bitter about the criticism of his "terror bombing" and the suggestion that he was acting like a crazy man. He told reporters that it "gags some of you" to acknowledge that he was right about "peace with honor." He also refused to discuss a possible amnesty for draft evaders. Kissinger, however, took a very different tack.[4] At his press conference on January 24 discussing the peace agreement, Kissinger voiced his hope that one result of the settlement would be that "we can begin to heal the wounds in America." After working the phones with various print journalists, Kissinger sat down with Marvin Kalb for a televised interview.[5] He emphasized that the bombing had avoided civilian residential areas and that it was designed to convince "both sides" in Vietnam that the war had to come to an end. He made sure to indicate his own personal "anguish" and described the bombing as a "very painful thing."[6] This conciliatory strategy seemed to work. *Time* proclaimed, "Kissinger is back on top now with his darkest days behind him."[7] It also annoyed Nixon, who believed Kissinger was continuing to distance himself to curry favor with the liberal establishment. Yet with the POWs returning and his own popularity still in the lofty 60 to 70 percent range, there was little that Nixon wanted to do about Kissinger's behavior except complain to Haldeman.

In early February, Kissinger departed Washington for an eleven-day trip to Southeast Asia, China, and Japan. Nixon made sure to send his communications director, Herbert Klein, along with Kissinger, with the instruction to make sure that "all of the credit for the end of the Vietnam War did not settle on Kissinger."[8] Arriving in Hanoi, Kissinger would later write, was like "stepping onto the moon."[9] Ironically, given the media attention to his other journeys, Kissinger's arrival in Hanoi did not even make the evening news.[10] Kissinger and the members of his staff took a brief walk in Hanoi before their first meeting, but when they returned to their guesthouse, the guards refused to allow Kissinger in. The North Vietnamese guard had never heard of the famous diplomat, and Kissinger did not have his required identity card. That incident seemed to set the tone of the meetings. Over the four days of talks, Kissinger was confronted by an unbowed North Vietnamese leadership that refuted his charges of violating the peace accords, resisted demands for withdrawal of their troops from Laos and Cambodia, and insisted on the details of promised economic aid. Kissinger tried to soften their stance by talking about the "new relationship" that America sought, joking about teaching at Hanoi University, and instructing the North Vietnamese on the congressional appropriations process. He also assured the North Vietnamese that if they cooperated with the United States in carrying out the agreement "in a spirit of reconciliation," that they could almost certainly "rely on historical evolution to achieve your objective."[11] He told Nixon, "If they showed restraint and honored their obligations, we were prepared to normalize relations as we are doing with Peking, and we would not interfere with the political self-determination of Indochina, no matter what its manifestations."[12]

Kissinger hoped the possibility of American economic aid might convince the North Vietnamese to moderate their behavior and demonstrate to them that they "cannot have their aid and eat Indochina too." He wanted them to understand that they should "now know unambiguously that they will have to choose between pressing their Indochina aims in an illegal manner and getting help in rebuilding their country."[13] Nonetheless, Kissinger's doubts about the settlement grew during this visit. Whether it was Lê Đức Thọ telling Kissinger that he was "too simple" to understand the Cambodia problem, or Pham Van Dong's evasions about north Vietnamese troops in Laos, Kissinger could see that Hanoi had not given up its ambitions.[14] Kissinger's one hope was to use Vietnam's giant neighbor to the north, China, to act as a check on Vietnamese ambitions. When Kissinger finally left Hanoi for China, he called it "the most oppressive atmosphere of any foreign capital I have ever visited."[15]

Kissinger and Nixon had both come to regard China as the outstanding success of the first term, and Nixon asked Kissinger to explore with the Chinese the possibility of another presidential visit. Nixon wanted to go at a warmer time of year, hoping for a "popular" reception from the Chinese people, something that "could be helpful" to him at home. The two men talked about the Chinese leaders as the "cold-blooded" realists they imagined themselves to be, while at the same time thinking that they enjoyed a "special relationship" with the Chinese.[16] Kissinger thanked Prime Minister Zhou Enlai for the polite reception, and when Zhou replied that this is "what we are supposed to do," Kissinger responded, "You are supposed to carry out foreign policy on the basis of interests, but there is also a strong feeling of warmth." He then began his talks with Zhou by emphasizing the progress the two countries had made by preparing to open liaison offices. The major topic of conversation was the shared assessment of the threat posed by the Soviet Union, and Kissinger found the Chinese far more direct now about their fears of Soviet aggression. A healthier Mao even told Kissinger, "We can work together to commonly deal with a bastard," insisting that "the goal of the Soviet Union is to occupy both Europe and Asia, the two continents."[17] Kissinger reassured Mao that the United States "will never knowingly cooperate in an attack on China." These Chinese fears reflected the tensions inherent to triangular diplomacy, but the national security adviser still believed that "we should be able to have our mao tai and drink our vodka too."[18]

After a brief stop in Japan to encourage the country to supply economic aid to Indochina, Kissinger returned to Washington. Nixon congratulated him and told him that they needed to find a liaison officer for China who was not from the State Department, and that "working with the Chinese can have great possibilities." Kissinger immediately answered, "But that really has to be done by you and me," and Nixon eagerly responded, "Alone!"[19] This confidence in their continued mastery of foreign policy was visible a few days later when the Israeli leaders visited Washington. Although Nixon told Al Haig that he continued to worry about Kissinger's "blind spot" on the Middle East, he was also certain that "we can't let State handle the Mideast: they'll screw it up."[20] Nixon began pressing Kissinger right after the election on the need to

"squeeze the old woman," a characteristically indelicate reference to the Israeli prime minister, Golda Meir.[21] Kissinger hesitated, believing that little
progress could be made until after the Israeli elections later in the year. Nixon
was insistent, and during Meir's visit he put the matter directly to her. After
reassuring Meir of his support for Israel's security and making a number of
pointed attacks on her "fellow Socialists" for their "naïve" views, Nixon told
her, "I would like Henry to explore privately with Egypt what might be possible." Kissinger was "a master of fuzzy language," Nixon added, and his efforts
to work toward a settlement on Israel's behalf could be "absolutely off-the-
record." Kissinger had already had exploratory talks with Hafez Ismail, one of
Anwar Sadat's closest advisers, and told Nixon that the Egyptians were "pant-
ing to get us involved." Meir quickly agreed to Kissinger's role, undoubtedly
encouraged by Nixon's willingness to continue supplying Israel with advanced military equipment and economic assistance.[22]

Toward the end of their meeting, Meir raised the issue of Soviet Jews.
Meir criticized the Soviet treatment of Jews trying to leave the country, telling Nixon that potential émigrés lost their jobs and ended up in prison. Nixon
listened to the concern but wanted a quid pro quo from the Israeli prime minister. Pending in Congress was legislation designed to grant the Soviet Union
"most favored nation" (MFN) status, a designation that would reduce the
tariffs on Soviet goods. Nixon and Kissinger hoped that expanding trade
with the Soviet Union would build support for the détente policy in both
countries, with both American business and Soviet bureaucracy more in-
vested in the relationship. The bill was in trouble, opposed by many American
Jews and their lobbying organizations because of the Soviet imposition of a
heavy emigration tax on Jews. Nixon told Meir he would take up the cause of
Soviet Jews privately, but to do so in a public manner, as Senator Henry Jackson and his allies wanted him to do, would be counterproductive. Nixon also
added his typical caveat when dealing with Israel and American Jews: that
such a lobbying effort would produce anti-Semitism in the United States and
that if it "continues to escalate, it will not help the Jewish Community."
Kissinger added that he hoped the Israelis would "restrain friendly Senators"
from supporting Jackson.[23] After Meir left, Kissinger flattered Nixon further,

telling him the Israelis had "a hell of a lot more confidence in you" than they had in Secretary of State Rogers when he proposed a peace plan. Agreeing with Nixon that Jewish emigration should not be allowed to affect policy toward the Soviet Union and was not "an objective of American foreign policy," Kissinger proclaimed—in what was an obvious attempt to show Nixon how "cold-bloodedly" objective he could be on a subject of concern to Jews—that "if they put Jews into gas chambers in the Soviet Union it is not an American concern. It may be a humanitarian concern . . ." Kissinger's voice trailed off and Nixon interjected, "But we can't blow up the world because of it."[24] Kissinger's willingness to hypothesize about a second Holocaust in order to criticize Rogers and defend détente was a low point in his obsequiousness to Nixon.[25]

If handling the world's most populous country as well as its most explosive region were not enough for *Time*'s Men of the Year, Nixon also announced in January, "The problems of Europe . . . will be put on the front burner." This was the beginning of the Year of Europe, which Kissinger proclaimed was necessary "because the era that was shaped by decisions of a generation ago is ending." Nixon had relatively little interest in the idea beyond its media impact and boosting his prestige.[26] Because of his background, both intellectual and personal, Kissinger took the Year of Europe initiative seriously, hoping to both reaffirm the solidarity of America's postwar alliance and prevent an increasingly united Europe from opposing America's policies. He had begun speaking about it with European leaders in the fall of 1972, in part as a reaction to the damage done to the relationship by Nixon's unilateral economic measures of August 1971. These conversations led him to believe that both the British and the French were sympathetic to the idea of greater American engagement with Europe. Kissinger's support for the plan did not come from any great sympathy for European leaders, and his perspective on them came close to the pot calling the kettle black. He told the Senior Review Group meeting in January 1973, "Present day Europe is not distinguished by great statesmanship. It is being run by a series of party bosses obsessed with domestic politics."[27] Both he and Nixon had come to doubt whether America should continue to support more European integration, with Nixon referring to a potential united Europe as "a Frankenstein monster, which could prove to be highly detrimental to our interests in the years ahead."[28]

Nevertheless, Kissinger surprised the British in particular by emphasizing the "domestic politics" behind the Year of Europe proposal. Kissinger told the British he feared the weakening of ties to Europe would undermine America's "national morale" and lead to a growth of radicalism on the left and the right. Kissinger suggested that the United States would become more isolated internationally without a strong tie to Europe and its position in the world would grow considerably weaker. He also admitted to the British that the "grandiose form of a 'new Atlantic Charter'" would be the best possible outcome of a presidential trip to Europe in the fall, acknowledging the possible domestic political benefits Nixon might achieve through the effort.[29] Unfortunately, by the time Kissinger actually delivered his Year of Europe speech, his first formal public foreign policy speech, the Watergate scandal was dominating coverage, and the substance of his speech was largely ignored in the American media.[30]

Despite their personal differences and resentments, Nixon hoped to continue to use a very willing Kissinger to accomplish his foreign policy objectives with maximum domestic political impact. However, when the White House counsel John Dean told Nixon, "We have a cancer within, close to the presidency, that is growing," the Watergate scandal began to overwhelm Nixon, preoccupying him day and night, eating away at his authority and legitimacy, and allowing Henry Kissinger to step into the breach.[31]

THE IMPACT OF WATERGATE

Kissinger dated his discovery of Watergate's impact to an April 14, 1973, conversation with Leonard Garment, who was then special consultant to the president. Kissinger recalled that the night before he had given a speech urging "national reconciliation" in the wake of the end of the Vietnam War, and that Garment began their conversation "by raising a question unlikely to receive an objective answer, 'Have you lost your mind?'" Garment proceeded to tell Kissinger that "Watergate was about to blow up" and that it "could not have developed without the cooperation of the highest levels of the Adminis-tration." Kissinger professed to be stunned by Garment's revelations and an-gered that these "acts that made no sense" would put at risk all that the administration had achieved. Foreign policy would be gravely affected, as the "political and moral authority" drained away from the presidency. Facing these challenges, Kissinger compared himself melodramatically to "a swim-mer who had survived dangerous currents only to be plucked from apparent safety by unexpected and even more violent riptides toward uncharted seas."[32]

Kissinger had been swimming in the secretive and even paranoid waters of the Nixon White House long enough to understand that environment. Al-though he insisted that "in the Nixon White House there was an almost total separation between the domestic and the foreign policy sides," he was also well aware that one of the primary aims of foreign policy was to secure domestic political victories. The obsession with leaks stemmed—at least in part—from the belief that they undermined the Nixon team's presentation of their for-eign policy.[33] Soon after he spoke with Garment, Kissinger called Nixon and told him that the most important thing was "to protect the presidency and your authority." Although he later described Haldeman and Ehrlichman as "men with a Gestapo mentality," he initially urged Nixon to try to contain the scandal and hold on to them, "if humanly possible."[34] When an inebriated Nixon lamented having to fire Haldeman and Ehrlichman and told Kissinger that instead he considered "throwing myself on the sword and letting Agnew take it," Kissinger responded immediately: "That is out of the question," and "I don't think the President has the right to sacrifice himself for an individ-ual." Their conversations now reflected the subtle shift in their positions of power, with Kissinger assuming the stronger position. Kissinger still told Nixon that he had "saved the country," but in the past tense, with frequent invocations of Nixon's eventual vindication by history. In response, Nixon repeatedly told Kissinger not to get discouraged, only to have his national security adviser tell him emphatically that he was not discouraged.[35] On April 30, the night he gave the national speech announcing Haldeman's and Ehrlichman's departures, Nixon called Haldeman and told him, "Kissinger's reaction is typical; he's waiting to see how it comes out."[36] The next day when Kissinger called again to console Nixon on his "unbelievably painful" and "tragic" decision to get rid of his two close associates, he reassured Nixon that the press would "scream for a few more days" but that Watergate would soon fade away "if there aren't any more major things coming out." Nixon interrupted with awkward laughter and said, "Oh there may be but what the hell," and quickly ended the conversation.[37]

The Watergate scandal had unfolded slowly after the arrest of five men in the Democratic National Committee headquarters in June 1972. The Nixon White House initially dismissed the story, in the famous words of Press Secretary Ron Ziegler, as a "third-rate burglary attempt," but *The Washington Post* investigated throughout the 1972 campaign, revealing the dimensions of the political sabotage as well as connections between the Watergate burglars and the Committee to Reelect the President (CREEP). The coverage did not dent Nixon's landslide, and many assumed that the landslide had also buried Watergate. However, the first convictions, on January 30, 1973, allowed Judge John Sirica to threaten long jail sentences and helped break the case wide open. John Dean, Nixon's White House counsel, began cooperating with prosecutors in early April. Following the money that had funded the Watergate Five led prosecutors and the FBI to the White House and ultimately forced Nixon to fire Haldeman and Ehrlichman. It also led to the revelation of the activities of the "plumbers" and the earlier break-in at the office of Daniel Ellsberg's psychiatrist. The noose around the president was beginning to tighten, and Nixon's overall popularity fell from 67 percent in January after the Vietnam peace treaty to only 45 percent in early May.[38]

Just as Nixon had feared, there were "more major things coming out." The week after he fired his two top aides saw the charges against Daniel Ellsberg in the Pentagon Papers case dismissed when the government's misconduct in the case, namely the White House "plumbers" Special Investigations Unit's burglary of Ellsberg's psychiatrist's office and the wiretaps that captured conversations between Ellsberg and Kissinger's former assistant Morton Halperin, was revealed. A week later Seymour Hersh published a story in *The New York Times* reporting that Kissinger had requested the wiretaps on members of his National Security Council staff and journalists. Alexander Haig, the new White House chief of staff, unsuccessfully tried to convince Hersh to delay the story until he could prove it wrong, asking him, "Do you honestly believe that Henry Kissinger, a Jewish refugee from Germany who lost thirteen members of his family to the Nazis, could engage in such police state tactics as wiretapping his own aides?" Thankfully for Kissinger's sake, Nixon helped defuse the impact of the story by taking responsibility for authorizing the wiretaps, even though, as he told his press secretary, Ron Ziegler, when it came to leaks, "Henry was the one that was, Christ, pounding the desks, squealing about it and so forth." Nixon believed Kissinger was "up to his ankles" in knowledge of the activities of the "plumbers" and had been fully in agreement with the administration's concerns about national security, but Nixon did not want to drag Kissinger into Watergate, hoping that keeping Kissinger active on foreign policy, the administration's success story, might somehow rescue his presidency.[39]

Unfortunately for Nixon, the strategy backfired, as Kissinger's foreign policy activism simply reinforced the perception that he was the real brains behind Nixon's diplomacy.[40] Kissinger's travels also kept him out of Washington as the news media's obsession with Watergate intensified. Only days after the firing of Haldeman and Ehrlichman, Kissinger headed to Moscow to prepare for the Washington summit with the Russians. Brezhnev treated Kissinger like a head of state, even inviting him out to Zavidovo, the politburo's hunting preserve. The Soviets desperately wanted an agreement on the prevention of nuclear war between the superpowers, but the Americans were cautious. Kissinger needed to soften the language enough so that it did not seem like either an alliance against the Chinese to Beijing or a U.S.-Soviet condominium to the European allies. To accomplish this, Kissinger had secretly enlisted one of the British Foreign Office's top diplomats, Sir Thomas Brimelow, to draft the agreement, leaving Rogers and the State Department completely in the dark.[41] Using Brimelow's draft, Kissinger successfully neutered the language and produced a "marginally useful text" for Nixon and Brezhnev to sign during their summit. However, the very symbolism of a U.S.-Soviet agreement still angered the allies, even the British—despite

Brimelow's role in shaping the agreement. The Chinese also remained suspicious, even though Kissinger tried mightily to convince them it amounted to nothing new.[42] More worrying to Kissinger was when Brezhnev managed to get him alone during their wild boar hunt and launched into a tirade against the Chinese, calling them "barbarians" and telling the American, "We have to prevent the Chinese from having a nuclear program at all costs."[43] To Kissinger, this sounded suspiciously like the preparations for a preventive attack on China.

Vietnam, however, still preoccupied him. Even as the story about his approval of wiretaps broke in mid-May, he was traveling back to Paris to negotiate again with Lê Đức Thọ. Since signing the agreements in January, Kissinger had tried to put on a public face of confidence even while he expressed private doubts. He told NBC's Barbara Walters in February that although the fighting had gone on a little longer than he expected, he was not worried about the cease-fire breaking down. When she asked directly if there was a possibility of a resumption of American involvement, he answered flatly, "No."[44] Privately he told a WSAG meeting that the attitude of the government "should be one of extreme vigilance" about the continuing communist infiltration. Two weeks later he recommended to Nixon "planning now for a 2–3 day series of intensive U.S. air strikes against the trail area of Southern Laos." But as Watergate began to preoccupy Nixon, Kissinger recognized that the president was growing reluctant to add any military action in Vietnam to his domestic troubles. On April 23 he told Nixon, "If we didn't have this god damn domestic situation, a week of bombing would put them . . . this Agreement in force."[45] On May 2, after Nixon's national speech on Watergate, Kissinger bluntly told the president, "We can't threaten them now."[46] Publicly Kissinger kept up his call for patience, saying about the chance that the Paris agreements would last, "We are not pessimistic."[47]

Kissinger arranged to meet with Lê Đức Thọ, and for almost a month they negotiated in Paris—allowing Kissinger to avoid the excitement in Washington generated by Senator Sam Ervin's hearings. The South Vietnamese were again reluctant to sign another agreement, and President Thiệu once again insisted that the North Vietnamese accept certain changes to the formula Kissinger negotiated. Kissinger later acknowledged, "Saigon's concerns were better founded than its presentation of them," adding that the South Vietnamese were "in a mortal struggle for survival."[48] At the time, however, he showed more anger toward Saigon, telling Nixon that Thiệu and his government were in a "suicidal mood." Kissinger told the South Vietnamese ambassador, "We are faced with a possibility of a Congressional Amendment to cut off all aid to Indochina," but that a successful agreement might serve to postpone action. "I grant that our domestic problems are none of your doing," Kissinger berated Ambassador Phuong, "but you should appreciate our present position."[49] The pressure worked, and Saigon "folded" and signed off on the joint communiqué drafted by Kissinger and Lê Đức Thọ. Kissinger said at a press conference that he believed both sides now understood that "nobody can have his way by force," and the press and television coverage stressed Kissinger's hope that this time the agreement would work.[50] But while he was sure Hanoi planned another offensive, the next day he told the South Vietnamese, "This is the last time I am going to get involved in negotiations on Vietnam," adding dramatically, "I am washing my hands of this."[51] Kissinger believed himself finally liberated from the "distraction" of Vietnam and now able to deal with the more significant issues of great power diplomacy.

Europe, the Soviet Union, China, Vietnam—the centrality of Kissinger to all these threads of American diplomacy made him seem like the indispensable man in the Watergate spring of 1973. A Gallup poll now showed him as the most admired man in America, surpassing Nixon and Billy Graham. The day after his star-studded fiftieth-birthday party on May 27 at New York's Colony Club, the commentator Eric Sevareid proclaimed on CBS Evening News that Kissinger's stature needed to be "protected," for he "has to keep on doing what he has almost alone among the Nixon entourage for four years, and that is keeping one foot in two cultures . . . the reigning political culture on one side and the intellectual-academic-press world on the other."[52] Joseph Kraft, who boycotted the party to protest Kissinger's role in the wiretapping of reporters, nevertheless titled a column "The Virtuoso at 50" and praised the "historic" diplomatic accomplishments of Kissinger. When he was asked what the best gift Kissinger received at the party was, the

CBS anchor Walter Cronkite, who attended along with other media stalwarts, joked, "They gave him a pardon," a comment that meant more than Cronkite might have intended.[53] When at a press conference on May 29 Kissinger acknowledged that his office "supplied" the names of those who were wiretapped in 1969, saying that it was a "painful matter" and that he did not find wiretapping a "particularly attractive procedure," both the NBC and CBS News anchors emphasized that this story was "unrelated to the Nixon reelection scandals."[54] ABC News did not even cover it, and the emphasis on all three networks was Kissinger's return to Paris to seek to rescue the Vietnam settlement.

By the time Kissinger returned from Paris, the wiretap story had largely disappeared. Talking to Nixon after he returned in June, Kissinger described his appearance in Congress to discuss the joint communiqué with Hanoi and argue against a cutoff in funding for military actions in Cambodia. Although the vote went against the administration, Kissinger proudly told Nixon that the reaction to his speech was "unbelievable," with a standing ovation and more than 150 congressmen wanting to have their pictures taken with him. A jealous Nixon seemed to choke out his reply, "Great, that's the stuff," expressing his forlorn view that this acclaim for Kissinger's work meant hope for his presidency.[55]

Leonid Brezhnev's visit to the United States in June 1973 provided Nixon with a brief respite from Watergate.[56] Kissinger assumed a prominent public role during the summit, briefing reporters about the expectations and trying to put its achievements in the most favorable light. When the two leaders agreed to try to sign a treaty for reductions in their nuclear arsenals by the end of 1974, basically striving for a SALT II agreement, Kissinger explained to reporters that defining equality in nuclear weapons would be a very complex matter, but that the United States would seek "strategic parity."[57] With the jovial atmosphere of the summit, in which Nixon and Brezhnev seemed to have a personal bond, Kissinger could not resist overselling its significance. He told reporters this was "the beginning of a new period of international relations," using the mixed metaphor of "a landmark on the road to the structure of peace." Kissinger proclaimed that this could lead to lifting from all nations "the fear of war itself." He did not discourage reporters from seeing "a sort of formalization of the end of the Cold War."[58]

Kissinger expressed this exaggerated optimism even though he had witnessed some difficult moments in the private talks between the two leaders. While out in the relaxed atmosphere of San Clemente, Brezhnev repeated his denunciations of "the sly and perfidious" Chinese and threatened war if the United States made an alliance with China. He also asked for an unscheduled late-night meeting with Nixon and Kissinger to insist that the Soviet Union and United States impose a peace settlement in the Middle East before another war broke out. Kissinger—who angrily noted in his own memo of the meeting, "Typical of Soviets to spring on us at last moment without any preparation"—should have realized that the contrast between his public presentation of superpower harmony and the true state of affairs was a recipe for eventual public disillusionment.[59]

Although most Americans welcomed the relaxation of tensions with the Soviet Union, in the summer of 1973 they were far more mesmerized by the Watergate hearings. Some 80 percent of all households watched some part of these broadcasts.[60] The impact on Nixon's public standing was devastating, and is reflected in the overwhelming congressional vote to end American bombing in Cambodia by August 15. Kissinger made it clear publicly that he opposed the deadline, but when it was enacted, the White House announced that Kissinger's "next assignment" would be to seek a cease-fire agreement in Cambodia before the deadline came into effect.[61] Privately Kissinger believed, "It is getting impossible to do anything in Indochina," and he sadly agreed when Defense Secretary James Schlesinger told him, "The responsibility for the pending collapse of Cambodia should be pinned on Congress."[62] Kissinger told a news conference on July 6 that he hoped China would use its "influence in the direction of restraint" and planned a trip to Beijing to try to get a cease-fire before the bombing halt went into effect.[63] By this point Prince Sihanouk had allied himself with the communist Khmer Rouge, and North Vietnam announced its support for his return to power. The Chinese, however, sent a note supporting Sihanouk's demand that the United States end its military involvement and postponing Kissinger's trip.

Reacting immediately, Kissinger saw this as an ominous sign. He told a small group of advisers that because "he and the President were the key men who embodied American support for China for the right reasons," that for the Chinese "to cancel a Kissinger trip was a major international event."[64] He suspected that they had changed policy because of Watergate and their perception of American weakness. A few days later, the Chinese sent a second note, suggesting only a ten-day postponement of Kissinger's trip. Kissinger had overreacted, personalizing triangular diplomacy and China's policy toward the United States far more than the Chinese had, showing that his "cold-blooded" realism could be trumped by his emotions and pride.

Even as he was pondering the motives behind China's policies, Kissinger was trying to maneuver Nixon into appointing him as secretary of state. Alexander Haig, now Nixon's chief of staff, was strongly pushing the appointment on a reluctant Nixon, who desperately wanted to avoid giving Kissinger the greater independence and stature that would come with the office. On July 13, in the middle of a discussion of Nixon's treatment for viral pneumonia at Bethesda Naval Hospital, CBS's Dan Rather reported that his sources confirmed that Nixon had decided to appoint Kissinger as secretary of state.[65] Secretary of State Rogers, who was on a trip to Japan for an economic summit, found himself besieged by questions about these rumors and refused to address them, adding fuel to the fire. While Kissinger claimed that Rather's leak came from those in the State Department who wanted to sabotage his appointment, the more likely scenario is the exact opposite, that the leak was intended to force Nixon's hand.[66] The implicit threat that the popular Kissinger would resign if Nixon appointed anyone else also weighed on the embattled president, who now had to confront the revelation of the White House taping system by Alexander Butterfield and the news that Vice President Spiro Agnew was under scrutiny for his financial dealings as governor of Maryland. To keep up the pressure, Kissinger continued to emphasize his importance to Nixon, telling him of a speech he gave extolling the virtues of the administration's foreign policy. "And it was a tremendous ovation, and I had to fight my way out of there," Kissinger proudly told Nixon. Perhaps remembering whom he was talking to, he added, "It just shows that basically you have a lot of strength in the country." Once again Nixon's awkward reply was revealing of his inner turmoil: "Yeah, ha, ha, right, right."[67] Nixon believed he had no choice but to replace Rogers with Kissinger. On August 22, at his first news conference in five months, Nixon told reporters that Rogers had resigned, praised him fulsomely, and then announced Kissinger's appointment with the simple sentence, "Dr. Kissinger's qualifications for this post, I think, are well known by all of you ladies and gentlemen, as well as those looking to [sic] us and listening to us on television and radio."[68] It was a begrudging and half-hearted acknowledgment that Henry Kissinger, Nixon's own Frankenstein monster, was now central to preserving his presidency.

THE FORTY-FOURTH SECRETARY OF STATE

Kissinger held a news conference the day after Nixon's announcement, and it was the lead item on all three network newscasts. He stressed that his appointment signaled a "new era" in cooperation between Congress and the president in foreign policy and that he would emphasize those aspects of foreign policy that enjoyed wide support. In this way he hoped the effects of Watergate on foreign policy would be "minimized." All three networks showed Kissinger's reply to the final question he was asked: whether he preferred to be called Mr. Secretary or Dr. Secretary. "I don't stand on protocol," Kissinger said, smiling. "If you just call me Excellency it will be okay," he added, as the press corps broke into laughter and the news anchors smiled.[69] Kissinger later wrote that, like Churchill when he became prime minister after Dunkirk, he felt "oddly relieved." Referring obliquely to the personal drama of his rivalry with Rogers, he believed that now "one's convictions would stand or fall on their merits, without being strained through the uncertainties of clashing personal ambitions."[70] As secretary of state he enjoyed unprecedented authority and the opportunity to implement his own ideas and plans for American foreign policy, subject only to the president's approval. In reality the besieged and preoccupied Nixon simply went along. Watergate made this possible, and Kissinger knew that. As Kissinger later said, "After the Watergate revelation, I was the glue that held it together in 1973—and I'm not being boastful."[71]

Although Kissinger described his Senate confirmation hearings as among the "most extensive ever," the outcome was never in doubt.[72] He had developed a friendly relationship with most of the senators on the committee, especially the chair, J. William Fulbright. The committee used the public hearings to air its chief complaint: the lack of consultation with Congress, while some of its members also grilled Kissinger about the secret bombing of Cambodia and the use of wiretaps. Kissinger knew he needed to separate himself from Nixon administration practices to win approval, but he did so carefully and in guarded language. He defended the Cambodia bombing but promised that in the future "we cannot conduct our foreign policy by deceiving the elected representatives and appropriate committees of the Congress." He philosophically described the wiretap issue as involving the "balance between human liberty and the requirements of national security" and stated that in his view the "weight should be placed on the side of human liberty." The committee wanted to see the FBI report on the wiretaps of Kissinger's staff and reporters but eventually agreed to allow just two senators to read it and report to the committee. After they reviewed the report, the NBC Nightly News anchor John Chancellor told viewers that Kissinger's confirmation was now certain since the story that Kissinger had simply provided names of people with access to secret information "was just as Kissinger told it."[73] When the full Senate confirmed him, Chancellor described Kissinger as a "country boy from Fürth, Germany, and the first secretary of state ever born in a foreign country."[74] Mentioning Kissinger's parents' flight from Nazi Germany, Chancellor described the "Harvard-educated" Kissinger as "the best explainer of foreign policy in the country," a "brilliant advocate who had posed the only serious challenge in the White House to the power of John Ehrlichman and Bob Haldeman," and who was close to the president but "escaped Watergate, tainted only by an involvement in secret wiretapping."[75] The positive media narrative, with its distortion of Kissinger's relationship with Haldeman and Ehrlichman, was now central to Kissinger's power. He was the indispensable man in the Nixon administration, the one figure rising above politics and serving the national interest.

The media glow would not have been as positive if there had been more knowledge of Kissinger's involvement in the "other September 11," the 1973 coup that overthrew the elected government of Salvador Allende in Chile. Kissinger had not paid much attention to Chile since the fall of 1970 and the attempt to prevent Allende from becoming president. Between 1970 and 1973, the CIA provided millions of dollars to Chilean opposition groups, helping business, labor, civic, and other groups organizing strikes and demonstrations against Allende. The CIA also cultivated contacts and relationships with the Chilean military in the event that it took action against Allende. Allende's own political and economic policies, including his close association with Castro's Cuba, contributed as well to the political polarization and economic chaos that fostered the conditions for the coup. The idea that "the CIA did it" is a vastly oversimplified conclusion, and as the Chilean historian Joaquín Fermandois writes, "The history of contemporary Chile was the result of choices made by Chilean actors."[76] Nevertheless, American involvement made the situation worse and ultimately proved counterproductive by providing a powerful rallying cry for anti-Americanism throughout the world. Because of its contradiction with American beliefs in self-determination, and its contribution to the ugly repression after the coup, in 2003 Secretary of State Colin Powell apologized for the American role.

Kissinger was at the time largely oblivious to these concerns. A few days after the coup began, and General Augusto Pinochet seemed to be taking charge, Kissinger told Nixon, "The Chilean thing is getting consolidated," but that the newspapers are "bleeding because a pro-communist government was overthrown." Nixon joined him in lamenting that unlike the Eisenhower era, when they would have been seen as heroes, now they had to conceal their role. Nixon remarked, "Our hand doesn't show on this one," and Kissinger added, "We didn't do it," but "we helped them, creating the conditions as great as possible."[77] Later in the month, after he had been confirmed as secretary, Kissinger made it a point to emphasize that in regard to the Pinochet government, "we should not support moves against them by seeming to disassociate ourselves from the Chileans and on the other hand should not be in a position of defending what they are doing in Santiago."[78] This formal posture belied the strong sympathy for the new government that Kissinger possessed. Kissinger was far more concerned with making sure the new regime knew of America's "good will" than with raising the issue of human rights, despite reports of summary executions and torture. When told that the regime was allowing the press access, Kissinger cynically remarked, "That demonstrates the total naiveté of the new government. If they think the press has any interest in the truth, they're mistaken. All they will want to do is horror studies."[79] Although he did act quietly to obtain the release of some of the junta's prisoners, including the Communist leader Luis Corvalán, Kissinger continued to insist, "However unpleasant they act, this government is better for us than Allende was."[80] As one critic of his policy put it, "almost overnight, Washington reopened the spigot of bilateral and multilateral economic assistance to Santiago."[81] The unseemly haste with which Kissinger wanted to help Pinochet's dictatorship consolidate its hold may constitute more of an indictment of Kissinger's record than his earlier role in trying to prevent Allende from assuming the presidency. Kissinger completely underestimated the extent to which the coup in Chile constituted "a watershed event" serving to "bring liberal human rights concerns . . . into mainstream public consciousness."[82] In the aftermath of Vietnam, however, Kissinger's view was that American foreign policy needed to be realistic, and even ruthless, in its willingness to ally with unsavory regimes to resist Soviet inroads.

On Chile, Kissinger followed a policy that was not different from the path that Nixon directed. A more distinctive Kissinger policy, however, emerged in a different region of the world, the Middle East. The "Yom Kippur" or "Ramadan" War of October 1973 caught American intelligence agencies flat-footed, as they had not predicted the sudden attack by Arab armies led by Egypt and Syria on Israel. Kissinger had met with Arab diplomats a week before the war and came away with the same impression, and the reassurances given to him by Israeli leaders further convinced him that he would have time after the Israeli elections for any peace initiative. When Assistant Secretary of State Joe Sisco awakened him early on Saturday morning, October 6, with word of an impending attack, Kissinger's first reaction was to call Soviet ambassador Dobrynin to tell him, in echoes of what he had said during the Indo-Pakistani war, "the President believes that you and we have a special responsibility to restrain our respective friends."[83] Kissinger had two major priorities in his mind at the beginning of the crisis. The first was to preserve détente with the Soviet Union, trying to limit the impact of the conflict and end it quickly. The second priority, however, was to use the conflict as a catalyst toward a peace settlement in the region, a settlement that Kissinger hoped would reduce Soviet influence.[84] During Nixon's first term, Kissinger had opposed the Rogers Plan, arguing that such efforts were premature and unlikely to win Israeli cooperation. He had created controversy with his background briefing in June 1970 that the United States hoped to "expel" the Soviet Union from its position in the region. Now that he was in charge of the process, Kissinger was determined to settle the conflict in a way that reduced Soviet influence without impairing détente, the diplomatic equivalent of threading the needle.

Kissinger sought to deal with the Middle East crisis on his own terms, displaying a personal confidence in handling the issues as well as refusing to allow Nixon to use the crisis for his own domestic political purposes. Although Kissinger kept Chief of Staff Al Haig well informed of his actions, he told Haig to discourage Nixon's desire to fly back to Washington from his Key Biscayne vacation in order to dramatize his role in the crisis. Haig replied that Nixon would soon face "a situation with Agnew," a careful way of informing Kissinger that the vice president would be resigning shortly, but that Nixon feared being seen as "sitting in the sun" while a war was going on. Kissinger was blunt and dismissive of Nixon's concerns, telling Haig to keep the president's "Walter Mitty tendencies under control." Kissinger explained that most Americans would see the conflict as a "local war" and that the administration needed to avoid looking "hysterical" in its reaction. After all, Kissinger noted, "this thing" might be over in twenty-four hours.[85] Kissinger even took a call from Prime Minister Edward Heath of Britain the night after Vice President Agnew resigned because the president was "loaded," an indication of the power that Kissinger now held.[86]

Kissinger's assumption was that Israel would score a clear and quick victory over the Arab armies, and this affected his reactions for the first three days of the crisis. Kissinger was willing to give the Israelis ammunition and supplies to replace what they expended, but only if they came to the United States to pick up the supplies. He was so confident of an Israeli victory that he also expected that any assistance the United States provided would come with the price tag of Israeli cooperation in the struggle with Henry Jackson over giving the Soviet Union MFN status. On Monday evening, October 8, Kissinger called to tell Nixon that he expected the war to be over in three days, adding, "If this thing ends without a blowup with either the Arabs or the Soviets, it will be a miracle and a triumph." Kissinger even told Nixon that he expected the Syrian front would be a "turkey shoot" by Wednesday, October 10. For his part, Nixon emphasized that even though he thought it was a good thing the Israelis were "clobbering the Egyptians and Syrians," it was vitally important that "this thing" not "hang over for another four years and have us at odds with the Arab world." Kissinger agreed, telling Nixon that their ability to manage the Soviet reaction was "a major triumph for our policy and we can use it in the MFN fight." Both men expected a cease-fire soon, with an Israeli return to their positions before the war. Kissinger concluded their conversation by telling Nixon, "If we can hold this present situation another 48 hours, Mr. President, it will be a great triumph for you."[87]

The Israeli ambassador, Simcha Dinitz, woke a sleepy Henry Kissinger twice during the early-morning hours of October 9 to ask him questions about the resupply of war matériel. When they met later in the morning in Kissinger's office, Dinitz told the secretary of state the shocking news that Israel had lost forty-nine planes and five hundred tanks in the first days of the war. Indeed, the Egyptian and Syrian forces, taking advantage of the element of surprise, successfully crossed the Suez Canal and penetrated into the Golan Heights, inflicting severe losses on the Israelis. In particular, the Egyptian forces, equipped with portable anti-tank weapons, had caused considerable damage. Kissinger was stunned, exclaiming, "500 tanks! How many do you have?" When the Israeli military attaché answered, "1800," Kissinger remarked, "So that's why the Egyptians are so cocky." Kissinger reminded

Dinitz of his personal assurance that the Israelis would be winning by now, and the ambassador replied, with great understatement, "Obviously something went wrong." Dinitz told Kissinger that Prime Minister Meir wanted to fly to Washington secretly to present Israel's case to Nixon, an idea Kissinger immediately discouraged. Kissinger now knew that his strategy was in trouble, that a "blowup" with the Arabs or Soviets was much more likely. The United States could not stand to witness an Israeli defeat by Soviet-supported enemies, let alone the implicit threat of how a nuclear-armed Israel might respond.[88] Kissinger also knew the Israelis were "scared if their losses get out, all the Arabs would jump in." Yet strong action by the United States in resupplying Israel risked a confrontation with the Soviet Union and the end of détente. It could also alienate the Arab countries and trigger the use of the "oil weapon." Domestically Israel commanded widespread support from Congress and the public, and a failure to address Israel's dire situation could further weaken Nixon politically. The expectation Kissinger expressed the night before of a foreign policy triumph must now have seemed to him the height of folly.

Although he recognized that the situation had changed, Kissinger still clung to the hope that the United States could escape from the crisis with détente and relations with the Arabs intact. He pushed for and got Nixon's agreement for a "quiet" resupply for the Israelis, telling Dinitz, "All your aircraft and tank losses will be replaced," and that Israel could take them from the United States by plane. He made it clear that the Israelis would have to do this themselves, and "you have to paint El Al out. This is for maximum security."[89] Perhaps sensing Dinitz's skepticism toward this makeshift solution, he added, "You have the additional assurance that if it should go very badly and there is an emergency, we will get the tanks in even if we have to do it with American planes."[90] (It would quickly become apparent that more would be needed, as Israel had only seven available transport planes for the resupply operation.) After offering such a powerful guarantee, Kissinger asked Dinitz to use his influence to keep senators and congressmen from criticizing the administration for its policies.

Others in the administration did not fully share Kissinger's two priorities.

Defense Secretary James Schlesinger was far more suspicious of Soviet motives, seeing in the outbreak of war a reason to question the value of détente. Schlesinger's determination to change American defense planning had already found him at odds with Kissinger. He also resented the degree to which Kissinger dominated the WSAG crisis discussions and excluded other cabinet secretaries from decision-making. At the same time Kissinger was reassuring Dinitz of American support, Schlesinger received a report from the Joint Chiefs chairman, Thomas Moorer, that the Soviets were about to commence with "a massive airlift into the Middle East." Schlesinger replied, "Okay, you are just watching the collapse of U.S. foreign policy."[91]

For his part, Kissinger deflected blame for his own miscalculations onto Schlesinger and the Defense Department, especially over the implementation of the airlift to Israel. He suspected that Schlesinger's skepticism had significant support within the bureaucracy, as complaints abounded about the lack of WSAG meetings and the secrecy with which Kissinger operated.[92] Kissinger continued to hope for a "successful outcome," which he defined as "one which both parties accept, though grudgingly, that does not get us into a confrontation with the Soviets, and it doesn't radicalize the moderate Arab countries."[93] To appease the Israelis and give the appearance of accelerating the delivery of supplies to Israel, Kissinger told Dinitz that he had ordered the military to charter twenty aircraft to transport the supplies, still hoping that the lack of a direct American role would avoid offending the Arabs. At a televised press conference on Friday, October 12, Kissinger was publicly optimistic about Soviet behavior in the crisis, comparing it with their actions during the 1967 war "as less provocative, less incendiary, and less geared toward military threats." He insisted that the current Soviet airlift to the Arab states did not constitute the "irresponsibility" that might threaten détente.[94]

Kissinger's public optimism belied his growing suspicions about Soviet behavior. Only a few hours after the press conference ended, he told the Israelis that he had information that the Soviets had mobilized three airborne divisions, possibly as a response to Israeli bombing raids on Damascus.[95] He was also concerned by reports that the Soviets were encouraging other Arab states, including Jordan, to enter the war. When Dinitz arrived late the same evening to complain that the slow pace of American deliveries was hindering Israel's military offensive, Kissinger told him it was a "disgrace" and blamed Schlesinger and the Defense Department, even though Schlesinger explained that the American charter companies were not eager for the business and that the "low profile" on American assistance was the official policy.[96] Kissinger then assured Dinitz that he had called Haig and Schlesinger every night to try to speed things up, although there is no record of such calls. Kissinger now pressed for action, telling Haig, "I do not believe for one minute that they can't get charters if they tell these charter companies that the next time they need a rate change they won't get it." Kissinger still did not want American planes bringing the supplies directly to Israel, insisting to Schlesinger that the "one thing we cannot have now given our relations with the Soviets is American planes flying in there. Anything else is acceptable."[97] Schlesinger told Haig that Kissinger's plan would not work, and urged him to go to Nixon and order direct American action. Although preoccupied with Watergate, Nixon seemed to draw energy from the need for a presidential decision, and he agreed with Schlesinger, telling Kissinger, "Do it now."[98]

Kissinger's complicated techniques for aiding Israel were too clever by half. Although continuing to express reservations, he now recognized that it was time to "fly in some US planes."[99] By the end of the WSAG meeting, Kissinger was calling Dinitz to tell him that the C-5As would be sent, as well as some C-141 transports, and that fourteen Phantom jets would be dispatched. Kissinger quickly adapted and tried to seize advantage from the new situation that went against his original preference. He now pushed Dinitz to use his influence to moderate Senator Henry Jackson's criticisms. The senator from Washington State was threatening a congressional investigation of the administration's handling of this crisis. Although Dinitz assured him that he told Jackson that Israel has "never had a better friend than Dr. Kissinger," Kissinger, with a mixture of self-pity and blackmail, told Dinitz, "Our whole foreign policy position depends on our not being represented as having screwed up a crisis, and with all affection for Israel, if it turns out that we are going to be under attack for mismanagement in a crisis, we will have to turn on you."[100] Continued success and the perception of highly skilled diplomacy were central to Kissinger's elevated public image, and he feared they could be undermined by any suggestion that the Nixon administration—or he personally—had "screwed up" on the Middle East. It was the epitome of the personalization of foreign policy that Kissinger had come to promote.

The American airlift transformed the war, with giant transport planes arriving on the hour in Tel Aviv with thousands of tons of equipment and supplies, and American pilots now arriving in F-4 Phantom jets to be given to the Israeli Air Force. The airlift had a profound psychological effect in Israel, lifting the morale of the citizenry, as more supplies arrived on the first day than the Soviets had delivered to their Arab allies over the previous four days. Television news reported ominously that the war had "widened dangerously," presenting the American resupply as an effort to "maintain the balance of power" in the region in response to Soviet efforts.[101] Now that the operation was underway, Kissinger sought to use it to gain leverage over Israel and convince the Arabs that the only way to a settlement was through dealing with the United States. This put him at odds with Nixon, who, even after authorizing the airlift, told Kissinger that after a cease-fire "we've got to squeeze [the Israelis] goddamn hard" and that "the Russians have got to know it."[102] Nixon was far more interested in a dictated peace by the superpowers than was Kissinger, who preferred a settlement that pushed the Soviets out of the region. "Even though the Israelis will squeal like stuck pigs," Nixon told Kissinger, "we ought to tell Dobrynin . . . that Brezhnev and Nixon will settle this thing."[103] When a group of Arab foreign ministers came to meet Nixon and Kissinger at the White House a few days later, Nixon assured them that his goal was a "just, equitable settlement in the Middle East." Kissinger promised that the United States would make a "major effort" for a Middle East peace settlement after a cease-fire. Nixon interrupted to promise the Arabs "a major and *successful* effort."[104] On NBC Nightly News that evening, the Saudi ambassador was shown remarking after the meeting that he hoped "the man who could solve the Vietnam War" would now devote his attention to the Middle East. Whether the ambassador meant Nixon or Kissinger was not clear, but the context suggested the latter.[105]

Kissinger called Nixon after the meeting to tell him that the "Arabs are floating on air," that they recognized Nixon was "a great man" who spoke to them with great "sincerity" and would do what he promised for Middle East peace. Kissinger's flattering of Nixon helped defuse the awkwardness that had been created between the two men by the awarding of the Nobel Peace Prize to him alone, rather than Nixon, something that Nixon deeply resented. (When Nixon called to congratulate Kissinger on the award, he suddenly mentioned the award money and said bluntly, "I would not put any in for Israel." Kissinger dutifully responded to Nixon's not-so-veiled anti-Semitism with "Absolutely not. That would be out of the question. I never give to Israel.")[106] Kissinger went on to tell Nixon that he had used the Vietnam negotiations in his discussions with the Arab foreign ministers, reminding them of the pressure that Nixon had put on Thiệu once the North Vietnamese had come up with an acceptable offer. Nixon relished the reminder of that triumph, with Kissinger adding that even having a meeting with the Arabs while the airlift to Israel was going on was an indication of the success of American diplomacy.[107] Neither man mentioned the news that Arab oil producers announced that day they were reducing oil production by 5 percent each month until Israel withdrew from the Arab territory it had occupied since 1967, and that the six Persian Gulf members of OPEC had unilaterally increased the price of oil by 70 percent and imposed an oil embargo against Israel's allies, most notably the United States.[108] The use of oil as a political weapon against the United States was just beginning.

By Thursday, October 18, the stalemate on the battlefield had broken, and Israeli forces were pouring across the Suez Canal and launching an offensive on the West Bank, threatening the destruction of Egypt's Third Army. With a humiliating defeat for Moscow's allies now a real possibility, Brezhnev sent an urgent message to Washington, noting that as the "events in the Middle East become more and more dangerous," the United States and the Soviet Union needed to take "prompt and effective decisions." Brezhnev then asked Nixon to send "the US Secretary of State and your closest associate Dr. Kissinger" to Moscow for talks. Kissinger now felt, "Everyone knows in the Middle East that if they want a peace they have to go through us." At the same time, he added, "We can't humiliate the Soviet Union too much." In a sign of how independent Kissinger had become from Nixon, and how unwilling he was to follow the patterns he had during the first Nixon term, Kissinger told Haig that he thought it would be a "cheap stunt" for the White House to couple the announcement of his trip to Moscow with Nixon's announcement of his proposed compromise in dealing with the White House tapes. In blunt terms, Kissinger told Haig, "It looks as if he is using foreign policy to cover a domestic thing," and added, "I would not link foreign policy with Watergate. You will regret it the rest of your life." Nixon reluctantly agreed to separate the announcements.[109]

Kissinger's trip to Moscow marked a turning point in his relationship with Nixon as well as in his personal conduct of diplomacy. It was the last trip he would take without the press, and it coincided with the infamous "Saturday Night Massacre," in which Nixon fired the Watergate special prosecutor, Archibald Cox, leading to the resignations of Attorney General Elliot Richardson and his deputy William Ruckelshaus. For the first time, significant congressional sentiment supported the president's impeachment, and the nationwide outcry against Nixon's action dominated media coverage and pushed the Middle East into the background. Nixon sent Kissinger to Moscow with a grant of full authority to negotiate with the Soviets; however, Nixon also informed the Soviets of this, which "horrified" Kissinger, since it "deprived [him] of any capacity to stall."[110] Kissinger also disliked Nixon's linking of an immediate cease-fire with an overall settlement of the Middle East conflict imposed by the superpowers. His initial meeting with Brezhnev revealed that their positions on a cease-fire were not far apart, although Kissinger resisted Brezhnev's invoking of his "full authority" and told the Soviet leader that he would still need to check with the president on any agreement he made. When Kissinger read the full text of Nixon's instructions, he angrily cabled Haig that the president's instructions "will totally wreck what little bargaining leverage I still have."[111] He also called Haig on an open line to complain, only to have the president's chief of staff tell him, "Get off my back. I have troubles of my own." When Kissinger angrily responded, "What troubles can you possibly have in Washington on a Saturday night?" Haig told him, "All hell has broken loose," in the wake of Nixon's decision to fire Cox.[112]

Kissinger and Brezhnev reached an agreement on a United Nations resolution for a cease-fire in place, beginning twelve hours after its approval at the UN. Kissinger then headed to Israel.[113] Kissinger was worried whether the Israelis, on the cusp of a complete victory, would accept the agreement. He was not averse to seeing them inflict an even more decisive defeat on the Arabs, although he also feared Soviet intervention if they went too far. When a communications breakdown in Moscow caused a four-hour delay in notifying Israel of the U.S.-Soviet agreement, Kissinger cabled Ambassador Dinitz and assured him that the "United States would understand if the Israelis felt they required some additional time for military dispositions before the cease-fire took effect." Kissinger also told Golda Meir that the Americans understood that "you have won the war, though at a very high cost." He added, "You won't get violent protests from Washington if something happens during the night while I'm flying."[114]

Israel continued its offensive despite the UN cease-fire resolution, determined to destroy the Egyptian Third Army. Brezhnev used the Washington–Moscow hotline to protest directly to Kissinger about the Israelis' "flagrant deceit" and called their behavior "absolutely unacceptable." The Soviet leader insisted that the Israelis withdraw their forces to the original cease-fire line.[115] The Egyptians added to this appeal, with Sadat urging Nixon to intervene immediately to stop Israel from its attempt to "change completely the situation on the military front." Concerned that the Israelis might advance farther and even threaten Cairo, Kissinger called Ambassador Dinitz and insisted that the fighting stop. Kissinger yelled at Dinitz, "Jesus Christ, you don't understand." Dinitz calmed him down and joked that his government might be more persuaded if he invoked a different prophet.[116]

Kissinger could probably have invoked Moses, Elijah, and Jeremiah, but the Israelis were in no mood to stop their advance. The next morning Kissinger again called Dinitz to complain that the Israelis broke the cease-fire and were attacking the Third Army. Dinitz tried to blame the Egyptians, but an exasperated Kissinger finally exploded, "Look, Mr. Ambassador, we have been a strong support for you, but we cannot make Brezhnev look like a goddam fool in front of his colleagues."[117] He told Dinitz that Sadat now wanted U.S. and

Soviet forces to intervene directly, sarcastically adding, "If the Soviets put some divisions in there you will have outsmarted yourselves." Kissinger said that the Soviets were now accusing him of having "gone from Moscow to Tel Aviv to plot with them the overthrow of the whole arrangement we've made."[118] Despite his worries over preserving détente, Kissinger confidently told his staff, "We have come out of this in the catbird seat. Everyone has to come to us since we are the only ones who can deliver." The Israelis, he said, learned that they could not fight a war without "an open US supply line," and while the Arabs "may despise us, or hate us," if they wanted a settlement, the United States is "the essential ingredient."[119]

Tensions mounted as the continuing Israeli violations of the cease-fire led the Russians to support a UN resolution calling for U.S. and Soviet troops to be deployed as peacekeepers. Ambassador Dobrynin told Kissinger that Soviet leaders were so angry that "you have allowed the Israelis to do what they wanted." Kissinger responded, "If you want confrontation we will have to have one. It would be a pity." Dobrynin denied wanting such a confrontation, but Kissinger's own thinking had clearly changed. He called Haig and told him that the Russians were now "taking a nasty turn" and that they "realize they were taken." Kissinger told Haig, "We have to be tough as nails now." Only two hours later, he called to tell Haig that Brezhnev had threatened that if the United States would not act jointly with the Soviets to enforce the cease-fire, the Soviets would intervene unilaterally. Kissinger told Haig, "We have to go to the mat on this one," although Haig cautioned, "I think they're playing chicken." Kissinger asked Haig whether he should wake the president, and Haig replied no. Kissinger now brought together a small group of officials, what was referred to later as a "curious little rump NSC meeting."[120] In Moorer's notes of the meeting, Kissinger emphasized his view that the hawks had prevailed over Brezhnev in the Kremlin, reversing his earlier policy. Kissinger believed, "*If the Democrats and the US public do not stop laying siege to their government, sooner or later, someone will take a run at us.*"[121] He returned to this sentiment later in the meeting, stressing that "*the overall strategy of the Soviets now appears to be one of throwing détente on the table since we have no functional President,*" and that "*we must prevent them from getting away with this.*" Kissinger's focus on the domestic political factors that encouraged a Soviet challenge overlooked many of the logistical problems, which Moorer stressed would make intervention difficult for the Russians. In the heat of the moment, however, the necessity to act was paramount, and Kissinger and the "little rump NSC" put the U.S. military forces on DEFCON 3, the highest stage of readiness since the Cuban Missile Crisis.[122]

Ironically, it was Brezhnev who added the line about unilateral action in the Soviet message, in what was essentially a bluff, as Haig had guessed. Incensed by the continuing Israeli attacks and dismayed by Sadat's desperation and Egyptian weakness, the Soviet leader had strengthened the message on his own.[123] The Soviet military was not prepared for action, and the politburo did not want a confrontation with the United States.[124] The crisis abated almost as quickly as it had arisen. The next day, Anwar Sadat accepted a UN force to supervise the cease-fire, and Brezhnev deliberately ignored the American action and indicated that he was dispatching seventy Soviet "representatives" to join with an American civilian team to observe the cease-fire. Now it was the United States that faced the charge of overreacting, as Kissinger discovered when he held a press conference to discuss the alert. To defend détente, Kissinger minimized the idea that the United States was confronting the Soviet Union and stressed that the alert was a "precautionary measure." However, reporters zeroed in on whether the American action was a "rational" response, and questioners implied that the alert was implemented for domestic political reasons in order to take attention away from Watergate. Kissinger's angry replies hinted at some of the reasons he had himself expressed at the late-night meeting. He accused the media of wanting to "create a crisis of confidence in foreign policy," implying, as he had told the NSC the night before, that it had created one domestically in its pursuit of the Watergate scandal.[125] He stressed that the decision was the unanimous recommendation of senior advisers, but also made it clear that the president had not taken part in the deliberations, a detail that did not escape notice. Later in the day he called Nixon to tell him, "Mr. President, you have won again," and proceeded to denounce the reporters, among them his friends Marvin Kalb, James Reston, and Colman McCarthy, who suggested the alert was done for political reasons. When Nixon mentioned his desire to hold a press conference the next day, Kissinger encouraged Nixon to "treat the bastards with contempt," and, in an unusual reference to the 1971 Indo-Pakistani war, reminded Nixon, "You were prepared to put forces in as you were prepared to go to nuclear war in Pakistan and that was way before you knew what was going to happen."[126]

Nixon took Kissinger's advice, but it did not work out well. Although Nixon hoped the press conference would allow him to bask in the glory of Kissinger's achievement, the reporters still focused on Watergate and the questions raised by the Saturday Night Massacre. Nixon was defiant and defensive about his Watergate decisions and the firing of the special prosecutor. But when one questioner asked whether his "Watergate troubles" might have encouraged "Soviet thinking about your ability to respond in the Mideast," Nixon stressed his military actions during the Vietnam War, when he had ordered the invasion of Cambodia, the bombing and mining of North Vietnam, and the Christmas bombing, and added, "Mr. Brezhnev knew that regardless of the pressures at home," he, Nixon, would do what is right, and that's "what made Mr. Brezhnev act as he did."[127] Kissinger called Haig right after the news conference ended and said, "The crazy bastard really made a mess with the Russians," stressing the contrast with his own approach of downplaying the confrontation. "He has turned it into a massive Soviet backdown," Kissinger added, with a public humiliation of Brezhnev. Kissinger asked Haig to call Dobrynin to try to soften Nixon's remarks, but added that Nixon "looked awful."[128]

On October 28, 1973, Egyptian and Israeli military commanders, in a moment replete with symbolism, met for the first time to discuss the ceasefire and the resupply of the Egyptian forces. The possibility of a new era in the Middle East was opening, but deft American diplomacy was required to seize this opportunity. The war had marked a turning point in the Nixon-Kissinger relationship, with Kissinger now acting essentially as the chief executive while Nixon struggled to survive and clung to Kissinger. Over the next several months, as Watergate continued to unfold and Americans waited in gasoline lines with prices skyrocketing, Kissinger engaged in a high-risk, crisis-driven foreign policy whose creativity and potential dangers would reverberate for decades to come.

THE KISSINGER STRATEGY TAKES SHAPE

The easing of the immediate crisis in the Middle East and the beginning of the cease-fire left Kissinger with new challenges.[129] Foremost, he needed to ensure that the fragile cease-fire held. Kissinger knew that Israel wanted to finish off Egypt's Third Army and that the Golan Heights remained equally volatile. Israel had been traumatized by the war—its casualty total of 2,668 killed was equivalent to an American death toll of 160,000.[130] The danger of a protracted war of attrition remained. Second, Kissinger needed to start negotiations between the parties, initially aimed at separating the military forces but ultimately toward a longer-term settlement. In contrast to Nixon's preference for a treaty dictated by the superpowers, Kissinger hoped to use these negotiations to push the Soviet Union out of the Middle East, demonstrating to the Arabs and Israelis that peace could come only through American power and mediation. Third, even though he wanted them out of the Middle East, Kissinger still wanted to preserve the advantages of détente with the Russians, especially in controlling the nuclear arms race and preventing a crisis like that in the Middle East, which could escalate dangerously. Fourth, the Arab oil embargo, begun in response to the American resupply of Israel on October 17, remained in place. As oil prices soared, temperatures fell, and Americans waited in long gasoline lines and shivered in homes without heating oil, the domestic political pressures would build. Nixon frequently pushed Kissinger on this issue, hoping that an end to the embargo would help him regain public support. Finally, along with the domestic political crises and pressures came serious tensions within the Western alliance. The Yom Kippur war had exposed the sharpest divisions within the West since the Suez crisis of the 1950s. Most European nations refused to allow American planes to use their facilities for the massive American airlift to Israel. Heavily dependent on imported oil, the European nations and Japan, led by France and its foreign minister, Michel Jobert, adopted a strong pro-Arab position, demanding Israeli withdrawal to its 1967 borders. The American nuclear alert also took Europe by surprise, and their vociferous complaint about a lack of consultation rang through the foreign offices. The "Year of Europe" now seemed hopelessly ironic, as Europeans challenged American leadership and seemed determined to forge their own Middle East and energy policies. The postwar Western alliance, America's greatest foreign policy success, was coming unglued.

Kissinger approached this combination of crises and dilemmas with extraordinary energy, intelligence, and guile. David Bruce, one of America's patrician diplomats from the early Cold War and still an active ambassador, captured an essential aspect of Kissinger's approach when he wrote in his diary that Kissinger's "physical and intellectual vigor amaze even those they discomfit... the spectacle of a fifty-year old German-born Jew, exercising the authority he does in coping with the end of an era complications of universal import elicits my sympathy, dazzles my imagination."[131] Kissinger devised a strategy, sensing how the various pieces of the jigsaw puzzle of world politics could be arranged to promote his vision of America's national interest.[132] He also recognized how his personal prestige could be harnessed to address these issues, and knew that success would further enhance his own personal power. Within days of the cease-fire, the TV networks were referring to Kissinger as the new "go-between" in dealings with Israel and the Arab world.[133] Planning a trip to the Arab states in the region, Kissinger told Golda Meir, "One thing the Arabs have achieved in this war—regardless of what they lost—is that they've globalized the problem. They have created the conviction that something must be done, which we've arrested only by my prestige, by my trip, by maneuvers." Kissinger argued to the Israelis that he had convinced the Egyptians that "the Russians can give them arms but only we can give them territory," but that he now needed to "get something started" in negotiations, in part to help lift the international pressure off Israel. His "nightmare" was "Russian helicopters going in there, and an enormous crisis which then forces you back anyway."[134] Presenting himself as Israel's protector, Kissinger pressured the Israelis to compromise.

After meeting with Meir and the Israeli delegation in Washington,

Kissinger went off for his first trip to the Arab world. Television coverage emphasized the possibility that war might break out again at any time, but also the historic nature of the "Jewish Secretary of State's visit."[135] In Egypt, Kissinger found an extraordinary negotiating partner in Anwar Sadat, a leader who grasped the significance of Kissinger's interest in the region and knew he could use it for his own objectives. Sadat wanted to reverse Egypt's previous position of hostility toward the United States and use American power to achieve his objectives.[136] He made it clear to Kissinger that he would accept the proposed "Kissinger Plan," which established a corridor to supply the trapped Third Army, set up United Nations checkpoints between the two sides, and allowed the release of Israeli prisoners of war. Sadat was emphatic: "Never forget, Dr. Kissinger. I am making this agreement with the United States, not with Israel."[137] This reversal of Egypt's position seemed to Kissinger as consequential as China's opening was to the geopolitics of the larger Cold War, and Kissinger was determined to nurture this change. Nixon cabled Kissinger to tell him he was "elated" by his accomplishment.[138]

The success of the Kissinger Plan in the Middle East contributed to the aura of Kissinger's sixth trip to China, his first as secretary of state. The Chinese enthusiastically embraced him, with Chairman Mao giving Kissinger a long and sustained handshake for the television cameras.[139] Behind the scenes, the Chinese leaders applauded the nuclear alert, leading Kissinger to remark, "The people who understand our foreign policy best are in Peking." Kissinger made it a point to discuss Brezhnev's threatening discussion of China at the summit earlier in the year and offered to share American intelligence with the Chinese on the Soviet threat to their country. Kissinger told the Chinese that the Russians had asked for American intelligence on China, particularly satellite photographs, something that Kissinger interpreted as meaning "they want us to accept the desirability of destroying China's nuclear capability or limiting it, rather than the information itself."[140] At the banquet after their talks, Kissinger offered a toast that reassured the Chinese that "no matter what happens" in Washington, the new American friendship with China would not change.[141] Reporters saw a Watergate-motivated tone in Kissinger's words, but Kissinger reassured Nixon in his report on the trip that the Chinese supported him. Mao remarked with his peasant humor that Watergate was "no more than a breaking of wind."[142] From Kissinger's point of view, the United States and China had become "tacit allies," sharing a similar view of the Soviet Union and a belief in the necessity of a "strong American world role and defense capability."[143]

The media celebrated Kissinger's nine-day, eight-country trip as one of frenetic negotiating, and this enhanced his stature in the midst of the gloomy news about Watergate. As Kissinger settled back into Washington, however, he found the Arab oil embargo the most pressing political issue. In a nationally televised speech, Nixon told Americans that they were facing the "most acute shortages of energy since World War II," and he invoked the Apollo moon landing to argue that Americans should strive for energy self-sufficiency by the end of the decade.[144] Nixon's "Project Independence" offered Americans a lofty goal, but for now their concerns were the more immediate ones of heating oil and gasoline. Kissinger's problem was how to get the Arab states to lift their embargo without seeming to succumb to the diplomatic blackmail. At times he postured in discussing the oil boycott with his staff, remarking, "I know what would have happened in the nineteenth century," then describing how the United States would have landed in the Arabian desert and divided up the oil fields. "But that obviously we cannot do," he sadly concluded.[145] At other times he vented his feelings more crudely: "It is ridiculous that the civilized world is held up by 8 million savages," he said in a White House meeting. Nevertheless, as angry as Kissinger was about the boycott, he opposed the suggestion of Defense Secretary Schlesinger to prepare a military contingency, describing his rival as "insane" and telling Haig, "I do not think we can survive these fellows in there at Defense—they are crazy." This did not keep Kissinger himself from implying the possibility of armed force at a press conference on November 21, when he said, "If pressures continue unreasonably and indefinitely, then the United States will have to consider what countermeasures it may have to take."[146] The Saudi reaction to Kissinger's words was swift, with Sheik Yamani, the leading Saudi representative, threatening to blow up the oil wells if there were any such military action. Contingency planning did proceed, however, and was extensive enough to create fears in

Britain that the Americans might actually follow their old imperialist methods.[147]

In reality, Kissinger knew the only way out of the problem was getting peace negotiations in the Middle East started, which would help convince the Arab nations that the United States genuinely sought a settlement. He told his staff, "We will have to pressure Israel, but if it looks like we do it under pressure, we won't even get credit for it." As a first step, Kissinger sought to use the auspices of the United Nations, with Soviet approval, to call for a Geneva Conference of the superpowers with Israel and the Arab nations. Kissinger's approach seems paradoxical. Geneva would be a multilateral conference that Kissinger wanted to use to promote bilateral negotiations between Israel and each of its adversaries. It would be hosted by the two superpowers, but with the goal of forcing the Soviets to the sidelines. Kissinger recognized, as he later wrote, that "Soviet cooperation was necessary to convene Geneva: afterward, we would seek to reduce its role to a minimum."[148] He might have added that his support for Geneva was also designed with Nixon in mind, as the president was much more inclined than Kissinger to want to work with the Soviet Union in the Middle East. The conference allowed Kissinger to appear to follow the president's wishes even as he planned a different policy.

Kissinger was less diplomatic in handling Nixon's ideas and suggestions, most of which grew out of the president's hope that a major triumph might defuse the outrage over Watergate. When Nixon considered sending a special envoy to Saudi Arabia to try to end the oil embargo, Kissinger told Brent Scowcroft, who was serving as deputy assistant on the National Security Council, "He [Nixon] does that and he is in deep trouble with me." Kissinger was also confident that Nixon would "calm down" and that he could persuade the president such a move would put the United States in the position of being a "supplicant" to the Saudis and "was hardly the best way to convey imperviousness to pressure."[149] He reacted in an equally vehement way when he found out that Nixon had met alone with Dobrynin to discuss the Middle East. Kissinger told Haig that such meetings damaged his ability to conduct diplomacy. Kissinger clearly feared that Nixon would give both countries a different sense of American policy, particularly regarding Soviet involvement in the process, than what Kissinger was trying to achieve. He complained that he was "flying blind" without knowing what Nixon had said, and emphatically told Haig that he must ensure "that this sort of thing does not happen again."[150]

At the same time he was trying to keep Nixon from undermining his policy, Kissinger directed his attention toward the Europeans, who wanted to arrange their own deals with the Arab oil producers. Europe's "disassociation" from America's policy in the Middle East was a rational response to its heavy dependence on oil from the region. Yet Kissinger's reaction had a sharp edge to it, combining his realism with a hefty element of historical memory and emotion. He saw their action in Cold War terms, arguing that it was "cowardly" and would "have disastrous consequences vis-à-vis the Soviet Union who, if allowed to succeed in the Near East, can be expected to mount ever more aggressive policies elsewhere."[151] He told the European foreign ministers that the Europeans "had done to us what we had done to them in 1956," evoking the memory of American action against Britain and France during the Suez crisis. He also shared in an American assessment of the Europeans as profoundly ungrateful to the United States, "the country that had restored their economies and on which they continued to rely for their security."[152] Kissinger connected the European action with their attempt to achieve greater unity, complaining, "Almost anything we do is used to organize Europe against us."[153]

Kissinger was determined to try to restore American leadership of the alliance and weaken the anti-American elements within Europe. His main opponent was the French foreign minister, Jobert, who advocated a European-Arab dialogue that Kissinger saw as a threat to his own strategy for the Middle East.[154] To counter Jobert and isolate the French, Kissinger sought to imitate the oil producers and their organization of OPEC. In a major speech delivered at Britain's prestigious Society of Pilgrims in London in December 1973, Kissinger proposed the "creation of an international consumers group to regulate world demand" for energy.[155] Such an "energy action group" among the oil-consuming nations would strengthen their hand in dealing with the oil producers. Along with convening the Geneva Conference, Kissinger's proposal for an organization of energy consumers was designed to regain the initiative for American diplomacy. It demonstrated to Europe that the Americans had a strategy to respond to both the Middle East crisis and the economic challenges facing the Western democracies.

The Geneva Conference convened December 21, 1973, and was immediately celebrated as a historic milestone. Although the Syrians decided not to take part, Kissinger convinced the Egyptians, Jordanians, and Israelis to attend. "For the first time since the creation of the state of Israel," NBC's Chancellor intoned, "Arabs and Israelis were sitting down together to discuss the prospects for peace."[156] The formal occasion allowed for tough speeches, with the Egyptian foreign minister threatening a return to war if the negotiations did not succeed. Kissinger was disappointed that the opening of the conference had not led the Saudis to end the oil embargo. In his report to Nixon, he stressed that although "the atmosphere could not be characterized as one of reconciliation, the parties were careful to keep all doors open." He went on to note, in words that reflected his continuing attempt to defuse Nixon's objections, "Your strategy is working well." That strategy, as Kissinger described it, was of being "the only participant who is in close touch with all the parties, the only power that can produce progress, and the only one that each is coming to in order to make that progress." This was a fair description of his strategy, not Nixon's plan.[157]

A NEW YEAR BEGINS: THE MIDDLE EAST AND THE ENERGY CONFERENCE

Flying out to San Clemente to see the president at New Year's 1974, Henry Kissinger took a regular commercial flight. This gesture, recognition that the energy crisis required public officials to economize, allowed Kissinger to joke at a news conference, "There are no stewardesses on Air Force One." Even though the humor about Kissinger as a ladies' man may have been growing stale—indeed, Kissinger would finally marry Nancy Maginnes, his longtime girlfriend, at the end of March—the reporters laughed along, with ABC's Stephen Geer remarking that the "famous Kissinger humor" was still in evidence "no matter how serious the problems" he faced. Those "problems" were now seen to be presidential ones, and Kissinger responded to one questioner who asked if he had assumed authority over foreign policy by stating, "I totally reject the idea I am attempting to conduct an independent policy." Even as Kissinger was denying it, ABC's Ted Koppel reported that the Israeli defense minister, Moshe Dayan, was bringing the terms of a disengagement agreement to Washington and that the Israelis believed "the hope for peace lies not in Geneva, but wherever Henry Kissinger is."[158]

The Israeli elections of late December 1973 weakened the government of Prime Minister Golda Meir, but not enough to prevent it from moving ahead with negotiations. The Israelis wanted Kissinger to conduct the negotiations bilaterally, fearing the pressure and isolation they would experience in a multilateral conference like the one in Geneva. They took the initiative with Dayan's disengagement proposal, which Kissinger thought "means that they have come 85 percent of the way to the Egyptian position on disengagement, and this without any demands for reciprocity." Kissinger knew that aspects of the Israeli proposal, especially concerning the distance of the withdrawal and the armaments allowed the forces, would be a hard sell to the Egyptians. He told Nixon that unless we "break the back of this thing in the next ten days," the momentum for peace would be lost and there would be a delay in ending the oil embargo.[159] Kissinger understood that an emphasis on speed played to Nixon's domestic political concerns and would override his interest in a U.S.-Soviet Geneva Conference settlement. Confessing that an "element of vanity" was present in his motivations, Kissinger wanted to manage these negotiations personally, hoping to score a success that would show the value of American power to the Arabs, push the Soviets out of the peace process, and enhance his own prestige.[160]

Kissinger's insight in handling these negotiations came in two ways: first, in understanding how he had become the essential mediator, the one person the Egyptians and Israelis trusted, at least for the moment; and second, in representing American power to both nations, with an authority to commit the United States to agreed-upon measures that gave him extraordinary leverage. Although his sympathy with Israel was more understandable, he bonded quickly with Anwar Sadat, whose goals as an Egyptian nationalist resonated with Kissinger. This meant that Sadat would not allow his alliance with Syria to prevent an agreement benefiting Egypt, and that he would try to get his Arab supporters to lift the oil boycott once the agreement was in place. At Kissinger's urging, Sadat was willing to set an early deadline to the talks.[161] Kissinger and Sadat were joined at the hip in pressuring the Israelis, whose messy and very democratic political system made them much more difficult negotiating partners than was the authoritarian Sadat. Kissinger pressed the Israelis hard, forcefully telling them that any resumption of the war would not be in their interest, no matter how strong their position appeared, and warning them that if they undertook extreme retaliation for any cease-fire violations, they risked "all hell break[ing] loose internationally."[162] Although he expressed understanding for Israeli concerns and recognized their vulnerability, he defended Sadat to the Israelis, pointing out that his "domestic situation" put limits on what he could concede.[163] Ultimately Kissinger thought Sadat had "gone beyond the outer edge of what he feels is safe." To finalize the agreement, Kissinger arranged for both Egypt and Israel to make their commitments to the United States rather than to each other, and he committed the United States to assure Egypt that Israel would not attack "the civilian areas to be established by Sadat in the Sinai."[164]

On January 17, 1974, Nixon announced the "historic" disengagement agreement in nationally televised remarks from the White House, calling it the "first significant step toward a permanent peace in the Middle East."[165] The president hoped that this diplomatic achievement, during a week when the controversy about the eighteen-and-a-half-minute gap in the Watergate tapes dominated the news, would be a welcome distraction. Nixon had tried to call Kissinger home two days earlier to provide "some publicized Presidential instruction and then complete the negotiation," but Kissinger ignored his request.[166] ABC News presented the agreement as a "personal triumph for Henry Kissinger," describing him as a "conquering warrior back from the negotiating wars." NBC's David Brinkley called him a "public hero" and celebrated his successful diplomacy as proving that "a Kissinger might often be worth more than divisions, carriers or bombers and a great deal cheaper."[167] Kissinger received a standing ovation when he briefed the congressional leadership, with Senator Fulbright calling this a "remarkable job." Kissinger described the larger goal of that policy in a way that proved misleading, telling the representatives, "We must be careful not to push out the Soviet Union—we will use Geneva to get their involvement and we have kept them partially informed." Nixon was even more solicitous of Soviet concerns, remarking, "We don't want to irritate the Soviet Union; we just want to play a constructive role."[168]

What Nixon really wanted was to be able to announce the end of the oil boycott in his State of the Union address, scheduled for January 30. Kissinger thought he had assurances from both Sadat and the Saudis that this would be possible. He tried to bluff the Saudis by threatening that if the boycott were not lifted, the United States might tell the Israelis not to withdraw and "would be forced to stop all further efforts toward peace in the Middle East."[169] When he told Nixon that he thought an announcement was near, the president replied, "This is the greatest thing we could possibly do," adding that without it, his speech "wouldn't amount to anything anymore."[170] The Saudis, however, decided not to act alone, and the other Arab oil-producing states were not willing to go along unless they saw Kissinger pushing the Israelis to withdraw from the new Syrian territory they had occupied during the war. Action on the Egyptian front was not enough. Kissinger was furious, saying to Brent Scowcroft, "If I was the President I would tell the Arabs to shove their oil and tell the Congress we will have rationing rather than submit," adding that this would get the embargo lifted in three days. Kissinger then joked, "But I am not President until this GD constitutional amendment," a revealing reference to Congressman Bingham's attempt to amend the Constitution on Kissinger's behalf. All Nixon could do in the State of the Union was to announce that a meeting would be taking place "to discuss the lifting of the embargo," not exactly the blockbuster Nixon wanted or needed.[171]

Nixon kept trying to influence the Saudis, and a week after the State of the Union he met with the Saudi ambassador without Kissinger present. Nixon emphasized to the ambassador that he was the "first President since Eisenhower who has no commitment to the Jewish community," and affirmed his own commitment to UN Resolution 242, calling for Israeli withdrawal from occupied territories. He distanced himself from Kissinger's public use of the term "blackmail" in referring to the oil embargo, calling it "unfortunate," and expressed the hope that after the embargo was lifted, he could strive for a "just peace." Nixon added, "I will have three years. My successor may be beholden to the groups here," a very unsubtle reference to American supporters of Israel. In contrast to Kissinger, Nixon stressed that the key to progress was the Geneva Conference and that he would do his best "to move the Israelis."[172]

Kissinger was aware of Nixon's maneuvers, but he continued to determine American strategy.[173] With his Washington conference of oil producers coming up in February, Kissinger targeted the oil embargo. Although the official American position was that an organization of oil consumers was not directed against the oil producers, Kissinger bluntly told his staff, "We have said it a hundred times and it's bullshit!" He went on to say, "Let's not kid ourselves. The purpose is to create a consumer group that improves the bargaining position of the consumers." Reaching into ancient history for an analogy, Kissinger remarked, "If we can't organize ourselves, then we really are in the condition of Greek cities facing Macedonia or Rome."[174] Kissinger knew that this approach faced stiff opposition from the French, who believed they had their own special relationship with the Arab countries. Foreign Minister Michel Jobert, who distrusted Kissinger as essentially a "politician above all else," called the Washington conference "a purely political act, a brilliant affirmation of American supremacy."[175]

The Frenchman was not far off in his assessment of Kissinger or his objectives. Kissinger himself would later admit, "Jobert was absolutely right when he said the energy conference was purely political. I don't give a damn about energy... The issue is to break the other Europeans away from the French."[176] Kissinger told Nixon that unless the United States took "tough action," it would "lose the pro-American people in Europe because they can't point out the bad consequences of anti-American actions."[177] Kissinger had already been meeting with other European representatives, particularly the British and the Germans, to convince them that the Americans had an energy plan that involved using supplies more rationally, promoting conservation, and developing alternative energy sources. Kissinger used his personal success in negotiating the first disengagement agreement to argue that the Americans could deliver in the Middle East and that this stood in contrast to the ineffectual European-Arab dialogue. Watching Kissinger's maneuvers, the French hesitated about whether to attend the Washington meetings. They finally agreed only a few days before the conference was set to begin, thinking that they had an understanding with the other European countries to stand against the Americans. However, European unity collapsed quickly after the conference began, and the French found themselves isolated.[178] In reporting the results to Nixon, Kissinger stressed, "We have broken the Community, just as I always thought I wanted to," noting that he had refused a compromise proposal from the French that "would be quite tolerable if I trusted the sons of bitches." Kissinger bragged that despite the American media's depiction of "that Titanic confrontation with Jobert," the French foreign minister "winds up having no votes and we have all of them. The communiqué is essentially the one we drafted."[179]

Kissinger was premature in thinking he had broken European resistance, and tensions grew worse over the next month. In early March the European Economic Community's rotating president, the German foreign minister Walter Scheel, told Kissinger that the EEC nations were going ahead with their dialogue with the Arab states, having reached the decision without consulting the Americans. Kissinger's anger was barely concealed as he told Scheel, "I say in all seriousness that the United States will not accept this procedure in the long run without its having a great effect on our relationship."[180] Kissinger accused the Europeans of undermining his diplomacy in the Middle East and ominously warned them, "Europe seems intent upon taking a path we will not accept. If Europe is determined to float its foreign policy, then the United States, too, will float its foreign policy. We will then have to see whose specific weight is the greatest." His hostility was particularly centered on the French, whom he believed were "organically hostile to the US and now clearly constitute the greatest global opposition to US foreign policy."[181] This was hyperbole and a considerable overreaction to the French efforts, but during the next month Kissinger would, in both public and private forums, make it clear that the United States was determined to stop a European Common Market that was "becoming organically anti-American." He even encouraged Nixon to weigh in on the subject, and in a speech in Chicago Nixon complained, "The Europeans cannot have it both ways. They cannot have the United States participation and cooperation on the security front and then proceed to have confrontation and even hostility on the economic and political front."[182] Nixon's speech, and the European reaction, led the American media to now designate the Year of Europe as a "bust."[183]

Nevertheless, the American pressure set off alarm bells among the Europeans, especially the Germans, who saw themselves in the most vulnerable position and needing America's security guarantee. About a week after Nixon's comments, Kissinger reported that he had the "best talks" with the German leaders, noting, "Both Brandt and Scheel say, and I think mean it, that Europe must unite within the context of close Atlantic relations, i.e., in close accord with us."[184] Kissinger was coming off two recent successes, the setting of a date for the beginning of Israeli-Syrian disengagement talks and the end of the oil embargo, both of which enhanced his image and power in Europe as well as diminished what he called "the sense of panic in Europe" over the energy crisis.[185] The easing of the tensions with Europe was also helped along by fate: the death of Georges Pompidou on April 2 meant that Jobert left the Foreign Ministry. The British prime minister, Heath, lost his election at the end of February, while the German chancellor, Brandt, resigned in a spy scandal in early May, replaced by Kissinger's friend Helmut Schmidt. The changing cast of characters, with the exception of Kissinger, removed some of the irritants in U.S.-European relations and allowed Kissinger to claim a modest success for the Year of Europe at NATO's Ottawa meeting in June, which reaffirmed the Atlantic alliance on its twenty-fifth anniversary.[186]

At the end of March 1974 Kissinger went to Moscow to prepare for a Nixon summit early in the summer. He told the press before he left that he hoped for a "conceptual breakthrough" on the issue of arms control and a possible SALT II treaty.[187] The Soviets were not in as conciliatory a mood as Kissinger might have hoped. They recognized that his strategy in the Middle East excluded them, and Brezhnev complained bitterly, "You have gone back on the understanding reached between us once on Egypt; now you want to do it on Syria. What other violations will there be?"[188] They complained as well about the failure of the administration to get their most-favored-nation status through Congress and the continued demands that they do more about Jewish emigration. Kissinger spent considerable time in his meetings trying to explain Senator Jackson's opposition, as well as the developing opposition of "certain circles in the United States" to the SALT I agreement and to détente in general.[189] When Brezhnev proposed an extension of the SALT I agreement, Kissinger told him, "We have come under strong attack in the United States for the existing agreement so extending it is not an easy matter."[190]

Kissinger recognized that one of the underlying difficulties in American-Soviet discussions was the different structure of their nuclear arsenals, with the American "triad" of land, sea, and airborne weapons, while the Soviet nuclear force was overwhelmingly still land-based missiles located on its territory. This made the creation of simple "equality" between the two superpowers a difficult issue to negotiate and an easy one for critics like Jackson to attack. It also made it difficult for the military services and government bureaucracies to unite around a unified American position in arms control negotiations. Kissinger was now aware that the Defense Department was less and less interested in another SALT agreement. The domestic politics of SALT were changing. Unlike with the SALT I agreement, which gave Nixon an important campaign boost in the 1972 election, Kissinger now acknowledged, "The President gets absolutely no political advantage from an agreement."[191] By this point Jackson had charged that Nixon wanted "a quick fix in Moscow" through a SALT agreement.[192] Kissinger thought that a new agreement might still be desirable for foreign policy reasons, but that an extension of the interim agreement in SALT I was the only political possibility. He put on a public show of defiance against Jackson, insisting in an April 26 news conference that the United States would neither "rush an agreement" for the summit nor turn down one that was desirable, merely because of "an intense domestic debate"—Kissinger's euphemistic description of the argument over Nixon's impeachment.[193]

At the end of April 1974, Kissinger again departed for the Middle East, hoping to negotiate a disengagement agreement between Israel and Syria. He stopped first in Geneva to meet with the Soviet foreign minister, Gromyko, determined to create at least the appearance of involving the Soviets in this negotiation.[194] Kissinger knew that the Soviets could undermine his Syrian negotiations if they came to believe it was worth the risk to détente. He was confident, however, that he could pull the diplomatic wool over their eyes with symbolic actions like meeting with Gromyko, especially since both the Syrians and the Israelis preferred direct American mediation. The problem was that this was about all that Israel and Syria could agree on, and the distrust between them was even greater than it was with Egypt. Kissinger told the press corps that in contrast with the Egyptian disengagement, "This is more delicate, more complicated, more uncertain than any other trip I have taken" and "has the potential of being an anguishing week."[195] It turned out to be an anguishing month.

Kissinger's skill as a negotiator rested on his intelligence, strategic vision, and pure physical stamina. He was, in the words of Abba Eban, the Israeli foreign minister, a "plenipotentiary" who would occasionally say he needed to discuss a matter with the president, but "clearly he was in charge."[196] He was also particularly adept at "explaining every situation in the manner most pleasing to the one who heard it."[197] This was only part of his talent. With the Israelis in particular, he was also able to paint realistic-sounding scenarios of what the consequences would be if his mission failed. Early in the negotiations he made it clear that he did not consider UN Resolution 242 calling for Israeli withdrawal from the occupied territories to be the guide to American policy. He told the Israelis that they "should not be asked to give up Golan," and that it was only a "narrow strip" that needed to be sacrificed to the Syrians.[198] The key, in Kissinger's view, was to "keep the Arabs divided." As the Israelis balked, however, at the concessions Kissinger suggested, he painted a dire scenario of cascading dangers. He began by describing how Israeli recalcitrance would reverse the trend toward moderation among the Arabs, which would in turn offer the Soviets a renewed opportunity to assert their leadership, throwing the negotiations into international forums like the UN that would then try to impose solutions on the Israelis. Even worse would be another oil embargo and another war, "in circumstances where the United States would be isolated and the likelihood that the kind of support necessary would be dependent on a most uncertain public and Congressional opinion."[199] These dire predictions of the future were difficult for the Israelis to refute.[200]

With the Syrian dictator, Assad, Kissinger adopted different tactics. Knowing Assad's basic suspicion and mistrust for both the United States and Israel, Kissinger was careful to present the negotiations in ways that played upon Assad's prejudices. In one of his first meetings, he told Assad that the "basic question" was "whether Israel will live in peace with its neighbors or behave like the Americans toward the American Indians." Knowing Assad believed that the Israelis and their supporters dictated American policies, Kissinger stressed his independence, arguing that his prestige allowed him to defy the pressure. He told Assad, "We have to use my prestige to put this over," and then cited Joseph Kraft, one of his critics in the press, to a puzzled Assad, who clearly had no idea who Kraft was. Kissinger used flattery on the Syrian leader, praising him for undertaking the talks and lauding the "courage and heroism of his soldiers" in forcing Israel to bargain. He also tried to convince Assad that from "his own selfish interest," it would be better for Kissinger to fail, since he was coming under such severe attacks from Israel's supporters, who accused him of being another "Chamberlain" and "working with the Soviets and Arabs to destroy Israel." When Assad made it clear he would not accept the initial Israeli proposal, Kissinger tried to convince him of the significance that "the Israelis would have withdrawn from strongpoints and territory which they did not lose in conflict."[201] Kissinger sought to convince Assad of the symbolism of an Israeli retreat from the town of Quneitra, which they had conquered in 1967. Although Kissinger himself may have doubted whether the Israelis would ever give up the entire Golan Heights, even such a modest withdrawal might strengthen the Syrian argument for a return to the 1967 borders. Assad was unmoved, but Kissinger's efforts may have planted a seed that flourished later.

Kissinger understood that America's real leverage came from pressuring Israel to make concessions, and he was determined to get Prime Minister

Meir to offer more to Syria. He told the Israelis that Assad was "very rational" and emphasized that Assad faced domestic difficulties, since "for 26 years the Syrian people had been taught that the Israelis were devils," and needed "tangible results" from peace. If the Israelis did not move further, especially on a more generous line of demarcation as well as giving the Syrians full control of the city of Quneitra, Kissinger threatened to go home and end his diplomacy. In the face of Meir's intransigence, Kissinger told her, "Your choice is not between absolute security and no security. Your choice will be to weigh the alternatives of the various courses of action."[202] His messages back to the United States were even more emphatic, expressing anger over the Israeli "lack of flexibility," which, in Kissinger's view, put at risk the American position in the Middle East because of "a kilometer here and there."[203] He told Scowcroft that he thought the Israelis were increasingly dismissive of pressure from Nixon to settle, believing that "presidential paralysis" had set in. He also feared that the Israelis were circumventing him because they believed "they had a direct pipeline to the Pentagon." He wanted Haig to call Defense Secretary Schlesinger and "hold up all new commitments" and "delay administratively pipeline items."[204]

What happened next shows how Kissinger often triggered reactions in Nixon that he came to regret. Nixon was clearly angered that the Israelis regarded him as too weakened to pressure them, and he told Scowcroft that he wanted to cut off all aid to Israel.[205] Just as Nixon was insisting on such a draconian measure, Palestinian terrorists attacked the town of Ma'alot and seized control of a school, taking ninety students and four teachers hostage. They demanded the release of twenty-six Palestinian prisoners held in Israeli jails. The drama transfixed Israel, lasting more than twenty-four hours before Israeli commandos stormed the school and killed the terrorists, but not before they had killed twenty-one students and wounded sixty-eight. Kissinger knew that the talks would be suspended but also took the occasion to oppose Nixon's cutoff in aid, arguing that it was "not the time for a public disassociation from Israel."[206]

In the aftermath of the attack, Kissinger sensed that the timing might now be right for an American initiative. Kissinger's new proposal would provide an American guarantee to Syria to police the limits on Israeli military forces in the hills around Quneitra. The United States would also provide assurances to Assad that it would continue its efforts toward a final settlement, as well as assuring the Israelis of "long term military supply." Kissinger now felt he was on the verge of a breakthrough and cabled Nixon, who was again ecstatic at the possibility. Nixon immediately asked Kissinger to begin planning a presidential trip to the Middle East after the agreement was signed.[207] However, a series of problems remained over the precise limitation of military forces in the area and the size of the UN forces that would be deployed. Kissinger asked Nixon for another letter to Meir, which he then drafted, warning that a failure of Kissinger's mission "would lead inevitably to a deterioration of Congressional support, renewed opportunities for Soviet intervention, and massive pressure for a reassessment of United States policy toward Israel."[208] Although the Israelis began to give way, they now raised the issue of terrorism, seeking a guarantee that any withdrawal would not open the way for terrorist attacks using Syrian territory. The capture of two terrorists and the killing of six others crossing the Golan Heights for an attack only intensified Israeli concerns.[209] These last-minute complications created an atmosphere of gloom, and on May 27, Kissinger's fifty-first birthday, he traveled to Damascus expecting to suspend the talks after a last discussion with Assad. Marvin Kalb reported on the likely failure of the talks, noting that unless there was some last-minute surprise, the chances of Kissinger "pulling a rabbit out of the hat were very slim indeed."[210]

In one of the most unusual episodes during his shuttle diplomacy, Kissinger met with Assad again, thinking that he would suspend the talks and try to salvage Nixon's visit to the Middle East. Assad lectured Kissinger on the evils of Zionism and how the philosophy of the Jewish state was incompatible with "logic and history and will never prevail." He also told Kissinger that their negotiations had convinced him that "Israel is as far away from wanting to pursue the path of peace as ever." Kissinger defended his efforts, telling the Syrian that previously most Americans rejected any involvement by the United States in the problems of the Middle East, but that "today in America it is quite different. And that is a big defeat for extreme Zionism in America." Assad pleaded with Kissinger for a public acknowledgment by the United States that it wanted the restoration of the 1967 frontiers. Kissinger rejected this, telling the Syrian leader, "We cannot have the president sign a letter that he cannot politically live with if it is published." Kissinger then went on to tell Assad that after the suspension of the talks, "You will see many attacks on me," especially from Israel's supporters. Once again, he brought up American newspaper columnists to the puzzled Syrian, telling Assad that there were ten articles saying he was "neglecting [his] duties in Washington." Assad suddenly used this moment in their talks to interrupt Kissinger and say sympathetically, "After having established this nice human personal contact, then out of loyalty, out of fondness, when we look at the imperative of Syrian-American relations, I'm particularly looking to the need not to harm you."[211]

Kissinger later wrote that "it was a stunning performance," but that the Syrian leader must have decided to settle the night before. He simply wanted to be sure he "had squeezed the last blood out of the stone."[212] Undoubtedly there was an underlying Syrian national interest at work, but Assad's gesture also demonstrates the degree to which the diplomacy of disengagement was intertwined with Henry Kissinger as the symbol of American power in the Middle East. Kissinger took Assad's new offers back to Israel, including a willingness to have the United States simply affirm Israel's right to defend itself from terrorist attacks. As in the Egyptian disengagement, both countries made their commitments to the United States, not to each other. On May 29, 1974, Nixon announced the agreements on national television, praising Kissinger and his team and stating "that based on the success in reaching this agreement in which the differences were so great that the prospects for reaching agreement on a permanent basis, I think, now are better than they have been at any time over the past 25 years."[213] Kissinger was now featured on the cover of both national news magazines again, with *Time* headlining a smiling Kissinger with "Mideast Miracle," while *Newsweek* simply dressed Kissinger as Superman and captioned the photo "It's Super K." On his return to Washington, Kissinger spoke of how Americans could take pride in the fact "that it was the United States that could play the role of the mediator," and that it was "the United States that was trusted by both sides" in the conflict.[214]

THE SALZBURG PRESS CONFERENCE AND
THE END OF THE NIXON PRESIDENCY

The uncritical adulation for Kissinger did not last very long. Although Kissinger thought the Syrian disengagement agreement a true "watershed" moment in the search for peace in the Middle East, the Watergate scandal had changed the atmosphere in Washington. As the hearings on the president's impeachment continued, Kissinger's own relative immunity from scrutiny fell away. In his first press conference after returning from the region, Kissinger found himself peppered not with questions about the Golan Heights but with pointed inquiries over his role in initiating wiretaps on his staff and journalists, as well as questions about his knowledge of the "Plumbers."[215] A reporter asked if Kissinger had retained counsel in case of a possible perjury investigation. Kissinger grew angry and replied, "I am not conducting my office as if it were a conspiracy." When the questioning continued about his role in the wiretaps, Kissinger avoided a direct response to the question of whether he had "recommended" the wiretaps and sounded increasingly defensive when he said this was a "press conference not a cross-examination."[216]

The problem Kissinger faced was that his own earlier replies had shaded the truth of his involvement in both issues. Kissinger had been outraged with the leaks over the Cambodian bombing and had gone along willingly and even enthusiastically with the wiretapping, wanting to reassure Nixon of his loyalty. He supplied the FBI director, Hoover, with the names of those on his staff who had access to the classified information. Similarly, Kissinger's anger at the Pentagon Papers leak and his emphasis on Ellsberg's psychological instability played a role in Nixon's determination to discredit Ellsberg by breaking into his psychiatrist's office. Given Kissinger's acute sensitivity to his position within the Nixon inner circle, his profession of complete ignorance about the activities of the Plumbers is hard to accept, even though he may not have known about all their activities. Kissinger's defensiveness reflected how close he was to some of the scandals that were threatening Nixon's presidency, even if he could still maintain his innocence.

Kissinger decided in this case that the best defense was a powerful offense.

Accompanying Nixon on his visit to the Middle East, Kissinger would not wait to address the charges against him until the trip was over. He carefully rehearsed his arguments with sympathetic reporters like the ABC anchor Howard K. Smith before he left the United States, and he decided to call a press conference in Salzburg, Austria, where the presidential party was stopping on its way to the Middle East.[217] In what the television newscasts referred to as the "strangest press conference ever held by an American Secretary of State," a serious and unsmiling Kissinger held forth in "the drawing room of the Kavalier House . . . in front of the tapestry of a medieval forest." Kissinger worked himself into an angry and defiant outrage against "unnamed sources" and other accusers who had challenged his "honor."[218] By focusing on some of the more extreme and largely unsubstantiated charges that had appeared, Kissinger sounded less defensive and far more defiant. He vigorously defended himself against the "innuendo" that he and his staff had read transcripts of the wiretaps, which included "salacious" information about "extramarital affairs or pornographic information."[219] Threatening to resign if he was not fully vindicated, Kissinger attacked the "poisonous" atmosphere created by the coverage of Watergate and spoke in an almost maudlin fashion about how he had hoped to "end division" in the United States, and that "when the record is written, one may remember that perhaps some lives were saved and that perhaps some mothers can rest more at ease, but I leave that to history."[220]

Kissinger's emotional tone and defiant anger made this a big story, and it led all the television newscasts and the major newspapers. After he left the press conference to attend a meeting with the German foreign secretary, the American ambassador to Germany, Martin Hillenbrand, who was accompanying Kissinger, expected him to still be in a highly emotional and agitated state. Instead, Hillenbrand noted, Kissinger was "completely calm and looking forward to the meeting." Hillenbrand wryly remarked, "I could only give him the highest marks for thespian ability."[221]

The act served him well. Kissinger's resignation threat overshadowed Nixon's hope for a triumphal journey, and the president resented being upstaged once again by his secretary of state. More important, it led to a chorus of bipartisan political support for Kissinger that only served to underscore the absence of such sentiment for Nixon. The Senate Democratic leader, Mike Mansfield, urged Kissinger to stay on the job, while Hubert Humphrey remarked that his friend should just "cool it." On the Republican side, Barry Goldwater vigorously defended Kissinger and attacked his critics.[222] The Senate Foreign Relations Committee immediately agreed to hold hearings again to evaluate the charges against Kissinger, even while its chair, J. William Fulbright, declared his continuing confidence in Kissinger. Newspaper columnists similarly spoke in support, with Joseph Alsop arguing, "Do we really want the responsibility of hounding from office the most admired public servant in the United States?" By the weekend, *The New York Times* headline was "Capital Rallying Around Kissinger," and it was clear that Kissinger had won the battle for public opinion.[223]

An uncomfortable Kissinger stayed in the background as Nixon traveled through the Middle East, cheered by almost a million people in Cairo—largely turned out by Sadat's security forces—and made the first visit by an American president to Damascus. Although Nixon, who was suffering from an acute case of phlebitis, also visited Tel Aviv and met with Israeli leaders, he expressed greater understanding for the Arab position in his meetings with those leaders, reflecting again his differences with Kissinger. Kissinger himself was still contemplating his next move, whether to work toward some type of Israeli-Jordanian agreement or continue his efforts on the Egyptian front.[224] Sounding somewhat jealous of the attention Nixon received, Kissinger noted in his memoirs that the president's press secretary, Ron Ziegler, "protected his notion of Presidential preeminence in news stories with the ferocity of a police dog."[225] The trip served to do little for the president's declining popularity, and a type of deathwatch began to infect Nixon's inner circle of advisers—what Kissinger later called the "grim, unspoken backdrop of the journey."[226]

The last days of the Nixon presidency also featured another trip to Moscow, though in a very different atmosphere than that of 1972. Senator Henry Jackson, whose ambition for the presidency aligned well with his Cold War suspicions of the Soviets, accused the administration of hiding secret agree-

ments made with the Soviets during the SALT I negotiations. Kissinger responded sharply, contending that Jackson's charges were "false in every
detail."[227] Senator Fulbright took up Kissinger's cause and attacked "hawks"
like Jackson for making another strategic arms agreement with the Soviets
impossible.[228] Kissinger quite deliberately lowered expectations for the
summit, conceding that any more substantial agreement would be subject to
special scrutiny in the United States because of the "contentious debate" surrounding Watergate. Kissinger himself knew that the Americans were going
to Moscow with a series of arms proposals he believed would be difficult for
the Soviets. Defense Secretary Schlesinger had strongly resisted a new SALT
agreement, even corresponding directly with Jackson and praising the senator's insistence that any new SALT agreement require absolute equality in
numbers, despite the various asymmetries between the American and Soviet
nuclear arsenals. To Kissinger, Schlesinger's alliance with a critic of the administration like Jackson should have led to his dismissal from the administration.[229] Nixon pleaded with the defense secretary for more flexibility in
negotiating, something that Schlesinger refused to provide. In a case of the
pot calling the kettle black, Kissinger accused Schlesinger of "patronizing"
Nixon by telling the president he had "great forensic skills" and should be able
to persuade Brezhnev to slow the Soviet MIRV program and achieve a "major
breakthrough."[230] Nixon himself felt Schlesinger's argument "was really an
insult to everybody's intelligence and particularly to mine," but there was little the president could do to overcome the resistance within his administration to another SALT agreement.[231]

Even before they got to Moscow, Kissinger engaged in a turf battle with
Al Haig on access to the president while there, upset when the chief of staff
insisted on having the quarters next to the president's suite. In another case of
the pot and kettle, Kissinger told his staff, "General Haig is out for himself and
when it comes to the crunch he puts himself first."[232] Once they were in
Moscow, it quickly became clear that the Russians were not interested in
emphasizing the importance of Brezhnev's "personal relationship" with Nixon,
leaving out Nixon's reference to this factor from their translations of his
dinner toast to Brezhnev.[233] As Kissinger understood, the "Soviets were cutting

their losses."[234] Kissinger's real achievement was getting the Soviets to agree to another meeting later in the year, by which time Nixon's fate would have been decided. Such a meeting could consider a new framework for SALT, one that would involve "the choice of either pursuing 'equal aggregates' or 'counterbalancing asymmetries' within a time frame relevant to military planning."[235] In practice this meant that a new president could decide which approach could be defended politically within the United States.[236]

The summit ended with only modest agreements on limiting ABMs and nuclear testing. With the nuclear arms race accelerating to extraordinary numbers of warheads and destructive power, Kissinger was becoming extremely frustrated with the complicated arguments being presented by the militaries of both countries. After talking about how difficult it was to get military leaders to think in terms of "restraint," Kissinger told reporters in Moscow, "What in the name of God is strategic superiority when you are at this level of warheads?"[237] Kissinger's plea was ironic given his own long history as a nuclear weapons expert who had often argued about the relative strategic advantages of competing nuclear arsenals, and it faced almost immediate criticism in the United States from Schlesinger, who disliked Kissinger's equating of both military establishments for their reluctance to compromise.

On July 24, 1974, when the Supreme Court ruled against the president and forced him to turn over the tapes, Nixon's fate was sealed. On August 5, Nixon revealed the existence of the "smoking gun" tape, in which Nixon tried to get the CIA to intervene with the FBI to stop its investigation of the Watergate case, proving that he was guilty of obstructing justice. The demand for his resignation now became overwhelming. The next day, in a story that was buried by the talk about Nixon's resignation, the Senate Foreign Relations Committee once again cleared Kissinger of the charge that he had "initiated" the wiretaps of his staff and journalists, and Kissinger announced that he would continue as secretary of state.[238] The very next evening Nixon summoned him to the White House to tell Kissinger that he would resign. As Kissinger told the story to Bob Woodward and Carl Bernstein for their bestseller The Final Days, he "really didn't like the President. Nixon had made him the most admired man in the country, yet the Secretary couldn't bring himself to feel affection for his patron."[239] That night Kissinger sought to console Nixon, telling him again that history would treat him more kindly than his contemporaries. Nixon was emotional when he began talking about facing a possible trial, and in one exchange that Kissinger did not share with the *Washington Post* reporters, Kissinger assured Nixon, "If they harass you after you leave office, I am going to resign as Secretary of State, and I am going to tell the world why!"[240] Nixon eventually broke down and began to sob. In a scene made famous by Woodward and Bernstein, Nixon asked Kissinger to kneel in prayer with him. Kissinger was so uncomfortable with this request—even as an Orthodox Jewish child he would not have kneeled to pray—that in his memoirs he claimed not to remember whether he kneeled. He did kneel with Nixon, although no prayers occurred to him, only "a deep sense of awe which seemed its own meaning."[241] After this he returned to his office and told his aides Lawrence Eagleburger and Brent Scowcroft how traumatic this experience had been. Nixon called again, this time asking Kissinger not to tell anyone he had cried.[242]

As secretary of state, Kissinger was the government official to whom Nixon addressed his letter of resignation. It was an ironic moment, as Nixon gave his resignation to the man whose authority and power he had largely created, nurtured, and then desperately grasped on to as a way to maintain his presidency. For the time being, Kissinger was the figure of continuity, the survivor of the Nixon administration, continuing to steer American foreign relations through a dangerous world. When Gerald Ford assumed the presidency on August 9, he and Kissinger arranged to meet with diplomats from fifty-seven countries to reassure them that there would be no basic changes in U.S. foreign policy. There was no question in the new president's mind that Kissinger needed to stay on. One of Ford's assistants told a reporter, "Kissinger *was* America's foreign policy."[243] As the NBC *Nightly News* correspondent Richard Valeriani summarized in his report on the meetings, the new president's approach to foreign policy would be to "leave it to Henry."[244]

6

"NO LONGER INDISPENSABLE"

Kissinger, Gerald Ford, and the Politics
of American Foreign Policy, 1974–1976

F OLLOWING THE "HALLOWEEN MASSACRE" of October 1975, when President Gerald Ford fired Secretary of Defense James Schlesinger and the CIA director, William Colby, and took away Kissinger's position as national security adviser, rumors circulated that Kissinger would soon resign as secretary of state. Barrie Dunsmore, ABC's diplomatic correspondent, started a report that contrasted Kissinger's position after the Syrian disengagement agreement, when he was "Super K," at the "height of his career" and "everybody's favorite," with his current situation, when he had become "everybody's favorite target." Dunsmore assembled an impressive list of attacks on Kissinger: the Senate Intelligence Committee's report criticizing Kissinger's role in the overthrow of the Chilean government; the congressional testimony of the former chief of naval operations Admiral Elmo Zumwalt, who accused Kissinger of lying about Soviet violations of the SALT treaty; and James Schlesinger's characterization of détente as weakness toward the Soviet Union. Comparing these with Kissinger's success in the Middle East and good relations with the Russians and Chinese, Dunsmore observed that Kissinger was now "more popular abroad than he was in the United States." The real meaning of the "so-called Halloween Massacre," Dunsmore intoned, was that Henry Kissinger was "no longer indispensable," adding that "while the thought of Gerald Ford being without Kissinger may have been unthinkable only a few months ago, many people are thinking about it today, including Henry Kissinger."[1] Over the coming months, the "Kissinger is about to resign" story was featured every few weeks, always based on the best in confidential sources.

Kissinger's tenure as secretary of state under Gerald Ford was controversial, but Dunsmore's prediction of Kissinger's demise proved very premature. Even if not "indispensable," Kissinger remained the central figure in American foreign policy until the very end of the Ford administration, actively trying to mediate the Rhodesian civil war, keeping a SALT agreement with the Soviet Union alive, and planning new proposals for the Middle East. Although his approach to foreign policy encountered ideological critiques from both ends of the political spectrum, Kissinger sought to navigate and adapt to the shifting tides of American public opinion, and to influence that opinion to keep Ford as president.

A "NORMAL" SECRETARY OF STATE:
THE FORD TRANSITION

"With Nixon's resignation, I became a 'normal' Secretary of State and lost my special status."[2] Kissinger later reflected that he was no longer "surrogate president for foreign affairs" and could resume a traditional role. Kissinger was being unduly—and uncharacteristically—modest about his status in the Ford administration. Kissinger's role and authority went well beyond that of a "normal" secretary of state, and he remained the most important official next to the president. Ford greatly admired the foreign policy of the Nixon

years, calling it "outstanding," and in one of his first official actions as president, he reaffirmed the "organization and procedures of the National Security
Council System."[3] Their early meetings underlined Kissinger's continuing
dominance of foreign policy. Kissinger explained the NSC structure to Ford,
noting, "Under President Nixon every paper from a Cabinet officer went into
him but through me, with a cover sheet," adding that "at the end Nixon only
read his memos."[4] Although Ford had been in Congress for fifteen years and
the House minority leader for almost a decade, his major focus had always
been on domestic affairs, and his foreign policy views were an uncomplicated
mix of Cold War shibboleths and traditional internationalism. He did not feel
confident in foreign policy matters. Providing Ford with an overview, Kissinger
alternately assumed the roles of teacher, political adviser, and motivational
coach, dispensing judgments and advice with an extraordinary confidence,
humor, and a self-assurance bordering on arrogance. Discussing the Middle
East, Kissinger told Ford that King Faisal of Saudi Arabia was "a kook but a
shrewd cookie," adding that on his last visit Faisal paid him the compliment
that "he didn't consider me a Jew but a human being." After providing a cap-
sule description of the personalities in the region, Kissinger told the president
that the Middle East was the "worst problem we face," and that the United
States could not afford another oil embargo. "If we are faced with that,"
Kissinger added ominously, "we may have to take some oil fields." Ford was
unfazed by Kissinger's suggestion of American military intervention, asking
only about the status of contingency plans. As their discussion drew to a close,
the president mentioned his involvement with the case of Simas Kudirka, a
Lithuanian sailor who sought to defect to the United States in 1970 but whom
the Coast Guard had handed back to the Soviets. As vice president, Ford
had written to the Soviet ambassador, Dobrynin, on the sailor's behalf but
received no answer. Kissinger assured the president he would talk privately
to Dobrynin and that his private channel offered the United States "great
opportunities with the Soviets," including another SALT agreement in 1975.
Ford replied, "That would help the election in '76."[5]

Years later Kissinger praised Ford as "an uncomplicated man tapped by
destiny for some of the most complicated tasks in the nation's history."[6] After

his first meeting with Ford, Kissinger left his office without feeling that there was any Nixon-like "hidden agenda," and that with Ford, "what one saw was what one got."[7] The most succinct summation of the Ford-Kissinger relationship is that Gerald Ford thought that Henry Kissinger was brilliant and that Henry Kissinger agreed.[8] Ford later wrote, "It would be hard for me to overstate the admiration and affection I had for Henry," adding the improbable observation that Kissinger had remained as secretary of state only "because I said I needed him."[9] Ford tried to convey the idea of a relationship of equals by saying that he "respected [Kissinger's] expertise in foreign policy and he respected my judgment in domestic politics," but Kissinger's dominance is hard to deny. He remained a powerful presence in Washington, with extensive connections to a sympathetic media. Foreign governments thought him equal to the president and treated him accordingly. Astute observers like George H. W. Bush, the American liaison in China, commented on his "imperiousness" and the almost "regal" way in which Kissinger traveled the globe.[10]

Kissinger also played an important role in two decisions that helped shape the Ford presidency: the selection of Nelson Rockefeller as vice president and Ford's pardoning of Richard Nixon.[11] In a way, Kissinger engineered his own personal trifecta: Ford as president, a pardon for Nixon, and his mentor Rockefeller as the vice president. Ford also identifies Kissinger as providing him with the counsel to back away from his earlier pledge not to seek the Republican nomination in 1976. Kissinger told him such a move would be "disastrous" and emphasized that foreign governments would view him as "a lame duck" and that it would have terrible consequences for dealing with Congress. "You can't reassert the authority of the Presidency if you leave yourself hanging out on a dead limb," Kissinger added.[12] Robert Hartmann, one of Ford's closest aides, regarded Kissinger as not just "the ablest diplomat" he had ever seen but also "as good a politician—internecine or international—as all but a formidable few," including on his list Winston Churchill, Franklin Roosevelt, Richard Nixon, and Golda Meir.[13]

Kissinger did face challenges to his position in the Ford administration. His continuing rivalry with Defense Secretary Schlesinger would now play out in front of the new president, and Schlesinger possessed considerable support on Capitol Hill. Like Kissinger, Schlesinger was the son of Jewish immigrants and a Harvard Ph.D., although unlike Kissinger, he converted to Lutheranism in his twenties and got his Ph.D. in economics rather than government. His academic specialty was in political economy, and he had entered the Nixon administration in the Bureau of the Budget but moved from there to the Atomic Energy Commission and then briefly to head the CIA. In his role as defense secretary, Schlesinger made important contributions to modernizing America's nuclear strategy and pushing for more defense contributions from European allies. His determination to strengthen nuclear forces brought him into an alignment and friendship with conservative Democrats like Henry Jackson and Reagan Republicans in the Senate. As brilliant, ambitious, and arrogant as Kissinger, Schlesinger would find his fatal flaw in his inability to avoid condescending to Ford, whom he did not fully respect.[14]

Ford's political advisers, including Hartmann, Philip Buchen, and L. William Seidman, worried that Kissinger's dominance of foreign policy weakened the president's political standing, and they were determined to help Ford assert his role. Ford's chief of staff, Donald Rumsfeld, was, as Kissinger described, the most "formidable new arrival" and "a special Washington phenomenon: the skilled full-time politician-bureaucrat in whom ambition, ability, and substance fuse seamlessly." This description from Kissinger's memoirs does not fully capture his sentiments at the time, which were decidedly more negative.[15] Rumsfeld was convinced that President Ford was far too dependent on Kissinger and deferential toward him, to the point of allowing his secretary of state to arrive late for meetings at the Oval Office, "sometimes by as much as twenty or thirty minutes."[16] Despite these rivalries, Kissinger retained his powerful position within the administration, keeping his dual role as secretary of state and head of the National Security Council. When a newspaper story appeared the day before President Ford's first speech to the United Nations, in September 1974, claiming that Kissinger would lose his NSC role, the president added a rebuttal line to his prepared speech. That line unequivocally praised Kissinger and said that he had the "unquestioned backing of the American people." In an indication of how positive the media remained toward Kissinger, NBC's John Chancellor said that beyond reassuring allies and "the Establishment," Ford praised Kissinger "because he deserved it."[17] Polls showed that Kissinger was America's most admired man for the second year in a row, and judged by 85 percent of Americans as doing a "splendid job."[18]

Nevertheless, cracks were appearing in the Kissinger image. During the first foreign policy crisis of the Ford administration, Kissinger became the target of critics. When the Greek military government supported a coup to annex the island of Cyprus in July 1974, Turkey launched a military invasion to protect the Turkish Cypriot population.[19] The initially modest Turkish action led to the collapse of the Greek junta, the return of democracy to Athens, and a shift in international sympathy to the Greek position. Peace talks in Geneva stalemated. Kissinger appealed to Turkey to give the negotiations more time, but Prime Minister Bülent Ecevit, a former student of Kissinger's, exploited nationalist passions to double down on a military solution and seize almost 40 percent of the island. Kissinger believed that Turkey was the more important NATO ally and feared that an American condemnation would weaken the United States in the eastern Mediterranean and the Middle East. His geopolitical reasoning proved extremely unpopular with Congress, many of whose members were strongly influenced by the powerful Greek-American lobby. On August 18, some twenty thousand demonstrated at the White House carrying signs that read, KISSINGER: THE BLOOD OF CYPRUS IS ON YOUR HANDS! A news reporter pointed out that none seemed to direct their anger at President Ford, only at Kissinger.[20] On Cyprus the next day, hundreds of Greek Cypriot demonstrators, screaming "Killer Kissinger," attacked the American embassy in Nicosia and killed the American ambassador, Rodger Davies.[21] Shaken by the ambassador's murder, Kissinger was largely resigned to the partition, hoping only to convince the Turks to give back some of the territory they had seized. Kissinger tried to prevent Congress from taking any action, fearing that it might push Turkey toward either "the Soviet Union or to a Qaddafi-type regime."[22] Kissinger emphasized to critics that American pressure had helped stop the war. Congress, however, responded with a vote to cut off all military aid to Turkey unless there was substantial progress toward a Cyprus settlement. The embargo on aid to Turkey went into effect in February 1975, and Kissinger saw it as his first defeat.[23]

The Cyprus question reflected the limits of America's power in the aftermath of the Vietnam War. Kissinger prevented the worst scenario of a full-scale war between Greece and Turkey but was unable to negotiate a reasonable settlement or prevent the violence and atrocities that occurred alongside partition. Within the domestic politics of American foreign policy, Kissinger was on the wrong side, supporting the Turks against the now democratic Greeks, who wanted a full Turkish withdrawal from Cyprus, free elections, and a restoration of the island's unity.[24] Kissinger now found himself increasingly challenged by those who sought greater morality and respect for human rights in U.S. foreign policy, as well as greater congressional control over that policy. Nowhere would this become more the case than with the Soviet Union.

DEFENDING DÉTENTE: THE JACKSON-VANIK AMENDMENT AND THE VLADIVOSTOK CONFERENCE

Gerald Ford fully supported détente, as the Soviet ambassador Dobrynin later recounted, even insisting on referring to it as "Kissinger's policy." One of Ford's first actions as president was to invite the Soviet cosmonauts and American astronauts who were training for a joint space mission to a town picnic in Alexandria, Virginia, where Ford had been living. During the helicopter ride back to the White House after the event, Ford told Dobrynin that he was looking forward to his meeting with Brezhnev and emphasized "the importance he attached to an agreement on limiting strategic arms, which was essential both for bilateral relations and for his presidential campaign."[25] Ford's time in Congress had made him sensitive to other issues, however, and while Dobrynin's description of him as "typical American congressman-patriot of the Cold War era" is condescending, it does capture Ford's political instincts. For this reason, he was particularly eager to work out a deal with Senator Henry "Scoop" Jackson over the issue of Jewish emigration from the Soviet Union, an issue that Ford both sympathized with and supported in a manner that Richard Nixon had not.[26] Ford respected the senator from Washington State, who had emerged from the Democratic Party's wreckage after 1972 as the clear front-runner for the nomination. Jackson combined an appeal to traditional Democratic supporters, the labor unions and working class, with a strong anti-communism and pro-defense-spending record designed to win back those voters alienated by McGovern's campaign. Ford told Kissinger, "We have to give Scoop his amendment." Kissinger replied cautiously, "If you get waiver authority, that Congress would have to veto it, it's okay," showing his own hope that Ford could hold on to presidential authority in judging Moscow's compliance.[27]

Kissinger believed strongly in the objectives of détente, both for its domestic political appeal, which he felt Nixon's landslide demonstrated, and for its foreign policy usefulness—reducing the danger of nuclear war, slowing the arms race, and stabilizing the relationship between the superpowers in ways that promoted trust and reduced the risk of armed conflict. For Kissinger, all these arguments for détente far exceeded in importance an issue like Jewish emigration or the persecution of Soviet dissidents. Kissinger justified the trade-off by maintaining that the Soviet Union might "evolve" or change internally in "an environment of decreasing international tensions." To Kissinger, this was another reason to continue détente and avoid the legislative tactics that Jackson recommended. Kissinger worked behind the scenes with his Soviet counterpart to facilitate Jewish emigration, and the numbers increased after 1969. While he never wavered in his conviction that "quiet diplomacy" was more effective than public demands, Kissinger followed Ford's lead in working for a compromise with Jackson. Recognizing the domestic politics at stake, he may have even hoped that by working with Jackson—at that time the front-runner for the Democratic nomination—they could defuse the issue before the 1976 election. When he testified before the Senate Foreign Relations Committee in September, Kissinger stressed that the Soviets had provided assurances that the education exit tax "is no longer being collected. We have been assured that it will not be reapplied." He went on to say that the volume of Jewish emigration was increasing and that "we are now moving toward an understanding that should significantly diminish the obstacles to emigration and ease the hardship of prospective emigrants."[28] Both the Soviet foreign minister, Andrei Gromyko, and Dobrynin had privately told Ford and Kissinger that their government would give him an assurance that it would allow some fifty thousand Jews a year to leave the Soviet Union.[29]

With Ford's support, Kissinger and Jackson ultimately agreed to exchange letters regarding their agreement. Kissinger's letter to Jackson reported on the assurances the administration had received about ending harassment and treating the emigrants fairly. It avoided any mention of specific numbers but did assume that "the rate of emigration from the USSR would begin to rise promptly from the 1973 level and would continue to rise to correspond to the number of applicants." Jackson's letter was much more specific, setting out a benchmark figure of sixty thousand for the number of emigrants and calling that "a minimum standard of initial compliance." In an Oval Office meeting on October 18, 1974, Kissinger and Jackson, along with the president, Senator Jacob Javits of New York, and Congressman Charles Vanik of Ohio, celebrated the signing of the Jackson-Vanik Amendment, prohibiting states that restricted the emigration rights of their citizens from being granted most-favored-nation status. A strangely quiet Kissinger sat in the background as Javits described the bill as "historic . . . like Moses leading his people out of bondage." Jackson praised the agreement as the "first major effort in bipartisan policy" in the administration, for which Ford "deserved a lot of credit." Although the tone of the event was celebratory, Jackson angrily noted that Brezhnev did not help with "that foul statement." He was referring to a recent Brezhnev comment to American business executives that the imposition of "utterly and unacceptable stipulations" on U.S.-Soviet trade were attempts at "intervention in internal affairs."[30] Jackson dismissed it as Soviet domestic posturing, while extolling the agreement as a "historic understanding in the area of human rights" and saying, "There has been a complete turnaround on the basic points that are contained in the two letters."[31] All three network newscasts made the same point, with NBC's John Chancellor proclaiming that the agreement amounted to a Soviet "cave-in to American congressmen led by Senator Jackson."[32]

Kissinger recognized that Jackson's comments would create problems for the Russians, and within three days the administration released a statement emphasizing that the Soviets had not agreed to specific numbers.[33] In his memoirs, Kissinger blames Ford for allowing Jackson to announce the agreement from the White House Briefing Room, thereby seeming to convey to the Russians that Jackson's approach was the official American position.[34] Kissinger's behavior, however, also raises questions. Why didn't he try to brief the media on what the agreement really meant, making sure that the Soviets did not misunderstand Jackson's boasting? Kissinger rarely shied away from such opportunities when they could advance his policies. Did he expect the Jackson approach to fail and hope that by his keeping a low profile, the blame might hurt the senator's presidential bid?

While such Machiavellian plotting was possible, another explanation is more likely, reflecting both Kissinger's calculations and his hubris. Kissinger was about to leave for a trip to Moscow to prepare for the summit meeting at Vladivostok. His primary attention had turned to the possibilities for a SALT II agreement, which Jackson and his allies would oppose.[35] Kissinger was supremely confident of his persuasive abilities on his arrival in Moscow, certain that as the most admired man in America, and the "incontestable captain of diplomacy," as Dobrynin referred to him, he could minimize the MFN controversy and get an agreement on SALT.[36] When Brezhnev began their Moscow talks by criticizing the Jackson-Vanik Amendment and Jackson's statements, Kissinger responded by pounding the table and proclaiming that Jackson's "manner is as humiliating for me as it is for you" and that the "press is saying that Kissinger has been defeated by Jackson." Then, in dramatic fashion, Kissinger said, "I'm as angry as you are," and stormed out of the room.[37] As with his Salzburg press conference, this was another example of Kissinger's theatrical approach to diplomacy. His strategy was to use Jackson to motivate the Soviets into making an agreement with him. Kissinger wanted Brezhnev to see him as the crucial ally against Senator Jackson and "the individuals and groups that oppose the betterment of Soviet-American relations," as Brezhnev himself put it.[38]

Kissinger personalized détente for the Soviets, arguing that he was both

Henry Kissinger, age eleven, with his brother,
Walter, age ten (BETTMANN / GETTY IMAGES)

A 1950 Harvard University
yearbook photo of Kissinger
(HARVARD UNIVERSITY)

Kissinger appeared on the cover of *Time* in
February 1969, less than a month after Richard
Nixon took office. (LOUIS GLANZMAN / *TIME*)

A caricature of Kissinger by David Levine in
a September 1969 issue of *The New York
Review of Books* (DAVID LEVINE / D. LEVINE INK)

Nixon and Kissinger
gazing out a window
in the Oval Office
(OLIVER ATKINS / WHITE
HOUSE PHOTO OFFICE
COLLECTION)

Kissinger and the
Soviet ambassador
Anatoly Dobrynin, his
counterpart in the
secret "back channel"
(U.S. DEPARTMENT OF STATE)

"Celebrity ladies' man" Kissinger with the actress Marlo Thomas in 1970 (FRANK EDWARDS / GETTY IMAGES)

Kissinger was on the cover of *Newsweek* in February 1972 when Nixon announced that he was negotiating with the North Vietnamese. (NEWSWEEK PUBLISHING LLC)

Nixon, Kissinger, and Secretary of State William P. Rogers negotiating with the Chinese premier Zhou Enlai in Beijing in February 1972 (OLIVER ATKINS / WHITE HOUSE PHOTO OFFICE COLLECTION)

Nixon and Kissinger walking through Red Square during the 1972 Moscow summit (OLIVER ATKINS / WHITE HOUSE PHOTO OFFICE COLLECTION)

Nixon and Kissinger meeting with Kissinger's first mentor, Fritz Kraemer, in October 1972 (OLIVER ATKINS / WHITE HOUSE PHOTO OFFICE COLLECTION)

Kissinger and Lê Đức Thọ in Paris in October 1972 (ROBERT L. KNUDSEN / WHITE HOUSE
PHOTO OFFICE COLLECTION)

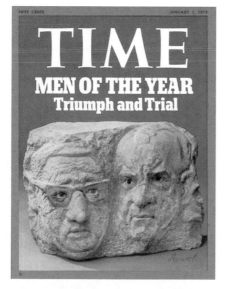

Nixon and Kissinger were named "Men of
the Year" by *Time* in January 1973. Kissinger,
aware that Nixon resented having to share
space on the cover with him, tried to get
the magazine to rescind the honor.
(ROB CRANDALL / *TIME*)

Kissinger depicted as Superman on a June
1974 cover of *Newsweek* after the success of
his "shuttle diplomacy" (JOHN HUEHNERGARTH /
NEWSWEEK PUBLISHING LLC)

Kissinger and the Soviet leader Leonid Brezhnev at Zavidovo in May 1973 (VLADIMIR
MUSAELYAN / TASS / GETTY IMAGES)

Kissinger and the Egyptian president Anwar Sadat (THE LIBRARY OF CONGRESS PRINTS AND
PHOTOGRAPHS DIVISION, WASHINGTON, DC)

Kissinger with President Gerald Ford and Vice President Nelson Rockefeller in the Oval Office
(DAVID KENNERLY / GERALD R. FORD PRESIDENTIAL LIBRARY)

Kissinger with President Ronald Reagan in June 1981 (REAGAN PRESIDENTIAL LIBRARY)

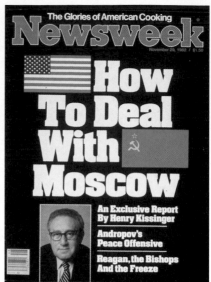

Kissinger's "World of Woes": playing the role of Gulliver on the cover of *Newsweek* in 1975 (JOHN HUEHNERGARTH / NEWSWEEK PUBLISHING LLC)

"How to Deal with Moscow": Kissinger on the cover of *Newsweek* in November 1982 (NEWSWEEK PUBLISHING LLC)

Kissinger with President Donald Trump (BLOOMBERG)

"Kissinger F---ing the World," by David Levine. Levine sold his cartoon to *The Nation* in 1984 after *The New York Review of Books* refused to print it. The caricature demonstrates the intense hostility that had developed toward Kissinger among many liberals and progressives. (DAVID LEVINE / D. LEVINE INK) its most important symbol and best advocate. In their next meeting after his walkout, he told Brezhnev that his personal popularity was at 80 percent— "which is extraordinary for a non-elected official." "Or an elected official," Dobrynin helpfully chimed in to say, adding, without any evident skepticism, "number one in history." Kissinger recounted how he had recently tried to engage Jackson in a debate over détente, but that Jackson "was afraid of a confrontation." Kissinger told the Russians that he, Kissinger, was not "considered a partisan political figure," and this meant he could not attack Jackson and play a direct role in the current midterm election campaign. Kissinger tempted the Soviets, saying if they "came to a SALT agreement in principle in Vladivostok" and Jackson attacked it, then Kissinger would be free to go around the country and defend the agreement and criticize Jackson. When Brezhnev asked how the Soviets could help, Kissinger answered, "The best way is if you and I are on the same side and Jackson is on the other." When Brezhnev replied, "I agree," Kissinger answered him with ringing solidarity, "Then we'll almost certainly win."[39]

Having established that they were, for all practical purposes, on the same side in this dispute with Jackson, Kissinger tried to deal with Brezhnev's other complaints in order to get to the SALT negotiations. He defended the trade agreement as the "best we can do" but acknowledged Brezhnev's criticisms as justified. He explained his own position on the proposed European Security Conference, largely dismissing its significance but predicting that the remaining issues would be resolved soon and the agreement would be signed in early 1975. Defending his shuttle diplomacy in the Middle East, Kissinger managed to get a smile from the normally reserved Gromyko by suggesting that Anwar Sadat might be playing a "double game" with the Americans and the Soviets, trying to extract more economic and military aid from both countries as he played them against each other. Kissinger also managed to keep a straight face in telling Brezhnev, "Especially in the Middle East, I think neither of us can gain a permanent advantage at the expense of the other, and any attempt by either of us to do so is going to be entirely futile."[40] Although it was unlikely that his Soviet counterparts were deceived, they allowed it to pass. Brezhnev moved on to his own concern, asking what Americans meant when they insisted that they "must be second to none in terms of strength," and what Kissinger thought about the possibility of an atomic war between their two countries. The Soviet leader then recessed the talks for the day to allow the American secretary of state to ponder his heavy questions, saying, "On that thought, I wish you pleasant dreams."[41]

Kissinger jokingly mentioned that he would ask Washington for instructions on how to answer Brezhnev. Actually, he cabled for a presidential message of support. Kissinger told Ford that he thought Brezhnev was not completely convinced of Ford's personal backing for the secretary. Whether this was a sign of Kissinger's perennial insecurity or a tactic designed to push Brezhnev toward talking more concretely about SALT, Ford sent a strong message of support, telling the Soviet leader that he had authorized "Secretary Kissinger to discuss with you the cardinal elements of a new agreement which we will address in our forthcoming meeting."[42] The next day Brezhnev waved Ford's cable at Kissinger but listened as Kissinger talked about the "objective realities of American defense planning." Brezhnev complained again that the United States was seeking nuclear superiority. Kissinger rejected this charge and then once again personalized the issue by proclaiming, "Any analysis of the U.S. scene would show that I alone have kept open the possibility of an agreement. Every proposal made to you in the last year has been made by me against the opposition of the majority in the U.S. government."[43]

What happened at their next meeting might have made for a skit on *Saturday Night Live*. Kissinger described how Brezhnev "interrupted his confidential and solemn presentation with periodic and futile attempts at making a toy artillery piece fire off a small explosive charge." As he played with the artillery piece, aiming it at Kissinger and his aide Helmut Sonnenfeldt, and periodically pulling the lanyard on the gun to fire, unsuccessfully, Brezhnev kept discussing his ideas for an agreement whereby the two superpowers would come to each other's assistance. As Kissinger finally summed up Brezhnev's idea, that "if either of us or one of our allies is attacked with nuclear weapons the other one would come to his assistance," the toy artillery gun went off with a loud bang, startling those present. Having succeeded in firing a shot, Brezhnev began to, in Kissinger's words, "strut about the room like a prizefighter who had just scored a knockout."[44] Brezhnev then pushed the toy gun aside and launched into a long discussion of his devotion to peace and his hope that his proposal would "guarantee a world free of nuclear war." Kissinger, however, saw Brezhnev's idea as similar to what the Soviets sought in the 1973 Prevention of Nuclear War Agreement, and feared its impact on both the U.S.-China relationship and NATO. He told Brezhnev that he could discuss it with President Ford at Vladivostok. After a brief recess, Brezhnev began their final session that evening with a question to Kissinger about whether "Jackson's invented something new?" Kissinger replied, "Any instructions Jackson sent me would have to be sent out to our Secret Service first. They might explode."[45] Brezhnev then made a new proposal, offering the United States equality in the aggregates of missiles and launchers by 1985, and accepting the equal number of MIRVs in the American proposal. Kissinger wrote to Ford that this was a "major step forward toward a SALT agreement in 1975 and perhaps a significant announcement at Vladivostok."[46]

Kissinger added an important note of caution to his cable advising Ford of the Soviet concession, telling him that in its present form, the Soviet proposal "would be shredded" by the Defense Department and leaked to the press and Jackson before "we can shape it." To accomplish that shaping, Kissinger appealed to Ford to avoid giving specific information to Schlesinger until he returned to Washington.[47] Gromyko also handed Kissinger a letter, which was "written not on Foreign Ministry stationery but on plain brownish paper," which rejected the letters concerning the trade bill that Kissinger had exchanged with Jackson.[48] The Russians were engaged in their own form of linkage, offering concessions in the SALT negotiations and hoping it would lead Ford and Kissinger to push back against Jackson on trade, most-favored-nation status, and even Jewish emigration. Kissinger decided to handle the issue differently, concealing the existence of the Gromyko letter from all but the president until after Vladivostok, hoping that an agreement there would lead the Soviets to back down. Kissinger told Ford that the Soviet reaction to Jackson's pressure "shows that what I predicted and warned Jackson about for months has now happened." Although he suspected the Soviets might publish the Gromyko letter, Kissinger still believed that they would accept the trade bill and allow emigration to proceed "for fear of strengthening Jackson."[49]

Kissinger was playing a complicated game, and the Soviets were no longer cooperating. He had hoped that the Soviets would see it as in their interest to swallow the "interference" in their internal affairs that the Jackson-Vanik Amendment meant for them, the degree to which it restricted how they controlled their own people, in order to help Ford and Kissinger politically win Senate approval for the SALT II treaty. Kissinger thought that the Soviets so feared strengthening Henry Jackson politically that they would follow Kissinger's advice on both the trade bill and SALT. It was a gamble on Kissinger's part, caused by his overweening sense of his importance to the Soviets, and it overestimated the degree to which Brezhnev could accept the foreign influence over Soviet domestic practices, which the Jackson-Vanik Amendment allowed.

In the short interval between Kissinger's Moscow trip and the Vladivostok summit, Kissinger sought to convince Ford that his assessment of the Soviet offer on SALT was correct, and that he himself was central to any agreement.[50] He emphasized the politics of détente, arguing that it divided the Democrats between the Jackson and Kennedy wings of the party, and that if Ford abandoned détente, the Democrats would reunite in opposition to the administration. As the summit approached, Kissinger gave Ford something of a pep talk, telling him that he need not worry about comparisons with Nixon, since Nixon "was a poor negotiator," and that he just needed to "act confident." When Kissinger suggested that it might help to "show you had an option and instinct to go to the right," Ford replied, "I have a tough and bombastic side." Kissinger immediately corrected him, telling the president, "I wouldn't do that. I would show him just a bit and then throttle it. Be firm but friendly." Ford's insecurity was painfully evident as he told Kissinger that he did not want any private meetings with Brezhnev without Kissinger present, since "we are a team." He added, "If you see things heading the wrong way, don't hesitate to set it straight."[51]

The Vladivostok conference proved the high point of détente during the Ford administration. Kissinger described the negotiations as something akin to a "Kabuki play—extremely stylized with a near-traditional script and fore-ordained outcome."[52] Kissinger was certain that Brezhnev wanted the summit to be a success, and that the concessions he made in Moscow on overall numerical equality for launchers and MIRVs would pave the way. Kissinger also recognized that what was being agreed to was a ceiling for the arms race, not anything approaching actual limitations or reductions. If they agreed to the 2,400 launchers for both and the 1,320 MIRVs for each, neither side would need to eliminate or scrap any weapons system. Much of the SALT discussion was "theological," arguments about systems planned for the distant future or weapons unlikely to be built. The United States would be hard-pressed to reach the ceilings with its current level of funding, and the new Congress was even less likely to spend for new weapons systems.[53] Encouraged by Kissinger, Ford's appeal to Brezhnev for an agreement rested heavily on the vicissitudes of American domestic politics. He told the general secretary that he planned to be a candidate in 1976 and that he wanted "a coordination of our foreign policies." Ford admitted he was "apprehensive that if others were elected the policy of 72–76 could be undercut." This comment elicited a joke from Brezhnev that "the Soviet Union is working for Jackson," to which Kissinger smilingly added, "Our intelligence reports say so." A humorless Ford defended Jackson's right to disagree but told Brezhnev, "I believe the American people wish us to pursue our present course." Ford added that he believed that "1975 is a crucial year," since an election year is not the best time for "serious negotiations," conveniently forgetting that Nixon's SALT agreement came in 1972.[54]

Ford was pleased with the "framework" agreement reached in Vladivostok, even if his spokesperson exaggerated the scale of the success.[55] Kissinger called the agreement a chance to "break the back of the arms race," and likely to lead to the signing of a new treaty during Brezhnev's scheduled visit in June 1975. Kissinger acknowledged that many technical issues remained, especially those of verification. He added that there were still very difficult negotiations ahead that "could fail," but that he thought they "were well down the road."[56] Reporters noted that Kissinger's "exuberant manner," more than his actual words, led some to think an agreement was near, although others reacted more skeptically to what was essentially an agreement to seek an agreement.[57] Kissinger himself did not return to the United States with Ford but rather went to Beijing, continuing to play the triangular diplomacy game, keeping the Soviets worried about the American relationship with China and the Chinese worried about his dealings with the Soviet Union. Despite his own confidence that the Vladivostok meeting provided him "leverage" with Beijing, Kissinger found that the Chinese were not in a cooperative mood.[58] From the start of the talks, when they invited Kissinger's rival, Defense Secretary Schlesinger, to come for a visit, the Chinese proved more difficult than Kissinger had experienced on earlier trips. They expressed displeasure with the Vladivostok location of the talks, an area of the Soviet Union in which Chinese had once settled. They also attacked the policy of détente with a fierceness that, as Kissinger described, would have pleased the "neoconservatives at *Commentary*."[59] The Chinese were coming to a more sophisticated understanding of American politics, and they recognized some of the disillusionment with détente in the United States, a disillusionment symbolized by a figure like Schlesinger. Kissinger's attempt to balance the two communist superpowers was in trouble. He sensed this even further when his interlocutor on this visit was not his favorite Zhou Enlai but rather Deng Xiaoping, whom Kissinger described as a "nasty little man." Moreover, on this visit Kissinger was not accorded his usual honor of a visit with Mao. It was a preview of the troubles ahead in the one diplomatic relationship over which Kissinger took an almost paternal interest.

Kissinger's major achievement of this trip was securing an invitation for President Ford to visit China, which, along with his hopes for a SALT agreement in 1975, was an attempt to steal from Nixon's playbook and repeat the same foreign policy maneuvers for the election in 1976.[60] Kissinger may have hoped that Ford's visit might end up being more substantive than Nixon's, with an agreement for the formal recognition of the People's Republic, something that Nixon had promised the Chinese by 1976. Progress on the normalization of relations was clearly stalled, with Deng repeating earlier Chinese demands for America to sever all its ties to Taiwan. Deng may have favored a more flexible approach, but in the bitter internal conflicts over the anticipated succession to Mao, he could not offer Kissinger any compromise. Kissinger brought with him intelligence on the latest in Soviet military moves in relation to Beijing, which his assistants shared with the Chinese military, and he continued to emphasize the threat posed by the "polar bear," as Deng referred to Russia.[61]

Kissinger returned from China in early December to testify before the Senate Finance Committee in support of the trade bill, which was in danger of not passing before Congress adjourned on December 20. Kissinger did not disclose the Gromyko letter to the committee, although he did repeat that the Soviet Union had not offered specific numbers of emigrants in its assurances. Kissinger made an impassioned pitch for the bill, saying that failure to pass it would be a "disastrous blow" to America's international position.[62] A little over a week later the bill passed the Senate, but when it was in the conference committee being reconciled with the House version, the Soviet Union publicly released the Gromyko letter, making it clear that they would not accept what they regarded as the "interference in internal affairs" of the Jackson-Vanik Amendment. The "Soviet rejection of the trade bill" story led the evening news on all three networks, with Senator Jackson defending his work, suggesting that the Russian action was for their own domestic consumption and that he was still confident they would hold to the agreement.[63] Kissinger told Ford that he now believed the Russians would reject the MFN deal, and that the Soviets did not consider the $300 million offered under the Export-Import Bank to be worth the sacrifice they were making in agreeing on emigration. Kissinger said that Dobrynin had told him they saw "a shift of Executive Power to the Congress," implying that agreements with the Ford administration were no longer seen as reliable or likely to be ratified. When Kissinger telephoned Dobrynin later that evening, he personalized the issue again, telling the Soviet diplomat that he had learned that this was the beginning of a Kremlin attack on him that was wholly unjustified, since Kissinger had "been trying to defend the Soviet point of view."[64] The Soviets did not relent, and Kissinger's hope to convince the Soviets to trust him and accept the trade bill as a necessary evil of American politics failed.[65]

As the year came to an end, the news for Kissinger did not get any better.

Both Ford and Kissinger were concerned that what Ford called "a new generation of wildass Democrats" in the recently elected Congress were determined to weaken and undermine presidential power, especially over foreign policy.[66] The new members of the "fighting ninety-fourth [Congress] were exultant in the muscle they had used to bring a President down, willing and able to challenge the Executive as well as its own Congressional hierarchy, intense over morality in government [and] extremely sensitive to press and public pressures."[67] The trade bill was only the tip of the iceberg, as Congress was increasingly determined to reassert its power against the "Imperial Presidency."[68] The cutoff of military aide to Turkey was a harbinger of this assertiveness, but the congressional role also reflected the shattering of the "Cold War consensus" and a willingness to question the trade-offs presidents had made in the name of national security. Representative Donald Fraser, who chaired the House Foreign Affairs Subcommittee on International Organizations and Movements, held hearings in 1973 and 1974 that highlighted human rights abuses among American allies such as Greece, Chile, and South Vietnam.[69] Kissinger warned Ford, "In the name of human rights, they will undermine national security."[70] In what might have been one of his more tone-deaf pieces of advice, Kissinger wanted the former congressman Ford "to go to the people against the Congress," promising that he would join him, and talk about "the Executive-Legislative relationship."[71]

Ford's position was made even more difficult by the outbreak of another set of scandals. On December 22, 1974, Seymour Hersh's article "Huge CIA Operation Reported in U.S. Against Anti-War Forces, Other Dissidents in Nixon Years" appeared and dominated the airwaves in the last days before Christmas. This story joined with another leaked CIA document, nicknamed the "family jewels," which detailed major CIA covert activities during the Cold War, including assassination plots against foreign leaders like Fidel Castro.[72] Together, as Kissinger later wrote, "the Hersh story and the discovery of the 'family jewels' had the effect of a burning match in a gasoline depot."[73] Although most of the revelations had to do with events well before the Nixon and Ford years, Kissinger worried about the revelations of the CIA's actions against Allende in Chile. To distance the administration from the "family jewels," Ford appointed a bipartisan commission, headed by Vice President Rockefeller, to investigate CIA misdeeds in the domestic arena. The Rockefeller Commission would not satisfy a Congress in the wake of Watergate, and in both the Senate and the House various committees began their investigations. Senator Frank Church and Congressman Otis Pike would lead the most important of these, and Kissinger would soon find himself both testifying before and battling against both committees. The year 1975 did not begin on an auspicious note for the Gallup Poll's most admired man in America.

THE BITTER TASTE OF FAILURE: THE SINAI NEGOTIATIONS AND THE FALL OF SAIGON

On January 15, 1975, Gerald Ford began his first State of the Union address by telling Americans that the "State of the Union is not good." The recession had thrown millions out of work, high oil prices aggravated inflation, and the federal budget deficit was growing at a record pace. Ford's speech focused on domestic affairs, but toward the end, he praised the foreign policy of recent years and warned, "This is not a moment for the American people to turn inward." Although he pledged to cooperate with Congress on foreign policy, he also insisted, "We cannot rigidly restrict in legislation the ability of the President to act." Such congressional restrictions, Ford noted, even if "intended for the best motives and purposes, can have the opposite result, as we have seen most recently in our trade relations with the Soviet Union."[74] The gentle reference to the failure of the Jackson-Vanik measure reflected Ford's restraint in dealing with Congress. Kissinger was much more critical. He told one interviewer that he thought "all the Western democracies at the present are suffering from a crisis of authority," and his pessimism about the future of the American political system was one of the worst-kept secrets in Washington. Kissinger was hardly alone in his sentiments, as Watergate, the oil crisis, and the economic problems of the Western democracies occasioned widespread concern. The Trilateral Commission, a nongovernmental group founded by

David Rockefeller to bring together leaders from the United States, Europe, and Japan, issued a report titled *The Crisis of Democracy*, which highlighted the problems of governing in the Western democracies.[75]

However, as common as these sentiments were in elite circles, Kissinger's pessimism would become a political issue, and complicate matters for President Ford and his presidential campaign. A little over a week after Ford's address, Kissinger spoke in Los Angeles, focusing on the need for a "new national partnership" in approaching foreign policy. The TV news coverage of his speech stressed his attack on "the growing tendency of Congress to legislate in detail the day-to-day or week-to-week conduct of our foreign affairs" and the threat that this "risks unraveling the entire fabric of our foreign policy." Kissinger brought up both the Soviet trade deal and the restrictions on aid to Turkey. Marvin Kalb reviewed the speech sympathetically, but noted that Kissinger's penchant for secrecy and his "elitist" practices had alienated many legislators. Congress now wanted more than a "hand-holding secretary of state."[76]

In the environment of January 1975, Henry Kissinger needed a success, and resuming his step-by-step diplomacy in the Middle East might provide one. Americans saw the Middle East as both the most dangerous part of the world and the most vital for America's economy.[77] Ford did not take much convincing when Kissinger laid out the various scenarios for him, even when he told Ford, "The American Jews will oppose you in 1976, because they think you would move in 1977 and with a new party they would have a crack at a better deal." Ford believed that "by next year energy and the economy will be in better shape," and step-by-step was the "responsible course." Kissinger stressed to Ford, "Only Sadat can make the concessions and he will do it only to you or me."[78] Kissinger used a press conference on January 28 to announce that he would soon take "an exploratory trip to the Middle East," designed to have talks with "all of the major participants." Although he tried to dampen expectations, he stated his personal belief that the interests "of Egypt, for the return of some territory, and of Israel, for some progress toward peace, can be reconciled."[79]

To Kissinger, the Israeli-Egyptian issue was the only part of the Middle

East tangle that looked negotiable. Earlier in 1974 Kissinger had hoped to follow the Syria disengagement with an agreement with Jordan, but the Arab leaders at the Rabat summit in October 1974 recognized the Palestine Liberation Organization as the representative of West Bank Palestinians.[80] The PLO's support for terrorism made it politically untenable as a negotiating partner, to both Israel and much of the American public. Syria was now largely rearmed by the Soviet Union and insisted on a reopening of the Geneva Conference and an Israeli withdrawal to its 1967 borders. The increasing violence along the Lebanese border, with Israel striking at Palestinian guerrillas, contributed to a sense that the region was a tinderbox. Kissinger told a meeting of the Washington Special Actions Group that he thought there was a possibility of a Soviet intervention in Syria designed to force the Israelis back to their 1967 borders. If the United States considered sending in military forces to help Israel, the CIA director, Colby, interjected, "we could write off the whole Arab world." General George Brown, chairman of the Joint Chiefs, said, "It would tear the country apart." Kissinger replied, "That's exactly my nightmare." He told the group, "If the Arabs win, with Soviet support, and we do nothing, we've had it."[81]

As pessimistic as Kissinger sounded on the future of the Middle East in general, he was reasonably optimistic that his shuttle diplomacy would work. Congress would be considering a major military and economic aid package for Israel, and as Kissinger put it, "You can't be willing to pay $3 billion for a stalemate."[82] Kissinger was also certain that the prospect of going back to the Geneva Conference would intimidate the Israelis. He presumed that the Israeli government under Yitzhak Rabin understood that "their specific terms are less important than continuation of this process—and they will have to take what they can get."[83] For the first time, however, Kissinger was traveling to the Middle East after having become the object of criticism at home. Senator Jackson argued that the secrecy Kissinger displayed during the final round of negotiations with the Soviets over the trade bill led to the collapse of that deal. On a more personal level, Nixon's former aide Charles Colson was released from jail at the end of January and began to give interviews. Among Colson's charges were that President Nixon regarded Kissinger as "unstable" during the Vietnam peace negotiations and that Nixon worried about Gerald Ford's ability to control Kissinger. Kissinger responded with an interview before leaving for the Middle East during which he remarked sadly on how foreign policy had been "insulated" from criticism during Watergate and that the attacks on him now "were a new experience."[84]

Kissinger started his "exploratory" trip in Israel, where the realities of the deeply divided and troubled Israeli political scene were starkly apparent. Kissinger quickly came to see that his attempt to use the Geneva Conference as a threat might backfire, as some in the Israeli cabinet saw Geneva "as an opportunity to maintain the present impasse." Kissinger also recognized that Israel's demand that Egypt formally commit "to end all acts of belligerency" might be too much for Sadat to accept in the present circumstances.[85] Kissinger's meeting in Egypt was "considerably more relaxed" than his time in Tel Aviv, and he had the impression Sadat would "do his best" to reach an understanding. Kissinger found Assad of Syria determined to "cause problems for Egypt both internally and in the Arab world if Egypt went it alone," but he believed he could manage the Syrian leader if he could produce another successful Israeli disengagement for the Egyptians.[86] Kissinger remained optimistic, telling reporters that the chances of another agreement were fifty-fifty at best, a calculation that understated what he really believed.[87] Unfortunately for Kissinger, he overestimated the Israeli willingness to exchange valuable territory, including the town of Ras Sudr and the Abu Rudeis oil fields, for a simple non-belligerency pledge from Sadat. For its own domestic political reasons, Israel was determined to drive a much tougher bargain.

Kissinger returned to the United States and reported on his trip to Ford in a manner that accentuated his own importance while downplaying the risks. He complained to the president about the weakness of the Israeli government and Prime Minister Rabin, shown in his saying, "I had to have lunch with the Cabinet to win them over." He told Ford, in words that sound similar to the way he once described the South Vietnamese, "You can't imagine the monomania, the hysteria in Israel. There is no sense of gratitude. They demand we put our whole policy in hock to them." When Ford asked Kissinger if he still suspected that "Israel was setting us up," the secretary of state replied that he believed Rabin wanted a deal. He then crudely added, "But they are in such a difficult domestic situation they could even prefer to go to Geneva and be raped."[88] Kissinger made sure to brief the congressional leadership and the American Jewish leaders in more decorous language. He told both groups that while the United States might eventually agree to going back to the Geneva Conference, "it makes an enormous difference under what conditions we go." Returning to Geneva with another successful agreement would help make the case that "moderation pays" and strengthen those forces against more radical elements. With the Jewish leaders, Kissinger also pleaded for support for "executive authority" against Congress. He complained of the current political environment, "There is a malaise here." The Jewish leaders assured him they supported his efforts at step-by-step diplomacy and took comfort when he responded to a question by saying, "I won't beat any world records to go to Geneva."[89]

When Kissinger returned to the Middle East in early March, he went with the conviction that he would conclude another disengagement agreement, strengthening the Ford administration against the increasingly assertive Congress. President Ford attached his personal prestige to Kissinger's mission, seeing Kissinger off at the airport and giving him carte blanche negotiating authority.[90] The outline of an agreement was broadly discussed— Israeli withdrawal from two key passes, Mitla and Giddi, in the Sinai and the Egyptian oil fields there, in return for some type of Egyptian assurance of non-aggression.[91] Even with these preconditions seemingly met, Kissinger discovered that the resistance in Israel was much stronger than he had anticipated. Once again, outside events played a role. A dramatic terrorist attack at Tel Aviv's Savoy Hotel dominated the news.[92] Kissinger had Ford quickly cable Prime Minister Rabin to tell him, "We cannot permit this act of terrorism to attain the goal it seeks—the disruption and collapse of our current peace efforts."[93] Kissinger recognized that he was trying to get the Israelis to make "a generous counterproposal which could convince Sadat of their seriousness," rather than a "rigid" point-by-point interrogation of each issue in any agreement.[94] It was an approach that also called for a great deal of trust in their mediator, and Kissinger personalized the negotiations in striking ways.

"The impact on our international situation could not be more serious," Kissinger told the Israeli leaders. "From the Shah to Western Europe, from the Soviet Union to Japan it will be hard to explain why the United States failed to move a country of less than three million totally dependent on it in the face of Egyptian proposals which seem extremely generous to them."[95] To Kissinger, whose belief in the interconnectedness of world events was always central to his thinking, his conviction that America was being challenged around the world made him ever more desperate for a success. As the Israeli position hardened, with an insistence that Sadat provide a written guarantee of non-belligerence, Kissinger tried to intimidate Tel Aviv. He drafted a note for Ford to send to Rabin threatening that "the failure to achieve an agreement is bound to have far-reaching effects in the area and on our relations."[96] It did not work, and Kissinger's sixteen-day peace mission to the Middle East was, as Tom Snyder, the anchor of NBC Nightly News on Sundays, reported, in "shambles."[97]

In public, Kissinger gave the impression of sadness at the collapse of the talks, and emphasized his exhaustion and weariness. The television coverage showed him meeting with the former prime minister Golda Meir and then speaking at the airport before his departure, his voice cracking with emotion as he thanked Rabin for his friendship.[98] Privately he told the Israeli cabinet before he left that it was "totally out of the question" for the United States to resume bilateral diplomacy and that now the Geneva talks must be resumed. Kissinger painted an exceptionally gloomy picture for the Israelis, telling them that this was "another lost opportunity," and that there was "a good possibility there will be another war in the next year." When Foreign Minister Yigal Allon challenged him to resume diplomacy in a few weeks, Kissinger once again personalized the issue, telling Allon that he could not, "Because I am no longer the figure who mesmerizes them in the Arab world, because in every area the United States is no longer a country that one has to take seriously." As the meeting ended, he grew philosophical, agreeing with Rabin that this was like a Greek tragedy: "Each side, following the laws of its own nature, reaches an outcome that was perfectly foreseeable."[99]

This was not how he talked in Washington. When he reported to President

Ford, his mood toward the Israelis was far angrier, even contemptuous, telling the president, "I am Jewish. How can I want this? I have never seen such cold blooded playing with the American national interest." He warned Ford that the Israelis would "get from Congress what they want and by-pass you," perhaps by playing "the Jackson game with the Soviet threat. If you don't give arms, you weaken an ally; if you give them arms, they get total freedom." The reference to domestic politics was deliberate, as Kissinger suspected that Jackson's courting of American Jews would link his anti-détente efforts with criticism of Kissinger's Middle East diplomacy. As he had done with Nixon, Kissinger taunted Ford when he told him, "Israel doesn't think they have to be afraid of you."[100] Ford's stern reply, "They will find out," marked the beginning of the "reassessment" that Ford had threatened, and Kissinger made sure to leak the message to the media that "if I were an Israeli, I'd be nervous."[101]

Kissinger wanted a tough policy, "a cooling of relations with Israel— which should be friendly but correct," to restore a sense of American leadership in the region, despite his thinking that "step-by-step is dead" and that the United States had "to consider whether we and the Soviet Union shouldn't make a global approach."[102] However, just as the reassessment toward Israel was beginning, Kissinger found himself faced with another disaster: the impending collapse of the American-supported regimes in Cambodia and South Vietnam. As he left a meeting with the congressional leadership, where he received bipartisan statements of support for his Middle East efforts, he went to attend a meeting of the National Security Council. There he listened as his assistant William Hyland described the chaotic evacuation of South Vietnamese forces, as President Thiệu hoped to create a new defensive line around the southern portion of the country. After Hyland reported, "We have no idea whatsoever what [Thiệu's] supply situation is," Kissinger plaintively asked, "What I want to know is how did this all happen?"[103]

Despite the appearance of being in control that he liked to present, Kissinger's surprised reaction was a reflection of how out of touch he was with the Indochina issue. He had paid little attention to the area once the Middle East became the focus of his diplomacy in October 1973. His instinctive reaction was to see Vietnam in light of his current difficulties: "No one thought the North Vietnamese would attack this year. They did it based on their assessment of American weakness."[104] Hearing that Thiệu's withdrawal from the northern provinces might have been spurred by the cutbacks in American assistance, Kissinger quickly decided that he would "make an all-out effort" to get a supplemental appropriation when Congress returned from its Easter recess. Although Kissinger was now prepared to concede on Cambodia—"Cambodia's finished," he bluntly told the group—he wanted to go to Congress to "ask for what is right and not worry if we get creamed. If we get creamed, we're going to get creamed asking for the right amount." The only thing Kissinger ruled out was a military response, citing the congressional prohibition and noting, with that law, "our hands are tied."[105]

Over the next six weeks, as the final tragedy of Indochina unfolded, Kissinger's mood ranged from intense anger and resentment at congressional opponents of any further assistance to the South Vietnamese, to defensiveness about his personal role in the tragedy, and finally to a resigned attempt to move America beyond Vietnam. The domestic politics of the issue, past and future, were never far from his mind. On March 26, 1975, he held a news conference and made an impassioned plea for assistance to South Vietnam, framing it as a "moral commitment" that would determine "what kind of people we are." For Kissinger to use the language of morality in discussing a foreign policy issue was unusual. Although he did not revive the domino theory, President Eisenhower's analogy describing the nations of Southeast Asia falling over like dominos to the Communists, Kissinger suggested that a failure to act would have dangerous consequences for the United States. The country could lose allies, find that the balance of power was shifting against it, and see its adversaries encouraged to attack American interests. He challenged, and clearly provoked, Congress and the Democrats by arguing that to deny assistance would "deliberately destroy an ally."[106]

This time it would not be just the "McGovern liberals" who responded, a sign that Kissinger had fundamentally misread public opinion. David Brinkley, who had so extravagantly praised Kissinger for his Middle East diplomacy, sharply rebuked him for talking about what "kind of people we are." Brinkley cataloged the long record of the American commitment to South Vietnam, but noted how little difference all the assistance and American lives lost had made. Now about 80 percent of Americans opposed any further aid, Brinkley said, since they were the kind of people who were willing to help but who, "having decided it was all a huge blunder, [are] refusing to go on with it."[107] Eric Sevareid, usually a friend to Kissinger, now took him to task by comparing him with the former chancellor Willy Brandt, whose optimism about the Western democracies contrasted with Kissinger's gloom, and who dismissed the idea that American influence would suffer if it did not give more aid to Vietnam.[108]

Such criticism from his friends in the media was not what Kissinger expected, and in the past it might have chastened him and sent him into overdrive trying to explain himself. This time it brought out a more aggressive and angry side of his personality, as well as his deep pessimism about the current state of the world. Along with frequent bitter comments like "To have the US as an ally is really a joy these days," and "We are a disgrace to be an ally," Kissinger tried to defend his past role in the Vietnam negotiations.[109] When *Newsweek*'s diplomatic correspondent Bruce van Voorst asked him about the 1973 Paris Peace Accords, he angrily replied, "You tell me, would any treaties have been maintained when no party was willing to enforce it?"[110] David Binder of *The New York Times* called to ask him about a rumored American negotiating initiative to "settle the Vietnam problem," and Kissinger replied, "Bullshit!" telling Binder that he couldn't quote his expletive but that no such efforts were now underway. Kissinger sarcastically added, "You know North Vietnam and you know diplomacy."[111] Kissinger told a meeting of the "Wise Men" group of the American foreign policy establishment—Dean Rusk, McGeorge Bundy, Averell Harriman, David Bruce, and John J. McCloy, among them—that while most foreign policy setbacks are inflicted by foreigners, "ours instead are being inflicted by ourselves." American authority had preserved the peace of the world for thirty years, but now it was acting like the unstable and ineffectual "French governments of the Third and Fourth Republics," and "inviting some misbehavior from the Soviets."[112]

Kissinger's unusual referencing of the French experience was not the only way this influenced his thought. He now advised Ford, as he once had Nixon, to start doing "what De Gaulle had with Algeria—be as tough as nails, and don't give ground anywhere. We have to be tough if challenged."[113] Kissinger had always admired how De Gaulle, in part through his rhetoric and his bearing, had made the French withdrawal from Algeria seem like an act of policy by the French, not a surrender to the Algerian rebels. After invoking the French leader, he continued with the most famous British statesman. He told the president to be tough in approaching Congress, recommending, "You need a Churchillean posture now."[114] The advice clashed with Ford's own instincts and those of his political advisers, who wanted him to be more conciliatory toward Congress and to distance himself from the Vietnam issue. Kissinger prevailed initially, and Ford gave a strong speech to Congress on April 10, 1975, pleading for $722 million in military and humanitarian assistance for South Vietnam. "There was not one clap of applause" in Congress for the speech, with two members even walking out in protest.[115] Kissinger remained defiant, telling Ford that the Democrats "will have no issue on Vietnam," since they "got us into it."[116] Congress would provide money only for the evacuation of the six thousand Americans and "some" South Vietnamese, and even this gesture was controversial. Concerned about "pulling the plug" too soon and creating panic among the Vietnamese, but hoping to get out as many Vietnamese who had worked for Americans as possible, Kissinger continued to press for the assistance, hoping to draw the political lines clearly. He told Brent Scowcroft, "Indochina is gone but we will make them pay for it. In my whole testimony today, I said twenty-five times that it was Congress's fault."[117] Kissinger rejected Senator Henry Jackson's charge that Nixon's letters to President Thiệu promising to take military action in the event of a North Vietnamese violation of the Paris agreements constituted a "secret" agreement. Kissinger confessed to Scotty Reston, "You know what agony we were going through to get out of that war. Everyone wanted us to get out; public opinion was to get the hell out of there. People think we had the opportunity to get the perfect agreement."[118] What Kissinger would not admit was that the "decent interval" he had expected between the agreement and the eventual collapse of South Vietnam was coming with indecent haste, and that there was no way to prevent it.

On April 23, President Ford gave a speech at Tulane University during which he announced that the Vietnam conflict was "a war that is finished as far as America is concerned." The standing ovation and enthusiastic reaction of the crowd turned Ford's phrase into a major news story, especially after Ford answered a question about whether Kissinger had anything to do with preparing the speech by saying, "No. Nothing at all."[119] Kissinger angrily told Ford, "This we don't need," but it was clear that the president recognized the direction of public sentiment.[120] Kissinger told sympathetic journalists that although he knew there were people around Ford who wanted to see Kissinger's influence "diminished," he was staying on with the administration "for two reasons—it is not fair to pass along the problems I now have and, second, I am trying to rally what can be rallied."[121]

As the final evacuation unfolded on American television screens, with scenes of helicopters leaving the roof of the embassy and images of panicked Vietnamese desperate to flee but being pushed back by Marine guards, the nightmare of Vietnam was seared deeper into the American imagination.[122] Against this backdrop, Kissinger held a news conference in which he described the evacuation and defended efforts to "rescue as many South Vietnamese that had worked with the United States for fifteen years in reliance on our commitments as we possibly could." He told reporters, "We had to make a judgment every day how many people we thought we could safely remove without triggering a panic and at the same time still be able to carry out our principal function and the remaining function," adding in a halting voice that he believed "our objectives were achieved."[123] He also used the occasion to echo Ford's view that this was not a "time for recrimination." Nevertheless, Kissinger also reiterated his own view that there was "no question that the outcome in Indochina will have consequences not only in Asia but in many other parts of the world."[124] He repeated his view that "the weakening of executive authority in the United States" was a major cause of the failure of the Paris peace treaties. Although he added, "I think it will be a long time before

Americans will be able to talk or write about the war with some dispassion" and "what lessons we should draw from it, I should reserve for another occasion," Kissinger almost immediately began a process of trying to frame the outcome in a way that would preserve his authority and help the Ford administration in the upcoming campaign.[125]

Even before Saigon's final collapse, Kissinger had arranged with the NBC News president, Herbert Schlosser, to give a lengthy interview to the *Today* show, broadcast over four days, to defend American foreign policy and his own position as a key architect of that policy. Ford was enthusiastic about the opportunity, telling Kissinger that it "burns me up" when people tried to focus on possible disagreements between the president and his secretary of state.[126] The interviewer, Barbara Walters, had become friendly with Kissinger, and her approach was gentle and deferential.[127] In such a comfortable setting, Kissinger defended the Ford administration's policies as well as his own personal role. While starting the interview by acknowledging that Vietnam was a "significant setback," Kissinger defended the administration's rescue of thousands of Vietnamese as part of America's "national duty."[128] He emphasized that it was the Nixon administration that found 550,000 American soldiers in Vietnam and withdrew them, and deflected a clumsy question from Walters about the "decent interval" by denying that there were "any very vocal statements" in 1973 that suggested it was only a "matter of time" before the North Vietnamese took over the South. He repeated his own version of why Saigon fell, stressing the effect of Watergate and the congressional cutbacks on aid and restrictions on U.S. military action to enforce the Paris agreements, although he also admitted, "We probably might have done nothing anyway."

When the subject turned to the Soviet Union, Kissinger acknowledged that the Soviets had provided the weapons for the North Vietnamese offensive and made the conquest "possible," but he emphasized that it was "the refusal of American arms [which] made the conquest of South Viet-Nam inevitable." Kissinger strongly defended détente based on the idea that "we have certain interests in common, such as the prevention of general nuclear war, such as limiting conflict in areas where both of us could get directly involved." He stressed, "Détente has never meant the absence of competition," a comment that hardly accorded with the way he once described it during the heady days of the first Nixon-Brezhnev summits. Kissinger also suggested a less sweeping and global interpretation of the fall of South Vietnam than he had expressed privately, telling Walters, "We might have perceived it more in Vietnamese terms rather than as the outward thrust of global conspiracy." Kissinger was trying to position himself as the exponent of a policy that would "gear American commitments to American capabilities and necessities," a recognition of the limits of American power. The problem with this positioning is that his personalization of the process often meant that he wanted to engage American power when he was in control of it, and Congress had interfered with that dynamic. When Walters probed about the allegation "that you are gloomy about what you see as the decline and erosion of the free world," Kissinger acknowledged, "It is partly true," and went on to say that "in many countries Marxist ideologies and perceptions of the world, which are contrary to our values, are gaining in strength."[129]

On the following Monday, May 12, at their morning meeting, President Ford asked Kissinger to be part of his election campaign in 1976. Kissinger responded with enthusiasm, telling Ford that this election would be "one of the most crucial ever." When Ford mentioned his potential rival within the Republican Party, Ronald Reagan, Kissinger immediately dismissed him as "incompetent," and agreed with Ford that any Democrat would be a "disaster."[130] On that same day Khmer Rouge forces, which had taken control of Cambodia the month before, seized the American container ship S.S. *Mayaguez* off the Cambodian coast, taking the crew prisoner and hauling the ship to Koh Tang, about thirty miles off the Cambodian coast. When Kissinger got word of the seizure, his reaction was angry and belligerent: "We are not going to sit here and let an American merchant ship be captured at sea and let it go into the harbor without doing a bloody thing about it."[131] At the NSC meeting later that same morning, Kissinger pushed hard for "a strong statement, a strong note and a show of force."[132] He was joined in his push by his mentor, Vice President Rockefeller, who argued, "If we do not respond violently we will get nibbled to death." President Ford, who feared a repeat of the *Pueblo* incident, in which North Korea seized a U.S. Navy intelligence ship, holding its crew hostage for almost a year, was determined to act quickly.[133] Kissinger's one hesitation was that undertaking military action from U.S. bases in Thailand would cause a crisis with the Thai government and lead to the quick closure of those bases. But he was certain that the United States must act, telling Ford, "At some point . . . the United States must draw the line . . . we must act upon it now, and act firmly."[134]

The timing of the crisis coincided with the beginning of Kissinger's efforts to "build a new consensus behind America's international role in the wake of Indochina." The secretary of state decided to keep two scheduled speaking appearances in St. Louis and Kansas City to avoid letting the *Mayaguez* incident give the impression "that the Southeast Asian nightmare would never end."[135] Kissinger's low profile changed the political imagery of the crisis, with President Ford appearing as far more important. Under the pressure of time, and fearing that the Cambodians would take the crew to the mainland as hostages, Ford ordered a marine assault on Koh Tang to rescue the crew as well as to seize the ship. In fact, the Cambodians had already released the crew on a fishing vessel. Because of faulty intelligence, the assault on Koh Tang faced much greater resistance and took greater casualties, with eighteen Americans killed and forty-nine wounded in the futile attempt to find the crew, who had been taken from the ship and then released by the Cambodians.[136] Nevertheless, the outcome of the crisis, with the crew safe and the *Mayaguez* freed, led to a feeling of elation at the White House, helped along by the extremely favorable media coverage of the operation.[137] Kissinger held a press conference and stressed that the crisis proved there were "limits to which the U.S. can be pushed," and the TV newscasts openly speculated on how much the crisis might benefit Ford politically at home.[138] As Ford himself later noted in his memoirs, "All of a sudden the gloomy national mood began to fade. Many people's faith in their country was restored and my standing in the polls shot up 11 points."[139] Kissinger recognized the dark irony in this, noting in his memoirs "that we had entered Indochina to save a country, and that we had ended by rescuing a ship."[140]

SUMMER 1975: THE MIDDLE EAST, SOLZHENITSYN, AND THE HELSINKI ACCORDS

The *Mayaguez* incident did lift Gerald Ford's standing in the country, with stories showing him ahead of his Democratic challengers as well as his prospective Republican foe, California's former governor Ronald Reagan.[141] This political strength led Kissinger to continue to encourage Ford to take a tough line toward Israel in the "reassessment" of Middle East policy. Privately, with President Ford and his deputy Scowcroft, Kissinger expressed his anger toward the Israelis, telling Ford that their behavior was an "outrage" and "an indignity to the United States." He wanted "psychological warfare against Israel," believing that they "blew up 18 months of U.S. diplomacy" with their refusal to reach an agreement with Egypt.[142] In a revealing comment, he complained bitterly that it was "damn humiliating" that the Israelis seemed to think "that I needed and the President needed this agreement ourselves. And the US desperately needed a success."[143] Kissinger often came back to the domestic politics of the issue and his own personal role. "I could keep the Middle East quiet through the '76 election," he told Ford. "I did the same in '72 when Israel did the same thing to Rogers in '71," a self-serving and selective memory of those events.[144]

There were certainly reasonable American fears that a collapsed peace process could lead to another war, another oil boycott, and even Soviet military intervention. Kissinger made the case that Sadat was essentially an "Egyptian bourgeois nationalist" interested in obtaining Egypt's land back from the Israelis, and that his talk of Arab solidarity was for public consumption. Kissinger recognized that an agreement with Egypt was "Israel's biggest opportunity . . . to turn Sadat away from the United Arab front and towards peace."[145] Kissinger also painted worst-case scenarios, especially when he spoke to various Jewish groups and supporters of Israel. He continually threatened to move the talks back to Geneva for an overall settlement, where Israel would be more isolated and face demands it withdraw to its 1967 borders. He told one group that if the Soviets were to send forces to support the

Syrians and Egyptians, Congress would likely refuse to intervene, but even if they did allow U.S. action, with "40 percent of our troops" being "Negroes," Kissinger added, "think of the possible race riots here, . . . a real Vietnam-type situation."[146] Kissinger also raised the specter of anti-Semitism, arguing, "If the Jewish community attacks the President you will see for the first time an American President attacking Israel, and this could unleash the most profound consequences." Kissinger cited none other than John Connally, the former treasury secretary, as telling him that if he were advising "somebody on how to sweep the midwest and the southwest in the next election," he would recommend "an anti-Semitic campaign."[147]

If Kissinger thought that his being America's first Jewish secretary of state might give him the political cover to be tougher against Israel, he quickly discovered otherwise. On May 22, 1975, shortly before Ford was planning a trip to Europe, where he would meet with Sadat to explore resuming negotiations, a letter written by Senator Jacob Javits and signed by seventy-five other senators urged the president to recognize that "preserving the peace requires that Israel obtain a level of military and economic support adequate to deter a renewal of war by Israel's neighbors." The letter warned Ford against any withholding of military aid to Israel and maintained that America's national interests stood "firmly with Israel in the search for peace in future negotiations, and that this premise is the basis of the current reassessment of U.S. policy in the Middle East."[148] Kissinger suspected that the Israeli embassy, and especially Ambassador Simcha Dinitz, were involved in organizing the letter.[149] He told Ford that it proved "Rabin's willingness to treat us as an antagonist."[150] Kissinger also realized that the Israelis had found the Achilles' heel of the American position, with Congress effectively asserting itself in foreign policy across the board against an unelected president. Kissinger feared that Sadat might see the letter as an indication that America would be unable to influence Israel toward any further concessions, and this might cause the Egyptian leader to back away from his newfound affection for the United States.

Yet Kissinger believed that America had potential leverage with Sadat, primarily because of the Egyptian leader's interest in Western economic aid and military assistance.[151] Kissinger did not object to having TV reporters portray the Ford meeting with Sadat as the president's attempt "to succeed where Henry Kissinger failed," and Kissinger prepared a toast for the president that saluted Sadat for his "statesmanship and wisdom," and proclaiming that America would not tolerate "stagnation" in its efforts for peace.[152] Sadat assured Ford that "my people have not lost confidence in Doctor Kissinger," and that the Egyptians wanted a "complete peace" and for the United States to achieve it, not the Soviet Union and not at Geneva.[153] Kissinger stressed to Sadat that the Israelis were trying to delay matters until after the American elections in 1976, while he and President Ford wanted "a result this year." Sadat offered to allow Americans to operate the monitoring stations in the Sinai and bluntly stated, "As far as I am concerned, Syria can go to war by itself. I am not intending to start a war." This was what Ford and Kissinger were hoping to hear. Sadat also asked for a "billion and a half dollars" in Western aid, and Kissinger understood that the United States would have to bankroll any agreement.

With Sadat's proposed concessions in mind, Kissinger became more optimistic about an interim agreement.[154] First, he needed to convince Prime Minister Rabin.[155] Kissinger told Ford that the Israeli leader and his entourage were the "world's worst shits," engaging in a "pattern of deception" that made negotiating with them an infuriating process. With Ford as a willing pupil, Kissinger provided detailed instructions before the president's meeting with Rabin, pushing him to be coldly correct to the Israeli leader and to threaten Rabin with a return to the Geneva Conference and negotiating based on Israel's 1967 borders. The meeting between the two leaders went badly, with Ford thinking there "was no give at all" in the Israeli position, and Kissinger coming to believe that they were simply "reselling their March proposal" and not moving any closer to compromising. Kissinger's anger was palpable when he confronted Rabin about what the Israeli leader claimed was a "misunderstanding" about maps of the Sinai they had presented, maps that seemed to indicate Israel would withdraw from the two passes. His voice dripping with sarcasm, Kissinger remarked to Rabin, "You must ask why should Joe [Sisco], Brent Scowcroft and I all have so substantial a misunderstanding.

You are right. We never used to have misunderstandings with the Israeli Government."[156] However, the Israelis held firm, with the result that Kissinger pushed Ford hard, telling him, "The tougher you are, the more chance there is to move them." Although Ford was pessimistic, Kissinger told him, "I think they will cave."[157] At the end of June, Ford delivered a harsh ultimatum to the Israeli government, calling the new Israeli suggestions "inadequate" and "counter to the interests of the United States and the world." This dispute, in Ford's words, went "to the very core of American-Israeli relationships."[158] Kissinger made sure this was leaked and the "American ultimatum" was the lead story on the network news.[159] The Israelis were shaken, and Ambassador Dinitz flew to the Virgin Islands, where Kissinger was on vacation, to assure the secretary that the Israeli government wanted to make a "serious effort" to prevent a crisis that would have "the gravest consequences for Israel, for the U.S., and for the world."[160]

Kissinger knew that Rabin's weak domestic position was at the heart of his obstinacy, and that the American pressure might help him overcome opposition within his cabinet to the interim agreement.[161] Indeed, Rabin told his cabinet that the American pressure was as great as that the Eisenhower administration had imposed after the 1956 Suez crisis.[162] Negotiations now moved ahead, with the United States pledging both significant economic and military assistance to both countries, but also the presence of Americans as monitors. Although Kissinger was able to compel the Israelis to compromise with Egypt, he was still walking a tightrope in trying to hold the different and at times competing strands of his foreign policy system together. As the Middle East discussions dragged on through the summer of 1975, Kissinger explained to Ford the politics of his approach: "The reason I reluctantly came to an interim agreement is that if you get it, plus a SALT agreement and one or two others, you'll be in good shape in foreign policy." Kissinger was intent on preserving and strengthening détente with the Soviet Union, believing that the threat to Ford's election in 1976 would come "if SALT blows up" and the Democrats moved to the left to attack the administration.[163]

Kissinger's political judgment was not as flawed as it might seem in retrospect. In July 1975, the future of relations with the Soviet Union still looked bright. On July 17, the Apollo-Soyuz rendezvous in space took place, covered extensively and positively by all three American television networks. Commentators made frequent reference to the symbolism of the meeting in space's coming thirty years after the American-Soviet meeting on the Elbe to end World War II, and speculated that this might one day symbolize the end of the Cold War.[164] Along with this public relations extravaganza went Ford's decision to attend the Conference on Security and Cooperation in Europe (CSCE) in Helsinki, a conference that would ratify a set of agreements that the Soviets considered a final settlement of World War II. Kissinger was never enthusiastic about the CSCE, telling Ford, "We never wanted it but we went along with the Europeans." To Kissinger, the whole thing was just a "grandstand play to the Left," and he considered many of the provisions for freedom of movement and information to be "meaningless."[165] Kissinger felt that the symbolism of the thirty-five-nation conference, along with Ford's additional trips to more independent-minded East European countries like Romania and Yugoslavia, could help bolster support for détente in the United States.

Kissinger's attempt to balance the cooperation and competition elements of détente occasionally led him to misjudgments, and none proved more damaging than the advice he gave to President Ford shortly before the CSCE to snub Aleksandr Solzhenitsyn, the famous Russian writer and dissident, who had been arrested and expelled from the Soviet Union in February 1974. Stanford University's Hoover Institution invited the Russian writer to come to the United States. Kissinger drew a distinction between Solzhenitsyn's prestige as an award-winning writer and his new role as both a critic of the Soviet system and an opponent of the policy of détente. Kissinger thought that a Ford meeting with Solzhenitsyn would further damage U.S.-Soviet relations, but he also disliked the way that American critics of détente were using the heroic writer to attack him and the Ford administration. Nevertheless, Ford's snub of Solzhenitsyn revealed divisions within the administration. Ford's young deputy assistant Dick Cheney argued that the United States had slipped over toward the appeasement of the Soviet system and given up "faith in our fundamental principles concerning individual liberty and democracy." Cheney argued vigorously that détente "should consist of agreements wherever possible to reduce the possibility of conflict, but it does not mean that all of a sudden our relationship with the Soviets is all sweetness and light."[166] Ford's failure to meet with Solzhenitsyn provided a campaign issue for both Scoop Jackson Democrats and Reagan Republicans.[167] It also contributed to the strong public criticism that Ford received when he did go to Helsinki, which Solzhenitsyn denounced as the "funeral of Eastern Europe." Both *The New York Times* and *The Wall Street Journal*, whose two editorial pages rarely agreed, attacked the president for going to the conference and signing the Helsinki Accords, thereby in their view legitimizing Soviet control over Eastern Europe.[168]

To try to increase public support for détente, Kissinger gave a series of talks, dubbed the "Heartland Speeches," because they were delivered in noncoastal cities like Atlanta, Minneapolis, Birmingham, and Cincinnati. Written largely by his assistant Winston Lord, Kissinger's speeches sought to explain his approach to foreign policy, respond to both critics of détente and those who attacked the "morality" of his policies, and rally support for the administration.[169] Kissinger acknowledged, "The American people will never be satisfied with simply reducing tension and easing the danger of nuclear holocaust." He stressed his hope that in the long term, "firmness in the face of pressure and the creation of incentives for cooperative action may bring about a more durable pattern of stability and responsible conduct." Citing the Apollo-Soyuz mission and the other achievements of détente, Kissinger posed questions he often asked in private meetings of critics: "What is the alternative they propose? What precise policies do they want us to change? Are they prepared for a prolonged situation of dramatically increased international danger?" Kissinger ended with one question that he often posed to his more conservative critics: "Can we ask our people to support confrontation unless they know that every reasonable alternative has been explored?" Kissinger's understanding of where American public opinion was, particularly its desire to spend less on defense and avoid military interventions, was one of the key justifications he used for his approach to the Soviet Union.

On human rights, Kissinger sounded conciliatory, even mentioning the work of Representative Donald Fraser of Minnesota, whose congressional

hearings, along with those of Senator Frank Church of Idaho and Representative Otis Pike of New York, had frequently targeted Kissinger's policies. He
claimed that the United States does not "and will not condone repressive
practices" and "will use our influence against repressive practices. Our tradi-
tions and our interests demand it." Kissinger, however, also tried to caution
his liberal critics. "Truth compels also a recognition of our limits," he intoned,
making it clear that he did not believe his listeners understood those limits. In
part, Kissinger saw it as a question of methods: "The question is whether we
promote human rights more effectively by counsel and friendly relations,
where this serves our interest, or by confrontational propaganda and discriminatory legislation." In a direct reference to the Cyprus issue, Kissinger
stressed, "Our alliances and political relationships . . . are not favors to other
governments, but reflect a recognition of mutual interests. They should be
withdrawn only when our interests change and not as punishment for some
act with which we do not agree." He also took aim at liberals who pushed for
withdrawal from Vietnam but wanted the United States to push harder on
human rights in South Korea and Indonesia. He noted, "It is the process of
American disengagement that has eroded the sense of security and created
a perceived need for greater internal discipline, and at the same time diminished our ability to influence domestic practices." As self-serving as that
defense was, Kissinger was both more truthful and more accurate when he
said, "Painful experience should have taught us that we ought not exaggerate
our capacity to foresee, let alone to shape, social and political change in other
societies." He concluded by restating the way he thought America should approach foreign policy: "The question is not whether our values should affect
our foreign policy but how. The issue is whether we have the courage to face
complexity and the inner conviction to deal with ambiguity; whether we will
look behind easy slogans and recognize that our great goals can only be
reached by patience, and in imperfect stages."[170]

The Heartland Speeches were a strong and persuasive defense of Kissinger's approach to foreign policy. But Kissinger's views on human rights were
much more hard-line than Winston Lord's gracious prose suggested. Indeed,
Kissinger's refusal to compromise with congressional opponents on human

rights issues "stirred a hornet's nest." His resistance to even modest reform legislation backfired and "played a pivotal role in moving human rights from the sidelines to the center of American diplomacy." Congressman James Abourezk later admitted that simple "dislike of Kissinger" got votes for human rights proposals.[171] Kissinger's personalization of "his" foreign policy, and his insistence on maintaining his tight control over it, proved counterproductive. He saw congressional criticism not as a rejection of the policy but as an attack on him personally. Although there was intellectual merit in his view of how best to advance American values and human rights, Kissinger's behavior toward his congressional opponents ultimately backfired.[172]

Despite the domestic protest over Solzhenitsyn and Helsinki, Kissinger continued to believe that détente was a winning political issue at home, and that to abandon it would invite a crisis with the Russians during an election year. Although they made little progress on the SALT negotiations when they met Brezhnev in Helsinki, in mid-August Dobrynin called Kissinger to tell him that Brezhnev wanted to set the date for his visit to the United States. The purpose of the trip would be to sign a SALT II agreement.[173] Although Kissinger welcomed Dobrynin's reassurance about SALT, he recognized that public opinion in the United States reflected growing fears that détente was "a one-way street." To signal his own displeasure with Soviet behavior, Kissinger publicly criticized the Soviets for seeming to take advantage of the political crisis in Portugal, where the Communist Party had shown considerable strength and organization. In words that the Soviets might have applied to Kissinger's approach to the Middle East, the secretary said that the United States has never accepted that the Soviet Union is "free to relax tensions selectively or as a cover for the pursuit of unilateral advantage."[174] Kissinger's speech led the evening news, and it was framed as an "aggressive" attack on the Soviet Union that sounded like a "warning."[175]

Domestic political considerations also played a role in Kissinger's determination to nail down the Sinai II Agreement and redeem his failure from earlier in the year. In this case, a combination of Sadat's suggestion of American technicians manning the monitoring stations, along with a hefty increase in military aid to Israel, helped produce a breakthrough in the talks. Kissinger told President Ford that his Democratic rival, Scoop Jackson, had earlier told the Israeli ambassador "not to make an interim agreement because it would only help you and me," and Kissinger clearly relished undermining Jackson by obtaining an agreement.[176] Kissinger also resented the degree to which the Israeli government told its own people it was under great American pressure to make concessions, or as he crudely told his assistant Joe Sisco, the Israelis are "putting out the word that they're being raped by us."[177] When Kissinger finally arrived in Israel in late August, he was met with "unprecedented hostility, mainly from right-wing opposition parties, and demonstrators accosted him at each stop."[178] Although he made progress with the Israelis on their withdrawal from the Mitla and Giddi passes, as well as relinquishing the Abu Rudeis and Ras Sudr oil fields, the scale of concessions and American commitments he was forced to make to Israel angered Kissinger. He told Ford that his talks with the Israelis had "taken on more the character of exchanges between adversaries than between friends,"[179] and described the Israelis as "treacherous, petty, and deceitful."[180]

The Sinai II agreement was signed on September 1, 1975, and was an important step toward the peace in the region, although the Ford administration made the same mistake it had with the Vladivostok summit and went overboard in presenting the agreement to the public. Ford's staff arranged a televised transmission of the phone call between Ford and Kissinger—transparently designed "to establish the President's primacy over Kissinger in foreign affairs," with the result that Ford hyperbolically described the agreement as "the most historic, certainly, of this decade and perhaps in this century." White House reporters broke into "unkind but justified laughter" as Ford attempted to assure Anwar Sadat over a malfunctioning telephone connection that "we're going to keep the momentum going" for more agreements.[181] In marked contrast to the media acclaim that greeted the Syrian disengagement agreement, NBC's Richard Valeriani simply remarked that the agreement was "modest good news" and concluded that it was the "best agreement that money could buy."[182] That negative tone continued in the television coverage, with reporting on the Senate leader Mike Mansfield's concerns that American technicians in the Sinai could be the first step to "another

Vietnam," and on Henry Jackson's insistence that Kissinger should swear "an oath" that there were no secret agreements in the settlement. Kissinger stressed in congressional testimony that the presence of Americans in the Sinai was a "reluctant" concession to the Israelis and Egyptians, and that their "peacekeeping" role was not comparable to their role in Vietnam.[183] Even the coverage of the actual signing in Geneva, with neither the Israelis nor the Egyptians acknowledging each other with words or a handshake, seemed to underscore the relative fragility of the peace, despite the administration's commitment of more than $2 billion in assistance to both Israel and Egypt.[184]

CHALLENGES MOUNT: THE HALLOWEEN MASSACRE, ANGOLA, AND THE DEMISE OF SALT

The restrained public reaction to Sinai II was a warning that foreign policy success had lost some of its appeal to an American public disillusioned with Washington. Kissinger angrily told Ford that even though the Sinai agreement was "the greatest achievement since the opening to China," Congress "was pissing all over it."[185] The deeper source of Kissinger's irritation was not Sinai II, which Congress ultimately approved, but the continuing challenges to his position and his policies. The congressional investigations, especially the House Intelligence Committee's, sought to call as witnesses State Department officials like Thomas Boyatt, who had dissented from Kissinger's Cyprus policy.[186] Kissinger's refusal to allow this led to a public confrontation and a citation of contempt, although Kissinger held his own in the television news coverage of the committee's hearings.[187] Along with this challenge came the clash with Defense Secretary Schlesinger over détente and the prospect of a SALT II agreement. In early October, a Department of Defense intelligence assessment leaked to *The New York Times*. The document was sharply critical of détente, concluding, "The Soviet Union is using the policy of détente to gain dominance over the West in all fields." In a clear reference to a possible SALT II agreement, the report maintained, "Soviet détente policy has facilitated Soviet strategic nuclear expansion and the canceling out of US superiority, without provoking extensive Western counterefforts."[188] ABC's Barrie

Dunsmore reported that conservative organizations supporting Ronald Reagan were circulating copies of the report.[189]

Ford was angry enough about the intelligence report to confront Schlesinger, telling him it was "amateurish." In his memoirs, Ford said that he had always found Schlesinger a difficult person to work with, noting, "His aloof, frequently arrogant manner put me off."[190] The disagreement over détente between Kissinger and Schlesinger fed the image of "internal anarchy" within the administration and weakened the president's public standing.[191] Ford's political advisers, led by Bryce Harlow, told him that he should fire both men. Even though Kissinger sensed his importance to Ford, he was chronically insecure. He played on the president's anger with Schlesinger, telling him that "DOD (Defense Department) should get out of foreign policy." He reminded Ford that "Vladivostok was a real achievement," and that while some of the criticism was directed at him, "it is going to get to you." Kissinger stressed the ways the Defense Department was making it more difficult for him to negotiate with the Soviets for SALT. He again warned Ford, "Schlesinger is making it tough for you with the Reagan bunch, but if you move to the right the liberals will kill you in the election for sabotaging détente." Ford agreed but told Kissinger he wanted to give Schlesinger another chance: "I want a SALT agreement. I want to let my conversation with [Schlesinger] sink in and then talk to him next week." Kissinger volunteered some talking points for the president on what "should be coming from the Pentagon" to support a pro-SALT position, adding a comment that was clearly designed to prod Ford to act: "Haig says he [Schlesinger] wants to be President."[192]

After this meeting with Ford, Kissinger left for China to finish the planning for Ford's trip to Beijing. Ford wanted Kissinger to help him to benefit politically without seeming to copy Nixon, and stressed that he should arrange "something different" from what Nixon had done on his trip but "dramatic" enough to attract extensive television coverage. Kissinger suggested visiting the ancient Chinese capital of Xi'an and told Ford he thought a communiqué that restated the Shanghai Communiqué of 1972 would be better for Ford domestically.[193] Unfortunately for Kissinger, he ran up against a

Chinese leadership determined to lecture him even more intently about the evils of détente. Deng Xiaoping, now the vice premier and taking Zhou En-lai's position, even compared détente with Chamberlain's appeasement policies before World War II.[194] The Chinese kept stressing American weakness, much to Kissinger's annoyance. Kissinger tried to spin the news coverage by telling reporters that the Chinese would love to see Americans and Russians "at each other's throats."[195] However, the coverage of Kissinger's trip focused on the Chinese critique of détente and emphasized the lack of progress in U.S.-China relations. It was a fitting prelude to what awaited Kissinger when he returned to the United States.

On Saturday morning, October 25, Kissinger arrived in the Oval Office to report to President Ford on his China trip, telling him that the relationship had "cooled" noticeably and that "Mao's theme is our weakness." Unaware of Ford's personnel plans, Kissinger added that Mao said, "He likes Schlesinger's view of the Soviet Union better than mine" and wanted the defense secretary to visit China to "drive the Soviet Union wild."[196] Later that afternoon, Ford called in Kissinger and Donald Rumsfeld to tell them that he had decided to fire Schlesinger and appoint Rumsfeld as defense secretary, while at the same time relieving Kissinger of his role as national security adviser by giving it to Kissinger's deputy, Brent Scowcroft. Kissinger tried to change the president's mind, arguing that he would be blamed for the firing and that losing his position as national security adviser might hurt his prestige in foreign capitals. But Ford was determined on the shake-up, hoping it would restore the sense that he was in command of his administration. He was unprepared for the negative reviews it received. *NBC Nightly News* went to Henry Jackson for comment, and he criticized the administration's "one-man operation" in foreign policy, portraying Schlesinger's firing as a triumph for Kissinger. However, if the firing of Schlesinger was a sign of Kissinger's strength, Ford's removal of Vice President Rockefeller from consideration as his running mate was a signal that Ford would try to appease conservative Republicans.

Kissinger shared in the Washington consensus that Donald Rumsfeld was behind the moves, seeking to advance his own power within the Ford administration.[197] In his first press conference after the shake-up, Kissinger stressed that his relationship with the president was excellent and "unchanged." In an attempt to undermine the view that Schlesinger's firing was his doing, Kissinger spoke very favorably of Schlesinger, describing him as "a man of outstanding ability and one of the best analysts of defense matters." ABC's Ted Koppel contrasted Kissinger's almost "lyrical" praise for Schlesinger with Kissinger's curt comment on Rumsfeld by saying that "heartfelt praise does not spring readily" to Kissinger when he speaks of Rumsfeld. Kissinger answered a reporter's question about Rumsfeld's qualification to be defense secretary in a hesitating and halting voice, finally saying that Rumsfeld is "a man who is very attuned to the political process," a damning compliment. When asked whether he would "last out" President Ford's term, Kissinger joked that he did not answer his phone on Sundays anymore, a not-so-subtle criticism of how the firings were handled, and allowed Koppel to remark that the "internal bickering" within the Ford administration was not over.[198] Kissinger also avoided a direct answer as to whether he had threatened to resign. Kissinger did indeed slip into a short depression, not unlike what he'd experienced when Nixon made him the scapegoat for his failed South Asian policy. Seeking both reassurance and sympathy, he brought together a group of friends, including Winston and Bette Lord, Lawrence Eagleburger, William Simon, and David Bruce.[199] Henry Brandon, the correspondent for the London *Times*, remarked that the dinner party seemed "like a gathering of the last loyalists."[200] They went over drafts of a resignation letter, which included goals Kissinger still hoped to see the administration achieve.[201] Ultimately, Kissinger simply decided to go to see the president, and Ford talked him out of it. As Ford wrote in his memoirs, "The country needed him—I needed him—to implement our foreign policy at this difficult time."[202]

Kissinger's loss of his national security advisor position did not prove to be a significant "demotion." Brent Scowcroft largely shared Kissinger's views on foreign policy and never interfered with Kissinger's access to the president.[203] Even though Kissinger insisted to the press that "the Secretary of State should play no political role in a Presidential election," and that he would "conduct [him]self in a non-partisan way," Kissinger knew that Ford still looked to him to produce the successes in foreign policy that Ford needed.[204] The most important of those was another SALT agreement. Kissinger used the same press conference in which he praised Schlesinger to say that he believed "that 90 percent of the SALT agreement is substantially agreed to," and that "with a serious effort on both sides, these differences can be bridged." Kissinger characterized the SALT talks as in "stagnation," however, claiming it was up to the Soviet Union to make a "reasoned response to our last proposal."[205]

Kissinger continued to campaign hard in support of détente and another SALT agreement. He cooperated with *Time*'s White House correspondent Hugh Sidey for an extremely sympathetic article that portrayed Kissinger as trying to prevent the country from going "back to the days of the cold war and bitter confrontation with the Soviet Union" and keeping "the new relationship" of détente alive. In Sidey's words, Kissinger was "simply brighter and more adept at the art of human persuasion than any of his adversaries," and Kissinger's reading of American politics, namely those Americans "in the farm areas [who] want Russian markets for their grain," might enable him to pull off "a miracle or two."[206] In a November 24 speech in Detroit celebrating the foreign policy achievements of the last six years, Kissinger stressed that "foreign policy must be based on reality, not rhetoric," and that "today's reality is that we live in a world of nuclear equality." Kissinger argued that in "place of continual crises" with the Soviet Union, there were now negotiations over all manner of issues, including arms control, economic relations, and international issues. Although he conceded that détente might have been oversold, he maintained that at its heart, the challenge for Americans was to "manage a fundamental conflict of values in the shadow of nuclear holocaust."[207]

After an exchange of letters with Brezhnev in mid-November, in which the Soviet leader promised "energetic efforts" to complete an agreement, both Ford and Kissinger were optimistic about a SALT II agreement and a successful summit meeting with the Soviet leader scheduled for April 1976. Their optimism led Ford's Republican opponent, Ronald Reagan, to be cautious in his attacks on Ford's foreign policy. In his speech announcing his candidacy for the Republican presidential nomination on November 20, 1975, Reagan stressed his opposition to big government, attacking the "buddy system" in

Washington, DC, and highlighting his role as an outsider. Rather than pro-claiming the United States was behind the Soviet Union, he remarked, "A de-cade ago we had military superiority. Today we are in danger of being surpassed by a nation that has never made any effort to hide its hostility to everything we stand for." He used the same equivocal phrasing about détente: "Through detente we have sought peace with our adversaries. We should con-tinue to do so but must make it plain that we expect a stronger indication that they also seek a lasting peace with us."[208] Reagan's caution is an important reminder that the electoral advantages of SALT were not a figment of Kissin-ger's imagination, and that the search for an agreement with the Russians made political sense at the time.

As they prepared to leave for China in late November, Kissinger was op-timistic that they could repeat the Nixon game plan for election year tri-umphs. Brezhnev's invitation to Kissinger to come negotiate after they returned from China was a positive sign. Kissinger even speculated that he could get the "Soviet-Chinese triangle working again."[209] After they arrived in China, Kissinger sought to convince the Chinese that he shared their ap-prehensions about the Soviets, but said, "We are promoting the strongest pol-icy against the Soviet Union that we can before the elections." He tried to convince the Chinese to cooperate in characterizing U.S.-Chinese relations as good and improving, because "our opponents will use any issue to under-mine the credibility of what we are doing."[210] The Chinese did restrict news coming out of the meetings, and Kissinger conducted the press briefing at the end of Ford's visit, presenting the discussions in the best possible light but leaving American reporters with the simple statement, "We are satisfied with the visit."[211] This approach largely worked. All three network news-casts reported Kissinger's statement that not much time was spent on dis-cussing détente, and on NBC Tom Brokaw even noted that Kissinger was successful in getting the Chinese to tone down their "bombastic rhetoric" about détente.[212]

Kissinger and Ford went from China to Indonesia, a country whose stra-tegic location and oil reserves had made it the most important American ally in Southeast Asia. During their meetings with the Indonesian dictator

Suharto, he indicated his intention to deal forcefully with the former Portuguese colony of East Timor, which had just declared its independence. Neither Kissinger nor Ford expressed any reservations about the Indonesian plan for conquest, with Ford telling the Indonesian leader, "We understand and will not press you on the issue." Remembering what happened with Turkey and Cyprus, Kissinger told Suharto that if they used American weapons, there could be problems with Congress. He asked that the Indonesians wait until they were back in Washington so that he and President Ford could "influence the reaction in America." Kissinger also expressed the hope that whatever they did, they would do it "quickly."[213] The next day, as the Americans' plane was in the air, the Indonesian army invaded East Timor, using American weapons and supplies, and completed the conquest in a particularly brutal and violent manner. Thousands of East Timorese were killed and imprisoned, with the army burning villages to the ground and committing widespread atrocities. Tragically, the issue received relatively little attention in the United States.[214] Kissinger saw Indonesia as a vital ally in a region where the United States had experienced serious setbacks. Questioning that ally's policies, especially over what seemed a "minor" territorial issue, was not on his agenda. Indonesia, like Turkey, Iran, and Chile, was an anti-communist ally in the Cold War, and Kissinger valued that allegiance far more than any concern over human rights within its territory. Neither Ford nor Kissinger thought the issue terribly significant either. Neither mentions it in their memoirs.[215]

When he did get back to Washington, it was not Portuguese East Timor that Kissinger was forced to address. The Portuguese colony of Angola gained its independence on November 11, 1975, and was immediately plunged into civil war.[216] Earlier in the year, Kissinger had played a key role in convincing Ford to authorize covert American financial support of the National Front for the Liberation of Angola (FNLA), led by Holden Roberto, a close ally of Zaire's leader, Mobutu Sese Seko—and a group that had also received assistance from China.[217] This American funding emboldened the FNLA to attack, encouraging the other factions to solicit outside aid. The Popular Movement for the Liberation of Angola (MPLA) enjoyed a strong position in the capital city of Luanda and had recruited Soviet and Cuban backing. In the south, the National Union for the Total Independence of Angola (UNITA) gained support from China and South Africa. Over the course of 1975, the United States and the Soviet Union gradually increased their support to their allies, with the United States now also aiding UNITA as well as the FNLA. Kissinger believed, "If all the surrounding countries see Angola go communist, they will assume the United States has no will."[218] In July the United States sent $14 million, and in early September provided an additional $10.7 million.

In pushing for even this modest amount of aid, Kissinger faced strong resistance within the State Department from the head of the Africa Bureau, Nathaniel Davis, who objected that U.S. vital interests were not at stake and the risks of intervention outweighed the potential benefits.[219] Davis also observed that the CIA measures in Angola were "inadequate to accomplish the purposes outlined."[220] Davis called out Kissinger's own caution about the domestic politics of the Angolan operation, arguing that if they could not find the political strength to make a major effort, then it would be much better to do nothing at all. Davis resigned after his objections to the Angolan intervention were overruled, and Kissinger complained to Ford that the African Bureau would leak its objections to the press. Convinced by Kissinger, Ford argued that if the United States did nothing, "we will lose Southern Africa," adding, "I won't let someone in Foggy Bottom deter me."[221]

Into the middle of the Angolan conflict came Fidel Castro in Cuba, with ambitions and dreams of his own. The Cuban leader's decision to intervene proved a crucial turning point. Over the course of 1974 and early 1975, Kissinger had begun reaching out to the Castro regime, using a variety of channels, including the possibility of "baseball diplomacy," with Bowie Kuhn, Major League Baseball's then commissioner, talking to Kissinger at a dinner party about scheduling exhibition games between American major league teams and Cuban teams.[222] Kissinger believed that the American attempt to isolate Cuba, with its trade embargo and economic boycott, had failed to change the Cuban regime. He decided to proceed toward normalization in a manner similar to what he and Nixon had used with China, cloaking the operation in various layers of secrecy. But Kissinger underestimated the ambitions of Castro. Emboldened by communist success in Vietnam and the "desire to establish himself as a great revolutionary leader on the world stage," Castro had dispatched military advisers to Angola early in the year to help the MPLA organize its forces. When the Americans escalated their support for the FNLA and UNITA in July, and the forces of the pariah regime of white South Africa crossed into southern Angola in August, Castro was determined to respond. He launched a massive air- and sealift with Soviet logistical support that would ultimately send some thirty-six thousand Cuban troops to rescue the MPLA and halt the South African advance.[223]

Kissinger reacted angrily to the Cuban intervention, believing them to be acting as surrogates for the Soviets, "paying back the Soviets for their military and economic support."[224] Referring to Castro as a "pipsqueak," Kissinger thought the Cuban leader was "thumbing his nose" at the United States.[225] Far more important to Kissinger than reconciliation with Cuba was the possible impact of Angola on détente and his effort to achieve a SALT agreement. When the dimensions of the Cuban assistance first became apparent in November 1975, Kissinger wanted the CIA to provide a significant increase in covert aid to match the Soviet-Cuban effort. He also delivered a stern public warning to the Soviets, proclaiming that they were in violation of the 1972 treaty on "Principles of Co-existence" and urging that there should be an "African solution to an African problem."[226] At the same time he also sought to provide the Soviets with a respectable way out of the crisis. He told Richard Valeriani of NBC that he believed their intervention was motivated by their competition with the Chinese and that they did not intend to challenge the United States. He added that Ford could not appear to "be soft" against the Russians, hoping that the politburo might consider Ford's domestic political problem.[227]

Along with his public efforts, Kissinger authored a secret message to the Soviets that deplored the "efforts [the Soviet Union] is now making to escalate the fighting in Angola," and argued that if these continued, they could "set back the progress of détente."[228] Kissinger's note stretched the truth when it asserted, "The United States for its part pursues no unilateral interests in

Angola and is exclusively concerned with seeing the people of that country live in peace, independence and well-being." As disingenuous as such claims were, they did indicate Kissinger's hope that Angola would not become an arena of competition with the Russians. Unfortunately for Kissinger, the Soviets found themselves in a winning situation in Angola, prevailing on the ground with their Cuban allies and in the court of African opinion through their opposition to the apartheid regime of South Africa. They defended their recognition of the MPLA as the legitimate government of Angola and matched the Americans in mendaciousness, claiming, "Not a single Soviet man is taking part in the hostilities in Angola."[229] Kissinger and Ford called in the Soviet ambassador, Dobrynin, and pleaded with him for help with his superiors in Moscow. Kissinger told the Russian, "We can't defend to our people your massive airlift and the Cuban troops." Ford added, "I am for détente but this is difficult for me to explain."[230]

During a year in which both the Senate and House were investigating the intelligence community, the idea that a $60 million covert effort to assist rebel forces in Angola could remain secret is bizarre. On December 13, 1975, Seymour Hersh detailed the full extent of the Angola program in a *New York Times* story. Senate Democrats, led by Richard Clark, began an effort to restrict funds for Angola. Media attention, particularly on *CBS Evening News*, explored parallels between the Angolan involvement and the beginning of the Vietnam intervention. In a five-day series of reports, Walter Cronkite was explicit about the connection, arguing "that America became so heavily involved in Vietnam because the government did not share enough of its decisions with the people," and that the purpose of this reporting was "to try to play our small part in preventing that mistake this time."[231] Senators raised the Vietnam comparison continuously during the debate over the Clark Amendment, which cut off funds for Angolan operations, and it passed in the Senate by a vote of 54 to 22.

Kissinger campaigned hard against the congressional measures, but he had little success in swaying sentiment. He told Ford, "We are living in a nihilistic nightmare," complaining about critics of SALT who talked of the Soviets having too many SS-19 missiles but then "caved" in Angola. Kissinger's outburst misses the degree to which his policies had served to energize critics on both the right and left of the political spectrum. Overselling détente helped the right to portray the continuing competition with the Soviets as a one-way street. Competing with the Soviet Union in a Third World country of no great strategic significance motivated the left. The road Kissinger walked between these two schools of criticism was made more difficult through his own personalization of all foreign policy questions as well as his penchant for secrecy and duplicity. Yet Kissinger's personal failings aside, he was not wrong about the problem facing American foreign policy. Kissinger told Ford that the task America faced was to "manage the emergence of the Soviets to a superpower status without a war." He feared that Congress was depriving the executive of "both carrot and stick," and in an echo of his own criticism of "massive retaliation" two decades earlier, he told Ford, "We will soon be in the position of nuclear war or nothing."[232]

As angry as Kissinger was about Angola, he still believed he could get a deal with the Russians on SALT. He postponed his trip to Moscow from December to January in order to provide more time for the American position to be decided, and especially to get the Defense Department's support. Kissinger continued to see SALT through the prism of détente and domestic politics. Mentioning Henry Jackson, still considered Ford's most likely Democratic opponent, Kissinger told Ford, "We have the SALT agreement within our grasp. We can smash our opponents." He asked the president for some flexibility in negotiating the range of various cruise missiles, both air- and sea-launched missiles, as well as flexibility in dealing with the Soviets over their Backfire bomber. Kissinger feared that the Defense Department was beginning to backtrack under Rumsfeld to a "stonewall position," and urged Ford to tell Rumsfeld that "you are determined to get an agreement and you want them to get with it." Ford's reply was revealing: "I want something very forthcoming because I happen to agree it is good substantively and good politically."[233]

"Good politically" was what Gerald Ford needed in January 1976. His approval rating had hit a low of 39 percent in mid-December. The Senate defeat over Angola did more damage, but Ford continued to support Kissinger and détente. Questioned on a special NBC program on American foreign policy, Ford insisted, "If the American people take a good, calculated look at the benefits from détente, I think they will support it rather than oppose it. And politically, I think any candidate who says abandon détente will be the loser in the long run."[234] Kissinger took a slightly different approach, seeking to place détente and his attempt to get a SALT agreement above any partisan considerations. He stressed that it would be a "tragedy' if "partisan controversy" interfered with his negotiations in Moscow. He also insisted that any SALT agreement would not be "a concession we make to the Soviet Union, but it is an objective that is in our own interest." Although acknowledging that the Angola issue was damaging relations, Kissinger insisted that SALT II was so important that it "bridges differences" between the superpowers.[235] He encouraged his friends in the media to report on the possibilities of an agreement and remind Americans of the importance of détente. Reston wrote a *New York Times* column arguing that even a "limited compromise" on SALT II would be "a political event in the [1976 presidential election] campaign." It would "help the President ease the pressure on détente, and the Russians, and this may have been what Moscow had in mind by inviting Mr. Kissinger to the Soviet Union in the first place."[236] On the eve of Kissinger's Moscow trip, ABC's Ted Koppel began a three-part series on détente, highlighting Kissinger's perspective on its significance in reducing the danger of nuclear war, and stressing the ways it served America's interest.[237]

Kissinger was overly dramatic in telling Anatoly Dobrynin that going to Moscow was committing "political suicide," but his negotiating position was the weakest since he had taken office.[238] He was bringing two different proposals from a divided American government, with an unelected president under siege politically, seeking to influence the Soviets on an issue, Angola, in which they held all the cards. The talks got off to a rocky start when a reporter yelled a question about whether Angola would be discussed, and Brezhnev replied, "I have no questions about Angola. Angola is not my country." Kissinger interjected that it would be discussed, but Brezhnev rudely dismissed this. In private, Kissinger continued to attempt to raise the subject, stating that it was "intolerable" that Cuba had launched an "invasion" and that the superpowers "must exercise restraint." Brezhnev kept demanding, "Are we here to discuss SALT? Or Angola?" He baldly asserted, "There is no Soviet military presence in Angola." At the end of the meeting, Brezhnev remarked in a conciliatory tone, "We hope we can achieve an agreement and that it will help Ford's situation." While welcoming that sentiment, Kissinger added, "I agree you have nothing to gain in Angola. We have nothing to gain in Angola. But 8000 Cubans running around..."[239]

Although annoyed by the Soviet leader's treatment of Angola, Kissinger believed that the talks on a SALT agreement had been fruitful and that a compromise was possible. The Soviets remained rigid on their Backfire bomber, insisting that it was not a long-range bomber and should not be counted under the agreement. Brezhnev even summoned a Soviet general to provide the Americans with a technical discussion of the bomber's capabilities. Moscow showed some flexibility in dealing with the different varieties of American cruise missiles. One possible compromise was a separate agreement to link the Soviet deployment of Backfire bombers with the U.S. right to deploy cruise missiles on twenty-five surface ships, and a willingness to forgo longer-range cruise missiles on submarines.[240] Brezhnev seemed favorably inclined and Kissinger and his team thought they might have a breakthrough.[241]

It was then, as William Hyland noted, that a "bombshell arrived from Washington."[242] The Moscow delegation received an extraordinary cable from National Security Adviser Brent Scowcroft—extraordinary in both what it described and Scowcroft's tone. President Ford had convened an NSC meeting on January 21, which was, as Scowcroft described it to Kissinger, "surreal." Scowcroft described how the Navy's representative, Admiral James Holloway, proceeded to reject any type of Backfire surface-ship cruise missile trade-off. Holloway insisted that the Navy had no "surface ship SLCM [submarine-launched cruise missile] at this time," a statement that blindsided President Ford. Neither Holloway nor Deputy Secretary of Defense William Clements would provide a "logical explanation" of their reversal from an NSC meeting two days earlier, when they accepted the negotiating position that Kissinger took to Moscow. Clements also launched an attack on Brezhnev's discussion of the Backfire bomber, arguing that the Soviet description of its characteristics was so different from American intelligence estimates as to call "into question Soviet good faith" in the negotiations. Scowcroft concluded his description of the meeting to Kissinger by remarking that it was a "complete debacle." His own hypothesis was that the Joint Chiefs did not want a SALT agreement and would come up with any arguments to prevent one. Scowcroft also suggested that an unholy alliance of the Joint Chiefs of Staff, the Arms Control and Disarmament Agency, and the Defense Department were now dug in on terms that would prevent a SALT agreement.[243] These agencies shared a conviction that the United States was falling behind the Soviet Union in its defense spending and nuclear weapons development, and that a SALT II agreement would further the Soviet advantage in strategic weaponry.

Kissinger believed that the Defense Department was "stonewalling" and urged the president to reconvene the NSC "and lay down the law." Ford was, however, reluctant to take on Rumsfeld and the Pentagon, and tried once again to find a compromise formula. Although he continued to promote the importance of a SALT treaty, Kissinger now realized that "he could no longer force the pace on SALT without building up an insurmountable opposition that would rebound against Ford in the election campaign."[244] Moreover, the opposition from the Defense Department was ultimately rooted in the suspicion of many in James Schlesinger's former domain that Kissinger and Ford wanted SALT for largely political and personal reasons, and that Kissinger in particular was willing to play fast and loose with technical issues to get an agreement.[245] Rumsfeld, in particular, believed the Soviets had been violating the first SALT treaty by concealing missile silos and other military infrastructure.[246] More important, he wanted to delay any treaty "that required restricting our cruise missile technologies as part of the deal."[247] To conciliate his opposition, Kissinger accepted a compromise proposal put forward by the Pentagon to set aside the Backfire and cruise missile issues and try to finish a treaty on other matters. When this was presented to the Soviets, Brezhnev told Ford it was a "step backward," and Ford concluded that a SALT treaty was probably impossible before the election.[248]

Kissinger remained focused on helping Ford to be reelected. He told

Ford that he worried about America's position in the world after the Angola debacle, which was "opening the Vietnam wounds again." Kissinger was still certain that "we have a damned good foreign policy" and that the administration needed to go on the offensive in proclaiming that fact. Perhaps remembering his experience with Nixon in the 1972 campaign, he told the president, "We have got to show you are a winner."[249] Privately, Kissinger harbored doubts about Ford and was not always discreet about expressing them. To British friends he mused, "I seem destined to work for losers."[250] At an off-the-record meeting with the *Boston Globe*'s editorial board, Kissinger harshly criticized Ford on Angola, suggesting that he should have imitated Nixon and gone around Congress. Fortunately for Kissinger, the criticism never appeared in print.[251]

KISSINGER'S LAST CAMPAIGN: RONALD REAGAN, AFRICA, AND THE 1976 ELECTION

In an April 1976 letter to his friend Isaiah Berlin, Peter Ramsbotham, the British ambassador in Washington, disagreed with Berlin's description of the "gloom and self-contempt" in the United States, but remarked, "Henry Kissinger has a split personality in Washington—or at least he enjoys the pretense of it." Ramsbotham noted that Kissinger often indulged the "Spenglerian side of his nature—as a historian he probably believes that the democratic pattern in the West, created by the British and Americans, cannot be sustained indefinitely." The ambassador observed, "In his role as Secretary of State, he is actively searching for new initiatives to assert the power of the United States in the world." Ramsbotham doubted whether there had ever been another secretary of state "so optimistically intent on trying to manipulate power in the national interest."[252]

Ramsbotham's insight captured the fundamental tension between the intellectual Kissinger and the political Kissinger. Kissinger spoke pessimistically in private, gloomy about America's political climate as well as his own personal situation. Kissinger's pessimism, especially his musings about America's decline, became "the only red-hot issue" in the race for the Republican nomination.[253] Yet if Kissinger worried about his job security and his legacy, it did not lead him to inactivity. As Ramsbotham noted, he actively searched for new places to apply the Kissinger magic, both to assert American power and, in a lesson he had learned from Nixon in 1972, to help Ford stay president. Kissinger also vigorously defended his foreign policy and attacked his critics, remaining a constant presence in the media. Although some of Ford's staff wanted him out, the president's personal support remained strong, and Kissinger wanted four more years on the job.[254]

There were considerable obstacles standing in Kissinger's path. His low standing with the "McGovernite Congress" marked him as a potential political liability to Ford. Only two days after Kissinger returned from Moscow, the House of Representatives voted overwhelmingly to cut off any covert assistance to pro-Western rebels in Angola. The NBC Nightly News reporter John Hart intoned that many representatives considered their vote a "personal rebuke of Secretary of State Henry Kissinger." Several told Hart that defeating Kissinger was something they would "thoroughly enjoy," and that "Kissinger's influence with Congress was never weaker."[255] Kissinger now sought to both conciliate and fight back, with John Chancellor referring to it as opening "diplomatic negotiations" with Congress. In the report on Kissinger's January 29 testimony, Hart noted that Kissinger left out of his prepared remarks his attack on Congress for not funding covert assistance to the Angolan rebels and went out of his way to state the administration's respect for congressional procedures.[256] When Senator Lowell Weicker, however, raised some damning allegations, including bribes to Italian lawmakers, the overthrow of Allende, and assassination plots, and called them a "national shame," Kissinger took a defiant stance, rejecting the assumptions behind Weicker's questions.[257] Kissinger also used his sense of humor to soften the public perception of his antagonism toward Congress. NBC Nightly News reported that as a "stand-up comedian" Kissinger performed well during a speech in Los Angeles, and the footage included his comment, in reference to the Pike Committee's recent attempt to cite him for contempt of Congress, that his friends thought this unfair—after all, he had "spent seven years concealing his contempt for Congress."[258]

Kissinger benefited from outside events. On December 23, 1975, left-wing terrorists in Greece assassinated the CIA station chief, Richard Welch. Although his killing was not directly connected to the congressional investigations, it allowed the Ford administration to push back against the attacks on the CIA, especially those of the House Intelligence Committee. In late January the full House voted not to release the Pike Committee's report. When the report leaked to *The Village Voice*, which published charges against Kissinger, Kissinger used a news conference to denounce it as a "new version of McCarthyism." When a reporter asked if Kissinger might resign, Kissinger displayed the same thespian ability he had shown eighteen months earlier in Salzburg. With anger in his voice, he said that he would resign if it "was in the interest of American foreign policy," but then asked "whether the style of public debate should be that any public figure can be destroyed by the most irresponsible and flagrant charges and that then the argument should be made that the effectiveness is affected because totally irresponsible and essentially untrue charges are made."[259] His aggressive refutation was the lead story on all three TV networks that evening, along with a story that President Ford told New Hampshire reporters that he would like Kissinger to remain his secretary of state in his next term. Richard Nixon called Kissinger to praise his "honest emotional outrage" and tell him, "I thought your press conference was splendid. It got a good play in the papers which is not important but it played very well on television."[260]

Nixon's phone call, although supportive in tone, was reflective of another problem for Kissinger. Although he had survived Watergate, Kissinger's association with Nixon was another political liability. In February 1976, for reasons that were probably related to their own internal power struggle, the Chinese government invited the disgraced Nixon to visit on the fourth anniversary of his original trip. Nixon reassured Kissinger he would support the administration's policy while in China, and Kissinger urged him "to get them off the idea we are soft on the Russians." Nixon also passed along political gossip that Reagan, who had given a speech two days earlier attacking détente, was getting advice from the former defense secretary Schlesinger. When Kissinger responded, "If [Reagan] keeps going after me I will have to get after him," Nixon counseled him, "Don't do anything by name," and "Stay above the battle."[261]

Although Kissinger wanted to treat Nixon's visit to China as potentially helpful to the administration, Ford and his political advisers worried about the perceptions. Ford's narrow victory over Reagan in the New Hampshire primary on February 24 was a surprise upset. Nevertheless, Ford blamed the Nixon visit to China for the close result, as it reminded voters of Watergate and his controversial pardon.[262] Kissinger was outraged, asking Scowcroft, "What possessed the President to pop off again?" He added that it "makes him look weak to say Nixon can hurt him." After blaming Ford's political advisers, Kissinger told Scowcroft that Ford was making a mistake in not "claiming a success in foreign policy," and in a self-pitying tone, Kissinger complained, "If he does not get out ahead soon in foreign policy I will be destroyed."[263] Scowcroft promised to convey the message, but Ford was thinking differently. In an interview with a Florida newspaper, Ford criticized again the "timing" of Nixon's trip to China. He then dropped a bombshell by saying he was removing the word "détente" from his vocabulary and from now on would talk about "peace through strength."[264] Although the president continued to defend Kissinger, Ford was clearly responding to public sentiment. NBC, in reporting Ford's decision, noted that according to its most recent poll, 64 percent of Americans thought that the Soviet Union was getting more out of détente than the United States was.[265]

Kissinger was disappointed with Ford's decision, expressing anger privately but also showing his sense of humor in public. During Senate hearings a week after Ford's interview, Senator Abraham Ribicoff of Connecticut criticized Kissinger for not joining with the Soviet Union to pressure France and Germany to restrict their sale of nuclear fuel to other countries. Ribicoff dramatically shouted that if we could not work with the Soviets in such a cooperative way, then "we should toss the whole concept of détente into a sewer." Kissinger smiled wryly and replied, "Well, Senator, there's great activity in that direction as it is," and the audience started to laugh. Later in the same testimony, Kissinger defended "the forbidden word" as necessary in a world where the superpowers could destroy each other.[266] Kissinger went on to say that there was no consistent standard for criticizing détente. On the one hand, some criticized the Ford administration for being too soft on the Soviet Union, while on the other hand, some complained that the United States did not work effectively with the Soviet Union against its traditional allies. Kissinger's juxtaposition of these attacks on détente was designed to highlight the middle ground the administration occupied and, by implication, the soundness of the policy.

Kissinger took the offensive with a speech in Boston titled "America's Permanent Interests." The speech came only a few days after the Florida primary, in which Ford handily defeated Reagan, and the White House thought Reagan's attacks on foreign policy had faltered.[267] While not uttering his name, Kissinger criticized Reagan for avoiding the complex issues of foreign policy through "nostalgic simplicities." Kissinger posed a series of questions targeted at both Reagan and the Democratic candidate Henry Jackson: "What do those who speak so glibly about one-way streets or preemptive concessions propose concretely that this country do? What precisely has been given up? What level of confrontation do they seek? What threats would they make? What risks would they run?" He ended his speech with an appeal for "national cohesion" and a grim warning: "The world watches with amazement—our adversaries with glee and our friends with growing dismay—how America seems bent on eroding its influence and destroying its achievements in world affairs through an orgy of recrimination."[268]

Both Reagan and Jackson responded by blasting Kissinger for descending into "partisan politics," with Reagan complaining to the Federal Election Commission, "If an incumbent is to be able to use individuals like Dr. Kissinger, paid for by the public, for campaign purposes, while these individual expenses are not charged against the incumbent's campaign limits, then the limitations in the law are a mere mockery."[269] President Ford reaffirmed in "unequivocal" terms that he wanted Kissinger to remain as secretary of state, and his victory in the Illinois primary four days later seemed to confirm the wisdom of his decision. Kissinger boasted to Ford that he had attended a dinner with Democratic liberals after the speech: "They attacked Jackson and congratulated me on my speech. If Jackson is to the right of you, I think you are in great shape.[270] Eric Sevareid weighed in with a commentary on *CBS Evening News*, citing Kissinger's continuing popularity and 58 percent approval rating, and defending his importance to dealing with the Russians and bringing about Middle East Peace. He was definitely not a "political liability," Sevareid argued.[271]

Then came the North Carolina primary. In the late stages of the Florida campaign, Reagan began attacking the administration over the Panama Canal and the negotiations Kissinger was then undertaking to return the canal to Panama. Although the issue had not turned the tide for Reagan in Florida, it did give him an emotionally powerful applause line: "It's ours! We built it! We paid for it! And we should keep it!"[272] The Panama Canal issue served as something of a substitute for what many Americans felt about the humiliation of the defeat in Vietnam.[273] Reagan stressed the issue in North Carolina, and it helped carry him to an unexpected victory. All three networks stressed the effectiveness of Reagan's attacks on the Panama Canal, Kissinger, and détente.[274] The *NBC Nightly News* reporter John Cochran, covering a Ford appearance in California, remarked that "a lot of Republicans just don't like Henry Kissinger" but that Ford's loyalty to Kissinger remained.[275] Reagan intensified the attack, buying a half hour of airtime on NBC on March 31. The former California governor started his speech focusing on the economy and government spending, but the parts that made the headlines dealt with foreign policy. Reiterating his attack on détente, Reagan quoted from former admiral Elmo Zumwalt's soon-to-be-published memoir. Reagan asserted that Kissinger told Zumwalt, "The day of the U.S. is past and today is the day of the Soviet Union," adding, "My job as Secretary of State is to negotiate the most acceptable second-best position available." Reagan kept the focus on Kissinger, noting that Kissinger's assistant, Helmut Sonnenfeldt, whom Reagan called "[Kissinger's] Kissinger," had expressed "the belief that, in effect, the captive nations should give up any claim of national sovereignty and simply become part of the Soviet Union," or as Reagan put it, "slaves should accept their fate."[276] Declaring that he was not prepared to consign America to the "dustbin of history," Reagan closed his talk with a characteristic appeal to American exceptionalism, "We're Americans and we have a rendezvous with destiny."[277] The speech raised more than $1.5 million.[278]

Kissinger knew that Reagan had hit upon a sensitive issue. Two days before Reagan's speech, Kissinger had gotten into an argument with Secretary of Defense Donald Rumsfeld in front of President Ford, telling Rumsfeld, "The impression that we are slipping is creating a bad impression around the world," with Rumsfeld replying, "But it's true." Kissinger appealed to the president, telling him, "I think the posture to take is that Reagan doesn't know what he's talking about and is irresponsible." Kissinger also wanted to take a tougher and more belligerent stance toward the Cubans. Kissinger had been warning the Cubans about possible American retaliation, including a blockade, if they undertook any more interventions in Africa.[279] Kissinger's harsh rhetoric, which some TV reporters dismissed as "election year toughness," irritated Rumsfeld.[280] The defense secretary told Ford, "I think we will kill ourselves if we make threats and the Congress passes a resolution forbidding any action." Ford responded that he did not want the "communists to get the idea that we would not take drastic action."[281]

Kissinger got a short political reprieve when Ford won the Wisconsin primary less than a week after the Reagan speech. Ford chose to interpret his victory as "fully justifying my faith in Henry Kissinger," and insisted that his staff also support "one of the greatest secretaries of state in American history."[282] Ford's insistence was necessary but not terribly effective. His campaign chair, Rogers Morton, said that Kissinger would leave the administration, and in anticipation of the Texas primary at the end of the month, Ford staffers floated rumors that John Connally would be Ford's choice to replace him.[283] Reporters even enjoyed comparing Ford's comments about Kissinger with the same things he had once said about Nelson Rockefeller before dumping him from the ticket.[284] Kissinger reacted angrily when asked about Morton, replying, "Is Morton running for President?" He was more effective with humor. Referring to the ways in which Deng Xiaoping's recent fall from grace in China was communicated to the West, Kissinger noted his sympathy for the Chinese leader, adding, "I'm in the wall-poster stage myself."[285]

Kissinger had a plan to avoid becoming a wall poster. Earlier in the year, Winston Lord sent Kissinger a memo comparing the current situation in southern Africa with what Kissinger faced in the Middle East in 1973. Noting the Soviet alignment with the "progressive" forces, the Arabs, and the American tie to Israel, the memo argued that Kissinger had successfully realigned that situation and managed to push the Soviets out of the Middle East.[286] Southern Africa now offered the same opportunity for American mediation.[287] In late March, the British had launched a new initiative to try to bring about a peaceful settlement in Rhodesia. However, Ian Smith, the white leader of the breakaway state, rejected it.[288] Despite strong international condemnation, Smith and his supporters had unilaterally declared independence in November 1965 and had weathered economic sanctions and political isolation. However, the collapse of the Portuguese empire and the independence of Angola and Mozambique, along with the increasing Cuban presence in the region, fundamentally changed the environment in which Rhodesia existed. Kissinger now believed that the United States was "the only power capable of affecting the calculations of the parties."[289] When the new head of the CIA, George H. W. Bush, briefed Kissinger with his assessment that the Cubans would be fighting in Rhodesia by the end of the year, Kissinger knew he needed to go to Africa. He told Ford, "Basically I am with the whites in Southern Africa, but in my comments I will support majority rule in Rhodesia. I will say the same about South Africa, but softer."[290]

Kissinger praised Ford for not considering domestic politics in changing his policy toward southern Africa.[291] But just as he had with détente, Kissinger was thinking of the general election. He saw the political benefit for the administration in embracing majority rule in southern Africa, thereby refuting a moralistic attack on foreign policy by the Democrats. With the guerrilla war against the Rhodesian government intensifying, and an explosion of unrest in South Africa's cities, predictions about a coming racial war were increasingly common, and an American effort to prevent this would attract voters.[292] The possibility that the Cubans would take an active role, supported by the Soviets, brought Cold War considerations into play as well, although Kissinger recognized that America could never intervene militarily to support racially discriminatory governments such as Rhodesia's or South Africa's. Kissinger now undertook significant efforts to build domestic support in favor of his initiatives.[293] This change in policy corresponded with Ford's own sense of right and wrong, his innate "decency," as well as his recognition that the American national interest would be better served by placing America foursquare in support of majority rule. But political motives were hardly absent. Martin Luther King, Jr., once remarked, "There are moments when the politically expedient can be morally wise."[294] Outside the moral issues at stake, Kissinger undoubtedly hoped that a diplomatic triumph in Africa would also restore some luster to his own reputation as well.[295]

In April 1976 in Lusaka, the capital of Zambia, Kissinger delivered one of his most important and moving speeches, affirming that America supported "self-determination, majority rule, equal rights, and human dignity for all the peoples of southern Africa—in the name of moral principle, international law, and world peace."[296] He went on to say, "Our support for this principle [majority rule] in southern Africa is not simply a matter of foreign policy but an imperative of our moral heritage," and that the Rhodesia regime would face America's "unrelenting opposition until a negotiated settlement is achieved." It was an uncommonly idealistic speech, leading the Zambian president, Kenneth Kaunda, to weep openly.[297] Despite concerns about how the African leaders might receive him, Kissinger handled the trip in a skillful fashion, winning accolades not only from Kaunda, who was considered pro-Western, but also from the more skeptical Julius Nyerere of Tanzania. Kissinger told Nyerere that the Arab countries were suspicious before 1973, but less so now that "we're giving $1 billion to Egypt in aid and [Sadat] has got more territory back than any other Arab leader." Kissinger added, "I like to think we can do the same with Africa on a cooperative basis, and work with you."[298] Nyerere later told a British diplomat that Kissinger might be able to push forward an agreement on majority rule and "there may yet be a chance for the war in Rhodesia to be brought to an end more quickly than had earlier seemed possible."[299] Avoiding the hubris he'd showed on other occasions, Kissinger told African leaders he was there to listen and learn, and insisted, "African problems should be solved by African solutions."[300]

Although Kissinger was thousands of miles away, Ronald Reagan kept his focus on him. Reacting to the Lusaka speech, Reagan said, "I'm afraid that we're going to have a massacre." He added even more somber language: "We seem to be embarking on a policy of dictating to the people of southern Africa and running the risk of increased violence and bloodshed in an area already beset with tremendous antagonism and difficulties." Reagan's attack appealed to racial backlash without touching on domestic issues like busing, crime, or affirmative action, and it connected to supporters of George Wallace, who could—and did—cross over to vote for Reagan in Texas.[301] Kissinger was blamed when Reagan won a sweeping victory in Texas on May 1. William Safire argued in his *New York Times* column that Ford's defeat had come from underestimating Reagan and not firing Kissinger.[302] Robert Michel, the assistant House Republican leader, said Kissinger's trip had a "devastating effect" in the South and that he should be "muzzled."[303] The Senate minority whip, Robert Griffin, said on *NBC Nightly News* that one Republican political adviser at a leadership meeting told Ford that Kissinger "ought to go."[304]

Kissinger returned from Africa on May 7, with only his wife and low-level State Department officials there to greet him. Marvin Kalb made the telling point that in the past, President Ford would have been there.[305] Kissinger told reporters that all things being equal, he would rather not stay on for another four years, a formulation that left open the possibility for change if the president asked him to stay. At the same time, Kissinger also marshaled a defense of his record and position, receiving considerable help from friends in the media. ABC's Ted Koppel delivered a commentary noting that Ford's campaign rested on the "twin pillars" of an improving economy and a successful "imaginative" foreign policy. Kissinger was key to the foreign policy, particularly in dealing with the Soviet Union and the Middle East, and firing him might cost the president support from middle-of-the-road voters.[306] NBC's Richard Valeriani, in a favorable summary of the Africa trip, remarked that despite the political controversies, polls showed that Kissinger remained "the most respected public figure in the country."[307] Some of Kissinger's fiercest critics also applauded the change in African policy. John Osborne in *The New Republic* praised the new policy, saying, "However ignoble its immediate origins and motivation, the revised African policy that Gerald Ford authorized and Henry Kissinger enunciated, is *right*. It is right morally, and I believe, will in the long run prove to be right politically and in terms of national security."[308] By the end of the month, Ford, despite being behind Reagan in the delegate count, said again, to the Los Angeles Press Club, that he wanted Kissinger to stay on as secretary of state in a Ford administration.[309]

In early June, Kissinger took a short break from his Africa initiatives to fly to a meeting of the Organization of American States (OAS) in Chile. Even though the Church Committee report had made clear that Nixon and Kissinger worked to overthrow the Allende regime, Kissinger used his trip to Santiago to try to reinforce in public his new image. With his African diplomacy in the headlines, Kissinger now spoke as a supporter of democracy in foreign policy and "referred to human rights in 40 percent of his speeches."[310] He delivered a speech at the OAS meeting in which he denounced the Chilean regime for its "violations of elemental international standards of human rights," and predicted that unless Chile undertook reforms, this would hurt relations with the United States.[311] Kissinger's public alignment with the cause of human rights was not, however, matched by any change in his personal diplomacy with dictators like General Pinochet. Privately he assured the Chilean leader, "We are sympathetic with what you are trying to do here." Kissinger explained that he faced "massive domestic problems, in all branches of the government especially Congress, but also in the Executive, over the issue of human rights."[312] Two days later Kissinger made the same appeal to the new Argentine military government of General Videla, which had come to power in a coup in March 1976. The regime declared martial law, and over the next years the "Dirty War" would take the lives of thousands of Argentines, many of whom were simply "disappeared." As with Indonesia and Chile, the United States was more concerned with supporting an anti-communist ally than defending human rights. Kissinger told Argentina's foreign minister, César Augusto Guzzetti, "We are aware you are in a difficult period. It is a curious time, when political, criminal, and terrorist activities tend to merge without any clear separation. We understand you must establish authority." Kissinger did try to encourage the Argentines to "get back quickly to normal procedures" and not focus on terrorism alone. Kissinger told the Argentine leader, "We want you to succeed. We do not want to harass you. I will do what I can. Of course, you understand, that means I will be harassed. But I have discovered that after the personal abuse reaches a certain level you become invulnerable." Kissinger did assure Guzzetti that "no matter what happens," he would come back to Argentina for the World Cup in 1978.[313]

After his return from South America, Kissinger arranged a meeting in Bodenmais, a remote Bavarian village in Germany, with the South African prime minister, John Vorster. Kissinger believed that South Africa held the key to progress in the region.[314] On June 16, 1976, South African police opened fire on children in Soweto protesting the use of Afrikaans in school. The shooting led to the worst rioting across South Africa in its history, with more than one hundred people killed during the first ten days of protests.[315] The United Nations condemned South Africa for the Soweto killings, and Kissinger's planned meeting with Vorster looked to be in doubt. Nevertheless, Kissinger went ahead with it, perhaps thinking that the domestic crisis might make Vorster even more amenable to abandoning Rhodesia and reducing South Africa's international isolation.[316]

Kissinger was sympathetic in his approach to Vorster, admitting that he was "a newcomer to Africa," but warning him that Rhodesia was "an unwinnable situation, no matter how long it takes, whether five or ten years." Comparing the situation with that in Algeria, whose French colonists had actually been there longer than the whites had been in Rhodesia, Kissinger predicted eventual defeat. He offered Vorster two choices: either work to promote majority rule in Rhodesia or play for time while the situation grew worse. It was, as Kissinger put it, "as fundamental a decision as any South African prime minister had ever faced."[317] Kissinger also made it clear that the United States could do little to help Smith's Rhodesia, referencing America's own racial politics. "With fifty percent of our combat troops being black because of our all-volunteer Army," there was really no "domestic situation in which we could support Smith."[318] Vorster wanted a "reasonable deal" for Rhodesia's whites that he could sell to both the Rhodesian prime minister, Ian Smith, and his own electorate in South Africa. This would have to involve financial inducements to prevent a rapid white exodus, some guarantees of "minority rights," a "moderate" black leader, and an end to the guerrilla war. The devil would be in the details of such a program, but Kissinger now thought his diplomacy might allow the United States to score a major success in Africa less than a year after one of its most humbling defeats.

Critics have attacked Kissinger for his dealings with the apartheid regime.[319] In Kissinger's defense, it is clear that he approached these negotiations as he had his Middle East talks, with a sense of what an agreement that would be in America's national interest and, coincidentally, in the political interest of the Ford administration, would look like. He hoped Zambia's Kaunda or Tanzania's Nyerere would play the role of Sadat, a moderate leader willing to engage with the despised white regime as Sadat had with the hated Jewish state. He would treat South Africa in a manner similar to how he'd treated Israel, offering the South Africans sympathy and reassurance but insisting that they make tough compromises, at first at the expense of the white Rhodesians, but in the future on such issues as Namibia, which South Africa still controlled, and the apartheid system itself. In the case of both the Middle East and South Africa, Kissinger was talking about step-by-step diplomacy, usually by creating a certain degree of "creative ambiguity" in the terms of the agreements he discussed, but pushing the process forward. Unfortunately, Kissinger's methods, and any gradual approaches to a moral issue, are always open to condemnation by those who want more immediate and sweeping action but who may underestimate the obstacles and the human costs that action might entail.[320]

Kissinger left his meeting with Vorster and returned to America, but not before stopping in Britain to brief Prime Minister James Callaghan and Foreign Secretary Anthony Crosland. Over the next two months the United States and Britain hammered out the details of the deal to offer the Smith government. Some of the British officials were concerned that with his eagerness to get an agreement before the American elections, Kissinger was misrepresenting the degree to which the white Rhodesians and the African states were willing to agree.[321] With the Ford-Reagan contest still unsettled, Kissinger did not seek to resolve the specifics, hoping to avoid anything that the Reagan opposition could denounce. In the weeks before the Republican National Convention in mid-August, he even went on a tour through remote Southwest Asia, visiting Pakistan and Afghanistan, and staying out of the news. He returned to attend the final day of the convention.[322] The convention's adoption of the "Morality in Foreign Policy" platform plank was a bitter blow to Kissinger, with its criticism of his détente policies and its extolling of Aleksandr Solzhenitsyn as a "great beacon of human courage."[323] Kissinger asked Rockefeller, "How can the President permit this to happen and not look like a weak coward?"[324] His anger is also seen in his bitter reaction to the North Korean "tree-cutting attack," when North Korean soldiers brutally attacked American soldiers who had come into the demilitarized zone to prune a tree, killing two men. Kissinger wanted a much more forceful response, including the possible shelling of the North Korean barracks. Ford rejected such choices in favor of simply going back into the DMZ and cutting down the tree. After making a tasteless joke about using the wood from the tree as coffins for the dead soldiers, Kissinger said to Scowcroft, "Do you think I made it clear to the president how unenchanted I was with him?"[325] As angry and disappointed as Kissinger was with Ford's response to the Korean incident and his refusal to defend Kissinger's foreign policy, Kissinger still wanted the president to win—desperately. At a meeting on August 30, with the convention now ended and the campaign beginning, Kissinger told Ford, "What we need to think about is your political situation. I don't think Americans like blacks. I don't want another Texas situation." Ford responded that if Kissinger could get South African cooperation, Americans would view things differently. He added, "I think if it is right, we should do it and the political consequences will come out alright." The president closed the meeting by telling his secretary of state: "Now that we've gotten rid of that son-of-a-bitch Reagan, we can do what's right."[326]

Kissinger left for Zurich to meet again with Vorster and get him to agree to deliver Ian Smith. Vorster accepted that responsibility, and Kissinger agreed he would come to South Africa and meet with Smith himself. At a press conference after the meeting, Kissinger tried to avoid any wording that might offer an uncomfortable comparison with "peace is at hand." "Should I say, 'progress' is at hand?" he joked with reporters. Although Kissinger certainly wanted an African success to help Ford's campaign, he also recognized that it would enhance his credibility if he could say his approach enjoyed bipartisan support. When he got back to Washington, he contacted the former secretary of state Dean Rusk, hoping to use him as a channel to the Carter campaign. Since one crucial factor in the negotiations was the American financial commitment to help fund the transition to majority rule, he wanted to see if Jimmy Carter might agree to avoid criticizing the administration's African policy. Carter asked for assurances that African leaders and Congress be kept informed of Kissinger's negotiations, and then agreed not to discuss the issue. Kissinger told Rusk to tell the Democratic contender, "I think he is behaving very patriotically." Carter's patriotism is clear, but it may have been an easier decision because, at the time of Kissinger's request, the Democrat was almost thirty points ahead of Ford in the polls.[327]

Kissinger headed back to Africa the following week, and his return to shuttle diplomacy was the lead story on all three TV networks. The importance of Kissinger's efforts was also clear in the reporting of the ongoing violence in South Africa itself, which had spread throughout the country. Two days before Kissinger was to arrive in Pretoria, Cape Town's harbor was shut down by a strike.[328] Kissinger made his way to the capitals of two of the African frontline states, facing hostile demonstrations in Tanzania and Zambia, and pessimism from their leaders about his chances of brokering a settlement. The evening news continued to highlight the dire possibilities of racial war in southern Africa. President Kaunda told American reporters that Kissinger had only "days left to avert a race war."[329] With this grim forecast, Kissinger then became the first American secretary of state to visit South Africa. Reporting back to Ford, he told the president that "after [his] seven painful hours of meetings with Ian Smith," the Rhodesians had "substantially accepted our proposals." The central concession was the agreement to achieve majority rule within two years. Negotiations would begin immediately on an interim government that "shares power, giving blacks a majority of the Cabinet but giving whites the safeguard of a 50–50 split on a key executive body, the Council of State." In return—and the Rhodesians and South Africans saw it as a "package" arrangement—UN sanctions and the guerrilla war would come to an end.

Kissinger came away from the negotiations with great respect for both Smith and Vorster, whom he felt "behaved honorably" in what could have ended up being a "disastrous" fate. His feelings about the black African leaders were not as warm, although he told Ford, "I believe we do all we can to see it through with care and make it work, for the sake of both communities." He continued to fear leaks and opposition from radical groups and the Soviets, who complained bitterly about his involvement in the region. Kissinger recognized that his "agreement" left many issues ambiguous and confused, though he did not fully acknowledge that to Ford. He did caution the president, however, "This is Africa, and one can never count on anything until it is completed."[330] If he were honest with himself, Kissinger would have acknowledged that there were multiple unresolved issues that could lead to a breakdown in the talks. Although the Israelis had driven him crazy in the Middle East negotiations, their insistence on the specifics of each kilometer withdrawn or number of troops allowed made the implementation of the agreement more durable. The American guarantees, especially in intelligence monitoring, were also significant in making the agreements hold. In the case of this agreement on Rhodesia, Kissinger was back in his Paris mode with the Vietnamese, using "creative ambiguity" and leaving a large number of issues unresolved and uncertain, subject to subsequent talks. He admitted to Bill Scranton, his friend and the ambassador to the United Nations, "My strategy, which is not heroic is to keep the thing sufficiently confused to exhaust them a bit . . . I am going to keep it confused until somebody's nerves go."[331]

On Friday, September 24, 1976, Ian Smith addressed his nation and accepted the proposals hammered out between Kissinger and the South Africans. In a speech that contained seven explicit references to "Dr. Kissinger," Smith made it clear that "this agreement doesn't give us the answer which we would have liked." Keeping Rhodesia "in the free world" was a goal shared with "Dr. Kissinger," and Smith made it clear he had "categorical assurance" from Kissinger that once this "package deal" was accepted, "there will be a cessation of terrorism." By describing the arrangement as a "package deal," Smith implied there would not be further negotiations. Smith also insisted that the agreement provided that in the interim government, the "Ministers of Defense and of Law and Order would be white," something the frontline presidents and guerrillas had not yet accepted.[332] Other provisions also angered the Africans, including Smith's description of the "trust fund" established to help whites during the transition. These would be among the many reasons that when the Rhodesia talks moved to Geneva, the British failed to broker a settlement. It would take more than three years and almost a completely different cast of characters before the newly named Zimbabwe would come into existence.[333]

Smith's acceptance of the principle and inevitability of majority rule was a Kissinger accomplishment.[334] Yet the domestic political impact of the Rhodesian achievement did not live up to Kissinger's hopes, and the television news coverage was nowhere as enthusiastic as it had been with his Middle Eastern diplomacy. *Time* magazine did call the agreement "the spectacular climax of a carefully and astutely planned push for peace."[335] *NBC News* described it as a "triumph for Henry Kissinger's shuttle diplomacy," while ABC's Howard K. Smith noted how this affirmed America's important role in the world. On CBS, Eric Sevareid credited Kissinger with getting "the train on the track," even though Britain would have to drive it toward an agreement.[336] President Ford issued a statement thanking everyone for their efforts, including the South Africans, but left out any reference to Kissinger.[337] The omission was an intended one, and reflected the Ford campaign's strategy against Jimmy Carter. Carter was an intelligent and disciplined campaigner who had courted diverse constituencies with great skill, avoiding offense and managing to be all things to all people. The Ford campaign saw him as an unprincipled opportunist, and thought Americans liked their candidate better but doubted his competence. What they believed they needed to do was "mobilize that good will" toward Ford and make sure that he personified "strong leadership." Mentioning Kissinger—whom Carter asserted was actually in charge of foreign policy—was not a way to personify such leadership.[338]

Kissinger intensely resented this, but Ford's handlers were right. Carter had long focused on Kissinger and his dominance of foreign policy as a political weakness for Ford, and his criticisms cut to the heart of Kissinger's style of foreign policy. In his first major foreign policy address, Carter had emphasized, "I believe that the foreign policy spokesman of our country should be the President, and not the Secretary of State." In what was a clear attack on the Kissinger style, Carter argued, "The conduct of foreign policy should be a sustained process of decision and action, and not a series of television spectaculars."[339] Carter described Kissinger as carrying out "a kind of secretive, 'Lone Ranger' foreign policy, a one-man policy of international adventure."[340] Carter claimed that he supported the objectives of détente but argued that "the Secretary of State has tied its success too closely to his personal reputation," and that as a result, Kissinger was "giving up too much and asking for too little." As Carter prepared for the foreign policy debate with Ford, Zbigniew Brzezinski, his chief foreign policy adviser, told him: "A major purpose of the debate on foreign policy would be *to leave the public with a clear impression that Ford has provided no leadership.* In other words, even if Ford claims successes for his foreign policy, the public should be left with the view—assuming he is convincing—that it was not due to him."[341] At the beginning of their October 6, 1976, foreign policy debate, Carter said, "As far as foreign policy goes, Mr. Kissinger has been the president of this country."[342]

Kissinger played a key role in preparing Ford for the foreign policy debate. Kissinger wanted the president to go on the offensive in defending "his" foreign policy, urging him to hit back hard at Carter's charges of a lack of a "moral basis." Ford emphasized how he would stress, "What is more moral than peace? What is more moral than bringing peace in the Middle East? What is more moral than what we're doing in Southern Africa?" Kissinger undoubtedly was pleased as Ford listed his diplomatic efforts, but then he warned Ford that Carter would charge that Kissinger himself was "running foreign policy." Kissinger, showing his own annoyance with Ford's political operatives, told the president, "The White House puts out that . . . you overrule me frequently. That makes you look weak, as if we compete." In Kissinger's view, Ford should tell the nation, "We are a partnership, with you making the decisions. We shape things in discussion—it is not a case of competing views." Ford did not respond directly to this bit of Kissinger advice, having been receiving the opposite advice from his political people.

The one section of the briefing where Ford may have listened too carefully came when Kissinger started talking about Eastern Europe and the "Sonnenfeldt Doctrine," the charge Reagan had used in the primaries. The Sonnenfeldt Doctrine suggested that the United States should accept Soviet control over Eastern Europe. Kissinger told Ford that there was no such thing, noting, "You visited three countries in Eastern Europe to symbolize our commitment to freedom in Eastern Europe." He added, "On Helsinki, the first point is there were 35 nations there, including the Vatican, not just the United States. Second, when he says it recognized sphere of influence, it shows Carter doesn't know what he is talking about. Helsinki says nothing about the Soviet Union in Europe. It says that borders can't be changed by force, but only by peaceful means. To whose advantage is this? Ours or the Soviet Union's, with 70 divisions on the border?" Kissinger was referring to the massive Soviet military presence in Eastern Europe and telling Ford that the Soviet acceptance of the idea that borders could only be changed peacefully disadvantaged them far more than it did the United States. What good was all that military power if it could not be used? At this point Kissinger confessed to Ford, "I am getting worked up. But this guy really burns me. He is super liberal and now he is turning tough."[343]

Kissinger's words always had a strong influence on Ford, and the president must have been impressed by how forcefully Kissinger defended Helsinki and the administration's policies on Eastern Europe.[344] When during the debate the *New York Times* reporter Max Frankel asked the question about Helsinki, in a way that implied the Soviet Union and communism were winning in Europe, Ford was ready to respond, but in a way that was a strange mashup of the advice he had received. He started out by defending his dealings with the Soviets, the Vladivostok accords, and the grain deals, but then switched to Helsinki: "If we turn to Helsinki—I am glad you raised it, Mr. Frankel—in the case of Helsinki, 35 nations signed an agreement, including the Secretary of State for the Vatican. I can't under any circumstances believe that His Holiness the Pope would agree, by signing that agreement, that the 35 nations have turned over to the Warsaw Pact nations the domination of Eastern Europe. It just isn't true. And if Mr. Carter alleges that His Holiness, by signing that, has done it, he is totally inaccurate." Along with saying the "Warsaw Pact" instead of the "Soviet Union," Ford jumbled some of Kissinger's points here—that Helsinki involved thirty-five nations, that the Vatican attended, and that Carter didn't know what he was talking about. But if he had stopped here, this might have gone unnoticed, and been seen as a rather clumsy appeal to Catholic voters. Ford continued: "Now, what has been accomplished by the Helsinki agreement? Number one, we have an agreement where they notify us and we notify them of any military maneuvers that are to be undertaken. They have done it in both cases where they've done so." And then he went on: "There is no Soviet domination of Eastern Europe, and there never will be under a Ford administration." Frankel's bemused reaction to Ford's last statement showed how quickly he recognized that Ford had misspoken, and his willingness to give the president another chance: "I'm sorry, could I just follow—did I understand you to say, sir, that the Russians are not using Eastern Europe as their own sphere of influence and occupying most of the countries there and making sure with their troops that it's a Communist zone, whereas on our side of the line the Italians and the French are still flirting with the possibility of communism?" Ford did not recognize the life preserver Frankel had tossed him and plunged further into the morass, again using some of Kissinger's formulations, but in the wrong way: "I don't believe, Mr. Frankel, that the Yugoslavians consider themselves dominated by the Soviet Union. I don't believe that the Romanians consider themselves dominated by the Soviet Union. I don't believe that the Poles consider themselves dominated by the Soviet Union. Each of those countries is independent, autonomous; it has its own territorial integrity. And the United States does not concede that those countries are under the domination of the Soviet Union. As a matter of fact, I visited Poland, Yugoslavia, and Romania, to make certain that the people of those countries understood that the President of the United States and the people of the United States are dedicated to their independence, their autonomy, and their freedom."

Jimmy Carter pounced quickly, arguing that Ford had just implicitly endorsed the Sonnenfeldt Doctrine by saying that the United States was accepting the current state of the relations between Eastern Europe and the Soviet Union even though it actually involved Soviet domination of these countries. He then translated Ford's answer into an effective political attack for an American ethnic audience: "I would like to see Mr. Ford convince the Polish Americans and the Czech Americans and the Hungarian Americans in this country that those countries don't live under the domination and supervision of the Soviet Union behind the Iron Curtain." Carter very cleverly substituted Czechoslovakia and Hungary for Yugoslavia and Romania, as both had been invaded by the Russians and both had sizable ethnic populations in the United States.

A newspaper headline the next day read, "Ford's Denial of 'Soviet Domination' Stands out as One of the Great Presidential Gaffes of the Past Century," although a majority of those sampled immediately after the debate called Ford the winner.[345] Kissinger certainly thought so, and called Ford to tell him what a great job he had done.[346] Unfortunately for Ford, the postdebate press conference focused on the "No Soviet domination" line, and the next day all three network newscasts led off with the story. John Chancellor began his newscast by saying it "was a bad news day for Gerald Ford" and that his comments about Eastern Europe had elicited "a storm of protest."[347] By the next evening, polls judged Carter the winner in the debate by a 61 to 19 percent margin.[348] The gap, which had been closing between Ford and Carter, now started to widen again. By the time Ford made a public apology and expressed his own regret that he "did not express [him]self clearly," the damage had been done. As one campaign chronicler put it, "There was no doubt that the engines of the president's comeback drive had stalled." One study concluded, "Ford's gaffe was significant, not because it alienated a narrow ethnic constituency, but because it seemed to prove the point stressed by Reagan and Carter, that Ford lacked the intelligence to govern."[349]

Meeting with Kissinger a few days after the debate, Ford asked him rather plaintively, "Are you going to resign because your president let you down?" Kissinger responded quickly, "Don't even think of what happened. One little glitch." Ford jumped at the compliment, telling Kissinger, "I thought I did well except for that one slip." Kissinger added, "You have confirmed in that debate the country's need for you and the disaster that Carter would be." Kissinger regretted only that Ford did not "get the chance to conceptualize."[350] What Kissinger politely ignored was that Ford had taken various parts of Kissinger's advice for answering the Sonnenfeldt Doctrine question but assembled them in the wrong way and with the wrong emphasis. Ford had faith in Kissinger and in Kissinger's concept of foreign policy, but he was not equipped to explain it. Kissinger's critics recognized this problem and were unmerciful. John Osborne wrote, "The President had been drenched for two years in the subtleties of Henry Kissinger's view that the US had to recognize the Soviet presence in Eastern Europe as a fact without either condemning or condoning it."[351] William Safire was even harsher: "The verbal gaffe was the President's, but the basic political blunder of Helsinki's was the Secretary of State's. Henry does not realize that to this day."[352] When Kissinger came to meet with Ford the day the Safire article appeared, Ford immediately said, "Before you say a word, I read the Safire article. He is a no good son-of-a-bitch. I don't believe a thing he said, so forget about it."[353] It was a touching gesture of loyalty from the president to his secretary of state, especially since Safire also noted that Kissinger had been denigrating Ford to close friends.

Ford's defeat on November 2, 1976, by only 2 percentage points, brought an end to Henry Kissinger's official role in shaping American foreign policy. Few would have predicted then that he would never return to the U.S. government in an official capacity shaping foreign policy. However, few also would have imagined that he would continue to exercise influence over foreign policy for the next four decades.

7

"WE DO NOT WANT HENRY KISSINGER ON THE COVER OF *TIME* MAGAZINE"

Citizen Kissinger and American Foreign Policy Since 1977

THE SUMMER OF 1983 was a low point for President Ronald Reagan. Although the economy was recovering from the worst recession since the 1930s, and his approval rating had inched up from its dismal 35 percent in January, Reagan's Central American policy was deeply unpopular. The Reagan team argued that the United States needed to support the government of El Salvador, despite that government's inability or unwillingness to control right-wing death squads. Reagan also backed the "contra" rebels, who fought against the Sandinista government of Nicaragua. With Vietnam a fresh memory, Congress reflected the public's skepticism, threatening to cut off funding for U.S. efforts in both countries. To avoid this clash, congressional leaders encouraged the president to follow a time-honored Washington tradition and set up a bipartisan commission to study the issue. Reagan accepted the idea and appointed the former secretary of state Henry Kissinger as its chair. Critics on the left, such as Congressmen Ed Markey of Massachusetts and David Obey of Wisconsin, argued that Kissinger could not be trusted and would simply endorse the White House's policy. Congressman Norman Mineta of California complained about appointing "the man who gave us the bombing of Cambodia."[1] On the right, Senator Jesse Helms remarked that he could think of "no one lower" on his list for such a position. Other politicians, however, praised the move, with Senator Charles Grassley of Iowa calling it a step toward peace, and even Henry Jackson, who had once been one of Kissinger's fiercest critics, saying the appointment was a "good beginning" to restoring bipartisan cooperation on foreign policy.

Kissinger continued to fascinate the media. In his commentary slot on *NBC Nightly News*, John Chancellor remarked that in 1980 when he asked one of Ronald Reagan's aides if there were a position for Kissinger in the new administration, the aide answered, "We want Ronald Reagan on the cover of *Time* magazine. We do not want Henry Kissinger on the cover of *Time* magazine." Things had certainly changed, Chancellor remarked, as the Reagan administration now "hitched its wagon to a star." Kissinger's appointment was, in Chancellor's words, "an admission of failure" in rallying the public behind their policy.[2] A few days later, Dan Rather on CBS reported Kissinger's meeting with President Reagan, noting there were more reporters and cameras there to cover Kissinger than could fit into the pressroom at the State Department. Both CBS with Rather and *NBC Nightly News* played a portion of the press conference where a reporter mistakenly referred to Kissinger as the current secretary of state, rather than George Shultz. Despite Kissinger's claim that he was not taking over policy on Central America, the underlying theme of the coverage was that "he's back"—that Henry Kissinger was ready once again to take the helm of American foreign policy.[3]

That did not happen. After finishing the report and presenting the findings to the president, Kissinger left the administration. At an off-the-record press conference in January 1984, he said he was not looking to stay in public life, implying that he realized that his role had been to help "sell" the Reagan policy in Central America, not shape it. With the exception of a brief moment

in 2002 when George W. Bush appointed him to chair the 9/11 Commission—
and then Kissinger withdrew less than two weeks later—Kissinger would, as
his biographer Walter Isaacson later put it, "remain on the sidelines, looming
large but never summoned back on the field."[4] This "retirement" from public
office was more akin to that of an ex-president than an ordinary cabinet officer, as Kissinger remained a celebrity figure of enormous influence and continuing media interest, commenting on the foreign policies of his successors
and opining on America's engagement in world politics. It may not have been
what he expected when he left power at age fifty-three in January 1977, but
American foreign policy after Kissinger would constitute a sustained dialogue with the policies and ideas he had propounded. Kissinger used the media and his political skills to remain relevant to the debates on American
foreign policy for the next four decades. Ultimately, he came to embody a
type of foreign policy, ruthlessly geopolitical in its pursuit of America's national interests, receiving the adjective "Kissingerian."

THE CARTER YEARS: KISSINGER AS
SHADOW SECRETARY OF STATE

Parliamentary systems have a group of opposition party members who serve
as the "shadow cabinet" to the government, providing an alternative perspective on policies and ready to assume power in the wake of an election. Henry
Kissinger assumed this role during the presidency of Jimmy Carter. He hovered over the shoulder of his friend Secretary of State Cyrus Vance, competed
with his rival National Security Adviser Zbigniew Brzezinski, appeared before congressional committees, and made pronouncements on foreign policy
that official Washington, and the rest of the world, listened to intently. As the
most prominent foreign policy analyst and commentator in the country,
Kissinger alternated between providing the Carter administration with
helpful political support for some policies and harshly criticizing others. The
expectation that he would be back in a position of power soon was widely
shared, and Kissinger cultivated it as well. In an interview on his last day in
office, he told *The New York Times* that he was passing on to his successor "a

world that is at peace, more at peace than in any previous transition, in which, in addition, in every problem area solutions can be foreseen even if they have not been fully achieved and the framework for solutions exist, in which the agenda of most international negotiations was put forward by the United States." He summarized this wordy description of his achievements by adding, "It cannot be entirely an accident, and it cannot be a series of tactical improvisations."[5] Network television assessments were also sympathetic and favorable, playing to Kissinger's celebrity image. ABC even covered Meadowlark Lemon of the Harlem Globetrotters presenting a jersey to Kissinger in honor of his 650,000 miles of "globe-trotting," as Kissinger remarked that the number "1" on the jersey accorded with his own assessment of himself.[6]

Kissinger found it hard to leave behind the perquisites of power. He borrowed Nelson Rockefeller's private plane for his first trip back to New York and held on to his Secret Service protection until April, when President Carter canceled it. Kissinger then hired the Secret Service agent who had been in charge of his protection.[7] It took a year before the NO PARKING signs were removed from in front of his Washington home, a delay the media interpreted as a sign of his continuing power.[8] Carter, who made it a point to be seen carrying his own luggage, told his cabinet that his administration would economize, avoiding the "ostentatiousness" of Kissinger's foreign travels.[9] Carter allowed the State Department to pay the $10,500 for Kissinger's official portrait to be painted, even though he decreed that in the future color photographs would be used. Kissinger, who rejected the first portrait because it made him look like "a dwarf," used the occasion of the unveiling to remark that it would undoubtedly be one of his most fulfilling moments, "at least until they do Mount Rushmore."[10]

With his sense of humor and the "force of his personality and mind," Kissinger was determined not to "recede into obscurity." Within the first months of his departure from office, he secured a $5 million contract for his memoirs, a five-year deal with NBC to provide commentary, and a professorship at Georgetown University. Along with these deals went consultant arrangements with Chase Manhattan and Goldman Sachs, the beginning of what would eventually become his own international consulting firm a few years later. The money stirred controversy, with *The Washington Post* characterizing Kissinger as a "mini-conglomerate by taking on a dazzling array of paid and unpaid positions."[11] The money helped sustain his costly lifestyle as well as the various legal battles he would engage in, fighting over the possession of his papers as well as the lawsuits of former colleagues like Morton Halperin, who felt Kissinger was responsible for the wiretaps used on him. Most important, Kissinger still commanded the national stage, remaining a dominant figure on issues related to American foreign policy. A *Washington Post* profile in January 1978 titled "Citizen Kissinger" captured his status in the headline: "Out of Office Isn't Out of Power."[12]

One reason Kissinger remained so central was that Jimmy Carter both encouraged and at times was unable to contain a variety of voices speaking about his foreign policy. While deliberately avoiding another "Lone Ranger," the main story of the Carter years quickly became the rivalry between Secretary of State Vance and National Security Adviser Brzezinski, with the UN ambassador, Andrew Young, also making his voice heard.[13] To some, this foreign policy cacophony contrasted negatively with Kissinger's domination of the previous administration. Carter wanted to embrace a moral vision in foreign policy, highlighting human rights issues and breaking with the secretive approach he identified with Kissinger. He expressed this idealism in his commencement address at the University of Notre Dame in May 1977, proclaiming, "I believe we can have a foreign policy that is democratic, that is based on fundamental values, and that uses power and influence, which we have, for humane purposes. We can also have a foreign policy that the American people both support and, for a change, know about and understand." The most famous expression from this speech, and the one that would come back to haunt him, was Carter's claim that America was now free "of that inordinate fear of communism" that had led the United States to embrace dictatorships for Cold War expediency.[14] At the same time, Carter also supported a number of objectives, including continuing détente with the Soviet Union, peace in the Middle East, and the normalization of relations with China, which were in continuity with Kissinger's policies.

Remarking that he had "developed great compassion for my successors,"

Kissinger was initially cautious in his comments on the administration's foreign policy. In a New York speech in September 1977, he remarked, "The new Administration deserves the opportunity to develop its policies without harassment and second guessing." Kissinger went on to extol the value of bipartisanship in foreign policy, making the case that "our country cannot uproot its whole foreign policy every four or eight years" without becoming a "major factor of instability in the world." Kissinger recognized that some might see in his plea for continuity in policy a self-serving appeal, since he was calling for the confirmation of his policies. "But the fact that there are also tactical benefits to the appeal to bipartisanship does not change the reality that to the world at large we are one nation which can only have one government."[15] To demonstrate his own commitment to the principle, Kissinger emphasized his support for Carter in the battle to ratify the Panama Canal treaties. The administration highlighted Kissinger's position, and all three networks showed a smiling Kissinger meeting with Carter in August 1977 to discuss the treaty.[16] Kissinger also generally endorsed the administration's moves in the Middle East and provided Carter with advice and ideas.[17] After Anwar Sadat's surprise visit to Jerusalem in November 1977, Kissinger was a frequent commentator on the network news, supportive of the moves toward peace that he saw as following in the footsteps of his earlier diplomacy.[18] The journalist Haynes Johnson wrote, "During that memorable weekend when Sadat flew into Jerusalem, it was Kissinger's measured commentary that gave the clearest insights into those dramatic happenings."[19] He was so prominent and supportive of the administration that in July 1978 Vice President Walter Mondale even suggested Kissinger as a possible negotiator before Carter decided to proceed himself with his Camp David talks with Anwar Sadat and Menachem Begin.[20]

Nevertheless, Kissinger also began to stake out some important differences with the administration. When Carter sent a delegation to Paris to talk with the "Socialist Republic of Vietnam" about normalizing relations, Kissinger supported normalization but criticized the idea of providing any economic aid, reminding his audience of Hanoi's violation of the Paris Peace Accords. Appearing before a congressional committee, Kissinger got a strong round of applause when he suggested that any request for aid from

Vietnam "should be placed in alphabetical order."[21] Kissinger also opposed the administration's plans to pull U.S. troops out of Korea and criticized the emphasis on human rights in Carter's first approach to negotiating a new SALT agreement with the Soviet Union. In his otherwise supportive New York speech, Kissinger questioned the administration's human rights policy by pointing out, "There are realities in the threats nations face, either from terrorism at home, such as in Argentina, or aggression across borders, such as Iran and Korea . . . We must take care, finally, that our affirmation of human rights is not manipulated by our political adversaries to isolate countries whose security is important for the future of freedom, even if their domestic practices fall short of our maxims."[22] At the same time he was criticizing the Carter administration for interfering with the "domestic practices" in friendly dictatorial countries, Kissinger was advocating intervention with America's democratic allies. He used his first "Segment 3" on *NBC Nightly News*, an extended interview with David Brinkley and Tom Brokaw, to urge the administration to take a tough stance against the Italian Communist Party's joining the government.[23] He followed that up with an hour-long NBC special on Eurocommunism, stressing again the importance of American "moral support" in helping Italy's Christian Democrats reject Communist participation in the government.[24] During a lunch in December 1977, Kissinger's liberal friend Arthur Schlesinger found him "mutedly critical" of the administration, remarking about Jimmy Carter, "There is something very weird about him."[25]

The American public increasingly shared Kissinger's reservations about Carter, with his popularity dropping over his first eighteen months in office. Kissinger, on the other hand, found himself enjoying a surge of positive media attention, especially in the nation's capital. *Washingtonian* magazine covered a Kennedy Center gala and wrote, "The biggest star in the super glittery assemblage, the star most oohed and aahed over, the star the TV cameras zeroed in on first when they panned the audience, was ex–Secretary of State Henry Kissinger."[26] *The Washington Post* covered his comings and goings relentlessly, noting his role on corporate boards, his trusteeship with the Rockefeller Brothers Fund, his role on the board of directors of the North American

Soccer League, and his attempt to bring the World Cup to the United States.[27] His views on foreign policy turned increasingly critical, especially as the Carter administration experienced setbacks in the Horn of Africa, in its relations with the European allies over the neutron bomb, and in finalizing the SALT II agreement. Interviewers from the German newsweekly *Der Spiegel* led off their session with Kissinger by noting a "certain feeling of dissatisfaction with America's leadership" and asking, "How does it feel to be a man of whom many people inside and outside America are saying this would never have happened . . . when Henry Kissinger was in office?" Kissinger politely reminded the interviewers that Carter was not elected to carry out Kissinger's policies, and that some change had to be expected. He emphasized, "I have been very careful not to make criticisms on essentially tactical issues and to give the Administration the sense that, on those items on which I agree, I will even give it public support."[28]

The Carter administration valued Kissinger's support, especially on the Panama issue, but many within the White House resented the "negative power" he enjoyed over the administration's foreign policy. They also resented his skill with the media. Hamilton Jordan, the White House chief of staff, contrasted the hardworking and self-effacing Cyrus Vance with Kissinger, who "valued above all his image as a world leader, and nothing was more important to him than the time he spent polishing that image." Jordan quoted a staffer who had watched Kissinger for many years and remarked: "He fed the press like they were a flock of birds. They ate well and they ate regularly, and they sang and sang Henry's song."[29] Carter officials also believed Kissinger undermined their policies with foreign leaders. When Kissinger kept his promise and returned to Argentina to attend the World Cup finals in June 1978, the American ambassador, Raúl Castro, feared that Kissinger's "repeated high praise for Argentina's action in wiping out terrorism and his stress on the importance of Argentina" would be used as justifications by the regime "for hardening its human rights stance." In a public speech in Buenos Aires, Kissinger implicitly criticized the Carter administration, arguing, "The United States owes you some understanding of the tragedies of your recent history."[30] Robert Pastor, the NSC official who handled Latin America, forwarded to

Brzezinski the Castro cable, warning that Kissinger's words were "the music the Argentine government was longing to hear." Pastor was concerned that Kissinger would speak out against the administration's human rights policy, but also recognized, "We don't want to get into a public argument with him on this subject when we will need his help on SALT, etc." He then suggested Brzezinski call Kissinger to see whether the administration could debrief him on human rights policy and some of the success they had in curbing the worst abuses of the Dirty War in Argentina.[31] Patricia Derian, the assistant secretary of state for human rights, echoed this idea in a note to Cyrus Vance. Noting that Vance was having "lunch with Henry," Derian explained that Kissinger "has a disturbing tendency, particularly in foreign lands, to make deprecating comments about our human rights policy." She urged Vance to tell "Henry" that this "message is counter-productive in terms of helping real, live human beings today." She also asked Vance to remind Kissinger of the "increased number of statutory constraints which would make it illegal for a subsequent Secretary of State to disregard human rights considerations in the implementation of foreign assistance programs."[32]

The reference to a "subsequent" secretary of state makes it clear how the Carter administration perceived Kissinger. Kissinger continued to try to have it both ways, presenting his views on foreign policy as above partisan politics while also developing a politically effective critique of the administration. His celebrity status made him "one of the Big Four fundraisers" for the Republicans for the midterm elections, in the same league as Ford, Reagan, and John Connally. His "shuttle politicking" raised over a million dollars early in the year.[33] He even flirted with the idea of running for the Senate himself from New York in 1980, as Jacob Javits, New York's liberal Republican senator, was seventy-four and in frail health.[34] Asked about his political ambitions on the CBS show *Face the Nation*, Kissinger joked that as long as Javits was "still playing tennis," he would surely run again.[35] Javits was the type of "Rockefeller Republican" with whom Kissinger felt most comfortable, and he did not challenge him when Javits did decide to run. Kissinger campaigned for liberal Republicans like John Anderson of Illinois and Edward Brooke of Massachusetts, the Senate's only African American member.

Friendly columnists like David Broder joked about "Kissinger the pol," and TV news showed the former secretary of state throwing himself into the political fray, shaking hands with Brooke's constituents and praising Brooke as a "man of integrity."[36] Kissinger's star power could not save Brooke, who went down to defeat to a liberal Democrat, Paul Tsongas. It was an unusual Republican loss in a midterm election that otherwise highlighted Carter's vulnerability. Brooke's defeat, followed two months later by the sudden death of Nelson Rockefeller, seemed symbolic of the gradual eclipse of that strain of Republican thought closest to Kissinger's own sentiments. Kissinger, who was jolted by the death of the man who was "like a father to me,"[37] eulogized Rockefeller in powerful words: "What a great President he would have been! How he would have ennobled us! What an extraordinary combination of strength and humanity, decisiveness and vision!"[38]

Kissinger closed his eulogy by reflecting on how Rockefeller would advise Americans, telling them to look to the future, "Do not look back!"[39] Kissinger himself was determined to campaign hard for a Republican victory in 1980. Arthur Schlesinger recorded a January 1979 dinner with the Kissingers at "their new and unlovely apartment at River House" in New York City, where it appeared to Schlesinger that Kissinger was "now turning his powerful intelligence to sharp and contemptuous criticism of the Carter Administration, though rather of a heads-I-win-tails-they-lose kind."[40] Kissinger's views, however, were more nuanced than simple partisanship.[41] Kissinger praised Carter's Camp David agreements on the Middle East and supported the administration's decision to recognize the People's Republic of China and cut ties to Taiwan.[42] But he attacked Carter's efforts in Africa, arguing that Ian Smith's "internal settlement" with Bishop Abel Muzorewa, who headed up the only African party that rejected violence and was willing to cooperate with Smith and the whites, should be supported.[43] Appearing on Face the Nation, he repeated his mantra that "foreign policy is a nonpartisan issue," while at the same time criticizing what he called Carter's support for "radical forces" fighting the Rhodesian government. He also argued that Carter had "needlessly exacerbated" relations with the Soviet Union by his "assault on the Soviet domestic structure."[44] Kissinger was now ambivalent on the SALT II agreement, insisting that the United States needed to increase defense spending in order to build up to the treaty's actual limitations. He also talked of trying to use a type of linkage to force the Soviets to limit their activities in Africa if they wanted a SALT II treaty. Yet at times he even sounded uncharacteristically optimistic, asserting that if America chose the right policies now, "by the late '80s we could be in a period of tremendous dynamism, while the Soviet Union could be in a period either of serious domestic crisis or at least ambivalence." His CBS interviewer remarked, "This isn't the Spenglerian pessimism that is so often associated with you."[45]

The issue that drove a lasting wedge between the Carter administration and Kissinger was the treatment of the shah of Iran. As the disorders in Iran peaked in the latter half of 1978, Kissinger was outspoken about the important contribution that the shah had made to the West. On *NBC Nightly News*, after images of rioting and disorder in Tehran, Kissinger appeared, stressing the shah's support for Israel, his actions during the Arab oil boycott, and the close relationship between the U.S. government and the shah over three decades.[46] Just as his comments about reconciling with Vietnam were connected to his own personal experience, Kissinger's passionate defense of the shah was linked to Nixon's 1972 decision to increase American weapons deliveries and effectively appoint the shah as guardian of the Persian Gulf. Kissinger and Nixon visited Tehran after their successful Moscow summit in May 1972, and were favorably impressed by the shah's modernization drive and his willingness, indeed eagerness, to act as a surrogate for the United States in the region. True to the Nixon Doctrine, Iran replaced Britain in the area as America's most important ally.[47]

Unfortunately the close relationship with the United States that encouraged the shah's military buildup and a rapid economic modernization also led to a blindness by American leaders like Kissinger to the political repression and violations of human rights that secured the regime. When an economic downturn hit Iran in 1977, these helped to create the conditions for political and social unrest and ultimately violent revolution. Nevertheless, Kissinger blamed the Carter administration's overall weakness in asserting American power and its policy of promoting human rights for undermining allies like the shah. After the shah left Iran, and the revolutionary regime of Ayatollah Khomeini seized power, Kissinger argued, "One of the reasons for the Shah's progressive demoralization was his very real doubt whether we were actually supporting him."[48] Kissinger claimed the collapse of the shah was "the biggest foreign policy debacle of the U.S. in a generation," a formulation that elicited ridicule from many who thought that Kissinger overlooked his own role in the Vietnam debacle.[49]

Throughout 1979, Kissinger actively lobbied the Carter administration on behalf of the shah, calling Brzezinski and President Carter directly to complain about the refusal to allow the shah to come to the United States for medical treatment.[50] He gave a widely publicized speech arguing that it was wrong for the United States to treat the shah "like a Flying Dutchman looking for port of call." Kissinger helped the shah obtain a ninety-day tourist visa to Mexico and traveled to have lunch with the deposed ruler in Cuernavaca.[51] Kissinger's liberal friends were not impressed. *The New York Times* recalled that Kissinger once refused to meet with Aleksandr Solzhenitsyn "lest he offend Soviet leaders."[52] Arthur Schlesinger remarked, "All very surprising on the lips of such a devotee of *Realpolitik*."[53] Nevertheless, Carter's political aides feared Kissinger's stance on the issue. As the shah's medical condition deteriorated, Hamilton Jordan told Carter, "Mr. President, if the Shah dies in Mexico, can you imagine the field day Kissinger will have with that? He'll say that first you caused the Shah's downfall and now you've killed him." Carter glared at him and said coldly, "To hell with Henry Kissinger . . . I am President of this country."[54]

Carter resented Kissinger but needed him. The president hoped a SALT II treaty would help in the general election, but it would be particularly valuable for Carter if he faced a liberal challenge within the Democratic Party from Edward Kennedy.[55] In June 1979, Carter traveled to Vienna to sign the accord with Leonid Brezhnev, extolling it as a "truly national achievement" of three presidential administrations and "tough painstaking negotiation."[56] There was fierce opposition, and Carter needed Kissinger's support if it were to have any chance for Senate approval. Kissinger's testimony that summer was widely covered in the media, with the network news posting a graphic of the conditions that Kissinger had set for his approval. Tom Pettit, NBC's Senate correspondent, called Kissinger's position on the treaty "Byzantine," saying that it had not left the administration "ecstatic," but at least it was not outright rejection. Kissinger may have tried his own form of linkage, tying his support for SALT II to help for the shah, but Carter remained defiant.[57]

When in October the shah's condition took a turn for the worse and Secretary of State Vance gave up his opposition, Carter decided to allow the Iranian leader to come to the United States for medical treatment. On November 4, radical students stormed the American embassy in Tehran, seized fifty-two American hostages, and set off a prolonged crisis that would define the Carter presidency. Public opinion rallied behind the president, but there was now increased scrutiny over the decision to admit the shah. Richard Valeriani of NBC reported that the State Department believed Kissinger had engaged in a form of "political blackmail" with his pressure on Carter, threatening that they would be accused of "murdering an old ally" by refusing the shah medical treatment. Asked about this at a press briefing, the assistant secretary of state for public affairs, Hodding Carter, replied curtly, "Ask Henry Kissinger."[58] Former undersecretary George Ball attacked Kissinger's "obnoxious" pressure on the Carter administration to admit the shah.[59] Kissinger defended his support for the shah but denied he had been involved in the final decision.[60] Schlesinger, watching Kissinger under attack, remarked: "[Henry] does appear ... a casualty of the Iranian affair ... When I was in Denver last week, the *Rocky Mountain News* (28 November) had a full-page headline on the editorial page: 'A Message to Kissinger: Shut Up.'"[61]

The controversy over the shah was not the only reason that the year 1979 did not turn out well for Kissinger. Kissinger planned the publication of the first volume of his memoirs for the fall of 1979, with excerpts published in *Time* magazine and a prime-time television special. Before his memoirs were published, two books appeared with distinctly different takes on Kissinger. In April, Joseph Heller, the author of the classic novel *Catch-22* and an important figure in New York literary circles, published *Good as Gold*, his third novel and a bitter takedown of Kissinger. The main character in the book, Bruce Gold, is a middle-aged, Jewish Columbia University professor whose essay "Nothing Succeeds as Planned" launches him on a political career. Along with satirizing contemporary American politics, Heller uses Kissinger to comment on the "American Jewish experience," from which Kissinger emerges as the "ultimate assimilationist . . . a man who sold his soul to get where he is."[62] Bruce Gold envies Kissinger and has set as one of his career projects to write Kissinger's biography. Gold collects numerous short newspaper clippings and commentaries on Kissinger, many of them caustic and unflattering. At one point a character in conversation with Gold remarks, "I have to confess I always thought of Kissinger as a greasy, vulgar, petulant, obnoxious contemptible, self-serving, social-climbing Jewish little shit."[63] *The New Republic* linked Heller's book to the publication of Kissinger's memoirs and characterized it as a "cultural event." It exclaimed, "A major novelist has taken on our greatest celebrity with all the power and wit and language at his command . . . Perhaps not since Tolstoy eviscerated Napoleon . . . has a central historical figure been so intimately castigated by the Word. Score one for literature."[64] Heller himself considered Kissinger "a great joke, one of the genuinely funny characters in American life. But he won't last."[65] In the book, his protagonist, Gold, tells his wife, "A society in which such a blithering hypocrite was lionized as a celebrity instead of shunned and despised was a society not worth its salt."[66] Heller's work captured the intense and growing rage against Kissinger among intellectuals and the left. Kissinger was, as Heller portrays him, "an odious *shlump* who made war gladly and did not often exude much of that legendary sympathy for weakness and suffering with which Jews regularly were credited." Indeed, in the character Gold's view, Kissinger is not even Jewish.[67]

The second important book published shortly before Kissinger's memoir was William Shawcross's *Sideshow: Kissinger, Nixon, and the Destruction of Cambodia*.[68] Shawcross, a British journalist, constructed a powerful narrative with the central message "Cambodia was not a mistake; it was a crime." The book argues that the Nixon administration's bombing and invasion of Cambodia were the proximate causes of that country's conquest by the Khmer Rouge and the subsequent genocidal policies. Stanley Hoffmann, Kissinger's former colleague, exuberantly praised the book, calling it "careful, detailed, and incisive." Hoffmann added a thinly veiled swipe at Kissinger's recent speeches: "For those who, ever since the debacle of 1975, keep worrying that American diplomacy's resolve, will, or position in the world will be permanently impaired by the motto 'No more Vietnams,' Shawcross's account of the pointless destruction of Cambodia should be compulsory reading."[69] The British journalist David Frost took Hoffmann's advice. Frost, who had achieved his own celebrity fame by interviewing Richard Nixon the year before, enlisted Shawcross to help him prepare for his network television interview with Kissinger, timed for the release of Kissinger's memoirs in October. Frost was determined, as he told *The New York Times*, "to test the Kissinger version of history and to show the real Kissinger in 3D."[70] When the interview was recorded, Frost's tough questions on Cambodia irritated and unsettled Kissinger. Kissinger believed he did not do as well as he should have and pressured NBC to allow another interview. Frost resisted, and the entire story ended up in *The New York Times*. NBC decided to broadcast the original interview, much to Kissinger's displeasure and anger. Frost pressed Kissinger on the bombing of "innocent Cambodia peasants" and challenged him for lying in a background briefing on previous American military actions in Cambodia.[71] Kissinger's angry reactions revealed the degree to which he had become accustomed to "gentle handling by the media." Even though Kissinger had legitimate defenses for his policies, the Frost interview left a decidedly negative impact on his relations with the media.[72] Tom Shales of *The Washington Post*, a media outlet that had provided Kissinger with some of his most positive coverage, criticized NBC for its arrangement with Kissinger and urged the network to fire him.[73]

The Heller and Shawcross books, along with Iran, all served to complicate and dim the celebrity aura around Kissinger. He remained powerful and influential but was now much more controversial as the election year of 1980 began. Kissinger did not endorse a Republican candidate initially, although observers thought him unlikely to support the early favorite, Ronald Reagan, who had been so critical of him in the 1976 primaries. In February 1980, Reagan won decisively in the New Hampshire primary, but some moderates in the party reached out to former president Gerald Ford, who originally declined to run, as the only hope of stopping Reagan. Ford announced that he was reconsidering his original decision, and Kissinger quickly went to see him, making the argument that a conservative like Reagan could not win against Carter. Scotty Reston, who remained one of Kissinger's most sympathetic media friends, speculated that Kissinger must have been convinced that Ford would run, because by "siding with Ford, he has infuriated Reagan, George Bush, and John Anderson, and minimized the chances they would ever nominate him to be Secretary of State—an ambition that no doubt occasionally crosses his mind."[74] Unfortunately for Kissinger, Ford decided that he had waited too long and that it would not be possible to stop Reagan, and on March 15 he announced he would not run. Two weeks later Kissinger told a college audience that he would be willing to serve in a Reagan administration and that he had actually met with Reagan to provide advice on a number of occasions. Kissinger said that he had "extensive conversations" with Reagan and that he was "impressed with my meetings with him." The *New York Times* report closed on the curious point that the only Republican candidate who stated publicly he would not appoint Kissinger as secretary of state was George H. W. Bush.[75]

As the convention approached in July, Kissinger's plans to attend became a source of controversy, with Senator Jesse Helms of North Carolina organizing conservatives against him. Kissinger canceled his appearance before the platform committee but still secured a position to address the convention on its second night. The Republican platform called for military superiority over the Soviet Union, strong backing for Taiwan, and a strict American interpretation of the Panama Canal treaty. It implicitly condemned Kissinger's détente policy and the SALT arms control negotiations. When Kissinger arrived in Detroit, reporters confronted him with uncomfortable questions. Marvin Kalb reminded Kissinger of his past statement about nuclear weapons, "What in God's name is superiority?" But Kissinger tried to argue that this statement was made in "a particular context in a particular negotiation." He was "not opposed to military superiority," because our "present defenses are inadequate." Kalb did not relent, asking Kissinger if he could be comfortable taking a job in a future Reagan administration with such a "hardline anti-

Soviet posture," but Kissinger insisted that it was now "imperative to prevent Soviet expansion."[76] The next day Kalb reported that Kissinger had met with Reagan for almost an hour, but that no photographs were permitted. Kalb also reported that Kissinger's speech that evening to the convention would likely be greeted with a chorus of boos.[77]

In fact, Kissinger received polite applause, and some delegates even stood up. His speech, however, did not begin until almost midnight eastern time. Judy Woodruff reported that the Reagan organizers grew complacent after their successful platform adoption the first night of the convention, and they failed to enforce speaker time limits. The result was that Kissinger's powerful attack on the Carter foreign policy, and his application for a return to power in a Reagan White House, did not cause much of a sensation. Cameras panned the audience during Kissinger's address, and at one of his more impassioned appeals for unity behind Reagan, several of the delegates were yawning.[78] Nancy Reagan and Nancy Kissinger were engrossed in a spirited discussion during Kissinger's address, with NBC's Garrick Utley commenting that "neither listened to a word he had to say." Many of Kissinger's strongest anti-Carter attack lines—"we are making the world safe for anti-American radicalism"; "if you do not know where you are going, any road will take you there"—fell "flat," David Brinkley wryly noted. The TV analysts also commented that such a partisan speech was "quite a turn for Henry Kissinger" since "he always emphasizes bipartisanship in foreign policy."[79]

Directly after his speech, Kissinger engaged in a very partisan activity: negotiating with Ronald Reagan's team about the unprecedented possibility that former president Gerald Ford would accept a place on the ticket as the vice president. Many Republicans saw this "dream ticket" as the only way the "extreme" Reagan could reassure moderates. Along with Alan Greenspan, who had been the chair of Ford's Council of Economic Advisers, Kissinger was enlisted by Reagan's people to see if Ford would consider the second spot on the ticket. Ford wanted "meaningful responsibilities" for a vice president, possibly including authority over the National Security Council. Ford later told the Kissinger biographer Walter Isaacson that he had insisted on Kissinger as secretary of state and that this was a deal breaker with Reagan.

According to Ford, Reagan replied, "I've been all over this country the last several years, and Kissinger carries a lot of baggage. I couldn't accept that. My own people, in fact, wouldn't accept it."[80] Kissinger claimed that he took his name out of consideration in order to facilitate an agreement, but Reagan decided against the arrangement after it was described as a "co-presidency."[81] Reagan determined then to select a different candidate, George H. W. Bush. The next day Kissinger told interviewers that the negotiators did not have enough time to "institutionalize" the type of arrangements Ford had demanded to give him real decision-making power.[82] The interview made it clear that Kissinger was deeply disappointed and that this was related to his own personal return to power. Reagan's people certainly believed Kissinger was attempting a "power grab," and they told Howell Raines of *The New York Times*, "Kissinger simply saw a Ford Vice Presidency as his ticket back to power."[83]

A disappointed Kissinger nevertheless campaigned actively for Reagan, even helping specifically with Jewish voters, a task he had done with great reluctance for Nixon.[84] Reagan called him early in the campaign to attack the Carter campaign for leaking information about the importance of the Stealth bomber in helping the United States stay ahead of the Soviet Union.[85] Kissinger also helped Reagan prepare for his debate with Carter.[86] To appeal to moderates, Reagan's people may have allowed the rumor to spread that Kissinger might be Reagan's choice to be secretary of state. In mid-October 1980, Arthur Schlesinger found himself on a flight to Washington sitting next to Bill Casey, a friend of his from their service in the wartime Office of Strategic Services, the forerunner of the CIA, and now Reagan's campaign manager. Schlesinger told Casey that Carter was having considerable success painting Reagan as a warmonger and said, "The one thing that [Reagan] could do that would instantaneously dispel international dismay and concern—" Casey interrupted him to say, "Henry." Casey told Schlesinger they were trying to bring Kissinger into the picture despite the attitude of "the right," which would not like it. Casey told Schlesinger, "The right had been disappointed in a number of things Reagan had done and would probably be more disappointed in the future."[87] The story appeared in *The New York Times* a few days later, with Bernard Gwertzman writing, "One of Ronald Reagan's most important assets in the final weeks of the campaign has been the visible support of Henry A. Kissinger . . . his endorsement has made Mr. Reagan more acceptable to the foreign policy establishment in this country and abroad."[88]

THE REAGAN AND BUSH YEARS: THE EXILE CONTINUES

The Reagan team thought floating Kissinger's name helped, but it did not take them long after Reagan's victory to end any speculation about Kissinger's return. Reagan appointed Kissinger to his transition team, and two days after Reagan's landslide win, NBC News featured a report with film of Reagan and Bush sitting with Kissinger and Al Haig. The correspondent Heidi Schulman discussed the importance of Kissinger's campaigning for Reagan, implying that it would lead to a job offer. But the next day the same network listed Shultz and Haig as the likely possibilities to lead the State Department, and Kissinger as a long shot. Hedrick Smith reported the comment of a Reagan insider: "If you have Kissinger in that job . . . you wind up by competing with your own Secretary of State and he takes over the world."[89] Another Reagan adviser stressed the Republican right's hatred of Kissinger: "If Henry Kissinger was put back into the State Department, Jesse Helms would commit hara-kiri on the White House lawn."[90] Kissinger did make a high-profile trip to the Middle East at the end of December, reported on *NBC Nightly News* as an "unofficial" trip with Reagan's approval. Roger Mudd reported Kissinger's journey as an effort to get back "into the center of power," part of his battle with the "New Right," which was trying to exclude him.[91] Kissinger called himself just a "sightseer," but the news anchor John Chancellor argued, "No one thought Kissinger just a sightseer." The trip showed Kissinger greeted with the pomp and ceremony usually reserved for heads of state, and the images were of Kissinger hugging and kissing Sadat of Egypt and sitting up until two in the morning to talk policy with Siad Barre of Somalia. The report ended by claiming that Kissinger's analysis of Middle Eastern policy, with an emphasis on resisting Soviet expansionism and aiding American allies in the region, would become the basis for the Reagan administration's approach to the region.[92]

Kissinger's prominence presented a dilemma to Reagan's advisers, and they aired these disagreements to the columnists Rowland Evans and Robert Novak in *The Washington Post*. "Reagan has never wanted any grandstanders in his diplomacy," one aide told the columnists. "But here is Henry holding daily press conferences about how Reagan intends to settle the Middle East and using his own agents to get invitations from countries like Oman that think he really is doing Reagan's bidding." Evans and Novak, however, came to Kissinger's defense by noting that he remained "the most glittering figure in America, sought out by statesman for confidential advice and talks." They recognized that this was a role best suited in an opposition position under the Democrats, not in a Republican administration, unless Kissinger was back, which "was not in prospect today." Nevertheless, a different Reagan insider admitted that Reagan's people still regarded Kissinger as "a valuable and important asset to us," with potential to carry out an important diplomatic mission in the future, perhaps to the Middle East or to the Soviet Union. For that reason, the insider said, "We don't want any hint of alienation between Reagan and Henry."[93]

Kissinger wanted to remain influential, but his own need for the limelight and media acclaim made him a controversial figure to Reagan's inner circle. They were divided over his role but determined not to have Reagan overshadowed, as Gerald Ford had been. When Kissinger returned from his trip, he met with Reagan quietly, but *The Washington Post* reported that sources in the Reagan White House said that the trip was a "flop" and that the "ambiguity surrounding [Kissinger's] standing in the Reagan Administration" led "Arab leaders to distance themselves from Kissinger." King Hussein, in particular, was still angry over his exclusion from Kissinger's earlier shuttle diplomacy and did not want to "lend his prestige" to Kissinger's mission. Richard Allen, Reagan's national security adviser, told the *Post* that Kissinger represented no one but himself.[94] However, throughout his first year in office, Reagan continued to meet with Kissinger far more regularly than Allen and his other conservative advisers liked. As Reagan described Kissinger's June 1981 return from a trip to the Middle East, "His amazing knowledge of all the 'players' and his report was most enlightening and helpful."[95] For his part, Kissinger regarded Reagan as "a nice man, a decent man,"

but could not resist telling Arthur Schlesinger, "He listens, and tries to understand, in so far as he is capable of understanding foreign policy. But I don't
have the impression that he ever ingests anything you tell him."[96]

Kissinger remained publicly supportive of the Reagan administration
throughout its first term, providing advice primarily on issues related to the
Middle East and the Soviet Union. His personal focus was on completing
the second volume of his memoirs, which would cover the last two years of the
Nixon administration, but he remained a highly visible figure. After almost
every crisis of that year—the failed Reagan assassination attempt, the shooting of Pope John Paul II, the American downing of two Libyan jets in the
Mediterranean, the Sadat assassination, and the declaration of martial law in
Poland—Kissinger was Ted Koppel's guest on ABC's *Nightline*. He was now
well on his way to becoming, as Isaacson described him, "the most ubiquitous
opinionmeister of the 1980s."[97] Kissinger still responded quickly to a presidential summons, such as when Reagan asked him to come to Washington to
appear with a group of former officials to support the sales of the Airborne
Warning and Control System (AWACS) to Saudi Arabia in October 1981. The
television news report showed Reagan speaking briefly and then turning to
Kissinger to continue the presentation. Reagan also asked Kissinger to attend
the funeral of Anwar Sadat. In an *NBC Nightly News* commentary about the
concern for the physical security of the participants, Paul Miller highlighted
the "former presidents and heads of state" in attendance, listing Ford, Carter,
Nixon, and Kissinger.[98] Such prominence could also bring danger. On a trip
to speak in Brazil and Peru in November 1981, Kissinger faced violent demonstrators screaming, "Murderer," forcing him to leave the speaking engagement in a police car.[99]

Kissinger occasionally faced the threat of physical violence in the United
States as well. Walking through the Newark, New Jersey, airport in February
1982, Kissinger encountered Ellen Kaplan, a supporter of Lyndon LaRouche,
a cultlike figure and political extremist. In the conspiracy thinking of
LaRouche and his followers, Kissinger was the central enemy, a homosexual,
a Nazi, and a murderer. Kaplan started shouting at Kissinger, "Is it true you
sleep with young boys at the Carlyle Hotel?" Kissinger's wife, Nancy, grabbed

the woman by the throat and pushed her away. Kaplan pressed assault charges, but Nancy was acquitted, with the judge saying that she had a "spontaneous, somewhat human reaction."[100] Kaplan claimed that the Kissingers were being treated like "British royalty," while "Bruiser" Nancy, as the tabloids called her, smiled through adult braces and laughed when asked whether she would do it again, saying only, "I don't know. Lord knows."[101] The incident occurred as Kissinger was heading to Boston for open-heart surgery. Kissinger gave a press conference before the procedure, with reporters remarking on his "un-dimmed sense of humor" when he joked that he wanted a quadruple bypass in order to have "one more than Al Haig," who had undergone triple bypass sur-gery in 1980. Kissinger was released from the hospital after only two weeks. A few days later, his father, Louis, died at age ninety-five.

Whether or not these intimations of his own mortality had an impact on his thinking, Kissinger did begin to make plans for a continuing career that did not include an immediate return to government. In July 1982 he turned Kissinger Associates, Inc. (KAI), into an active company, bringing along his former deputy Brent Scowcroft as one of his first associates, followed shortly thereafter by Larry Eagleburger. "For a retainer reported in economic circles to be $250,000 per client," the Kissinger firm would provide "strategic plan-ning advice to a small number of clients in the corporate world."[102] Over time KAI came to represent a very prominent group of more than two dozen cor-porations. The list was secret, and companies were forbidden from discussing their relationship with KAI. But because some of Kissinger's group ended up reentering government—Scowcroft and Eagleburger both entered the George H. W. Bush administration in 1989—financial disclosure forms shed light on some of the major clients. They included banks like Chase Manhat-tan and S. G. Warburg, automobile manufacturers like Fiat and Volvo, insur-ance companies like AIG, and conglomerates like Daewoo and Union Carbide. To these privileged and powerful companies, Kissinger dispensed his foreign policy wisdom, undertook diplomatic assignments, and was a "personal national security adviser to their chairmen."[103] Kissinger's plunge into the world of international business consulting was ironic, since as secre-tary of state he often joked about how little he understood international economics. His work at KAI, however, not only provided him with a considerable income but also allowed him to promote the economic side of globalization.

Kissinger remained largely supportive of Reagan's foreign policy throughout his first term, welcoming the replacement of Richard Allen by William Clark as national security adviser and his friend George Shultz as secretary of state when Al Haig resigned in June 1982. He did criticize what he perceived as their relative lack of response to the Polish crisis, arguing that the administration was in a "better position to challenge our allies over Poland, with respect to which I suspect European publics are more clear-sighted than their governments, than over the Middle East or Central America." Kissinger concluded by arguing, "It is we who must lead in this alliance." Kissinger did make it clear that he remained supportive of Reagan "and continued to believe that the Administration embodies the best chance for free peoples; that its success is of vital importance for our country and those who depend on it."[104] Although Kissinger's criticism in this instance may have irritated the State Department, this may have had the opposite effect with Reagan, who behind the scenes was far angrier with the European allies and wanted to act more decisively on behalf of Poland.[105]

Kissinger continued to advise the administration on the Middle East in the aftermath of the June 1982 Israeli invasion of Lebanon and was rumored to be considered for a diplomatic mission at the time.[106] His friendship with Shultz and knowledge of the Middle East brought frequent consultations, and some observers professed to see his hand in the administration's September 1982 peace proposals.[107] He continued to back Reagan on taking a tough stance toward the Soviet Union, although the growing nuclear freeze movement was creating significant political pressure on the administration. Kissinger criticized the Western Allies when they protested the administration's attempt to prevent the building of a pipeline for natural gas imports from the Soviet Union. He was in favor of cutting off credits to the Soviets to build the gas pipeline, fearing the political "manipulation" the Russians could exercise through controlling energy supplies. He called the Soviet Union a "disintegrating empire," a formulation close to Reagan's heart.[108] Yet at the same time he also criticized some of those hard-line conservatives who had complicated his life when he was in government. In a widely publicized essay in *Newsweek* after the death of Leonid Brezhnev in November 1982, Kissinger attacked those "who luxuriate in the myth of diabolic Soviet planners implementing a detailed master plan for world revolution." Invoking his own experience, he remarked, "No one who has actually dealt with the Soviet leadership has encountered such types." Although recognizing the continued military power of the regime, Kissinger stressed, "The Soviet system is an economic disaster." In words that might be seen as predicting Mikhail Gorbachev's rise, Kissinger argued, "The instinct for self-preservation of Soviet leaders should lead at least some of them to the conclusion that the country is overextended and must somewhere retrench. This is not psychology; it is reality." This offered real possibilities for the West, and Kissinger urged the Reagan administration to develop a policy that would "combine military strength with a strategy for peace."[109]

Privately Kissinger was more critical of Reagan's team, although Arthur Schlesinger realized that some of this was Kissinger "playing to a liberal house."[110] He criticized Vice President Bush as "a very weak man," and thought George Shultz had "no knowledge of foreign policy" and would be "at the mercy of the State Department bureaucracy." He told Schlesinger that he was trying to work on Shultz to "bring him around on arms control." With Reagan, he lamented, "If you talk to him alone, you can be sure nothing will ever happen."[111] At the same time he was making these comments to Schlesinger, Kissinger came to Washington for lunch with Reagan and the CIA director, Casey, and was "most complimentary" about policy in the Middle East.[112] He also warmly praised Secretary of State Shultz before his visit to China, arguing against the "conventional wisdom" that the Reagan administration was at fault for current difficulties. In fact, Kissinger contended, "The Administration has gone to extraordinary lengths—even more remarkable given its starting point—to emphasize its commitment to close ties with Peking."[113]

Kissinger's own proclivity for talking out of both sides of his mouth and for double-dealing became a major public conversation in May 1983, with the publication of Seymour Hersh's *The Price of Power: Kissinger in the Nixon White House*, a study of Kissinger's role as national security adviser during

Nixon's first term in office. The book received national attention in the media and several "best book of the year" awards from major newspapers and magazines. Stanley Hoffmann once again wrote a favorable review, calling it the "Kissinger anti-memoirs." Although the book discusses many of the foreign policy issues of the first Nixon term, laying out its attack on the administration's Vietnam, Chile, and other Cold War policies, the topic that got the most immediate attention was Hersh's portrayal of Kissinger's duplicity at dealing with both the Humphrey and the Nixon campaigns in 1968. The NBC report on the book highlighted the charge that Kissinger was a "power hungry double dealer" who had offered the Humphrey campaign the "derogatory" materials that the Rockefeller campaign had collected on Nixon, but when Nixon appeared to be winning, offered Nixon "invaluable" secret information on the Paris peace talks. When the race tightened, Kissinger supposedly wrote to Humphrey criticizing Nixon and offering his service to a Humphrey administration. Ironically, the report featured Seymour Hersh on camera providing a type of backhanded praise for Kissinger, noting that Kissinger was positioning himself to become the national security adviser no matter who won, and that "you have to admire the man's ingenuity." The report went on to interview Norman Sherman, an aide to Humphrey, who confirmed the contacts with Kissinger but also said that Humphrey, if he had won the election, would have appointed Kissinger national security adviser.[114] Nevertheless, Kissinger called the charges against him a "slimy lie" and fumed about the book with his friends.[115]

Schlesinger recognized that the Hersh book clearly "struck a nerve" with Kissinger, adding, "There are even those who say that Henry took on the [Central American] commission in order to distract attention from the book."[116] Whatever Kissinger's motivations for accepting Reagan's offer to head the commission, its timing was fortuitous. Reagan knew from his frequent meetings with Kissinger that he would likely support the administration's policy, especially in its anti-Soviet overtones. On May 24 they had lunched together with the CIA director, and Kissinger argued that the United States should consider taking an action that "would put down a marker" to the Soviets— Kissinger even suggested "blockading Nicaragua."[117] When Reagan announced

in a July 18 speech that he was appointing a commission to lay "the foundation for a long-term, unified, national approach to the freedom and independence of the countries of Central America," he praised Kissinger as a "very
distinguished American, outstanding in the field of diplomacy, virtually a
legend in that field."[118] Even though Kissinger may have recognized that his
role would be to sell the administration's policy, not to shape it, the appointment was an opportunity for him to return to the public spotlight
dealing with an issue of great public concern. Some even suspected that
Reagan had unknowingly "put the Lone Ranger of American diplomacy back
in the saddle."[119]

Kissinger approached his role with his own experience foremost in mind,
wanting to remove the perception that the United States was about to enter
into another Vietnam. He told Schlesinger that his aim was "to rebuild a foreign
policy consensus by getting a unified report," which Schlesinger dismissed as
impossible, since the Reagan administration was "militarizing" policy toward
the region. Kissinger responded that he hoped the commission could obtain
agreement on "the diagnosis," leaving room "for disagreement on tactics,"
dodging Schlesinger's objection but keeping open the idea that he could accomplish something constructive.[120] Kissinger did work effectively toward
bridging differences within the twelve-person group, gaining praise from one
of its prominent Democrats, Henry Cisneros, the mayor of San Antonio, for
his "patient and fair" approach to the committee's workings. Between August
and December 1983, the commission held thirty full days of hearings and
heard from over four hundred witnesses.[121] Largely because of Kissinger's
presence, the commission's tour of Central America drew great media attention. Kissinger was treated as a star in the countries they visited, with the
networks noting that he was "applauded in the hotel" and hugged by national
leaders.[122] In El Salvador, Kissinger gave an uncharacteristically strong defense of human rights and democracy and attacked right-wing death squads,
a stance that won him support from even the conservatives on the commission.[123] The Nicaraguan government's heavy-handed approach to the commission, with leaders haranguing it and even using Soviet-supplied maps and
reports, made it easier for Kissinger to convince some commission members

of the importance of criticizing "Sandinista support for insurgency and subversion in neighboring countries."[124]

The Kissinger Commission's report was impressive in reaching consensus about the problems the United States faced in Central America. It recognized the "indigenous" roots of the unrest, and called for $400 million more in immediate military aid and a five-year, $8 billion economic and humanitarian program of assistance.[125] The report gave a tacit endorsement to the contras, although two members dissented from that recommendation. On one of the most important questions the commission examined, military aid to El Salvador, the report's consensus, which Kissinger endorsed, was "conditionality," or tying military aid to El Salvador to improvement in the human rights situation of the country. Kissinger, however, did attach a note giving his own understanding of conditionality. In this note, Kissinger supported "conditionality as applied to military aid to El Salvador but ask[ed] that it not be interpreted in a way that would lead to a Marxist-Leninist victory in El Salvador, thereby damaging vital American interests and risking a larger war."[126] Asked about his formulation, Kissinger argued, "It is inherently illogical in the name of human rights to bring into power people who have never demonstrated the slightest concern for human rights and who have never permitted their governments to change from their totalitarian way in any country in which they were in office." Following up, the reporter asked, "Aren't you saying to the death squads that 'you people who have killed 30,000 of your own citizens, bad as you are, you are preferable to Marxist-Leninists'?" Kissinger responded, "I am confident that we can take care of the death squads without going to the other extreme."[127]

Media coverage of the Kissinger report highlighted the issue of conditionality, and whether the Reagan administration would accept the commission's recommendations.[128] After some initial confusion, Reagan embraced the report and praised the commission's "positive recommendations to support democratic development, improve human rights, and bring the long-sought dream for peace to this troubled region so close to home."[129] Reagan, however, continued to insist that the White House would have the final word on whether the Salvadoran government had met its obligations on human rights, a position that Kissinger endorsed but that the Democrats continued to reject. The Kissinger Commission helped Reagan turn down the overall political temperature of the Central American crisis, and the Salvadoran question did not matter to presidential politics in 1984. The victory of the moderate Christian Democrat José Napoleón Duarte in the May elections over the right-wing candidate Roberto D'Aubuisson helped the administration win congressional approval of continued aid to the government. Kissinger recognized how this would affect his recommendations, telling reporters during the background briefing in January, "I am not giving away any secret if I tell you that it was the unanimous conviction of the Commission that a victory for Duarte would be compatible with the objectives of the process of democratization."[130]

When asked at his briefing of reporters if he would take on any other assignments from the president, Kissinger replied with a rare, unequivocal, "No. I absolutely do not expect to take on any other assignments." He then explained that he would do the requisite briefings and congressional testimony to explain the commission's report, but "it will be the administration that will have to defend its programs . . . I'm going back to private life." When a reporter pressed him further, using the formulation that Nixon had once used and asked, "We're not going to have you to kick around anymore?" Kissinger seemed for a moment to qualify his earlier remark: "I'm not saying that—I certainly have no aspirations."[131]

Although one account argues, "By this point, Kissinger had most likely abandoned any serious thought about returning to government," in reality Kissinger always kept his options open.[132] His media profile remained high.[133] A LexisNexis survey from 1975 through 1987 showed 10,187 mentions of Kissinger in the press, behind only President Reagan and Elizabeth Taylor.[134] After his contract with NBC ended in 1982, he began to appear regularly on ABC programs, including Ted Koppel's *Nightline* and *This Week with David Brinkley*.[135] When the nuclear apocalypse movie *The Day After* was shown on ABC to more than a hundred million viewers in November 1983, Kissinger was on Koppel's show immediately following it, lamenting the fact of nuclear weapons but arguing for their necessity.[136] (He and Gerald Ford even found time to appear on an episode of ABC's highly rated evening soap opera *Dynasty* in December 1983.)[137] Although he admitted that he was "less than enthusiastic" at first about President Reagan's proposal for the Strategic Defense Initiative, nicknamed "Star Wars," a defensive shield against nuclear missiles, he now gave it support as a way to increase deterrence with the Soviets and protect against "third nuclear countries," like a nuclear-armed Libya.[138] This support came in one of Kissinger's regular newspaper op-eds, about a dozen a year, for the *Los Angeles Times*, which were syndicated throughout the country, including in *The Washington Post* and the *New York Post*. He maintained his warm relationship with Reagan, receiving an appointment to the President's Foreign Intelligence Advisory Board, a distinction Kissinger relished, as it took him back to his early career in intelligence. He advised Reagan on his September 1984 meeting with the Soviet foreign minister, Gromyko, and Reagan wrote in his diary that they were "tracking very close on the approach to take."[139] Kissinger attended the Republican National Convention and publically endorsed Reagan for reelection, though he did tell Arthur Schlesinger how much he liked a critical article that Schlesinger had written about Reagan, only to add, "The only trouble is that the alternative is worse, so grudgingly, I am going to have to support Reagan."[140] Though he might have wanted to appear to be a grudging Reagan backer to his liberal friends in New York, publically he was enthusiastic. After Reagan's landslide victory, Kissinger wrote an op-ed for *The Washington Post* titled "Ronald Reagan's Great Opportunity," which praised the "Great Communicator" and urged him to become the "Great Educator," taking "bipartisanship beyond the least common denominator." Kissinger believed, "Not since the immediate postwar period has a president had such an opportunity to shape a more benign international order."[141] In comparison with the usual tenor of Kissinger's gloomy writing, it was an extraordinarily optimistic statement.

Kissinger was likely disappointed not to get a position in Reagan's second-term administration, but he continued to meet with Reagan and support the president's foreign policy positions. Although he had once been identified with détente, Kissinger now evinced a tough stance on the Cold War, emphasizing skepticism toward the Soviet Union, support for America's close relationship with China, and the importance of overall firmness toward challenges like terrorism, which might be exploited by the Soviets. He met with Reagan after the Soviet leader Konstantin Chernenko died in March 1985, reassuring him that it was best not to go to the funeral.[142] He advised Reagan to meet with the younger and more dynamic Mikhail Gorbachev "in due course," but told the press not to be deceived by Gorbachev's attractive style or personality: "The first thing one has to remember is that you don't get to be the head of the politburo by being a choirboy."[143] Kissinger disassociated himself from a critical report issued by the Georgetown Center for Strategic and International Studies attacking the Star Wars program. Kissinger also supported Reagan's trip to the Bitburg cemetery in Germany, even though members of the Waffen-SS were buried there. In Kissinger's view, loyalty to the West German chancellor, Helmut Kohl, who had supported the United States in the deployment of medium-range nuclear missiles during that crisis in 1983, overrode the domestic outcry over Reagan's visit.[144] He praised Reagan's meeting with Gorbachev in November and once again argued that it made it possible for him to achieve great things in foreign policy.[145]

The administration also brought Kissinger in on another major foreign policy problem it faced in 1985—international terrorism. Kissinger took a tough stance when he briefed the vice president's task force on terrorism in the wake of July's hijacking of TWA Flight 847. The briefing paper for Vice President Bush noted that Kissinger "has adopted an increasingly hardline position on combatting terrorism," and that this was related to the "superpower implications of the U.S. response." If the United States appeared uncertain or vulnerable in its actions against terrorism, and capable of being swayed by public opinion, the Soviets would "exploit our perceived weakness and ultimately destabilize the strategic balance." Kissinger advocated a rigid policy of no concessions to terrorists, fully understanding that "innocent lives must and will be sacrificed in pursuit of this higher purpose."[146]

Kissinger's assessment of the terrorist issue offers some insight into a bizarre moment in January 1986 when he considered running for governor of New York.[147] Kissinger's frustration with his exile from power during the Reagan years, coupled with the desperate search of Republican leaders for a candidate to take on the popular Mario Cuomo, combined to produce a brief flurry of interest in a Kissinger candidacy.[148] Isaacson dismisses the idea by noting, "The notion of him as governor, milking cows at state fairs and wrestling with legislators over highway funds, was on the face of it ridiculous."[149] However, just as important to Kissinger's consideration may have been the politically difficult task of defending positions like his hard-line stance on terrorism to a New York public. Kissinger understood the significance of domestic politics in the American system much better than he is normally given credit for, but he remained better at providing ideas to others than he was at advancing them on his own behalf.

With no position in the administration, and no political office to run for, Kissinger was reduced to commenting on the foreign policy actions he once had the power to shape and determine. In April 1986, during what he thought was a private session at the Library of Congress, Kissinger disparaged the arguments that the administration and its opponents were making over aid to the contra rebels in Nicaragua, saying both sides spoke in "platitudes." But then he went on to tell the group of scholars, including a reporter, that although Ronald Reagan was not the "trivial" figure most intellectuals thought he was, that when you met him, "You ask yourself, how did it ever occur to anybody that he should be Governor, much less President?" This derision was what Kissinger had been saying about Reagan to his liberal friends for years, but to have it in *The New York Times* and on ABC News was another matter altogether. Kissinger seemed aware of what he had done when he said to the reporter, "Did I kill myself in there?" He may not have been quite as regretful as he sounded, since he also told the scholars, "The Reagan Administration has been more personally offensive to me than any others."[150]

Kissinger's tone toward the Reagan administration's foreign policy shifted markedly toward the end of 1986. When Reagan went to Iceland to meet Gorbachev in October 1986, Kissinger warned that although the United States was in a "very favorable negotiating position," it was in danger of "frittering away this opportunity." He thought that Reagan was too enamored of the idea of creating a "personal chemistry" with Gorbachev and that the arms control agreements that might come out of the summit "would not reduce any significant danger."[151] Kissinger was appalled when it became clear after the summit that Reagan had almost agreed to Gorbachev's proposal to eliminate all nuclear weapons. He told a television audience that it was "preposterous" and "outrageous" for Gorbachev to spring such a proposal on Reagan.[152] Kissinger worried that Gorbachev's proposal, if serious, would leave the United States at a significant disadvantage in the conventional balance of arms in Europe, as well as potentially facing challenges from smaller nuclear powers. More important, Kissinger saw the Reykjavík summit as an example of the amateurishness of the Reagan foreign policy team, with the president poorly prepared and the Soviet leader able to dictate the proceedings.[153]

The revelation in early November 1986 that the Reagan administration was involved in trading arms for hostages, the Iran-Contra scandal, further intensified Kissinger's critique of the administration. The scandal, which originated in the Reagan National Security Council and involved selling weapons to Iran in return for the release of hostages in Lebanon, and then circumventing congressional restrictions by using the money to fund the contra rebels in Nicaragua, threatened to bring down the administration. Kissinger became a frequent guest of the TV news programs, using his experience as a former national security adviser to explain how the scandal occurred.[154] His criticism of the administration was sharp and severe, and he feared a "disintegration" of the administration's foreign policy. In Kissinger's words, on both the Reykjavík and Iran issues, Reagan "lacked a reasoned statement of options and consequences," which in Kissinger's language meant the administration had no idea what it was doing.[155] Kissinger also thought this was the case when Reagan moved toward accepting what appeared to be Soviet agreement on the "Zero Option," which involved removing all American tactical nuclear weapons from Europe in return for Soviet removal of its SS-20 missiles. This led to an awkward confrontation with Reagan at the March 1987 meeting of the President's Foreign Intelligence Advisory Board. Reagan, who rarely mentioned unpleasant disagreements in his diary, noted that Kissinger's ideas on arms control were ones "I do not agree with."[156] (The well-briefed Gorbachev knew about Reagan's annoyance with Kissinger. At their meeting in Moscow in May 1988, he joked that "he could give the

President some free advice—even though Henry Kissinger would have charged him millions for the favor.")[157]

Kissinger's opposition to Reagan's arms control policy even led him to work together again with Richard Nixon. His relationship with his former boss had remained testy, with occasional phone conversations when Nixon was in San Clemente. The two men had never socialized together, but after Nixon moved to New York in 1979, they did have the occasional lunch. (Nixon's house was just over the back fence from that of Kissinger's friend Arthur Schlesinger.) The two had traded barbs against each other in their memoirs, with Kissinger's contempt for Nixon's thinly veiled anti-Semitism and Nixon's dismissal of Kissinger's attempt to take credit for foreign policy being the most salient clashes. Their respective David Frost interviews had also created more rifts between them. Kissinger went with Nixon to Sadat's funeral in October 1981 and upon his return told Schlesinger, "As soon as we got on the plane, Nixon was his old self again, trying to manipulate everybody and everything, dropping poisonous remarks, doing his best to set people against each other." He added that when he was in the car with Gerald Ford alone, Ford said to him, "Sometimes I wish I had never pardoned that son of a bitch."[158] Despite all this, the two men still shared the "frustration of being out of power, but reveled in the ability to affect policy with a well-placed word or a strategically timed column."[159] Kissinger and Nixon joined forces to criticize the pursuit of the "Zero Option," suggesting that such a proposal would leave the Soviets with an unacceptable advantage in conventional forces, as well as allow them to threaten America's Asian allies with their remaining shorter-range nuclear missiles. In Nixon and Kissinger's words, the "wrong kind of deal" could jeopardize the NATO alliance, an alliance "sustained by seven administrations of both parties." The two men also took a thinly veiled shot at President Reagan when they wrote, "Any Western leader who indulges in the Soviets' disingenuous fantasies of a nuclear-free world courts unimaginable perils."[160]

Kissinger was a critic of the popular Intermediate-Range Nuclear Forces Treaty, signed by Reagan and Gorbachev in December 1987, although he argued that renegotiating it would be worse and that it should be ratified.[161] He remained convinced that the removal of theater nuclear forces in Europe would favor the Soviets, in large part because the Western democracies were lulled into complacency by arms control and would not make the fiscal sacrifices necessary to build up their conventional forces. Consequently, "strategy and arms control are on different, potentially incompatible tracks, each with its own constituency." Ironically, at least for someone like Kissinger who realized how Nixon used foreign policy for domestic purposes, he ended his point by claiming, "Sooner or later, a grave price will have to be paid for the paramountcy of domestic politics over national security considerations." Kissinger also criticized what he saw as the growing willingness to interfere in the domestic practices and policies of other nations around the globe. The second Reagan term had witnessed the administration's willingness to push nations like Haiti, the Philippines, Taiwan, and South Korea in a democratic direction. Kissinger accepted that the United States should prefer democracies, but he raised the objection, "As American resources are shrinking, the drive toward global intervention seems to be increasing." He closed this long lament about the direction of U.S. foreign policy by recalling his November 1984 article about the great opportunity that Ronald Reagan had to "reconcile the American domestic debate and to take bipartisanship beyond the least common denominator. This has not happened." Still, he hoped that a lame-duck President Reagan might raise the issue of the "relationship between power and diplomacy, of the content of peace and the nature of global progress." He also hoped that the presidential candidates might participate in such a national debate rather than rely on "gimmicks" in their treatment of foreign policy.[162]

Kissinger's criticism of Reagan was a move to the right of the political spectrum, courting that faction of Republicans who had always been hostile to his personality and policies. Kissinger "realized it was the true believers on the Right rather than his old academic colleagues on the Left who had the power to prevent him from serving in another Republican administration."[163] While this was undoubtedly part of Kissinger's motivation, his foreign policy views also reflected a certain innate caution, concern for stability, and criticism of American crusading that had been with him since his time in office. To some extent, these views were ideally suited for him to work with Vice President George H. W. Bush, who quickly became the front-runner for the Republican nomination. Kissinger may well have known that many of his negative comments about Bush being "weak" would have gotten back to the vice president. He noticed that he was the only person "criticized" by name in Bush's campaign biography.[164] Kissinger sought to make amends in every way possible. He praised Bush repeatedly in his television interviews, describing the "rather courageous step" Bush had taken in encouraging Nixon to resign and remarking on how Bush had gained "the respect of all of the Chinese leaders" during his service there. In an indirect criticism of his former deputy Alexander Haig, who was also running for president, Kissinger recalled how at the time of the assassination attempt on Ronald Reagan, Bush "behaved very well, with great dignity." (Haig's famous "I'm in charge here" remained one of his most public missteps.) Kissinger even tried to make an asset of Bush's frequent attendance at state funerals as vice president, arguing that it allowed him to get a reading of the new leaders.[165] He harshly criticized Bush's Democratic rival, Michael Dukakis, as "completely unqualified" on foreign policy, adding, "It is a myth that you can learn in office."[166] Dukakis's silence on foreign policy, Kissinger said, made him "very nervous."[167] The Bush team even made sure Kissinger was at the presidential debate, thinking his presence might unnerve and intimidate Dukakis.[168]

Kissinger not only sang the praises of George Bush, he also helped him in what proved one of his most controversial moves: selecting Dan Quayle as his running mate. The impression that Quayle was intellectually ill-equipped to become president was widely shared in the media, reinforced by the Democratic vice presidential candidate Lloyd Bentsen's famous "You're no Jack Kennedy" put-down in their debate. Kissinger praised Quayle as "one of the best informed senators on National Security affairs that I know" and "unusually well informed in the areas that we discussed which dealt mostly with national security issues and arms control and negotiations with the Soviets."[169] Kissinger coached Quayle on foreign policy for the vice presidential debate, and they maintained a friendship after the election. Kissinger told Arthur Schlesinger that he found Quayle to be "well-informed and intelligent," which Schlesinger took to mean, "That Quayle listens reverently to Henry and that Henry thinks Quayle may be President someday."[170]

Kissinger's all-out dedication to the Bush-Quayle ticket came from his hope that Bush would select him as secretary of state, though he told intimates that would be only for a year, while James Baker, as Bush's chief of staff, got the White House in order.[171] In fact, Bush selected Baker as secretary of state and took two members of Kissinger Associates, Brent Scowcroft and Lawrence Eagleburger, as his national security adviser and deputy secretary of state, respectively. Although disappointed he was not selected, Kissinger thought this ensured his access to the administration in a way that he'd never possessed during the Reagan years. Almost immediately, he suggested to President-elect Bush that he would travel to Moscow to meet with Gorbachev to discuss some type of deal with the Soviets about the future of Eastern Europe. In Kissinger's plan, the Soviets would promise not to use violence to suppress the liberalization of Eastern Europe, as they had in Hungary in 1956 and Czechoslovakia in 1968, in return for which the West would not exploit the changes to damage "legitimate" Soviet security interests. The idea would bring a type of "Finlandization" of Eastern Europe, something that most observers in early 1989 thought very desirable. As one account put it, "The proposal was classically Kissingerian: the use of secret high-level diplomacy to reach a bargain based on the balance of power." Bush was intrigued enough by the idea to authorize Kissinger to take a letter from him to Gorbachev, assuring Gorbachev that his administration would continue in the spirit of the Reagan administration. It would need some time to assess the situation, and he hoped the Russian leader could be patient.[172]

Kissinger met first with Alexander Yakovlev, one of Gorbachev's closest aides. Yakovlev noted that Kissinger "made a statement about his closeness to the new President of the USA, George Bush, and to the people comprising his inner circle." Kissinger went on to tell Yakovlev that the administration wanted to move forward with the Soviets to deal with the "unpredictability" of the future of Europe. He quoted Kissinger as saying, "G. Bush, as President, would be willing to work on ensuring conditions in which a political evolution could be possible, but a political explosion would not be allowed [to happen]." In Kissinger's view, this was about the United States and the Soviet Union learning "to live in balance with each other." Kissinger added, in a characteristic formulation, "We should not be trying to reform you and you [should] agree to live in conditions of relative and not absolute security. I do not believe that you have any plans for world revolution, and the Soviet Union does not have capabilities for that either."[173] The Bush administration was willing to talk about these things with the Soviets in a "confidential manner." The next day Kissinger gave much the same message to Gorbachev. The Soviet leader told Kissinger that he would like to see the Americans allow the Soviet Union greater access to their market and repeal restrictions dating to the 1970s. Kissinger responded, "The Jackson-Vanik Amendment was directed against me in the first place, and only then against the Soviet Union."[174] Kissinger also assured Gorbachev that he could send messages through him to the Bush administration, although Gorbachev may not have been as taken with him as Kissinger thought. Gorbachev later told his advisers that he thought Kissinger "hinted at the idea of a USSR-USA condominium over Europe."[175] The Soviet leader did send a letter back to Bush through Kissinger. Bush called a few days later and thanked Gorbachev for being "very generous in his time with Henry Kissinger." He assured Gorbachev that he would listen to what Kissinger reported, but then added, "They would not necessarily believe everything because this was, after all, Henry Kissinger, but they knew the General Secretary had been generous with his time, and they would listen attentively to what Dr. Kissinger said."[176] Unaware that Bush was already distancing himself from him and his mission, a cheerful Kissinger returned to Washington with Gorbachev's letter and met with Bush, joking with reporters that he didn't know what was in the letter since "it was in Russian so I couldn't read it."[177]

Critics later referred to Kissinger's approach as "Yalta II," which was unfair but not wholly inaccurate. Kissinger was in accord with Bush in wanting to prevent a violent Soviet crackdown. Bush shared with Kissinger the belief that the Russians had to show their goodwill through more than "cosmetic changes," and that until they did, Gorbachev's "peace offensive" in Europe was a threat to the Western alliance. Bush used Kissinger's mission to feel out Gorbachev's response, but he also maintained his distance from the former secretary of state, whom he clearly mistrusted, a mistrust that he did not hesitate to share with Gorbachev. Ultimately, the Kissinger proposal was overtaken by the speed of events in Eastern Europe, and when State Department officials reviewed it, they made the case that the Kissinger Plan legitimized a Soviet presence in Eastern Europe that was eroding on its own. "Why buy what history is giving you for free?" was how one official put it. Borrowing this approach, Secretary of State Baker talked about Kissinger's idea with the *New York Times* columnist Thomas L. Friedman and implied it was unnecessary, given the favorable trends already unfolding in Eastern Europe. Kissinger reacted angrily to what he felt was Baker's distortion of his approach, and the Yalta II controversy it stirred. He wrote an op-ed in which he insisted, "It goes without saying that the goal of American policy should be the reversal of Yalta, not the revival of Yalta." Baker implied diplomacy was unnecessary unless anarchy broke out. Kissinger's fear was that "once there is anarchy and the tanks roll, it is too late for diplomacy."[178]

Kissinger's biographer wrote, "From the Yalta II incident on, Kissinger's relations with Bush and Baker were chilly ... and they made no effort to involve Kissinger in the administration's momentous decisions as the Soviet hold on Eastern Europe crumbled."[179] Another writer called this the "worst indignity" inflicted on Kissinger in his attempt to return to policy making.[180] These judgments exaggerate the degree to which the Bush administration marginalized Kissinger. Bush may not have liked or trusted Kissinger, but he knew his value. The former secretary of state continued to play a role, both in policy issues and opinion making. In late 1989, Kissinger advised President Bush that a "two-Germanys policy" would be "disastrous," warning that "if the Germans see us as obstructing their aspirations, we'll pay a price later on." Kissinger encouraged Bush to move "in virtual lockstep" with the West German chancellor.[181] This advice accorded with Bush's own instincts, but in reinforcing them, Kissinger played a role in one of the great successes of the administration: the peaceful reunification of Germany. Kissinger also continued to have a role in policy toward China. After the Tiananmen Square massacre, when Chinese soldiers crushed the student protests, many Americans wanted the Bush administration to enact tough measures against Chinese trade to punish the Beijing government. Kissinger counseled moderation and faced harsh criticism; he was accused of "kissing Deng Xiaoping's bloodied hand."[182] Kissinger never failed to argue for the importance of the U.S.-China relationship, and he remained a key interlocutor between the two countries. Both he and Nixon undertook separate trips to China later in the year to work to repair relations, with Kissinger arguing that it was necessary for the United States to have a "strategic dialogue" with Beijing.[183] The Kissinger and Nixon trips prepared the ground for Scowcroft's second visit to Beijing in December 1989, and helped settle some of the most difficult issues coming out of the Tiananmen Square repression and the U.S. reaction.[184]

During the Bush years, Kissinger was also called on frequently to comment on policies in the Middle East and toward the Soviet Union. He was an outspoken supporter of Bush's policies after the Iraqi invasion of Kuwait and backed his decision to send forces to Saudi Arabia. He was a strong supporter of using force to oust Saddam Hussein, appearing frequently on the evening news. He was critical of the administration only when it looked as though it would back away from a confrontation with Saddam.[185] Kissinger called Bush shortly after the war began in January 1991 and told him, "Thank you for saving us all from this demon Saddam Hussein."[186] During the conflict, he was a frequent presence on both the networks and that newer presence in the media world, CNN, providing commentary and analyzing the diplomatic situation of the United States.[187] After the war, he backed the administration's efforts at the Madrid conference to encourage negotiations between the Israelis and the Palestinians. He was skeptical of President Bush's claim of a "new world order" in the wake of the Persian Gulf War, and worried that the United States could become overextended in its commitments.[188] Kissinger was also a frequent commentator in the aftermath of the failed Soviet coup and the resulting collapse of the Soviet Union. Once again, he joined with his former boss Richard Nixon in criticizing what he regarded as the Bush administration's inadequate response to Russia and its need for economic assistance from the West.[189]

Kissinger also assumed a particularly high profile on terrorism issues. With Americans being taken hostage in Lebanon, the issue was frequently in the public eye and subject to emotional debate. After the kidnapping and execution of Colonel William Higgins, there was an even greater public outcry. On a special *Nightline* on August 3, 1989, Ted Koppel hosted a mock meeting of the National Security Council, replete with elderly foreign affairs experts assembled around a table. Their task was to handle a hostage crisis, proposing and debating possible solutions. Kissinger chaired the meeting and made a point of saying he would have begun an NSC meeting when he was national security adviser by asking, "What are we trying to do? What are we trying to accomplish? Are we trying to retaliate for the murder of an American colonel? Are we trying to prevent an additional hostage from being executed? Are we trying to tackle the hostage situation in its totality?"[190] Kissinger dominated the discussion, leading the mock NSC toward many of his own stated positions on how to respond to terrorism. The hourlong show, largely uninterrupted by Koppel, was a small indication of the key role Kissinger still occupied in any national discussion of foreign policy issues.

Kissinger supported Bush for reelection in 1992, although he told his friend Schlesinger that the president was "a very petty man," and if Kissinger still had hopes of an official return, they probably lay with Quayle's ascendancy.[191] Compared with his role in 1988, Kissinger was involved only minimally in the reelection efforts. In fact, in September 1992 he found himself in the national spotlight over an issue that he must have thought had long been resolved. The Senate Select Committee on POW/MIA Affairs held widely covered hearings over the possibility that American prisoners were left behind in Southeast Asia. In the 1980s, the hit movie *Rambo II: First Blood* had popularized the idea that hundreds of American prisoners had been abandoned in Indochina, and polls showed that some 70 percent of Americans believed there were still American prisoners in Southeast Asia. Ross Perot, who was prominent at the time as a third-party candidate for president, had also highlighted this issue. When the committee met in September 1992, Defense Secretaries Melvin Laird and James Schlesinger both testified that they believed there was intelligence that some American prisoners might have been left behind in Laos. For his part, Kissinger strongly rejected the idea and bristled at the suggestion there was a conspiracy to hide the fact. In a sharp exchange with Senator John Kerry, Kissinger said he knew that the accusation the United States abandoned POWs was a "flat-out lie," adding, "There is no excuse, two decades after the fact, for anyone to imply that the last five presidents from both parties, their White House staffs, secretaries of state and defense, and career diplomatic and military services either knowingly or negligently failed to do everything they could to recover and identify all of our prisoners and MIAs."[192] Kissinger admitted it was possible the Vietnamese had kept prisoners, and he actually hoped that Kerry's committee would put the issue to rest. He said angrily, "It did not occur to me that American officials would become the victims of such investigations."[193] Kissinger's testimony was effective in calming the committee's inquiry, and when its report was issued in January 1993, it received relatively little notice or attention. The passage of time and the opening up of Vietnam and the rest of Southeast Asia casts doubt on this widely believed "myth" of the Vietnam War, but the controversy reflected how Vietnam continued to haunt Kissinger.

The POW/MIA issue was not the only irritant Kissinger felt in late 1992. Walter Isaacson, the editor of *Time*, published *Kissinger: A Biography*, and Kissinger's reaction proved the truth of Gerald's Ford's observation that Kissinger had the thinnest skin of anyone he knew in public life. Isaacson's picture of Kissinger, while generally favorable, was "warts and all," and it was clear that many of Kissinger's staff and former staff members shared memories of their boss. *Newsweek* summarized the book as portraying Kissinger "as a masterful and farsighted diplomat, but also a manipulative, deceitful, and paranoid bureaucratic infighter." "He is insane over this book," one former associate told the magazine, and Kissinger was also furious over positive reviews of the book. He angrily called his former assistant William Hyland, who had praised the book's "balanced objectivity," and subsequently did not attend a dinner honoring Hyland's retirement as editor of *Foreign Affairs*.[194] Theodore Draper's favorable review of the book in *The New York Times Book Review* led Kissinger to encourage his friend Stephen Graubard to write a four-page single-spaced letter to the *NYTBR* attacking the book's treatment of Kissinger's Harvard years—only a small fraction of the almost nine-hundred-page study.[195] One former staff member remarked that the book was just "a long overdue correction to his Superman image," but to Kissinger, for whom his Superman image was central to his self-promotion as well as his power and influence, it was an unwelcome affront.[196]

THE ELDER STATESMAN: SCHOLAR, EULOGIST, ADVISER

The election of Bill Clinton, the first Democrat in the White House in over a decade, did not augur well for Kissinger's influence in Washington. Clinton believed Kissinger played a disreputable role in the 1968 election, passing information about the progress of the Paris peace talks to Richard Nixon.[197] Only a few days after the election, Leslie Gelb, a former undersecretary of state during the Carter years and the New York Times foreign affairs correspondent, accused Kissinger and others in the Republican establishment of "undermining Bill Clinton with foreign diplomats and businessmen—just as they did with Jimmy Carter." Gelb, who studied under Kissinger at Harvard, said of Kissinger, "I've never known a man so admired and distrusted at the same time." Gelb accused Kissinger of telling foreign representatives that Clinton was "dangerously inexperienced in world politics," surrounded by naive former Carter officials and, with only 43 percent of the vote, lacking a mandate for change. Gelb urged the president-elect to "send out the word that he knows who they are—and that he will settle accounts soon."[198] Kissinger rejected Gelb's charges, professing to be shocked at Gelb's "mean-spirited injunction to the new President to 'settle accounts.'"[199] It is not hard to imagine, however, that Gelb was right about what was being said by Kissinger. His article was a preemptive shot at Kissinger, coming from those Democrats who remembered the struggles Jimmy Carter faced.

With the end of the Cold War and the decreased importance of foreign policy to the electorate, the Clinton administration did not face the type of Republican reaction on foreign policy that Jimmy Carter had confronted. For his part, Kissinger remained an active commentator on foreign policy during the Clinton administration, critical of some policies, such as on Somalia and Haiti, but supportive of others, including the Clinton initiatives toward China and the Middle East and the trade agreement with Mexico and Canada. He was invited to the White House when Clinton reversed his campaign pledge and renewed China's most-favored-nation status, and he supported Clinton's successful effort to normalize trade with the People's Republic of China. Kissinger promoted the idea that China's economic development and integration into the world economy was in America's national interest, and he consistently downplayed concerns about human rights and Chinese political authoritarianism. The Kissinger of the Clinton years was also distinctly opposed to the use of U.S. military force abroad, particularly in the Balkans. He was skeptical about humanitarian intervention, and criticized the administration for the "mission creep" of its intervention in Somalia as well as in Haiti. *Nightline* with Ted Koppel was still one of Kissinger's preferred media outlets, and he appeared on extended segments dealing with Serbia, the Middle East, Somalia, and Russia.[200] His eulogy for Richard Nixon was on all three networks and cable in April 1994, and afforded him the opportunity to praise Nixon as a "seminal president" and highlight their foreign policy successes.[201] As the 1990s went on, Kissinger appeared more frequently on CNN, particularly for its "Breaking News" segments. An obviously distressed and emotional Kissinger talked of Yitzhak Rabin hours after his assassination, praising his role as a "soldier and a thinker," a man of peace who "walked a lonely road."[202] He provided commentary throughout the Republican National Convention of 1996, as well as the Clinton summits on Russia and the Middle East.[203]

Along with his role in commenting on foreign policy and running Kissinger Associates, Kissinger returned to writing in the 1990s, producing three major books. The first was *Diplomacy* in 1994, which quickly became a bestseller. At more than eight hundred pages, the book begins with the story of modern international relations with Cardinal Richelieu in the seventeenth century but focuses most of its attention on the issues, personalities, and movements of the twentieth century. In interpreting the history of American diplomacy, Kissinger juxtaposes two presidents, Theodore Roosevelt and Woodrow Wilson, as representing the poles of realism and idealism. While acknowledging the importance of Wilsonian ideals in the appeal of America in the world, Kissinger expresses a decided preference for Theodore Roosevelt, who understood the importance of conducting foreign policy "in the national interest." Some of Kissinger's passages about Roosevelt are essentially identical to the way he would describe his own foreign policy: "Roosevelt was impatient with the pieties which dominated American thinking on foreign policy." "Nothing annoyed Roosevelt as much as high sounding principles backed by neither power nor the will to implement them." "To [Roosevelt], peace was inherently fragile and could be preserved only by eternal vigilance, by the arms of the strong, and by alliances among the like-minded."[204] Not surprisingly, the book's survey of the rest of twentieth-century American diplomacy finds that only during the Nixon-Ford years did leaders conduct foreign policy in proper and realistic consideration of America's interests and capabilities. Ernest R. May, a former colleague of Kissinger's, praised the book for its "marriage of vision and shrewdness" in treating the subject of diplomacy, but also noted that the book is "a book of maxims disguised as a history of statecraft. The maxims are often splendid. The history is not."[205] Showing his thin skin had not grown any thicker, Kissinger wrote a long response in which he argued that May's generally favorable review was filled with "petty distortions and personal aspersions."[206]

Diplomacy was representative of Kissinger's determination to assert his position as the foremost American scholar-diplomat of his generation, and place his own work in the Nixon and Ford administrations in the broad historical sweep of twentieth-century American diplomacy. It also compelled Kissinger to complete the third volume of his memoirs, covering the years of Gerald Ford's presidency. *Years of Renewal*, published in 1999, lacks the rich narrative, the many personal portraits, and the careful attention to detail of the earlier works. Although it has the benefit of greater perspective, it suffers from Kissinger's heavy-handed determination to fit the Ford presidency into a grand narrative of America's triumph in the Cold War. Kissinger even manages to frame the Ford administration, whose top leaders unanimously despised Ronald Reagan, as laying the groundwork for Reagan in the 1980s. Kissinger is most concerned with defending himself from his neoconservative critics, arguing, "By depicting the diplomatic strategy of the Nixon and Ford Administrations as a form of appeasement and our resistance to communist expansion in various theaters as a diversion from the main struggle, the neoconservatives undercut the real foreign policy debate, which was not with them but with the liberals." In Kissinger's view, the Ford presidency was more successful and more accomplished than previously believed, and Reagan's policy was, "in fact, a canny elaboration of the geopolitical strategies of the Nixon and Ford administrations combined with the rhetoric of Wilsonianism—a quintessentially American combination of pragmatism and idealism."[207]

Completing his memoirs did allow Kissinger the luxury of quoting Winston Churchill's famous adage, "History will be kind to me for I intend to write it." As the documents and records of the Nixon and Ford years became available, however, historians took a hard look at Kissinger's policies, and they were not kind. While he could ignore many of the scholarly and academic monographs, Kissinger had a much more difficult time addressing the inflammatory and polemical work of the British essayist Christopher Hitchens. Hitchens was a supremely gifted writer whose personal political journey took him from being on the left and seeing America as the "evil empire" to supporting the invasion of Iraq and George W. Bush. Throughout his political evolution, however, he maintained his distaste for Nixon's "indescribably loathsome deputy Henry Kissinger."[208] Hitchens published *The Trial of Henry Kissinger*, a book that charged Kissinger with a series of crimes in Cambodia, Chile, and East Timor, and argued, "It is time for justice to take a hand."[209] A year later, the BBC released a documentary based on Hitchens's book, giving the charges against the former secretary of state an even wider audience. For the first time Kissinger faced a real limit on his ability to travel, as a judge in Paris sent officials to serve a summons on Kissinger while he was staying at the Ritz hotel, forcing him to leave the country quickly.[210]

To say that the Hitchens book is one-sided and distorted is beside the point. Much of what he offered to an American and a world audience was already present in the books by Heller, Shawcross, and Hersh. Hitchens, nevertheless, distilled the indictment of Kissinger into a passionate jeremiad that was as much about the moral compromises and expediency embedded in America's Cold War policies as it was about the personal responsibility of Henry Kissinger. Because Kissinger sought to be America's diplomat and world statesman, to promote himself as the heroic negotiator bringing peace and stability through his efforts, brilliantly using the media to sustain this Superman image, he was the obvious and most convenient target of the rage against the impact of those Cold War policies. That his own philosophy of international relations held that in a tragic world, a statesman was not able to choose between good and evil, but only among different forms of evil, made the Hitchens indictment all the more persuasive among those who possessed a more idealistic, noble, and even pacifist vision of international affairs. Kissinger's choices were, in their view, simply evil, and he was a war criminal, no different from those sentenced at Nuremberg.

On September 10, 2001, Hitchens told a campus audience at the University of Washington that the next day, the family of a murdered Chilean general, General René Schneider, would bring a lawsuit against Henry Kissinger in a federal court in Washington. Hitchens boasted, "So comrades and friends, brothers and sisters, we shall be able to say tomorrow—September 11, 2001—will long be remembered as a landmark day in the struggle for human rights."[211] As Hitchens himself remembered, the terrorist attacks of that day did not diminish the fervor with which he argued for Kissinger's criminality, but he recognized that it changed the climate of public opinion within the United States. Although the parallel is an inexact one, just as Kissinger had emerged to chair the Central America committee in the wake of Seymour Hersh's book and its attack on him, the 9/11 attacks afforded Kissinger the opportunity to reemerge as an elder statesman in an America at war. The possibility of war crimes trials for Cold War–era diplomats faded away as America's "holiday from history" ended and the "war on terror" commenced. The lawsuit was eventually dismissed.

Kissinger was in Germany on September 11, and when reached by phone he told CNN that the Bush administration would need to retaliate swiftly. At age seventy-seven as the presidential campaign of 2000 began, Kissinger no longer entertained thoughts of a government role, but he swiftly signed on to George W. Bush's campaign, mending fences with former rivals like Donald Rumsfeld and developing a close relationship with Vice President Dick Cheney. Along with Colin Powell, Kissinger helped prepare Bush for the foreign policy debate with Vice President Al Gore. The famous Watergate journalist Bob Woodward was exaggerating when he wrote, "Former Secretary of State Henry Kissinger had a powerful, largely invisible influence on the foreign policy of the Bush Administration," but Kissinger certainly found his advice and counsel welcomed by Cheney, Rumsfeld, and the younger Bush, who did not have the resentments his father carried from previous encounters with Kissinger.[212] Both Cheney and Rumsfeld met regularly with Kissinger, and Kissinger was an outspoken supporter of the administration's policies. As early as September 17, 2001, he told CNN, "If [Iraq has] ties to any of these terrorist networks, they should be attacked." Kissinger did not share the neoconservative perspective about liberating Iraq or establishing democracy there, but he was persuaded that an Iraqi regime with weapons of mass destruction posed a threat to the United States. When his former deputy Brent Scowcroft criticized the Bush administration's drive toward war from a realist perspective, Kissinger privately sympathized but publicly continued to support the administration.

On November 27, 2002, President Bush signed the bill creating the bipartisan September 11 Commission and selected Kissinger as chair, with the former Democratic senator George Mitchell as co-chair. Bush called Kissinger "one of our Nation's most accomplished and respected public servants," insisting that "Dr. Kissinger will bring broad experience, clear thinking, and careful judgment to this important task."[213] The lead story that night on all three networks was a somber Kissinger assuring journalists that the president supported him going "where the facts lead us," and that he was "not restricted by any foreign policy considerations." Tom Brokaw noted that Kissinger was a "controversial selection" because of his past, "from Vietnam, to Chile, to China."[214] Sandy Berger, who served as Clinton's national security adviser, called Kissinger's selection a "very good choice," and even William Safire, who had been harshly critical of Kissinger in the Ford administration, argued that Kissinger's long experience in government would give him the ability to study the complex intelligence bureaucracy and explain how it had failed to prevent the 9/11 attacks. Safire dismissed both what he called the "hate-Henry industry" for raising issues from the Vietnam era and the idea that his business contacts from Kissinger Associates might influence his findings. "He is working for his historic reputation, not his clients." Walter Isaacson, Kissinger's biographer, now the chairman and chief executive officer of CNN, acknowledged the controversy about Kissinger but believed that he was "capable of being analytically brilliant and intellectually honest, even brutally so." He echoed Safire's argument that the seventy-nine-year-old Kissinger saw this as a chance "to burnish his reputation for history."[215]

Twenty years earlier Kissinger's appointment to chair the Central American commission brought praise and criticism, but the praise quickly drowned out the naysayers. This was not the case in 2002. Almost immediately Senator John Kerry, who had tangled with Kissinger over the POW/MIA issue and was planning to run for president in 2004, insisted that Kissinger sever any business relationships from Kissinger Associates that might make his objectivity suspect. Kissinger promised to do so, insisting that "no foreign government'" would affect his judgment. The editorial page of *The New York Times* called Kissinger a "consummate Washington insider" and doubted that a man like him, with his "affinity for power and the commercial interest he has cultivated" could ever be "the staunchly independent type that is needed for this critical post." The editors reasoned that the Bush administration appointed Kissinger to "contain an investigation" the administration had originally opposed.[216] Kissinger also faced a new generation of media pundits who regarded his historical record with deep disdain. No longer having friends at *The New York Times* like Scotty Reston or Max Frankel to sing his praises, Kissinger faced a torrent of criticism, often reflecting the pervasive influence of the Hersh, Shawcross, and Hitchens books. The liberal columnist Molly Ivins, famous for her humor as much as her journalism, wrote, "Good grief. I turn my back for 10 minutes and they bring back the old War Criminal. I try not to hold grudges, but I must admit I have never lost one ounce of rancor toward Henry Kissinger, that cynical, slithery, self-absorbed pathological liar." Frank Rich called Kissinger the "strangest player" in an administration bent on war with Iraq and "predictably" engaged in a cover-up of his various business associates who might be connected to the investigation.[217] *The New York Times'* Maureen Dowd accused Kissinger of thinking "the greatest threat to the country was the prying eyes of the public, the press, and Congress."[218] She referenced Kissinger's reputation for secrecy and cover-ups: "If you want to get to the bottom of something you don't appoint Henry Kissinger. If you want to keep others from getting to the bottom of something, you appoint Henry Kissinger." Kissinger angrily responded that the *Times* would eventually apologize for judging him that way after the commission's report was finished. But the criticism intensified, with Clarence Page of the *Chicago Tribune* noting, "From Cambodia to Chile," Kissinger was "widely reviled." Even older journalists, ones Kissinger had once courted, joined in. Helen Thomas, who had once traveled with Kissinger in the Middle East, attacked the secrecy and way Kissinger protected the "government establishment."[219]

Two weeks later Kissinger quit the chairmanship abruptly, with his professed reason being that it would take a long time for him to divest from his various business associations and that the commission needed to begin its work promptly. Kissinger also did not want to provide Congress with information regarding the clients of Kissinger Associates, especially the foreign governments. The timing of his resignation ended up linking it in the evening news to the Senate majority leader Trent Lott's refusal to step aside because of racist comments he made about the 1948 election, a double set of embarrassments for the Bush administration.[220] The quick appointment of the former New Jersey governor Thomas Kean and the former congressman Lee Hamilton brought the 9/11 Commission back into order, and Kissinger's resignation, as Jussi Hahnhimäki later wrote, "became a footnote in history as the Bush Administration geared up for its war against Iraq."[221]

Kissinger remained a voice in support of that policy, appearing frequently on CNN, and less frequently on the traditional networks, in support of the president. After Colin Powell presented the American case to the United Nations, Kissinger told CNN's Aaron Brown that Powell had "closed the deal" on the issue of Iraq's violation of UN sanctions. He called Saddam a "maniac" who had killed members of his own family and he criticized France's refusal to follow the American lead.[222] As the countdown to war came closer, Kissinger remained supportive of Bush's approach, insisting that no last-minute compromise could make a difference, since the Iraqi president, Saddam Hussein, "has had twelve years to comply."[223] After what seemed like a rapid American military victory, and the setting up of an occupation government, Kissinger was back on the evening news to discuss his protégé Paul Bremer, who became the top administrator in Iraq.[224]

As the insurgency within Iraq continued and grew over the next three years, Kissinger became increasingly concerned over the parallels he perceived with Vietnam. He disliked Bush's second inaugural address, with its emphasis on promoting democracy and freedom throughout the Middle East. He was careful to put a more positive spin on his criticism when he met with the White House adviser Michael Gerson, recognizing that Bush's ideological approach might help with American public opinion and sustain a longer military campaign. Nevertheless, Kissinger worried that the administration was floundering in Iraq, promoting the elections it had sponsored and talking about America "standing down" as Iraqis "stood up." The determination to withdraw seemed to promote a willful blindness toward the deteriorating situation. Kissinger believed that the Bush administration lacked a strategy to defeat the insurgency, and he told the former general Jack Keane, with whom he served on the Defense Policy Board Advisory Committee, "We will lose."[225] In a widely read newspaper column in August 2005, Kissinger cautioned the administration that waning public support for the war could produce a Vietnam-like situation. The line in his column that made the most impact among Bush's advisers was actually drawn from Kissinger's reading of the French experience in Algeria, not the American one in Vietnam: "Victory over the insurgency is the only meaningful exit strategy." Kissinger repeatedly warned of the dangers of starting to withdraw troops before securing such a victory. As Cheney recalled, Kissinger told him, "Once you start . . . the Democrats' demands for more will never end." He shared with Cheney and Bush his famous "salted peanuts" memo of September 1969, telling them, "Withdrawals are like salted peanuts. Once you start, you can't stop." He told Gerson, "The president can't be talking about troop reductions as a centerpiece . . . You may want to reduce troops. But troop reduction should not be the objective; this is not where you put your emphasis."[226]

Bob Woodward portrayed Kissinger as something akin to the evil genius behind Bush's failed Iraq policy when he published *State of Denial* in late 2006.[227] The book appeared shortly before the Iraq Study Group, the bipartisan panel Bush had created in March 2006, issued its report. That report, which provided a number of possible diplomatic options for facilitating an American withdrawal, also suggested the possibility of increasing the number of American soldiers in order to stabilize Iraq. Nevertheless, the over-whelming Democratic victories in the November 2006 midterm elections, coupled with Bush's decision to replace Defense Secretary Rumsfeld, seemed to indicate a change of strategy in Iraq. Kissinger changed his advice, now arguing publicly that it was not possible to achieve victory in Iraq. In echoes of the "decent interval" strategy he had employed in Vietnam, Kissinger, in var-ious newspaper columns and on interview shows, advised the Bush adminis-tration to seek some larger diplomatic arrangement with Iraq's neighbors, especially Syria, that would allow for the withdrawal of American forces.[228] Kissinger was genuinely surprised when President Bush decided instead on the "surge" strategy, increasing the number of American combat troops with the goal of stabilizing the country. Kissinger never became a vocal critic, but he remained pessimistic about the surge strategy well into 2007, especially as he perceived the violence in Iraq spiking and the president's political support weakening in the United States.[229] Kissinger wrote, "The war in Iraq is ap-proaching a kind of self-imposed climax."[230]

As Tom Ricks points out in his book on the surge, Kissinger was right that the "war was approaching a climax—but not the sort [Kissinger] envi-sioned."[231] In fact the insurgency was beginning to run out of steam, and the American surge was beginning to work. Coupled with the "Sunni awakening"—the various alliances American military commanders forged with Sunni leaders—the level of violence in Iraq declined precipitously. For his part, despite his initial skepticism, Kissinger supported the administration and remained in its good graces. He provided advice to Secretary of State Condo-leezza Rice in her decision to restart the Six Power Talks and attempt to end North Korea's nuclear program. Rice used Kissinger to reinforce the message to China's President Hu that the United States was serious in these efforts.[232] Kissinger continued to enjoy enormous prestige within China, and he at-tended the 2008 Olympics as an honored guest with President Bush. Kissinger also was outspoken about the idea of curbing Iran's nuclear program, which he argued risked destabilizing the entire Middle East.

It would be on this issue that Henry Kissinger would have his name used by both presidential candidates during the first debate between Barack

Obama and John McCain. McCain had sought to portray Obama as danger-ously naive about American foreign policy, taking up a point Hillary Clinton had raised against the Illinois senator during the heated Democratic prima-ries. Clinton criticized Obama when he said he would meet with America's enemies—Iran, North Korea, and Cuba—without preconditions. Clinton focused on the idea of meeting with the most loathsome of these at the time, the Iranian president, Mahmoud Ahmadinejad. Ahmadinejad's anti-Semitism and Holocaust denial had made him particularly unacceptable, and Clinton had attacked Obama for this. During the presidential debate, when asked about dealing with Iran, McCain used the analogy of Nixon's trip to China and brought up how this had first been prepared by Henry Kissinger's visits. This was the proper way to handle diplomacy, McCain emphasized in his attack on Obama. Obama jumped at the opportunity to invoke Kissinger, noting that the famous statesman had, along with other secretaries of state, agreed that the United States should meet with Iran. And Obama added, "Guess what—without preconditions." His Democratic rival's invoking of Kissinger's words seemed to unsettle McCain, who found himself telling Obama that he had misunderstood. "My friend Dr. Kissinger, who's been my friend for 35 years, would be interested to hear this conversation and Sena-tor's Obama's depiction of his positions on the issue. I've known him for 35 years."[233] (Indeed, McCain had even arranged for his vice presidential candi-date, Sarah Palin, to meet with Kissinger. Maureen Dowd caustically wrote, "Kissinger probably explained détente and Metternich to Palin, while she explained the Iditarod and moose carving to him.")[234]

Thirty-two years after he had left his last public office, two U.S. presiden-tial candidates were still invoking Henry Kissinger's name and claiming his approval for the diplomatic strategies they would use with America's adver-saries. It was a remarkable testament to the degree to which Kissinger had become identified in history and legend as a symbol of American foreign policy—a hotly contested one, but a symbol nevertheless.[235]

EPILOGUE:
HENRY KISSINGER—CELEBRITY
DIPLOMAT, COLD WAR ICON

L ATE-NIGHT TELEVISION VIEWERS in the summer of 2013 expected that
 Stephen Colbert, the popular host of Comedy Central's *The Colbert Report*,
would reveal the song of the summer with his guests the French electronic
music duo Daft Punk. At the last minute, the group canceled their appearance
because Viacom, the owner of both Comedy Central and MTV, had booked
them for a "surprise appearance" on the following month's Video Music
Awards. Colbert told his audience that Daft Punk's "peeps" feared that if the
group were on Colbert's show, no one would watch them the next month. He
then explained, with his tongue planted firmly in his cheek, "That's how music works. You love a band, you see them once, you never want to see them
again. That's why when the Beatles went on *Ed Sullivan*, they dropped off the
face of the earth." After the laughter subsided and the audience was suitably

primed for a different and improvised show, Colbert brought on some new guests, including the actors Ashton Kutcher, Hugh Laurie, and Robin Thicke, and eventually proceeded to do his own dance number with Radio City Music Hall's famous Rockettes. Colbert danced his way out of the studio and through the streets of Manhattan, and at one point into the Park Avenue office of Henry Kissinger. Kissinger was clearly in on the joke, but sat at his desk and looked on seriously as Colbert danced merrily around his office. Eventually Kissinger picked up his phone and said in his distinctive voice, "Security."[1]

Colbert, who hosted his show in character as a bloviating, right-wing news host, had come to like and respect Henry Kissinger and considered him a "friend of the show."[2] Colbert had Kissinger on his program often, and the interviews mixed serious topics with humorous revelations.[3] In June 2011 he got the "grandpa" secretary of state to admit that he would not play chess any longer with his eight-year-old grandson because the boy was beating him. "You negotiated with Mao Zedong but you're scared of your grandson," Colbert teased. Three years later, when Kissinger came on to promote his fifteenth book, *World Order*, Colbert assumed his right-wing persona and told Kissinger that all the disorder in the world was "Obama's fault," only to have Kissinger defend the president. Colbert, who had become a liberal favorite after his 2006 appearance at the White House Correspondents' Association Dinner and eviscerating attack on the Bush administration, even had Kissinger on his final show in December 2014 before he left to take over David Letterman's *Late Show*. Colbert's friendly approach to Kissinger elicited a furious backlash. Paul Rosenberg, a columnist for *Salon*, could not believe that Colbert consorted with the "monstrous" Henry Kissinger and allowed him to "laugh his sins away." A writer at the radical magazine *Mother Jones* criticized Colbert for "dancing with a war criminal." The list of atrocities and murders attributed to Kissinger by these critics approached Nuremberg-type numbers, with Rosenberg concluding that Kissinger was no ordinary war criminal but a man who had helped "systemically derange the entire world order in ways so profound and far-reaching that it will probably take another fifty years or so until they are properly understood."[4]

Although Kissinger would object to the word "derange," he might be

pleased that Rosenberg considered him such a world-changing historical figure. Determined not to "fade away" from public life Douglas MacArthur–
style, Kissinger waged an extraordinarily successful campaign to remain
politically relevant. With the election of the Democrat Barack Obama in
2008 over his friend John McCain, Kissinger knew the White House was unlikely to call on him as George W. Bush had. Even though Obama had invoked him during the debates, and spoke approvingly of a foreign policy of
limits and "realism," the Democrat was also an outspoken critic of the Iraq
War Kissinger had supported; Obama's foreign policy approach emphasized
multilateralism and was suspicious of past exercises of American power. Proclaiming the advent of "smart power" in contrast to the "stupid wars" of the
Bush era, Obama had little use for Kissinger or the foreign policy establishment "Blob," as his aide Ben Rhodes described it.[5] For his part, Kissinger, although cloaking his words in careful and even sympathetic language, was a
critic of most of the Obama foreign policy agenda, including the Iranian nuclear deal and the decision to pull back from the Middle East, best captured
when Obama refused to enforce his chemical weapons "red line" in Syria in
2013. From Kissinger's perspective, Obama's decision not to act against the
Assad government and Russian intervention in Syria put an end to the policy
he himself had initiated forty years earlier. When the Israeli ambassador, Michael Oren, complained to Kissinger that Obama's policies meant "the end of
American hegemony in the Middle East," Kissinger replied, "And what makes
you think anybody in the White House still cares about American hegemony
in the Middle East?"[6]

Kissinger was skeptical about Obama, even seeing similarities between
the first African American president and his famously bigoted boss. In 2010,
Kissinger called Kati Marton, the wife of Ambassador Richard Holbrooke, to
offer condolences after Holbrooke's sudden death. In one of his last public
appearances, Holbrooke had been onstage with Kissinger at a State Department conference marking the publication of the last volume of historical documents on the Vietnam War. The two men had despised each other, with
Holbrooke considering Kissinger "a liar, an immoral and deeply cynical man
with an overblown reputation," while Kissinger viewed Holbrooke as "the

most viperous character I know around this town."[7] But for this event, and although they had been on different sides of the Vietnam debate, they pretended that time had helped heal most of the wounds. Holbrooke, whose skill in negotiating the Dayton Agreements ending the Yugoslav war led many to see him as a Democratic version of Kissinger, and who wanted to be seen that way, had struggled to connect with Obama, who had kept him at a distance. As a favor to Hillary Clinton, Obama gave Holbrooke a vaguely defined assignment to try to end the war in Afghanistan. Holbrooke's frustration with his peacemaking attempts and the president's disdain for him were widely known in Washington. In his condolence call, Kissinger told Marton that Obama reminded him of Richard Nixon because both Nixon and Obama were loners, resistant to friendships with Washington politicians and officials. He added, "The key difference is that Nixon liked to have big personalities around him, Obama does not."[8] The point, of course, was that Nixon could tolerate a "big personality" of ambition and talent like Kissinger, while Obama could not handle his equivalent in Holbrooke. Left unspoken was that every president after Nixon learned that empowering a Henry Kissinger came with great risks as well as rewards.

The Obama administration personality with whom Kissinger quickly connected was Holbrooke's friend and supporter Secretary of State Hillary Clinton. Although Hillary's husband had never warmed to him, "Hillary and Henry" developed a mutual-admiration society. In her role as senator from New York and member of the Foreign Relations Committee, she and Kissinger had become friendly with each other, despite their political differences. Kissinger wrote approvingly of her direction of the Department of State, and they did interviews together discussing their relationship with their respective presidents and the difficulties of managing diplomacy.[9] They also appeared together on the *Charlie Rose* show in early 2011, again discussing their common experiences as secretary of state.[10] Clinton praised Kissinger's secret diplomacy toward China in the 1970s and tried to connect it with her own efforts as secretary of state to deal with hostile regimes.[11] Her favorable review in *The Washington Post* of Kissinger's *World Order* raised some eyebrows among Democrats, especially those progressives who never forgot or forgave

Kissinger.[12] Her rival in the Democratic primaries, Vermont's Bernie Sanders, denounced Clinton for taking foreign policy advice from Kissinger, describing him as "one of the most destructive Secretaries of State in the modern history of our country." As the election approached and Kissinger sat for extensive interviews with *The Atlantic*'s Jeffrey Goldberg, he joked that unlike other Republican leaders who endorsed Hillary out of their disgust over Donald Trump's candidacy, Kissinger decided that it might hurt more than help Clinton if he endorsed her.[13]

Kissinger was one of the first major foreign policy figures President-elect Donald Trump called in after his surprising victory. As different as their styles might be, Kissinger expressed praise for Trump's achievement and a cautious optimism about the real estate developer's potential to be a transformative president. Trump's particular interest in relations with Russia and China, and Kissinger's extensive knowledge and personal relations with both countries' leaders, made the ninety-four-year-old former secretary of state a surprisingly frequent visitor to the White House.[14] Kissinger sensed an opportunity with Trump and continued to write and opine on foreign policy questions.[15] In August 2017, Kissinger wrote a *Wall Street Journal* op-ed on dealing with North Korea, advising Trump "that an understanding with China is needed for maximum pressure and workable guarantees." He appeared that same evening on the *Charlie Rose* show, laying out his ideas and cautiously defending Trump on foreign policy, without endorsing the president's fiery rhetoric.[16] (Neither Rose nor Kissinger took note of the remarkable fact that this was the sixtieth anniversary of the publication of *Nuclear Weapons and Foreign Policy*.)

Kissinger, however, was not done with trying to influence American foreign policy and international affairs. In January 2018 he appeared before the Senate Armed Services Committee, asked to comment on the "international challenges" facing America. Kissinger's testimony turned into a defense of the "liberal world order," which many commentators feared that Donald Trump was undermining. Kissinger praised it as "flexible, open, cooperative, and able to make mid-course corrections as needed." But he added that the world order "is not self-executing," and that much depended on "America's initiatives and its integrative approach." Receiving the Alexis de Tocqueville Prize for political literature in Paris three months later, in April, he reiterated this defense of the liberal world order, arguing that it represented "a synthesis of the American and European visions."[17] Both public events found Kissinger carefully avoiding any direct criticism of Donald Trump. After Trump's strange summit with Vladimir Putin in July in Helsinki, the journalist Edward Luce of the *Financial Times* arranged an interview with Kissinger and told him directly that he seemed to go "to great lengths to preserve access to people in power at the expense of not speaking plainly in public." Kissinger responded by acknowledging that friends wanted him to speak more plainly, but what came out remained carefully ambiguous. He told Luce, "Trump may be one of those figures in history who appears from time to time to mark the end of an era and to force it to give up its old pretenses," adding, "I think we are in a very, very grave period for the world."[18]

Kissinger's determination to remain a public figure opened him up to protests and unpleasant shouting matches. His appearance at the dedication of the Schwarzman Center at MIT and for an event at New York University were met by student protests and strident denunciations of him as a "war criminal." The NYU protest, which prevented Kissinger from speaking, provoked the Kissinger critic William Shawcross to rebuke the students, arguing that whatever his own disagreements with Kissinger had been over Cambodia, "he is an extraordinary man who deserves respect."[19] Kissinger continued to garner that respect from more established figures, with books appearing that lauded his prowess as a negotiator and a diplomat even as academic historians continued to question and denounce the policies he supported and the legacy he bequeathed.[20] He was honored when Senator John McCain chose him as one of the eulogists at his funeral, joining former presidents Bush and Obama in paying tribute to the former Vietnam POW and presidential candidate. For his part Kissinger published two extended articles in *The Atlantic* on the challenge that artificial intelligence posed to human society.[21] From nuclear weapons to artificial intelligence, the ninety-six-year-old Henry Kissinger remained a voice in American public life.

. . .

ANY DISCUSSION OF the historical importance and legacy of Henry Kissinger, his successes and failures, triumphs and tragedies, confirms the wisdom of the eminent Dutch historian Pieter Geyl, who described history and historical writing as an "argument without end."[22] Perspectives on Kissinger will remain extremely polarized for generations to come, and this book is but a modest intervention, not an attempt to end the debate. Early in this project, I had lunch with a group of Harvard professors, including some who had gone to Washington in May 1970 after the invasion of Cambodia to meet with Kissinger. One of them remarked, in a reference to Secretary of State Dean Acheson, who had played such a decisive role in shaping U.S. foreign policy in the Cold War that he titled his memoirs *Present at the Creation*, that I should title my study of Kissinger *Present at the Destruction*. Many of my academic colleagues in the historical field have been similarly hostile as well, seeing Kissinger as symbolic of the worst features of America's Cold War foreign policy, especially his cynicism about democracy in Chile and ruthless willingness to victimize small countries like Cambodia and Bangladesh in pursuit of his objectives.[23] By contrast, a survey of scholars of international relations, a less ideological group, ranked Kissinger as the most effective secretary of state in the past fifty years by a wide margin.[24] Kissinger still enjoys considerable prestige among Washington policymaking elites, the establishment media, and the general public, many of whom remember, or have learned, of his masterful diplomacy with the then Soviet Union and in the Middle East, but most important, his role in the opening of China, a country that now looms very large in the American imagination. His continued presence in American public life, with appearances on news shows, frequent newspaper columns, and well-publicized meetings with the president, all testify to this prestige. Abraham Wagner, in a 2019 study of Kissinger, argues that Kissinger "remains the most significant foreign policy intellectual in the world whose advice is still sought by world leaders, corporate executives and the news media."[25] With it now being more than forty years since Kissinger held public office, one could hope there would be some middle ground in interpretation about such an important historical figure. It is clear that is still not the case.

I am convinced that it is not necessary to render a moral judgment on Henry Kissinger in order to learn from his career, especially the critical insights Kissinger's biography offers into America's role as a world power and the international system America fostered and developed. My original title for this study was *Henry Kissinger and the Dilemmas of American Foreign Policy,* and I planned to emphasize the ways in which Kissinger faced certain timeless and structural dilemmas in attempting to conduct American foreign policy. This was in keeping with the idea of using his biography as a prism through which to tell a larger story of American diplomacy in the twentieth century. "Dilemmas" was a theme inspired by the great French writer Alexis de Tocqueville, whose classic nineteenth-century work *Democracy in America* still resonates today. Tocqueville believed that democracies, unlike aristocracies, lacked the capacity to act with the necessary resolve, secrecy, and speed. These qualities, which were inherent to aristocracies, are essential to success in foreign policy. He further questioned whether a democratic nation could ever possess the long-term perspective required to undertake complicated international initiatives whose results would not be known for decades. Tocqueville also recognized that during the first years of the American republic, foreign policy issues were extraordinarily divisive, and the political unity of the country was fractured by the contrasting sympathies of Federalists and Republicans with the warring powers of Britain and France. At the time that Tocqueville wrote in the 1830s, the United States was a very marginal player in the world of international relations, then dominated by the great European powers. Tocqueville famously predicted that the United States would rise to great power status and eventually confront the autocratic Russian empire, but he doubted American democracy's competence in handling foreign relations.

So did Kissinger. Kissinger's concerns about the American political system, which became a campaign issue in 1976, were consistent with criticisms he had expressed about America's leadership and foreign policy from very early in his career. Some writers have even traced Kissinger's distrust of mass democracy and its "self-destructive elements" to his family's experiences with the Weimar Republic and Nazi Germany.[26] At least as far as the conduct of American foreign policy went, Kissinger, as the dutiful agent of Richard

Nixon, was nevertheless quite successful in overcoming the procedural weaknesses and dilemmas that American democracy created for the conduct of foreign policy. Tocqueville and other critics would have been impressed with how Nixon and Kissinger effectively centralized decision-making in the White House, and were, for at least a few years, able to conduct a pragmatic and flexible foreign policy that proved popular with the American people. The secrecy with which they were able to operate kept their rivals within government off guard and allowed the impact of "big plays"—as Nixon called them—such as the opening to China to impress friends and foes alike. Kissinger provided the intellectual "framing" to the foreign policy using the language of geopolitical realism in rationalizing and justifying a policy that was largely driven by domestic politics, particularly the intense desire of a majority of Americans to pull back after the disaster of Vietnam.[27] Anthony Hartley, a British journalist and a perceptive observer of American political and cultural life, wrote in 1972, "Military failure is traditionally the most brutal of shocks for any governing class," and America's failed war in Southeast Asia was just such a shock.[28] Disillusioned by the costs of the war in blood and treasure, Americans were open to a foreign policy shorn of Wilsonian rhetoric and Kennedy idealism.[29] Manipulating the balance of power and playing off the communist giants of the Soviet Union and China, as well as relying on allies, even unsavory ones like Iran or Pakistan, as surrogates for American power—these measures appealed to a country that only a few years earlier cheered President Kennedy when he talked of "paying any price, bearing any burden" to assure the "survival and success of liberty."[30]

With his skill in communicating with both print and television journalists, along with an intellectual firepower that impressed and intimidated politicians, Kissinger played a crucial role in selling this foreign policy, giving the impression of an unusual intelligence and design behind American actions in the world. He became the voice and symbol of American foreign policy on the television evening news, as important, if not more important, than the president. This perception, that Americans had a strategy, that they knew what they were doing as they recalibrated and retrenched from the expansive foreign policy, was crucial to the appeal of Kissingerian foreign policy. This gave foreign policy during the Kissinger years a perception of both reliability and creativity that Americans and foreign leaders could all appreciate, even when they disagreed with various measures and actions. During the contentious political year of 1976, when critics on the left and the right of the political spectrum attacked Kissinger, polls still showed that both he and his foreign policy retained the approval of the majority of Americans.[31] From the perspective of 2020, in light of the consternation stirred by Donald Trump and his challenge to the liberal international order, Kissinger and Nixon helped rescue that liberal world order when it came under challenge after the Vietnam War, when the slogan "Come Home, America" resonated with many Americans the way "America First" has in recent times.

Nevertheless, the design Kissinger presented to the world was not always that intelligent, and even his control over much of the foreign policy machinery did not prevent short-term thinking, ill-conceived reactions to exaggerated fears, and simply disastrous mistakes. Kissinger liked to argue that he and Nixon sought to create a new "architecture of peace," a structure for international relations based around triangular diplomacy and détente. Even his most recent book highlights his continuing interest in achieving some type of "world order," a search for a global "equilibrium" that would promote peace and prevent great power conflict.[32] The problem is that the analogy itself is flawed, giving the misleading impression that relations between states can somehow be fixed or made permanent, when the real pattern of international relations is one of constant change and development. Kissinger was far more a tactician than a strategist, and his real skill was in his ability to react and respond to international events and trends, such as when he shifted American policy in southern Africa toward support for majority rule. Although never one to acknowledge any weakness, Kissinger recognized some of the limitations in his diplomacy. He told a group of Foreign Service officers in 1977, "When you are in these positions you can't really reflect about their meaning because as you rise through the policy process your actions become really more and more like those of an athlete . . . You have to react almost instinctively and you have to worry later about the significance of what you have done."[33] There were real achievements in Kissinger's diplomacy, most notably his success in dealing with China and the Soviet Union and engaging in the Middle East peace process. But the administration's failed policy on the Vietnam War was the product of internal battles within the administration, domestic political pressures, and Nixon's own conflicting impulses. American policies in Chile and the India-Pakistan conflict were at odds with long-standing American principles, and were ill-considered and ultimately disastrous. The appearance of intelligence, control, and competence was as important, if not more important, to Kissinger than the reality of that control; or as one historian put it, Kissinger's "greatest exertions . . . were directed toward the tactical manipulation of perceptions."[34] Kissinger's great fear, which he candidly expressed to the Israeli ambassador during the Yom Kippur War, was to be exposed as being incompetent, to having "screwed up" a crisis. When things started to go wrong for Kissinger, with the Jackson-Vanik Amendment, the fall of Saigon, and the fiasco in Angola, it was important for him to be able to blame Congress, to deflect responsibility away from the misjudgments and miscalculations he had made. The techniques Nixon and Kissinger used, especially the centralization and secrecy with which they operated, produced an inevitable political backlash. The backlash was also caused by genuine policy mistakes and failures, which the administration had sought to conceal.

In fact, the real dilemma Kissinger faced, and the larger lesson that his experience in conducting foreign policy teaches, was not what Tocqueville outlined. The Frenchman did not anticipate how, as it became the world's first superpower and stood at the center of international order, America's foreign policy would remain interwoven with domestic politics and the struggle for political ascendancy at home. When the Cold War political consensus fractured in the wake of Vietnam, foreign policy emerged as a central political issue, a critical component in assembling a political coalition, sharpening differences with opponents, appealing to swing voters, and winning elections. One of the central lessons in observing Henry Kissinger's career is the inherent tension between the domestic politics of foreign policy—the need to appear in control of events, project strength and resolve, assert American values, and "do something" when faced with a crisis or challenge—and the real limits of

American power, both in the danger of intervention in countries whose conflicts were poorly understood and in the frequent and difficult choices faced in a world of violent and competing national states.[35] Kissinger understood and recognized, even if he occasionally regretted, that "the conduct of international relations is and should be, like other facets of policy, part of the rough and tumble of electoral politics."[36] Kissinger certainly sought to convey the image of the nonpolitical expert, enhanced by his Harvard background and German accent, explaining the intricacies of foreign policy to provincial, naive American politicians and the public at large. He served Nixon well in this role, helping him control foreign policy as a tool for electoral advantage. Nixon's relative success as "the first modern Republican president to reach out specifically to cultural and national security conservatives across party lines" owed much to Kissinger's efforts.[37] When Watergate crippled Nixon, Kissinger's mastery over the foreign policy machinery and skill with the American media contributed to his own ascendancy and status as effectively "president for foreign policy." Kissinger sought to help Gerald Ford in the same manner he had Nixon, with foreign policy achievements like SALT II or a settlement in Zimbabwe. The irony was that his previous successes, especially détente with the Soviet Union, the opening to China, and ending the Vietnam War—reduced the relative importance of foreign policy as an electoral consideration. Although, as the historian Colin Dueck puts it, "Kissinger's realism, competence, and success always played better with the general public than with the ideological activists in either party, and the secretary of state remained a respected asset to Ford going into the fall election," the electorate was far more concerned with economic issues.[38] Even so, Carter only barely won the election, and Kissinger came very close to maintaining his position of power. The reputation Kissinger earned—and helped create—as a successful foreign policy practitioner contributed greatly to his continuing public influence over the next four decades, as well as his financial success in the private sector as a consultant to governments and multinational companies.

Kissinger understood the American political system he operated within, but this did not keep him from trying to make the case that American leaders should treat foreign policy differently and with less of a focus on short-term political gains. His "Heartland Speeches" of 1975 attempted this argument, trying to convince Americans to move away from Wilsonian democratic crusading toward an understanding of the inherent limits of power and the need to approach foreign policy objectives in stages rather than from an absolute moral position. In what was a careful criticism of American exceptionalism, Kissinger insisted, "Today we find that—like most other nations in history—we can neither escape from the world nor dominate it. Today we must conduct diplomacy with subtlety, flexibility, maneuver, and imagination in the pursuit of our interests. We must be thoughtful in defining our interests. We must prepare against the worst contingency and not only plan for the best. We must pursue limited objectives and many objectives simultaneously."[39]

Although these speeches are sophisticated and measured in their approach to foreign policy, they were also self-serving and defensive, making the case for Kissinger's approach as the ideal Goldilocks mean between a McGovern-style liberal idealism and a Reaganite hard-line anti-communism. Ironically, Kissinger's lamentations about American foreign policy and critique of exceptionalism were undermined by his own position and actions as secretary of state. His phenomenal ascent to the heights of power as an immigrant and Jewish refugee seemed as much a testament to American exceptionalism as a criticism of it. Kissinger's willingness to advise presidents to use American power abundantly, from bombing in Vietnam, mediating in the Middle East, and playing off the Soviet Union and China, hardly seemed a call for its limitation. As the British ambassador Peter Ramsbotham had observed in 1976, Kissinger's Spenglarian pessimism about the decline of the West, and the congressional restraints he faced, coexisted with his continuing search for new areas, like sub-Saharan Africa, to exercise American power. Just as Kissinger could dismiss the importance of personal diplomacy, except when he himself was at the center of it, so, too, did his lectures about foreign policy and the limits of power seem contradicted by his own career and behavior.

Kissinger's "personalization" of foreign policy, his emphasis on how diplomatic and political issues related to him personally, is one of the most revealing aspects in studying his behavior in office. As much as the theorist in Kissinger stressed the role of impersonal "national interests" in determining the foreign policies of states, Kissinger the policymaker saw issues through a personal lens. To the Chinese, he was the symbol of the new relationship with the United States; to the Russians, he was their ally against Henry Jackson and critics of détente; to the Chilean and Argentine dictators, he would hold off the congressional liberals and their human rights demands; and to the Israelis and Arabs, he was their honest broker, even as he told each how much he sympathized with their claims. A British analysis produced for the incoming Labour government in March 1974 saw this tendency in Kissinger: "Despite his high intelligence and his conceptual approach to foreign policy, by no means [do] all [Kissinger's] actions form part of a coherent master plan aimed at promoting the United States' political advantage. Mood, emotion and the circumstances of his own background—he is the first immigrant ever to become US Secretary of State and is very conscious of the dignity of his office—are powerful conditioning factors. They on occasion lead him to personalize his dealings with foreign countries, and to inflate specific issues into the 'touchstone of relations' with them."[40]

Kissinger's personalization of power was further encouraged and augmented through his successful exploitation of both the print and electronic media. Kissinger cultivated, nourished, and charmed journalists, reporters, and media executives with extraordinary energy, and was willing to spend hours explaining his policies, answering their questions, and calming their worries. Journalists reciprocated, treating him far more favorably than other administration figures, especially Nixon, whose own attitude toward the media was one of general contempt and loathing. Kissinger even recognized that within the relatively colorless Nixon administration, his image as a "playboy" or "swinger" increased the media attention devoted to him. He had a personal interest in Hollywood and the entertainment industry, and his newfound prominence led Hollywood to reciprocate the interest. Kissinger did not carefully plot his ascent as a pop icon and celebrity, but he took steps during his time in office that made this development more likely. Achieving that stature and worldwide celebrity contributed to the power and influence he exercised as an American representative, especially in the Middle East, where he seemed the "indispensable" man to the peace negotiations. Even if he could never become what one letter writer to *Time* magazine proposed, "president of the planet earth," Kissinger understood how his celebrity status brought with it a form of political power.[41] Kissinger himself was one of the most successful self-promoters in late twentieth-century American public life.

In his early career, Kissinger often referenced the Greek goddess Nemesis, "which defeats man by fulfilling his wishes in a different form or by answering his prayers too completely."[42] Kissinger's celebrity status and the personalization of foreign policy he encouraged may have answered his prayers too completely, for they have also led to the degree to which Kissinger himself is held personally responsible, in a moral sense, for the outcome of many policies and actions over which he had relatively limited influence or control. One of the most significant and underappreciated stories of the Nixon-Ford-Kissinger years is the retrenchment of American power, the most significant retrenchment since the beginning of the Cold War.[43] To some extent, Nixon's media-oriented foreign policy events, including the trips to China and the Soviet Union, served to obscure this development and create a misleading impression of American global activism. The Nixon Doctrine, however, fundamentally rested on the principle that the United States would no longer, as Nixon put it, "conceive all the plans, design all the programs, execute all the decisions, and undertake all the defense of the free nations of the world."[44] As American power receded, its reliance on allies limited its ability to control and regulate their behavior. Whether it was Pakistan in Bangladesh, Indonesia in East Timor, Iran and the Kurds, or Turkey in Cyprus, the United States often found itself confronting difficult choices created by the actions of its allies. This is not to excuse the fact that Kissinger was often supportive of allies, like Pakistan and Indonesia, whose actions were abhorrent. The tendency of writers to place responsibility on Kissinger for the body counts in these situations creates a misleading impression of much greater American control and involvement than was the case.

Where Kissinger had more direct involvement and authority, such as in Vietnam policy, the bombing of Cambodia, and the policy toward Chile, he was, and remains, a determined Cold Warrior, maintaining that, as his biographer

Niall Ferguson puts it, "arguments that focus on loss of life in strategically marginal countries . . . must be tested against this question: how, in each case, would an alternative decision have affected U.S. relations with strategically important countries like the Soviet Union, China, and the major West European powers? . . . The maker of grand strategy in the Cold War had to consider all cases simultaneously in the context of a prolonged struggle against a hostile and heavily armed rival."[45] This assertion is problematic. Kissinger may have presented himself in his memoirs as a detached "maker of grand strategy" who weighed all the relevant factors in his decisions. Domestic political advantage and personal ambition, even when they served to advance America's national interest and a Cold War strategy, were far more important factors in the approach of policymakers like Nixon and Kissinger than grand strategy. Even if one believes and supports the moral distinction that existed between a democratic United States and a dictatorial Soviet Union during the Cold War—which I do—the use of that conflict to excuse any and all mistakes and flawed policies over more than four decades is not very persuasive. Kissinger does have a point: that historians should consider what and where alternative policies may have led the United States. It is also the case that critics often revile Kissinger as uniquely evil for conducting policies that were not substantially different from those carried out during the Eisenhower, Kennedy, or Johnson years, when Cold War considerations fostered assassination plots and other covert actions. In Cambodia, the extensive use by the North Vietnamese of the sanctuaries to attack American soldiers should weigh as a factor in any assessment of the decision to bomb the country, and the atrocities of the Khmer Rouge should remain their responsibility, even if American policies contributed to the tragic circumstances that allowed this group to seize power. Chile poses different questions, and the cynicism and politics behind the Nixon-Kissinger approach to intervening in a "strategically marginal" country to overturn a democratic election did serious damage to American interests. The callous indifference toward the post-1973 repression in Pinochet's Chile, as well as the willful ignorance toward Argentina's Dirty War, are aspects of the Kissinger record that are hard to justify, even though there were earlier precedents in Eisenhower's overthrow of the

Arbenz government in Guatemala and the Kennedy campaign against Castro in Cuba.

Unlike Robert McNamara, whose apology for his role in the Vietnam War stirred a national debate in the 1990s, Henry Kissinger remains unapologetic about his decision-making role in foreign policy, even expressing disdain for McNamara's public regrets.[46] That Kissinger left office but remained a prominent figure in American public life, that he earned a fortune in the private sector from the reputation he had developed, and that he continued to influence foreign policy incensed those like Christopher Hitchens who thought he deserved a punishing historical reckoning.[47] Kissinger, however, did not back down. I had the opportunity to watch him at a State Department conference on Vietnam in 2010. Sitting in front of the flag of the Socialist Republic of Vietnam, with a number of its diplomatic and military representatives sitting in the front rows, Kissinger expressed no second thoughts about his own role, and regretted only that the American-supported Republic of Vietnam, South Vietnam, did not survive. The Vietnamese did not challenge him, and actually crowded around him after his talk for pictures! Americans are far less forgiving. Kissinger continues to face confrontations over his past, even in unlikely circumstances. In a hearing before John McCain's Senate committee in 2015, as Kissinger was preparing to testify about American national security policy, Code Pink protesters attempted to perform a "citizen's arrest" of Kissinger and had to be removed from the committee room. Promoting his book *World Order* in a public radio interview in 2014, Kissinger suddenly found Todd Zwillich, the host of the program *The Takeaway*, asking him, "Was it the case that realism trumped democratic idealism there when you engineered the coup against Salvador Allende?" Kissinger reacted angrily, only to have the discussion move to the bombing of Cambodia, when Zwillich commented, "There were hundreds of thousands of people killed in that campaign." An exasperated Kissinger replied, "Wait a minute. Ignorance is no excuse for being insulting." But Kissinger could not escape Zwillich's determination to press the "war criminal" charge.[48]

When the Democratic presidential candidate Bernie Sanders attacked Kissinger during his primary debate with Hillary Clinton, their exchange captured the ambivalence about Henry Kissinger that exists in the American public's memory. In the previous week's debate, Clinton had boasted of her association with Kissinger. Sanders, aware of the criticism that he was a foreign policy lightweight, used his attack on Kissinger to challenge Clinton's judgment, especially her vote in favor of the Iraq War. After Sanders denounced Kissinger for his role in the Vietnam War and the destruction of Cambodia, Clinton tried to defend her association with Kissinger by praising his role in the opening to China. Sanders responded by again referencing Kissinger's Vietnam role, particularly his adherence to the domino theory and "the great threat of China." Sanders linked Kissinger to the trade agreements with China that he believed had cost American workers their jobs, and concluded, "The terrible, authoritarian, Communist dictatorship he warned us about, now he's urging companies to shut down and move to China."[49] The Sanders critique reminds us that Kissinger has managed to live long enough, and been in the public realm long enough, to be condemned for both the unthinking anti-communism of the early Cold War and the harmful effects of the globalization of the post–Cold War era. Kissinger continues to symbolize America's world power and prominence, a role and position many Americans now find too costly and burdensome and wish to reject.

Henry Kissinger was and is a complicated man—brilliant, devious, suspicious, arrogant, insecure, obsequious, paranoid, thoughtful, tenacious, domineering, vulnerable, direct, deceptive, insensitive, eloquent, petty, turgid, witty, thin-skinned—in short, the *polytropos* that Hans Morgenthau recognized when Kissinger was at the height of his world fame. Kissinger is also a truly significant historical figure and symbol of America's international power, a man who played a critical role in American foreign policy and whose long life after his government service has allowed him to try to shape both the understanding of that era and America's subsequent history. Henry Kissinger both exercised *and* symbolized twentieth-century American power, leaving a legacy that twenty-first-century Americans are still seeking to understand.

NOTES

Introduction: Henry Kissinger and American Power

1. Niall Ferguson, *Kissinger: The Idealist, 1923–1968* (New York: Penguin, 2015), p. xii.
2. Kissinger's divorce and his complicated relationship with his younger brother, Walter, receive very little attention in the book, an understandable omission since many of the principals, including Kissinger's ex-wife and his brother, are still alive.
3. Greg Grandin, *Kissinger's Shadow: The Long Reach of America's Most Controversial Statesman* (New York: Metropolitan Books, 2015), p. 227.
4. Robert Kaplan, "In Defense of Henry Kissinger," *The Atlantic*, May 2013, the atlantic.com/magazine/archive/2013/05/the-statesman/309283. Winston Lord and K. T. McFarland have recently contended that "the Nixon-Kissinger foreign policy remains the standard by which all subsequent administrations have been measured." Winston Lord, *Kissinger on Kissinger: Reflections on Diplomacy, Grand Strategy, and Leadership* (New York: All Points Books, 2019), p. xvii.
5. I wrote a short commentary on this point. "Kissinger at 90: Still a Force to Be Reckoned With?," E-International Relations, July 10, 2013, e-ir.info/2013/07/10/kissinger-at-90-still-a-force-to-be-reckoned-with.

6. The archive was created because Paul Simpson, a Nashville insurance executive, doubted the objectivity of the national media and was shocked to learn that their evening newscasts were not saved. Paul C. Simpson, *Network Television News: Conviction, Controversy, and a Point of View* (Franklin, TN: Legacy, 1995), p. 15.

7. David Greenberg, "Do Historians Watch Enough TV? Broadcast News as a Primary Source," in *Doing Recent History*, ed. Claire Potter and Renee Romano (Athens: University of Georgia Press, 2012), p. 191.

8. Nixon's press secretary wrote, "[Nixon's] first instructions to me on the morning after the 1968 election were, 'I want you to do a lot more television.'" Herbert G. Klein, *Making It Perfectly Clear* (New York: Doubleday, 1980), p. 76.

9. CBS News convention coverage, August 22, 1972, Vanderbilt Television News Archive (VTNA).

10. Michel Jobert, *Memoires D'Avenir* (Paris: Grasset, 1974), p. 275.

11. Thomas Alan Schwartz, "'Henry, . . . Winning an Election Is Terribly Important': Partisan Politics in the History of U.S. Foreign Relations," *Diplomatic History* 33, no. 2 (2009).

12. Hedrick Smith, *The Power Game: How Washington Works* (New York: Random House, 1988), p. 600.

13. George F. Kennan, *The Kennan Diaries*, ed. Frank Costigliola (New York: W. W. Norton, 2014), pp. 333–34. Kennan later published a version of this argument in his book *Realities of American Foreign Policy* (Princeton, NJ: Princeton University Press, 1954), pp. 42–49.

14. Hans J. Morgenthau, "Henry Kissinger, Secretary of State: An Evaluation," *Encounter* 43 (November 1974), p. 57.

1. The Making of Henry Kissinger, 1923–1968

1. "Kissinger Appointment," *ABC News*, *CBS Evening News*, and *NBC Nightly News*, December 2, 1968, VTNA.

2. Niall Ferguson, *Kissinger: The Idealist, 1923–1968* (New York: Penguin, 2015), pp. 857–59.

3. "Kissinger: The Uses and Limits of Power," *Time*, February 14, 1969.

4. Arthur Schlesinger, Jr., *Journals: 1952–2000* (New York: Penguin, 2007), p. 302.

5. Tom Wicker, "In the Nation: The More Things Change . . . ," *The New York Times*, December 12, 1968, p. 46. There was some dissent, but it came from the political extremes. Arno Mayer, a leftist Princeton historian and an antiwar critic, denounced the "orgy of celebration" that greeted Kissinger's selection, although he acknowledged that Kissinger was "at least as qualified for the advisory post as so many of his predecessors," including McGeorge Bundy and Walt Rostow, but added that that "does not really inspire confidence." Mayer's voice was rare in 1968.

6. "Kissinger: The Uses and Limits of Power," *Time*, February 14, 1969.

7. Jeremi Suri, *Henry Kissinger and the American Century* (Cambridge, MA: Belknap, 2007), p. 2.

8. Ferguson, *Kissinger*, pp. 42ff. I have relied heavily on Ferguson's discussion of Kissinger's early life and his Army service.

9. Ferguson, *Kissinger*, p. 67.

10. Bruce Mazlish, *Kissinger: The European Mind in American Policy* (New York: Basic Books, 1976), p. 19.

11. Walter Isaacson, *Kissinger: A Biography* (New York: Simon & Schuster, 1992), p. 26.

12. Hoffmann quoted in William Shawcross, *Sideshow: Kissinger, Nixon, and the Destruction of Cambodia* (New York: Simon & Schuster, 1979), p. 78.

13. Evi Kurz, *The Kissinger Saga: Walter and Henry Kissinger, Two Brothers from Fürth, Germany* (London: Weidenfeld & Nicolson, 2009), p. 95.

14. Isaacson, *Kissinger*, p. 34.

15. Walter Laqueur, *Generation Exodus: The Fate of Young Jewish Refugees from Nazi Germany* (Hanover, NH: Brandeis University Press, 2001), p. 143.

16. Ferguson, *Kissinger*, p. 107.

17. Ferguson provides an extensive quote of a Kissinger letter to another girl he was interested in, Edith, and praises "its analytical precision and psychological penetration." Ferguson, *Kissinger*, pp. 108–110. In fact, the letter is somewhat cringeworthy, employing some of the language Kissinger would later use in his work on Cold War politics to describe a romantic triangle. He cautions Edith against a friendship with one of his rivals, "because of his desire to dominate you ideologically and monopolize you physically."

18. Isaacson, *Kissinger*, p. 38.

19. Stephen Richards Graubard, *Kissinger: Portrait of a Mind* (New York: W. W. Norton, 1974), p. 2.

20. For an overview, see Michael J. Bennett, *When Dreams Came True: The GI Bill and the Making of Modern America* (Washington, DC: Brassey, 1996), especially pp. 277–310.

21. Mazlish, *Kissinger*, p. 53.

22. Ferguson, *Kissinger*, p. 116, reproduces the whole letter.

23. Louis E. Keefer, *Scholars in Foxholes: The Story of the Army Specialized Training Program in World War II* (Jefferson, NC: McFarland, 1988), pp. 27ff.

24. This is the date given in the documents provided to the Senate for his confirmation as secretary of state.

25. Keefer, *Scholars in Foxholes*, p. 99, and Ferguson, *Kissinger*, p. 120.

26. Ralph Blumenfeld, *Henry Kissinger: The Private and Public Story* (New York: New American Library, 1974), p. 47.

27. Deborah Dash Moore, *GI Jews: How World War II Changed a Generation* (Cambridge, MA: Harvard University Press, 2004), p. 49.

28. Isaacson, *Kissinger*, p. 43.

29. Ferguson, *Kissinger*, p. 127.

30. Ferguson, *Kissinger*, pp. 128–29.

31. Kissinger's eulogy of Kraemer is at henryakissinger.com/remembrances/fritz-kraemer. Kraemer cut off contact with Kissinger in November 1975 after the so-

called Halloween Massacre and the firing of Kraemer's superior, Secretary of Defense James Schlesinger. This is covered in chapter 6.

32. Ferguson, *Kissinger*, pp. 141–42.

33. Ferguson, *Kissinger*, pp. 146–52, provides a detailed description of the dangers Kissinger faced during this period, even with what was, by most standards, a much more comfortable job than an ordinary infantryman.

34. Isaacson, *Kissinger*, p. 48.

35. Ferguson, *Kissinger*, p. 156. Although a very sympathetic biographer, Ferguson points out there is no evidence to support later claims, especially by Kraemer, that Kissinger played a key role in getting Krefeld back on its feet. See also Holger Klitzing, *The Nemesis of Stability: Henry A. Kissinger's Ambivalent Relationship with Germany* (Trier, Germany: WVT, 2007), pp. 46–47.

36. Ferguson, *Kissinger*, p. 183. See also Klitzing, *Nemesis of Stability*, p. 48.

37. Ferguson, *Kissinger*, p. 164.

38. Ferguson, *Kissinger*, pp. 167–68.

39. Ferguson, *Kissinger*, p. 180. For an earlier account, see Blumenfeld, *Henry Kissinger*, p. 72.

40. Ferguson, *Kissinger*, p. 175. See also Isaacson, *Kissinger*, pp. 53–54.

41. Isaacson, *Kissinger*, p. 54.

42. Moore, *GI Jews*, p. 254.

43. David Landau, *Kissinger: The Uses of Power* (Boston: Houghton Mifflin, 1972), p. 16.

44. An early critical book is Harold Zink, *The United States in Germany, 1944–1955* (Princeton, NJ: Val Nostrand, 1957). Later accounts include John Gimbel, *The American Occupation of Germany, 1945–1949* (Stanford, CA: Stanford University Press, 1968); Edward N. Peterson, *The American Occupation of Germany: Retreat to Victory* (Detroit: Wayne State University Press, 1977); and John H. Backer, *Winds of History: The German Years of Lucius DuBignon Clay* (New York: Van Nostrand, 1983).

45. Ferguson, *Kissinger*, p. 189.

46. Ferguson, *Kissinger*, p. 199.

47. Isaacson, *Kissinger*, p. 55.

48. Ferguson, *Kissinger*, pp. 202–203.

49. Blumenfeld, *Henry Kissinger*, p. 80.

50. Harvard's flexibility may have reflected the attitudes of its president, James Bryant Conant, who had been a driving force behind the historic GI Bill. Suri, *Henry Kissinger*, pp. 100–101.

51. Ferguson, *Kissinger*, p. 211. When Kissinger thought the dog would arrive before him, he sent his parents a six-and-a-half-page letter of instructions on caring for Smokey.

52. In a long letter he wrote to his parents in 1945, he recounted a trip back to the places of his youth. In Leutershausen, where he had enjoyed summers with his brother and their maternal grandparents, he recounted how he "drove very slowly, past the ghosts of all the men who lived and died in the hatred of the years. I thought of the little boy who played football in the yard and the old man who used

to stand in the window to watch him. All the years came back and for a moment time stood still." For a moment, Kissinger reflected, "the valley was alive with the people I used to know." But in a few seconds, "the illusion faded . . . I said goodbye to my grandparents." Kissinger then drove to Fürth, and even visited the school where his father had taught. He went on to see the bombed-out ruins in Nuremberg and closed his letter with a biblical reference—curiously to the New Testament—and an unusual personal note: "Those who live by the sword shall perish by the sword. There on the hill overlooking Nuremberg I said farewell to my youth." Isaacson, *Kissinger*, pp. 50–51.

53. Isaacson, *Kissinger*, p. 52–53, quoting Kissinger's letter, 1946.
54. Professor Stanley Hoffmann, who spent World War II as a Jewish child in hiding in France, warned about some of the speculation about Kissinger, noting that "anyone who goes through the Nazi experience loses some levity," but that Kissinger never was "a gloomy person, never humorless." Hoffmann, who met Kissinger in 1955 and was his colleague in Harvard's Government Department, added, "These experiences have to have an effect. But the lessons one derives are not predictable." Blumenfeld, *Henry Kissinger*, p. 68.
55. Suri, *Henry Kissinger*, p. 109.
56. Blumenfeld, *Henry Kissinger*, p. 82.
57. Graubard, *Kissinger*, p. 4.
58. Isaacson, *Kissinger*, p. 68.
59. Blumenfeld, *Henry Kissinger*, p. 88. Suri called him a "condescending windbag." Suri, *Henry Kissinger*, p. 304.
60. Ferguson, *Kissinger*, p. 233.
61. Ferguson, *Kissinger*, p. 235. Kissinger thought that Elliott saw himself as a "talent scout." Blumenfeld, *Henry Kissinger*, p. 88.
62. Isaacson, *Kissinger*, p. 63. Years later, after he had become famous, Kissinger told the Italian journalist Oriana Fallaci, "If you want to know who has influenced me the most, I'll answer with the names of two philosophers: Spinoza and Kant." Oriana Fallaci, *Interview with History* (Boston: Houghton Mifflin, 1977), p. 40.
63. Graubard, *Kissinger*, p. 6.
64. Kissinger would imitate this formulation in one of his frequent critiques of the advice offered by bureaucracies. With every foreign policy problem, Kissinger said, the bureaucracy would come up with three choices: nuclear war, surrender, or its preferred solution.
65. Ferguson, *Kissinger*, p. 237.
66. Peter W. Dickson, *Kissinger and the Meaning of History* (Cambridge, UK: Cambridge University Press, 1978), p. 53.
67. Dickson, *Kissinger*, p. 52.
68. Dickson, *Kissinger*, p. 75–78. In a recent critique of Kissinger's influence, the historian Greg Grandin sees the key to understanding all of Kissinger's later foreign policy actions through his senior thesis, particularly in what he calls its "radical relativism: there is no such thing as absolute truth, [Kissinger] argued, no truth at all other than what could be deduced from one's own solitary perspective." Grandin

says that Kissinger's "relativism was a tool of self-creation and hence self-advancement as well," arguing that since Kissinger believed in nothing, he was skilled at being all things to all people. Grandin, *Kissinger's Shadow*, pp. 9–11. In contrast, Jeremi Suri regarded Kissinger's thesis simply as a reflection that "history is about both conflict and opportunity, decline and renewal." In Suri's view, Kissinger is for free will and arguing against determinism, contending that leaders "must turn conflict and decline into opportunity and renewal." Jeremi Suri, "Henry Kissinger, the Study of History, and the Modern Statesman," in *The Power of the Past: History and Statecraft*, ed. Hal Brands and Jeremi Suri (Washington, DC: Brookings, 2016), p. 43. In my view, Grandin's reading is shaped much more by what he perceives Kissinger became and did than by what the text of the thesis argues.

69. Ferguson, *Kissinger*, p. 237. In contrast, the historian Bruce Kuklick termed Kissinger's thesis the "most intellectually creative and sustained piece of work that [Kissinger] wrote," and "arguably a work of genius." Bruce Kuklick, *Blind Oracles: Intellectuals and War from Kennan to Kissinger* (Princeton, NJ: Princeton University Press, 2006), p. 184.

70. A similar development occurred at Stanford. Rebecca Lowen, *Creating the Cold War University: The Transformation of Stanford* (Berkeley: University of California Press, 1997).

71. Ferguson, *Kissinger*, p. 260.

72. William Y. Elliott, foreword, *Confluence* 1, no. 1 (March 1952), p. 1.

73. Kissinger, memo, December 12, 1950, quoted in Suri, *Henry Kissinger*, p. 114 (emphasis in the original).

74. Ferguson, *Kissinger*, p. 315. Ferguson somewhat excuses this as "a young man's sweeping self-assurance."

75. The full text of the document can be found on the Truman Library's website: trumanlibrary.gov/library/research-files/report-national-security-council-nsc-68.

76. Ferguson suggests that one reason Kissinger put up with Elliott, who could be an "overbearing windbag," was Elliott's ability to help him with both the International Seminar and *Confluence*. Ferguson, *Kissinger*, p. 274.

77. Suri, *Henry Kissinger*, p. 117.

78. In 1962 he used his friendship with Schlesinger to arrange an audience with President Kennedy. Kissinger to Schlesinger, August 17, 1962, White House Files (WHF), Arthur Schlesinger Papers, Box WH-39, John F. Kennedy Library (JFKL).

79. Elliott, *Confluence* 1, no. 1, p. 1.

80. Henry Kissinger, editor's note, *Confluence* 1, no. 2 (June 1952), p. 1.

81. The quote is from Thomas Schelling, a Nobel Prize–winning economist who was originally a friend but split with Kissinger over Vietnam. Isaacson, *Kissinger*, p. 73.

82. "New Quarterly Planned, International Magazine Slated for January by Harvard," *The New York Times*, August 26, 1951, p. 56.

83. Klitzing, *Nemesis of Stability*, p. 78.

84. Kissinger to Bundy, January 21, 1952, McGeorge Bundy Papers, Box 14, JFKL. Mazlish later wrote, "It is extraordinary how many of the people to whom I talked

about Henry Kissinger traced their acquaintance with him back to an invitation to contribute an article to *Confluence*." Mazlish, *Kissinger*, p. 71.

85. Kissinger's response to Stone was the same as one he sent to Adam Ulam, a professor in the Government Department at Harvard. Kissinger to Ulam, reprinted in *Confluence* 3, no. 4 (1955), p. 499.

86. Kissinger to Salomon, January 28, 1954, *Confluence*, General Records, 1951–1969, Box 3, Harvard University Archives.

87. Kissinger to Kraemer, November 19, 1954, quoted in Ferguson, *Kissinger*, p. 289.

88. In April 1961, when he was already established as a bestselling author, Kissinger wrote to Arthur Schlesinger that the seminar "was literally flat broke (to put it crudely) and that we will have to close down this summer if we do not receive any further support." Kissinger to Schlesinger, April 19, 1961, Schlesinger Papers, WHF, Box WH-13, JFKL.

89. Kissinger to Stone, May 11, 1954, International Seminar Records 1951–1969, Box 15, Harvard University Archives.

90. Hugh Wilford, *The Mighty Wurlitzer: How the CIA Played America* (Cambridge, MA: Harvard University Press, 2008), p. 127.

91. Ferguson, *Kissinger*, p. 281. Suri makes more of the CIA's role, arguing that it was part of "a web of academic programs around the world dependent on U.S. intelligence agencies, as well as philanthropic foundations, for their basic sustenance." Suri, *Henry Kissinger*, p. 122. Some writers also argue that the seminar points to "the role of the CIA in the rise of Henry Kissinger." One piece of evidence is a letter from Kissinger to Richard Nixon in 1955 inviting him to speak to the seminar. The author does not add that Nixon could not attend, and would not meet Kissinger for another twelve years. "A Document from the Harvard International Summer School," annotation by Scott Lucas, in *Culture and International History*, ed. Jessica C. E. Gienow-Hecht and Frank Schumacher (New York: Berghahn, 2003), pp. 259–60.

92. Ferguson, *Kissinger*, p. 267.

93. James Hershberg, *James B. Conant: Harvard to Hiroshima and the Making of the Nuclear Age* (New York: Knopf, 1993), p. 511.

94. Ferguson, *Kissinger*, p. 271.

95. Thomas A. Schwartz, *America's Germany: John J. McCloy and the Federal Republic of Germany* (Cambridge, MA: Harvard University Press, 1991).

96. Kissinger, "Notes on Germany," undated (conveyed in a memo from W. Y. Elliott to Raymond B. Allen, July 11, 1952, records of the Psychological Strategy Board, Harry S. Truman Library, Box 6.

97. Ferguson, *Kissinger*, p. 936.

98. John G. Stoessinger, *Henry Kissinger: The Anguish of Power* (New York: W. W. Norton, 1976), pp. 1–3.

99. Kissinger was not fondly regarded by many of his fellow graduate students, disliked for his tendency to play up to professors. Behind his back, they referred to him as Henry Ass-Kissinger. Isaacson, *Kissinger*, p. 104.

100. Henry Kissinger, "Peace, Legitimacy, and the Equilibrium: A Study of the States- manship of Castlereagh and Metternich," preface, Ph.D. dissertation, Harvard University, 1954, Harvard University Archives.

101. Michael Joseph Smith, *Realist Thought from Weber to Kissinger* (Baton Rouge: Louisiana State University Press, 1986), p. 200.

102. Henry Kissinger, *A World Restored* (London: Weidenfeld & Nicolson, 1957), p. 5.

103. Kissinger, *World Restored*, p. 323.

104. Ferguson, *Kissinger*, p. 291, and Fallaci, *Interview with History*, p. 40.

105. Paul W. Schroeder, *Metternich's Diplomacy at Its Zenith, 1820–1823* (Austin: Uni- versity of Texas Press, 1962), p. 241.

106. Mazlish argues that Kissinger's hopes were "dashed, much to his shock and disap- pointment." Mazlish, *Kissinger*, p. 79.

107. Kissinger told Danielle Hunebelle, "The prospect of staying [at Harvard] for eight years, dependent on full professors, on their good will, instead of being productive yourself—that prospect terrified me." Danielle Hunebelle, *Dear Henry* (New York: Berkley Press, 1972), p. 45.

108. Ferguson, *Kissinger*, pp. 325–26.

109. Kissinger, *World Restored*, quoted in Ferguson, *Kissinger*, p. 294.

110. Richard Aldous, *Schlesinger: The Imperial Historian* (New York: W. W. Norton, 2017), p. 3.

111. Ferguson, *Kissinger*, pp. 330–36. Kissinger told this story in his eulogy of Schlesinger on April 23, 2007, henryakissinger.com/remembrances/eulogy-for-arthur-m -schlesinger-jr.

112. Ferguson, *Kissinger*, p. 351.

113. Rockefeller to Kissinger, August 16, 1955, Rockefeller Special Assistant Papers, RG 4, Box 68, Nelson Rockefeller Papers (NRP).

114. Isaacson, *Kissinger*, p. 91.

115. Kissinger eulogy to Nelson Rockefeller, February 2, 1979, henryakissinger.com /remembrances/nelson-rockefeller.

116. Isaacson, *Kissinger*, p. 90.

117. Kissinger to Stephen Graubard, July 9, 1956, International Seminar Papers, Box 13, Harvard University Archives.

118. Joseph E. Persico, *The Imperial Rockefeller: A Biography of Nelson A. Rockefeller* (New York: Simon & Schuster, 1982), p. 82.

119. Ferguson, *Kissinger*, p. 359, and Blumenfeld, *Henry Kissinger*, p. 180.

120. Kissinger to Rockefeller, December 21, 1955, Rockefeller Special Assistant Papers, RG 4, Box 93, NRP.

121. Rockefeller to Kissinger, December 30, 1955, Rockefeller Special Assistant Papers, RG 4, Box 60, NRP.

122. Kissinger to Stephen Graubard, June 25, 1956, International Seminar Papers, Box 13, Harvard University Archives.

123. Kissinger to Max Millikan, June 20, 1956, Special Studies Project, RG V4A, Box 8, NRP.

124. Kissinger to Harvey W. DeWeerd, December 14, 1956, Special Studies Project, RG V4B, Box 15, NRP.

125. Kissinger to Nancy Hanks, April 1, 1957, Special Studies Project, RG V4A, Box 1, NRP (emphasis in the original).

126. Henry Kissinger, *Nuclear Weapons and Foreign Policy* (New York: Harpers, 1957), p. 7.

127. Mazlish, *Kissinger*, p. 95.

128. As one historian later wrote, "Kissinger was a masterful popularizer of themes developed by a corps of thinkers who advocated thoughtful United States participation in world affairs. Robert D. Schulzinger, *Henry Kissinger: Doctor of Diplomacy* (New York: Columbia University Press, 1989), pp. 4–5.

129. Russell Baker, "U.S. Reconsidering 'Small War' Theory," *The New York Times*, August 11, 1957, p. 1.

130. Ferguson, *Kissinger*, p. 379.

131. The British analysis is in Ramsbotham to de Zulueta, December 11, 1957, Prime Minister's Office Records (PREM) 11/4223, Public Record Office (PRO), London.

132. Kissinger to Kintner, August 11, 1956, Special Studies Project, RG V4B, Box 14, NRP.

133. Henry Kissinger, "Reflections on American Diplomacy," *Foreign Affairs*, October 1956.

134. Kissinger to Berle, December 19, 1956, Special Studies Project, RG V4A, Box 1, NRP. That this criticism flies in the face of the *realpolitik* for which Kissinger is famous is understandable only if one recognizes its political usefulness for critics of the Eisenhower administration, both Republican and Democratic presidential hopefuls.

135. Summary, *International Security: The Military Aspect*, January 5, 1958, Special Studies Project, RG V4A, Box 18, NRP.

136. Nancy Hanks to Bill Kintner, January 9, 1958, Special Studies Project, RG V4B, Box 14, NRP. See also Marvin Kalb and Bernard Kalb, *Kissinger* (Boston: Little, Brown, 1974), p. 56.

137. "Interview with Henry Kissinger," Harry Ransom Center, July 13, 1958, hrc.contentdm.oclc.org/digital/collection/p15878coll90/id/67/rec/37.

138. Percy to Rockefeller, July 2, 1958, Special Studies Project, RG V4F, Box 42, NRP.

139. Kissinger to General C. H. Bonesteel, September 18, 1957, Special Studies Project, RG V4F, Box 43, NRP.

140. Kissinger to Stephen Graubard, June 25, 1956, International Seminar Papers, Box 13, Harvard University Archives.

141. "Interview with Henry Kissinger," hrc.contentdm.oclc.org/digital/collection/p15878coll90/id/67/rec/1. When he heard that Bundy had described him to a student as leaning Republican, he wrote to Bundy, "[I] guarded my independence fiercely." Ferguson, *Kissinger*, p. 436.

142. Isaacson, *Kissinger*, p. 104.

143. Acheson to Kissinger, March 14, 1960, Papers of Dean Acheson, Correspondence, Folder 226, Microfilm Edition, Yale University.

144. Arthur M. Schlesinger, Jr., *Journals 1952–2000* (New York: Penguin, 2007), p. 84. In his interview with Mike Wallace two years earlier, Kissinger had actually singled out Nixon for praise as a leader who had "shown awareness of the situation" that America found itself in. The interview is available at hrc.utexas.edu/multimedia /video/2008/wallace/kissinger_henry_t.html.

145. Henry A. Kissinger, *The Necessity for Choice* (New York: Harper & Brothers, 1961), p. 2. McGeorge Bundy later observed that Kissinger "had an enormous capacity for gloom about the future of the republic when he was not in charge." Isaacson, *Kissinger,* p. 114.

146. Wallace used this expression in his interview at hrc.utexas.edu/multimedia/video /2008/wallace/kissinger_henry_t.html.

147. Isaacson, *Kissinger,* p. 105.

148. Ferguson, *Kissinger,* p. 468.

149. Bundy to Kissinger, February 18, 1961, National Security Files (NSF) 320, JFKL.

150. Ferguson, *Kissinger,* p. 457. Ferguson suspects that Kennedy would have offered Kissinger a full-time position, and that it was Bundy who kept Kissinger more distant, largely because he suspected his ties to Rockefeller.

151. Henry Kissinger, *White House Years* (Boston: Little, Brown, 1979), pp. 13–14.

152. Isaacson, *Kissinger,* p. 111.

153. Memorandum, Kissinger to Kennedy, April 6, 1961, Re. Visit of Chancellor Adenauer—Some Psychological Factors, NSF, Box 79, Germany, Subjects, Adenauer visit 2/1/61–4/6/61, JFKL. Klitzing, *Nemesis of Stability,* stresses the degree to which Kissinger's ambivalence toward Germany and the Germans persisted throughout his career.

154. Meeting with Adenauer, May 18, 1961, NSF, Henry Kissinger, Box 462b, JFKL.

155. Aldous, *Schlesinger,* p. 254.

156. Memorandum, Kissinger to Bundy, July 14, 1961, NSF, Box 320, JFKL.

157. McGeorge Bundy, "Covering Note on Henry Kissinger's Memo on Berlin," July 7, 1961, NSF, Box 81, Germany, JFKL.

158. Landau, *Kissinger,* p. 71, argues that Kissinger wanted a military response to the Wall, but his source is Daniel Ellsberg, by then a critic of Kissinger.

159. Kissinger argued that any weakening of the American commitment to German reunification would be "an enormous Communist victory" and a "staggering blow" to the Federal Republic. Such an abandonment of the principle of self-determination could not be countenanced. Kissinger, *Necessity for Choice,* p. 144.

160. Kissinger raised the stakes even further when he concluded, "Retaining Germany as a willing member of the Western Community is important not only for the future of Germany but it is even more vital for the peace of the world." Kissinger to Bundy, August 18, 1961, NSF, Box 462b, JFKL. Kissinger's "nightmare" was "a resurgence of nationalism in Germany and to Soviet-German deals on a national basis, wrecking the achievements of fifteen years of European integration." Kissinger to Arthur Schlesinger, October 3, 1961, WHF, Box WH-13, JFKL.

161. Kissinger to Schlesinger, September 12, 1961, WHF, Box WH-13, JFKL.

162. Kissinger to Schlesinger, November 3, 1961, WHF, Box WH-13, JFKL.

163. Adenauer's continual expression of concerns about American weakness and strategic inferiority were particularly grating to the Kennedy administration. In an annoyed and almost rude tone, Bundy asked Kissinger, "If you can think of any way in which your own very influential voice might be brought to the Chancellor's ear, in order to get it through his head that the current strategic balance is, in fact, as represented by both his professionals and ours." Bundy to Kissinger, December 17, 1961, WHF, Box WH-13, JFKL. Kissinger complained that he was representing a policy he didn't really understand or agree with. Kissinger to Schlesinger, April 9, 1962, Box WH-39, JFKL.

164. Isaacson, *Kissinger*, p. 114.

165. Ferguson, *Kissinger*, pp. 562–63.

166. Memorandum, Kissinger to Rockefeller, November 4, 1963, and December 23, 1963, Rockefeller Family Papers, RG 15, Box 4, NRP.

167. Kissinger to Schlesinger, July 12, 1963, WHF, Box WH-39, JFKL.

168. Mazlish, *Kissinger*, p. 122. Ferguson makes it clear how negative Kissinger's assessment of Kennedy was, I would argue for largely partisan reasons. Ferguson, *Kissinger*, pp. 562–77.

169. Memo, Kissinger to Rockefeller, May 13, 1964, Rockefeller Family Collection, RG 15, Box 3, NRP.

170. See Ferguson, *Kissinger*, p. 605–611, for a moving account of Kissinger's dislike of the right wing.

171. Kissinger to Bundy, November 27, 1964, National Security Files (NSF), Files of McGeorge Bundy, Box 15, LBJ Library.

172. I have analyzed this issue in my *Lyndon Johnson and Europe* (Cambridge, MA: Harvard University Press, 2003), pp. 39–46. See also Klitzing, *Nemesis of Stability*, pp. 166–97. His reports on his conversations with German leaders during his frequent visits to Bonn would become one of the more important ways the White House kept its finger on the pulse of German developments during the Johnson years. Klitzing, *Nemesis of Stability*, pp. 187–96.

173. Kissinger to Bundy, March 30, 1965, NSF, Files of McGeorge Bundy, Box 15, LBJ Library.

174. Bundy to Kissinger, April 12, 1965, NSF, Files of McGeorge Bundy, Box 15, LBJ Library.

175. Bundy to Kissinger, April 30, 1965, NSF, Files of McGeorge Bundy, Box 15, LBJ Library.

176. Bundy to Kissinger, July 6, 1965, NSF, Files of McGeorge Bundy, Box 15, LBJ Library.

177. Ferguson, *Kissinger*, p. 624.

178. Ferguson, *Kissinger*, p. 635.

179. Kissinger, *White House Years*, pp. 232–33.

180. The tape is edited—perhaps because Johnson and McNamara discussed Kissinger's personality—but it can be heard on the Miller Center's website. It is dated November 2, 1965. millercenter.org/the-presidency/educational-resources/assessing-the-war.

181. Kissinger to Bundy, November 6, 1965, and McGeorge Bundy Memo to William Bundy, November 10, 1965, NSF, Files of McGeorge Bundy, Box 15, LBJ Library. See also Isaacson, *Kissinger*, pp. 117–19.

182. Ferguson, *Kissinger*, p. 661.

183. Kissinger to Clifford, November 10, 1965, NSF, Files of McGeorge Bundy, Box 15, LBJ Library. Clifford wrote about the incident in his memoirs, noting how "it threatened to make Kissinger unemployable as an adviser." Clark Clifford, *Counsel to the President* (New York: Random House, 1991), p. 432.

184. Ferguson, *Kissinger*, p. 665. He did add, "Our deepest challenge then is to discover how a nation can be built when the society is torn by internal schisms and in the middle of a civil war." Kissinger, *White House Years*, pp. 118–19. Isaacson actually misreads Kissinger's handwritten letter, which emphasized that his pessimism was *not* because of the weakness of the Saigon government. Or at least that's what he wrote. Isaacson, *Kissinger*, p. 119.

185. Ferguson, *Kissinger*, pp. 671–72.

186. Ferguson writes, "Vietnam had awakened the man of action long dormant inside the professor." Ferguson, *Kissinger*, p. 683.

187. Cable, Rusk to Lodge, July 11, 1966, NSF, Country File Vietnam, Box 34, LBJ Library. Kissinger was disappointed by the lack of progress that he could see in securing the countryside. He had visited the province of Vinh Long in October 1965 and was told it was 80 percent pacified. In July 1966 when he returned, the same province chief told him that "enormous progress had been made" and that 70 percent of the province was pacified. Kissinger, *White House Years*, p. 233.

188. While the Chinese Communists continued to denounce the United States in vehement terms and provide men and material to support Hanoi, the Johnson administration was increasingly seeking to deal with the more "moderate" Soviet Union, also an ally and supporter of North Vietnam, on such issues as East–West trade, a nuclear nonproliferation agreement, and arms control negotiations. To engage the Russians required drawing a distinction between fighting communists in Vietnam and negotiating with them in Moscow. Kissinger faithfully reflected the administration's policy. As his first biographers put it, "Kissinger's opposition to an American pullout was an uncritical reflection of the official wisdom of those days." Kalb and Kalb, *Kissinger*, p. 69.

189. Arthur Schlesinger, Jr., "Schlesinger Suggests That We Recover Our Cool and Follow a Middle Way Out of Vietnam," *The New York Times Magazine*, September 18, 1966, p. 116.

190. Michael Palliser to J. Murray, May 3, 1966, and A. M. Billise to C. M. MacLehose, October 3, 1966, PREM 12/1270, PRO, London.

191. Isaacson, *Kissinger*, p. 121. Kissinger's opportunity for such diplomacy came about because of his involvement with the Pugwash conferences on nuclear disarmament. Named after the location of its first meeting in Nova Scotia, the Pugwash group was an association of scientists from both sides of the Iron Curtain committed to nuclear disarmament and arms control. Kissinger's Harvard colleague, the

chemist Paul Doty, was a founding member, and Kissinger had been attending the conferences for a number of years, one of the few real opportunities for intellectuals from East and West to meet for meaningful dialogue.

192. The fact that Nancy Maginnes, the future Mrs. Kissinger, was on sabbatical at the Sorbonne was also a factor in encouraging Kissinger to pursue his search for negotiations. Ferguson, *Kissinger*, p. xvii.

193. Schlesinger, *Journals*, p. 296. Kissinger's efforts did help pave the way for what became known as the "San Antonio Formula," the American offer to stop the bombing of North Vietnam in return for the beginning of negotiations.

194. Telegram, Kissinger to Dean Rusk, January 4, 1968, NSF, Country File Vietnam, Box 140, LBJ Library.

195. Kissinger's initiative did eventually reach the Soviet leadership, but according to Georgi Arbatov, the director of the Institute of the USA and Canada, it "did not make a great impression on anyone." Richard A. Moss, "Behind the Back Channel: Achieving Détente in U.S.-Soviet Relations, 1969–1972," Ph.D. dissertation, George Washington University, August 2009, p. 39. I am indebted to Dr. Moss for his insight into Kissinger's first attempt at secret diplomacy with the Russians. Moss also covers this in less detail in his book. Richard A. Moss, *Nixon's Back Channel to Moscow: Confidential Diplomacy and Détente* (Lexington: University Press of Kentucky, 2017), pp. 4–5.

196. Graubard, *Kissinger*, p. 241.

197. Kissinger to Hugh Morrow, November 8, 1967, NAR Papers, Folder 25, Box 1, NRP.

198. Isaacson, *Kissinger*, pp. 125–26.

199. Kissinger, "The Need to Belong," *The New York Times Book Review*, March 17, 1968, p. 34.

200. Isaacson, *Kissinger*, pp. 127–28.

201. Ambassador Winston Lord, a good friend of Kissinger's and an admirer, made this point. Foreign Affairs Oral History Project, adst.org/OH%20TOCs/Lord,%20Winston.pdf, p. 87.

202. The most detailed and fascinating account of this comes in Ken Hughes, *Chasing Shadows: The Nixon Tapes, the Chennault Affair, and the Origins of Watergate* (Charlottesville: University of Virginia Press, 2014). As impressive as this work is, it still underestimates the North and South Vietnamese and overestimates the value of what Kissinger provided. Pages 175–77 give details on Kissinger's role.

203. Nguyen Xuan Oanh, an economist and a Republic of Vietnam official, quoted in Robert Brigham, *Reckless: Henry Kissinger and the Tragedy of Vietnam* (New York: Public Affairs, 2018), p. 5. He added, "We did not need a college professor from Harvard telling us how to solve our diplomatic problems."

204. Jonathan Aitken, *Nixon: A Life* (London: Weidenfeld & Nicolson, 1993), p. 363.

205. Ferguson, *Kissinger*, p. 796.

206. Richard M. Nixon, *RN: The Memoirs of Richard Nixon* (New York: Grosset & Dunlap, 1978), pp. 323–29.

207. John A. Farrell, *Richard Nixon: The Life* (New York: Doubleday, 2017), p. 342. Farrell argues, "Of all Richard Nixon's actions in a lifetime of politics, this was the most reprehensible."

208. See the excellent discussion based on new LBJ tapes in Robert "KC" Johnson, "Did Nixon Commit Treason in 1968? What the New LBJ Tapes Reveal," hnn.us/articles/60446.html (accessed February 3, 2010).

209. Evan Thomas argues that the "evidence suggests that Nixon, through layers of deniability, took measures to make sure that Thiệu would not agree to the peace talks in time to swing the 1968 election to Humphrey." Evan Thomas, *Being Nixon: A Man Divided* (New York: Random House, 2015), p. 181. Ken Burns's eighteen-hour documentary on Vietnam, released in 2017 to great fanfare, also asserts Nixon's collusion with Saigon to prevent peace talks and defeat Humphrey as a simple statement of fact, without any consideration of other contingencies or possibilities.

210. Kissinger, *White House Years*, pp. 11–16.

211. Ferguson, *Kissinger*, p. 831, is correct that it really is impossible to see, in light of the North Vietnamese demands, how a chance for peace was lost. It is also the case that Thiệu and Humphrey had met, and it is likely that Thiệu realized Humphrey's impatience with the progress of his government. Humphrey expressed that in careful terms when he came back to the United States in November 1967. *Foreign Relations of the United States, 1964–1968*, vol. 5 (Washington, DC: GPO, 2006), pp. 997–1002. I owe this point to Luke Nichter, one of the foremost students of this issue.

212. Ferguson, *Kissinger*, pp. 830–32. Pierre Asselin is completely dismissive of the idea that there was a chance for peace, arguing, "Hanoi was toying with Washington and winning." Pierre Asselin, *Vietnam's American War: A History* (Cambridge, MA: Cambridge University Press, 2017), p. 170. In her otherwise critical account of Kissinger's behavior, Catherine Forslund makes this point, noting that it was both Moscow and Hanoi that took the initiative in October 1968. Catherine Forslund, *Anna Chennault: Informal Diplomacy and Asian Relations* (Wilmington, DE: Scholarly Resources, 2002), p. 66.

213. In a taped conversation with Nixon in April 1972, Kissinger agreed when Nixon said, "You have to realize too that they [the North Vietnamese] are quite aware of American political things because there isn't any question but that they agreed to the bombing halt before the election because Johnson convinced them that was the only chance of defeating Nixon." Kissinger went on to add, "As I told you all that fall, what the game was." *FRUS*, vol. 14, *Soviet Union, October 1971–May 1972*, p. 447.

214. Ferguson, *Kissinger*, p. 826.

215. Isaacson, *Kissinger*, p. 133.

216. Seymour M. Hersh, *The Price of Power: Henry Kissinger in the White House* (London: Faber, 1983), pp. 14–15.

217. William Safire, *Before the Fall: An Insider's View of the Pre-Watergate White House* (Garden City, NY: Doubleday, 1975), p. 160.

218. In speaking once to Nixon, who asked him why academics hated the United States—a very loaded question, certainly—Kissinger described the difficult travails

of the ordinary assistant professor, dependent on the approval of senior colleagues for advancement. He then remarked that academics "believe in manipulation," and perhaps for no one was this more true than Kissinger himself. Ferguson, *Kissinger*, p. 329. In his recent biography of Nixon, Evan Thomas suggests that Kissinger was very skilled at "how to play off Nixon against Nixon," in effect manipulating the president's insecurities to his own advantage. Thomas, *Being Nixon*, p. 193.

219. Kissinger, *White House Years*, p. 43. Nixon may have forgotten to offer Kissinger the position of assistant to the president for National Security Affairs, but it may also have been the case that he simply did not want to risk a rejection.

220. Ferguson, *Kissinger*, p. 854. Most of Kissinger's colleagues had little doubt that his consulting was more for show, so his liberal Harvard friends would not think he had sold out to Nixon. Kissinger undoubtedly wanted to keep a foot in both camps, as had been his pattern politically as well. He asked Carl Kaysen, a Harvard colleague who had worked for Kennedy, "Am I equal to the task, Carl? . . . I'm so scared." Kissinger desperately wanted to be told to take the position with the man he had only recently called "unfit" to be president. Hersh, *Price of Power*, p. 24.

221. Kissinger, *White House Years*, pp. 11–16.

222. Ferguson, *Kissinger*, p. 854.

223. Author's personal interview with Henry Kissinger, December 5, 2006.

224. Rostow to LBJ, December 5, 1968, NSF, Memos to the President, Walt Rostow, Box 43, LBJ Library.

225. Ferguson, *Kissinger*, pp. 855–56.

226. Richard Reeves, *President Nixon: Alone in the White House* (New York: Simon & Schuster, 2001), p. 33; and Andrew L. Johns, *Vietnam's Second Front: Domestic Politics, the Republican Party, and the War* (Lexington: University Press of Kentucky, 2010), p. 238.

227. Kissinger also recommended eliminating the National Security Action Memoranda (NSAM) of previous administrations and replacing it with both the National Security Decision Memoranda (NSDM) and the National Security Study Memoranda (NSSM). National Security Decision Memoranda 2, January 20, 1969, accessed at the Nixon Library's website, nixonlibrary.gov/virtuallibrary/documents/nsdm /nsdm_002.pdf. The NSDM would report presidential decisions to the agencies and provide a means for Kissinger and the NSC to follow the implementation of such decisions. The NSSM would "direct that studies be undertaken" by the appropriate agencies. NSDM 1, January 20, 1969, nixonlibrary.gov/virtuallibrary /documents/nsdm/nsdm_001.pdf. See also Schulzinger, *Henry Kissinger*, pp. 24–25.

228. The numerous NSSMs that Kissinger and the NSC issued in the first months allowed the Nixon-Kissinger team to get a fresh look at the problems they faced— an early NSSM was designed to stimulate new thinking about China. NSSM, US Policy Toward China, February 5, 1969, nixonlibrary.gov/virtuallibrary/documents /nssm/nssm_014.pdf. But they also helped Nixon and Kissinger tie up the bureaucracy's energy with answering the questions posed, and helped them assess and understand where the various agencies stood on policies, knowledge that gave

the president and his national security adviser a better way to gauge the advice they were receiving and control their choices. Ambassador Winston Lord made this point in an extensive oral history he did for the Foreign Affairs Oral History Project, adst.org/OH%20TOCs/Lord,%20Winston.pdf, pp. 74–75.

229. Kissinger clearly dominated access to the president in the first one hundred days of the administration, having 198 meetings with Nixon compared with Rogers's and Defense Secretary Melvin Laird's combined total of 30. Robert Dallek, *Nixon and Kissinger: Partners in Power* (New York: HarperCollins, 2007), p. 100.

230. Roger Morris, *Uncertain Greatness* (New York: Harper & Row, 1977), p. 46.

231. Dale Van Atta, *With Honor: Melvin Laird in War, Peace, and Politics* (Madison: University of Wisconsin Press, 2008), p. 136. Nixon's press secretary Herbert Klein later wrote, "Kissinger, I think, felt he could control Rogers. To him, Laird was more like a loose football, he did not know where he would stop on an issue." Klein, *Making It Perfectly Clear*, p. 311.

232. H. R. Haldeman, *The Haldeman Diaries* (New York: Putnam, 1994), August 14, 1969, p. 98. Kissinger never enjoyed any real personal connection to Nixon, remarking in later interviews that he wished they had gone to a baseball game together. Interview with Henry Kissinger, December 6, 2006.

233. Henry Kissinger, *Years of Upheaval* (Boston: Little, Brown, 1982), p. 98.

234. Telcon, Kissinger and Elliot Richardson, February 19, 1970, Box 4, Nixon Presidential Materials Staff (NPMS), National Archives (NARS).

235. Kissinger, *Years of Upheaval*, p. 94.

2. "You Can't Lose Them All"

1. Harvard had a rule that limited professors to two years away without resigning their positions.

2. *CBS Evening News*, January 16, 1971, VTNA.

3. Haldeman, *Diaries*, January 15, 1971, p. 281.

4. *CBS Evening News*, January 13, 1971, VTNA.

5. "A Tale from the Underground," *The New York Times*, January 15, 1971, p. 42.

6. *CBS Evening News*, November 7, 1969, VTNA.

7. Nixon, *RN*, p. 497.

8. Telcon, Kissinger and Margaret Osmer, September 25, 1970, Box 7, NPMS, NARS.

9. Richard Nixon, "Inaugural Address," January 20, 1969, accessed at presidency .ucsb.edu/node/239549.

10. "Kissinger: The Uses and Limits of Power," *Time*, February 14, 1969 (accessed online).

11. Ambassador Freeman to John Graham, 12 September 1969, FCO 73/40, PRO London.

12. *Time*, February 14, 1969 (accessed online).

13. *CBS Evening News*, January 29, 1969, VTNA. In his speech building up Rogers, Nixon even suggested that Rogers might be his successor as president or the chief justice of the Supreme Court. Richard Nixon, "Remarks to Key Personnel at the

Department of State," January 29, 1969, presidency.ucsb.edu/documents/remarks
-key-personnel-the-department-state.

14. "From Fürth to the White House Basement," *Time*, February 14, 1969. What is interesting about the *Time* article is the lack of any mention that Kissinger was Jewish, even though his family's origins as refugees is discussed. Given his sensitivity about the issue, Kissinger may very well have asked that this not be mentioned.

15. Richard Nixon, "The President's News Conference," February 6, 1969, presidency .ucsb.edu/documents/the-presidents-news-conference-151.

16. Kissinger, *White House Years*, p. 235.

17. Henry Kissinger, "The Vietnam Negotiations," *Foreign Affairs*, January 1969, p. 216.

18. *FRUS 1969–1976*, vol. 1, pp. 80–81.

19. *FRUS 1969–1976*, vol. 1, p. 121. Nixon would say something similar to a reporter after the Cambodian invasion: that what mattered would be "how it turned out." *NBC Nightly News*, May 1, 1970, VTNA.

20. Hersh, *Price of Power*, p. 51.

21. This is one way to understand Nixon's comment at the NSC meeting on March 28, 1969, that "there is no doubt that U.S. forces will be in Vietnam for some time, something like a large military assistance group, but our public posture must be another thing." *FRUS 1969–1976*, vol. 6, p. 173.

22. *FRUS 1969–1976*, vol. 1, p. 60.

23. Ken Weisbrode notes that one result of the trip was that "the Europeans and the European Desk were put on notice: This was a man (Kissinger) who required attention—and on their home turf." Kenneth Weisbrode, *The Atlantic Century* (Cambridge, MA: Da Capo Press, 2009), p. 209. Weisbrode stresses that Kissinger's coolness toward European unity was the major reason.

24. Weisbrode, *Atlantic Century*, p. 215.

25. *FRUS 1969–1976*, vol. 1, pp. 62–63.

26. Memo, Kissinger to Nixon, March 5, 1969, President's Trip Files, National Security Confidential File (NSCF), NPMS, NARS. In the first months of the administration, Kissinger worried obsessively about his standing with the president. He knew that he embodied many of the establishment groups and institutions Nixon hated. William Safire observed, "To the president, [Kissinger] was more deferential than any of us [were]; we excused this on the grounds that he was a newcomer to the group, had never called Nixon by his first name or been made to feel needed by a man struggling to come back." Safire, *Before the Fall*, p. 157. Kissinger's incessant and obsequious flattery of presidential news conferences and speeches reflected this insecurity. The most well known was Kissinger's call to Nixon after his speech of April 7, 1971, available at nixontapes.org/hak/1971-04-07_Nixon_001-010 .mp3. Occasionally it could backfire. At one point, after the Nixon administration set forth a plan to get rid of America's stocks of chemical and biological weapons, Kissinger came to the White House and proudly told Nixon of all the wires he had received from his friends at Harvard who congratulated him and praised the administration for taking this move. Nixon replied, "Henry, the wires would really

pour in from Harvard if I surrendered the United States to [Soviet premier] Kosygin." Haldeman, *Diaries*, November 26, 1969, p. 133.

27. Luke A. Nichter, *Richard Nixon and Europe: The Reshaping of the Postwar Atlantic World* (New York: Cambridge University Press, 2015), makes the best case for Nixon's attention to Europe, but even he acknowledges that the administration's priorities were elsewhere.

28. Telcon, Kissinger and Rogers, March 12, 1969, Box 1, NSCF, NPMS, NARS.

29. Kissinger had written, "The central task of American foreign policy is to analyze anew the current international environment and to develop some concepts which will enable us to contribute to the emergence of a stable order." And Kissinger doubted this could be done with the United States still engaged in Vietnam. Henry Kissinger, "The Central Issues of American Foreign Policy," in *Agenda for the Nation*, ed. Kermit Gordon (Washington, DC: Brookings, 1968), p. 610.

30. Telcon, Kissinger and Robert Ellsworth, January 27, 1969, Box 1, NSCF, NPMS, NARS. Kissinger also tried to appeal to the Soviet Union's own self-interest by making it clear that President Nixon was not like Eisenhower in an important respect, that of the concept of "rollback." He told Dobrynin, "President Nixon takes into account the special interests of the Soviet Union in Eastern Europe, and does not intend to do anything there which could be evaluated in Moscow as a 'challenge' to her position in that region." Memorandum of Conversation, Dobrynin and Kissinger, June 12, 1969, quoted in Jeffrey Kimball, *The Vietnam War Files* (Lawrence: University Press of Kansas, 2004), pp. 70–71.

31. MemCon (USSR), Kissinger to Dobrynin, March 3, 1969, in *Soviet-American Relations: The Détente Years, 1969–1972* (Washington, DC: GPO, 2007), p. 34. Kissinger was careful in explaining in his press background briefings that Nixon did not seek "a settlement of all political issues" with the Russians, but that the president wanted "enough movement" to "indicate that there is enough good faith in the direction of trying to reduce the intensity of political conflict." He summed this up by saying that he would like "to deal with the problem of peace on the entire front in which peace is challenged and not only on the military one." *FRUS 1969–1976*, vol. 1, p. 59.

32. Kissinger, *Nuclear Weapons and Foreign Policy*, p. 51.

33. *FRUS 1969–1976*, vol. 6, p. 44.

34. *FRUS 1969–1976*, vol. 6, p. 121.

35. Haldeman, *Diaries*, March 17, 1969, CD-ROM.

36. *FRUS 1969–1976*, vol. 6, p. 121.

37. William Beecher, "Raids in Cambodia by U.S. Unprotested," *The New York Times*, May 9, 1969, nytimes.com/1969/05/09/archives/raids-in-cambodia-by-us-unprotested-cambodia-raids-go-unprotested.html.

38. Telegram, Dobrynin to Soviet Foreign Ministry, April 15, 1969, in *Soviet-American Relations*, pp. 53–56.

39. Haldeman, *Diaries*, April 19, 1969, p. 65.

40. CBS coverage highlighted Kissinger's role, noting his responsibility for the fact-finding and reporting incorrectly that Kissinger was counseling "caution and no retaliation." *CBS Evening News*, April 15, 1969, VTNA.

41. Reeves, *President Nixon*, p. 69.

42. Richard Nixon, "Address to the Nation on Vietnam," May 14, 1969, presidency .ucsb.edu/documents/address-the-nation-vietnam-0. To ensure this speech was only a White House product, Nixon waited until Secretary of State Rogers left on a trip to Southeast Asia to have Kissinger draft it.

43. Reeves, *President Nixon*, p. 73.

44. *CBS Evening News*, May 1, 1969, VTNA. There were also reports on ABC and on both networks on April 29, 1969, that quoted Kissinger.

45. *CBS Evening News*, May 5, 1969, VTNA.

46. Rick Perlstein, *Nixonland: The Rise of a President and the Fracturing of America* (New York: Scribner, 2008), p. 387.

47. Haldeman, *Diaries*, April 8, 1969, p. 60.

48. Richard A. Hunt, *Melvin Laird and the Foundation of the Post-Vietnam Military, 1969–1973* (Washington, DC: GPO, 2015), p. 400.

49. Richard F. Kaufman, "We Must Guard Against Unwarranted Influence by the Military-Industrial Complex," *The New York Times*, June 22, 1969, p. 10.

50. Hunt, *Melvin Laird*, p. 98. Hunt's discussion of Laird's role is close to definitive.

51. Kissinger perceived Laird "as his one substantial threat to total domination of the bureaucracy." Hersh, *Price of Power*, p. 71.

52. Richard Nixon, "The President's News Conference," June 19, 1969, presidency .ucsb.edu/documents/the-presidents-news-conference-150.

53. Haldeman, *Diaries*, June 19, 1969, p. 80.

54. Hunt, *Melvin Laird*, p. 111.

55. Isaacson, *Kissinger*, p. 213.

56. Isaacson, *Kissinger*, p. 215.

57. Lord remained loyal to Kissinger, and believed Kissinger defended him when he made an error on a report on Laos in early 1970. Foreign Affairs Oral History Project, adst.org/OH%20TOCs/Lord,%20Winston.pdf, p. 210.

58. Peter Rodman remarked in a later interview, "[Kissinger] was very insecure about his own position . . . The fact that he had people like Mort Halperin, Win Lord, Lake and all these doves and intellectuals. Henry himself was, in a sense, the target of this suspicion." adst.org/OH%20TOCs/Rodman,%20Peter%20W .toc.pdf. Kissinger also later said that he had not thought the wiretaps to be illegal. Kissinger, *White House Years*, p. 253.

59. Telcon, Kissinger and Nixon, August 5, 1969, Box 2, NSCF, NPMS, NARS.

60. Kissinger had taught Sainteny's wife in the International Seminar.

61. Nixon, *RN*, p. 393.

62. William Burr and Jeffrey P. Kimball, *Nixon's Nuclear Specter: The Secret Alert of 1969, Madman Diplomacy, and the Vietnam War* (Lawrence: University Press of Kansas, 2015), pp. 179ff. The Burr and Kimball book is the definitive account of Duck Hook.

63. *FRUS 1969–1976*, vol. 6, pp. 418–23.

64. Haldeman, *Diaries*, July 7, 1969, CD-ROM.

65. Haldeman, *Diaries*, August 18, 1969, p. 99.

66. *NBC Nightly News*, August 5, 1969, VTNA. Brinkley's remarks were very strong and not reserved for a clearly "editorial" moment.

67. Reeves, *President Nixon*, p. 129.

68. Kissinger was angry about this, telling Nelson Rockefeller, the man who appointed Goodell to fill Robert Kennedy's Senate term, that Goodell was "playing cheap politics with the lives of people over there and our country." Telcon, Kissinger and Rockefeller, September 24, 1969, Box 2, NSCF, NPMS, NARS.

69. Burr and Kimball, *Nixon's Nuclear Specter*, pp. 224–25.

70. *FRUS 1969–1976*, vol. 6, pp. 370–74. This memo took on a new life when the noted political writer Bob Woodward stated that Kissinger had given the memo to President George W. Bush when he was considering whether to withdraw troops from Iraq in 2006. Bob Woodward, *State of Denial* (New York: Simon & Schuster, 2006), p. 409.

71. Reeves, *President Nixon*, p. 132.

72. Telcon, Nixon and Kissinger, September 16, 1969, Box 2, NSCF, NPMS, NARS.

73. Telcon, Kissinger and Nixon, September 27, 1969, Box 2, NSCF, NPMS, NARS.

74. Burr and Kimball, *Nixon's Nuclear Specter*, pp. 246–49. I have relied heavily on their account.

75. Haldeman, *Diaries*, October 3, 1969, p. 114.

76. Burr and Kimball, *Nixon's Nuclear Specter*, p. 249. See as well their earlier treatment, William Burr and Jeffrey Kimball, "Nixon's Nuclear Ploy," in *Bulletin of the Atomic Scientists* 59, no. 1 (January–February 2003), pp. 28–37, 72–73.

77. Haldeman, *Diaries*, October 9, 1969, pp. 116–17.

78. Memo, Kissinger to Nixon, September 27, 1969, in *Soviet-American Relations*, pp. 77–78.

79. Burr and Kimball, *Nixon's Nuclear Specter*, pp. 255–93, is the definitive account.

80. Telcon, Nixon and Kissinger, October 20, 1969, Box 2, NSCF, NPMS, NARS.

81. *FRUS 1969–1976*, vol. 6, pp. 468–69.

82. Memo, Dobrynin to Moscow, October 20, 1969, in *Soviet-American Relations*, p. 97.

83. Why were the Russians unmoved by the Nixon-Kissinger nuclear alert? We know now that the Soviets had other issues they may have considered more pressing, including an extraordinarily tense phase in their relations with China. Burr and Kimball, *Nixon's Nuclear Specter*, pp. 308–309. It may even have been the case that Soviet officials connected the alert to U.S. warnings against possible Soviet attacks on China. At least this is the implication of the Chinese historian Liu Chen-shan's work: that the Soviets were convinced in mid-October that the United States would attack them if they moved against China. "USSR Planned Nuclear Attack on China in 1969," *Daily Telegraph*, May 13, 2010.

84. Ilya V. Gaiduk, *The Soviet Union and the Vietnam War* (Chicago: Ivan R. Dee, 1996), pp. 215–18.

85. *NBC Nightly News*, October 15, 1969, VTNA. CBS and ABC were similar in tone.

86. Reeves, *President Nixon*, pp. 137–39.

87. Telcon, Kissinger and Tom Braden, October 10, 1969, Box 2, NSCF, NPMS, NARS.
88. Telcon, Kissinger and Adam Walinsky, October 9, 1969, Box 2, NSCF, NPMS, NARS.
89. Haldeman, *Diaries*, October 9, 1969, p. 117.
90. Kissinger, *White House Years*, p. 306.
91. Richard Nixon, "Address to the Nation on the War in Vietnam," November 3, 1969, presidency.ucsb.edu/documents/address-the-nation-the-war-vietnam.
92. Kissinger, *White House Years*, p. 307.
93. Kissinger, *White House Years*, pp. 306–307.
94. *NBC Nightly News*, November 13, 1969, VTNA, contained a report on a youth group protesting as the silent majority and singing patriotic songs. ABC's coverage on November 13, 1969, consisted of noting that attendance at the New York demonstration was significantly less than expected, and Howard K. Smith highlighted the polls showing Nixon's overwhelming support in the country.
95. Haldeman, *Diaries*, December 16, 1969, p. 138.
96. Kissinger, *White House Years*, p. 307.
97. A French documentary producer, Danielle Hunebelle, interviewed him in late 1969 for French television, and would come to fall in love with him and write about it. Hunebelle, *Dear Henry*.
98. Maxine Cheshire, "The Clutched Envelope Puzzle," *The Washington Post*, November 4, 1969. Kissinger had flirted with Howar, a Democrat with an acid tongue, earlier in the year, telling her that he was headed to the meeting at Midway with Nixon to negotiate withdrawals from Vietnam, but that when he got back, he would like to call her for dinner. "If you bring about a withdrawal from Vietnam," Howar told him, "you can call me and do whatever you want with me." Kissinger deadpanned, "Dinner will be sufficient." Isaacson, *Kissinger*, pp. 369–70.
99. Telcon, Kissinger and Rowland Evans, December 3, 1969, Box 3, NSCF, NPMS, NARS. Kissinger's comment was an allusion to the fate of his predecessor, Walt Rostow, who went to the University of Texas after his stay in the Johnson White House. The rumor was that Rostow was not welcome back in liberal and antiwar Cambridge.
100. Kissinger, *White House Years*, p. 20.
101. David R. Young, "The Presidential Conduct of Foreign Policy, 1969–1973," unpublished doctoral dissertation, Oxford University, 1981, p. 398. Young was a special assistant to Kissinger in the NSC and was one of the original "Plumbers," but he was granted immunity for his testimony and never convicted of a crime.
102. Telcon, Kissinger and Peter Flanigan (of *Newsweek*), June 10, 1969, Box 2, NSCF, NPMS, NARS.
103. Joseph Kraft, "In Search of Kissinger," *Harper's Magazine*, January 1971, p. 54. Despite his criticism, Kraft closed the article by praising Kissinger's "mastery of foreign policy."
104. Telcon, Kissinger and Cheshire, December 11, 1969, Box 3, NSCF, NPMS, NARS.
105. Dorothy McCardle, "Lenin's Birthday Party," *The Washington Post*, April 23, 1970.

106. Telcon, Kissinger and Sander Vanocur, January 28, 1970, Box 4, NSCF, NPMS, NARS, turning down an offer to appear on the *Today* show.

107. Gregg Herken, *The Georgetown Set: Friends and Rivals in Cold War Washington* (New York: Knopf, 2014), p. 332.

108. Safire, *Before the Fall*, pp. 158–59.

109. Safire, *Before the Fall*, p. 161.

110. Haldeman, *Diaries*, January 8, 1970, p. 142.

111. The term was coined by the Norwegian historian Geir Lundestad. See Geir Lundestad, *The American "Empire" and Other Studies of US Foreign Policy in a Comparative Perspective* (New York: Oxford University Press, 1990).

112. *FRUS 1969–1976*, vol. 1, pp. 153–58, 195–203.

113. Memo, Kissinger to Nixon, October 20, 1969, Box 2, NSCF, NPMS, NARS.

114. Memo, Kissinger to Nixon, February 16, 1970, Box 4, NSCF, NPMS, NARS.

115. *FRUS 1969–1976*, vol. 1, p. 186.

116. Haldeman, *Diaries*, February 20, 1970, p. 156.

117. Haldeman, *Diaries*, March 17, 1970, p. 167.

118. For an extensive discussion of Kissinger as a negotiator, see James K. Sebenius, R. Nicholas Burns, and Robert H. Mnookin, *Kissinger the Negotiator: Lessons from Dealmaking at the Highest Level* (New York: HarperCollins, 2018). The authors recognize that Vietnam was not one of the more successful Kissinger negotiations, although they do give him credit for the Paris agreements.

119. *FRUS 1969–1976*, vol. 6, pp. 596–601.

120. *FRUS 1969–1976*, vol. 6, p. 625.

121. Nixon, *RN*, p. 446.

122. *FRUS 1969–1976*, vol. 6, pp. 785–86.

123. Asselin argues that the Hanoi regime "played for time." Their strategy was predicated on the idea that Nixon would not escalate as long as the secret discussions were underway. Asselin, *Vietnam's American War*, p. 179.

124. Whether or not American officials on the ground in Cambodia were as surprised remains a matter of debate. Kenton Clymer, *The United States and Cambodia: A Troubled Relationship* (London: Routledge, 2014), pp. 22ff.

125. *FRUS 1969–1976*, vol. 6, p. 565.

126. *FRUS 1969–1976*, vol. 6, p. 703.

127. Nixon, *RN*, p. 447.

128. *FRUS 1969–1976*, vol. 6, pp. 818–19.

129. Kissinger, *White House Years*, p. 183.

130. By questioning CIA agents just returned from Cambodia, Kissinger learned that the North Vietnamese "were rolling up the smaller Cambodian posts to get freedom of movement," but there was still nothing to indicate yet whether they would move out of the sanctuaries. If they did, the CIA agents disagreed about whether the Cambodians would fight or simply collapse. *FRUS 1969–1976*, vol. 6, pp. 828–31.

131. *FRUS 1969–1976*, vol. 6, p. 834.

132. Kissinger, *White House Years*, pp. 491–92.
133. Young, "Presidential Conduct," p. 41.
134. Haldeman, *Diaries*, April 24, 1970, CD-ROM.
135. Haldeman, *Diaries*, April 23, 1970, p. 184.
136. Richard Nixon, "Address to the Nation on Progress Toward Peace in Vietnam," April 20, 1970, presidency.ucsb.edu/documents/address-the-nation-progress-toward -peace-vietnam-0.
137. *FRUS 1969–1976*, vol. 6, p. 838.
138. *FRUS 1969–1976*, vol. 6, p. 853. Lord provides a good description of the conflicts within Kissinger's NSC staff. Foreign Affairs Oral History Project, adst.org /OH%20TOCs/Lord,%20Winston.pdf, pp. 200ff.
139. Safire, *Before the Fall*, p. 183.
140. Haldeman, *Diaries*, April 30, 1970, p. 189. In his book, Buchanan notes the contrast between what Kissinger said at the time and how he wrote about Nixon's speech in his memoirs. Patrick J. Buchanan, *Nixon's White House Wars: The Battles That Made and Broke a President and Divided America Forever* (New York: Crown Forum, 2017), p. 159.
141. The activities of COSVN were disrupted by the invasion, but as with most insurgent operations, it was extremely mobile and the Communist military leaders simply outran their American pursuers deeper into Cambodia. Matthew M. Aid, *The Secret Sentry: The Untold History of the National Security Agency* (New York: Bloomsbury Press, 2009), p. 124. Winston Lord makes this point in his oral history. Foreign Affairs Oral History Project, adst.org/OH%20TOCs/Lord,%20 Winston.pdf, pp. 192ff.
142. Safire, *Before the Fall*, p. 187. Nixon's April 30, 1970, speech can be found at presidency.ucsb.edu/documents/address-the-nation-the-situation-southeast -asia-1.
143. Nixon complained to Kissinger, "We have been praised for all the wrong things— Okinawa, SALT, germs, Nixon Doctrine." Now, in Nixon's mind, he was not retreating, not negotiating, and not giving away something—he was acting and doing the "right thing." Haldeman, *Diaries*, April 27, 1970, CD-ROM.
144. On May 8, some 250 Foreign Service officers sent a letter of protest to Secretary Rogers, confirming Nixon's own view of the unreliability of the State Department. Asaf Siniver, *Nixon, Kissinger, and U.S. Foreign Policymaking* (Cambridge, UK: Cambridge University Press, 2008), p. 104.
145. Young, "Presidential Conduct," p. 52. Young cites his own contemporary notes of May 9, 1970, as his source for this observation.
146. *ABC News*, May 6, 1970, VTNA.
147. Nixon, *RN*, p. 457.
148. Safire, *Before the Fall*, p. 192.
149. I have largely followed the story as it is recorded in Mike Kinsley, "I Think We Have a Very Unhappy Colleague-on-Leave Tonight," *The Harvard Crimson*, May 19, 1970 (online version).

150. Kissinger, *White House Years*, p. 515.
151. Haldeman, *Diaries*, May 18, 1970, p. 200.
152. Hersh wrote, "Kissinger had cracked the inner circle." Hersh, *Price of Power*, p. 202. Kissinger's nickname is an allusion to the famous play *The Playboy of the Western World* by John Millington Synge.
153. Richard Nixon, "Report on the Cambodian Operation," June 30, 1970, presidency .ucsb.edu/documents/report-the-cambodian-operation. Winston Lord wrote the report describing the results of the incursion. Foreign Affairs Oral History Project, adst.org/OH%20TOCs/Lord,%20Winston.pdf, pp. 192ff. As devastating as the domestic impact had been, the military results were positive. One study concludes that "the incursion was thus militarily necessary and reasonably well conducted despite its hurried nature." John Shaw, *The Cambodian Campaign* (Lawrence: University Press of Kansas, 2005), p. 153.
154. Kissinger, *White House Years*, p. 516.
155. Kalb and Kalb, *Kissinger*, p. 191.
156. Memo, Kissinger to Nixon, July 19, 1969, quoted in David Stout, "Nixon Papers Recall Concerns on Israel's Weapons," *The New York Times*, November 29, 2007.
157. Memo, Kissinger to Nixon, October 7, 1969, retrieved on National Security Archive website, nsarchive.gwu.edu.
158. Young, "Presidential Conduct," p. 157. Young argues that Nixon knew of these Kissinger-Rabin meetings but did not take much interest in them.
159. Nixon claimed later to be skeptical about the Rogers Plan, writing in his memoirs "in strictly practical terms, the provision for return of occupied territory meant that the Rogers Plan had absolutely no chance of being accepted by Israel." Nixon, *RN*, p. 478.
160. MemCon, Kissinger to Nixon, February 10, 1970, in *Soviet-American Relations*, p. 122.
161. A recent book has even dated the introduction of Soviet ground personnel to late 1969. Isabella Ginor and Gideon Remez, *The Soviet-Israeli War, 1967–1973: The USSR's Military Intervention in the Egyptian-Israeli Conflict* (New York: Oxford University Press, 2017), pp. 101ff.
162. MemCon, Dobrynin to Politburo, February 10, 1970, in *Soviet-American Relations*, p. 125.
163. MemCon, Dobrynin to Politburo, June 10, 1970, in *Soviet-American Relations*, p. 151.
164. MemCon, Dobrynin to Politburo, June 10, 1970, in *Soviet-American Relations*, p. 152.
165. Telcon, Kissinger and Haldeman, March 2, 1970, Box 4, NSCF, NPMS, NARS.
166. Kissinger, *White House Years*, p. 581.
167. Kissinger, *White House Years*, p. 580. Young makes the point that this expulsion would likely take place in the context of a negotiated settlement, and that Kissinger exaggerated the degree that he was already looking toward excluding the Russians from the region, which he would achieve in 1974. Young, "Presidential Conduct," pp. 199–200.
168. Telcon, Kissinger and Max Frankel, July 7, 1970, Box 6, NSCF, NPMS, NARS. Kissinger even thought that Rogers was planting stories in the press about him dating the Hollywood actress Jill St. John as a way to hurt his standing with Nixon.

169. Telcon, Kissinger and Ron Ziegler, July 15, 1970, Box 6, NSCF, NPMS, NARS.

170. Safire, *Before the Fall*, p. 170.

171. Haldeman, *Diaries*, July 16, 1970, CD-ROM.

172. Kissinger, *White House Years*, p. 590.

173. Chalmers Roberts, "State's Most Happy Fella," *The Washington Post*, August 2, 1970, p. 39.

174. Herken, *Georgetown Set*, p. 334. Herken argues that Alsop's column led to a blackmail attempt by Russian intelligence.

175. Safire, *Before the Fall*, p. 406.

176. Haldeman, *Diaries*, August 17, 1970, CD-ROM.

177. Haldeman, *Diaries*, September 1, 1970, CD-ROM.

178. *CBS Evening News*, September 12, 1970, VTNA. Coverage of the hijacking crisis dominated all three networks over the first half of the month.

179. Nixon, *RN*, p. 483.

180. Telcon, Kissinger and Marvin Kalb, September 16, 1970, Box 7, NSCF, NPMS, NARS.

181. *FRUS 1969–1976*, vol. 1, pp. 247–57; and Kissinger, *White House Years*, pp. 614–15.

182. *FRUS 1969–1976*, vol. 24, p. 717.

183. *FRUS 1969–1976*, vol. 24, p. 719.

184. Haldeman, *Diaries*, September 21, 1970, CD-ROM.

185. Kissinger had an almost casual assumption of Israeli military prowess, especially compared with that of the United States. As he once said to Safire, "There'll be no more ten year wars. The Israelis have it right—if you can't win a war in six days, the hell with it." Safire, *Before the Fall*, p. 568.

186. Assad then ruled Syria for almost thirty years, even leaving his son Bashar in power after his death.

187. Reeves, *President Nixon*, p. 255.

188. Telcon, Kissinger and Nixon, September 23, 1970, Box 7, NSCF, NPMS, NARS.

189. Telcon, Kissinger and Nixon, September 23, 1970, Box 7, NSCF, NPMS, NARS.

190. Hersh, *Price of Power*, p. 250; and Grandin, *Kissinger's Shadow*, p. 143.

191. Hersh, *Price of Power*, p. 250; and H. R. Haldeman, *The Ends of Power* (New York: Times Books, 1978), pp. 85–86.

192. MemCon, Dobrynin to Politburo, September 25, 1970, in *Soviet-American Relations*, p. 197. I have also relied on Moss, *Nixon's Back Channel to Moscow*, pp. 54–60. The book is a shorter version of his dissertation, and I have consulted that as well. Richard A. Moss, "Behind the Back Channel: Achieving Détente in U.S. Soviet Relations, 1969–1972," Ph.D. dissertation, George Washington University, 2009, pp. 85–95. There is an inherent uncertainty in dealing with a crisis that involves the "intentions" of an opposing state. The certainty that Hersh and Grandin have that the Soviets would never have acted if the United States did nothing is not a certainty that any responsible decision maker can have. That this crisis also benefited Kissinger does not automatically mean it was an invented one.

193. Kissinger, *White House Years*, p. 641.

194. Asaf Siniver, "The Nixon Administration and the Cienfuegos Crisis of 1970: Crisis-Management of a Non-Crisis?," *Review of International Studies* 34 (2008), p. 82.

195. A submarine tender is a type of ship that supplies and supports submarines.

196. MemCon, Kissinger to Nixon, September 25, 1970, in *Soviet-American Relations*, pp. 193–94.

197. MemCon, Dobrynin to Politburo, October 9, 1970, in *Soviet-American Relations*, p. 207.

198. Kissinger feared that otherwise public opinion "will ascribe it to Soviet benevolence." Telcon, Kissinger and Nixon, October 12, 1970, Box 7, NSCF, NPMS, NARS.

199. Telcon, Kissinger and Chuck Bailey (*Chicago Sun Times*), October 16, 1970, Box 7, NSCF, NPMS, NARS.

200. Moss, *Nixon's Back Channel to Moscow*, pp. 59–60.

201. Jonathan Haslam, *The Nixon Administration and the Death of Allende's Chile* (London: Verso, 2005), p. 55. The literature on Allende, Chile, and the United States during this period is considerable and politically polarized. Among the most important works are Peter Kornbluh, *The Pinochet File: A Declassified Dossier on Atrocity and Accountability* (New York: New Press, 2003); Lubna Z. Qureshi, *Nixon, Kissinger, and Allende: U.S. Involvement in the 1973 Coup in Chile* (Lexington: Rowman & Littlefield, 2009); and Kristian Gustafson, *Hostile Intent: U.S. Covert Operations in Chile, 1964–1974* (Washington, DC: Potomac Books, 2007). For a broad overview, I have examined Simon Collier and William F. Sater, *A History of Chile, 1808–2002*, 2nd ed. (New York: Cambridge University Press, 2004); and Mark Falcoff, *Modern Chile 1970–1989* (New Brunswick, NJ: Transaction, 1989). Among the best recent books is Tanya Harmer, *Allende's Chile and the Inter-American Cold War* (Chapel Hill: University of North Carolina Press, 2011).

202. Korry's cable is cited by Kissinger in *White House Years*, p. 653.

203. Harmer, *Allende's Chile*, p. 9.

204. Telcon, Nixon and Kissinger, September 12, 1970, Box 7, NSCF, NPMS, NARS.

205. Isaacson, *Kissinger*, p. 291.

206. Richard Helms, *A Look Over My Shoulder: A Life in the Central Intelligence Agency* (New York: Random House, 2003), p. 404.

207. In the Christopher Hitchens book and the BBC documentary *The Trials of Henry Kissinger*, Chile is joined with Cambodia and East Timor as one of three counts of the indictment of Kissinger as a war criminal.

208. Dallek, *Nixon and Kissinger*, pp. 228–29.

209. Isaacson, *Kissinger*, p. 290.

210. Telcon, Kissinger and Don Kendall, September 14, 1970, Box 7, NSCF, NPMS, NARS.

211. Kissinger, *White House Years*, p. 653; and Kristian C. Gustafson, "CIA Machinations in Chile in 1970," *Studies in Intelligence* 47, no. 1 (2003), p. 39.

212. Telcon, Kissinger and Rogers, September 14, 1970, Box 7, NSCF, NPMS, NARS.

213. Dallek, *Nixon and Kissinger*, p. 232. Vaky's reservations were powerful, as was the implicit argument that the United States, which claimed to be standing up for self-determination in South Vietnam, could not afford to compromise that principle in Chile. Vaky could also have cited Kissinger's own writings on Germany.

214. Christopher Andrew and Vasil Mitrokhin, *The World Was Going Our Way: The KGB and the Battle for the Third World* (New York: Basic Books, 2005), p. 72.

215. Harmer, *Allende's Chile*, pp. 38–39. Harmer's book is the most sober and judicious account of the Cuban role in Chile.

216. Kissinger, *White House Years*, p. 654.

217. The idea was to have the congress select Jorge Alessandri, of the right-wing National Party, which had received 35.3 percent of the vote. The idea of this "Rube Goldberg" gambit was that Alessandri would serve briefly, perhaps only one day, but thereby provide a break in presidential succession, which would legally allow the more popular current president, Eduardo Frei, to be selected for another presidential term. Chilean law did not allow a president to serve two consecutive terms. This approach collapsed from a lack of cooperation from the key participants. Although Frei was concerned about what an Allende presidency might mean for Chile, he was reluctant to participate in such a transparent scheme to deny Allende his electoral victory. Even more telling was the fact that his political party, the Christian Democrats, had moved to the left, and its candidate for president, Radomiro Tomic, who got 28 percent of the vote, had already recognized Allende as president-elect on election night. Mark Falcoff, "Kissinger and Chile: The Myth That Will Not Die," *Commentary*, November 2003, p. 5.

218. Dallek, *Nixon and Kissinger*, p. 232.

219. *FRUS 1969–1976*, vol. 21, pp. 372–73. Nixon also insisted that the Hickenlooper Amendment, which prohibited assistance to governments that nationalized U.S. companies without compensation, be applied to Chile.

220. Haslam, *Death of Allende's Chile*, p. 69. The clear parallel here is with the South Vietnamese generals who in the fall of 1963 plotted the military coup against President Diem, knowing that the Kennedy administration, which had originally supported the idea, would have no choice but to help them if they succeeded.

221. *FRUS 1969–1976*, vol. 21, p. 439.

222. *FRUS 1969–1976*, vol. 21, pp. 444–45.

223. NSDM 93, Policy Towards Chile, November 9, 1970, in *FRUS 1969–1976*, vol. 21, pp. 451–52.

224. *FRUS 1969–1976*, vol. 21, p. 453.

225. Kornbluh, *Pinochet File*, p. 88.

226. The verdict of many Chilean historians is that Allende's downfall was largely of his own making. As one historical account puts it, "Sad as it is to have to say this, the real 'destabilization' of Chile was the work of Chileans." Collier and Sater, *History of Chile*, p. 355.

227. Nixon, *RN*, p. 490.

228. This was the theme of Nixon's inaugural address, January 20, 1969, presidency .ucsb.edu/documents/inaugural-address-1.

229. All three television news shows covered Kissinger's September 25, 1970, visit to Paris, but the lead of their story was that he was telling the South Vietnamese vice

president, Ky, not to attend a pro-war rally that was being held in the United States. *NBC Nightly News*, September 25, 1970, VTNA.

230. Luu Van Loi and Nguyen Anh Vu, *Le Duc Tho–Kissinger Negotiations in Paris* (Hanoi: Thê Giôi Publishers, 1996), p. 147. Kissinger's attempt to get the North Vietnamese to accept an electoral outcome may have been a "silly position" to take with "a doctrinaire revolutionary movement," as one biographer argued, but it was also a position far more consistent with American principles than the administration's secret behavior in Chile. Isaacson, *Kissinger*, p. 287.

231. MemCon, Kissinger and Jean Sainteny, September 27, 1970, Box 7, NSCF, NPMS, NARS.

232. Loi and Vu, *Le Duc Tho–Kissinger Negotiations in Paris*, pp. 145–55.

233. Telcon, Kissinger and Safire, October 6, 1970, Box 7, NSCF, NPMS, NARS.

234. Kissinger, *White House Years*, p. 980.

235. Richard Nixon, "Address to the Nation About a New Initiative for Peace in Southeast Asia," October 7, 1970, presidency.ucsb.edu/documents/address-the-nation -about-new-initiative-for-peace-southeast-asia.

236. *ABC News*, October 8, 1970, VTNA. The ABC report highlighted the idea that Vietnam would not be an issue in the midterm elections.

237. Telcon, Kissinger and Mankiewicz, October 8, 1970, Box 7, NSCF, NPMS, NARS; Ang Cheng Guan, *Ending the Vietnam War: The Vietnamese Communists' Perspective* (London: Routledge, 2004), p. 59. Ironically enough it was the Chinese communists who encouraged the Vietnamese in their rigid diplomatic position. Mao complimented the Vietnamese on their "policy for the diplomatic struggle" and told them that the reason the United States had not attacked China was because the Vietnamese communists were doing a successful job of pinning them down. Mao read the transcripts of the secret negotiations and commented, "Kissinger is a University professor who does not know anything about diplomacy. I think he is not someone who can compete with Xuan Thuy, even though I have not met Xuan Thuy." Guan, *Ending the Vietnam War*, pp. 55–56.

238. Rick Perlstein, in *Nixonland*, pp. 524ff, makes this argument about the campaign of 1970.

239. Safire, *Before the Fall*, p. 319.

240. Telcon, Kissinger and Finch, October 8, 1970, Box 7, NSCF, NPMS, NARS.

241. Telcon, Kissinger and Jim Cannon, October 22, 1970, Box 7, NSCF, NPMS, NARS.

242. Telcon, Kissinger and Berger, November 3, 1970, Box 7, NSCF, NPMS, NARS.

243. Reeves, *President Nixon*, p. 272.

244. Nixon to Haldeman, December 1, 1970, Memoranda from the President, President's Personal File, Nixon Materials Project, Box 2, Folder 4, National Archives.

245. Nixon to Haldeman, December 4, 1970, Memoranda from the President, President's Personal File, Nixon Materials Project, Box 2, Folder 4, National Archives.

246. Barbara Walters, *Audition* (New York: Vintage, 2009), p. 179. This December 1970 interview was also the source of one of Kissinger's most famous quotes:

"The nice thing about being a celebrity is that if you bore people, they think it's their fault."

247. It would be a major loss, but Haldeman thought, "We can survive anything, and the battle [between Kissinger and Rogers] is too much to contend with." Haldeman, *Diaries*, September 26 and 27, 1970, CD-ROM.

248. Haldeman, *Diaries*, December 3, 1970, CD-ROM.

249. Haldeman, *Diaries*, December 12, 1970, CD-ROM.

250. Isaacson, *Kissinger*, p. 314.

251. Telcon, Kissinger and Nixon, October 7, 1970, Box 7, NSCF, NPMS, NARS.

252. Telcon, Kissinger and Nixon, December 24, 1970, Box 8, NSCF, NPMS, NARS.

253. Telcon, Kissinger and Nixon, December 10, 1970, Box 8, NSCF, NPMS, NARS.

254. Telcon, Kissinger and Nixon, January 5, 1971, Box 8, NSCF, NPMS, NARS.

255. Telcon, Kissinger and Shearer, December 21, 1970, Box 8, NSCF, NPMS, NARS.

256. *FRUS 1969–1976*, vol. 1, pp. 284–91.

3. "Nixon's Secret Agent"

1. *CBS Evening News*, January 26, 1972, VTNA. In his commentary on NBC, David Brinkley, who was a harsh critic of the war, thought that the North Vietnamese were basically being offered a chance to return to the situation before the Americans intervened. Brinkley said that "very little" was being asked of the North Vietnamese in the president's proposals, and that if they accepted them, "they can then return to what they were doing before the Americans came, conquering the South." *NBC Nightly News*, January 26, 1972, VTNA.

2. *NBC Nightly News*, January 26, 1972, VTNA. Herbert Klein explains the rule as originating with Nixon and Haldeman, who feared "that his German accent would remind too many of the Nazi war machine at a time when we were in the midst of the Vietnam emotions." Klein, *Making It Perfectly Clear*, p. 325.

3. *CBS Evening News*, February 7, 1972, and *ABC Evening News*, January 26, 1972, VTNA.

4. Haldeman, *Diaries*, December 21, 1970, p. 267.

5. Richard Nixon, "Address to the Nation on the Situation in Southeast Asia," April 7, 1971, presidency.ucsb.edu/documents/address-the-nation-the-situation-southeast-asia-0.

6. Kissinger, *White House Years*, p. 994.

7. *FRUS 1969–1976*, vol. 7, p. 283.

8. Kissinger, *White House Years*, p. 999, and *FRUS 1969–1976*, vol. 7, p. 329.

9. Hendrick Smith, "Foreign Policy: Kissinger at Hub," *The New York Times*, January 18 and 19, 1971. The stories had inside sources, probably including Kissinger.

10. Haldeman, *Diaries*, January 18, 1971, pp. 282–83.

11. In classic Kissinger revisionism, he told his first biographers that he lacked enthusiasm for the operation. Kalb and Kalb, *Kissinger*, p. 176.

12. *FRUS 1969–1976*, vol. 7, p. 395.
13. "Indochina: The New Optimism," *Newsweek*, March 1, 1971, p. 18.
14. *FRUS 1969–1976*, vol. 7, p. 407.
15. Safire, *Before the Fall*, p. 390 (emphasis in the original).
16. *NBC Nightly News*, March 21, 1971, and *NBC Nightly News*, March 22, 1971, VTNA. *ABC Evening News* had many of the same images.
17. The best treatment of the invasion is in John Prados, *The Blood Road: The Ho Chi Minh Trail and the Vietnam War* (New York: John Wiley & Sons, 1999), pp. 311–79, especially pp. 359–60.
18. *CBS Evening News*, February 26, 1971, VTNA.
19. *FRUS 1969–1976*, vol. 7, p. 440.
20. William M. Hammond, *Public Affairs: The Military and the Media, 1968–1973*, The United States Army in Vietnam (Washington, DC: Center for Military History, 1996), p. 458. Among antiwar activists the sentiment was even stronger. Art Hoppe, a columnist for the *San Francisco Chronicle*, commented that when he heard the news that the Laos invasion had bogged down, he thought, "Good," and then proclaimed that "because I hate what my country is doing in Vietnam, I emotionally and often irrationally hope that it fails." Art Hoppe, "To Root Against Your Country," March 5, 1971, in *Deadline Artists, America's Greatest Newspaper Columns*, ed. John Avlon, Jesse Angelo, and Errol Louis (New York: Overlook Press, 2011), p. 38. The Senate Democratic caucus also voted to set a deadline for the withdrawal of all American forces from Vietnam. Senator Henry Jackson, later to become one of Kissinger's adversaries, called him. "I really tried to help you out in the caucus. Not many of us left," Jackson concluded, a reference to the diminished number of war supporters in the Senate. Telcon, Kissinger and Henry Jackson, February 26, 1971, Box 9, NSCF, NPMS, NARS.
21. *FRUS 1969–1976*, vol. 7, p. 450.
22. Kissinger Briefing, March 11, 1971, quoted in Hammond, *Public Affairs*, p. 468.
23. *FRUS 1969–1976*, vol. 7, p. 467.
24. Telcon, Kissinger and Moorer, March 18, 1971, quoted in Hammond, *Public Affairs*, p. 474. According to Moorer, Kissinger implied that the United States could simply leave the ARVN in Laos rather than helicopter them out. Moorer, however, told them that this would make even more political problems.
25. Hammond, *Public Affairs*, p. 476.
26. Alexander M. Haig, Jr., *Inner Circles: How America Changed the World: A Memoir* (New York: Warner Books, 1992), p. 274. Haig attributed Kissinger's reaction to his rivalry with Defense Secretary Laird.
27. Nixon, *RN*, p. 499.
28. Haldeman, *Diaries*, March 3, 1971, p. 306. Nixon also began taping his conversations around the end of February 1971, perhaps to ensure that Kissinger could not claim credit for the administration's actions. Haldeman, *Ends of Power*, p. 195.
29. *FRUS 1969–1976*, vol. 7, p. 490.
30. Kissinger, *White House Years*, pp. 1015–1016. Kissinger calculated that he had seventy-eight meetings with opponents of the war over a yearlong period.

31. When Kissinger defended himself to Haldeman by remarking, "I don't know whether it hurts us to show humanity toward these people," Nixon's chief of staff replied coldly, "It doesn't do us any good. It dignifies them. They should be decapitated." TelCon, Kissinger and Haldeman, March 13, 1971, Box 9, Folder 4, NSCF, NPMS, NARS.

32. Kalb and Kalb, *Kissinger*, p. 178.

33. *CBS Evening News*, March 13, 1971, VTNA; Telcon, Kissinger and Dan Rather, March 12, 1971, Box 8, NSCF, NPMS, NARS.

34. Kissinger believed exchanges "would help create more popular understanding for the administration's unpopular policy and buy more time, in effect, for the United States to wiggle its way out of Indochina." Kalb and Kalb, *Kissinger*, p. 179.

35. *FRUS 1969–1976*, vol. 7, p. 516.

36. Van Atta, *With Honor*, p. 365. The Calley case also exploded at the same time. On March 29, Lieutenant William Calley was found guilty in the My Lai massacre case. There was a huge public outcry, and telegrams flooded the White House and Congress at a rate of almost 100–1 against the verdict. Four days later Nixon intervened in the case, removing Calley from the stockade and putting him under house arrest until his appeals could be heard. The intervention cooled public emotions, but it also underlined the continuing political weight of Vietnam.

37. Nixon, "Address to the Nation on the Situation in Southeast Asia," April 7, 1971, presidency.ucsb.edu/documents/address-the-nation-the-situation-southeast -asia-0.

38. Ken Hughes, "Fatal Politics: Nixon's Political Timetable for Withdrawing from Vietnam," *Diplomatic History* 34, no. 3 (June 2010), pp. 497–506; Ken Hughes, *Fatal Politics: The Nixon Tapes, the Vietnam War, and the Casualties of Reelection* (Charlottesville: University of Virginia Press, 2015), especially pp. 11–20. Hughes locates the decision for a decent interval in the February–April 1971 period, during which he analyzed the White House tapes. His conclusions accord with those in Kimball, *The Vietnam War Files*.

39. This frequently quoted conversation can be listened to at nixontapes.org/hak /1971-04-07_Nixon_001-010.mp3.

40. Available at nixontapes.org/hak/1971-04-07_Nixon_001-026.mp3.

41. Haldeman, *Diaries*, April 8, 1971, p. 325. Nixon exaggerated the lack of support. Rogers also called him, as did Vice President Agnew and a host of other figures, including Governor Nelson Rockefeller, Billy Graham, and Ronald Reagan.

42. Lord Cromer's memo, titled "United States: First Impressions—No Longer God's Own Country," reads in part that "what Americans have had forced upon them is a realization of the limitations of power and money." July 21, 1971, FCO 82/46, PRO, London.

43. *NBC Nightly News*, May 3, 1971, VTNA.

44. Kissinger himself played the strategic board game Diplomacy. The game was invented in the 1950s by a Harvard student, Allan Calhamer, and was known as the "thinking man's Risk." chicagomag.com/Chicago-Magazine/May-2009/All-in -the-Game.

45. *CBS Evening News,* April 17, 1971, VTNA.

46. "The Ping Heard Round the World," *Time,* April 26, 1971.

47. Haldeman, *Diaries,* April 12, 1971, p. 327.

48. At nixontapes.org/hak/1971-04-14_Nixon_001-091.mp3. Nixon and Kissinger recognized the public fascination with China, although Nixon worried it might have an impact on his attempt to get a summit with Moscow. They also recognized that the change in policy would have an impact on relations with Taiwan. Both men lamented the "tragedy" that a change in China policy would mean for its aged leader, Chiang Kai-shek, but as Kissinger put it, "We have to be cold about it." Douglas Brinkley and Luke Nichter, *The Nixon Tapes: 1971–1972* (New York: Houghton Mifflin Harcourt, 2014), pp. 64–70.

49. Nixon's article is reprinted in *FRUS 1969–1976,* vol. 1, pp. 10–21.

50. *FRUS 1969–1976,* vol. 17, p. 7.

51. Winston Lord provides some background on the thinking of both Nixon and Kissinger on China, although he does not mention Kissinger's doubts about the opening. Foreign Affairs Oral History Project, adst.org/OH%20TOCs/Lord,%20 Winston.pdf, pp. 110–11.

52. Ferguson, *Kissinger,* p. 727, talks about Kissinger's skepticism toward China before he entered government. It is true that he wrote speeches for Rockefeller's 1968 campaign that indicated an openness toward China, but how deeply he believed that is open to question.

53. Haig, *Inner Circles,* p. 257. It is a legitimate question as to whether Kissinger was as dismissive as Haig—and Haldeman—make him out to be about Nixon's China opening. I confess that I tend to believe them, in part because the comments sound like the type of flippant remark Kissinger occasionally made about Nixon's ideas when they seemed to him far-fetched. And going to China must have seemed that way.

54. Haldeman, *Ends of Power,* p. 91.

55. Asselin, *Vietnam's American War,* p. 138.

56. Memorandum, Kissinger to Nixon, March 19, 1969, in *Soviet-American Relations,* p. 34.

57. Allen S. Whiting, a former State Department official and China expert, briefed the NSC on the extensive Soviet threat to China, and this influenced Kissinger's sense of the opportunities created for the United States by the Sino-Soviet conflict. Hersh, *Price of Power,* p. 357.

58. *FRUS 1969–1976,* vol. 12, p. 226.

59. *FRUS 1969–1976,* vol. 17, p. 181.

60. Odd Arne Westad, *The Cold War: A World History* (New York: Basic Books, 2017), p. 407.

61. Kuisong Yang and Yafeng Xia, "Vacillating Between Revolution and Détente: Mao's Changing Psyche and Policy Toward the United States, 1969–1976," *Diplomatic History* 34, no. 2 (April 2010), pp. 401–402. Mao viewed the student turmoil in the United States after Kent State in this light, hoping that it signaled the

prospect of weakening the imperialist enemy. When the Chinese actually accepted Nixon's offer to visit, it was justified in the politburo as the result of pressures from "the broad masses of the people" who were against the "Vietnam War and racial discrimination." But as Odd Arne Westad notes, "China's leaders concluded that 'since there is no way to be sure that an armed revolution would break out in the United States,' Nixon's offer should be accepted." Odd Arne Westad, *Restless Empire: China and the World Since 1750* (New York: Basic Books, 2012), pp. 368–69.

62. *FRUS 1969–1976*, vol. 17, p. 222 (emphasis in the original). Kissinger speculated there were radical elements in the Chinese air force who opposed any rapprochement with the United States.

63. Ironically enough, Mao was deciding to signal his own renewed interest in talks by inviting the American journalist Edgar Snow to join him on the reviewing stand celebrating the anniversary of the founding of the People's Republic in October. Snow was considered a left-wing apologist for China, and Mao's signal failed to receive attention in Washington. John H. Holdridge, *Crossing the Divide* (Lanham, MD: Rowman & Littlefield, 1997), p. 41.

64. "Nation: I Did Not Want the Hot Words of TV," *Time*, October 5, 1970.

65. *FRUS 1969–1976*, vol. 17, pp. 249–52. Kissinger did offer some other names as well—Ambassador Robert Murphy, Governor Thomas Dewey, or Ambassador David Bruce—as possible emissaries.

66. Chris Tudda, *A Cold War Turning Point: Nixon and China, 1969–1972* (Baton Rouge: Louisiana State University Press, 2012), p. 63.

67. *CBS Evening News*, February 26, 1971, VTNA.

68. *FRUS 1969–1976*, vol. 17, p. 301.

69. Kissinger, *White House Years*, p. 715.

70. Brinkley and Nichter, *Nixon Tapes: 1971–1972*, pp. 106–111, nixontapes.org/hak 1971-04-27_Nixon_002-052-1.mp3. There is a transcript in *FRUS 1969–1976*, vol. 17, pp. 303–308.

71. Kissinger, *White House Years*, p. 717.

72. *FRUS 1969–1976*, vol. 17, p. 304.

73. Only a couple of days after they received the message from Pakistan, Rogers was criticizing the Chinese government's behavior, and Nixon and Kissinger worried this would send the wrong signal to China. Tudda, *Cold War Turning Point*, p. 72.

74. Richard Nixon, "The President's News Conference," April 29, 1971, presidency .ucsb.edu/node/239908.

75. *FRUS 1969–1976*, vol. 17, p. 313.

76. *FRUS 1969–1976*, vol. 17, p. 318 (emphasis in the original).

77. Kissinger, *White House Years*, p. 725.

78. Kissinger called Nixon's attention to a *Washington Post* article that labeled him the "peace candidate." *FRUS 1969–1976, Vietnam*, vol. 7, p. 674. I have developed this argument much more thoroughly in Thomas Schwartz, "The Peace Candidate:

Richard Nixon, Henry Kissinger, and the Election of 1972," in *US Presidential Elections and Foreign Policy*, ed. Andrew Johnstone and Andrew Priest (Lexington: University Press of Kentucky, 2017), pp. 203–228. Nixon even tried to rename America's "armed forces" as her "peace forces," but it didn't catch on.

79. Nixon, *RN*, p. 415.
80. These Nixon quotations are drawn from his comments at NSC meetings on February 12, 14, and 19, 1969. *FRUS 1969–1976*, vol. 34, pp. 8–29.
81. MemCon, Dobrynin to Politburo, July 9, 1970, in *Soviet-American Relations*, p. 175. This was, of course, Dobrynin's interpretation of the American interest in a summit meeting, but it probably is not far off the mark.
82. *FRUS 1969–1976*, vol. 32, p. 403.
83. *FRUS 1969–1976*, vol. 32, p. 476. Nixon and Kissinger also thought that conditions in Europe in early 1971 would also make a move toward the Soviets effective. Both the Germans and the Soviets wanted an agreement that would regularize and stabilize access to West Berlin, the city that had been at the center of so many East–West crises earlier in the Cold War. The Soviets had already indicated in many conversations that an agreement on Berlin was a high priority for them, a way to stabilize their western front as they faced the Chinese threat in the east. A Soviet note echoing the German interest in a Berlin agreement soon followed, stressing that "it would be desirable to know the point of view of the White House" and emphasizing "the importance which the West Berlin question has assumed in our relations." Riots in Poland in December 1970 made Kissinger wonder whether the Soviets might pay a higher price for the potential stabilizing effect of a Berlin settlement. William Hyland, one of his advisers, speculated that the Soviets seemed to have come under pressure from the East Germans, and perhaps from groups within the politburo, for investing too heavily in Brandt's *Ostpolitik*. The Soviet leadership may have feared going to their party conference in March "with their Western policy in a shambles—no Berlin progress, no move to ratify the German treaties, no prospect for economic assistance from the West Germans— but that we hold the key to this increasingly complicated tangle of issues." *FRUS 1969–1976*, vol. 40, pp. 493–96. Hyland's analysis was on the mark, as the Soviet leader, Leonid Brezhnev, in consolidating his position at the party congress, proclaimed a policy oriented toward peace with the West and "openly identified himself with the Soviet response to Brandt's Ostpolitik." Vladislav Zubok, *A Failed Empire* (Chapel Hill: University of North Carolina Press, 2007), p. 214. Kissinger now suggested that the United States "insist on Soviet guarantees of access and a clearly defined legal status for West Berlin" and, resurrecting his idea of linkage, couple the offer on Berlin with progress in the SALT negotiations, especially a freeze on the Soviet nuclear buildup. Kissinger, *White House Years*, 802.
84. MemCon, Dobrynin to Politburo, January 9, 1971, in *Soviet-American Relations*, pp. 250–51.
85. MemCon, Dobrynin to Politburo, January 9, 1971, in *Soviet-American Relations*, p. 263.

86. Kissinger, *White House Years*, p. 841.

87. The irony was that the embarrassing news about SALT came only days after Rogers returned from a successful Middle East trip and was the subject of a profile in *The New York Times* with the headline "Rogers Enjoying Job These Days as Never Before." *The New York Times*, May 15, 1971.

88. Gerard Smith, *Doubletalk: The Story of the First Strategic Arms Limitation Talks* (New York: Doubleday, 1980), pp. 223–24.

89. nixontapes.org/hak/1971-05-19_Nixon_003-071.mp3. In a subsequent phone conversation, Nixon told Kissinger that even the "selfish and partisan" liberal journalists and indeed "any guy with any sense of decency is interested in world peace." nixontapes.org/hak/1971-05-21_Nixon_003-114.mp3.

90. *CBS Evening News*, May 20, 1971, VTNA.

91. It is worth noting here that in the middle of the Pentagon Papers controversy, Nixon telephoned Haldeman to see if he could get a letter-writing campaign to replay his daughter Trisha's wedding in prime time. Prados and Porter, *Inside the Pentagon Papers*, pp. 107–108.

92. nixontapes.org/hak/1971-05-21_Nixon_003-110.mp3.

93. nixontapes.org/hak/1971-05-21_Nixon_003-114.mp3.

94. *FRUS 1969–1976*, vol., 32, p. 510.

95. Haldeman, *Ends of Power*, pp. 110–11. Ellsberg later denied the claims, and James Rosen makes the point that Haldeman later felt that this book was more his coauthor's than his, and that many points were exaggerated. James Rosen, *The Strong Man: John Mitchell and the Secrets of Watergate* (New York: Doubleday, 2008), p. 530. *The Washington Post*'s managing editor, Howard Simmons, would later remark he harbored the "delicious thought" from time to time that "a temper tantrum by Henry Kissinger resulted in Watergate." Quoted in Max Holland, *Leak: Why Mark Felt Became Deep Throat* (Lawrence: University Press of Kansas, 2012), p. 223.

96. John Prados and Margaret Pratt Porter, *Inside the Pentagon Papers* (Lawrence: University Press of Kansas, 2004), p. 79.

97. nixontapes.org/amh.html 005-050-1.mp3.

98. nixontapes.org/hak/1971-06-13_Nixon_005-059-2.mp3. Both he and Nixon suspected that one motive for the story was to influence that week's congressional debate over setting a deadline for withdrawal from Vietnam in the Hatfield-McGovern Amendment.

99. Rosen, *Strong Man*, pp. 158–59.

100. Oval Office Conversation 525-001, June 17, 1971, nixonlibrary.gov/white-house-tapes/525/conversation-525-001.

101. *Newsweek*, June 28, 1971, p. 16. Ellsberg said that Kissinger told him he did not need to read the study because "we make decisions very differently now."

102. Hersh, *Price of Power*, p. 385.

103. Oval Office Conversation 524-027, June 17, 1971, nixonlibrary.gov/white-house-tapes/525/conversation-524-027.

104. Oval Office Conversation 526-002, June 18, 1971, nixonlibrary.gov/white-house -tapes/526/conversation-526-002.

105. Oval Office Conversation 536-016, July 3, 1971, nixonlibrary.gov/white-house -tapes/536/conversation-536-016.

106. Oval Office Conversation 537-004, July 5, 1971, millercenter.org/the-presidency /educational-resources/nixon-the-jews-are-born-spies.

107. Prados and Porter, *Inside the Pentagon Papers*, p. 221, for speculation on Kissinger's motives.

108. "Interior Secretary Morton Dines with Former Secretary Hickel: German Secrets," *The Washington Post*, June 24, 1971, C4.

109. "Ecumenical Party: 'A Housewife,'" *The Washington Post*, June 30, 1971, B2.

110. Kissinger, *White House Years*, p. 735.

111. *FRUS 1969–1976*, vol. 17, pp. 355–56.

112. *FRUS 1969–1976*, vol. 17, p. 357.

113. *CBS Evening News*, July 10, 1971, VTNA.

114. *FRUS 1969–1976*, vol. 17, p. 361.

115. *FRUS 1969–1976*, vol. 17, pp. 453–55.

116. It is true that Kissinger developed a type of friendship with Anatoly Dobrynin, but this was always coupled with expressions of disdain for the Russians and Russian behavior. See Barbara Keys, "Henry Kissinger: The Emotional Statesman," *Diplomatic History* 35, no. 4 (September 2011), pp. 587–609.

117. Schlesinger, *Journals*, p. 341.

118. *FRUS 1969–1976*, vol. 17, pp. 361–78. An excellent description of the talks is also in Winston Lord's long oral history. Foreign Affairs Oral History Project, adst.org /OH%20TOCs/Lord,%20Winston.pdf, pp. 127–34.

119. *FRUS 1969–1976*, vol. 17, pp. 414–15.

120. *NBC Nightly News*, July 15, 1971, VTNA.

121. Margaret MacMillan, *Nixon and Mao: The Week That Changed the World* (New York: Random House, 2007), p. 202.

122. Annotated News Summary, July 19, 1971, President's Office Files, Box 32, NPMP, NARS.

123. Isaacson, *Kissinger*, p. 347.

124. Haldeman, *Diaries*, July 16, 1971, p. 388.

125. Louis Harris, "Public Approves China Trip of President by 68% to 19%: The Harris Survey," *The Washington Post*, September 20, 1971, A6.

126. Robert Mason, *Richard Nixon and the Quest for a New Majority* (Chapel Hill: University of North Carolina Press, 2004), p. 137.

127. *FRUS 1969–1976*, vol. 13, pp. 870–71. Kraemer's pessimism was stark: In Europe, Germany was on the road to "Finlandization," and it was "impossible to meet any Western European who is *not* convinced that under U.S. internal pressures (Mansfield Resolution and Amendment) we will within the foreseeable future withdraw a considerable part of our troops from Germany." Kraemer argued that the Soviet military position in the eastern Mediterranean had been "enormously strengthened" and that in the Middle East, "as a result of our policy of Negotiation

instead of Confrontation, we are leaving a strategic vacuum with neither friend nor foe believing that we would intervene militarily, which will lead to the outbreak of Arab-Israeli hostilities within perhaps eight months." On this last point, Kraemer was off by only a year.

128. *FRUS 1969–1976*, vol. 13, p. 871 (emphasis in the original).

129. *FRUS 1969–1976*, vol. 13, pp. 874–75.

130. Winston Lord made this point. Foreign Affairs Oral History Project, adst.org /OH%20TOCs/Lord,%20Winston.pdf, p. 135.

131. "The Inscrutable Occidental: Henry Alfred Kissinger," *The New York Times*, July 17, 1971.

132. Isaacson, *Kissinger*, p. 349.

133. Isaacson, *Kissinger*, p. 359.

134. The reference to Kissinger's children was in the People section of *Time*, September 13, 1971, p. 40.

135. Telcon, Kissinger and Nixon, August 16, 1971, Box 9, NSCF, NPMS, NARS.

136. Winston Lord notes that the Soviets were hesitating on setting a date before the China trip was announced. Foreign Affairs Oral History Project, adst.org/OH%20 TOCs/Lord,%20Winston.pdf, p. 273. He discusses this at length on pp. 273–76.

137. *NBC Nightly News*, October 20, 1971, VTNA. There were about a dozen stories on the networks during Kissinger's visit. Most were quite short, but one dealt with the increased demand for instruction in the Chinese language. *NBC Nightly News*, October 24, 1971, VTNA. Dallek comments that the trip "gave Henry visibility on a level with heads of states and celebrities that he craved but could not have imagined attaining as the president's national security adviser." Dallek, *Nixon and Kissinger*, p. 330.

138. Event Summary by George H. W. Bush, December 10, 1971, George Bush Presidential Library, George H. W. Bush Collection, Series: United Nations File, 1971– 1972, Box 4, nsarchive.gwu.edu/NSAEBB/NSAEBB79/#docs. Bush's comment came as he reflected on both the China vote and the India-Pakistan War. Bush respected Kissinger's intelligence and ability, but never fully trusted him. Their relationship would remain strained, even after, as president, Bush appointed many of Kissinger's friends and associates—including Lawrence Eagleburger and Brent Scowcroft—to important positions in his administration.

139. *NBC Nightly News*, October 28, 1971, VTNA.

140. Barnard Law Collier, "The Road to Peking, or, How Does This Kissinger Do It?," *The New York Times Magazine*, November 14, 1971, pp. 34, 35, and 111.

141. Mark Feldstein, *Poisoning the Press: Richard Nixon, Jack Anderson, and the Rise of Washington's Scandal Culture* (New York: Farrar, Straus and Giroux, 2010), p. 166. In his memoirs Kissinger used a Watergate expression to describe how Nixon and the administration left him twisting "slowly, slowly in the wind." Kissinger, *White House Years*, p. 918.

142. *FRUS 1969–1976*, vol. 11, p. 45.

143. Blood was subsequently transferred as retribution for his outspoken involvement in the dissent against official policy. Gary J. Bass, *The Blood Telegram: Nixon,*

Kissinger, and a Forgotten Genocide (New York: Knopf, 2013), pp. xi–xiii. The Bass book is an impassioned and devastating attack on American policy during this period, and it singles out Nixon and Kissinger for the greatest responsibility. The book should be read along with Srinath Raghavan, *1971: A Global History of the Creation of Bangladesh* (Cambridge, MA: Harvard University Press, 2013).

144. *FRUS 1969–1976*, vol. 11, p. 65. Kissinger would later concede in his memoirs that the "ungenerous spirit" of Nixon's reaction shows there was "some merit to the charge of moral insensitivity." Kissinger, *White House Years*, p. 854.

145. *FRUS 1969–1976*, vol. 11, p. 98.

146. *FRUS 1969–1976*, vol. 11, p. 140, and Raghavan, *1971*, p. 101. Raghavan makes the argument that if the United States had used its economic leverage on Pakistan early in the crisis, it could have mitigated the situation. Unfortunately this early period overlapped with the secret China initiative, and Nixon was not about to risk such a politically important move to pressure Pakistan.

147. *Time* ran a multipage story titled "Pakistan: The Ravaging of Golden Bengal," replete with photos of starving children and cholera victims in Indian camps, and the claim that there were now 7.5 million refugees in India. *Time*, August 2, 1971, pp. 24–29.

148. Nixon and Kissinger on *The Concert for Bangla Desh*, Nixon Presidential Materials Project, Conversation Oval 553, August 2, 1971, 9:45 a.m., Oval Office, The White House, nsarchive.gwu.edu/NSAEBB/NSAEBB79/Bangladesh.mp3.

149. *FRUS 1969–1976*, vol. 11, p. 265.

150. *FRUS 1969–1976*, vol. 11, p. 164. Bass notes that Nixon liked very few people, but he "spoke of Yahya with an uncharacteristic blend of admiration and affection." Bass, *Blood Telegram*, p. 7.

151. Nixon Presidential Materials Project, Conversation Oval 553, August 2, 1971, 9:45 a.m., Oval Office, The White House, nsarchive.gwu.edu/NSAEBB/NSAEBB79 /Bangladesh.mp3. Before his secret trip to China, Kissinger stopped in New Delhi and met with Prime Minister Gandhi. He told Gandhi that he had been "impressed with the intensity of Indian feeling in regard to the present situation," though he tried to reassure her that "a strong India is in the interest of the United States" and that "he could not conceive of India and the United States having serious clashing interests on a global scale." *FRUS 1969–1976*, vol. 11, pp. 222–25.

152. Holdridge, *Crossing the Divide*, p. 62.

153. *FRUS 1969–1976*, vol. 11, p. 316.

154. MemCon, Kissinger to Nixon, October 9, 1971, in *Soviet-American Relations*, p. 487.

155. *FRUS 1969–1976*, vol. 11, pp. 493–99.

156. Conversation Among President Nixon, the President's Assistant for National Security Affairs (Kissinger), and the President's Assistant (Haldeman), Washington, November 5, 1971, *FRUS 1969–1976*, vol. E-7, Document 150, history.state .gov/historicaldocuments/frus1969-76ve07/d150. Kissinger later wrote that the two meetings between Nixon and Gandhi "were without doubt the two most unfortunate meetings Nixon had with any foreign leader." Kissinger, *White House Years*, p. 878.

157. Raghavan, *1971*, p. 228.

158. Before Dobrynin returned to Moscow for a meeting of the Central Committee in mid-November, Kissinger again urged him to push for "parallel actions by the USSR and the US to prevent" a war in South Asia. MemCon, Dobrynin to Politburo, November 18, 1971, in *Soviet-American Relations*, p. 527.

159. Raghavan, *1971*, p. 232.

160. Sultan M. Khan, *Memories and Reflections of a Pakistani Diplomat* (Oxford: Alden Press, 1997), pp. 368–69.

161. *FRUS 1969–1976*, vol. 11, pp. 556–57.

162. *FRUS 1969–1976*, vol. 11, p. 597.

163. *FRUS 1969–1976*, vol. 11, p. 612.

164. Bass, *Blood Telegram*, p. 293.

165. Transcript of Telephone Conversation Between Secretary of the Treasury Connally and the President's Assistant for National Security Affairs (Kissinger), Washington, December 5, 1971, *FRUS 1969–1976*, vol. E-7, Document 159.

166. *FRUS 1969–1976*, vol. 11, p. 649.

167. *FRUS 1969–1976*, vol. 11, p. 677.

168. *CBS Evening News*, December 14, 1971, VTNA, provides a representative example.

169. Haldeman, *Diaries*, December 7, 1971, p. 463.

170. Background Briefing with Henry Kissinger, December 7, 1971, NPMP, NSC Files, Indo-Pak War, Box 572, nsarchive.gwu.edu/NSAEBB/NSAEBB79/BEBB30.pdf.

171. The ABC correspondent Bill Gill did reproduce Kissinger's arguments without any qualification, although NBC and CBS were more skeptical. *ABC Evening News*, December 8, 1971, VTNA.

172. At nixontapes.org/hak/1971-12-07_Nixon_016-037.mp3.

173. This is one of the more controversial aspects of the crisis. Seymour Hersh later identified the source as Moraji Desai, a political opponent of Gandhi's who was not in the cabinet and would not have been privy to her plans. Desai sued Hersh for libel over the allegation, but Hersh won. Hersh, *Price of Power*, pp. 449–50. It remains unclear to this day how reliable this intelligence was, and even Bass is reluctant to dismiss it entirely. Bass, *Blood Telegram*, pp. 289–90. Bass accepts that Nixon and Kissinger were sincere in their belief that India sought to destroy West Pakistan, although he attributes this to a very selective and prejudicial reading of the evidence by them.

174. Nixon and Kissinger considered various measures to "scare" off the Indians and send a "tough warning" to the Russians. To avoid both legal and congressional restrictions, they wanted to get third parties, particularly Iran and Jordan, to send military supplies to the Pakistanis. Bass, *Blood Telegram*, pp. 293–96.

175. *FRUS 1969–1976*, vol. 11, p. 705. Kissinger told Nixon that canceling the summit was too drastic, and the two men went back and forth on this. Kissinger encouraged Nixon's speculation that if he could "play it out toughly," he could go to the summit. Clearly this planted a seed in Kissinger's mind about using this threat later in the crisis.

176. Conversation Between President Nixon and His Assistant for National Security Affairs (Kissinger), Washington, December 9, 1971, *FRUS 1969–1976*, vol. E-7, Document 168, history.state.gov/historicaldocuments/frus1969-76ve07/d168.

177. Conversation Among President Nixon, His Assistant for National Security Affairs (Kissinger), and His Deputy Assistant for National Security Affairs (Haig), Washington, December 9, 1971, *FRUS 1969–1976*, vol. E-7, Document 168, history.state.gov/historicaldocuments/frus1969-76ve07/d177.

178. MemCon, Kissinger for President's File, December 9, 1971, in *Soviet-American Relations*, p. 537. Raghavan describes how this conversation got Moscow's attention and led them to pressure India to restrict its war aims. Raghavan, *1971*, pp. 251–52. The description of the Russian diplomat is from Isaacson, *Kissinger*, p. 376.

179. Conversation Among President Nixon, His Assistant for National Security Affairs (Kissinger), and His Deputy Assistant for National Security Affairs (Haig), Washington, December 12, 1971, *FRUS 1969–1976*, vol. E-7, Document 177, history.state .gov/historicaldocuments/frus1969-76ve07/d177.

180. Robert McMahon, "The Danger of Geopolitical Fantasies: Nixon, Kissinger, and the South Asia Crisis of 1971," in *Nixon in the World*, ed. Fredrik Logevall and Andrew Preston (New York: Oxford University Press, 2008), p. 266.

181. Richard Moss makes the point that the frequent contact with the Soviets during the crisis makes it difficult to see the crisis as being as dangerous as some have argued. Moss, *Back Channel to Moscow*, p. 148.

182. Conversation Between President Nixon and His Assistant for National Security Affairs (Kissinger), Washington, December 12, 1971, *FRUS 1969–1976*, vol. E-7, Document 178, history.state.gov/historicaldocuments/frus1969-76ve07/d178.

183. *CBS Evening News*, December 14, 1971, VTNA.

184. Bass thinks that Kissinger did not check with Nixon on this threat, but that seems unlikely. Bass, *Blood Telegram*, p. 311. On the other hand, this could be a case of Kissinger thinking he intuited Nixon's wishes, only to have the president cut him off at the knees.

185. Haldeman, *Diaries*, December 15, 1971, p. 469.

186. One of Indira Gandhi's top aides describes Kissinger's description of India's war aims as a "complex exercise in scenario building which has nothing to do with the facts." P. N. Dhar, *Indira Gandhi, the Emergency, and Indian Democracy* (New Delhi: Oxford University Press, 2000), p. 180.

187. *FRUS 1969–1976*, vol. 11, pp. 851–52.

188. *CBS Evening News*, December 16, 1971, VTNA.

189. *ABC Evening News*, January 5, 1972, VTNA.

190. James Rosen, "Nixon and the Chiefs," *The Atlantic*, April 2002, theatlantic.com /magazine/archive/2002/04/nixon-and-the-chiefs/302473.

191. John Ehrlichman, *Witness to Power: The Nixon Years* (New York: Simon & Schuster, 1982), p. 307.

192. Moss, *Back Channel to Moscow*, p. 194. In the dissertation on which the book is based, Moss provides a detailed transcript that makes it clear it was Erlichman who suggested therapy for Kissinger, although Nixon did not object. Moss, "Behind the Back Channel," pp. 290–92.

193. Kissinger, *White House Years*, p. 918 (emphasis in the original).

194. Kalb and Kalb, *Kissinger*, p. 263.

195. *ABC Evening News*, January 5, 1972, VTNA.

196. Haldeman, *Diaries*, January 10, 1972, p. 479.

197. Haldeman, *Diaries*, January 13, 1972, CD-ROM.

198. "Nixon: Determined to Make a Difference," *Time*, January 3, 1972, pp. 10–13, 16–19.

199. Perlstein, *Nixonland*, p. 618.

200. Telephone conversation, Nixon and Kissinger, January 1, 1972, nixontapes.org /hak/1972-01-01_Nixon_017-125.mp3.

201. Safire, *Before the Fall*, p. 400.

202. Isaacson, *Kissinger*, pp. 397–98. *CBS Evening News*, January 27, 1971, VTNA, played the serious quote from Kissinger, while ABC ran the humorous statement about Steinem. The CBS segment included an argument by Kissinger that the administration sought a lasting peace that was greater than the simple absence of war.

203. Russell Baker, "Mister Professident," *The New York Times*, January 30, 1972, p. 13.

4. "Peace Is *Really* at Hand"

1. *ABC Evening News*, special coverage, January 24, 1973, VTNA.

2. *CBS Evening News*, *NBC Nightly News*, and *ABC Evening News*, January 24, 1973, VTNA.

3. *NBC Nightly News*, April 5, 1972, VTNA.

4. Haldeman, *Diaries*, February 14, 1972, p. 498.

5. *FRUS 1969–1976*, vol. 17, pp. 663–64.

6. Brinkley and Nichter, *Nixon Tapes: 1971–1972*, pp. 398–404; and *FRUS 1969–1976*, vol. 17, pp. 661–72. Nixon's comment about being more Chinese can be heard on the tape. Oval Office conversation no. 671–1, February 14, 1972, Nixon Library.

7. Kissinger, *White House Years*, pp. 774–75.

8. Hersh, *Price of Power*, p. 490. It is remarkable he could say this with a straight face.

9. For an excellent treatment of this subject, and the importance of television coverage and diplomatic spectacle for Nixon, see Tizoc Chavez, "'One Picture May Not Be Worth Ten Thousand Words, but the White House Is Betting It's Worth Ten Thousand Votes': Richard Nixon and Diplomacy as Spectacle," in *The Cold War at Home and Abroad: Domestic Politics and U.S. Foreign Policy Since 1945*, ed. Andrew Johns and Mitch Lerner (Lexington: University Press of Kentucky, 2018), pp. 146ff. The title quote comes from a commentary by Eric Sevareid on *CBS Evening News*, February 11, 1972, VTNA.

10. Chapin's approach was painstaking and deliberate. He outlined it in a conference in 2010. "The Week That Changed the World," USC U.S.-China Institute, November 10, 2010, china.usc.edu/ShowArticle.aspx?articleID=2283.

11. Hersh, *Price of Power*, p. 495. Television personnel dominated the 155-member press delegation.

12. MacMillan, *Nixon and Mao*, p. 121.

13. Hersh, *Price of Power*, p. 494.

14. *ABC Evening News*, February 22, 1972, VTNA. Rogers subsequently called Haldeman because of these reports and demanded he be included in any other meetings with Mao. Haldeman, *Diaries*, p. 509.

15. *FRUS 1969–1976*, vol. 17, p. 732.
16. For some full accounts, see Tudda, *Cold War Turning Point*, and MacMillan, *Nixon and Mao*. Winston Lord provides an excellent account in his extensive oral history, Foreign Affairs Oral History Project, adst.org/OH%20TOCs/Lord,%20 Winston.pdf, pp. 135–70.
17. *FRUS 1969–1976*, vol. 17, p. 699.
18. Holdridge, *Crossing the Divide*, p. 92. Holdridge gives "maximum credit" to Kissinger for devising the formulation.
19. Lord has an interesting account of this. Foreign Affairs Oral History Project, adst .org/OH%20TOCs/Lord,%20Winston.pdf, pp. 167–69.
20. Tudda, *Cold War Turning Point*, p. 200.
21. *NBC Nightly News*, February 27, 1972, VTNA.
22. Kissinger, *White House Years*, p. 1092.
23. Haldeman, *Diaries*, February 28, 1972, p. 514.
24. Kissinger also spoke with Nancy Reagan and told Nixon that she's "got a hell of a lot more brains than he has." Telephone conversation, February 28, 1972, nixontapes .org/hak/1972-02-28_Nixon_020-106.mp3.
25. Haldeman, *Diaries*, March 2 and March 8, 1972, CD-ROM.
26. Kissinger to Haldeman, April 12, 1972, quoted in Sarah Thelen, "A Summit Meeting with God," *Passport*, January 2014, pp. 74–75. I want to thank Sarah Thelen for sending me an original copy of this memo.
27. *FRUS 1969–1976*, vol. 8, pp. 143–46.
28. Lien-Hang T. Nguyen, *Hanoi's War: An International History of the War for Peace in Vietnam* (Chapel Hill: University of North Carolina Press, 2012), p. 241.
29. Asselin, *Vietnam's American War*, p. 192.
30. Stephen P. Randolph, *Powerful and Brutal Weapons: Nixon, Kissinger, and the Easter Offensive* (Cambridge, MA: Harvard University Press, 2007), pp. 28–29.
31. *CBS Evening News*, April 3, 1972, VTNA. Coverage of the offensive was extensive and pessimistic about the South Vietnamese.
32. *FRUS 1969–1976*, vol. 8, pp. 162–63.
33. *FRUS 1969–1976*, vol. 8, p. 169.
34. In my judgment, the only two measures Nixon excluded were the use of nuclear weapons and sending American combat troops back into Vietnam. The nuclear weapons issue is controversial, since Nixon did raise the issue in a conversation with Kissinger on April 25, 1972. However, the context of this conversation, and several other references to nuclear weapons that appear on the tapes, indicate that this was never a serious possibility. This had far more to do with Nixon's "madman" bluff that he had tried to use earlier in the war without much success. See the treatment in Moss, *Back Channel to Moscow*, p. 226, and his long footnote on p. 353. I disagree on this point with my colleague and friend Jeffrey Kimball, but I would allow that this is a matter of opinion.
35. Randolph, *Powerful and Brutal Weapons*, p. 114. Randolph also makes clear that this imposed considerable costs, including taking many forces from other important areas of the world.

36. Moss, *Back Channel to Moscow,* pp. 227–33, makes it clear that Kissinger frequently threatened to use American influence to scuttle Moscow's treaties with the Germans.

37. Telephone conversation, Kissinger and Nixon, nixontapes.org/hak/1972-04-12 _Nixon_022-119.mp3.

38. These diary references are in Nixon, *RN,* p. 589.

39. *FRUS 1969–1976,* vol. 14, pp. 429, 449.

40. In his memoirs, Kissinger wrote, "Vanity can never be completely dissociated in high office from the perception of national interest." Kissinger, *White House Years,* pp. 1120–21.

41. *FRUS 1969–1976,* vol. 14, pp. 401, 434.

42. *FRUS 1969–1976,* vol. 14, pp. 454–55. When Treasury Secretary John Connally came by for a scheduled meeting, Nixon told him that he suspected the Russians misjudged him, that they thought he was subject to the same domestic pressures that weakened Connally's old friend Lyndon Johnson. "And they read I'm a political man," Nixon told Connally. "They're quite correct. But what they didn't realize is that I know that nobody can be President of this country, and have a viable foreign policy, if the United States suffers a defeat fighting the miserable, little Communist country, fueled by Soviet arms, and that the world is going to be a very dangerous place." The Soviets would then pressure America and its allies in the Middle East and around the world. Vietnam, in Nixon's telling, was "the supreme test."

43. *FRUS 1969–1976,* vol. 14, pp. 475–504. The Brezhnev Doctrine was a Soviet foreign policy position that called for military intervention to prevent any communist country from flirting with political pluralism that might threaten party rule. It was invoked against Czechoslovakia in 1968, and that is what Kissinger was referencing.

44. Kissinger, *White House Years,* p. 1154.

45. *FRUS 1969–1976,* vol. 14, p. 561. Kissinger tried to blame Nixon's attitude on the presence of Bebe Rebozo and implied that the two men drank too much and encouraged each other's bellicosity. But Nixon's attitude about Kissinger's approach to the trip had more to do with domestic politics than with alcohol and Rebozo. *FRUS 1969–1976,* vol. 14, p. 599.

46. *CBS Evening News,* April 24, 1972, VTNA.

47. Haldeman, *Diaries,* April 24, 1972, p. 543.

48. Given that Nixon had asked his friend Bebe Rebozo to set Kissinger up with younger women after the China trip, one wonders if Kissinger's story was intentionally manipulative.

49. Nixon and Kissinger conversation, April 25, 1972, EOB Conversation No. 332–22. My thanks to Richard Moss for his transcript of this conversation.

50. Telephone conversation, Nixon and Kissinger, April 25, 1972, nixontapes.org /hak/1972-04-25_Nixon_023-070.mp3.

51. *NBC Nightly News,* April 25, 1972, VTNA.

52. Kalb and Kalb, *Kissinger,* p. 296.

53. His speech followed the same pattern as those on Cambodia: an optimistic speech about ending the war and withdrawals, followed two weeks later by an escalation of the war.

54. Richard Nixon, "Address to the Nation on Vietnam," April 26, 1972, presidency .ucsb.edu/documents/address-the-nation-vietnam.

55. "Richard Nixon Vietnam War Speech (Post-Speech Analysis Only)," CBS Evening News, April 26, 1972, VTNA.

56. Isaacson, Kissinger, p. 416.

57. FRUS 1969–1976, vol. 8, p. 345.

58. In answer to a question while in Texas, Nixon made a veiled threat to bomb the dikes in North Vietnam, acknowledging the "enormous number of civilian casualties" that might cause but also stressing that "we are prepared to use our military and naval strength against military targets throughout North Vietnam, and we believe that the North Vietnamese are taking a very great risk if they continue their offensive in the South. I will just leave it there, and they can make their own choice." Nixon's comments can be found at presidency .ucsb.edu/documents/remarks-and-question-and-answer-session-with-guests -following-dinner-secretary-connallys. See also Kalb and Kalb, Kissinger, p. 298.

59. Haldeman, Diaries, May 1, 1972, pp. 547–48 and CD-ROM.

60. Haldeman, Diaries, May 1, 1972, pp. 547–48 and CD-ROM. Kissinger angrily called the Abrams cable a "self-serving, egg-sucking, panicky lecture" that might "demoralize Thiệu and convince him that the U.S. was going to sell out Saigon." FRUS 1969–1976, vol. 8, p. 392.

61. Haldeman, Diaries, May 1, 1972, p. 547.

62. Kissinger, White House Years, p. 1173.

63. Anatoly Dobrynin, In Confidence: Moscow's Ambassador to Six Cold War Presidents (Seattle: University of Washington Press, 1995), p. 246. Kissinger told Nixon that his talks were "thoroughly unproductive." FRUS 1969–1976, vol. 8, p. 386; and Kissinger, White House Years, p. 1169.

64. Nixon, RN, p. 600.

65. Nixon asked Haldeman to do a poll, and when the results came back, it showed that 60 percent of Americans favored going ahead with the summit. Haldeman, Diaries, May 2, 1972, p. 549.

66. The May 5 conversation is recorded in Moss, Back Channel to Moscow, p. 285.

67. Winston Lord makes it clear that Kissinger's staff thought they would lose the summit. Foreign Affairs Oral History Project, adst.org/OH%20TOCs/Lord,%20 Winston.pdf, p. 242.

68. Kissinger would later face considerable criticism for his dealing with the SLBM issue. Moss, Back Channel to Moscow, p. 261.

69. In a conversation with Nixon on March 31, 1972, Kissinger urged Nixon to reach out to the academic community after the election, although he disparaged the group, remarking that they could be bought cheaply. nixonlibrary.gov/white -house-tapes/699/conversation-699-001.

70. Isaacson, Kissinger, p. 420.

71. *FRUS 1969–1976*, vol. 8, pp. 434–46. Nixon's political calculations about the price he would pay for his Vietnam decisions went back and forth, often depending on his mood and audience. On the one hand, he believed that defeat in Vietnam meant the end of his hopes for a second term. On the other hand, he thought the military escalation might be unpopular enough to cause him to lose as well, to fall on "my sword." *FRUS 1969–1976*, vol. 8, pp. 458. His actions were a gamble, but one in which the domestic political calculus was never far from his mind.

72. *FRUS 1969–1976*, vol. 8, pp. 456–70.

73. MemCon, Dobrynin to Politburo, May 5, 1972, in *Soviet-American Relations*, p. 796.

74. Richard Nixon, "Address to the Nation on the Situation in Southeast Asia," May 8, 1972, presidency.ucsb.edu/documents/address-the-nation-the-situation-southeast-asia.

75. Safire, *Before the Fall*, p. 428, captures the very negative response.

76. "Richard Nixon Speech Re: Vietnam War (Post-Speech Analysis Only)," *CBS Evening News*, May 8, 1972, VTNA.

77. Stephen Ambrose, *Nixon: The Triumph of a Politician, 1962–1972* (New York: Simon & Schuster, 1987), pp. 540–41.

78. Columbia University was on strike when I visited there in May 1972 as an admitted senior, but classes were being held outside rather than in campus buildings.

79. *CBS Evening News*, May 9, 1972, VTNA.

80. Kalb and Kalb, *Kissinger*, p. 308.

81. Telcon, Kissinger and Dobrynin, May 9, 1972, in *Soviet-American Relations*, pp. 804–805. Bundy is convinced that the German situation was central to the Soviet decision to proceed with the summit. William Bundy, *A Tangled Web* (New York: Hill and Wang, 1998) p. 321.

82. Zubok, *A Failed Empire*, pp. 220–21.

83. *NBC Nightly News*, May 11, 1972, VTNA.

84. *FRUS 1969–1976*, vol. 14, p. 817.

85. *FRUS 1969–1976*, vol. 14, pp. 829–30. The change in Kissinger's mood and demeanor was striking. Before Patolichev's visit on May 11, Kissinger subtly distanced himself with sympathetic journalists from Nixon's decision to mine Haiphong harbor. Marvin Kalb later recorded how Kissinger used the phrase "the President felt" that the mining was necessary, rather than his customary "we," and how he compared the lack of opposition to the mining in Nixon's cabinet meeting with that in Stalin's politburo. Kalb and Kalb, *Kissinger*, p. 304. Although reports of Kissinger's doubts about his policies and double-dealing with the media must have reached him, Nixon did not allow them to affect his use of Kissinger's talents. Leonard Garment, a special counsel to Nixon—a liberal Republican and Jew, like Kissinger—argued that Kissinger served to "extend" Nixon's powers, with such qualities as "the European sophistication, the urbane brilliance, the self-mocking wit, the skill with the press, the unmistakable Jewishness." Leonard Garment, *Crazy Rhythm: My Journey from Brooklyn, Jazz, and Wall Street to Nixon's White House, Watergate, and Beyond . . .* (New York: Random House, 1997), p. 187.

86. *FRUS 1969–1976*, vol. 14, p. 943.
87. *FRUS 1969–1976*, vol. 14, p. 939.
88. *FRUS 1969–1976*, vol. 14, p. 948.
89. *FRUS 1969–1976*, vol. 14, p. 949.
90. *FRUS 1969–1976*, vol. 14, p. 947.
91. *FRUS 1969–1976*, vol. 14, p. 835.
92. *FRUS 1969–1976*, vol. 14, p. 965.
93. Kissinger, *White House Years*, pp. 1217ff.
94. Jussi Hahnhimäki, *The Flawed Architect: Henry Kissinger and American Foreign Policy* (London: Oxford University Press, 2004), p. 220.
95. *ABC Evening News*, May 22, 1972, VTNA.
96. This was particularly the case with *CBS Evening News*, where Walter Cronkite was a space enthusiast. See the CBS broadcast of May 24, 1972, VTNA.
97. Kalb and Kalb, *Kissinger*, p. 314.
98. *NBC Nightly News*, May 22, 1972, VTNA.
99. MemCon, May 24, 1972, in *Soviet-American Relations*, p. 903. Kissinger was convinced that the Russian hostility was designed to produce a written transcript for Hanoi, evidence that the Soviets remained in solidarity with their Third World socialist brethren under attack by the imperialists. Kissinger, *White House Years*, p. 1228.
100. *ABC Evening News*, May 25, 1972, VTNA. Congressman John Ashbrook, a conservative critic of Nixon's, gave reporters the details of the basic numbers of missiles under consideration in the SALT discussions, criticizing the agreement as one that would "doom the United States to nuclear inferiority." Senator Henry Jackson pronounced himself "greatly disturbed" over the agreement, which was "unbelievable" in delivering not parity between the two superpowers but "sub-parity." Bernard Gwertzman, "Accord Expected to Offset Missile Totals and Power," *The New York Times*, May 24, 1972; and *CBS Evening News*, May 26, 1972, VTNA.
101. Kissinger, *White House Years*, p. 1233.
102. Nixon, *RN*, p. 615.
103. There is a clear account of this in Isaacson, *Kissinger*, pp. 432–36. The other problem was the assumption that the U.S. lead in MIRV technology would be long-lasting. Once the Russians began to MIRV their larger missiles, the U.S. advantage in this area disappeared and became a key concern for the SALT II negotiations.
104. John Osborne, *The Fourth Year of the Nixon Watch* (New York: Liveright, 1973), p. 93.
105. Kalb and Kalb, *Kissinger*, p. 328.
106. The "Basic Principles" agreement can be found in *FRUS 1969–1976*, vol. 1, pp. 389–91.
107. *CBS Evening News*, May 29, 1972, VTNA.
108. The idea for such a dramatic return came from the legendary public relations man Tex McCrary, who had mentored both Nixon speechwriter William Safire and advance man Dwight Chapin. Charles J. Kelly, *Tex McCrary: Wars, Women, Politics: An Adventurous Life Across the American Century* (Lanham, MD: Hamilton Books, 2009), p. 195.

109. *FRUS 1969–1976*, vol. 1, p. 399.

110. "Richard Nixon Address to Congress Re: His Trip to the USSR," *CBS Evening News*, Special, June 1, 1972, VTNA.

111. Isaacson, *Kissinger*, pp. 437–38; and *CBS Evening News*, May 31, 1972, VTNA. Kissinger's swinger image was further enhanced when a group of Playboy bunnies voted him "the man I'd most like to go out on a date with"—over the rock star Eric Clapton and the actor Burt Reynolds—with one bunny, Lynn Cole, "breathlessly describing how 'his eyes are so penetrating they make him look like he knows what's on your mind before you even say it.'" "'A Snobbish Image Abroad': Personalities," *The Washington Post*, July 8, 1972, C3.

112. Isaacson, *Kissinger*, p. 437.

113. Kalb and Kalb, *Kissinger*, p. 328. The reference to Hasty Pudding, the name of the Harvard theatrical society, captures how Kissinger's Ivy League background connected him to many elite journalists; he was one of them in a way that Nixon could never be.

114. *CBS Evening News*, June 15, 1972, VTNA.

115. "Kissinger, Often Seen, Is Finally Heard on TV," *The New York Times*, June 25, 1972. It is often incorrectly noted that his "peace is at hand" news conference in October was the first time the White House allowed him to be recorded.

116. *CBS Evening News*, August 15, 1972, VTNA.

117. *CBS Evening News*, convention coverage, August 22, 1972, VTNA; and Kalb and Kalb, *Kissinger*, pp. 343–44.

118. Safire, *Before the Fall*, p. 459.

119. At npr.org/2012/08/04/157670201/the-thomas-eagleton-affair-haunts-candidates-today.

120. There is some debate over whether Kissinger's push for a settlement before the November election clashed with Nixon's reluctance, something attributed to either the president's aggressive character or his political fear that a settlement would allow conservative Democrats to drift back to McGovern on economic issues. This distorts the dynamic between the two men and misses their basic agreement on the need to end the war, which both viewed as a distraction from their larger ambitions. Isaacson, *Kissinger*, pp. 440–41. Isaacson's book was used as the basis for the 1995 television film *Kissinger and Nixon*, which dramatized the conflict between the two men in an almost cartoonish fashion. The Nixon character wants to keep the war going to "score a touchdown," Kissinger wants to settle because of his personal vanity, and Al Haig is presented as a tormented moralist. It is Hollywood at its worst. imdb.com/title/tt0113554.

121. This discussion is reproduced in Hughes, *Fatal Politics*, pp. 85–86.

122. Kissinger, *White House Years*, p. 1319.

123. Nguyen, *Hanoi's War*, pp. 261–76.

124. Chen Jian, "China and the Indochina Settlement at the Geneva Conference of 1954," in *The First Vietnam War*, ed. Fredrik Logevall and Mark Lawrence (Cambridge, MA: Harvard University Press, 2007), p. 260. The Chinese premier, Zhou Enlai, believed the Eisenhower administration had been held back by the

public before the elections, and this perception of American public opinion seems to have been accepted by the Vietnamese as well.

125. Kissinger, *White House Years*, p. 1325. Kissinger comes dangerously close to expressing a traditional racial prejudice about "inscrutable Orientals," but his ultimate conclusion about the tragic character of the relationship is fair-minded.

126. *FRUS 1969–1976*, vol. 8, p. 962.

127. Since Nixon had assured the two communist superpowers that the United States sought to end its involvement in the war, continuing seemed to defeat the purpose of triangular diplomacy. *FRUS 1969–1976*, vol. 8, pp. 953–54.

128. Nixon was quite direct with Kissinger on this point in a conversation the day before Kissinger left for Paris on October 6. nixonlibrary.gov/white-house-tapes /793/conversation-793-006.

129. *FRUS 1969–1976*, vol. 8, p. 1072.

130. *FRUS 1969–1976*, vol. 8, p. 1073.

131. Kissinger, *White House Years*, pp. 1345–46.

132. Winston Lord provides a description of this moment. Foreign Affairs Oral History Project, adst.org/OH%20TOCs/Lord,%20Winston.pdf, p. 246.

133. *FRUS 1969–1976*, vol. 9, p. 25.

134. Hughes, *Fatal Politics*, pp. 101–103, has an excellent analysis of McGovern's misreading of Nixon.

135. *FRUS 1969–1976*, vol. 9, pp. 120–21.

136. Reeves notes that Nixon "took wine very seriously" and that "he drank the best." Reeves, *President Nixon*, p. 267.

137. This was the judgment of Kissinger's aide John Negroponte, who was most skeptical of the agreement. George W. Liebmann, *The Last American Diplomat: John D. Negroponte and the Changing Face of American Diplomacy* (New York: I. B. Tauris, 2012), p. 58.

138. Haldeman, *Diaries*, October 13, 1972, p. 630. To put more pressure on Thiệu, Kissinger may have leaked the basic elements of the agreement to CBS News's Marvin Kalb. After Kalb's report on October 13, Kissinger told Nixon he suspected Rogers was responsible—not the most likely scenario. Kissinger's relationship with Kalb makes his role in this leak far more likely than Rogers's. nixontapes.org /hak/1972-10-13_Nixon_031-041.mp3; Kissinger called Rogers after talking to Nixon, and Rogers replied, with barely veiled sarcasm, "He couldn't have gotten anything from us because Christ nobody knows it." He went on to tell Kissinger that Kalb was writing a book about him and had been trying to interview Rogers. Telcon, Kissinger and Rogers, October 13, 1972, Box 16, NSCF, NPMS, NARS.

139. *FRUS 1969–1976*, vol. 9, pp. 144–53.

140. Nixon asked Haldeman to conduct a poll on the different scenarios for a settlement. Haldeman, *Diaries*, October 22, 1972, CD-ROM.

141. Telcon, Kissinger with Lloyd Shearer, October 16, 1972, and with Max Frankel, October 13, 1972, Box 16, NSCF, NPMS, NARS.

142. The "my Leader" references pop up in Telcon, Kissinger and Pete Peterson, October 13, 1972, and with Hugh Sidey, October 30, 1972, Box 16, NSCF, NPMS,

NARS. His conversation with Nixon, Telcon, November 6, 1972, Box 17, Box 7, NSCF, NPMS, NARS.

143. Safire, *Before the Fall*, p. 136.

144. Haldeman, *Diaries*, October 17, 1972, p. 635.

145. Kissinger, *White House Years*, p. 1377.

146. Winston Lord charitably describes Kissinger as "optimistic" before meeting Thiệu, "although we knew he would huff and puff." Foreign Affairs Oral History Project, adst.org/OH%20TOCs/Lord,%20Winston.pdf, p. 249.

147. Kalb and Kalb, *Kissinger*, p. 363.

148. Larry Berman, *No Peace, No Honor: Nixon, Kissinger, and Betrayal in Vietnam* (New York: Touchstone, 2001), p. 164.

149. *FRUS 1969–1976*, vol. 9, p. 251.

150. *FRUS 1969–1976*, vol. 9, pp. 262–63.

151. *CBS Evening News*, October 26, 1972, VTNA.

152. Kalb and Kalb, *Kissinger*, p. 384.

153. Haldeman, *Diaries*, October 26, 1972, p. 638.

154. Nixon and Kissinger phone conversation, October 26, 1972. This conversation is particularly revealing in how well the two men understood the domestic political implications of this step. nixontapes.org/hak/1972-10-26_Nixon_032-063.mp3. In his memoirs, Kissinger remarks blandly, "Nixon and I did not discuss the domestic political implications." Kissinger, *White House Years*, p. 1398. In one of his rare misreadings of the evidence, Isaacson says that Nixon was "enraged" by Kissinger's pronouncement. Isaacson, *Kissinger*, p. 460.

155. Kissinger, *White House Years*, p. 1400.

156. "Goodbye Vietnam," *Newsweek*, November 6, 1972.

157. Kissinger, *White House Years*, p. 1409.

158. Oriana Fallaci, *Interview with History*, trans. John Shepley (Boston: Houghton Mifflin, 1977), pp. 30–44. The original interview appeared in *The New Republic*, December 16, 1972, pp. 17–22.

159. *NBC Nightly News*, November 6, 1972, VTNA.

160. Nixon, *RN*, p. 715.

161. Kissinger and Nixon phone conversation, November 8, 1972, nixontapes.org/hak/1972-11-08_Nixon_033-060.mp3.

162. Haldeman, *Diaries*, November 19, 1972, p. 656.

163. *FRUS 1969–1976*, vol. 9, p. 381.

164. *FRUS 1969–1976*, vol. 9, p. 397.

165. *FRUS 1969–1976*, vol. 9, pp. 399–400. I've also used the tape of the conversation: nixontapeaudio.org/chron5/153-028.mp3.

166. Nixon told Kissinger to get the best agreement he could, although he also kept adding that a bilateral agreement with Hanoi was "repugnant" to him. *FRUS 1969–1976*, vol. 9, pp. 420–21.

167. *NBC Nightly News*, November 19, 1972, VTNA.

168. Kissinger, *White House Years*, p. 1417.

169. Kissinger, *White House Years*, p. 1419. Kissinger also notes that his relations with Nixon were "wary and strained," suffering in the aftermath of the Fallaci interview.

170. *FRUS 1969–1976*, vol. 9, p. 492. Both Kissinger and Nixon now expected they could get a settlement. *FRUS 1969–1976*, vol. 9, p. 499; and *NBC Nightly News*, November 29, 1972, VTNA.

171. *NBC Nightly News*, December 4, 1972, VTNA.

172. *FRUS 1969–1976*, vol. 9, pp. 509–513.

173. Kissinger, *White House Years*, p. 1433.

174. Ehrlichman, *Witness to Power*, pp. 314–15.

175. *FRUS 1969–1976*, vol. 9, p. 561.

176. *FRUS 1969–1976*, vol. 9, p. 579.

177. *FRUS 1969–1976*, vol. 9, p. 617.

178. James Reston, "Current Peace Session Near End," *The New York Times*, December 13, 1972, p. 1.

179. Kissinger, *White House Years*, p. 1448. Kissinger writes that it was difficult to reconstruct their decision-making because there wasn't a written record. But in the tape of the meeting, Kissinger's role emerges more clearly, showing him eager to justify his path during the negotiations, defending himself from what he suspected were Nixon's criticisms, and advocating the renewal of bombing against North Vietnam. Kissinger defended his own conflicting reports and changing moods, referring again to the negotiations as "a roller coaster. Up and down, the whole time." In Kissinger's view, this pattern made it difficult for the Americans to tell whether the North Vietnamese were serious.

180. *FRUS 1969–1976*, vol. 9, p. 648. This reference to the North Vietnamese has to be read as a reference to Thiệu as well. By this point, Kissinger saw all the Vietnamese this way.

181. *FRUS 1969–1976*, vol. 9, pp. 635–79. The meeting on December 14 is so important that the editors of the *Foreign Relations* series included the entire thing. The two men play off each other, but Kissinger is also a genius at striking the right chords with Nixon, from mentioning the April 1969 Korean incident, which had always bothered Nixon, to using the word "impotent," which clearly got at Nixon's insecurities. One can listen to the tape at nixonlibrary.gov/white-house-tapes/823 /conversation-823-001.

182. Haldeman, *Diaries*, December 15, 1972, p. 677.

183. Kissinger, *White House Years*, p. 1451. Kissinger said that Nixon gave him seven single-spaced pages of instructions and that he referred to the president so often because of these instructions. Critics would jump on the word "charade," tying it to the "peace is at hand" optimism Kissinger had encouraged.

184. Kalb and Kalb, *Kissinger*, p. 413.

185. *NBC Nightly News*, December 17, 1972, VTNA.

186. For the details on Linebacker II, I rely on the article by Earl H. Tilford, Jr., in *Encyclopedia of the Vietnam War*, ed. Spencer Tucker (New York: Oxford University Press, 2000), pp. 233–34.

187. Kalb and Kalb, *Kissinger*, pp. 416–17.

188. *NBC Nightly News*, December 18, 1972, VTNA.

189. Charles Colson, *Born Again* (Old Tappen, NJ: Chosen Books, 1976), p. 77.

190. *NBC Nightly News*, December 20, 1972, VTNA.

191. "Nixon and Kissinger: Triumph and Trial," *Time*, January 1, 1973, p. 13.

192. Haldeman, *Diaries*, December 15, 1972.

193. Telcon, Kissinger and Jerry Schecter, December 1, 1972, Box 17, NSCF, NPMS, NARS. Kissinger asked the *Time* editor, "Can you at least write the goddamn thing to make my subordinate position clear?"

194. *FRUS 1969–1976*, vol. 9, pp. 775–92.

195. Berman, *No Peace, No Honor*, p. 217. I find myself in partial agreement with Larry Berman's argument that Nixon believed the threat of American airpower might serve as a guarantee for South Vietnam's existence as long as he was president. I disagree with his argument that Nixon and Kissinger expected to have to use American military force frequently in Vietnam after the settlement. What I see from their talks is the desire to get out and let the Vietnamese fight it out among themselves.

196. Kissinger, *White House Years*, p. 1456.

197. Isaacson, *Kissinger*, p. 472.

198. Colson, *Born Again*, pp. 79–80.

199. Kissinger, *White House Years*, p. 1456.

200. Asselin argues that Linebacker II devastated North Vietnam and compelled it to return to the peace negotiations. Asselin, *Vietnam's American War*, p. 203.

201. Winston Lord mentions the importance of the bombing as a message to President Thiệu. Foreign Affairs Oral History Project, adst.org/OH%20TOCs/Lord,%20 Winston.pdf, p. 257.

202. Nguyen, *Hanoi's War*, pp. 295–97.

203. *FRUS 1969–1976*, vol. 9, pp. 851–52.

204. *FRUS 1969–1976*, vol. 9, pp. 862–65.

205. Telephone conversation, January 5, 1973, nixontapes.org/hak/160-004.mp3.

206. Thiệu tried to send representatives to lobby Congress on his behalf. Kissinger met with Ambassador Tran Kim Phuong to tell him, "Your government has managed to enrage the President almost beyond belief." He also told the hapless ambassador that the South Vietnamese had "put out a pack of lies" about him. Kissinger's tone was both resigned and threatening as he told the ambassador, "The party is over. We have taken everything we are going to take." But his resentment bubbled up when he blurted out, "No one here wants the Nobel Prize. Saigon has attacked me for betraying you, and I am attacked here as a murderer." When Phuong replied, "I have never heard President Thiệu say anything to me like that or about you wanting the Nobel Prize," Kissinger responded, "It makes no difference. It is not a personal matter. I happen to admire President Thiệu. It is a tragedy. We have produced a horrible tragedy." *FRUS 1969–1976*, vol. 9, pp. 882–92.

207. *NBC Nightly News*, January 10, 1973, VTNA.

208. Winston Lord underlines the point that there were no major differences with the October agreement. Foreign Affairs Oral History Project, adst.org/OH%20 TOCs/Lord,%20Winston.pdf, p. 258.

209. *FRUS 1969–1976*, vol. 9, p. 1006.

210. *FRUS 1969–1976*, vol. 9, p. 1051.

211. *FRUS 1969–1976*, vol. 9, p. 1141.

212. Richard Nixon, "Address to the Nation Announcing Conclusion of an Agreement on Ending the War and Restoring Peace in Vietnam," January 23, 1973, presidency.ucsb.edu/documents/address-the-nation-announcing-conclusion-agreement-ending-the-war-and-restoring-peace.

213. Kissinger's press conference was covered by all three networks live on January 24, 1973. It shows him at the height of his powers, but it is also clear that he was minimizing and avoiding certain delicate issues, especially the question about assurances given to Thiệu in the event of a treaty violation. "Henry Kissinger Press Conference Re: Vietnam War Cease Fire Agreement," *ABC Evening News*, January 24, 1973, VTNA.

214. *NBC Nightly News*, January 24, 1973, VTNA.

215. Winston Lord stresses this as well. Foreign Affairs Oral History Project, adst.org/OH%20TOCs/Lord,%20Winston.pdf, pp. 262–63.

216. Kissinger, *White House Years*, p. 1472.

217. Ehrlichman, *Witness to Power*, p. 316.

218. Haldeman, *Diaries*, January 14, 1973, CD-ROM.

219. Haldeman, *Diaries*, January 27, 1973, CD-ROM.

220. *ABC Evening News*, January 31, 1973, VTNA. Nixon's reaction is in Haldeman, *Diaries*, February 2, 1973.

5. "Henry Kissinger Did It"

1. *NBC Nightly News*, May 29, 1974, VTNA.

2. Kissinger, *Years of Upheaval*, p. 5.

3. Other writers have insisted that Nixon planned to fire Kissinger well before the end of the year. Colson, *Born Again*, p. 80.

4. Richard Nixon, "The President's News Conference," January 31, 1973, presidency.ucsb.edu/documents/the-presidents-news-conference-86.

5. Only a week before, on January 23, 1973, Nixon had told Kissinger that because Marvin Kalb could not bring himself to congratulate the president on the air, Kissinger should "never, never, never" meet with him for another interview. nixontapes.org/hak/036-099.mp3.

6. *CBS Evening News*, February 1, 1973, VTNA.

7. Jerrold Schecter, "A View of Henry Kissinger Riding High," *Time*, February 5, 1973.

8. Klein, *Making It Perfectly Clear*, p. 391.

9. Kissinger, *Years of Upheaval*, p. 23.

10. TV coverage during this period focused on the return of the POWs. Washington had not arranged with Hanoi the extensive coverage it had with China, as 1973 was not an election year.

11. *FRUS 1969–1976*, vol. 10, p. 77. Pierre Asselin notes that Vietnamese historians enjoy telling a story of Kissinger visiting the National History Museum and rec-

ognizing the long history of Vietnamese resistance to foreign intervention. They see this as a type of "apology," although Kissinger had said similar things before. Asselin, *Vietnam's American War*, pp. 215–16.

12. Kissinger, *Years of Upheaval*, p. 43.

13. *FRUS 1969–1976*, vol. 10, p. 120. The cringeworthy humor points to the authorship of Winston Lord, who freely confesses to this failing. Interview with Winston Lord, February 17, 2006.

14. Indeed, at the same time Kissinger was meeting with the North Vietnamese, the Soviet ambassador in Hanoi was cabling Moscow that the "Vietnamese comrades" planned in the near future to "replace the reactionary regimes of Saigon, Vientiane, and Phnom Penh with progressive ones," with the goal of creating a "Federation of Indochinese countries." Hahnhimäki, *Flawed Architect*, p. 263.

15. Kissinger, *Years of Upheaval*, p. 42.

16. At a meeting with David Bruce in Beijing in November 1973, Kissinger said, "On every trip we have gone through protestations of emotional ties. But there are no illusions. I think the Chinese are impressive because they are tough, unsentimental, calculating. They understand the overall world situation better than I would say anyone else I have dealt with—not because they love us sentimentally, but precisely because they can overcome their sentiment in order to deal with us and to understand the necessities." Priscilla Roberts, ed., *Window on the Forbidden City: The Beijing Diaries of David Bruce, 1973–1974* (Hong Kong: Centre of Asian Studies, 2001), pp. 354–55. To what extent Nixon and Kissinger appreciated this contradiction between their belief in a special relationship and this cold-blooded calculation is not clear.

17. *FRUS 1969–1976*, vol. 18, pp. 125, 137. Kissinger had been afraid the Chinese would not arrange a meeting with Mao, and one night he was "pacing one of the halls of the guesthouse letting off steam by swearing and denouncing the Chinese bureaucracy for failing to arrange a meeting with Mao." Klein notes that it was almost as if the Chinese were listening in on them, as they quickly set up the meeting. Klein, *Making It Perfectly Clear*, p. 137.

18. Kissinger knew that balance would soon be tested by Brezhnev's intense desire for a "nuclear understanding" with the United States, the Prevention of Nuclear War Agreement. The Chinese believed this effort at U.S.-Soviet cooperation was targeted at them and found it "anathema." *FRUS 1969–1976*, vol. 38, Part 1, p. 11.

19. *FRUS 1969–1976*, vol. 18, p. 196.

20. *FRUS 1969–1976*, vol. 25, p. 8.

21. *FRUS 1969–1976*, vol. 25, p. 8.

22. *FRUS 1969–1976*, vol. 25, pp. 105–115.

23. *FRUS 1969–1976*, vol. 25, pp. 112–14.

24. National Archives, White House Tapes, March 1, 1973, Conversation No. 866–16.

25. The subsequent release of this tape in December 2010 led to great public embarrassment for Kissinger and a public apology for this statement. Kissinger tried to put the tape into context, arguing against critics like Michael Gerson who contended that it represented the administration's "moral insensitivity." He defended

the Nixon efforts to gain freedom for Soviet Jews and criticized the Jackson-Vanik Amendment restrictions. Henry A. Kissinger, "Putting the Nixon Tape in Context," *The Washington Post*, December 26, 2010, washingtonpost.com/wp-dyn /content/article/2010/12/23/AR2010122304552.html.

26. Nixon, *RN*, p. 787.

27. *FRUS 1969–1976*, vol. E-15, Part 2, Document 5, Minutes of a Senior Review Group Meeting, January 31, 1973.

28. *FRUS 1969–1976*, vol. E-15, Part 2, Document 9, Memorandum, President Nixon to Kissinger, March 10, 1973.

29. Discussion in the British Embassy in Washington, April 19, 1973, PREM 15/1362, PRO, London.

30. Kissinger, *Years of Upheaval*, 153. When Kissinger complained about the coverage of the speech, an editor at *The Washington Post* told him that it was "not General Marshall at Harvard." Herken, *Georgetown Set*, p. 366.

31. Stanley Kutler, *Abuse of Power: The New Nixon Tapes* (New York: Simon & Schuster, 1997), p. 243.

32. Kissinger, *Years of Upheaval*, pp. 75–76.

33. In my opinion, wiretapping journalists over the bombing of Cambodia was not designed to prevent a secret from being revealed to an enemy government, since they knew all about the bombing. It could only have been designed to control what the American people learned about the policies undertaken on their behalf.

34. Kalb and Kalb, *Kissinger*, p. 443; and Kutler, *Abuse of Power*, p. 314. Kissinger told Haldeman that he, too, would resign if Haldeman was forced out, and Haldeman took him seriously. Haldeman, *Diaries*, April 13, 1973, p. 773. Given Haldeman's repeated role in defending Kissinger against Rogers, his comment to the Kalbs was an act of ingratitude.

35. Kutler, *Abuse of Power*, p. 322. According to Isaacson, Alexander Haig, after he became Nixon's chief of staff on May 2, 1973, alerted Kissinger to the White House taping system. This may have led Kissinger to tone down some of his more unctuous flattery, although he continued to reassure Nixon that history would vindicate him. Isaacson, *Kissinger*, p. 494.

36. Haldeman, *Diaries*, April 30, 1973, p. 826.

37. Telephone conversation 45-130, May 1, 1973, Nixon Library.

38. The statistics in the Gallup poll are striking for the decline. historyinpieces.com /research/nixon-approval-ratings.

39. Kutler, *Abuse of Power*, p. 553.

40. Fallaci, *Interview with History*, p. 38.

41. Lord Cromer, the British ambassador in Washington, angrily remarked, "We were struck by the astonishing anomaly of the most powerful nation in the world invoking the aid of a foreign government to do its drafting for it, while totally excluding its own Ministry of Foreign Affairs." His comments of March 7, 1973, can be found in his letter to Brimelow, FO73/135, PRO, London.

42. Kissinger, *Years of Upheaval*, p. 286.

43. *FRUS 1969–1976*, vol. 15, p. 451.

44. *NBC Nightly News*, February 25, 1973, VTNA.

45. *FRUS 1969–1976*, vol. 10, p. 207.

46. Nixon tapes, May 2, 1973, Conversation 909–6, Nixon Library.

47. *NBC Nightly News*, May 3, 1973, VTNA.

48. Kissinger, *Years of Upheaval*, p. 334.

49. *FRUS 1969–1976*, vol. 10, pp. 331, 353.

50. *NBC Nightly News*, June 13, 1973, VTNA.

51. *FRUS 1969–1976*, vol. 10, pp. 354–56.

52. *CBS Evening News*, May 28, 1973, VTNA.

53. Isaacson, *Kissinger*, pp. 502–503.

54. *NBC Nightly News*, May 29, 1973, VTNA.

55. Telephone conversation, Nixon and Kissinger, 40–117, June 14, 1973, Nixon Tapes, Nixon Library.

56. The Ervin Committee agreed to postpone its hearings while the Soviet leader was in the country. However, the hearings resumed the very day of his departure, giving Brezhnev, as Kissinger caustically wrote, "an unprecedented personal opportunity to watch the public indictment of the President with whom they had just been negotiating." Kissinger, *Years of Upheaval*, p. 288.

57. *NBC Nightly News*, June 21, 1973, VTNA.

58. Kalb and Kalb, *Kissinger*, p. 442; and *NBC Nightly News*, June 22, 1973, VTNA.

59. *FRUS 1969–1976*, vol. 15, pp. 534–42.

60. This estimate comes from the Associated Press: apnews.com/6f36c34ab6b845bf8b279db3ac559897.

61. *NBC Nightly News*, June 29, 1973, VTNA.

62. *FRUS 1969–1976*, vol. 10, p. 360.

63. *NBC Nightly News*, July 6, 1973, VTNA.

64. *FRUS 1969–1976*, vol. 18, p. 301.

65. *CBS Evening News*, July 13, 1973, VTNA.

66. Kissinger, *Years of Upheaval*, p. 422. Kissinger claims that Rather assured him that the story came from opponents of his nomination in the State Department. If it did, these opponents were undoubtedly among the dumbest State Department officials to have ever been in the Foreign Service.

67. *FRUS 1969–1976*, vol. 10, p. 392.

68. Richard Nixon, "The President's News Conference," August 22, 1973, presidency.ucsb.edu/documents/the-presidents-news-conference-87.

69. *NBC Nightly News*, August 23, 1973, VTNA.

70. Kissinger, *Years of Upheaval*, p. 423.

71. Alistair Horne, *Kissinger 1973: The Crucial Year* (New York: Simon & Schuster, 2009), p. 187.

72. Kissinger, *Years of Upheaval*, p. 426.

73. *NBC Nightly News*, September 7, 10, and 12, 1973, VTNA.

74. Technically this was not true. Eisenhower's second secretary of state, Christian Herter, was born of American parents in Paris. Kissinger was the first naturalized citizen to become secretary of state.

75. *NBC Nightly News*, September 21, 1973, VTNA.
76. Joaquín Fermandois, "The Persistence of a Myth: Chile in the Eye of the Cold War," trans. Mark Falcoff, *World Affairs* 167, no. 3 (Winter 2005), p. 112. This conclusion is shared by other historians of Chile as well, even those intensely critical of Nixon and Kissinger. Collier and Sater, *History of Chile*, p. 355.
77. *FRUS 1969–1976*, vol. 21, pp. 923–24.
78. Department of State, Memorandum, "Secretary's Staff Meeting, October 1, 1973: Summary of Decisions," October 4, 1973, accessed in "Kissinger and Chile: The Declassified Record," nsarchive.gwu.edu/NSAEBB/NSAEBB437.
79. *FRUS 1969–1976*, vol. 21, p. 930.
80. Kissinger, *Years of Upheaval*, p. 412.
81. Kornbluh, *Pinochet File*, p. 204.
82. This is the very persuasive argument in Barbara J. Keys, *Reclaiming American Virtue: The Human Rights Revolution of the 1970s* (Cambridge, MA: Harvard University Press, 2014), p. 148. Keys notes that the extensive media coverage of the repression, which included a *Newsweek* story on the "slaughterhouse in Santiago," energized liberals to press human rights concerns in Congress.
83. Henry Kissinger, *Crisis* (New York: Simon & Schuster), 2004, p. 16.
84. *FRUS 1969–1976*, vol. 25, p. 338. Admittedly, he is telling the Chinese ambassador this, but his objective to reduce the Soviet presence in the Middle East became clear as the crisis proceeded.
85. *FRUS 1969–1976*, vol. 25, pp. 312–14.
86. *FRUS 1969–1976*, vol. 25, p. 441.
87. *FRUS 1969–1976*, vol. 25, pp. 389–91. Using the word "triumph" three times within this short conversation with Nixon may well have been what Kissinger meant when he wrote later in his memoirs that "the gods are offended by hubris." Kissinger, *Years of Upheaval*, p. 491.
88. *FRUS 1969–1976*, vol. 25, pp. 393–96. Reports indicated that Golda Meir had ordered the arming and alerting of Jericho missiles, Israel's principle nuclear delivery system. Avner Cohen, "Nuclear Arms in Crisis Under Secrecy: Israel and the Lessons of the 1967 and 1973 Wars," in *Planning the Unthinkable: How New Powers Will Use Nuclear, Biological, and Chemical Weapons*, ed. Peter R. Lavoy, Scott D. Sagan, and James J. Wirtz (Ithaca, NY: Cornell University Press, 2000), esp. pp. 117–19.
89. *FRUS 1969–1976*, vol. 25, p. 413.
90. *FRUS 1969–1976*, vol. 25, p. 414.
91. *FRUS 1969–1976*, vol. 25, p. 424.
92. *FRUS 1969–1976*, vol. 25, pp. 448–50. In the discussion between Joint Chiefs Chair Moorer and Deputy Secretary of Defense Clements, the anger toward Kissinger's decision-making style is abundantly expressed.
93. *FRUS 1969–1976*, vol. 25, p. 430.
94. *NBC Nightly News*, October 12, 1973, VTNA.
95. *FRUS 1969–1976*, vol. 25, p. 454.

96. *FRUS 1969–1976*, vol. 25, pp. 458–66. Kissinger was trying to make Schlesinger seem the impediment to Dinitz, but Schlesinger was not being wholly cooperative.

97. *FRUS 1969–1976*, vol. 25, p. 467.

98. *FRUS 1969–1976*, vol. 25, p. 486; and Kissinger, *Years of Upheaval*, p. 514.

99. *FRUS 1969–1976*, vol. 25, p. 484.

100. Kissinger, *Crisis*, p. 229.

101. *NBC Nightly News*, October 15, 1973, VTNA.

102. *FRUS 1969–1976*, vol. 25, p. 496.

103. *FRUS 1969–1976*, vol. 25, p. 499.

104. *FRUS 1969–1976*, vol. 25, p. 569.

105. *NBC Nightly News*, October 17, 1973, VTNA. I would wager the Saudi ambassador meant Kissinger.

106. Suri, *Henry Kissinger and the American Century*, p. 208. Suri notes that Kissinger left this part of the conversation out of his book *Crisis*.

107. *FRUS 1969–1976*, vol. 25, pp. 573–74.

108. Kissinger, *Years of Upheaval*, pp. 536–37.

109. *FRUS 1969–1976*, vol. 25, p. 623. In a small concession to Nixon, both announcements were made by the White House.

110. Kissinger, *Years of Upheaval*, p. 547.

111. *FRUS 1969–1976*, vol. 25, p. 632.

112. Kissinger, *Years of Upheaval*, p. 552.

113. *FRUS 1969–1976*, vol. 25, p. 640.

114. *FRUS 1969–1976*, vol. 25, p. 658. Kissinger later wrote that he had a "sinking feeling that I might have emboldened them." Kissinger, *Years of Upheaval*, p. 569.

115. *FRUS 1969–1976*, vol. 25, p. 676.

116. Michael K. Bohn, *Nerve Center: Inside the White House Situation Room* (Washington, DC: Brassey's, 2003), p. 74.

117. *FRUS 1969–1976*, vol. 25, pp. 704–705.

118. *FRUS 1969–1976*, vol. 25, p. 706.

119. *FRUS 1969–1976*, vol. 25, p. 714.

120. There were six other officials—Defense Secretary Schlesinger, CIA chief William Colby, Joint Chiefs chairman Thomas Moorer, NSC deputy Brent Scowcroft, chief of staff Haig, and NSC member Jonathan Howe.

121. *FRUS 1969–1976*, vol. 25, p. 740 (emphasis in the original).

122. *FRUS 1969–1976*, vol. 25, p. 741 (emphasis in the original).

123. For "overreacting," see the statement by Victor Israelyan in Richard B. Parker, *The October War* (Gainesville: University of Florida Press, 2001), pp. 224–25.

124. Victor Israelyan, *On the Battlefields of the Cold War*, trans. Stephen Pearl (University Park: Penn State University Press, 2003), pp. 250–52.

125. *NBC Nightly News*, October 25, 1973, VTNA.

126. *FRUS 1969–1976*, vol. 25, p. 753.

127. Richard Nixon, "The President's News Conference," October 26, 1973, presidency.ucsb.edu/documents/the-presidents-news-conference-84.

128. *FRUS 1969–1976*, vol. 25, p. 764. In his memoirs Kissinger tones down his reaction and notes that "it was not the most propitious moment to summon Brezhnev to a test of manhood." Kissinger, *Years of Upheaval*, p. 606.

129. For a similar assessment of the challenges Kissinger faced, but with a different judgment of his performance, see Salim Yaqub, *Imperfect Strangers: Americans, Arabs, and U.S.–Middle Eastern Relations in the 1970s* (Ithaca, NY: Cornell University Press, 2016), especially pp. 145–82. Yaqub is far more critical of Kissinger than I am, although we agree that Kissinger did not want to return Israel to its 1967 borders.

130. Aaron David Miller, *The Much Too Promised Land* (New York: Bantam, 2008), p. 134.

131. Roberts, *Window on the Forbidden City*, p. 396.

132. Miller, *Much Too Promised Land*, p. 131.

133. *NBC Nightly News*, November 2, 1973, VTNA.

134. *FRUS 1969–1976*, vol. 25, pp. 858–69.

135. *NBC Nightly News*, November 6, 1973, VTNA. The newscast included a David Brinkley editorial discussing how necessary Kissinger's mission was, primarily because of the oil embargo.

136. Miller, *Much Too Promised Land*, p. 137.

137. Kissinger, *Years of Upheaval*, p. 643.

138. *FRUS 1969–1976*, vol. 25, p. 911. Nixon asked Kissinger not to announce any easing of the oil embargo if Kissinger should achieve that as well, believing that the White House should make such an announcement, as it could help "in dramatically healing recent wounds." Unfortunately this agreement did not lead to a lifting of the embargo.

139. *NBC Nightly News*, November 13, 1973, VTNA. The handshake lasts at least thirty seconds.

140. *FRUS 1969–1976*, vol. 18, pp. 327–37.

141. *NBC Nightly News*, November 14, 1973, VTNA.

142. *FRUS 1969–1976*, vol. 18, p. 435.

143. *FRUS 1969–1976*, vol. 18, p. 431.

144. Richard Nixon, "Address to the Nation About Policies to Deal with the Energy Shortages," November 7, 1973, presidency.ucsb.edu/documents/address-the-nation-about-policies-deal-with-the-energy-shortages.

145. *FRUS 1969–1976*, vol. 36, p. 643.

146. *FRUS 1969–1976*, vol. 36, pp. 690–93, 706.

147. *FRUS 1969–1976*, vol. 36, p. 692.

148. Kissinger, *Years of Upheaval*, p. 755.

149. *FRUS 1969–1976*, vol. 36, p. 693; and Kissinger, *Years of Upheaval*, p. 881.

150. *FRUS 1969–1976*, vol. 15, pp. 630–31.

151. Kissinger, *Years of Upheaval*, p. 715.

152. Kissinger, *Years of Upheaval*, p. 733.

153. *FRUS 1969–1976*, vol. E-15, Part 2, Document 40, history.state.gov/historical documents/frus1969-76ve15p2/d40. The reference to the 1956 Suez crisis is in this document.

154. Mallory Martin Hope, "Year of Discord: French-U.S. relations, April 1973–June 1974," undergraduate honors thesis, Vanderbilt University, 2015, pp. 38–39.

155. *FRUS 1969–1976*, vol. 15, p. 630.

156. "Geneva Peace Conference," *NBC Nightly News*, December 21, 1973, VTNA.

157. *FRUS 1969–1976*, vol. 15, p. 1190.

158. "Oil Embargo / Kissinger President," *ABC Evening News*, January 3, 1974, VTNA.

159. *FRUS 1969–1976*, vol. 26, pp. 2–3.

160. Kissinger, *Years of Upheaval*, p. 803.

161. Kissinger, *Years of Upheaval*, p. 811. In his memoirs, Kissinger attempts to downplay how important this agreement was to him as well as Sadat.

162. *FRUS 1969–1976*, vol. 26, p. 21.

163. *FRUS 1969–1976*, vol. 26, p. 23.

164. *FRUS 1969–1976*, vol. 26, pp. 68–69.

165. Nixon, "Remarks About an Egyptian–Israeli Agreement on Disengagement of Military Forces," January 17, 1974, presidency.ucsb.edu/documents/remarks -about-egyptian-israeli-agreement-disengagement-military-forces.

166. Kissinger, *Years of Upheaval*, p. 830.

167. *NBC Nightly News*, January 24, 1974, VTNA.

168. *FRUS 1969–1976*, vol. 26, pp. 97–101.

169. *FRUS 1969–1976*, vol. 36, p. 803.

170. *FRUS 1969–1976*, vol. 36, p. 816.

171. *FRUS 1969–1976*, vol. 36, pp. 820–21.

172. *FRUS 1969–1976*, vol. 36, pp. 866–69.

173. Kissinger may even have been certain Nixon's days were numbered. NBC broadcast a report that he told two Israeli ministers that Nixon would resign within six months. *NBC Nightly News*, January 22, 1974, VTNA.

174. *FRUS 1969–1976*, vol. 36, pp. 822–33.

175. Jobert, *Memoires*, quoted and translated in Hope, "Year of Discord," p. 85. Jobert himself was also very political, recognizing that once Pompidou was gone, new elections might offer him a chance for further advancement among the Gaullists. His candidate, Jacques Chaban-Delmas, finished third in the May 5 election.

176. *FRUS 1969–1976*, vol. E-15, Part 2, Document 50, history.state.gov/historical documents/frus1969-76ve15p2/d50.

177. *FRUS 1969–1976*, vol. 36, pp. 880–81.

178. The American coverage stressed the French "obstructionist" tactics. *NBC Nightly News*, February 12, 1974, VTNA.

179. *FRUS 1969–1976*, vol. 36, pp. 900–901. Nixon told Kissinger that he tried to tell the Europeans "the facts of life" in his after-dinner toast. In a reflection of how irreverent he had become toward Nixon, Kissinger told Haig before the conference dinner that he hoped Nixon "does not dribble over them too much tonight." *FRUS 1969–1976*, vol. 36, p. 895.

180. *FRUS 1969–1976*, vol. E-15, Part 2, Document 49, history.state.gov/historical documents/frus1969-76ve15p2/d49.

181. *FRUS 1969–1976*, vol. E-15, Part 2, Document 52, history.state.gov/historical documents/frus1969-76ve15p2/d52.

182. Nixon, "Question-and-Answer Session at the Executives' Club of Chicago," March 15, 1974, presidency.ucsb.edu/documents/question-and-answer-session-the-executives -club-chicago.

183. *NBC Nightly News*, March 21, 1974, VTNA.

184. *FRUS 1969–1976*, vol. E-15, Part 2, Document 55, history.state.gov/historical documents/frus1969-76ve15p2/d55.

185. Kissinger, *Years of Upheaval*, p. 933.

186. The Declaration was not another Atlantic charter, but it was the best Kissinger could do. nato.int/cps/en/natohq/official_texts_26901.htm?.

187. Kissinger, *Years of Upheaval*, p. 1021.

188. *FRUS 1969–1976*, vol. 15, p. 757.

189. *FRUS 1969–1976*, vol. 15, p. 704.

190. *FRUS 1969–1976*, vol. 15, p. 710. Kissinger reported to Nixon that their discussions were "inconclusive" and that there was a "desultory quality to the rest of the Soviet performance." *FRUS 1969–1976*, vol. 15, p. 794.

191. *FRUS 1969–1976*, vol. 33, p. 252.

192. *CBS Evening News*, April 26, 1974, VTNA.

193. *CBS Evening News*, April 26, 1974, VTNA.

194. Kissinger told American Jewish leaders before he left that it was "pathetic" for Gromyko, whose country had put between $15 and $20 billion into the Middle East, to be reduced to this "humiliating show of impotence." *FRUS 1969–1976*, vol. 26, p. 203.

195. Richard Valeriani, *Travels with Henry* (Boston: Houghton Mifflin, 1979), p. 215.

196. Valeriani, *Travels with Henry*, p. 209.

197. Valeriani, *Travels with Henry*, p. 208.

198. *FRUS 1969–1976*, vol. 26, p. 227.

199. *FRUS 1969–1976*, vol. 26, p. 216.

200. Some did try to counter Kissinger. The political opposition, led by the Likud leader Menachem Begin, began calling any government softening "Kissinger concessions." *ABC Evening News*, May 10, 1974, VTNA.

201. *FRUS 1969–1976*, vol. 26, pp. 244–45.

202. *FRUS 1969–1976*, vol. 26, pp. 268 (the entire meeting is on pp. 252–69).

203. *FRUS 1969–1976*, vol. 26, p. 271.

204. *FRUS 1969–1976*, vol. 26, p. 277.

205. Kissinger, *Years of Upheaval*, p. 1078.

206. Kissinger, *Years of Upheaval*, p. 1079. Kissinger does not make the connection in his memoirs between his message about Nixon's "paralysis" and his insistence on an aid cutoff.

207. *FRUS 1969–1976*, vol. 26, p. 290. In a sign of how dependent he was on Kissinger now, Nixon also assured him that, contrary to published reports, he had never

used the terms "Jew boy" or "wop" in the Watergate tapes. That he felt the necessity to reassure Kissinger on this point is interesting in and of itself.

208. *FRUS 1969–1976*, vol. 26, p. 295.
209. *NBC Nightly News*, May 23, 1974, VTNA. Kissinger writes incorrectly that Assad "had never encouraged, or for that matter permitted, guerrilla raids from Syrian territory." Kissinger, *Years of Upheaval*, p. 1090.
210. *CBS Evening News*, May 27, 1974, VTNA.
211. *FRUS 1969–1976*, vol. 26, pp. 300–334, records this extraordinary meeting with Assad.
212. Kissinger, *Years of Upheaval*, p. 1098.
213. Richard Nixon, "Remarks About a Syrian–Israeli Agreement Leading to the Disengagement of Forces," May 29, 1974, presidency.ucsb.edu/documents/remarks-about-syrian-israeli-agreement-leading-the-disengagement-forces.
214. *NBC Nightly News*, May 31, 1974, VTNA.
215. One of the Nixon tapes had the president commenting that Kissinger had requested a wiretap on his former aide Anthony Lake. The opening of John Ehrlichman's trial had reignited the issue of how much Kissinger knew about the role of his former aide David Young in the scrutiny of Daniel Ellsberg after the Pentagon Papers were leaked.
216. *NBC Nightly News*, June 6, 1974, VTNA.
217. *ABC Evening News*, June 11, 1974, VTNA.
218. Isaacson, *Kissinger*, p. 585. Some of Kissinger's aides "cringed" at this, recognizing that Kissinger's credibility had been called into question by FBI memos and the Nixon tapes, not "unnamed sources." Bob Woodward and Carl Bernstein, *The Final Days* (New York: Simon & Schuster, 1976), p. 211.
219. *NBC Nightly News*, June 11, 1974, VTNA.
220. Isaacson, *Kissinger*, p. 585.
221. Martin J. Hillenbrand, *Fragments of Our Time: Memoirs of a Diplomat* (Athens: University of Georgia Press, 1998), p. 342.
222. *NBC Nightly News*, June 11, 1974, VTNA.
223. Isaacson, *Kissinger*, p. 586.
224. Kissinger, *Years of Upheaval*, pp. 1123–43.
225. Kissinger, *Years of Upheaval*, p. 1142.
226. Kissinger, *Years of Upheaval*, p. 1142.
227. *NBC Nightly News*, June 24, 1974, VTNA.
228. *CBS Evening News*, June 26, 1974, VTNA.
229. When Kissinger heard that Jackson was going to China at the end of June, he cabled David Bruce, the American envoy there, and asked him to tell Jackson not to criticize Kissinger in front of Chinese leaders. This was because "our relationship with the Chinese depends on their confidence and faith in me as a person." Kissinger went on to add, "I consider the possible damage which Jackson could do with a few ill chosen words of such transcendental importance to our relationship with the Chinese that it is essential to head it off with steps I have mentioned

above." Roberts, *Window on the Forbidden City*, p. 505. Interestingly enough, Kissinger, the realist, emphasized the significance of personal diplomacy—when that diplomacy involved him.

230. Kissinger, *Years of Upheaval*, p. 1158.
231. Nixon, *RN*, p. 1024.
232. Woodward and Bernstein, *Final Days*, p. 224.
233. *NBC Nightly News*, June 18, 1974, VTNA.
234. Kissinger, *Years of Upheaval*, p. 1163.
235. Kissinger, *Years of Upheaval*, p. 1172.
236. *FRUS 1969–1976*, vol. 15, p. 984.
237. *NBC Nightly News*, July 3, 1974, VTNA.
238. *NBC Nightly News*, August 6, 1974, VTNA.
239. Woodward and Bernstein, *Final Days*, p. 422.
240. Nixon, *RN*, p. 1076.
241. Kissinger, *Years of Upheaval*, p. 1210; and Isaacson, *Kissinger*, p. 599.
242. Isaacson, *Kissinger*, p. 600.
243. Barry Werth, *31 Days: The Crisis That Gave Us the Government We Have Today* (New York: Doubleday, 2006), p. 16.
244. *NBC Nightly News*, August 9, 1974, VTNA.

6. "No Longer Indispensable"

1. *ABC Evening News*, December 5, 1975, VTNA.
2. Henry Kissinger, *Years of Renewal* (New York: Simon & Schuster, 1999), p. 189.
3. *FRUS 1969–1976*, vol. 38, p. 210.
4. MemCon, Ford, Kissinger, and Scowcroft, August 13, 1974, Scowcroft Papers, Box 4, Gerald R. Ford Library (GRFL).
5. MemCon, Ford, Kissinger, and Scowcroft, August 12, 1974, Scowcroft Papers, Box 4, GRFL. As a result of Ford's intervention, the Soviets allowed Kudirka to emigrate. In 1980 he was arrested in Washington at an anti-Soviet demonstration. At people.com/archive/he-risked-his-life-to-leave-russia-now-simas-kudirka-faces -trial-in-his-adopted-u-s-vol-14-no-15.
6. Kissinger, *Years of Renewal*, p. 17.
7. Kissinger, *Years of Renewal*, p. 25. The Kissinger critic and former aide Roger Morris recognized that with Ford, Kissinger "felt an obvious warmth, candor, and ease," which was certainly not present in his tortured relationship with Nixon. Morris, *Uncertain Greatness*, p. 292.
8. Peter Rodman, Kissinger's assistant, said in a later interview: "The relationship between Kissinger and Ford was the most normal, healthy, uncompelled relationship because Ford thought Kissinger was the greatest." adst.org/OH%20TOCs /Rodman,%20Peter%20W.toc.pdf.
9. Gerald R. Ford, *A Time to Heal* (New York: Harper & Row, 1979), p. 129. Donald Rumsfeld recently wrote that Ford's "strong desire to keep Kissinger on board created . . . a worrisome perception of dependency that would linger." Donald Rumsfeld, *When the Center Held* (New York: Free Press, 2018), p. 12.

10. Jon Meacham, *Destiny and Power: The American Odyssey of George Herbert Walker Bush* (New York: Random House, 2015), p. 184. This even held for his wife. *NBC Nightly News* featured a report on a Kissinger trip to India, with Nancy Kissinger visiting the Taj Mahal and being treated as a "virtual First Lady." *NBC Nightly News*, October 30, 1974, VTNA.

11. Rumsfeld notes that Kissinger told Ford that the trial of a former president would "damage America's standing abroad." As Rumsfeld was U.S. ambassador to NATO at the time, he caustically notes that he "was not aware of any of these discussions or considerations." Rumsfeld, *When the Center Held*, p. 42.

12. Ford, *A Time to Heal*, p. 146.

13. Robert T. Hartmann, *Palace Politics: An Inside Account of the Ford Years* (New York: McGraw-Hill, 1980), p. 287.

14. Bob Woodward, *Shadow: Five Presidents and the Legacy of Watergate* (New York: Simon & Schuster, 1999), pp. 30–31, also makes it clear that Schlesinger was insubordinate to Ford, refusing to follow his orders on a number of occasions.

15. In his memoirs Kissinger includes a long passage from the Washington journalist John Osborne, who wrote about the "depth and ferocity of the animosities" generated by Rumsfeld. Kissinger, *Years of Renewal*, pp. 175–76.

16. Donald Rumsfeld, *Known and Unknown: A Memoir* (New York: Sentinel, 2011), p. 180. Rumsfeld viewed Kissinger's prominence in the Ford administration as a problem from the very start.

17. *NBC Nightly News*, September 18, 1974, VTNA. The line that he "deserved it" is in Chancellor's discussion with Richard Valeriani immediately after Ford's address. Kissinger still received very sympathetic and even fawning media coverage.

18. Sebenius, Burns, and Mnookin, *Kissinger the Negotiator*, p. xi.

19. Kissinger's actual role in the Cyprus diplomacy was not extensive, and a recent scholarly treatment has largely praised his success in preventing a full-scale war between Greece and Turkey. The best recent treatment of the crisis is Aykut Kilnic, "Ancient Passions and Ethnic Rivalries: The Limits of U.S. Foreign Policy During the Cyprus Crisis of 1974," doctoral dissertation, University of New Hampshire, June 2014. Along with *FRUS 1969–1976*, vol. 30, I have relied heavily on this account for my interpretation of the crisis.

20. *NBC Nightly News*, August 18, 1974, VTNA.

21. *NBC Nightly News*, August 19, 1974, VTNA.

22. *FRUS 1969–1976*, vol. 30, p. 462.

23. Kissinger, *Years of Renewal*, p. 236.

24. When Ford gave his speech at the United Nations, demonstrators appeared with anti-Kissinger signs. *ABC Evening News*, September 18, 1974, VTNA.

25. Dobrynin, *In Confidence*, pp. 323–27.

26. Less than a week into his presidency, Ford arranged a breakfast meeting including Kissinger, Jackson, and other political figures concerned with the trade bill and Jewish emigration, indicating his own view of the importance of a compromise. Paula Stern, *Water's Edge: Domestic Politics and the Making of American Foreign*

Policy (Westport, CT: Greenwood Press, 1979), p. 146. Stern's account shows re-markable insight into the congressional politics that shaped this issue.

27. MemCon, Ford, Kissinger, and Scowcroft, August 17, 1974, Scowcroft Papers, Box 5, GRFL.

28. Kissinger Testimony, September 19, 1974, Department of State Office of Media Services (Washington, DC: GPO, 1974), p. 15.

29. Dobrynin, *In Confidence*, p. 334.

30. *FRUS 1969–1976*, vol. 16, pp. 163–69, provides a copy of the letters and the tran-script of the meeting.

31. Stern, *Water's Edge*, p. 163.

32. *NBC Nightly News*, October 18, 1974, VTNA.

33. Stern, *Water's Edge*, p. 166.

34. Kissinger blamed this on Ford's "excess of generosity" toward his prospective presidential rival. Kissinger, *Years of Renewal*, p. 259.

35. Kissinger states in his memoirs that in October 1974, the "existing Soviet-American relationship was hanging by a thread." But this is not how he actually behaved in Moscow, and the record shows he was more confident. Kissinger, *Years of Renewal*, p. 269.

36. Dobrynin, *In Confidence*, p. 320.

37. *FRUS 1969–1976*, vol. 16, p. 191.

38. *FRUS 1969–1976*, vol. 16, p. 198.

39. *FRUS 1969–1976*, vol. 16, pp. 198–99.

40. *FRUS 1969–1976*, vol. 16, p. 209.

41. *FRUS 1969–1976*, vol. 16, p. 217.

42. *FRUS 1969–1976*, vol. 16, p. 219.

43. *FRUS 1969–1976*, vol. 16, p. 247.

44. Kissinger, *Years of Renewal*, p. 282.

45. *FRUS 1969–1976*, vol. 16, p. 262.

46. *FRUS 1969–1976*, vol. 16, p. 276.

47. Before leaving on the trip, Kissinger had warned Ford that Schlesinger was "the big problem" for a SALT agreement and that unlike past defense secretaries like Robert McNamara, who protected the president, "Jim is in the business for him-self." MemCon, Ford, Kissinger, and Scowcroft, October 21, 1974, Scowcroft Pa-pers, Box 6, GRFL.

48. Kissinger, *Years of Renewal*, p. 284.

49. *FRUS 1969–1976*, vol. 16, p. 278.

50. He had some help in this. Donald Kendall, the CEO of PepsiCo and a frequent visitor to the Soviet Union, called Scowcroft to relate a conversation he had with President Ford. Kendall had been in Moscow in mid-October and met with Brezh-nev, who expressed concern about reports that Kissinger might lose his NSC job. Brezhnev made clear "the deep reliance they placed on [Kissinger] as the symbol of U.S. policy and of relationships with the Soviet Union." Kendall told Scowcroft how he conveyed this to Ford, and that Ford reassured him of his "total confi-dence" in Kissinger. *FRUS 1969–1976*, vol. 16, p. 280. Kendall was a good friend

of Richard Nixon's, and Nixon had represented the company as a lawyer. He is often mentioned as the person who triggered Nixon's decision to try to stop Salvador Allende from coming to power in Chile in September 1973.

51. *FRUS 1969–1976*, vol. 16, pp. 316–17.

52. Kissinger, *Years of Renewal*, p. 292.

53. Brezhnev wanted a success and overrode his military advisers in not counting British and French nuclear forces under the American total. Zubok, *A Failed Empire*, p. 245. Brezhnev also suffered a seizure during the conference, the beginning of the health problems that would affect his powers during his last years in office.

54. *FRUS 1969–1976*, vol. 16, pp. 327–28.

55. Ron Nessen, President Ford's press secretary and a former NBC reporter, proclaimed that Ford would return to America "in triumph" and that "it was something that Nixon couldn't do in three years, but Ford did it in three months," which strained the credulity of the Washington press corps. John Osborne, *White House Watch: The Ford Years* (Washington, DC: New Republic Books, 1977), p. 31. Isaacson notes that Nessen's comment came after several glasses of vodka and stirred up controversy in the United States with former Nixon aides like William Safire, who blamed Kissinger. Isaacson, *Kissinger*, p. 627.

56. *NBC Nightly News*, November 24, 1974, VTNA.

57. Osborne, *White House Watch*, p. 35.

58. William Burr, ed. *The Kissinger Transcripts* (New York: New Press, 1999), p. 286.

59. Kissinger, *Years of Renewal*, p. 872.

60. George H. W. Bush, who had become the head of the liaison office in Beijing as his consolation for not being selected as Ford's vice president, noted Kissinger's expressed interest in his plans for 1980, with Kissinger clearly assuming that the ticket of Ford-Rockefeller was set for 1976. Meacham, *Destiny and Power*, p. 185.

61. Burr, *Kissinger Transcripts*, p. 286.

62. *NBC Nightly News*, December 3, 1974, VTNA.

63. *NBC Nightly News*, December 18, 1974, VTNA.

64. *FRUS 1969–1976*, vol. 16, p. 388.

65. Golden also argues that Kissinger thought he could convince the Soviets to accept Jackson-Vanik and the limitation on export-import loans. Peter Golden, *O Powerful Western Star!: American Jews, Russian Jews, and the Final Battle of the Cold War* (Jerusalem: Geffen Books, 2012), pp. 307–308.

66. Kissinger, *Years of Renewal*, p. 36.

67. Randall B. Woods, *Shadow Warrior: William Egan Colby and the CIA* (New York: Basic Books, 2013), p. 413.

68. Arthur Schlesinger, *The Imperial Presidency* (Boston: Houghton Mifflin, 1973).

69. Sarah B. Snyder, *From Selma to Moscow: How Human Rights Activists Transformed U.S. Foreign Policy* (New York: Columbia University Press, 2018), pp. 105ff.

70. MemCon, Ford, Kissinger, and Scowcroft, December 3, 1974, Scowcroft Papers, Box 7, GRFL.

71. MemCon, Ford, Kissinger, and Scowcroft, December 3, 1974, Scowcroft Papers, Box 7, GRFL.

72. Woods, *Shadow Warrior,* pp. 403–404. In May 1973, James Schlesinger, when he was heading the CIA, requested a report from the agency on any activities related to Watergate. William Colby, Schlesinger's successor, continued this probe, and the result was the "family jewels."

73. Kissinger, *Years of Renewal,* p. 320.

74. Gerald Ford, "Address Before a Joint Session of the Congress Reporting on the State of the Union," January 15, 1975, presidency.ucsb.edu/documents/address -before-joint-session-the-congress-reporting-the-state-the-union-1.

75. The full text of the report can be found at archive.org/stream/TheCrisisOf Democracy-TrilateralCommission-1975/crisis_of_democracy_djvu.txt.

76. Kissinger's speech, "A New National Partnership," January 24, 1975, is available from the Department of State, Bureau of Public Affairs, Office of Media Services. The coverage comes from *CBS Evening News,* January 24, 1975, VTNA.

77. The fear of another war and Arab oil embargo even led Kissinger to suggest again that the United States might consider using force to seize oil supplies if an embargo threatened "the actual strangulation of the industrialized world." *FRUS 1969–1976,* vol. 37, p. 108.

78. MemCon, Ford, Kissinger, and Scowcroft, January 6, 1975, Scowcroft Papers, Box 8, GRFL.

79. *NBC Nightly News,* January 28, 1975, VTNA.

80. Kissinger, *Years of Renewal,* p. 382.

81. *FRUS 1969–1976,* vol. 26, p. 486. Brown's comment is particularly interesting, since he had already caused controversy by talking about how Israel was becoming a burden to the Pentagon and blaming Jewish control over the banks and newspapers in the United States. "Brown's Bomb," *Time,* November 25, 1974.

82. *FRUS 1969–1976,* vol. 26, p. 504.

83. *FRUS 1969–1976,* vol. 26, p. 503.

84. *NBC Nightly News,* February 9, 1975, and *CBS Evening News,* February 7, 1975, VTNA. This is speculation, but Kissinger's tendency to personalize foreign policy makes one wonder whether even the tiniest chink in his armor may have made him less confident in dealing with these negotiations.

85. *FRUS 1969–1976,* vol. 26, pp. 505–507.

86. *FRUS 1969–1976,* vol. 26, pp. 508–509.

87. *NBC Nightly News,* February 13, 1975, VTNA.

88. *FRUS 1969–1976,* vol. 26, p. 516.

89. *FRUS 1969–1976,* vol. 26, pp. 517–26.

90. *NBC Nightly News,* March 5, 1975, VTNA.

91. *FRUS 1969–1976,* vol. 27, p. 311. The oil issue also puts into partial relief Kissinger's simultaneous but secret acquiescence to the shah of Iran's decision to make a deal with the Iraqi leader Saddam Hussein, which led to his withdrawal of support for the Kurdish resistance in Iraq. The shah's Iran had expressed a willingness to sell Israel oil to make up for the possible loss of the Egyptian fields. Kissinger did not want to abandon the Kurds but had little choice once the shah had decided. The American use of Iran as a surrogate power to defend its interests in the Persian

Gulf, the essence of the Nixon Doctrine, also captured Kissinger's personal conviction that the shah was a reliable and loyal American ally. See the excellent study by Roham Alvandi, *Nixon, Kissinger, and the Shah: The United States and Iran in the Cold War* (New York: Oxford University Press, 2014), especially pp. 114–25. Alvandi sees the shah as far more proactive here, wanting to cut his losses and get a deal with the Iraqis.

92. Palestinian guerrillas arrived in small boats and shot their way to the Savoy Hotel, taking hostages and battling Israeli soldiers. The death toll was seven guerrillas, five hostages, and three Israeli soldiers, and reporters speculated that the raid was designed to damage Kissinger's chances for an agreement. *NBC Nightly News, ABC Evening News*, and *CBS Evening News*, March 6, 1975, VTNA. The *NBC Nightly News* report did feature Rabin saying that efforts toward peace would go on, although the PLO itself was not an organization with which Israel would negotiate.

93. *FRUS 1969–1976*, vol. 26, p. 526.

94. *FRUS 1969–1976*, vol. 26, p. 531.

95. *FRUS 1969–1976*, vol. 26, p. 545. Portugal had just experienced a failed coup by right-wing generals, and a left-wing junta seemed to be firmly in control. *NBC Nightly News* even speculated that if another Middle East war broke out, the new Portuguese government would not allow American planes to refuel in the Azores, which they had done in 1973. *NBC Nightly News*, March 12, 1975, VTNA.

96. The note went on to say that Ford had "directed an immediate reassessment of U.S. policy in the area, including our relations with Israel, with a view to assuring that the overall interests of America in the Middle East and globally will be protected." It was the beginning of the famous "reassessment," which would dominate the headlines for the next several months. *FRUS 1969–1976*, vol. 26, p. 553.

97. *NBC Nightly News*, March 23, 1975, VTNA.

98. *NBC Nightly News*, March 23, 1975, VTNA.

99. *FRUS 1969–1976*, vol. 26, pp. 555–63.

100. *FRUS 1969–1976*, vol. 26, pp. 564–68.

101. *NBC Nightly News*, March 24, 1974, VTNA.

102. *FRUS 1969–1976*, vol. 26, p. 568.

103. *FRUS 1969–1976*, vol. 10, p. 687.

104. MemCon, Ford, Kissinger, and Scowcroft, March 24, 1975, Scowcroft Papers, Box 10, GRFL.

105. *FRUS 1969–1976*, vol. 10, pp. 687–94.

106. *NBC Nightly News*, March 26, 1975, VTNA.

107. *NBC Nightly News*, March 26, 1975, VTNA.

108. *CBS Evening News*, March 27, 1975, VTNA.

109. *FRUS 1969–1976*, vol. 10, pp. 691, 717.

110. Kissinger, *Crisis*, p. 437.

111. Kissinger, *Crisis*, p. 432. It may not have helped him at this time that it was reported that Richard Nixon, still a pariah in official Washington, told advisers and former aides like the columnist William Safire to go easy on Kissinger in the "interests of peace." *CBS Evening News*, March 28, 1975, VTNA.

112. *FRUS 1969–1976*, vol. 38, pp. 278–80.
113. MemCon, Kissinger, Schlesinger, and Scowcroft, April 2, 1975, Scowcroft Papers, Box 10, GRFL.
114. Kissinger, *Crisis*, p. 439.
115. Isaacson, *Kissinger*, p. 643.
116. MemCon, Ford, Kissinger, and Scowcroft, April 11, 1975, Scowcroft Papers, Box 10, GRFL.
117. Kissinger, *Crisis*, p. 471.
118. Kissinger, *Crisis*, p. 445.
119. Hartmann, *Palace Politics*, p. 322.
120. Kissinger, *Years of Renewal*, pp. 535–36. Even after more than twenty years, Kissinger made it a point to say that Ford did not refer to the Tulane speech in his memoirs.
121. Kissinger, *Crisis*, pp. 491–95.
122. *CBS Evening News*, April 30, 1975, VTNA, contains many of these images.
123. *NBC Nightly News*, April 29, 1975, VTNA.
124. *CBS Evening News*, April 29, 1975, VTNA.
125. *FRUS 1969–1976*, vol. 10, pp. 947–48.
126. MemCon, Ford, Kissinger, and Scowcroft, April 14, 1975, Scowcroft Papers, Box 10, GRFL.
127. At one point she exclaimed, "I like your questions much better than mine. They are more understandable."
128. The historian in Kissinger mentioned the War of 1812 as another possible defeat in America's almost two-hundred-year history.
129. Kissinger interview, *Today* show, May 5–8, 1975. All these quotations are taken from the transcript provided by the Department of State's Bureau of Public Affairs (Washington, DC: GPO, 1975). Kissinger also took the opportunity to defend himself against what was becoming the most common criticism that he faced, namely excessive secrecy in conducting diplomacy. He used some humor: "I am certain that if I read top secret documents in front of the Washington Monument to a public assembly I would still be accused of conducting foreign policy too secretly."
130. MemCon, Ford, Kissinger, and Scowcroft, May 12, 1975, Scowcroft Papers, Box 11, GRFL.
131. *FRUS 1969–1976*, vol. 10, p. 974.
132. *FRUS 1969–1976*, vol. 10, p. 979.
133. Kissinger, *Years of Renewal*, p. 551.
134. Ford, *A Time to Heal*, p. 276.
135. Kissinger, *Years of Renewal*, p. 554.
136. Robert J. Mahoney, *The Mayaguez Incident: Testing America's Resolve in the Post-Vietnam Era* (Lubbock: Texas Tech Press, 2011), p. 180.
137. The television coverage was almost uniformly positive, and any doubts about the cost of the operation came over the next weeks and had relatively little impact on the polling numbers. NBC, CBS, and *ABC Evening News*, May 12–16, 1975, VTNA.
138. *CBS Evening News*, May 16, 1975, and *NBC Nightly News*, May 15 and 16, 1975, VTNA.

139. Ford, *A Time to Heal*, p. 284.

140. Kissinger, *Years of Renewal*, p. 575.

141. The Harris Poll reported that Ford was preferred by Republicans 40–17 over Reagan. *NBC Nightly News*, June 30, 1975, VTNA.

142. *FRUS 1969–1976*, vol. 26, pp. 572, 576.

143. *FRUS 1969–1976*, vol. 26, p. 619.

144. *FRUS 1969–1976*, vol. 26, p. 573. Kissinger's role at the time may have led to his neglect of the signals being sent from Sadat that he wanted the United States to play a more active role in promoting a settlement.

145. *FRUS 1969–1976*, vol. 26, p. 627.

146. *FRUS 1969–1976*, vol. 26, p. 604.

147. *FRUS 1969–1976*, vol. 26, p. 601.

148. *FRUS 1969–1976*, vol. 26, p. 647. *NBC Nightly News* had a filmed report on the letter but included the reservations of the Senate majority leader, Mike Mansfield. *NBC Nightly News*, May 22, 1975, VTNA.

149. I have relied on the doctoral dissertation by Kenneth Kolander, "Walking Out of Step: U.S.-Israel Relations and the Peace Process, 1967–1975," University of West Virginia, 2016. Kolander did extensive research in the archives of the Israeli Foreign Ministry.

150. *FRUS 1969–1976*, vol. 26, p. 649. The pressures generated by the American Jewish community are also discussed in Peter Golden, *Quiet Diplomat: A Biography of Max M. Fisher* (New York: Cornwall Books, 1992), pp. 312–26. Fisher was one of the most prominent Republican Jewish leaders of the era.

151. Kissinger personally had more affection for Assad of Syria than he did for Sadat, once telling Ford that Assad was "fantastic" and wanting the president to meet him. MemCon, Ford, Kissinger, and Scowcroft, June 6, 1975, Scowcroft Papers, Box 12, GRFL. Kissinger's affection for Assad raises once again the uncomfortable question about his preference for ruthless authoritarian leaders over more democratic figures. This may also reflect the occupational hazard of preferring leaders who didn't have the same domestic constraints he faced.

152. *NBC Nightly News*, June 1, 1975, VTNA. The report from Garrick Utley also referred to Kissinger's failure in March as "a setback for his reputation for infallibility," an unusual formulation but reflective of the media's high regard for Kissinger.

153. *FRUS 1969–1976*, vol. 26, p. 653.

154. Kissinger thought another Middle East agreement would strengthen Ford against any Democrat in 1976, even Ted Kennedy, who now led among Democratic voters despite disavowing his interest in running. Kissinger told Ford that Abraham Ribicoff, the senator from Connecticut, had told him that only Ted Kennedy could beat Ford, but Kissinger commented that Kennedy's life was such a mess that it would be a problem for him to run. *FRUS 1969–1976*, vol. 26, p. 666.

155. In his memoirs, written after Rabin's tragic assassination in 1995, Kissinger's assessment of Rabin was extremely generous, praising his courage and "aloof integrity," as well as his commitment to the peace process. Kissinger, *Years of Renewal*, pp. 374–82.

156. *FRUS 1969–1976*, vol. 26, p. 701.

157. *FRUS 1969–1976*, vol. 26, p. 741.

158. *FRUS 1969–1976*, vol. 26, p. 748.

159. *NBC Nightly News*, June 29, 1975, and *ABC Evening News* and *NBC Nightly News*, June 30, 1975, VTNA.

160. *FRUS 1969–1976*, vol. 26, p. 752.

161. Kissinger told one pro-Israeli group of Jewish Americans that he thought Rabin would agree to 98 percent of his position. *FRUS 1969–1976*, vol. 26, p. 720.

162. This was reported by John Chancellor as coming from Israeli radio. *NBC Nightly News*, July 1, 1975, VTNA.

163. *FRUS 1969–1976*, vol. 16, p. 719.

164. The reference to the end of the Cold War was explicit in the NBC broadcast, but all had a positive theme. NBC, CBS, *ABC Evening News*, July 17, 1975, VTNA.

165. MemCon, Ford, Kissinger, and Scowcroft, August 15, 1974, Scowcroft Papers, Box 5, GRFL. Some historians have argued that Kissinger's disdain for the CSCE might have led the Soviets to believe that the human rights provisions within the agreement would not be enforced and, ironically, led them to put up less resistance to them. Weisbrode, *Atlantic Century*, p. 241.

166. *FRUS 1969–1976*, vol. 16, p. 612.

167. The report on July 15, 1975, gave particular attention to the Russian's attack on détente. *NBC Nightly News*, July 15, 1975, VTNA.

168. Kissinger, *Years of Renewal*, p. 653.

169. Winston Lord wrote many of these, and he discusses the process in adst.org /OH%20TOCs/Lord,%20Winston.pdf, pp. 340ff.

170. All the quotations are from Kissinger's speech, July 15, 1975, Bureau of Public Affairs, Department of State.

171. Keys, *Reclaiming American Virtue*, pp. 153–55.

172. An example of this "personalization" is in Roberts, *Window on the Forbidden City*, p. 505.

173. *FRUS 1969–1976*, vol. 16, p. 728.

174. Kissinger insisted that "80 percent of the Portuguese people have declared unmistakably their desire for a democratic system," but he also threatened that if there were "major Communist influence" in a Portuguese government, that government could not remain part of the NATO alliance. All the quotations are from Kissinger's speech, August 14, 1975, Bureau of Public Affairs, Department of State. Weisbrode makes the point that Kissinger's concerns about Portugal had a strong domestic component: "The last thing [Kissinger] wanted to give [the political right] was a political victory for the Left anywhere on his watch." Weisbrode, *Atlantic Century*, p. 262.

175. *NBC Nightly News*, August 14, 1975, VTNA. The speech was also a sign that Kissinger had accepted the U.S. ambassador Frank Carlucci's advice to support the moderates in Portugal against the Communist elements. This was a distinct change from Kissinger's earlier pessimism and belief that Portugal was doomed to fall to

communism and should be isolated from the rest of NATO. Bernardino Gomes and Tiago Moreira de Sá, *Carlucci Versus Kissinger: The US and the Portuguese Revolution*, trans. Susana Serras Pereira (Lanham, MD: Lexington Books, 2011), pp. 171–80. For a critical look at Kissinger's approach to Eurocommunism and particularly with what he sees as Kissinger's obsession with bipolarity, see Mario del Pero, *The Eccentric Realist: Henry Kissinger and the Shaping of American Foreign Policy* (Ithaca, NY: Cornell University Press, 2006), pp. 92–100. Kissinger was indicating that any Soviet assistance to Communist parties in Portugal endangered détente. American diplomats in Europe saw the situation differently. They recognized that the Europeans, particularly the Germans, were providing significant support to the democratic forces in Portugal and played a much more important role in preventing a Communist seizure of power in that country than the United States did. Hillenbrand, *Fragments*, p. 341.

176. *FRUS 1969–1976*, vol. 26, p. 796.
177. *FRUS 1969–1976*, vol. 26, p. 798.
178. William B. Quandt, *Peace Process: American Diplomacy and the Arab-Israeli Conflict Since 1967*, 3rd ed. (Washington, DC: Brookings, 2005), p. 168. Quandt served on the National Security Council during these negotiations.
179. *FRUS 1969–1976*, vol. 26, p. 807.
180. *FRUS 1969–1976*, vol. 26, p. 840. Israel got increases in military and economic aid as well as Washington's pledge to consult closely before any further diplomatic moves. The United States also promised not to talk with or recognize Yasser Arafat's Palestinian Liberation Organization until it recognized Israel, an important concession, although, given Kissinger's track record in secret negotiations, hardly ironclad. Yaqub, *Imperfect Strangers*, p. 171.
181. Osborne, *White House Watch*, p. 183.
182. *NBC Nightly News*, September 1, 1975, and September 4, 1975, VTNA.
183. *NBC Nightly News*, September 5, 1975; September 8, 1975; October 3 and 8, 1975; VTNA.
184. *NBC Nightly News*, September 2 and 4, 1975, VTNA.
185. *FRUS 1969–1976*, vol. 26, p. 851.
186. The clash between the Ford administration and the Pike committee came close to producing a constitutional crisis over congressional access to classified information. See the National Security Archive's treatment of the investigations at nsarchive.gwu.edu/NSAEBB/NSAEBB596-Pike-Committee-and-White-House-clashed-over-access-to-CIA-secrets.
187. *CBS Evening News*, October 31, 1975, VTNA. David Schoumacher's report contains a humorous exchange between Congressman Ron Dellums and Kissinger, wherein Dellums levels a whole series of allegations and attacks on Kissinger and asks for Kissinger's comment. Kissinger dryly replies, "Except for that there is nothing wrong with my operation?" The people in the committee room laughed. Schoumacher then notes that the committee, "bested in the public give and take," was glad to move to a private session and work out some type of arrangement with

Kissinger. Even Grandin, no fan of Kissinger's, remarks that Kissinger's response was "pitch-perfect, delivered with just a hint of borscht-belt syntax." Grandin sees this as a case where Kissinger's "crime" was converted into "procedural question" or "domestic drama." Underlying Grandin's thinking is a moral rejection of the use of American power in international affairs, a legitimate position, but one fraught with its own dangers. Grandin, *Kissinger's Shadow*, pp. 139–40.

188. *FRUS 1969–1976*, vol. 16, pp. 740–42.

189. *ABC Evening News*, October 9, 1975, VNTA.

190. Ford, *A Time to Heal*, p. 324.

191. Hartmann, *Palace Politics*, p. 360.

192. *FRUS 1969–1976*, vol. 16, pp. 831–32.

193. *FRUS 1969–1976*, vol. 18, p. 752.

194. *FRUS 1969–1976*, vol. 18, p. 771.

195. *NBC Nightly News*, October 23, 1975, VTNA.

196. *FRUS 1969–1976*, vol. 18, p. 832.

197. Rumsfeld believed Kissinger was influenced by his mentor Rockefeller's antagonism toward Rumsfeld. Rumsfeld, *Known and Unknown*, p. 223. But Rumsfeld also notes that he and Cheney submitted their resignations to Ford, an act that precipitated the Halloween firings. Rumsfeld, *When the Center Held*, p. 222.

198. *ABC Evening News*, November 10, 1975, VTNA.

199. Winston Lord provides an account of this in his oral history. adst.org/OH%20 TOCs/Lord,%20Winston.pdf, p. 366–67.

200. Henry Brandon, *Special Relationships* (New York: Scribner, 1989), p. 318.

201. Isaacson, *Kissinger*, p. 671. Isaacson recounts this as happening immediately after the events. Ford remembered it as happening almost two months later.

202. Ford, *A Time to Heal*, p. 354. Kissinger did incur one profound personal loss from the Halloween massacre. His first great mentor, Fritz Kraemer, worked in the Pentagon and had become a fan of Schlesinger's, admiring his hard line against détente and his criticism of Kissinger's "defeatism" toward the Russians. Kraemer came to believe that Kissinger had orchestrated Schlesinger's firing and decided to cut off all contact with Kissinger, refusing to speak with him ever again. Despite the efforts of numerous intermediaries, including Nancy Kissinger and Kraemer's son, Kraemer held on to his vow. The family, however, allowed Kissinger to eulogize Kraemer when he died in 2003. "Like the ancient prophets," Kissinger said of Kraemer, "he made no concessions to human frailty or to historic evolution; he treated intermediate solutions as derogation from principle." For Kissinger, who conceived of himself as the policymaker, a clash with the prophet was inevitable: "The prophet thinks in terms of crusades; the policymaker hedges against the possibility of human fallibility. The policymaker, if he wants to avoid stagnation, needs the prophet's inspiration, but he cannot live by all the prophet's prescriptions in the short term; he must leave something to history." Kissinger's October 8, 2003, eulogy to Kraemer, a remarkably moving talk, can be found at henryakissinger.com/remembrances/fritz-kraemer.

203. Bartholomew Sparrow, *The Strategist: Brent Scowcroft and the Call of National Security* (New York: Public Affairs, 2015), p. 183. I agree with Sparrow on Scowcroft's integrity and independence, but on the major issues, he worked with Kissinger as a team.

204. Press conference, Department of State Bureau of Public Affairs, November 10, 1975.

205. CBS, NBC, and ABC all had similar reports on the Kissinger press conference on November 10, 1975, VTNA. I have supplemented this with the transcript of Kissinger's press conference, Department of State Bureau of Public Affairs, November 10, 1975. The same broadcast also highlighted the farewell ceremony held at the Pentagon for Defense Secretary Schlesinger, where he warned that détente should be pursued "without illusion" and that only the United States could serve as an effective counterweight to the Soviet Union.

206. Hugh Sidey, "Why Kissinger Survives," *Time*, November 17, 1975 (online version).

207. Henry Kissinger, "Building an Enduring Foreign Policy," November 24, 1975, Department of State Bureau of Public Affairs.

208. Reagan's announcement can be accessed at fordlibrarymuseum.gov/library/exhibits/campaign/020400452-001.pdf.

209. Kissinger believed that the prospects for an agreement had brightened because the Soviet's Backfire bomber and cruise missiles could be considered "peripheral systems" and not included in the SALT II agreement. Kissinger hoped that if the agreed Vladivostok total of 2,400 delivery systems could be reduced to 2,300, "it would take the Soviets out of cruise missiles." *FRUS 1969–1976*, vol. 16, p. 859. Kissinger was likely basing his approach on the memo from Denis Clift of the NSC in *FRUS 1969–1976*, vol. 33, pp. 492–94. Clift suggested regarding the Backfire and cruise missiles as "peripheral."

210. *FRUS 1969–1976*, vol. 18, p. 871. Controlling the information allowed them to prevent knowledge of a minor gaffe that Ford made with Mao. When Mao said once again that he would soon be receiving an invitation from God, his elliptical way of talking about his death, Ford went up to Mao and said something to the effect of: "I'm going to overrule Kissinger and make sure that you get that invitation from God very soon." Winston Lord Oral History, adst.org/OH%20TOCs/Lord,%20Winston.pdf, p. 387.

211. Ron Nessen, *It Sure Looks Different from the Inside* (New York: Playboy Press, 1978), p. 140. As press secretary, Nessen took intense criticism for the relative absence of news from the meeting, and he blamed Kissinger.

212. *NBC Nightly News*, December 4, 1975, VTNA.

213. The conversation between Kissinger, Ford, and Suharto can be found in Document 141, *FRUS 1969–1976*, vol. E-12, *Documents on East and Southeast Asia, 1973–1976*, history.state.gov/historicaldocuments/frus1969-76ve12/d141.

214. Although there were stories in the newspapers, only one story was on the nightly news during December 1975, and it presented the issue in a pro-government fashion. *CBS Evening News*, December 5, 1975, VTNA.

215. It is the basis for one of the three "war crimes" alleged by Hitchens against Kissinger. Christopher Hitchens, *The Trial of Henry Kissinger* (London: Verso, 2001), pp. 90–107.

216. One of the better treatments of this subject is John Prados, *Safe for Democracy: The Secret Wars of the CIA* (Chicago: Ivan R. Dee, 2006), p. 441.

217. *FRUS 1969–1976*, vol. 28, p. 235.

218. *FRUS 1969–1976*, vol. 28, p. 280.

219. On a personal level, Kissinger may have felt let down by Davis. He makes it a point to mention in his memoirs his vigorous defense of Davis, who had been the American ambassador in Chile during the Allende years. Kissinger, *Years of Renewal*, p. 801.

220. Kissinger called the observation by Davis "prescient." Kissinger, *Years of Renewal*, p. 811.

221. *FRUS 1969–1976*, vol. 28, p. 286.

222. This history is well documented in William M. LeoGrande and Peter Kornbluh, *Back Channel to Cuba: The Hidden History of Negotiations Between Washington and Havana* (Chapel Hill: University of North Carolina Press, 2014), especially pp. 126–45.

223. As the historian of the Cuban mission Piero Gleijeses concluded, "The Cuban role in Africa was unprecedented. What other Third World country had ever projected its power beyond its immediate neighborhood?" Piero Gleijeses, *Conflicting Missions: Havana, Washington, and Africa 1959–1976* (Chapel Hill: University of North Carolina Press, 2002), p. 9.

224. He quotes America's UN ambassador at the time, Daniel Patrick Moynihan, who called the Cubans "Moscow's Gurkhas." Kissinger, *Years of Renewal*, p. 786.

225. LeoGrande and Kornbluh, *Back Channel to Cuba*, p. 145.

226. *NBC Nightly News*, November 25, 1975, VTNA.

227. *ABC Evening News*, November 25, 1975, VTNA.

228. *FRUS 1969–1976*, vol. 28, p. 354.

229. *FRUS 1969–1976*, vol. 28, p. 358.

230. *FRUS 1969–1976*, vol. 28, p. 366.

231. *CBS Evening News*, December 15, 1975, VTNA. Almost a third of the broadcast was devoted to Angola.

232. *FRUS 1969–1976*, vol. 28, p. 395.

233. Telcon, President/Secretary, December 10, 1975, accessed at the National Security Archive's website, nsarchive.gwu.edu/NSAEBB/NSAEBB454.

234. Gerald Ford, "Interview for an NBC News Program on American Foreign Policy," January 3, 1976, presidency.ucsb.edu/documents/interview-for-nbc-news-program-american-foreign-policy.

235. *NBC Nightly News*, January 14, 1976, VTNA.

236. James Reston, "Kissinger's Mission," *The New York Times*, January 21, 1976, p. 35, cited in *FRUS 1969–1976*, vol. 16, p. 915.

237. *ABC Evening News*, January 20, 21, and 22, 1976, VTNA. Koppel became close to Kissinger, and his reporting frequently echoed Kissinger's views.

238. *FRUS 1969–1976*, vol. 16, p. 908.

239. *FRUS 1969–1976*, vol. 16, pp. 917–32.

240. *FRUS 1969–1976*, vol. 16, pp. 933–46. This was also connected to an attempt to lower the overall aggregates from the Vladivostok treaty to a strategic ceiling of

2,300 or even 2,200 overall strategic weapons. I have also relied on the excellent account by Kissinger's deputy, William G. Hyland, *Mortal Rivals* (New York: Random House, 1987), pp. 158–60.

241. *NBC Nightly News*, January 22, 1976, VTNA.

242. Hyland, *Mortal Rivals*, p. 161.

243. Scowcroft's description of the meeting is in *FRUS 1969–1976*, vol. 16, pp. 946–48. The NSC meetings of both January 19 and January 21, 1976, are in *FRUS 1969–1976*, vol. 33, pp. 534–70.

244. Hyland, *Mortal Rivals*, p. 162.

245. Kissinger had already been accused publicly by the former admiral Elmo Zumwalt of deliberately concealing intelligence on Soviet violations of the SALT I treaty, a charge that received widespread TV coverage and that Kissinger angrily denied. *ABC Evening News*, December 9, 1975, VTNA.

246. Rumsfeld, *When the Center Held*, p. 182.

247. Rumsfeld, *Known and Unknown*, p. 231.

248. *FRUS 1969–1976*, vol. 16, p. 1023.

249. *FRUS 1969–1976*, vol. 16, pp. 992–93

250. Brandon, *Special Relationships*, p. 319.

251. Isaacson, *Kissinger*, p. 683.

252. Peter Ramsbotham to Isaiah Berlin, April 15, 1976. I want to thank my friend and colleague Dr. Raj Roy, who interviewed Ambassador Ramsbotham, for providing me with a copy of this letter.

253. "The Kissinger Issue: Whose Alamo?," *Time*, April 19, 1976 (online edition).

254. "The Kissinger Issue: Whose Alamo?," *Time*, April 19, 1976 (online edition).

255. *NBC Nightly News*, January 26 and 27, 1976, VTNA. Hart was more explicit than the reporters on other networks in calling this a defeat for Kissinger.

256. *NBC Nightly News*, January 29, 1976, VTNA.

257. Sam Donaldson remarked that he was "running out of friends on Capitol Hill." *ABC Evening News*, February 5, 1976, VTNA.

258. *NBC Nightly News*, February 4, 1976, VTNA.

259. NBC, *ABC Evening News*, and *CBS Evening News*, February 12, 1976, VTNA. *CBS Evening News* even closed with Eric Sevareid's commentary expressing support for Kissinger staying on as secretary of state.

260. Telcon, Nixon and Kissinger, February 13, 1976, accessed at nsarchive.gwu.edu /NSAEBB/NSAEBB454.

261. Telcon, Kissinger and Nixon, February 13, 1976, accessed at nsarchive.gwu.edu /NSAEBB/NSAEBB454. *The Wall Street Journal* got hold of the transcripts of a conversation Kissinger had with Nixon after he returned from his trip to China, in which Kissinger praised Nixon's report of the trip, but after he hung up with Nixon, he called Nelson Rockefeller to report that Nixon was still an "egomaniac" who wrote the report about himself. The conversation reflected the wariness between the two men, with Kissinger still showing respect for his old boss's political judgment but disparaging him behind his back. Shawcross, *Sideshow*, p. 75.

262. *NBC Nightly News*, February 26, 1976, VTNA. John Chancellor even stressed how rare it was for a sitting president to criticize a former president.

263. Telcon, Scowcroft and Kissinger, February 27, 1976, accessed at nsarchive.gwu .edu/NSAEBB/NSAEBB454.

264. *FRUS 1969–1976*, vol. 16, p. 1014.

265. *NBC Nightly News*, March 1, 1976, VTNA.

266. *NBC Nightly News* and *CBS Evening News*, March 9, 1976, VTNA.

267. *NBC Nightly News*, March 10, 1976, VTNA.

268. James Reston, "Kissinger and Jackson," *The New York Times*, March 12, 1976. The speech was the lead story on all three network news shows on March 11, 1976. On CBS, Bernard Kalb commented that Kissinger might now have crossed the line between explaining diplomacy and campaigning. *CBS Evening News*, March 11, 1976, VTNA.

269. Jon Nordheimer, "Kissinger Scored on Campaign Role," *The New York Times*, March 14, 1976, p. 44.

270. MemCon, Kissinger, Ford, and Scowcroft, March 15, 1976, NSF, Scowcroft Files, Box 18, GFPL.

271. *CBS Evening News*, March 16, 1976, VTNA.

272. Ray Nothstine, "The Spirit of '76, Reagan Style," December 7, 2007, blog.acton .org/archives/2089-the-spirit-of-76-reagan-style.html.

273. For an excellent treatment of this subject, see Adam Clymer, *Drawing the Line at the Big Ditch: The Panama Canal Treaties and the Rise of the Right* (Lawrence: University Press of Kansas, 2008), especially pp. 10–32.

274. *NBC Nightly News*, March 24, 1976, VTNA.

275. *NBC Nightly News*, March 26, 1976, VTNA.

276. Weisbrode notes that the reference to Sonnenfeldt's talk to the ambassadors was leaked to *The Wall Street Journal* by Paul Nitze's son-in-law. Nitze was a longtime Kissinger antagonist. Weisbrode, *Atlantic Century*, p. 243.

277. Ronald Reagan, "To Restore America," March 31, 1976, Reagan Library, reaganlibrary.gov/3-31-76.

278. Jules Witcover, *Marathon: The Pursuit of the Presidency, 1972–1976* (New York: Viking Press, 1977), p. 417.

279. Kissinger's aggressive rhetoric did lead to planning for military contingencies, but this is one of those cases where Kissinger's bark was worse than his bite. LeoGrande and Kornbluh, *Back Channel to Cuba*, pp. 148–49, provide the details, but, in my opinion, exaggerate the likelihood of anything happening.

280. *CBS Evening News*, March 25, 1976, VTNA.

281. *FRUS 1969–1976*, vol. 35, pp. 310–11.

282. *NBC Nightly News*, April 7, 1976, VTNA.

283. *ABC Evening News*, April 16, 1975, VTNA.

284. *NBC Nightly News*, April 5, 1976, VTNA.

285. *NBC Nightly News*, April 8, 1976, VTNA.

286. I have relied heavily on both Nancy Mitchell, *Jimmy Carter in Africa: Race and the Cold War* (Palo Alto, CA: Stanford University Press, 2016), pp. 44–116, and the

outstanding dissertation by William Bishop, "Diplomacy in Black and White: America and the Search for Zimbabwean Independence, 1965–1980," Vanderbilt University, 2012, pp. 47–100.

287. Winston Lord discusses this in his oral history. adst.org/OH%20TOCs/Lord,%20 Winston.pdf, p. 359ff. The memo was authored by Tom Thornton, one of Lord's aides.

288. Bishop, "Diplomacy in Black and White," 58.

289. Kissinger, *Years of Renewal*, p. 915.

290. Mitchell, *Carter in Africa*, p. 48. In his memoirs, Kissinger left out this expression of sympathy for the white regimes, but he was anxious to stress how little domestic political considerations played in his decision to go to Africa. He begins the chapter on this by remarking, "It would not have been predicted by any observer of American politics that a Republican administration would take the lead in bringing about a breakthrough to majority rule in Southern Africa." Kissinger, *Years of Renewal*, p. 903.

291. Kissinger even indirectly references NSSM 39 of 1969, called the "tar baby option" by Anthony Lake, which called for American acceptance of the white minority regimes of southern Africa for the foreseeable future. Anthony Lake, *The "Tar Baby" Option: American Policy Toward Southern Rhodesia* (New York: Columbia University Press, 1976). Lake, of course, had served on Kissinger's NSC staff and resigned after Cambodia. Kissinger deliberately refers to NSDM 38, which simply gave Africa a low priority, rather than to the more well-known NSSM 39, which embraced the white regimes. See Kissinger, *Years of Renewal*, pp. 903–916, for his discussion of the topic.

292. Bishop, "Diplomacy in Black and White," pp. 50–51.

293. Kissinger, *Years of Renewal*, p. 921.

294. This was in reference to the famous phone call that Robert Kennedy made to get King released from jail shortly before the 1960 election. Larry Tye, *Bobby Kennedy: The Making of a Liberal Icon* (New York: Random House, 2016), p. 129.

295. Mitchell, *Carter in Africa*, p. 38.

296. Kissinger speech, April 27, 1976, Department of State, Bureau of Public Affairs.

297. Bishop, "Diplomacy in Black and White," pp. 47, 49–50. Kaunda had long wanted the United States to take an active role, and he believed America could prevent what Kaunda believed would be a terrible conflict. As historic as the speech was in committing the United States to majority rule in Rhodesia within two years, and to insisting that South Africa begin to dismantle apartheid, the actual coverage of the speech on the American television networks was sparse, with no direct reporting on the evening news. NBC, ABC, and CBS all gave it about one minute of treatment in their reports by the anchors. April 27, 1976, VTNA. Reporters did travel with Kissinger, and Richard Valeriani did a long report on the Kissinger visit after he returned. But none of this had any of the immediacy of the Middle East coverage. Part of the reason for this was technical: the film of the Lusaka speech was flown to Kinshasa, in what was then Zaire, a satellite point, but the technicians there were unable to get the signal to London. Valeriani, *Travels with Henry*, p. 372.

298. *FRUS 1969–1976*, vol. 28, p. 485.

299. Bishop, "Diplomacy in Black and White," pp. 71–72.

300. Michael T. Kaufman, "Kissinger Meets 2 African Leaders," *The New York Times*, April 26, 1976, p. 1. Kissinger also insisted that America's previous indifference to Africa was no longer relevant. He even scheduled a trip to the Senegalese island of Gorée, which had served as a key location in the transatlantic slave trade. There was very little TV coverage of this part of the trip. Ted Koppel filed a report, but the focus was on Kissinger's response to Reagan's charges. *ABC Evening News*, May 1, 1976, VTNA.

301. Mitchell's analysis of this is excellent. Mitchell, *Jimmy Carter*, p. 59. Kissinger's support for the repeal of the Byrd Amendment—which had allowed the United States to import Rhodesian chrome and weakened the sanctions against the Ian Smith government—allowed Reagan to link his attack on Kissinger's African initiative with his criticism of détente, as he claimed that this would increase U.S. dependence on chrome from communist countries.

302. CBS released a poll showing that in the upcoming Indiana primary, more than half of Republican voters thought Kissinger made too many concessions to the Russians. *CBS Evening News*, May 4, 1976, VTNA. Republican congressman John Rhodes called the timing of Kissinger's trip "unfortunate." Mitchell, *Jimmy Carter*, pp. 60–61.

303. Osborne, *White House Watch*, p. 326.

304. *NBC Nightly News*, May 6, 1976, VTNA.

305. *CBS Evening News*, May 7, 1976, VTNA.

306. *ABC Evening News*, May 8, 1976, VTNA.

307. *NBC Nightly News*, May 10, 1976, VTNA.

308. Osborne, *White House Watch*, p. 328 (emphasis in the original). When Kissinger appeared before the Senate Foreign Relations Committee, Senator George Mc-Govern praised his support for majority rule. Senator Harry Byrd, who showed up at the committee meeting to denounce Kissinger for suggesting the repeal of the amendment with his name, wildly accused Kissinger of "embracing" the Soviet Union and endangering America's national security, allowing Kissinger to reply, "Absolutely wrong!" and to deliver a sober and statesmanlike prediction. "If the men with the guns triumph," Kissinger warned, America's import of chrome could be more severely affected than if it approved the sanctions. *NBC Nightly News*, May 13, 1976, VTNA.

309. *ABC Evening News*, May 25, 1976, VTNA.

310. Keys, *Reclaiming American Virtue*, p. 221.

311. *NBC Nightly News*, June 8, 1976, VTNA. The report went on to mention that Chile tortured and killed political prisoners.

312. MemCon, Kissinger to Pinochet, June 8, 1976, NSF Files, Box 20, GRFL.

313. The discussion between Kissinger and Guzzetti is in Document 48, *FRUS 1969–1976*, vol. E-11, Part 2, *Documents on South America, 1973–1976*. Their talk began with a discussion of the recently completed California primary, and when Guzzetti mentioned that in the nineteenth century an Argentine battleship made a claim

on Hawaii and California, Kissinger quickly said, "I want you to know that we bought Hawaii, we paid for it, and we intend to keep it forever."

314. Mitchell, *Jimmy Carter*, p. 74. The controversy over the new African policy might have intensified domestically, but conservative attacks softened when Reagan stumbled before the California primary. In answering a question, the former California governor suggested that the United States might actually send military forces to defend the Ian Smith regime to prevent a "bloodbath." In the anti-military intervention atmosphere of the period, the Ford campaign perceived an opening to raise doubts about Reagan's judgment. It quickly put up TV ads comparing the situation to Vietnam with the slogan, "Governor Reagan couldn't start a war. President Reagan could." Mitchell, *Jimmy Carter*, p. 63.

315. Mitchell, *Jimmy Carter*, pp. 74–75.

316. Bishop, "Diplomacy in Black and White," p. 79. Mitchell is very critical of Kissinger and Vorster, seeing in them "powerful white men discussing the future of Africa." Mitchell, p. 75.

317. Bishop, "Diplomacy in Black and White," p. 80.

318. MemCon, Kissinger to Vorster, June 23, 1976, NSF Files, Box 20, GFPL.

319. Andrew Young, who would be Jimmy Carter's UN ambassador, compared Kissinger's talks with Vorster to dealing with Bull Connor, the Southern sheriff who used firehoses on Birmingham schoolchildren, rather than Martin Luther King, Jr. Nancy Mitchell, in her recent study, accuses Kissinger of going beyond diplomatic niceties and colluding with Vorster, rather than putting pressure on him to change apartheid and condemn him for Soweto. Mitchell, *Jimmy Carter*, p. 75.

320. A recent study makes many of these points in celebrating Kissinger's achievement in the southern African negotiations. Sebenius, Burns, and Mnookin, *Kissinger the Negotiator*, pp. 3–64.

321. Bishop, "Diplomacy in Black and White," p. 83. In a discussion with South Africa's ambassador to the United States, Kissinger argued, "We are not trying to reform you. We are trying to prevent the radicalization of Black Africa and a race war." When the South African responded, "We have nowhere to go. We are not like the British or Portuguese. We will fight to the last man," Kissinger told him, "I think history is against you, but we want to buy time at least." The hope that Kissinger held out was that "we can get the black states involved in development rather than organizing against the whites." He had offered this to Sadat's Egypt with some success, but he had also done so with the North Vietnamese to complete failure. In the Lusaka speech, Kissinger had proposed the United States "triple our support for development programs in southern and central Africa." To help deal with the economic effect of the tougher sanctions on Rhodesia, Kissinger was even willing to propose $12.5 million in assistance for Mozambique, even though its government was a leftist regime aligned with the MPLA of Angola. Kissinger's argument to the South African whites rested on one of the oldest American strategies in foreign policy, namely that economic development and progress could overcome the national and racial hatreds of the region.

322. Kissinger was attempting to convince Pakistan to stop its nuclear program. Sebenius, Burns, and Mnookin, *Kissinger the Negotiator*, p. 90.

323. Isaacson, *Kissinger*, p. 698.

324. Telcon, Kissinger and Rockefeller, August 17, 1976, NSF Files, Box 20, accessed at nsarchive.gwu.edu/NSAEBB/NSAEBB526-Court-Ordered-Release-of-Kissinger -Telcons/documents/11%2008-17-76%20Nelson%20Rockefeller.pdf.

325. Telcon, Kissinger and Scowcroft, August 20, 1976, NSF Files, Box 20, accessed at nsarchive.gwu.edu/NSAEBB/NSAEBB526-Court-Ordered-Release-of-Kissinger -Telcons/documents/12B%2008-20-76%20Scowcroft.pdf.

326. MemCon, Ford, Kissinger, and Scowcroft, August 30, 1976, NSF Files, Box 20, GRFL.

327. Mitchell, *Jimmy Carter*, pp. 93–94. Mitchell also makes clear that Africa was not a high priority for Carter, and there was not much difference between Republican and Democratic views on policy toward Africa.

328. Mitchell, *Jimmy Carter*, p. 97.

329. *ABC Evening News*, September 16, 1976, VTNA.

330. *FRUS 1969–1976*, vol. 28, pp. 574–75.

331. It was a dangerous strategy, which Ambassador Ramsbotham, a Kissinger admirer, later described to the Foreign Office, concluding that Kissinger had been "misled by his own exuberance and arrogance." Quoted in Mitchell, *Jimmy Carter*, pp. 102–103.

332. *FRUS 1969–1976*, vol. 28, pp. 588–93. It is striking how often Smith mentions Kissinger's name. Ian Smith later told a young Rhodesian, Donald McKenzie, that Kissinger was one of the smartest people he had ever dealt with. Author's interview with Donald McKenzie, May 25, 2017.

333. Mitchell details the reasons for the breakdown in talks. Mitchell, *Jimmy Carter*, pp. 104–116. For an outstanding treatment of the American role in making of Zimbabwe, see Bishop, "Diplomacy in Black and White," especially chapters 4 and 5.

334. Bishop, "Diplomacy in Black and White," pp. 97–100, provides a balanced judgment of Kissinger's contribution.

335. Isaacson, *Kissinger*, p. 691.

336. *NBC Nightly News*, September 24, 1976; *CBS Evening News*, September 27, 1976; and *ABC Evening News*, September 30, 1976; VTNA.

337. In his memoirs, Kissinger claims this is when he decided he would leave office if Ford won. However, he always left himself the out that if the president asked him to stay, he would have to consider the request. Kissinger, *Years of Renewal*, p. 1012. Gerald Ford, "Remarks on Diplomatic Negotiations in Southern Africa," September 24, 1976, presidency.ucsb.edu/documents/remarks-diplomatic-negotiations -southern-africa.

338. Leo P. Ribuffo, "Is Poland a Soviet Satellite? Gerald Ford, the Sonnenfeldt Doctrine, and the Election of 1976," *Diplomatic History* 14 (Summer 1990), p. 396.

339. *FRUS 1977–1980*, vol. 1, p. 25.

340. Isaacson, *Kissinger*, p. 700. Ironically enough, commentators did not mention that the cowboy imagery corresponded to the infamous interview Kissinger had given to Oriana Fallaci back in 1972. Since the speechwriter was Zbigniew Brzezinski, it is almost certain it was a deliberate reference.

341. *FRUS 1977–1980*, vol. 1, pp. 49–50 (emphasis in the original).

342. Isaacson, *Kissinger*, p. 701.

343. That Kissinger would use the word "partnership" is a sign of how tone-deaf he was on this issue, but it is also revealing as to how he saw his own elevated role in the administration. *FRUS 1969–1976*, vol. 38, pp. 467–71.

344. Isaacson, *Kissinger*, p. 701. At another debate preparation session, Kissinger's assistant William Hyland had also pushed Ford hard on Eastern Europe, so much so that the president started to get angry.

345. Ribuffo, "Is Poland a Soviet Satellite?," p. 386.

346. Isaacson, *Kissinger*, 702.

347. *NBC Nightly News*, October 7, 1976, VTNA. Both CBS and ABC also led off their broadcast with the Ford gaffe, although the bad economic news was also damaging to the president.

348. Osborne, *White House Watch*, p. 417.

349. Ribuffo, "Is Poland a Soviet Satellite?," p. 403.

350. MemCon, Ford to Kissinger, October 11, 1976, NSF Files, Box 21, GFPL.

351. Osborne, *White House Watch*, p. 416.

352. Safire, quoted in Isaacson, *Kissinger*, p. 703.

353. MemCon, Ford to Kissinger, October 18, 1976, NSF Files, Box 21, GFPL 7.

7. "We Do Not Want Henry Kissinger on the Cover of *Time* Magazine"

1. Isaacson, *Kissinger*, p. 724.

2. *NBC Nightly News*, July 19, 1983, VTNA.

3. CBS and *NBC Nightly News*, July 25, 1983, VTNA.

4. Isaacson, *Kissinger*, p. 715.

5. *FRUS 1969–1976*, vol. 38, Part 1, pp. 477–78.

6. *ABC Evening News*, December 21, 1976, VTNA. At the end of the report, Harry Reasoner even joked with Barbara Walters about Kissinger's status as a sex symbol. The awkwardness between the two anchors is palpable.

7. Isaacson, *Kissinger*, p. 706.

8. *NBC Nightly News*, January 8, 1978, VTNA.

9. *CBS Evening News*, January 31, 1977, VTNA; and Isaacson, *Kissinger*, p. 706. Kissinger traveled with a fairly large entourage, and he did not spare any expense. Carter was determined to appear frugal by comparison.

10. *NBC Nightly News*, December 20, 1978, VTNA. Kissinger also remarked that they had painted over his "scepter."

11. Jack Egan and Lee Lescaze, "Kissinger, Simon: Visible, Wealthy," *The Washington Post*, February 19, 1978, H1.

12. Bob Reiss, "Citizen Kissinger," *The Washington Post*, January 8, 1978, A1.

13. Zbigniew Brzezinski, *Power and Principle* (New York: Farrar, Straus and Giroux, 1983), p. 58.

14. Carter, "Address at Commencement Exercises at the University of Notre Dame," May 22, 1977, presidency.ucsb.edu/documents/address-commencement-exercises-the-university-notre-dame.

15. Henry Kissinger, *For the Record: Selected Statements 1977–1980* (Boston: Little, Brown, 1981), pp. 71–77.

16. NBC, *ABC Evening News*, CBS, August 15, 1977, VTNA. Carter later wrote a note to Kissinger saying, "Without your personal help, approval of the treaties would not have been possible." Carter note to Kissinger, May 1, 1978, Papers of Jimmy Carter, Name File—Henry A. Kissinger, White House Confidential Files, Carter Presidential Library. See also Jimmy Carter, *Keeping Faith: Memoirs of a President* (New York: Bantam, 1982), p. 171.

17. Carter, *Keeping Faith*, p. 305. *ABC Evening News* reported that Kissinger was advising Carter before Menachem Begin's visit in September 1977. *ABC Evening News*, September 29, 1977, VTNA.

18. *NBC Nightly News*, November 15, 1977, and *NBC Nightly News*, December 19, 1977, VTNA. Kissinger was a go-to source for television news on any Middle East story.

19. Haynes Johnson, "Our Man in Versailles: Elegant Backdrops and Flashes of Wisdom," *The Washington Post*, January 13, 1978, D1.

20. Brzezinski, *Power and Principle*, p. 249.

21. *NBC Nightly News*, July 19, 1977, and an earlier use of the same line by Kissinger, *NBC Nightly News*, May 3, 1977, VTNA.

22. Kissinger, *For the Record*, p. 85.

23. *NBC Nightly News*, October 24, 1977, VTNA. This was the first appearance in his consulting agreement with NBC. His first news special aired January 13, 1978, and got terrible TV ratings. Isaacson, *Kissinger*, p. 711.

24. Murrey Marder, "Italy's Plight Intensifies U.S. Criticism of Eurocommunism," *The Washington Post*, January 13, 1978, A10. On this issue, the Carter administration moved toward Kissinger's position, issuing a strong statement against Communist participation. Brzezinski believed U.S. pressure worked. Brzezinski, *Power and Principle*, p. 312. He does not give any credit to Kissinger.

25. Schlesinger, *Journals*, p. 438.

26. The *Washingtonian* story is quoted in Isaacson, *Kissinger*, p. 706.

27. "Kissinger Becomes Board Chairman of NASL," *The Washington Post*, October 5, 1978, D2.

28. Kissinger, *For the Record*, pp. 129–30. On pp. 129–72 is a long interview Kissinger gave in July 1978 to the editors of *Der Spiegel* in which he laid out his foreign policy criticisms in careful detail.

29. Hamilton Jordan, *Crisis: The Last Year of the Carter Presidency* (New York: G. P. Putnam, 1982), pp. 48–49.

30. Charles A. Krause, "Kissinger Hits U.S. Stance on Anti-Terrorism," *The Washington Post*, June 26, 1978, A18. ABC covered his trip. *ABC Evening News*, June 22, 1978, VTNA.

31. Memo, Pastor to Brzezinski, "Kissinger on Human Rights in Argentina and Latin America," July 11, 1978, in National Security Archive posting, nsarchive.gwu.edu/dc.html?doc=3010641-Document-04-National-Security-Council-Kissinger.

32. *FRUS 1977–1980*, vol. 2, Document 189.

33. Bill Curry, "Republicans Are Feasting on Super K: Republicans Feasting on Super K's Drawing Power," *The Washington Post*, August 27, 1978, A1.

34. Jim Hoagland, "Kissinger, Hinting '80 Senate Race, Attacks President's Foreign Policy," *The Washington Post*, September 25, 1978, A17.

35. CBS, *Face the Nation*, September 24, 1978. I accessed a copy of this tape at the Carter Presidential Library.

36. *NBC Nightly News*, October 26, 1978, VTNA.

37. *NBC Nightly News*, January 27, 1979, VTNA. Kissinger's emotions were clearly on the surface as he remembered Rockefeller.

38. Kissinger's February 2, 1979, eulogy to Rockefeller can be found at henryakissinger.com/remembrances/nelson-rockefeller/.

39. *NBC Nightly News*, February 2, 1979, featured a long excerpt from Kissinger's eulogy.

40. Schlesinger, *Journals*, p. 459.

41. Kissinger could be very partisan in unguarded moments. In August 1980 he told the actor Richard Burton that Carter's election would be "a world catastrophe . . . because Carter was totally ignorant of foreign politics. He was a peanut farmer and a fool and a megalomaniac." Richard Burton, *The Richard Burton Diaries*, ed. Chris Williams (New Haven, CT: Yale University Press, 2012), p. 620.

42. Carter, *Keeping Faith*, p. 188, makes it clear that Carter asked Kissinger for advice on China even before he became president.

43. Mitchell, *Jimmy Carter*, p. 677.

44. CBS, *Face the Nation*, September 24, 1978.

45. "An Interview with Kissinger," *Time*, August 13, 1979.

46. *NBC Nightly News*, November 6, 1978, VTNA.

47. The best treatment of this subject is Alvandi, *Nixon, Kissinger, and the Shah*.

48. Kissinger, *For the Record*, p. 178.

49. Isaacson, *Kissinger*, p. 715.

50. Brzezinski, *Power and Principle*, p. 473. Brzezinski agreed with Kissinger, and it caused significant tension between him and Carter. Carter, *Keeping Faith*, p. 452. The campaign to pressure Carter to admit the shah, orchestrated by Chase Manhattan Bank's president, David Rockefeller, has been described in detail. David D. Kirkpatrick, "Bank's Secret Campaign to Win Entry into U.S. for Shah of Iran," *The New York Times*, December 29, 2019, p. 10. Kirkpatrick was able to use the papers of David Rockefeller, who passed away in 2017, in this article.

51. *The Washington Post*, August 14, 1979, A16.

52. William Shawcross, *The Shah's Last Ride* (New York: Simon & Schuster, 1988), p. 155.

53. Schlesinger, *Journals*, p. 465.

54. Jordan, *Crisis*, p. 31. It is worth noting that Carter also praised Kissinger for calling him immediately after he announced the April 1980 failure of the mission to rescue the hostages, noting that he was "full of praise and approval of our attempt, and offering to help me in any possible way." Carter, *Keeping Faith*, p. 518.

55. Schlesinger, *Journals*, p. 465.

56. Jimmy Carter, "Address Delivered Before a Joint Session of the Congress on the Vienna Summit Meeting," June 18, 1979, presidency.ucsb.edu/documents/address-delivered-before-joint-session-the-congress-the-vienna-summit-meeting.

57. Brzezinski, *Power and Principle*, p. 474. Brzezinski felt that when he reported Kissinger's "subtle" linkage, it was counterproductive and only made Carter angry at the pressure. Carter did keep his channels to Kissinger open, bringing him on an ad hoc committee the president established in September to study the presence of a Soviet brigade in Cuba. *NBC Nightly News*, September 27, 1979, VTNA. The Cuban brigade had been in Cuba well before the SALT agreement, and Carter ultimately tried to dismiss the issue.

58. *NBC Nightly News*, November 26, 1979, VTNA. This was a particularly biting report by Valeriani, who was normally quite sympathetic to Kissinger.

59. Bill Richards, "Ball Asserts Kissinger's 'Obnoxious' Pressure Preceded Entry of Shah," *The Washington Post*, November 26, 1979, A8.

60. Henry Kissinger, *Observations: Selected Speeches and Essays 1982–1984* (Boston: Little, Brown, 1985), pp. 255–56.

61. Schlesinger, *Journals*, p. 480.

62. Tracy Daugherty, *Just One Catch: A Biography of Joseph Heller* (New York: St. Martin's Press, 2011), p. 345.

63. Joseph Heller, *Good as Gold* (New York: Simon & Schuster, 1979), p. 262.

64. Daugherty, *Just One Catch*, p. 346.

65. Daugherty, *Just One Catch*, p. 345.

66. Heller, *Good as Gold*, p. 361.

67. Heller, *Good as Gold*, p. 348.

68. William Shawcross, *Kissinger, Nixon, and the Destruction of Cambodia* (New York: Simon & Schuster, 1979).

69. Stanley Hoffmann, "The Crime of Cambodia," *The New York Review of Books*, June 28, 1979, accessed at nybooks.com/articles/1979/06/28/the-crime-of-cambodia.

70. Edwin Diamond, "I Want Kissinger to Think on Camera," *The New York Times*, October 7, 1979.

71. "Henry Kissinger: An Interview with David Frost," *NBC Nightly News*, October 11, 1979, VTNA.

72. Shawcross, *Shah's Last Ride*, p. 343, has an account from Shawcross himself of the background to the interview.

73. Tom Shales, "Kissinger's Frostbite: and NBC's Million-Dollar Headache," *The Washington Post*, October 11, 1979, D1.

74. James Reston, "Why Kissinger Jumped," *The New York Times*, March 12, 1980, A27.

75. "Kissinger Is Willing to Go Back to Service in Reagan Presidency," *The New York Times*, March 30, 1980, p. 18.

76. *NBC Nightly News*, July 14, 1980, VTNA.

77. *NBC Nightly News*, July 15, 1980, VTNA.

78. Robert G. Kaiser, "Kissinger for Reagan—with Reservations," *The Washington Post*, July 16, 1980, A16.

79. *NBC Nightly News*, convention coverage, July 15, 1980, VTNA.

80. Isaacson, *Kissinger,* p. 719.
81. Meacham, *Destiny and Power,* pp. 247–51. George H. W. Bush certainly thought the deal would work and was convinced he would not get the call from Reagan.
82. *NBC Nightly News,* July 17, 1980, VTNA.
83. Howell Raines, "Top Advisers to Reagan Recount Hard Bargaining with Kissinger," *The New York Times,* July 22, 1980, p. 24.
84. Rowland Evans and Robert Novak, "Reagan's Carter Country," *The Washington Post,* October 8, 1980, A19.
85. *NBC Nightly News,* September 5, 1980, VTNA.
86. Robert G. Kaiser and Peter Milius, "A Stream of Statistics—and Some Fudging," *The Washington Post,* October 29, 1980, A9.
87. Schlesinger, *Journals,* p. 505.
88. Bernard Gwertzman, "Reagan Advisers Ponder Kissinger Foreign Policy Role," *The New York Times,* October 31, 1981, A17.
89. Hendrick Smith, "Reagan Seeks to Emphasize Role of Cabinet Members as Advisers," *The New York Times,* November 8, 1980, p. 1. This insider sounds very similar to the one who told John Chancellor he did not want Henry Kissinger's picture on the cover of *Time* magazine.
90. Richard Burt, "Three Being Weighed for Reagan's Secretary of State," *The New York Times,* November 16, 1980, p. 34.
91. *NBC Nightly News,* December 29, 1980, VTNA.
92. *NBC Nightly News,* January 5, 1981, VTNA.
93. Rowland Evans and Robert Novak, "Kissinger Without Portfolio," *The Washington Post,* January 7, 1981, A23.
94. David Ottaway, "Shuttled Off: Kissinger, Once Held in Awe by Arabs, Now Finds Himself Held at Arm's Length; 'Private' Kissinger Found Arab Potentates Less Eager to See Him," *The Washington Post,* February 3, 1981, A1. Allen was a longtime rival of Kissinger's, who blamed his exclusion from the Nixon administration's foreign policy team on Kissinger.
95. Ronald Reagan, *The Reagan Diaries,* ed. Douglas Brinkley (New York: Harper-Collins, 2007), p. 24.
96. Schlesinger, *Journals,* pp. 512 and 519.
97. Isaacson, *Kissinger,* p. 711.
98. *NBC Nightly News,* October 9, 1981, VTNA.
99. *CBS Evening News,* November 18, 1981, VTNA.
100. Joyce Wadler, "Nancy Kissinger Acquitted of Assault in 'Throttling' of Woman at Airport," *The Washington Post,* June 11, 1982.
101. *NBC Nightly News,* June 10, 1982, VTNA.
102. Don Oberdorfer, "Kissinger's New Team: Kissinger, Other Superstars Establish a Consulting Firm," *The Washington Post,* August 24, 1982, A1.
103. The best treatment of KAI is in Isaacson, *Kissinger,* pp. 730–59. I have relied heavily upon it.
104. Henry Kissinger, "Poland's Lessons for Mr. Reagan," *The New York Times,* January 17, 1982.

105. Gregory F. Dombar, *Empowering Revolution: America, Poland, and the End of the Cold War* (Chapel Hill: University of North Carolina Press, 2014), p. 47.
106. *NBC Nightly News*, July 18, 1982, VTNA.
107. Jack Anderson, "Kissinger Seen Aiming for a Comeback," *The Washington Post*, January 17, 1983, C13.
108. *NBC Nightly News*, January 24, 1982, VTNA.
109. Kissinger, *Observations*, pp. 116–21.
110. Schlesinger, *Journals*, p. 546.
111. Schlesinger, *Journals*, pp. 530, 537–38.
112. Reagan, *Diary*, p. 124.
113. Kissinger, *Observations*, p. 141.
114. *NBC Nightly News*, June 2, 1983, VTNA.
115. Isaacson, *Kissinger*, p. 713. When Kissinger asked Schlesinger what he thought of Hersh's book, the historian replied he hadn't read it. But he added in his journal entry that later in the week he had run into Robert McNamara, who was carrying the book and remarked that it was "a prosecutor's brief, but interesting." Schlesinger, *Journals*, p. 555.
116. Schlesinger, *Journals*, p. 555.
117. Reagan, *Diaries*, p. 155.
118. Ronald Reagan, "Remarks at the Quadrennial Convention of the International Longshoremen's Association in Hollywood, Florida," July 18, 1983, presidency .ucsb.edu/documents/remarks-the-quadrennial-convention-the-international -longshoremens-association-hollywood.
119. Steven Strasser, "The Return of Kissinger," *Newsweek*, August 1, 1983.
120. Schlesinger, *Journals*, p. 554.
121. Hahnhimäki, *Flawed Architect*, p. 463.
122. *NBC Nightly News*, October 16, 1983, VTNA.
123. *NBC Nightly News*, October 12, 1983, VTNA.
124. Kissinger, *Observations*, p. 196.
125. Isaacson, *Kissinger*, p. 725.
126. *The Report of the President's National Bipartisan Commission on Central America* (New York: MacMillan, 1984), p. 156. He was joined in this reservation by Nicholas Brady and John Silber.
127. Background Briefing, a Commission Official (Kissinger), January 10, 1984, Small-Stringer, Karna, Files, White House Media Relations, Box 15, Reagan Library. This dialogue captured Kissinger's acceptance of the Jeanne Kirkpatrick argument about the difference between authoritarian and totalitarian governments, and why the United States could work with the former against the latter. Schlesinger, *Journals*, p. 554, notes that Kissinger told Schlesinger he regarded Kirkpatrick as the "evil genius" behind the Reagan Central American policy.
128. *NBC Nightly News*, January 10, 1984, VTNA.
129. Ronald Reagan, "Radio Address to the Nation on Recommendations of the National Bipartisan Commission on Central America," January 14, 1984, presidency

.ucsb.edu/documents/radio-address-the-nation-recommendations-the-national
-bipartisan-commission-central.

130. Background Briefing, a Commission Official (Kissinger), January 10, 1984, Small-
Stringer, Karna, Files, White House Media Relations, Box 15, Reagan Library.

131. Background Briefing, a Commission Official (Kissinger), January 10, 1984, Small-
Stringer, Karna, Files, White House Media Relations, Box 15, Reagan Library.

132. Hahnhimäki, *Flawed Architect*, p. 464.

133. The journalist Murray Mauder wrote a two-part series at the beginning of the year
that celebrated Kissinger as the "Shadow Secretary of State." Murrey Marder,
"Spotlight Stays on Kissinger, 'Shadow Secretary of State,'" *The Washington Post*,
January 2, 1984, A1.

134. Chuck Conconi, "Personalities," *The Washington Post*, April 24, 1987, B3.

135. Isaacson, *Kissinger*, p. 711.

136. *Nightline*, ABC, November 20, 1983, VTNA.

137. Tom Shales, "Dropping in on 'Dynasty,'" *The Washington Post*, December 21, 1983, C1.

138. Henry Kissinger, "Should We Try to Defend Against Russia's Missiles: The U.S.-
Soviet Relationship," *The Washington Post*, September 23, 1984, p. 82.

139. Reagan, *Diaries*, p. 269.

140. Schlesinger, *Journals*, p. 571.

141. Henry Kissinger, "Ronald Reagan's Great Opportunity," *The Washington Post*,
November 20, 1984, A15.

142. Reagan, *Diaries*, p. 308.

143. "Kissinger, Reagan Confer," *The Washington Post*, March 14, 1985, A23.

144. David Hoffan, "President Supported on Trip: Nixon and Kissinger Back Cemetery Visit," *The Washington Post*, April 29, 1985, A1.

145. Henry Kissinger, "An Opportunity for a Breakthrough," *The Washington Post*, November 17, 1985, p. 44; and Henry Kissinger, "The Long Journey," *The Washington
Post*, December 17, 1985, A19.

146. Briefing Memo, Admiral Holloway to Vice President Bush, Meeting with
Kissinger, November 11, 1985, Oliver North Files, Box 32, Reagan Library.

147. Fred Kaplan harshly criticized Kissinger for his hard-line stance on the terrorist
issue, mocking him for his "no-concessions" stance. Fred Kaplan, "For This We
Need Kissinger?," *The Washington Post*, July 14, 1985, B5.

148. Margot Hornblower and David S. Broder, "Kissinger Considers Race for New
York Governor," *The Washington Post*, January 31, 1986, A3.

149. Isaacson, *Kissinger*, p. 726.

150. "'Off Record' Kissinger Talk Isn't," *The New York Times*, April 20, 1986, p. 20; and
ABC World News Tonight, April 19, 1986, VTNA.

151. David Hoffman, "President Faces Test in Iceland," *The Washington Post*, October
9, 1986, A1.

152. *NBC Nightly News*, October 14, 1986, VTNA. Those sympathetic to Gorbachev's
initiative have referred to Kissinger as the "leading obtusenik" in denouncing nuclear abolition. Svetlana Savranskaya and Thomas Blanton, eds., *The Last Superpower Summits* (New York: Central European Press, 2016), p. 135.

153. Henry Kissinger, "Fundamental Agreements Do Not Happen Overnight," *The Washington Post*, October 19, 1986, A1.

154. Kissinger was on all three networks on November 25, 1986, and made frequent appearances throughout the month.

155. Henry Kissinger, "Not Its Power but Its Weakness," *The Washington Post*, December 21, 1986, D8; and *NBC Nightly News*, November 25, 1986, VTNA.

156. Reagan, *Diaries*, p. 483.

157. Quoted in Savranskaya and Blanton, eds., *Last Superpower Summits*, p. 409.

158. Schlesinger, *Journals*, p. 530. Schlesinger noted that Kissinger told the story repeatedly, and that Nancy Kissinger told him that Nixon, "though highly intelligent, was an awful man." Schlesinger, *Journals*, p. 546.

159. Monica Crowley, *Nixon in Winter* (New York: Random House, 1998), p. 231.

160. Richard Nixon and Henry Kissinger, "An Arms Agreement—on Two Conditions," *The Washington Post*, April 26, 1987, p. 67.

161. Helen Dewar, "Kissinger Backs Pact, with Misgivings," *The Washington Post*, February 24, 1988.

162. Kissinger, "The Great Foreign Policy Divide," *The Washington Post*, November 24, 1987, A23.

163. Isaacson, *Kissinger*, p. 721.

164. Michael R. Beschloss and Strobe Talbott, *At the Highest Levels: The Inside Story of the End of the Cold War* (Boston: Little, Brown, 1993), p. 13. Bush would have been particularly sensitive to this criticism of being "weak." As *Newsweek* put it, "Bush suffers from a potentially crippling handicap—a perception that he isn't strong enough or tough enough for the challenges of the Oval Office. That he is, in a single mean word, a wimp." Margaret Garrad Warner, "Bush Battles the 'Wimp' Factor," *Newsweek*, October 19, 1987, accessed at newsweek.com/bush-battles-wimp-factor-207008.

165. *NBC Nightly News*, August 11 and 12, 1988, VTNA. This was Ken Bode, the NBC political correspondent's long biographical story on Bush, and Kissinger emerges as one of the most flattering people interviewed about the vice president.

166. CBS and *NBC Nightly News*, April 25, 1988, VTNA.

167. *NBC Nightly News*, August 14, 1988, VTNA.

168. Meacham, *Destiny and Power*, p. 346.

169. *NBC Nightly News*, convention coverage, August 17, 1988, VTNA.

170. Schlesinger, *Journals*, p. 729.

171. Beschloss and Talbott, *Highest Levels*, p. 13.

172. Beschloss and Talbott, *Highest Levels*, p. 16.

173. The conversation between Yakolev and Kissinger is reproduced in Svetlana Savranskaya, Thomas Blanton, and Vladislav Zubok, eds., *Masterpieces of History: The Peaceful End of the Cold War in Europe, 1989* (New York: Central European Press, 2010), p. 343.

174. Savranskaya, Blanton, and Zubok, *Masterpieces of History*, p. 346.

175. Savranskaya, Blanton, and Zubok, *Masterpieces of History*, p. 351. The editors of the volume note that Gorbachev, in conversations with his aides, referred to Kissinger as "Kisa," which is a diminutive term for a cat and contained connota-

tions of "slinking around." It was also the name of a pretentious Soviet aristocrat in a classic 1960s Soviet movie. Both could certainly have applied to the former secretary of state.

176. Quoted in Savranskaya and Blanton, *Last Superpower Summits*, p. 493.

177. *CBS Evening News*, January 28, 1989, VTNA.

178. Henry Kissinger, "Reversing Yalta," *The Washington Post*, April 16, 1989, B7. See the account in Isaacson, *Kissinger*, pp. 728–29.

179. Isaacson, *Kissinger*, p. 729.

180. Hahnhimäki, *Flawed Architect*, p. 464.

181. Beschloss and Talbott, *Highest Levels*, p. 138.

182. Sparrow, *The Strategist*, pp. 362–66.

183. Daniel Southerland, "Beijing Reverting to Secretive Ways," *The Washington Post*, November 8, 1989, A38.

184. Grandin argues, "Kissinger played a key role guiding the White House's forgiving response." Grandin, *Kissinger's Shadow*, p. 197.

185. *ABC World News Tonight*, December 1, 1990, VTNA.

186. Meacham, *Destiny and Power*, p. 460.

187. The TV archive holdings indicate he was on CNN for the first five days of the war, and then intermittently through the end of February 1991, VTNA.

188. Sparrow, *The Strategist*, p. 481.

189. *NBC Nightly News*, March 10, 1992, VTNA.

190. *Nightline*, ABC, August 3, 1989, VTNA. The other retired policy types were Assistant Secretary of State Richard Murphy; David Aaron, who was deputy national security adviser under Carter; Admiral James Lyons, who had been deputy chief of naval operations; and Pat Buchanan, one of Nixon's speechwriters and a soon-to-be presidential candidate.

191. Schlesinger, *Journals*, p. 729.

192. *NBC Nightly News*, September 22, 1992, VTNA.

193. Crowley, *Nixon in Winter*, p. 263.

194. Margaret Garrard Warner, "Kissinger: Betrayal of the Apostles?," *Newsweek*, October 4, 1992, p. 50.

195. Stephen Graubard, "Henry Kissinger's Harvard Years," *The New York Times Book Review*, October 25, 1992.

196. In the second edition of the book, Isaacson notes that Kissinger would not speak to him for a while after the book appeared. But after Isaacson became managing editor of *Time*, he received a phone call from Kissinger, who said, "Well Walter, even the Thirty Years War had to end at some point. I forgive you." Isaacson, *Kissinger* (New York: Simon & Schuster, 2005), p. 11. The book also led to the television movie *Kissinger and Nixon*, which was released in December 1995. The background to the film can be found at imdb.com/title/tt0113554.

197. Bill Clinton, *My Life* (New York: Vintage, 2004), pp. 185–86.

198. Leslie Gelb, "Is Clinton Tough Enough?," *The New York Times*, November 8, 1992, p. 152.

199. Henry Kissinger, "No G.O.P. Bad-Will Ambassadors on Tour," *The New York Times*, November 15, 1992, p. 18.

200. *Nightline*, ABC, April 22, 1993; September 3, 1993; October 6, 1993; and January 7, 1994; VTNA.

201. ABC, CBS, NBC, CNN, April 27, 1994, VTNA.

202. CNN coverage of the Rabin assassination, November 5, 1995, VTNA.

203. CNN, August 12, June 17, October 2, and November 25, 1996, VTNA.

204. Henry Kissinger, *Diplomacy* (New York: Simon & Schuster, 1994), pp. 40, 45, and 54.

205. May's review is in *The New York Times*, April 3, 1994.

206. Kissinger's response is in *The New York Times*, April 24, 1994.

207. Henry Kissinger, "The Old Left and the New Right," *Foreign Affairs* 78, no. 3 (1999), pp. 114–15. Kissinger published a third book during this period, *Does America Need a Foreign Policy? Toward a Diplomacy for the 21st Century* (New York: Touchstone, 2001). Published shortly before the September 11 attacks, it was largely lost in the changed attitude toward foreign affairs that the attack created.

208. Christopher Hitchens, *Hitch 22: A Memoir* (New York: Twelve, 2010), p. 221.

209. Hitchens, *The Trial of Henry Kissinger*, p. xi.

210. Hahnhimäki, *Flawed Architect*, p. 479.

211. Hitchens, *Hitch 22*, p. 240.

212. Bob Woodward, *State of Denial*, p. 406.

213. George W. Bush, "Remarks on Signing the Intelligence Authorization Act for Fiscal Year 2003," November 27, 2002, presidency.ucsb.edu/documents/remarks -signing-the-intelligence-authorization-act-for-fiscal-year-2003.

214. *CNN Evening News*, November 27, 2002, and *NBC Nightly News*, November 27, 2002, VTNA.

215. Hahnhimäki, *Flawed Architect*, pp. 479–80.

216. "The Kissinger Commission," *The New York Times*, November 29, 2002, A38.

217. Frank Rich, "Pearl Harbor Day 2002," *The New York Times*, December 7, 2002, A21.

218. Maureen Dowd, "Disco Dick Cheney," *The New York Times*, December 11, 2002, A35.

219. Hahnhimäki, *Flawed Architect*, p. 481.

220. *CBS Evening News*, December 13, 2002; and *NBC Nightly News*, December 13, 2002, VTNA.

221. Hahnhimäki, *Flawed Architect*, p. 481.

222. *CNN Evening News*, February 5, 2003, VTNA.

223. *CNN Evening News*, March 11, 2003, VTNA.

224. *NBC Nightly News*, May 12, 2003, VTNA.

225. Thomas Ricks, *The Gamble: General Petraeus and the American Military Adventure in Iraq* (New York: Penguin, 2009), p. 81.

226. Woodward, *State of Denial*, p. 409.

227. Woodward, *State of Denial*, pp. 406–410. Woodward's book also attracted considerable media attention, with Kissinger's role emphasized. NBC, September 28, 2006, VTNA.

228. *NBC Nightly News*, November 20, 2006, VTNA.

229. Gallup's measure of Bush's approval can be found at gallup.com/interactives /185273/presidential-job-approval-center.aspx.

230. Ricks, *Gamble*, p. 188.

231. Ricks, *Gamble*, p. 191.

232. Condoleezza Rice, *No Higher Honor: A Memoir of My Years in Washington* (New York: Crown, 2011), p. 526.

233. The transcript of the debate can be accessed at debates.org/index.php?page=2008 -debate-transcript. I have also relied on Del Pero, *Eccentric Realist*, pp. 1–2.

234. Maureen Dowd, "Park Avenue Diplomacy," *The New York Times*, September 24, 2008.

235. This issue is explored fully in David M. Wight, "Henry Kissinger as Contested Historical Icon in Post 9/11 Debates on US Foreign Policy," *History and Memory* 29, no. 2 (Fall/Winter 2017), pp. 125–60.

Epilogue: Henry Kissinger—Celebrity Diplomat, Cold War Icon

1. A recap can be found at colbertnewshub.com/2013/08/07/august-6-2013-stephest -colbchella-013.

2. Colbert's affection for Kissinger had not prevented him from satirizing the former secretary of state, especially in 2006 after the publication of Woodward's *State of Denial*. The October 3, 2006, episode is no longer available online.

3. This can be found at imdb.com/title/tt0458254/fullcredits?ref_=tt_cl_sm#cast.

4. These articles can be found at salon.com/2014/12/22/stephen_colberts_one _mistake_the_monstrous_henry_kissinger_shouldnt_get_to_laugh_his_sins _away; and motherjones.com/politics/2013/08/stephen-colbert-henry-kissinger -daft-punk-video.

5. Rhodes channeled much of Obama's critique: nytimes.com/2016/05/08/magazine /the-aspiring-novelist-who-became-obamas-foreign-policy-guru.html.

6. Michael B. Oren, *Ally: My Journey Across the American-Israeli Divide* (New York: Random House, 2015), p. 94. Oren's complaint focused on the Iranian nuclear deal, but the conversation captures Kissinger's sense that one of his singular achievements was being undermined.

7. George Packer, *Our Man: Richard Holbrooke and the End of the American Century* (New York: Knopf, 2019), pp. 166–67.

8. Mark Leibovich, *This Town* (New York: Blue Rider Press, 2013), p. 242.

9. For example, "Meeting of the Diplomats," by Jon Meacham, *Newsweek*, December 21, 2009, from the magazine dated January 4, 2010.

10. The show was dated April 20, 2011: charlierose.com/videos/15398. Kissinger also appeared on the show to discuss the World Cup. His role as a soccer commentator came from his genuine personal enthusiasm for the game and contributed to softening his image as a cold-blooded diplomat. His contribution to promoting soccer within the United States is an underappreciated aspect of his legacy.

11. Wight, "Kissinger as Contested Historical Icon," pp. 148–49.

12. Hillary Rodham Clinton, "Hillary Clinton Reviews Henry Kissinger's 'World Order,'" *The Washington Post*, September 4, 2014, washingtonpost.com/opinions

/hillary-clinton-reviews-henry-kissingers-world-order/2014/09/04/b280c654
-31ea-11e4-8f02-03c644b2d7d0_story.html?utm_term=.3a4f64ba2516.

13. Kissinger gave extensive interviews to Goldberg, including this postelection one. He expected Hillary to win. theatlantic.com/magazine/archive/2016/12/the -lessons-of-henry-kissinger/505868.

14. Wight, "Kissinger as Contested Historical Icon," pp. 153–54. Kissinger also developed a close relationship with Jared Kushner, Trump's son-in-law. Michael Wolff, *Fire and Fury: Inside the Trump White House* (New York: Henry Holt, 2018), p. 41.

15. Kissinger has even been seen as being behind Trump's outreach to Russia as a way of containing China, a new version of triangular diplomacy. thedailybeast.com /henry-kissinger-pushed-trump-to-work-with-russia-to-box-in-china?ref=home.

16. At charlierose.com/videos/30895.

17. These can be found on Kissinger's own website: henryakissinger.com/speeches.

18. This appeared in the *Financial Times*, July 20, 2018. ft.com/content/926a66b0 -8b49-11e8-bf9e-8771d5404543.

19. Shawcross's comment can be found at realclearpolitics.com/articles/2018/11/20 /kissinger_and_i_were_once_at_odds_but_let_him_speak_138694.html.

20. Sebenius, Burns, and Mnookin, *Kissinger the Negotiator: Lessons from Dealmaking at the Highest Level* (New York: Harper, 2018); Winston Lord, *Kissinger on Kissinger: Reflections on Diplomacy, Grand Strategy, and Leadership* (New York: All Points Books, 2019); and Abraham R. Wagner, *Henry Kissinger: Pragmatic Statesman in Hostile Times* (New York: Routledge, 2019). For much more critical treatments of Kissinger, see Robert Brigham, *Reckless: Henry Kissinger and the Tragedy of Vietnam* (New York: Public Affairs, 2018); and Stephen G. Rabe, *Kissinger and Latin America: Intervention, Human Rights, and Diplomacy* (Ithaca, NY: Cornell University Press, 2020).

21. At henryakissinger.com/articles.

22. Robert McNamara used this as the title of one of his retrospective views of the Vietnam War. Robert S. McNamara, *Argument Without End: In Search of Answers to the Vietnam Tragedy* (New York: Public Affairs, 1999).

23. Both Grandin, *Kissinger's Shadow*, and Hahnhimäki, *Flawed Architect*, are representative of this tendency, although Hahnhimäki's book is far more balanced. Nevertheless, it includes a serious consideration of whether Kissinger should be considered a war criminal. Hahnhimäki, *Flawed Architect*, pp. 491–92. For a more recent example of this style, see Robert Brigham, *Reckless: Henry Kissinger and the Tragedy of Vietnam* (New York: Public Affairs, 2018).

24. Almost a third of the more than one thousand scholars surveyed by *Foreign Policy* magazine ranked him this way. washingtonpost.com/blogs/in-the-loop/wp/2015 /02/05/scholars-votes-kerry-dead-last-in-terms-of-effectiveness.

25. Wagner, *Henry Kissinger*, p. 2.

26. Suri, *Henry Kissinger and the American Century*, p. 51.

27. On the concept of "framing the news," I have relied on Robert M. Entman, *Projections of Power: Framing News, Public Opinion, and U.S. Foreign Policy* (Chicago: University of Chicago Press, 2004), especially pp. 1–22.

28. Anthony Hartley, "The American Crisis: Between Old Idealism and New Despair," *Encounter* 39 (May 1972), p. 36.

29. This is also the argument put forth by Mario del Pero in his excellent book, Del Pero, *Eccentric Realist*, p. 5.

30. JFK's inaugural pledge can be found at presidency.ucsb.edu/documents/inaugural-address-2at.

31. *The Gallup Poll: Public Opinion, 1972–1977* (Wilmington, DE: Scholarly Resources, 1978), vol. 2, pp. 881–82, 887–88, and 902–11.

32. Henry Kissinger, *World Order* (New York: Penguin, 2014), p. 2.

33. Meeting of Secretary Kissinger with Representatives of Foreign Service Officer Class, January 6, 1977, Kissinger Meetings, NARS.

34. Weisbrode, *Atlantic Century*, p. 270.

35. For a recent examination of these issues, see Helen V. Milner and Dustin Tingley, *Sailing the Water's Edge: The Domestic Politics of American Foreign Policy* (Princeton, NJ: Princeton University Press, 2015).

36. Miroslav Nincic, "Elections and U.S. Foreign Policy," in *The Domestic Sources of American Foreign Policy*, ed. Eugene R. Wittkopf and James M. McCormick, 4th ed. (Lanham, MD: Rowman and Littlefield, 2004), p. 117.

37. Colin Dueck, *Hard Line: The Republican Party and U.S. Foreign Policy Since World War II* (Princeton, NJ: Princeton University Press, 2010), p. 142.

38. Dueck, *Hard Line*, p. 184.

39. Henry Kissinger, "The Moral Foundations of Foreign Policy," speech, July 15, 1975, in Henry Kissinger, *American Foreign Policy*, pp. 195–213. This is emphasized in John Lewis Gaddis, "Rescuing Choice from Circumstance: The Statecraft of Henry Kissinger," in *The Diplomats 1939–1979*, ed. Gordon A. Craig and Francis L. Loewenheim (Princeton, NJ: Princeton University Press, 1998), pp. 564–92.

40. Visit of the US Secretary of State, March 27, 1974, PREM 167182, PRO, London.

41. The *Time* magazine quote can be found at content.time.com/time/magazine/article/0,9171,942862,00.html.

42. Kissinger, *World Restored*, p. 1. He used the same quote in *Nuclear Weapons and Foreign Policy*.

43. This pattern in American foreign policy is discussed in Stephen Sestanovich, *Maximalist: America in the World from Truman to Obama* (New York: Knopf, 2014).

44. Richard Nixon, "First Annual Report to the Congress on United States Foreign Policy for the 1970's," February 18, 1970, presidency.ucsb.edu/documents/first-annual-report-the-congress-united-states-foreign-policy-for-the-1970s.

45. Ferguson, *Kissinger*, p. 24.

46. According to Stephen Talbot, Kissinger faked tears and said, "Boo-hoo," about McNamara. "He's still beating his breast, right? Still feeling guilty." Talbot was appalled. Stephen Talbot, "The Day Henry Kissinger Cried," December 6, 2002, salon.com/2002/12/05/kissinger_3. There is no question that the lack of remorse greatly irritates those who see Kissinger as the equivalent of a war criminal. For a more recent reflection, connected with the release of documents about Kissinger on Argentina, see Jon Lee Anderson, "Does Henry Kissinger Have a

Conscience?," *The New Yorker*, August 20, 2016, newyorker.com/news/news-desk/does-henry-kissinger-have-a-conscience.

47. Not just Hitchens. The Harvard professor Frederik Logevall compared Kissinger unfavorably with McNamara, noting that Kissinger would admit to only "tactical mistakes." "Rethinking McNamara's War," *The New York Times*, November 28, 2017, nytimes.com/2017/11/28/opinion/rethinking-mcnamaras-war.html?smprod=nytcore-ipad&smid=nytcore-ipad-share.

48. At wnyc.org/story/transcript-kissinger-talks-isis-confronts-his-history-chile-cambodia.

49. This debate is described in Wight, "Kissinger as Contested Historical Icon," pp. 151–52.

SELECTED BIBLIOGRAPHY

Future historians studying Henry Kissinger will go to Yale University and the Library of Congress to consult his voluminous personal papers. Although parts are available today, these collections will become fully available five years after the death of Dr. Kissinger. In the meantime, scholars must use a variety of other sources. For this book, I have relied heavily on the collections produced by the Office of the Historian at the Department of State, the deservedly famous *Foreign Relations of the United States*. Having had the privilege of serving for a term as the representative of the Organization of American Historians on the Historical Advisory Committee to the Office of the Historian, I was thoroughly impressed with the high quality of work done by the scholars in this office. These historians also had access to the Kissinger papers. Below, I list the main volumes I used.

Foreign Relations of the United States (FRUS) for the Richard M. Nixon and Gerald R. Ford Administrations (1969–1976). Washington, DC: Government Printing Office. All these volumes can be accessed electronically at history.state.gov /historicaldocuments/nixon-ford.

1: *Foundations of Foreign Policy, 1969–1972*
5: *United Nations, 1969–1972*
6: *Vietnam, January 1969–July 1970*
7: *Vietnam, July 1970–January 1972*
8: *Vietnam, January–October 1972*
9: *Vietnam, October 1972–January 1973*
10: *Vietnam, January 1973–July 1975*
11: *South Asia Crisis, 1971*
12: *Soviet Union, January 1969–October 1970*
13: *Soviet Union, October 1970–October 1971*
14: *Soviet Union, October 1971–May 1972*
15: *Soviet Union, June 1972–August 1974*
16: *Soviet Union, August 1974–December 1976*
17: *China, 1969–1972*
18: *China, 1973–1976*
21: *Chile, 1969–1973*
25: *Arab-Israeli Crisis and War, 1973*
26: *Arab-Israeli Dispute, 1974–1976*
27: *Iran; Iraq, 1973–1976*
28: *Southern Africa*
30: *Greece; Cyprus; Turkey, 1973–1976*
32: *SALT I, 1969–1972*
33: *SALT II, 1972–1980*
34: *National Security Policy, 1969–1972*
36: *Energy Crisis, 1969–1974*
37: *Energy Crisis, 1974–1980*
38: *Foundations of Foreign Policy, 1973–1976*
40: *Germany and Berlin, 1969–1972*
E-7: *Documents on South Asia, 1969–1972*
E-12: *Documents on East and Southeast Asia, 1973–1976*
E-15, Part 2: *Documents on Western Europe, 1973–1976*

In addition to the regular *FRUS* volumes, I also made use of the special volume on the so-called back channel between Kissinger and the Soviet ambassador Anatoly Dobrynin: *Soviet-American Relations: The Détente Years, 1969–1972*. Washington, DC: Government Printing Office, 2007.

I first encountered the Nixon papers when they were still held in College Park, Maryland. They have subsequently been moved to the Nixon Library in Yorba Linda, California. The Gerald R. Ford Library is in Ann Arbor, Michigan.

National Archives and Records Administration
    White House Tapes
    Nixon Presidential Materials
    National Security Council Files

Chronological File
Indo-Pak War
President's Office Files
President's Trip Files
Richard Nixon Presidential Library and Museum
Nixon Tapes
Public Papers of the President (online)
Gerald R. Ford Presidential Library
Brent Scowcroft Papers

The Nixon Library has made the Nixon tapes accessible online. I have also used the excellent website of Luke Nichter, nixontapes.org.

The Miller Center at the University of Virginia has also been of great use to me in this project: millercenter.org/the-presidency/secret-white-house-tapes/about-nixons -secret-white-house-tapes.

I have also benefited enormously from the work of the National Security Archive in Washington, DC, particularly the research of William Burr, Peter Kornbluh, and Svetlana Savranskaya. Their postings can be found at nsarchive.gwu.edu.

KISSINGER'S WRITINGS

Although Henry Kissinger's writings must be used with caution, they are indispensable to any examination of his career. In particular, the first two volumes of his memoirs are extraordinary works of history, even when they are quite creative in their portrayal of events.

Unpublished

"The Meaning of History: Reflections on Spengler, Toynbee and Kant," undergraduate thesis, Widener Library, Harvard University, 1950.

Published

A World Restored. London: Weidenfeld and Nicolson, 1957.
Nuclear Weapons and Foreign Policy. New York: Harpers, 1957.
The Necessity for Choice. New York: Harper and Brothers, 1961.
White House Years. New York: Simon and Schuster, 1979.
For the Record: Selected Statements 1977–1980. Boston: Little, Brown, 1981.
Years of Upheaval. New York: Simon and Schuster, 1982.
Observations: Selected Speeches and Essays 1982–1984. Boston: Little, Brown, 1985.
Diplomacy. New York: Simon and Schuster, 1994.
Years of Renewal. New York: Simon and Schuster, 1999.
Does America Need a Foreign Policy? Toward a Diplomacy for the 21st Century. New York: Simon and Schuster, 2001.
Ending the Vietnam War: A History of America's Involvement in and Extrication from the Vietnam War. New York: Simon and Schuster, 2003.

Crisis: The Anatomy of Two Major Foreign Policy Crises. New York: Simon and Schuster, 2004.

On China. New York: Penguin, 2011.

World Order. New York: Penguin, 2014.

OTHER ARCHIVAL COLLECTIONS

Harry S. Truman Library, Independence, Missouri
    Psychological Strategy Board
John F. Kennedy Library (JFKL), Boston, Massachusetts
    National Security Files (NSF)
    Germany
    McGeorge Bundy Papers
    White House Folder
    Schlesinger Papers
Lyndon Baines Johnson Library, Austin, Texas
    National Security Files (NSF)
    Henry Kissinger
    Country File
    Vietnam
    Files of McGeorge Bundy
    Memos to the President
Rockefeller Brothers Fund Archives, Sleepy Hollow, New York
    Nelson Aldrich Rockefeller Papers
    Rockefeller Family Collection
    Rockefeller Family Papers
    Rockefeller Special Assistant Papers
    Special Studies Project
Public Records Office, London, England
    Federal Records Center
    Prime Minister's Office Records
Yale University, New Haven, Connecticut
    Papers of Dean Acheson

PERSONAL INTERVIEWS

I did not rely heavily on personal interviews, although I am grateful for the opportunity I had to talk with Dr. Kissinger and a few of those associated with him.

Interview with Henry Kissinger, December 5, 2006

I also spoke more informally with Helmut Sonnenfeldt, Richard Smyser, Marvin Kalb, Winston Lord, and Brent Scowcroft.

TELEVISION NEWS

The Vanderbilt Television News Archive has been in existence since August 1968 and provided a rich record of Kissinger's media exposure.

Vanderbilt Television News Archive (VTNA), Nashville, Tennessee
ABC Evening News
CBS Evening News
NBC Nightly News

NEWSPAPERS AND PERIODICALS

Commentary
The Daily Telegraph
The Harvard Crimson
Newsweek
The New York Times
The New York Times Magazine
Time
The Washington Post

DIARIES AND OTHER PUBLISHED PRIMARY SOURCES

Brinkley, Douglas, and Luke Nichter. *The Nixon Tapes: 1971–1972*. New York: Houghton Mifflin Harcourt, 2014.

———. *The Nixon Tapes: 1973*. New York: Houghton Mifflin Harcourt, 2015.

Burr, William, ed. *The Kissinger Transcripts: The Top-Secret Talks with Beijing and Moscow*. New York: New Press, 1999.

Haldeman, H. R. *The Haldeman Diaries: Inside the Nixon White House*. New York: G. P. Putnam, 1994.

———. *The Haldeman Diaries: Inside the Nixon White House. The Complete Multimedia Edition*. Santa Monica, CA: Sony Imagesoft, 1994. CD-ROM.

Lord, Winston. Oral history. adst.org/OH%20TOCs/Lord,%20Winston.pdf.

Lưu, Văn Lợi, and Anh Vũ Nguyễn. *Lê Đức Thọ–Kissinger Negotiations in Paris*. Hanoi: Thế Giới, 1996.

Roberts, Priscilla, ed. *Window on the Forbidden City: The Beijing Diaries of David Bruce, 1973–1974*. Hong Kong: Centre of Asian Studies, 2001.

Schlesinger, Arthur M., Jr. *Journals: 1952–2000*. New York: Penguin, 2007.

UNPUBLISHED DISSERTATIONS AND UNDERGRADUATE THESES

Bishop, William. "Diplomacy in Black and White: America and the Search for Zimbabwean Independence, 1965–1980." Ph.D. dissertation, Vanderbilt University, 2012.

Hope, Mallory Martin. "Year of Discord: French-U.S. Relations, April 1973–1974." Undergraduate thesis, Vanderbilt University, 2015.

Jeffrey, Samuel R. "A Most Divisive Year: The Year of Europe and Anglo-American Relations in 1973." Honors thesis, Vanderbilt University, 2016.

Kolander, Kenneth. "Walking Out of Step: U.S.-Israel Relations and the Peace Process, 1967–1975." Ph.D. dissertation, University of West Virginia, 2016.

Moss, Richard A. "Behind the Back Channel: Achieving Détente in U.S.-Soviet Relations, 1969–1972." Ph.D. dissertation, George Washington University, August 2009.

Talley, Mark Christian. "Forgotten Vanguard: The Origins and Mission of the National Council for United States–China Trade, 1972–1980." Honors thesis, Vanderbilt University, 2016.

MEMOIRS

Colson, Charles. *Born Again*. Old Tappen, NJ: Chosen Books, 1976.

Dobrynin, Anatoly. *In Confidence: Moscow's Ambassador to Six Cold War Presidents*. Seattle: University of Washington Press, 1995.

Ehrlichman, John. *Witness to Power: The Nixon Years*. New York: Simon and Schuster, 1982.

Ford, Gerald. *A Time to Heal: The Autobiography of Gerald R. Ford*. New York: Harper and Row, 1979.

Garment, Leonard. *Crazy Rhythm: My Journey from Brooklyn, Jazz, and Wall Street to Nixon's White House, Watergate, and Beyond . . .* New York: Random House, 1997.

Haig, Alexander M., Jr. *Inner Circles: How America Changed the World: A Memoir*. New York: Warner Books, 1992.

Haldeman, Harry R. *The Ends of Power*. New York: Times Books, 1978.

Hartmann, Robert. *Palace Politics: An Inside Account of the Ford Years*. New York: McGraw-Hill, 1980.

Helms, Richard. *A Look Over My Shoulder: A Life in the Central Intelligence Agency*. New York: Random House, 2003.

Hillenbrand, Martin J. *Fragments of Our Time: Memoirs of a Diplomat*. Athens: University of Georgia Press, 1998.

Holdridge, John H. *Crossing the Divide: An Insider's Account of the Normalization of U.S.-China Relations*. Lanham, MD: Rowman and Littlefield, 1997.

Klein, Herbert G. *Making It Perfectly Clear*. New York: Doubleday, 1980.

Nessen, Ron. *It Sure Looked Different from the Inside*. New York: Playboy Press, 1978.

Nixon, Richard M. *RN: The Memoirs of Richard Nixon*. New York: Grosset and Dunlap, 1978.

Rumsfeld, Donald. *Known and Unknown: A Memoir*. New York: Sentinel, 2011.

Safire, William. *Before the Fall: An Insider's View of the Pre-Watergate White House*. Garden City, NY: Doubleday, 1975.

Zumwalt, Elmo R. *On Watch: A Memoir*. New York: Quadrangle, 1976.

SECONDARY SOURCES: BOOKS

Aitken, Jonathan. *Nixon: A Life*. London: Weidenfeld and Nicolson, 1993.

Alvandi, Roham. *Nixon, Kissinger, and the Shah: The United States and Iran in the Cold War*. New York: Oxford University Press, 2014.

Ambrose, Stephen. *Nixon: The Triumph of a Politician, 1962–1972*. New York: Simon & Schuster, 1987.

Andrew, Christopher, and Vasil Mitrokhin. *The World Was Going Our Way: The KGB and the Battle for the Third World*. New York: Basic Books, 2005.

Ang, Cheng Guan. *Ending the Vietnam War: The Vietnamese Communists' Perspective*. London: RoutledgeCurzon, 2004.

Bass, Gary J. *The Blood Telegram: Nixon, Kissinger, and a Forgotten Genocide*. New York: Knopf, 2013.

Berman, Larry. *No Peace, No Honor: Nixon, Kissinger, and Betrayal in Vietnam*. New York: Touchstone, 2001.

Blumenfeld, Ralph. *Henry Kissinger: The Private and Public Story*. New York: New American Library, 1974.

Bohn, Michael. *Nerve Center: Inside the White House Situation Room*. Washington, DC: Brassey's, 2003.

Brandon, Henry. *Special Relationships: A Foreign Correspondent's Memoirs from Roosevelt to Reagan*. New York: Scribner, 1989.

Burr, William, and Jeffrey P. Kimball. *Nixon's Nuclear Specter: The Secret Alert of 1969, Madman Diplomacy, and the Vietnam War*. Lawrence: University Press of Kansas, 2015.

Clymer, Adam. *Drawing the Line at the Big Ditch: The Panama Canal Treaties and the Rise of the Right*. Lawrence: University Press of Kansas, 2008.

Collier, Simon, and William F. Sater. *A History of Chile, 1808–2002*, 2nd ed. New York: Cambridge University Press, 2004.

Dallek, Robert. *Nixon and Kissinger: Partners in Power*. New York: Harper Perennial, 2007.

Del Pero, Mario. *The Eccentric Realist: Henry Kissinger and the Shaping of American Foreign Policy*. Ithaca, NY: Cornell University Press, 2006.

Dhar, P. N. *Indira Gandhi, the Emergency, and Indian Democracy*. New Delhi: Oxford University Press, 2000.

Dickson, Peter. *Kissinger and the Meaning of History*. Cambridge, UK: Cambridge University Press, 1978.

Fallaci, Oriana. *Interview with History*. Boston: Houghton Mifflin, 1977.

Ferguson, Niall. *Kissinger: The Idealist, 1923–1968*. New York: Penguin, 2015.

Forslund, Catherine. *Anna Chennault: Informal Diplomacy and Asian Relations*. Wilmington, DE: Scholarly Resources, 2002.

Garthoff, Raymond. *Détente and Confrontation: America Soviet Relations from Nixon to Reagan*. Washington, DC: Brookings, 1985.

Gleijeses, Piero. *Conflicting Missions: Havana, Washington, and Africa 1959–1976*. Chapel Hill: University of North Carolina Press, 2002.

Golden, Peter. *O Powerful Western Star!: American Jews, Russian Jews, and the Final Battle of the Cold War*. Jerusalem: Geffen Books, 2012.

———. *Quiet Diplomat: A Biography of Max M. Fisher*. New York: Cornwall Books, 1992.

Gomes, Bernadino, and Tiago Moreira de Sá. *Carlucci Versus Kissinger: The US and the Portuguese Revolution*. Translated by Susana Serras Pereira. Lanham, MD: Lexington Books, 2011.

Grandin, Greg. *Kissinger's Shadow: The Long Reach of America's Most Controversial Statesman*. New York: Metropolitan Books, 2015.

Graubard, Stephen Richards. *Kissinger: Portrait of a Mind*. New York: W. W. Norton, 1974.

Gustafson, Kristen. *Hostile Intent: U.S. Covert Operations in Chile, 1964–1974*. Washington, DC: Potomac Books, 2007.

Hahnhimäki, Jussi. *The Flawed Architect: Henry Kissinger and American Foreign Policy*. London: Oxford University Press, 2004.

———. *The Rise and Fall of Détente: American Foreign Policy and the Transformation of the Cold War*. Washington, DC: Potomac Books, 2013.

Hammond, William. *Public Affairs: The Military and the Media, 1968–1973*. The United States Army in Vietnam. Washington, DC: Center for Military History, 1996.

Harmer, Tanya. *Allende's Chile and the Inter-American Cold War*. Chapel Hill: University of North Carolina Press, 2011.

Haslam, Jonathan. *The Nixon Administration and the Death of Allende's Chile*. London: Verso, 2005.

Herken, Gregg. *The Georgetown Set: Friends and Rivals in Cold War Washington*. New York: Knopf, 2014.

Hersh, Seymour M. *The Price of Power: Henry Kissinger in the White House*. London: Faber, 1983.

Hershberg, James. *James B. Conant: Harvard to Hiroshima and the Making of the Nuclear Age*. New York: Knopf, 1993.

Hitchens, Christopher. *The Trial of Henry Kissinger*. London: Verso, 2001.

Hoffmann, Stanley. *Primacy or World Order: American Foreign Policy Since the Cold War*. New York: McGraw-Hill, 1980.

Holland, Max. *Leak: Why Mark Felt Became Deep Throat*. Lawrence: University Press of Kansas, 2012.

Horne, Alistair. *Kissinger 1973: The Crucial Year*. New York: Simon and Schuster, 2009.

Hughes, Ken. *Chasing Shadows: The Nixon Tapes, the Chennault Affair, and the Origins of Watergate*. Charlottesville: University of Virginia Press, 2014.

———. *Fatal Politics: The Nixon Tapes, the Vietnam War, and the Casualties of Reelection*. Charlottesville: University of Virginia Press, 2015.

Hunebelle, Danielle. *Dear Henry*. New York: Berkley Press, 1972.

Hyland, William G. *Mortal Rivals: Superpower Relations from Nixon to Reagan*. New York: Random House, 1987.

Isaacson, Walter. *Kissinger: A Biography*. New York: Simon and Schuster, 2005.

Israelyan, Victor. *On the Battlefields of the Cold War*. Translated by Stephen Pearl. University Park: Penn State University Press, 2003.

Johns, Andrew. *Vietnam's Second Front: Domestic Politics, the Republican Party, and the War*. Lexington: University Press of Kentucky, 2010.

Kalb, Marvin, and Bernard Kalb. *Kissinger*. Frankfurt am Main, Germany: Ullstein, 1974.

Kaufman, Robert C. *Henry M. Jackson: A Life in Politics*. Seattle: University of Washington Press, 2000.

Keefer, Louis E. *Scholars in Foxholes: The Story of the Army Specialized Training Program in World War II*. Jefferson, NC: McFarland, 1988.

Kelly, Charles J. *Tex McCrary: Wars, Women, Politics: An Adventurous Life Across the American Century*. Lanham, MD: Hamilton Books, 2009.

Keys, Barbara J. *Reclaiming American Virtue: The Human Rights Revolution of the 1970s*. Cambridge, MA: Harvard University Press, 2014.

Khan, Sultan. *Memories and Reflections of a Pakistani Diplomat*. Oxford: Alden Press, 1997.

Kimball, Jeffrey. *The Vietnam War Files: Uncovering the Secret History of Nixon-Era Strategy*. Lawrence: University of Kansas Press, 2004.

Klitzing, Holger. *The Nemesis of Stability: Henry A. Kissinger's Ambivalent Relationship with Germany*. Trier, Germany: WVT, 2007.

Kornbluh, Peter. *The Pinochet File*. New York: New Press, 2003.

Kuklick, Bruce. *Blind Oracles: Intellectuals and War from Kennan to Kissinger*. Princeton, NJ: Princeton University Press, 2006.

Kurz, Evi. *The Kissinger Saga: Walter and Henry Kissinger, Two Brothers from Fürth, Germany*. London: Weidenfeld and Nicolson, 2009.

Kutler, Stanley. *Abuse of Power: The New Nixon Tapes*. New York: Simon and Schuster, 1997.

Lake, Anthony. *The "Tar Baby" Option: American Policy Toward Southern Rhodesia*. New York: Columbia University Press, 1976.

Laqueur, Walter. *Generation Exodus: The Fate of Young Jewish Refugees from Nazi Germany*. Hanover, NH: Brandeis University Press, 2001.

LeoGrande, William, and Peter Kornbluh. *Back Channel to Cuba: The Hidden History of Negotiations Between Washington and Havana*. Chapel Hill: University of North Carolina Press, 2014.

Liebmann, George W. *The Last American Diplomat: John D. Negroponte and the Changing Face of American Diplomacy*. New York: I. B. Tauris, 2012.

MacMillan, Margaret. *Nixon and Mao: The Week That Changed the World*. New York: Random House, 2007.

Mason, Robert. *Richard Nixon and the Quest for a New Majority*. Chapel Hill: University of North Carolina Press, 2004.

May, Ernest. *American Cold War Strategy: Interpreting NSC-68*. Boston: Bedford/St. Martin's, 1993.

Mazlish, Bruce. *Kissinger: The European Mind in American Policy*. New York: Basic Books, 1976.

McPherson, James Brian. *Journalism at the End of the American Century, 1965–Present*. Westport, CT: Praeger, 2006.

Meacham, Jon. *Destiny and Power: The American Odyssey of George Herbert Walker Bush*. New York: Random House, 2015.

Miller, Aaron David. *The Much Too Promised Land*. New York: Bantam, 2008.

Mitchell, Nancy. *Jimmy Carter in Africa: Race and the Cold War*. Palo Alto, CA: Stanford University Press, 2016.

Moore, Deborah Dash. *GI Jews: How World War II Changed a Generation*. Cambridge, MA: Harvard University Press, 2004.

Morris, Roger. *Uncertain Greatness*. New York: Harper and Row, 1977.

Moss, Richard A. *Nixon's Back Channel to Moscow: Confidential Diplomacy and Détente*. Lexington: University Press of Kentucky, 2017.

Nguyen, Lien-Hang T. *Hanoi's War: An International History of the War for Peace in Vietnam*. Chapel Hill: University of North Carolina Press, 2012.

Osborne, John. *The Fourth Year of the Nixon Watch*. New York: Liveright, 1973.

————. *White House Watch: The Ford Years*. Washington, DC: New Republic Books, 1977.

Perlstein, Rick. *Nixonland: The Rise of a President and the Fracturing of America*. New York: Scribner, 2008.

Persico, Joseph E. *The Imperial Rockefeller: A Biography of Nelson A. Rockefeller*. New York: Washington Square Press, 1983.

Prados, John. *The Blood Road: The Ho Chi Minh Trail and the Vietnam War*. New York: John Wiley and Sons, 1999.

Quandt, William. *Peace Process: American Diplomacy and the Arab-Israeli Conflict Since 1967*. 3rd ed. Washington, DC: Brookings, 2005.

Qureshi, Lubna Z. *Nixon, Kissinger, and Allende: U.S. Involvement in the 1973 Coup in Chile*. Lanham, MD: Lexington Books, 2009.

Raghavan, Srinath. *1971: A Global History of the Creation of Bangladesh*. Cambridge, MA: Harvard University Press, 2013.

Randolph, Stephen P. *Powerful and Brutal Weapons: Nixon, Kissinger, and the Easter Offensive*. Cambridge, MA: Harvard University Press, 2007.

Reeves, Richard. *President Nixon: Alone in the White House*. New York: Simon and Schuster, 2001.

Rodman, Peter. *Presidential Command*. New York: Knopf, 2009.

Rosen, James. *The Strong Man: John Mitchell and the Secrets of Watergate*. New York: Doubleday, 2008.

Savranskaya, Svetlana, and Thomas Blanton, eds., *The Last Superpower Summits*. New York: Central European Press, 2016.

Schroeder, Paul W. *Metternich's Diplomacy at Its Zenith, 1820–1823: Austria and the Congresses of Troppau, Laibach, and Verona*. Austin: University of Texas, 1962.

Schulzinger, Robert D. *Henry Kissinger: Doctor of Diplomacy*. New York: Columbia University Press, 1989.

Schwartz, Thomas. *America's Germany: John J. McCloy and the Federal Republic of Germany*. Cambridge, MA: Harvard University Press, 1991.

————. *Lyndon Johnson and Europe: In the Shadow of Vietnam*. Cambridge, MA: Harvard University Press, 2003.

Siniver, Asaf. *Nixon, Kissinger, and U.S. Foreign Policymaking*. Cambridge, UK: Cambridge University Press, 2008.

Smith, Michael J. *Realist Thought from Weber to Kissinger*. Baton Rouge: Louisiana State University Press, 1986.

Snyder, Sarah B. *Dictators, Diplomats, and Dissidents: United States Human Rights Activism in the Long 1960s*. New York: Columbia University Press, forthcoming.

Sparrow, Bartholomew. *The Strategist: Brent Scowcroft and the Call of National Security*. New York: Public Affairs, 2015.

Stern, Paula. *Water's Edge: Domestic Politics and the Making of Foreign Policy*. Westport, CT: Greenwood Press, 1979.

Stoessinger, John George. *Henry Kissinger: The Anguish of Power.* New York: W. W. Norton, 1976.

Suri, Jeremi. *Henry Kissinger and the American Century.* Cambridge, MA: Belknap, 2009.

Thomas, Evan. *Being Nixon: A Man Divided.* New York: Random House, 2015.

Tudda, Chris. *A Cold War Turning Point: Nixon and China, 1969–1972.* Baton Rouge: Louisiana State University Press, 2012.

Valeriani, Richard. *Travels with Henry.* Boston: Houghton Mifflin, 1979.

Walters, Barbara. *Audition.* New York: Vintage, 2009.

Weisbrode, Kenneth. *The Atlantic Century.* Cambridge, MA: Da Capo Press, 2009.

Werth, Barry. *31 Days: The Crisis That Gave Us the Government We Have Today.* New York: Doubleday, 2006.

Westad, Odd Arne. *The Global Cold War.* New York: Cambridge University Press, 2005.

———. *Restless Empire: China and the World Since 1750.* New York: Basic Books, 2012.

Wilford, Hugh. *The Mighty Wurlitzer: How the CIA Played America.* Cambridge, MA: Harvard University Press, 2008.

Witcover, Jules. *Marathon: The Pursuit of the Presidency, 1972–1976.* New York: Viking, 1977.

Woods, Randall B. *Shadow Warrior: William Egan Colby and the CIA.* New York: Basic Books, 2013.

Woodward, Bob. *State of Denial.* New York: Simon and Schuster, 2006.

Woodward, Bob, and Carl Bernstein. *The Final Days.* New York: Simon and Schuster, 1976.

Yaqub, Salim. *Imperfect Strangers: Americans, Arabs, and U.S.–Middle Eastern Relations in the 1970s.* Ithaca, NY: Cornell University Press, 2016.

Zanchetta, Barbara. *The Transformation of American International Power in the 1970s.* New York: Cambridge University Press, 2014.

Zubok, Vladislav. *A Failed Empire: The Soviet Union in the Cold War from Stalin to Gorbachev.* Chapel Hill: University of North Carolina Press, 2007.

SECONDARY SOURCES: ARTICLES

Cohen, Avner. "Nuclear Arms in Crisis Under Secrecy: Israel and the Lessons of the 1967 and 1973 Wars." In *Planning the Unthinkable: How New Powers Will Use Nuclear, Biological, and Chemical Weapons,* edited by Peter R. Lavoy, Scott D. Sagan, and James J. Wirtz. Ithaca, NY: Cornell University Press, 2000.

Fermandois, Joaquín. "The Persistence of a Myth: Chile in the Eye of the Cold War." Translated by Mark Falcoff. *World Affairs* 167, no. 3 (2005).

Gustafson, Kristian. "CIA Machinations in Chile in 1970." *Studies in Intelligence* 47, no. 3 (2003).

Hoppe, Art. "Root for Your Country." In *Deadline Artists, America's Greatest Newspaper Columns,* edited by John Avlon, Jesse Angelo, and Errol Louis. New York: Overlook Press, 2011.

Hughes, Ken. "Fatal Politics: Nixon's Political Timetable for Withdrawing from Vietnam." *Diplomatic History* 34, no. 3 (2010).

Jian, Chen. "China and the Indochina Settlement at the Geneva Convention of 1954." In *The First Vietnam War*, edited by Fredrik Logevall and Mark Lawrence. Cambridge, MA: Harvard University Press, 2007.

McMahon, Robert. "The Danger of Geopolitical Fantasies: Nixon, Kissinger, and the South Asia Crisis of 1971." In *Nixon in the World*, edited by Fredrik Logevall and Andrew Preston. New York: Oxford University Press, 2008.

Tilford, Earl H., Jr. Entry in *Encyclopedia of the Vietnam War*, edited by Spencer Tucker. New York: Oxford University Press, 2000.

Yang, Kuisong, and Yafeng Xia. "Vacillating Between Revolution and Détente: Mao's Changing Psyche and Policy Towards the United States, 1969–1976." *Diplomatic History* 34, no. 2 (2010).

ACKNOWLEDGMENTS

I have long been interested in the career of Henry Kissinger. When I first applied to Harvard University for college, my local interviewer mentioned in an offhand manner that he had taken a course with Kissinger. I wanted that opportunity myself. However, after I finally arrived as a graduate student in history, Henry Kissinger did not return following his service in government. Kissinger did remain an influence on campus, however. I took a course on German politics from Dr. Guido Goldman, a Kissinger friend, and was fortunate enough to work with professors Charles Maier and Alan Brinkley, both of whom knew Kissinger and occasionally told me stories about their encounters with him. My doctoral adviser, Professor Ernest May, had been a contemporary of Kissinger at Harvard. While he admired aspects of Kissinger's career, he was definitely not a Kissinger fan. Professor Francis Bator, with whom I later worked on a different project, was also generous in sharing his stories about Kissinger.

This book has taken me a very long time to write, and consequently I have many people to thank. I live in fear that I will forget to mention someone, and I want to make a preemptive plea for forgiveness! Many of the names here deserve much fuller descriptions of their contributions to this book, but that will have to wait until I can inscribe their copies.

This book came about at the suggestion of Louis Masur, the editor of *Reviews in American History*. Originally, I began at Farrar, Straus and Giroux with the generous help and encouragement of Thomas LeBien, and then of editor Alexander Star and his assistant, Ian Van Wye.

Many institutions have assisted me along the way. The Vanderbilt University Research Council provided financial support. The Rockefeller Archive and the Gerald R. Ford Presidential Library provided me with financial assistance to visit their archives. I enjoyed a fellowship at the Woodrow Wilson International Center for Scholars (now called the Wilson Center) in their History and Public Policy program, under the leadership of Christian Ostermann. My research assistant there, Erin Robinson, did an excellent job in compiling material on Kissinger. I also spent time at the Norwegian Nobel Institute, then under the leadership of Geir Lundestad. Both Christian and Geir have been extraordinarily helpful in my research for this book, and I remain in their debt.

My friend Greg Mark of DePaul University's College of Law took on the onerous job of reading this entire manuscript and helping me to edit it to a reasonable length. I am immensely grateful to him for that assistance. Sahr Conway-Lanz, who is now at the Library of Congress, read several chapters and provided excellent advice in addition to catching a number of mistakes. I greatly appreciate his help.

I want to thank the archivists at the Nixon Project, especially John Powers, as well as those at the Rockefeller and Ford Archives. Special thanks to Dan Caldwell of Pepperdine University, who gave me a complete collection of Kissinger's State Department news conferences and speeches.

My brief and eventful service with the State Department's Advisory Committee on Historical Diplomatic Documentation was influential in my understanding of Kissinger. I thank all the members I served with for their friendship during a difficult time: William Roger Louis, Robert McMahon, Tom Zeiler, Carol Anderson, Katie Sibley, Margaret Hedstrom, and Edward Rhodes. My service on the advisory committee also enabled me to get to know the enormously talented staff of the State Department's Office of the Historian. They were and are a remarkable group of scholars: Edward Keefer, David Geyer, Erin Mahan, Chris Tudda, Adam Howard, Doug Selvage, Steve Randolph, John Carland, Kristin Ahlberg, Myra Burton, Melissa Jane Taylor, James Wilson, Craig Daigle, Kathy Rasmussen, M. Todd Bennett, William McAllister, and the late Peter Kraemer.

I taught with, and learned a great deal about writing from, *The Washington Post*'s David Maraniss. Professor Klaus Larres at the University of North Carolina hosted me for a talk about the book, as did Professor Joseph Siracusa at RMIT University in Melbourne, Australia, and Professor Darlene Rivas at Pepperdine University.

I also want to thank the community of Cold War scholars and diplomatic historians who have been supportive of this effort. Jussi Hahnimäki, Jeremi Suri, Mario del Pero, Max Holland, Mark Moyar, Svetlana Savranskaya, William Burr, Michael Creswell, Frank Gavin, Frank Costigliola, Andreas Daum, Dan Klingensmith, Jeffrey Herf, Peter Hahn, Barbara Keys, Mark Atwood Lawrence, Zach Levey, Effie Pedaliu, Sarah Snyder, Andrew Johns, Amy Sayward, Günter Bischof, James Hershberg, Hope Harrison, Daniel Sargent, Bernd Schaefer, Robert Bothwell, Robert "KC" Johnson, Deng Feng, and Liu Shu. I owe special thanks to University of Notre Dame's Professor Wilson "Bill" Miscamble, C.S.C., who talked me through an inordinate number of crises in completing this book. "Father Bill" is both a scholarly colleague and one of my dearest friends.

My professional colleagues at Vanderbilt have helped me along the way. Gary Gerstle, Sarah Igo, Joel Harrington, Michael Bess, Marshall Eakin, Bill Caferro, Frank Wcislo, Jane Landers, Dennis Dickerson, Dan Usner, Richard Blackett, Helmut Smith, Meike Werner, Katherine Carroll, Emily Greble, Vereen Bell, Robert Driskill, John Geer, Erwin Hargrove, Jefferson Cowie, Jim Epstein, Leor Halevi, Lauren Clay, David Carlton, Peter Lorge, Christopher Loss, Kevin Kim, Moses Ochonu, Paul Conkin, Ruth Rogaski, Devin Fergus, and Matthew Ramsey. The staff of the History Department has always made it a pleasure to go to work, especially Heidi Welch, Susan Hilderbrand, and Meagan Artus.

I have had an extraordinarily able group of Vanderbilt research assistants. I can not say enough about their skill, hard work, and dedication: Jaidza Butler, Samuel Jeffrey, Tyler Bitner, Aaron Crist, Parkes Brittain, Justin X. DeMello, Mallory Hope, Phillip W. Field, Analise Obremsky, Christopher Zhang, and Jacob Schroeder.

I have also benefitted enormously from the graduate students with whom I have worked at Vanderbilt. They include Werner Lippert, Justin Wilson, Adam Wilsman, Lu Sun, Will Bishop, Steve Harrison, Aileen Teague, Zoe LeBlanc, Breck Walker, Mike Davis, Appu Soman, Caroline Pruden, Tizoc Chavez, Jaideep Prabhu, Rachel Donaldson, Frances Kolb, Mario Rewers, Johnathon Speed, Danielle Stubbe, Mary Bridges, Kangzhi Chen, Anthony Siracusa, Henry Gorman, Tiago Fernandes Maranhao, Kayleigh Whitman, Salam Alsarhan, Bernes Karacay, Lu Hongmou, Yin Mengmeng, Mark Vertuli, Carrie Lee Smith, and Sean Smith.

I have also had the good fortune to work with graduate students from other universities over the course of this project. They have now advanced in their own careers, but I am grateful for their help: Kenny Kolander, Stephan Kieninger, Steve Brady, Luke Nichter, Aykut Kilinc, and Raj Roy.

There have been several outstanding Vanderbilt students who asked great questions about Henry Kissinger and helped me think more deeply about the subject: Christian Talley, Selden Hunnicutt, Matt Sturgell, Camille Parker, Gabrielle Grys, Claire Holloway, Anela Mangum, Jake Zellner, Matt Genova, Andrea Messner,

Nicholas DeNuzzo, Matthew DeNuzzo, Lauren O'Neil, Sebastian Peskind, Stephen Vaden, Chetan Immanneni, Ty Johannes, Nihar Patel, Mary Gwin, Laura Grove, Alexander Boyd, Jeremy Bloomstone, Eric Turner, Henry Goldberg, Temple Baker, Bradley Cordes, Won Ki Lee, Blake Hall, Stephanie Freeman, Luke Julian, Mark Hand, Chad Burchard, Tommy Goodman, Daniel Yan, Neil Booher, Abby Miller, Sebastian Arango, Frank Martin, Katelin Olson, Justin Memmott, Alex Sweet, Lawrence Waller, Jonathan Feldman, Winston Du, John Cliburn, Robin Arnett, Garrett Sweitzer, J.J. Alexander, Jordan Janis, Margaret Pless, Rudy Wu, Andrew Barge, and Josh Burgener.

Over the years I have probably bored my friends to death with Kissinger stories. They have been kind enough to listen: George Paine, Art Jacobs, Austin Triggs, Peter Brush, Donna Johnson, Ann Marie Owens, Willy Stern, Lyn Fulton-John, Lisa Katchka, Richard and Sherry Chriss, Joe Sestak, Monica Walker, Lindsay Collins, Alan Bookbinder, Rebecca Rubin, Sissy Frank, Katie Gravens, Mike Mahoney, Guy Reed, John Sesek, Lou Ellen Heckman, Karen Flanagan McCarthy, John Yoo, Melanie Billings-Yun, Diane Kelly, Diane Kunz, Clare McHugh, Lisa Mihaly, Sharon Meers, Joann and Bill Marianetti, Pat Tomasso, Joe Zicari, Charles Crimi, and Frank Longo.

I owe very special thanks to my dear friend Marie Keeler, who always believed in me even when I had my doubts.

With great sadness I remember those who did not live to see me finish this book. Professors May, Brinkley, and Bator, along with my Vanderbilt colleagues Hugh Graham and Sam McSeveney, were always supportive. My parents, John and Mary Schwartz, and my siblings, John, Bob, and Gerianne Schwartz, would have enjoyed seeing me finish this tome. My uncle, Richard Leland, and aunt, Rosemary Stamos, got to see a draft, but I greatly regret that they are not here for the finished product.

My extended family has always been there for me, and were even kind enough to stop asking, "When will the book come out?" at every holiday celebration. My siblings Mary, Joe, Rose, and Carol; in-laws Tom, Ed, Donna, John, and Patty; as well as Jane Bruce, Barbara Leland, Melissa Stockdale, Amy Kirschke, Bonnie Bruce, Mike Peterson, and my growing collection of nieces and nephews: Johnny and Christine; Eric and Michelle; Jenny and Mario; James, Edna, Nic, and Alexandra; Michael, Elizabeth, and Mike; Landon, Brianna, Miles, Lucy, Nora, Jayda, and our newest entry, John Harrison.

This book is dedicated to my three daughters—Helene, Evie, and Marigny—who grew up with this project, and always gave me the love and encouragement I needed to make it through the tough times and the good times. They are the true treasures of my life.

INDEX

A NOTE ABOUT THE AUTHOR

Thomas A. Schwartz is Distinguished Professor of History at Vanderbilt University, where he specializes in the history of the foreign relations of the United States. He has served on the U.S. State Department's Historical Advisory Committee and as president of the Society for Historians of American Foreign Relations. *Henry Kissinger and American Power* is his third book.